W9-BXH-627

To Jennifer, whose good taste is apparent! May you have many happy times in the kitchen!

"To have good

taste is to find

in things the good

taste they have."

—St. Bernard

Anne Coppenham
March 18, 2000

French FARM HOUSE

COOKBOOK

SUSAN HERRMANN LOOMIS

Foreword by Patricia Wells

ILLUSTRATIONS BY JULIE ECKLUND

WORKMAN PUBLISHING • NEW YORK

Copyright © 1996 by Susan Herrmann Loomis
Illustrations © 1996 by Julie Ecklund
All rights reserved. No portion of this book may be reproduced—
mechanically, electronically, or by any other means, including photocopying—without written permission of the publisher.
Published simultaneously in Canada by Thomas Allen & Son Limited.

Loomis, Susan Herrmann.
French farmhouse cookbook / by Susan Herrmann Loomis; illustrated by Julie Ecklund.
p. cm.
Includes index.
ISBN 1-56305-488-4 (pbk. : alk. paper)
1. Cookery, French. I. Title
TX719.L662 1996
641.5944—dc20   96-41092
CIP

Cover design by Lisa Hollander
Cover illustration by Robbin Gourley
Cover photograph by Elizabeth Watt
Book design by Lisa Hollander and Lori S. Malkin with Natsumi Uda

Workman books are available at special discounts when purchased in bulk for premiums and sales promotions
as well as for fund-raising or educational use. Special editions or book excerpts can be created to specification.
For details, contact the Special Sales Director at the address below.

Workman Publishing Company, Inc.
708 Broadway
New York, NY 10003-9555

Manufactured in the United States of America
First printing October 1996
10 9 8 7 6 5 4 3 2 1

This book is dedicated to

Doris Bain and Joseph Francis Herrmann,

who continue to inspire in me

a respect for good food, good people,

and traditions worth honoring.

Acknowledgments

➤•••◄

Writing the *French Farmhouse Cookbook* has fulfilled a long-held dream. When I left France in 1983 after four years of culinary study and work, I had hoped to return and live there. That came to pass, and I have countless people to thank.

I first want to give thanks to two dear friends who have encouraged and nurtured the dream:

Patricia Wells helped me get started in this delightful profession and has been a constant and generous friend and colleague for more than fifteen years. She and her husband, Walter, have never ceased to be there for me in every way, and I thank them both with all my heart.

Edith Leroy, my *âme-soeur*, has taught me so much about France, flavors, freshness, the French aesthetic, and simple ways to make a house a home. Without Edith, her husband, Bernard, and their family, whose friendship and broad view of French and American cultures has helped me enormously, life would be incomplete.

Remerciements • Acknowledgments

I thank the farmers I have spent the past three years visiting. Their dedication and hard work provide a constant source of inspiration. You will meet many in this book, but there are a great number of people, farmers and others, who deserve special thanks.

Dany Dubois opened her home and her life fifteen years ago to my husband, Michael, then to me. With Dany, her husband, Guy, and their children, Gilles and Kathie, I have gained intimate insight into French farm life.

Thank you to Jean-Pierre Xiradakis of La Tupina in Bordeaux, who set me on the trail of exceptional farmhouse fare and folk in Gascony.

A heartfelt thanks to Marie-Claude Gracia, who is, I believe, one of the best chefs in France, and who gives real meaning to the phrase "cooking from the heart."

Thank you to the Daguins, whose cheer, generosity, and knowledge have given me an enduring admiration for Gascons and their food.

In the Pays Basque I thank Marie-Agnès and Michel Carricaburu, who instilled in me a deep affection for their region and for themselves. In Espelette I thank André Darraidou, owner of Euzkadi and tireless promotor of Basque culture and cuisine, and Mari Txu Garacotche, president of the Espelette pepper growers' association, for her helpful introduction.

In Provence, thank you to Jacqueline and Louis Priaulet for their friendship and olive oil; Mme. Suzy Ceysson, director of the Coopérative Oléicole de la Vallée des Baux, in Maussane, for her help; Monique Tourrette, a source of vast information and delectable recipes, and valued friend; George Illy, protector of all that is traditional in Provence; and David and Beverly Crofoot, wonderful friends and Provenceaux at heart.

In Normandy, my second home, I thank the Dugords—particularly Isabelle—for their warmth and generosity; to Philippe Marche, postman and historian of Le Neubourg, who generously gave of his time and knowledge; to M. Clet and his *équipe* at our neighborhood *épicerie;* to Babette at Herboristerie Margat, for her remedies and recipes; to Odette and René Plassart for their warm and generous hospitality.

In Brittany, thanks go to Patrick Jeffroy, a most talented chef who shared generously of his time, his memories, and his friends; to Olivier Roellinger, for his suggestions; to Michel Coze, grower of *roses de Roscoff*, and M. Chapelin, one of the world's foremost artichoke researchers. In southern Brittany, thank you to the Cadorets; to Germaine and

Jean Plassart for their continued and warm interest; to the Larhantecs for the evening we spent amidst crêpes and cider; to the le Rhun family for their delicious buckwheat flour.

To Helene Bourillon in Burgundy I give a triple kiss on each cheek for good company on many trips into the French countryside.

In the Beauce, I thank Lawrence Sevestre and Marie-France Gossard for their help; thank you to Yves Devisme for the introduction. Thank you also to M. Pauget, in Paris.

Thank you to everyone involved in Terre de Semences; to Didier Blain at Interprofession Bio; and to everyone at Biocoop.

Thank you to Jean-Louis Palladin in Washington, D.C., for offering the names of his favorite French regions and friends within them.

Wines were chosen with the distinguished and thoughtful help of Alain Dumergue; thanks go to him and to Philippe Marquent and Claude Udron for their helpful tips and hints, and for their friendship.

Thank you to Jane Martin, for her careful checking of the French in this book.

Barbara Leopold tested recipes with her usual perceptiveness and skill, and I thank her immensely, as well as Cynthia Nims.

I owe much to Marion Pruitt, who stepped in at a critical moment to recipe-test and quickly became indispensable. She has tested, retested, and tested again, and her midnight faxes have often had me in stitches. Thank you, Marion.

Steven Rothfeld steered me in many good directions, and I thank him for his good taste and humor.

There are many people who have, knowingly and unknowingly, helped me pursue this and other work and who deserve many thanks: Zanne Stewart at *Gourmet* magazine; Janet Piorko and Nancy Newhouse at *The New York Times;* Patsy Jamieson and Susan Stuck at *Eating Well;* everyone at *Bon Appétit* magazine, particularly William Garry and my dear friend Karen Kaplan; Carole Lalli, Pamela Mitchell, and Tina Ujlaki; and everyone at *Sesame Street Parents Magazine.*

And I cannot possibly forget Anne Willan, who made it easy for me to first come and live in France, and to all those at La Varenne in Paris; and to Barbara Kafka, who has helped me in the most valuable of ways, and remains an admired friend and colleague.

I have enjoyed a long and fruitful relationship with Workman Publishing, and I thank Peter Workman for his belief in me; Suzanne Rafer, my editor, for her patience and humor; Kathie Ness for her careful copyediting; Margery Tippie for coordinating the details; Lisa Hollander for her

inspired design; and publicist Andrea Glickson for everything.

I am grateful to M. Michel Devisme, who is a valued neighbor and responsible for many of the wonderful people in my life; and to Miche Devisme for her wise and interesting view of life.

Thank you to our friends Christian and Nadine Devisme, and their delightful children; to Annie Grodent for many things, including her eager sharing of family, markets, cuisine, and lore, and to Jean for his humor; to Bernadette and Laurent Martin for their unbeatable phraseology and friendship; to Heloise Tuyéras for her friendship and caring; to Marcel and Françine Leborgne for their help and gentle teasing; to Florence and Edouard Labelle for making our first year in France so pleasant; to Brigitte and Marc Emeric for their hospitality and the way they add beauty to the world; to Magaly and Marco Baude for adding artful comfort to our lives; to Mark and Honorine Tepfer for being stalwart friends with humor, exceptional palates, and deep interest; to Philippe Lignon for his friendship; to Gabriell Peltre for his insight on quinces; and to Judy and Billy Kao for their contribution to the better parts of life, namely friendship and comics.

Ellen Cole faithfully stayed up late into the night going over the manuscript and helping me laugh about it all; Megan White was an exceptional addition to our household and helped in every way; Mike and David were willing and hungry tasters. Thanks, too, to Anne Hurley, Cathy Burgett, Jerry Lyman, and Tom and Alyssa Putnam.

I couldn't have done this book without the love and support of my parents Doris and Joseph Herrmann; my sister Mary, brothers Jeff and John with Gayle and Mollie; and my sister Kate and her family. Thank you, too, to Mary Lou Suckling.

Finally, but not finally at all, I thank my husband, Michael, who gives such richness to my life, in every way. And thank you to our son, Joseph, who brightens every single day.

Contents

>···<

THE SALAD BOWL
Le Saladier
55

Crisp green salads refresh your palate after a hearty main course and flavorful composed salads serve as inviting starters. Enjoy Dandelion Green Salad with Croutons, Curried Cauliflower Salad, and a Warm Lentil and Bacon Salad.

THE DAIRY
La Laiterie
91

Fromage Blanc, Warm Camembert Tart, and Fried Egg Crêpes are some of the easy cheese and egg dishes that are as much at home here as they are in France.

THE FARMYARD
La Basse-Cour
115

Luscious chicken and duck preparations reign supreme on the farm table and include simple roasts and stews, a savory Chicken Braised in Beer, and a Duck with Artichokes and Spring Onions.

THE PASTURE
Le Pâturage
161

On the French farm, meat is reserved for special occasions and what delicious occasions they are. Celebrate with Jacqueline Priaulet's Daube, Roast Lamb with Sage, Roast Pork with Potatoes and Onions, and Rillettes Baked in Brioche.

THE SEA
La Mer

France is a seafood-loving country, and Poached Fish with Aïoli, Basque-Style Cod, Pickled Mackerel, and Mussels Cooked in Cider are just a few of the farm favorites included here.

THE FIELD
AND THE GARDEN
Le Champ et le Jardin

Fresh vegetables, at their peak of flavor, are beautifully prepared in the farm kitchen. Savor Asparagus with Two Sauces, Broccoli with Snail Butter, Eggplant with Tomato Coulis, Noémie's Leeks in Red Wine, and perfect French Fries.

THE BREAD OVEN
Le Four à Pain

The breads and tarts in this chapter are reminiscent of the time when most farms had their own bread ovens. Here crusty loaves and bubbling, savory tarts, Quick Brioche, and Tomato and Sweet Pepper Pizza emerge hot and fragrant and irresistible.

TIME FOR
A SNACK
Le Goûter

The four o'clock snack is a French institution, indulged in on farms and in cities, by adults and by children. When late afternoon hunger strikes, do as the French do: Serve up Walnut Butter Cookies, Crêpes with Sugar, Alsatian Coffee Bread, or Hazelnut Pound Cake.

THE CELLAR AND THE PANTRY
La Cave et l'Armoire
393

Homemade wines and liqueurs and jars of jams and jellies line the shelves of the farm cellar and pantry. Brighten your morning toast with such favorites as Apricot and Red Currant Jam and Quince Jelly, and begin dinner with an apéritif of Cherry Wine or Lemon Vebena Liqueur.

EVERYTHING SWEET
Tous ce qui est Sucré
431

No farm meal is complete without a sweet finale. Normandy Apple Tart, Lemon Cake with Strawberries, Sautéed Beignets with Sugared Plums, Cinnamon Rice Pudding, Floating Island, and Chocolate and Cheese Taluas are just a few perfect endings.

THE BASICS
Les Bases
503

Stocks, pastries, Crème Fraîche, and Vanilla Sugar—they're all basics of a farm kitchen.

VISITING THE FARM
522

Here are some tips for planning an overnight stay on some of the farms featured in this book.

INDEX
523

Foreword

>···<

Susan Loomis is a dreamer with the perseverance and determination to follow her dreams. Lucky for us, she generously allows us to tag along on her odysseys. In this, Susan's latest farm adventure, she delivers us to the doorstep of salt-marsh lamb farmers in Normandy, to the fertile olive orchards of Les Baux in Provence; she helps us weather a storm in Brittany in the company of ruddy-faced oyster fishermen, and takes us to the source of all good French food—as everyone knows—the farm kitchen itself. It is here, through Susan, that we learn to make our own red wine vinegar and fashion perfect farm pastry, add a touch of tarragon cream to our cauliflower, and douse steamed fresh zucchini with garlic and parsley. We bathe lentils in white wine with herbs and add a spoonful of black currant liqueur to our baked apples as we fetch them from the oven.

A trained cook and journalist with an insatiable curiosity, the eye of a careful reporter, and an ear tuned in on the latest farm "astuce," Susan Loomis obviously shares with the French farmer a respect and deep adulation for the land and the satisfaction of a job well done. She writes as well as she cooks, not simply saying that the hard-laboring men and women we meet are wonderful and special, but telling us what gives

salt-marsh lamb its delicate flavor (it's their diet of tender grass, diluted with dew) or why the green beans of France simply taste better than those grown anywhere else (it's the French soil).

In an increasingly homogenous and standardized world, Susan opens the door to a universe of real-life farmers imbued with zeal and no lack of modern-day problems. Despite her own love for the country, Susan does not gloss over the realities of today's world and does not paint an overly romantic view of French farm life.

She reminds us, again and again, that the source of pleasure in food comes from flavor. Flavor comes from fruits, vegetables, cheese, fish, meat, and poultry not by accident but only as a result of centuries of respect for the soil and what it will—and what it will not—give of itself. Just as a meal cooked with true love cannot be bad, food grown with passion and attention to detail must almost certainly reap discernible benefits for the farmer as well as the consumer.

French Farmhouse Cookbook encourages us to reflect upon this France so many of us love, this compact and sometimes frustratingly rigid world that often turns inflexibility to its advantage. Where would the glories of French gastronomy be without its tenacious farmers, who so wisely understand the value of tradition? Think of French cuisine without the regal delicacy of the Bresse poultry, the intense salinity of the Breton oyster, the heady grass-green sharpness of its first-of-season olive oil, the soothing warmth of the *tarte Tatin*. Susan shows us once again that this food of legends is also the food of reality. It is a cuisine that fits naturally into everyday modern life and one that can be shared as easily in Galveston as in Gascony, that is as welcome in Cincinnati as it is in Carcassone, and as rewarding in Seattle as it is in Strasbourg.

The crux of the book is, of course, the valuable font of recipes, and it is here that Susan Loomis's voluminous knowledge and sheer love of the land, of gardening, food, cooking, and of course feasting shines through. Many recipes may contain only three or four ingredients, but often it is just that added pinch of salt, the juniper berries the farmer stirs into the carrots, or the extra dose of water the farm wife adds to her pastry that makes the difference between a dish that's ordinary and one that opens our eyes and our palates to gratifying, unanticipated pleasures and flavors.

Susan's vivid writing makes us want to put down the book, head to the market, and race to the kitchen in hopes of sharing her own thrill of seeing that "almost black and toothsome, gelatinous beef glisten" as we serve up another portion of Provençal beef daube.

Susan Loomis has France in her bones. Like a good farm wife who saves every scrap of food, Susan Loomis saves every scrap of information that comes her way, and we, her grateful readers, are the fortunate beneficiaries. This very, very good book is her finest work to date.

—Patricia Wells
Paris, September 1996

Seeking Out the Farmer

➤···❖

The hours I spent squeezing past farm vehicles on tiny French roads and avoiding rocket-powered cars on the *autoroute* afforded me time to think about why I search out food producers where they live and work.

Part of the answer is that I love to meet people, and I am intensely curious about the way they live. I am drawn to farmers because I feel that their work is fundamental. They grapple every day with things that make a difference. They must second-guess the elements and the market, and try to control them both. They balance work and family life, generally exquisitely. They have an ingrained ability to relax at mealtime, tell stories, have fun.

Being with people who are intensely involved in what they do, and who have passions, is compelling enough, but finding individuals who want to share those passions is thrilling. Farmers are like that, for farming is based on sharing, anticipating the needs of others, and producing to meet them.

I enjoy nothing more than spending a day with farmers in field or kitchen, then sitting down to a meal with them. It is a rare privilege that allows me, albeit briefly, to be a part of their lives. It gives me a sense of urgency about where societies are going, and the value placed on tilling the soil.

And that is where my deeper interest lies. For I believe that good-quality soil, respect for those who work it, and vital rural communities are essential to a balanced society. In the world I am familiar with, which comprises the United States and Europe, I feel we are moving so fast and in such helter-skelter fashion that we do more than take such things for granted, we often overlook them entirely.

In our competitive race for progress and advancement, we are demanding more goods, more excitement, more food. Yet, we have become terribly cavalier about quality—that is, flavor and texture. We opt to go along with those who pull the strings of international food production, including the developers of seed varieties, hybridized plants, fertilizers, and other synthetic chemicals used in agriculture, those who are interested solely in quantity, durability, attractiveness in the marketplace.

Technologically, these developments

produce miracles, yet they do nothing for the fabric of rural life, nor for the quality of our food. In fact, as growers turn to hybrids in order to satisfy increasingly narrow demands by the consumer, produce becomes less interesting, less flavorful.

There has always been another side to agriculture in France. Farmers on small family farms growing produce from seeds they have saved themselves have always been the backbone of French agriculture, and much of what is wonderful about France—its villages, stunning markets, gorgeous rural vistas, unparalleled restaurants—all exists thanks to these farms.

As one drives from beautiful village to beautiful village, all appears well. But scratch the surface and the same developments we've seen in American agriculture exist in France. The official byword in French agriculture—and one can't really discuss French agriculture without including the European Economic Community, the EEC—has become quantity. Large farms are buying up small ones, which heralds the gradual decline of the small family farm.

As an official in the French ministry of agriculture in Paris told me, "I'm sorry to say, money reserved for agriculture is going increasingly to larger concerns. We've got to think about quantity. Small farmers don't really interest the government." This young man, from a small farm himself, went on to say: "It's all related to money, and we've got to be competitive."

He spoke with a regret he readily admitted. He also told me no one else he knew in the ministry shared his regret. All efforts are focused on becoming a more powerful economic world power.

Watching these developments over the past several years, talking with farmers late into the evening about how they are faring, I fear for France. France has always been an agricultural society, the breadbasket of Europe. Within its borders one experiences a tremendous variety of climates, and the foods that go with them. I find it dispiriting that the French government and citizenry are willing to let their agricultural wealth, their very identity, melt into the grand technological age of "progress."

I see more and more farmers opening their homes to tourists, which in itself is a wonderful development. It allows people to get to know the country where it truly lives. But I worry that French farms will become "toy" farms, where tourism prevails over actual production. I've already been to farms where farmers have given up tilling the soil in favor of offering more rooms to visitors, simply because the latter pays better. One cannot blame the farmer, who does what must be done to survive. But this development does not bode well for the future, as farmers increasingly encourage their children to either leave the farm or become innkeepers instead of producers, and as one member of a couple works outside the home and supermarket complexes replace the village center.

My spirits rise when I go to my market, however, and buy stunning produce from the hands of the people who produce it.

As France swings one way, I can only hope it will swing the other; that if there is a farm crisis it will awaken the French public to what it is in danger of losing. France must begin to work hard to save its farms, not just for tourists, but for its own health and well-being.

This is my fervent hope, as I walk by stalls of fragrant produce. I feel a personal investment in the health of agriculture, in both the U.S. and France. My research is personally satisfying, of course, but I also feel compelled to try and bring the producer and consumer together in a way that might make a difference. I like to tell their stories, to introduce them through the easy and delicious vehicle of food.

In France, tradition informs every aspect of food, from its production to the rousing meals around the farm table. Pride in that tradition, and in good hard work that produces fabulous food, is still vital and alive. Tradition can be a beautiful thing, for it can act as a springboard for development. In France, tradition gives the French, and French producers particularly, the confidence to go forward. It lives in them.

I have tried to communicate this within the pages of this book. I hope that the richness, the fabric, the color of French farm life comes through, tempts you, makes you want to run to the kitchen and bring the aromas and flavors of France to your table. I hope that by meeting some of the producers in this book you will appreciate even more keenly their hard work, their vital role in society, their wonderfully flavorful food.

I hope, too, that everyone who reads this book will be infused with the desire to buy from farmers whenever they can, and that the experience of going to markets in places where they exist will be enriching.

THE FOOD

The food in this book is the basis of French cuisine. It is the *cuisine du terroir*, and it is to these recipes and the people who produce them that the great chefs of France return for inspiration.

Here you will find familiar recipes, each with the stamp of the person who gave it to me. You may be surprised at how simple they really are. But it follows, for on the farm there is no "kitchen help." French farm food offers intense and pure flavor; what counts in French farm cooking is the quality of the ingredients, the nuances of their combination.

Where is the beef, you might ask? Beef producers in France don't keep the meat they raise, they sell it. Beef was, and still is, reserved for special occasions. Aside from a few classics—*daube, pot-au-feu, grillades de boeuf, baekeoffe*—there were few beef recipes to be had.

Why so much poultry? Every farm has a *basse-cour,* or farmyard, where chickens, ducks, and geese run free. Poultry is easy and inexpensive to raise, so it is a standard on the French farm table. And as for vegetables, well, they grow right next to the farmhouse, and are there for the picking.

THE RECIPES

So many times when I was with a farm cook in the kitchen, furiously taking notes, she'd laugh. "I don't know how much I add, I just do what my mother, my neighbor, my grandmother showed me to do," she'd say.

Nonetheless, I measured and remeasured, tasted and fussed to get these recipes as exact as possible, to faithfully reproduce the flavors of the French farm kitchen. I then sent them to the U.S. to be tested again, and the faxes that flew with questions and comments all had one single aim—to make the food in this book simpler, more delicious, more authentic for you.

I guarantee if you follow these recipes to the letter you'll be satisfied beyond measure. But don't feel confined. Use them as a guide, adjusting where you like. A recipe is a method of procedure, and within there is a

great deal of room to move. So do as the great chefs of France do—go to the farm for inspiration. Cook the real food of France, with the French farm cook at your elbow.

ASTUCE

An *astuce* is a clever trick, and it is the *astuces* of the French farm cook that give farm food its depth of flavor. You will find astuces sprinkled throughout the pages of this book: Transmitted directly from the farm, they will help you simplify, and teach you to encourage the best from your ingredients.

The most important *astuce* of all is to obtain quality ingredients, and to use them while they are still fresh. Freshness is the key to wonderful food, and what you invest in it will be saved in time and effort in the kitchen. Your reward will be flavor.

This book is a personal journey to the French farm. I lost count of the number of farms I visited and kilometers I traveled. All I know is that I could spend the rest of my life researching, and even now, as I approach the end, I have a list of unvisited farms. But as I've already learned to say, a book is never finished, merely abandoned to meet a deadline.

Enjoy this "visit" to the French farm. You will experience some fabulous meals and rousing good times. This is my promise to you. *Bon appétit!*

—Susan Herrmann Loomis
Louviers, September 1996

VENEZ PRENDRE L'APERO

Come Have a Drink and a Bite

On the French farm, the apéritif is served at table, and as soon as guests take their places, the bottles come out of the armoire, like family treasures: *vin de pêche, vin de noix, vin de cerises, vin d'orange* . . . home-made apéritifs, usually accompanied by the obligatory bottles of whiskey, pastis, and Picon (a bitter orange drink).

Glasses clink with an *"A la santé"* ("To health"), and everyone takes a sip. If food is served, it is simple and light, like the little dishes in this chapter.

More often than not, *l'heure d'apéritif* stretches on into the evening, and the snacks that accompanied that first drink somehow evolve into a full meal. In fact, I've learned that being invited over for *un verre* often means an invitation for dinner. It is as though the hosts are hedging their bets. If they find themselves tired or ready to end the evening, then *un verre* and an assortment of snacks will be it, and no one will feel slighted or disappointed. But if they find themselves relaxed and in good company, then the meal stretches on, and soon whatever was to be served to the family emerges from the kitchen and everyone settles in. It's a pleasant tradition, with an element of surprise, and one that is easy to adopt.

So if you'd like to do as they do on the French farm, make an assortment of apéritif wines to stock your armoire (recipes for several are included in the pantry chapter—"La Cave"), and have some of these little dishes on hand to "open the appetite."

Monique's Anchoïade
Anchoïade de Monique

→ ••• ←

You have to love anchovies to love this Provençal appetizer. It tickles your palate awake and makes it dash in three directions at once—toward the anchovies, the fruity olive oil, the pungent garlic. And there is even a fourth, if you include the delicate slash of vinegar that brings everything up a notch.

This recipe is from the kitchen of Monique Tourrette (see also her Tapenade on page 4), who serves it as a dip for fresh vegetables, traditionally at Christmastime. In winter I serve it with fresh, crisp slices of fennel or celery, both then at their sweetest. In spring and summer there are no limits: red and green bell peppers, fat slices of cucumber, wedges of not-quite-soft ripe tomatoes, fava beans, green beans, carrot rounds . . . I always also serve small, thick slices of freshly baked country bread for dipping—on them, the purity of the *anchoïade* becomes almost sinful.

When I'm really in the mood for anchovies, I follow an old Provençal tradition and toast a good-size slice of bread for each guest, then top each slice with an anchovy fillet or two. The procedure is this: Dip a small piece of untoasted bread into the *anchoïade*, pass it over your slice of anchovy-topped toast so any excess *anchoïade* drips onto the toast, and then, stopping to mash a bit of the anchovy off the toast onto the bread, eat the bread.

When all of the *anchoïade* is gone, you are left with a luscious garlic-, anchovy-, and oil-soaked piece of toast.

I prefer salt-cured anchovies to those preserved in oil because they are firm, and the integrity of their meat gives a rustic quality to this *anchoïade*. They are still quite salty after being soaked, though as a friend put it, "It's such a good saltiness." However, your own taste for salt will determine what you use. Milk is the preferred soaking liquid because it absorbs salt without making the fillets watery.

Serve this with a lightly chilled Collioure.

ASTUCE . . . .

• Anchoïade is not a vision of loveliness—the anchovies tend to sink while the oil tends to rise. Nonetheless, there are few things more enjoyable for dipping fresh crisp vegetables and freshly toasted bread. My suggestion for serving? Use a smallish dark-hued bowl, and the looks won't matter a bit. All you'll notice is the fine, sharply attuned flavor.

. . . .

FOR THE ANCHOÏADE

40 anchovy fillets or 20 whole anchovies
*   preferably in salt, washed and, if whole,*
*   bones removed*
½ cup (125 ml) milk
½ cup (125 ml) extra-virgin olive oil
2 cloves garlic, peeled, green germ
*   removed, and minced*
1 teaspoon best-quality red wine
*   vinegar*

FOR SERVING

12 anchovy fillets
2 tablespoons milk
6 large slices plus 18 strips (2 x 1 inch;
*   5 x 2½ cm) country bread*
4 fennel bulbs, trimmed and cut into
*   ½-inch-wide (1¼ cm) strips*
Freshly ground black pepper

1. Preheat the broiler.

2. Prepare the *anchoïade:* Place the 40 anchovy fillets in a small shallow bowl and cover with the ½ cup (125 ml) milk. Let sit for 15 to 20 minutes. Then drain the anchovies and rinse them quickly under running water. Gently pat them dry.

3. Transfer the anchovies to a small saucepan and place it over medium heat. Slowly add the oil, breaking up the anchovies as you stir so they form a paste.

4. Add the garlic, then the vinegar. Cook, stirring, just until the mixture is blended, 2 to 3 minutes. The anchovies won't be entirely smooth and the sauce won't be emulsified—it will be a somewhat rough-looking mixture. Keep warm over very low heat.

5. Prepare the toasts: Place the 12 anchovy fillets in a small shallow bowl and cover with the 2 tablespoons milk. Soak, drain, and pat dry as in step 2 above.

6. Toast the 6 large slices of bread on both sides under the broiler. Top each of the toasts with 2 anchovy fillets. Place the anchovy-topped toasts in a basket lined with a linen or cotton napkin and keep warm.

7. Arrange the fennel strips on a large serving platter.

8. To serve, generously season the *anchoïade* with pepper, stir, then transfer it to a warmed serving bowl. Serve the fennel, bread, and toast alongside. (Note that the *anchoïade* will not be emulsified, and that the oil will rise to the surface.)

9. To eat the *anchoïade*, dip the fennel and the untoasted bread into the *anchoïade*, stirring as you dip so you get anchovies and garlic as well as oil. Follow the instructions in the headnote to make the most of your toast.

6 appetizer servings

Tapenade

→ ··· ←

Tapenade is certainly the most popular appetizer in Provence. There are dozens of varieties at every Provençal market—large inky mounds of this fragrant and luscious purée. Made with aged Provençal olives, which themselves are served as appetizers, it keeps for many days in the refrigerator—if you can manage to resist it for that long.

I love to make it because it evokes all the heat and aromas of summer in Provence, when the taste buds ache for salt and gutsy flavor. Monique Tourrette, who lives in Venasque, shared this basic recipe with me. Though the heat was bouncing off the soil, we were both salivating as we talked about tapenade. "You can even freeze this if you want," she said.

It is delicious served as is, with freshly toasted country bread. Once you've had it that way, experiment with it—spread it under the skin of a chicken just before you roast it, or use it in poultry stuffing. Try tossing a couple of tablespoons with some freshly steamed new potatoes, or using it on pizza with sun-ripened tomatoes. The possibilities are nearly endless.

ASTUCES . . . .

• *Soaking canned anchovy fillets in milk is the surest way to ease the salt out of them. While it won't take away all the salt, the milk absorbs a great deal of it, leaving the flavor and texture of the anchovy intact. (You can also rinse them in cool running water, which will remove some salt, but not much.)*

• *If you've kept tapenade in the refrigerator for several days, taste it before serving. Garlic fades slightly over time and you may need to add a lot more.*

. . . .

8 to 10 anchovy fillets (see Note)
¼ cup (60 ml) milk
2 cups (300 g) Greek or French black olives, pitted
1 tablespoon capers, drained
1 teaspoon Dijon mustard
1 clove garlic, peeled, green germ removed, and minced
Freshly ground black pepper
6 tablespoons olive oil

1. Place the anchovies in a small shallow bowl and cover them with the milk. Let them

sit for 15 minutes. Then quickly drain them, rinse with water, and pat dry.

2. Place all the ingredients except the olive oil in a food processor and process to form a thick purée. With the processor running, add the oil in a thin stream until it is thoroughly incorporated into the mixture. Taste for seasoning, and adjust if necessary.

1⅓ cups (325 ml) tapenade

NOTE: The recipe calls for 8 to 10 anchovy fillets. If you like anchovy flavor, which can be pungent but here adds an earthy, undeniably fish-flavored dimension, use 10 fillets. If you're unsure about your penchant for them, start with 8 and then add more if you like.

Tapenade with Tuna
Tapenade au Thon

Adding freshly cooked tuna to tapenade, a common Provençal practice, gives it substance, amplifies its flavor, turns it into something quite different from plain tapenade. I like to include this in a trio of tapenades to serve as an appetizer, along with freshly toasted bread and such vegetables as fennel, new carrots, and fresh green beans.

Since the olives and the anchovies are already salty, it is doubtful you will need to add any salt to your tapenade. However, it's best to taste and season according to your preference.

Serve a chilled Jurançon Sec along with this.

ASTUCE . . . .
• *To pit an olive, slit it down one side and press on it. The pit should just pop out.*

. . . .

1 recipe Tapenade (see preceding recipe)
4 ounces (125 g) fresh tuna
3 tablespoons water
3 sprigs fresh thyme, or ¼ teaspoon dried
1 clove garlic, peeled
1 small shallot, quartered
11 small fresh basil or flat-leaf parsley leaves, for garnish

1. Prepare the tapenade as directed and set aside in a serving bowl.

2. Place the tuna in a small skillet. Add the water, thyme, garlic, and shallot. Cover and cook over medium heat, checking occasionally to be sure the tuna doesn't dry out, until it is opaque through, 4 to 5 minutes. Remove from the heat and let cool.

3. When the tuna has cooled, flake it into the tapenade, then mix well so it is thoroughly incorporated into the mixture. Garnish with basil or parsley leaves, and serve.

2 cups (500 ml)

Basil Tapenade

Tapenade au Basilic

>···←

It's hard to choose a favorite tapenade—I love them all. But this one speaks most of a Provençal market, where one wanders amidst the aromas of basil, pungent garlic, and fragrant, shiny olives.

I make this in summer, when basil is plentiful in the garden. It keeps for at least a week in the refrigerator, though some of the basil flavor dissipates. If necessary, I add a bit more basil just before serving, and I always serve it on a bed of large fresh basil leaves. Serve this as part of a trio of tapenades, along with freshly toasted bread.

Try a Jurançon Sec or a Bandol Rosé alongside.

1 recipe Tapenade (page 4)
1 cup (loosely packed) fresh basil leaves

1. Prepare the tapenade as directed, adding the basil leaves after the oil and processing until they are thoroughly incorporated and all you can see in the tapenade is tiny green flecks. Taste for seasoning, and adjust if necessary.

2. Transfer the tapenade to a small bowl, and serve.

About 1⅓ cups (325 ml)

N O T E : The tapenade will keep well for several weeks in an airtight container in the refrigerator, though it will lose some of its flavor. To serve, remove it from the refrigerator at least 1 hour ahead of time.

Stuffed Prunes
Prunes Farcis

Marie Fuméry lives near the city of Agen, a small paradise surrounded by low-growing plum trees. She and her husband, Etienne, have six children, help run a nursery school in one of the outbuildings of the farm, and raise and sell prunes, wheat, and garbanzo beans, which they raise biodynamically.

Despite a schedule that would daunt most people, Marie, who is slight, blond, and demure, cooks food with surprising depth and variety. Because she has a ready supply of prunes at hand, many of her dishes incorporate them.

These she serves as an appetizer, and I have adopted them because the combination is perfect—the tart creaminess of blue cheese plays perfectly off the dense sweetness of the prunes. I like to serve these with a glass of Champagne, though any good-quality dry white wine makes a wonderful accompaniment.

While these are best heated for an instant in a searing oven, they are wonderful at room temperature, too.

4 ounces (125 g) blue cheese, such as Bleu
  d'Auvergne or Fourme d'Ambert
26 pitted prunes
Small handful of flat-leaf parsley leaves

1. Preheat the oven to 450°F (230°C).
2. Break off bite-size pieces of the cheese and stuff them into the prunes, wrapping the prune around the cheese so it stays inside. You will have to judge how much cheese to put in each prune—roughly ½ teaspoon per prune. But if you find yourself running out, just use less—if you have too much, place more in each prune.

3. Set the prunes on a heatproof serving dish—just about any plate will do, as it will be in the oven for less than 1 minute.

4. Mince the parsley.

5. Place the stuffed prunes in the oven just long enough for them to heat slightly—the cheese shouldn't melt at all—about 30 seconds. Remove from the oven, sprinkle lightly with the parsley, and serve. If necessary, reheat them before offering seconds.

26 stuffed prunes

NOTE: If you can't find imported French blue cheeses, use either Oregon blue or Maytag blue, or, in a pinch, Danish blue. They will all be quite delicious!

Chestnuts in Gascony

In Gascony, chestnut season arrives just after the corn has dried on the stalks, when night falls quickly and turns chill. Traditionally, farm families assembled in the evenings at that time of year for *despelocaire*, shucking the ears. Work was the theme of the evening, socializing the rhythm that made the hours fly by.

"Often we'd be twenty to thirty people in the barn," says Denise Lascourrèges, a farmer from Poudenas, a tiny Gascon village. "Those were the days—we'd shuck the ears, and when the whole pile was finished, we'd eat chestnuts, melon jam and baguette, and drink *le bourrat*." *Le bourrat* is young wine that Gascons look forward thirstily to each fall. It's really just slightly fermented grape juice—the sugars have only just begun to give it a gentle fizz. It's always well chilled, drawn right from huge vats, usually out in the barn.

"*Le bourrat* is just the thing to help with the *étouffé chrétien* that chestnuts give you,"

says Mme. Lascourrèges, referring to the smothering thirst engendered by chestnuts.

It goes down easily. "So easily that even I, who don't drink wine, would have a spinning head by the end of the evening," she adds, laughing.

When the neighbors had finished at one farm, they'd go on to the next the following night, until all the corn in the neighborhood was shucked and stored.

Now corn is mechanically harvested and shucked, which allows farmers time for other things. While she welcomes the efficiency, Mme. Lascourrèges mourns the passing of those crisp fall evenings with neighbors and friends.

Her husband, André, agrees. "The old days may have been harder, but they were more sociable," he says.

The Lascourrèges and their friends still indulge in chestnuts, boiled with a fig leaf or star anise (page 10), and *le bourrat* now and then, although instead of shucking corn, the men play cards and the women sit in the parlor and talk, often about the old days. "In other parts of the world I suppose people eat peanuts or popcorn," Mme. Lascourrèges says. "For us it's chestnuts and *le bourrat*."

THE CHESTNUT

Chestnut trees are magnificent, their leaves spreading gracefully, their fruit bunched among the limbs by twos and threes. The fruit is ripe when the spiky outer casings have a golden hue, and it takes just a quick tap to release a shower. The chestnut trees that grow in France are native to Italy, brought by Romans. Now they grow naturally, particularly in the Ardèche region.

Today the fruit of the *châtaignier* is regarded as something of a luxury, but the chestnut used to be called *le pain des pauvres*, bread for the poor. Families with little else were able to harvest chestnuts in abundance and lived on them throughout the year. Those that weren't consumed fresh were dried and later ground into flour to produce a heavy bread, or were used in soups or porridges. They were even used as a form of currency in certain parts of the country.

Parmentier, the man who made the potato accessible to the French in the 18th century, attempted to do the same with the chestnut. He gave directions for harvesting and processing chestnuts, though with uncertain success.

Chestnuts still have an unstable place in French agriculture, in part because they are produced less expensively in other countries. Production has dwindled in the past ten years by about one third. Many of the chestnuts in the French marketplace are imported from other European countries, notably Italy.

Much research is being done in France, however, and several new chestnut varieties have been introduced in the past twenty years. Though they still take four years to produce a viable crop, in general the production is larger. A movement is afoot to encourage farmers and gardeners to plant chestnut trees. While they may take time to come into production, they will thrive for centuries. Not a bad investment.

Regardless of where the chestnuts come from, the moment the air turns crisp, gorgeous, shiny brown mounds are displayed in the markets. In Paris and other cities around the country, the air is filled with the woodsy aroma of chestnuts roasting over coals.

At the market, chestnuts are sold under two different names: *marron* and *châtaigne*. The fruits are essentially the same, and they both issue from the same tree. But when cut open, the *châtaigne* has a thin skin dividing its meat into two pieces. The meat of the *marron* is whole, and thus is much more highly sought after for candying and roasting because it keeps its shape. It is impossible to tell which is which without cutting into them, though myths abound about ways to tell the difference!

In order to discover the composition of a crop, a sample is taken and cut into. If the crop is no more than twelve percent *châtaignes*, it can be sold as *marrons*. Any more than that and it must be sold as *châtaignes*, which fetch a lower price.

Boiled Chestnuts with Star Anise
Châtaignes Bouillies aux Anis Étoilé

≻···≺

66 "Mme. Châtaignes" (Denise Lascourrèges, see page 8) from Gascony gave me this little hint for boiling chestnuts: "Add star anise, and you'll have a taste you'll never forget." It is wonderful, indeed—the star anise echoes the sweetness of the chestnuts and gives them the tiniest hint of the Middle East. The cuisine of Gascony owes much to the Middle East for it was on the spice route, and many exotic spices that are not found in other areas of France have made an indelible mark here.

Serve these as an appetizer, with Champagne or other sparkling wine. Failing the curve-bladed chestnut knives, paring knives are useful for peeling the chestnuts.

1 pound (500 g) unshelled chestnuts
4 whole star anise

Place the chestnuts in a large saucepan and cover them with water. Add the star anise, cover, and bring to a boil. Reduce the heat so the chestnuts are boiling gently, and continue cooking until they are tender (pierce one with a skewer), about 17 minutes. Drain, discard the star anise, and serve, with a paring knife alongside (see "Peeling Chestnuts," page 45).

About 6 servings

Springtime's Best Little Dish
Le Meilleur Petit Plat du Printemps

On those fine spring days when generous radishes have pushed their leaves through the soil and their small red bulbs into the ground, there is nothing better than to indulge in one of France's finest snacks.

1 bunch fresh radishes, rinsed well
 and patted dry
Unsalted butter
Fine sea salt
Freshly made Sourdough Bread
 (page 316), thickly sliced

1. Leave the radishes intact, with leaves and roots still attached. Arrange them in a flat basket or on a large serving platter.

2. Place the butter in a small dish, packing it in firmly. Place the salt in another small dish.

3. To eat, slather a slice of bread with butter. Pick up a radish, dip it in salt, and eat it, with bites of buttered bread in between.

Never enough

Pickled Eggplant
Aubergines en Vinaigre

❧ • • • ❧

Eggplant looks so beautiful at the market, with its tight purplish-black skin and seductive shape, that I can never resist buying lots of it. Then I get it home and sauté, grill, bake it—and still have leftovers. Here is a preparation that takes care of those, in true Provençal tradition.

This pickled eggplant is based on a recipe from a wonderful collection published by the Farmer's Insurance Cooperative in the Vaucluse department of Provence. It is tart and herb-rich, making it a nice appetizer served with fresh Sourdough Bread (see Index) or as a dip with fresh vegetables. You might also want to dab it on cooked pizza or toss it into pasta. It will keep well for several months, and it improves with age.

4 medium eggplants, ends trimmed,
 cut into ½-inch (1¼ cm)
 cubes
4 teaspoons coarse sea salt
3 cups (750 ml) best-quality red wine
 vinegar
4 cloves garlic, 2 unpeeled, 2 peeled
10 black peppercorns
15 sprigs fresh thyme, rinsed and patted
 dry
3 imported bay leaves
1½ cups (375 ml) olive oil

1. Place the eggplant cubes in a colander, sprinkle them with the salt, and let drain for 1 to 1½ hours. Rinse the eggplant quickly and pat dry.

2. Place the eggplant in a large heavy saucepan and add the vinegar, unpeeled garlic cloves, 5 of the peppercorns, 1 handful of the thyme, and 2 of the bay leaves. Bring to a boil over medium-high heat. Then reduce the heat and simmer for 20 minutes. Drain and set aside to cool.

3. When the eggplant is cool, place it in a jar large enough to hold it comfortably. Add the remaining handful of thyme, the peeled garlic cloves, and the remaining bay leaf and 5 peppercorns, gently pushing the ingredients down into the eggplant. Slowly pour in the olive oil, inserting a chopstick or stainless-steel knife down along the side of the jar, pushing aside the eggplant pieces as necessary so the oil will penetrate everywhere. Cover and refrigerate for 3 to 4 weeks before serving. Check occasionally to be sure the eggplant is covered with a thin layer of oil; add more oil if necessary.

About 3 cups (750 ml)

Oysters on the Half Shell
Les Huîtres

There are many ways to eat and enjoy an oyster, but freshly shucked on the half shell has to be the best! Here follow ideas for oysters, best shared with a crowd of oyster fans.

2 dozen oysters, shells well rinsed
Fresh seaweed or greens, such as Swiss chard or escarole
1 lemon, cut into 8 wedges
Freshly ground black pepper
Fine sea salt, preferably fleur de sel *from Brittany*

1. No longer than an hour before serving, shuck the oysters. Place them, each on a half shell, on a bed of crushed ice that is covered with either seaweed or greens (you may set them directly in the ice if you're going to serve them immediately; if they're going to

And the Best Oyster Is . . .

>·<

*A*s for which French oyster is best, well, the best is what you have in front of you at the moment. For although the French have a complex system to denote an oyster's size and quality, a certain cynicism surrounds it. The label claires, *which refers to fattening beds in the Marennes-Oléron area, is considered a sign of high quality. Today, however, an oyster with that label might actually have been raised elsewhere and have stopped in Marennes-Oléron*

only long enough to pick up a label, without ever actually dipping its shell in a claire.

This doesn't mean that the quality of French oysters has diminished. It just means the old labeling systems are being tampered with and it's the quantity of top-quality oysters that has diminished. As is always true, if you're going to eat oysters and you're not right on the bay, know your vendor. A trustworthy oyster vendor will give you good, reliable quality.

---

sit, they will get too cold and must be protected from direct contact with the ice).

2. Place the lemon wedges, the pepper, and the salt in separate dishes and pass them

along with the oysters, to be used, if desired, *separately, not together.*

4 servings

Oyster Stew
Blanquette d'Huîtres

>···<

This is an oyster stew unlike any you've ever tasted. François Cadoret of Locmariaquer in southern Brittany gave me the idea (an uncle in his family makes this regularly), and I find it brilliant. A typical blanquette because of the cream and egg yolk, it is actually quite unusual, since oysters in France are rarely cooked and even more rarely served in this fashion.

I suggest shucking your own oysters for this dish, to get the best, most intense flavor. However, you may use shucked oysters if they are impeccably fresh. You will notice that there is no salt or pepper in this recipe—none is needed.

ASTUCE . . . .

• *Strain the oyster liquor through dampened cheesecloth. That way, the cheesecloth won't absorb the liquor; since it is already dampened, it will release it all.*

. . . .

¾ cup (185 ml) oyster liquor, strained if
    necessary
¼ cup (60 ml) water
½ cup (125 ml) Crème Fraîche (page 520)
    or heavy (whipping) cream
2 large egg yolks
24 medium oysters, shucked
1 tablespoon minced fresh chives

1. Place the oyster liquor and the water in a medium-size saucepan over medium heat, and bring slowly to a simmer. Whisk

Ancient Finds
➔•←

O ne of M. Cadoret's favorite activities is strolling on the sand right in front of his office, before the tide covers it. There he can stub the end of his boot on the remnants of ancient wooden pilings. He showed me one, jagged but firm, that stuck six inches out of the sand.

"We've found wooden boxes with grillwork in the bottom that date to Roman times," he said. "The Romans filled them with oysters and set them on these pilings. It gives you a funny feeling."

That is Brittany, full of ancient echoes and mystery. For M. Cadoret, such finds keep life in perspective.

together the crème fraîche and the egg yolks; then whisk them into the oyster liquor. Reduce the heat to medium-low and whisk the mixture constantly until it thickens, about 4 minutes.

2. Add the oysters to the mixture, and stir gently until they are hot through and their mantles (the edges of the oysters) are loosely furled, 2 to 3 minutes.

3. Immediately divide the blanquette among four warmed shallow serving bowls. Top each with a sprinkling of chives, and serve.

4 servings

A Little Story About Oysters

It was a blustery January morning in Locmariaquer, on the southern coast of Brittany, and the sun was putting on a spectacular light show among the clouds.

"You know what they say about the Breton climate," said François Cadoret, an oyster grower. "You can have all four seasons in a day."

M. Cadoret was leading me through his oyster flats in the Baie de Quiberon, his collar turned up, his hat pulled down, only his gray-streaked beard and wild strands of hair showing. The spray was cold on my face. Through the thick rubber of my boots and a double layer of socks, I could still sense the frigid water of the bay.

We stopped to talk with a yellow-slickered colleague, Alain Boderin, who raises the deep-cupped oyster (*Crassostrea gigas*) referred to in France as *japonaise* or *creuse*. The oysters are grown in plastic mesh bags set on metal tables about 8 inches (20 cm) above the gravelly sea bottom.

When the tide is out, as it was that morning, the oysters are exposed to the air. Sensible creatures, they keep their shells shut so their lifeblood—the salt water they need for survival—doesn't drain out. When they're underwater again, they open and gulp up to 400 gallons (1500 l) a day, filtering plankton for sustenance.

This method allows the oysters to eat in the most plankton-rich area of the bay, without fear of predators or overcrowding. It also teaches them to keep their shells shut, a skill which will prove vital later on as they travel from bay to market. If the shell stays shut, an oyster can live out of water for up to three weeks.

Like many who cultivate the *creuse*, M. Boderin gets the babies, or *naissans*, from Arcachon, near Bordeaux, where the natural production is plentiful. To give them room, he transfers them to larger mesh bags as they grow. They are ready for market in about three years.

Until 1860 the only oyster in France was *Ostrea edulis*, the flat, or *plate*, oyster, an indigenous species. That year a ship filled with cupped oysters from Portugal dis-

(continued)

charged its cargo during a storm, and from then on the *plates* had company, which were then called *portugaises*.

In the 1970s the *portugaises* were destroyed by disease. Growers who had become dependent on this fast-growing species turned to Japan for replacements. Now the *creuse*, hardier and faster-growing than the *plate*, is the mainstay of the industry.

M. Boderin cultivates only the *creuse*. M. Cadoret raises both varieties.

Discussing the oyster industry in France with M. Cadoret, one thing becomes clear: It has undergone unimaginable catastrophes and survived to tell the tale.

He is the third generation to cultivate oysters in this same spot, and he shakes his head when he talks about the freezes, diseases, competition, and other difficulties the industry has suffered just in his lifetime.

"I see it as very simple," he said. "We've done some stupid things. We've survived and learned. Now we keep it simple."

He doesn't buy oyster seed from hatcheries, as many growers still do, because he's convinced diseases come from that source. Instead, he collects his own wild *plate* seed and buys wild *creuse* seed from Arcachon.

Right after capture, the *naissans* are brought to the shallow waters of the bay, placed in plastic mesh tubes that are attached to metal tables much like those belonging to M. Boderin, and left to grow for eighteen months.

We walked farther out into the water toward one of the Cadoret barges, where a crew hefted tables from the water and tapped off the oysters. That afternoon it would "sow" them in the bay.

There they stay for eighteen months, until barges dredge them from the bay bottom and bring them to holding containers in shallow water, where they are calibrated and sold.

The *plates* raised naturally on the bay bottom, where they filter a mere 100 gallons (375 l) of water a day, grow to full size in four to five years. Highly prized, they are extremely delicate and very susceptible to weather and disease.

The *plate* is most familiarly known as the Belon oyster, named for a nearby estuary. Many consumers are under the impression that only *plates* from that estuary can be called "Belons," a name which holds much cachet in France. But the name can be applied to any flat oyster.

"Relatively few oysters are now raised in the Belon," M. Cadoret said. "It would be impossible to limit the production to that estuary."

He scooped up a *plate*, pried it open, and handed it to me. I slid the oyster into my mouth, and as its exquisite flavor flooded my taste buds, I could hardly tell where the sea ended and I began.

The tide was coming in and we headed back. "If we stay out much longer, the water will be over our heads," M. Cadoret said with a laugh.

YVON MADEC

In northern Brittany, not far from Morlaix, the oyster situation is different. There Yvon Madec raises *plates* and *creuses* in a tiny community called Prat-ar-Coum, using methods evolved through three generations of his family's involvement in the industry.

M. Madec is proud of his *plates*, for he raises them with few casualties. His secret is to buy them nearly mature from Great Britain, when they are sturdy and essentially disease-resistant. He puts them in *parcs aux huîtres*, or fattening beds, on the river outside his office and six months later, after they've gotten a veneer of Prat-ar-Coum flavor, he harvests them. The resulting oyster lacks the gutsiness of its southern cousin, but is pleasant nonetheless.

Though M. Madec is one of the best known names in Breton oysters, he long ago branched out into other shellfish, recognizing the difficulty of depending on one capricious crop. He markets a variety of shellfish by mail, some of which he raises himself, others which he buys and resells.

Both kingpins in the Breton oyster business, M. Cadoret and M. Madec have their individual methods, their beliefs about oysters, and an undeniable passion and dedication. Each has survived similar difficulties—storms, disease, water pollution, the grounding of the oil tanker *Amoco Cadiz*—to emerge strong, committed, and wily in the ways of business.

Despite what nature has brought, they continue in a precarious profession. They're prospering, to be sure, but each has other motives. M. Madec is a deeply concerned environmentalist. M. Cadoret wants the profession to survive and wants the Cadoret family, which began oystering in 1880, to remain a part of it.

Thanks to the courage and persistence of these men and their Breton colleagues, Breton oysters are increasingly available and their quality remains high. Oyster lovers in France can continue to enjoy the succulent fruits of their labor, and the waters of Brittany look bright for the future.

Warm Oysters with Balsamic Vinegar

Les Huîtres Tièdes au Vinaigre Balsamique

I got this recipe from François Lecallo while we were standing on the banks of his salt marsh on the Breton shore. We were talking about favorite things to eat, and this ranked high on his list. "I usually like my oysters raw, on the half shell," he said. "But this—you've got to try this."

I did, and I agree with him. It allows the oysters' fresh, briny flavor to shine right through.

Giving specific quantities here is difficult, and the amounts of butter and vinegar are really too large for the number of oysters. But any less and it becomes too awkward for serving, so unless you want to season the oysters directly from the bottle and the pan (which I don't recommend since everyone will want to do their own), try these amounts. You can easily double the number of oysters and still serve the same amounts of vinegar and butter.

Remember that less is more. You want just a touch of vinegar and butter so the heavenly flavor of oysters comes through.

2 dozen small to medium oysters, scrubbed,
  in the shell
4 tablespoons (½ stick; 60 g) unsalted
  butter, melted
¼ cup (60 ml) best-quality balsamic vinegar

1. Preheat the oven to 450°F (230°C).

2. Arrange the oysters on a baking sheet, cup side down (if necessary, set them on a bed of coarse salt to keep them stable).

3. Place the oysters in the oven and bake just until the shells open, about 5 minutes. Remove them from the oven and, using an oyster knife, cut the muscle inside the top shell of each oyster to free the shell, and discard the shell.

4. To eat the oysters, first drizzle just a touch (less than ⅛ teaspoon) of butter into an oyster, then 2 to 3 drops of vinegar, and slurp it up!

2 to 4 servings, depending on the enthusiasm of the eaters

Extraordinary Grilled Cheese
Croûtes de Fromage

→•••←

This flavorful appetizer comes straight from the mountains of Jura, where Comté cheese reigns supreme. Hearty yet sophisticated, it fits with the craggy mountains where hikers crowd the slopes in summer and winter brings cross-country and downhill skiers.

Sometimes I make this for lunch, for it is popular with all ages. You must use a hearty bread, either Sourdough Bread or a *pain de campagne* with a close crumb, so that it can soak up the custard without falling apart. Cut the "croûtes" in pieces, as described, or serve the sandwiches whole, along with a crisp green salad.

Try a Vin de Jura or a Riesling alongside.

2 large eggs
1 cup (250 ml) lightly fruity white wine,
*   such as Vin de Jura or Riesling*
Sea salt and freshly ground black pepper
3 long slices Sourdough Bread (page 316),
*   cut in half crosswise*
1 tablespoon unsalted butter
1 tablespoon mild vegetable oil
2 cups (210 g) grated Gruyère or
*   Comté cheese*
½ cup (loosely packed) flat-leaf parsley leaves

1. Whisk together the eggs, the wine, a generous amount of salt, and a touch of pepper in a small bowl; then transfer the mixture to a shallow dish that's large enough to hold the bread slices in one layer. Place the bread slices in the dish and leave them there for several minutes so they become thoroughly soaked with the mixture (without falling apart). Turn the slices over, if necessary, so they evenly soak up the mixture.

2. Heat the butter and oil in a nonstick skillet over medium heat. Add 3 slices of the bread. Top each slice with one third of the grated cheese, and then with a slice of the remaining bread.

3. Cook on one side until the bread is golden and the cheese is half melted, about 3½ minutes (adjust the heat as needed so the bread turns a lovely gold color). Turn and cook on the other side until the bread is golden and the cheese is fully melted, an additional 3½ minutes.

4. Meanwhile, mince the parsley.

5. Remove the sandwiches from the skillet, and cut them crosswise into 1-inch-wide (2½ cm) strips. Arrange them on a warmed platter and sprinkle with the minced parsley.

4 to 6 servings

Little Cheese Puffs

Gougères

➤•••◄

You can hardly set foot in Burgundy without being served a *gougère* at some time. *Choux* pastry delicately flavored with Gruyère cheese, it is the quintessential accompaniment to a kir (white wine with a drizzle of crème de cassis), but it is even better as an accompaniment to Champagne.

Though widely ascribed to Burgundy, there remains some mystery surrounding the origin of the *gougère*. Apparently, as long ago as the 14th century, the Flemish were eating little cheese pastries that they called *goieres*. It's possible that at one point or other in French history, *gougères* and the right to make them were a gift of fealty from the Flemish to the Burgundian rulers. It makes sense—while some cultures deal in gold and rubies, the French ascribe that value to recipes.

Whatever the origin, *gougères* are light and delicious, and so easy to make. I've added chives to my version, but they are delicious simply made with cheese. On the other hand, you might get very creative and add other herbs, black pepper, Parmesan cheese. The dough is willing to accept whatever you put into it.

Gougères are best served at room temperature. For added convenience, these can be made ahead, frozen once baked, then crisped, while still frozen, in a hot oven before serving.

ASTUCES . . . .

• *Many recipes for* choux *pastry call for it to be pricked once it's removed from the oven, or for it to be baked with the oven door left slightly ajar. Neither is necessary. The trick to keeping these puffy is to bake them thoroughly.*

• *Be sure that the butter is well chilled before melting it in the water. If it is warm or soft at all, the batter will be oily and the* gougères *will not puff up as they are supposed to.*

. . . .

1¼ cups (175 g) unbleached all-purpose flour
¼ teaspoon freshly grated nutmeg
1 cup (250 ml) water
¾ teaspoon sea salt
7 tablespoons (105 g) unsalted butter, chilled, cut into chunks
4 large eggs
¾ cup (75 g) grated Gruyère or Comté cheese
¼ cup minced fresh chives

1. Preheat the oven to 400°F (205°C).

Line two baking sheets with parchment paper.

2. Sift the flour and the nutmeg together onto a piece of waxed or parchment paper.

3. Combine the water, salt, and butter in a medium-size pan and bring to a boil over medium-high heat. Let the mixture boil for 30 seconds. Then remove it from the heat and add the flour all at once. Beat the mixture vigorously with a wooden spoon. It will go together easily, creating a sort of thick paste. Continue beating until the mixture comes away from the side of the pan and forms a homogeneous ball of dough, 20 to 30 seconds. The dough should not be sticky—it will be slippery from the melted butter—but it should hold together well and not stick to the pan or the wooden spoon. If it does, return it to the heat and continue beating until it dries out (a matter of seconds).

4. Remove the pan from the heat and let the dough cool slightly. Then add the eggs, one at a time, beating well after each addition. When they are incorporated, beat in the cheese, then the chives.

5. Using a tablespoon, place walnut-size portions of the dough on the prepared baking sheets, leaving about 1 inch between them. Bake in the center of the oven until the *gougères* are puffed, golden, and crisp, 35 to 40 minutes.

6. Remove from the heat, remove from the parchment paper, and let cool on a wire cooling rack.

35 to 40 gougères

N O T E : You may fill these with your choice of fillings. Try Fromage Blanc with Herbs (see Index), for example. To fill a *gougère*, cut off the top and spoon in the filling. Or better yet, use a pastry bag: pierce the bottom with a knife, insert a pastry tip, and gently squeeze in the filling.

Pork and Duck Rillettes
Rillettes de Porc et de Canard

Rillettes. Those who have tasted them swoon at the mention. Like pâté but lighter and more flavorful, there is something about their heavenly texture and gently spiced flavor that wins the heart and palate.

A more country-style dish doesn't exist. *Rillettes* were born out of the farmwife's instinct to use every single part of a newly butchered animal. When a pig had been dispatched and hung in the barn, all the bits that had been cut away from the major pieces went into a giant cast-iron kettle over a huge fire. All farms had poultry, so a duck or goose was thrown in for flavor, along with fresh thyme, bay, and allspice.

Treated like pâté, *rillettes* are served at room temperature, with fresh crusty bread.

Try a Brouilly, a Cahors, or a Touraine Gamay alongside.

FOR SALTING THE DUCK
1 duck (3 to 3½ pounds; 1½ to 1¾ kg),
   giblets discarded
1 teaspoon sea salt

FOR THE RILLETTES
1 pound (500 g) salt pork
1 pound (500 g) pork shoulder
2 pounds (1 kg) fatty pork (such as the
   trimmings from loin roasts)
1½ cups (375 ml) water
3½ teaspoons sea salt (see Note)
10 black peppercorns
10 allspice berries
1 very large handful fresh thyme sprigs, or
   2 teaspoons dried
3 imported bay leaves

1. Salt the duck: Cut the duck into 6 pieces (2 breasts, 2 wings, 2 legs and thighs) and carefully rinse off any blood. Cut as much meat from the bones as possible.

Discard any bones that are free of meat, and keep any that still have a good amount of meat on them. Place the duck meat and the remaining bones in one layer in a flat nonreactive dish, and sprinkle ½ teaspoon of the salt over all. Turn the meat and bones, and sprinkle with another ½ teaspoon salt. Cover tightly and refrigerate for 24 hours.

2. Prepare the *rillettes:* Place the salt pork in a large saucepan, add water to cover, and bring to a boil. Drain and rinse.

3. Cut the duck meat, pork shoulder, and fatty pork into ½-inch (1¼ cm) cubes and place them in a large kettle or stockpot. Add the water, the 3½ teaspoons salt, and the herbs and spices. Stir, cover, and bring to a boil over medium-high heat. Reduce the heat so the water is just simmering. Cook, stirring now and then to be sure that the meat is cooking evenly and not sticking, until the meat is extremely tender and any meat on the duck bones has fallen off, about 5½ hours.

4. When the meat is cooked, remove the pot from the heat. When the ingredients are cool enough to handle, use your fingers to go through them carefully, discarding the bones, herb stems, and bay leaves, and breaking up any large pieces of meat. You will actually need to mash the *rillettes* with your fingers (it's wonderful—kind of like playing in warm mud) to be sure you remove all bits of bone and gristle. The goal is to reduce the *rillettes* to a homogeneous mixture. But leave any bits of skin that you find, as they add great texture.

5. Transfer the *rillettes* to a 6-cup (1½ l) terrine. Let the *rillettes* cool completely.

Then store them, covered, in the refrigerator. They will keep for 1 to 2 weeks if well covered and chilled. Remove them from the refrigerator at least 1 hour before serving. You can also sterilize them in jars.

12 to 16 servings (6 cups; 1¾ kg)

N O T E : Don't be concerned that there is too much salt here; as the *rillettes* chill, the seasonings blend to give a perfectly flavored result.

A Fond Memory

I remember first making these rillettes *on a farm in the Dordogne more than fifteen years ago.*

Before my time, the rillettes *had cooked over a wood fire in the* cuisine, *a fancy name for a funny old stone building with a huge fireplace, tile floors, and whitewashed walls. By the time I arrived, a large gas burner sat where the fire once burned, but that was the only innovation in a process hundreds of years old.*

Making rillettes *was simple and satisfying, for they required only cutting, chopping, tossing in the kettle, and seasoning. They cooked slowly, and each time I'd pass the door of the* cuisine, *I would inhale their luscious aroma.*

And then that wondrous moment came when they were prepared.

*We'd haul the kettle outside into the freezing air (*rillettes *are most often made in winter) to cool enough for us to handle them. Then whichever women were available from the village—it was a tiny one, so there were just four or five—would gather round the kettle, hands would go in, and we'd mash the contents, on the hunt for bits of bones and herb stems.*

I loved the feeling of the rillettes *squishing through my fingers and the laughing conversation that accompanied the work. It was a magic moment, one when all the women were together doing a simple task that occupied our hands but left our minds free to wander. Though it was cold outside, we didn't feel a thing, absorbed in our mindless task and our rolling conversation.*

When the rillettes *were smooth, and before they'd cooled and hardened into a pâté-like texture, someone would scoop up a dishful to take to the farmhouse, where everyone would gather later on. No matter how often* rillettes *were served during the year, they were always welcomed, always enjoyed with gusto.*

I still go to visit the farm, and I still see all the same faces. They are more weathered, as is my own, the hair that frames them more gray. Although we come from backgrounds as different as could be, we pick up conversation as easily as if we'd never been apart. And I know that if a batch of rillettes *were in process, we'd all eagerly roll up our sleeves.*

Smoked Sausage on Salad

Jésus de Morteau sur Sa Salade

→ · · · ←

The best Jésus de Morteau, a fat smoked sausage, I know comes from a small town in the Doubs, near Russey, where the Guillaume family smokes their own inside their farm's tall, wide chimney, or *tuyé*. I bought several of the sausages, and discovered that my favorite way to eat them was poached, atop a salad. *"Miam, miam,"* as they would say on the farm.

This salad, with its rosette of reddish rounds of sausage, is an excellent start to a meal. It can also be a meal in itself, with a fine dessert such as Upside-Down Caramelized Apple Tart (see Index) afterward. Don't forget to serve plenty of crusty bread alongside.

Try a Sancerre Blanc or Rouge, a Bourgueil, or a lightly chilled Beaujolais alongside.

FOR THE SAUSAGES

2 smoked sausages, such as kielbasa
(each 8 ounces; 250 g)
2 cups (500 ml) white wine, such as a
Sancerre Blanc

FOR THE SALAD

1 scant tablespoon best-quality red wine vinegar
Sea salt and freshly ground black pepper
1 heaping tablespoon minced shallot
¼ cup (60 ml) extra-virgin olive oil
7 ounces (210 g) escarole or curly endive
leaves (8 cups, loosely packed), rinsed,
patted dry, and torn into bite-size pieces

1. Place the sausages in a medium-size saucepan and add the wine. Add enough water to cover the sausages (you may use all white wine if you like). Bring to a boil, reduce the heat, and simmer the sausages, partially covered, until they are cooked through, 20 to 30 minutes.

2. About 10 minutes before the sausages are cooked, make the salad: Whisk the vinegar, salt, pepper, shallot, and olive oil together in a large bowl. Add the escarole, toss so it is thoroughly coated with the dressing, and taste for seasoning. Divide the salad among four dinner plates.

3. Remove the sausages from the poaching liquid, and discard the liquid. Slice the sausages on the diagonal into ¼-inch-thick (½ cm) slices and arrange them in a rosette pattern atop each salad. Serve while the sausage is piping hot, with plenty of bread alongside.

4 servings

Claude Udron's Foie Gras Terrine
La Terrine de Foie Gras de Claude Udron

I learned about this simple yet sumptuous terrine at the country home of Claude Udron, formerly chef of the reputed restaurant Pile ou Face, in Paris. Claude's house was not far from us, in Normandy, and there he raised the herbs, many of the lettuces, and most of the eggs used at the restaurant. Much of his weekend was spent harvesting this bounty.

He also spent a good part of each weekend visiting other producers, and collecting fat chickens, fresh cream, gorgeous vegetables, and foie gras.

One day, not too long before Christmas, I was discussing foie gras with Claude and he invited me to watch him prepare the terrine he served at the restaurant. When I arrived at his home, a small group of neighbor women were already there. "I decided to do a class," Claude said with a wide smile. "That way you can all have the terrine ready in time for Christmas."

Claude had the terrine in various stages of preparation, so he could walk us through it step-by-step. He deftly denerved the foie gras, patted it back into shape, and poured the marinade over it. He showed us how to pack a marinated foie gras into a mold, then went to the oven and returned with one that had just finished cooking. It was a rapid, skillful performance, giving us all the confidence to return home and make our own terrines, so prized during the holiday season.

Claude's recipe follows, and you will see it is simple to prepare. Take your time, and all will go well. Wait the fifteen days, then assemble your family and friends for the "unveiling." Accompany the terrine with thinly sliced, toasted bread and a lovely, lightly chilled Sauternes, Champagne, or Barsac.

As the terrine cooks, the foie gras will melt into golden fat at the edges. If your oven won't hold a temperature as low as 225°F (105°C), you may cook the terrine as hot as 250°F (120°C), though check it for doneness after 55 minutes.

A S T U C E . . . .

• When scraping the liver and removing the nerves, save any scraps. Work quickly but gently so that you handle the liver as little as possible—the heat from your hands will gradually melt it. Also, be careful to keep the liver in large pieces, which gives a better result to the terrine.

. . . .

2 pounds (1 kg) foie gras
  (fattened duck liver)
6 tablespoons hearty red wine
6 tablespoons dry white wine
6 tablespoons water
1½ teaspoons sea salt
1 teaspoon sugar
Freshly ground black pepper to taste
  (about ¼ teaspoon)

1. Remove the liver from the refrigerator about 2 hours before you plan to prepare it, so it has time to come to room temperature.

2. Check over the liver and remove and discard any greenish coloring (bile) you may see, which is most likely to be where the two lobes of the liver join. It is very important to remove all traces of the bile, which will give a bitter flavor to the liver. Remove and discard any reddish areas for they will lend bitterness as well. Gently scrape the surface of the liver to remove the transparent skin, which is thicker on some livers than others. Reserve the skin.

3. The next step, and perhaps the most important in the preparation of the liver, is to remove the nerves. Gently separate the two lobes by pulling them apart—they are attached by a network of nerves. Make a ½-inch (1¼ cm) cut two thirds of the way down the center of the larger lobe. Gently open up the foie gras, pulling the flesh back with your fingers, and begin lifting out the nerve, fol-lowing it the length of the lobe. You may need to make shallow cuts in the liver to reveal all of the nerve, which tends to wander the length of the lobe. The nerve branches two thirds of the way down the lobe, sloping down around either edge. Continue to follow and remove it, all the way to its end. If it snaps, make a shallow cut in the liver to find it again. Work carefully so you don't break the liver into small pieces—your goal is to keep it in as large pieces as possible. After you have carefully inspected the lobe to be sure all of the large nerve has been removed, gently fit it back into shape. Reserve the nerve. The smaller lobe also has a large nerve in it, the end of which attached the two lobes together. Cut into the small lobe near the end of the nerve that emerges from it, gently opening it up and removing it right to its end, following the nerve as you did in the large lobe. Reserve this nerve as well. You may see a network of smaller nerves, which are not necessary to remove.

4. In a small bowl whisk the wines, water, salt, sugar, and pepper together.

5. Place the liver in a nonreactive dish and pour the marinade over it. Press the reserved skin and nerves of the liver through a fine-mesh sieve, and add any exuded liver to the liver in the dish. Turn the pieces of liver so they are moistened all over. Cover with aluminum foil and refrigerate for 24 hours, turning once again about halfway through if you can do so without them falling apart. If the pieces seem too fragile, leave them as they are in the marinade.

6. The next day, preheat the oven to

225°F (105°C). Place a colander in a dish or bowl large enough to accommodate any liquid that might drain from it.

7. Fit the liver, which will have absorbed most of the liquid, into a large (8 cup; 2 l) terrine or nonaluminum baking dish, pressing on it gently but firmly so it is well packed. Cover the terrine. Discard any remaining marinade.

8. Place the terrine in a large baking pan with sides that are at least 3 to 4 inches (7½ to 10 cm) high, and fill the pan with cold water so that it comes several inches up the sides of the terrine. Cook until the liver is soft and just warm through, and a shallow pool of yellow fat has formed around the edge of the terrine, 1 hour to 1 hour and 5 minutes. The best test for doneness is to stick a finger right in the center of the terrine to the bottom. If it is warm all the way through but slightly cooler at the bottom, it is cooked enough.

9. Remove the liver from the oven and gently turn it into the colander to drain, which will take 10 to 15 minutes. Occasionally, turn it carefully with a large spatula to help it drain.

10. When no more fat is draining from the liver, place it in a 4-cup (1 l) rectangular mold. Cover it with aluminum foil, shiny side down. Cut a piece of cardboard to fit just inside the mold. Place it directly on top of the foil, then place a 2-pound (1 kg) weight on top. Refrigerate for 2 weeks before eating. Once you've served the terrine, you must eat it up within 2 to 3 days.

10 to 12 servings

Salted Foie Gras
Foie Gras Salé

>···<

The first time I tried foie gras prepared this way, I was astonished. Germaine Souillard, who lives in the town of Albi, in the Tarn, gave me a thick slice on a piece of toast, and it melted in my mouth with a rich, nutty flavor. She told me all she'd done was let the foie gras sit in salt for seven hours, then season it liberally with pepper. I must have looked doubtful, for she assured me several times it was true.

This preparation is very different from the other foie gras recipe in this book, which is more refined, yet equally good. I can't decide which is my favorite—each is wonderful in a totally different way. I love the pepper on this, which heightens the nutty, full-flavored yet hauntingly subtle taste of the foie gras. It is wonderful accompanied by slices of hot toasted baguette, a tossed green salad, and a sweet Bergerac Blanc.

ASTUCE . . . .

• *The warm milk helps the foie gras absorb the salt evenly. It also softens the foie gras, so handle the liver quickly and with care.*

. . . .

1 medium (1½ pounds; 750 g) foie gras
  (fattened duck liver)
6 to 8 cups (1½ to 2 l) milk
6 cups (about 2½ pounds; 1¼ kg) coarse
  sea salt
2 tablespoons coarsely ground black pepper

1. Remove the foie gras from the refrigerator 2 hours before you plan to work with it, so it has time to come to room temperature.

2. Follow the instructions on page 26, steps 2 and 3, for cleaning the foie gras and removing the nerves (see Note). Discard the nerves. Pat the liver back into shape.

3. Heat the milk over low heat to just lukewarm (see Note). Place the liver in a large bowl and cover it with the warmed milk. Let it sit in the milk, turning it if necessary so it is evenly covered with the milk, until it has softened substantially, about 5 minutes.

4. Remove the foie gras from the milk and wrap it firmly in a single layer of tightly woven cheesecloth (if the cheesecloth is loosely woven, fold it over to make a double layer), tying the ends together so the foie gras is firmly bound.

5. Sprinkle a ½-inch-thick (1¼ cm) layer of salt on the bottom of a shallow bowl or terrine large enough to hold the foie gras generously. Completely cover the foie gras with salt, making sure it fills in all the holes around the foie gras. If the ends of the cheesecloth are quite long and you don't want to cut them, just let them hang outside the container.

6. Cover the container with aluminum foil and refrigerate for 7 hours.

7. Remove the foie gras from the salt, brushing it lightly to remove any salt clinging to it. Unwrap and discard the cheesecloth. Gently press the pepper all over the outside of the foie gras, so it is black on the surface. You may either serve the foie gras immediately, or return it to the refrigerator for an hour or so before slicing and serving.

8. To serve, thinly slice the foie gras

after you've removed it from the refrigerator, and arrange it on a lightly chilled serving plate.

10 to 20 servings, depending on appetites

NOTES: When removing the large nerve from the foie gras, work slowly and carefully.

Ideally, the foie gras should stay in large pieces. Reassemble it after it has soaked in the milk, and wrap it firmly in cheesecloth—it will magically glue itself back together.
• The milk shouldn't be so hot it melts the foie gras. Test it on the inside of your wrist for temperature; if you can't feel the drop you put there, the temperature is perfect.

Garlic and Liver Pâté
Pâté de Foie à l'Ail

>···<

I'm very choosy about pâtés in general, and I love this one because of its rich, true flavor. The combination of liver, garlic, pork, and *quatre épices*, or "four spices," is heavenly. It jolts your taste buds awake with its ample, gutsy flavor.

With the aid of a food processor, this goes together in a minute. And once it's made, you've got pâté at your disposition for a week. I love to serve it as an appetizer, with cornichons, the tiny French pickles. I also enjoy it for lunch, with fresh bread. And when it comes to picnics, I'm not sure there is anything better than slabs of pâté with a wonderful, lightly chilled Côtes d'Aix-en-Provence Rosé and plenty of bread.

This pâté is tender and moist, yet it holds together well. Once you've tried it you'll be tempted to make it often.

ASTUCE . . . .

• *When a recipe calls for minced garlic, it means minced with a knife, not with a garlic press. When minced by hand, the garlic stays in nice little pieces that have some texture and give pure, clear flavor. When pressed, the garlic becomes more of a purée, and the flavor is not as clean.*

. . . .

1 square piece of caul fat (16 inches;
　40 cm) or 6 thin slices salt pork
　(see Note), for lining the mold
12 large cloves garlic, peeled, green germ
　removed, and minced
2 pounds (1 kg) fresh pork liver
1 pound (500 g) ground pork
Sea salt and freshly ground black pepper
¼ teaspoon Quatre Epices (page 519)
Cornichons, for garnish

1. Preheat the oven to 350°F (175°C).

2. Line an 8-cup (2 l) loaf pan with the caul fat or the salt pork, leaving the ends to hang over the sides of the pan.

3. Place the garlic and the liver in a food processor. Process until the liver is almost a purée, with some chunky texture. Add the pork, process until blended, then add the seasonings. Place a bit of the pâté in a small skillet and sauté it over medium-high heat until it is cooked through. Taste for seasoning, remembering that the pâté will be served cold and the flavors will calm down; be sure it is well seasoned.

4. Pack the loaf pan with the pâté mixture and place it in a deep roasting pan. Pour enough boiling water into the roasting pan to reach halfway up the sides of the loaf pan. Bake in the center of the oven until the pâté registers 162°F (72°C) in the center, 1¼ to 1½ hours.

5. Remove the pâté from the oven and let cool, in the mold, to room temperature. At this point you may either unmold it or cover it with parchment paper and a sheet of aluminum foil, place two 1-pound (500 g) weights on it, and refrigerate overnight. To serve, unmold the pâté on a serving platter and garnish with cornichons.

8 to 10 servings

NOTE: If using salt pork, place it in a casserole, cover it with water, and bring to a boil. Drain, repeat, and let cool, then use as directed.

Confit of Chicken Gizzards
Confit de Gésiers

→ • • • ←

Yes, gizzards. Call them *gésiers*, if you like—it makes them sound so much more delicate and refined! *Confit de gésiers*, loosely translated as "gizzards poached in fat," are an integral part of French cuisine, tender delicacies tossed into salads and soups, occasionally wrapped in an omelette, added to a sauce. Typically, the gizzards come from fattened ducks or geese, and they are oversize, extemely tender, wonderfully flavorful.

The *gésiers* in this confit—a Norman rendition of a southwestern classic—are from simple barnyard chickens, and they are cooked long and slowly in pork fat and herbs until they soften and become tender, aromatic morsels.

I remember the first time I tasted confit of chicken gizzards. It was a crisp fall day, and I had walked into the charcuterie in our neighboring village, Le Vaudreuil, only to be enveloped in the most wonderful aroma. On the shelf above all of the chunky pâtés, homemade sausages, and terrines was a steaming container. Inside were warm *gésiers*, fresh from the stove.

"Try one," Francine Leborgne insisted, and I popped one into my mouth. It was succulent, tender, rich with flavor. "These are chicken gizzards?" I asked, incredulous, then asked for some to take home.

I sliced and sautéed them and added them to salad—they were fantastic. I returned to the charcuterie, notebook in hand. Mme. Leborgne saw me coming, and was ready with the ingredients when I walked in the door. It took me a few tries, all of which she graciously sampled. She didn't give me her imprimatur until I got them right—and here they are. The recipe that follows has the right balance of flavor and tenderness.

To keep the *gésiers*, I cover them completely with fat, place them in the refrigera-tor, and generally use them within a month.

In the U.S., gizzards tend to be sold in pieces, though if you check through packages, you can often find those that are whole. This recipe was tested with the most intact gizzards I could find at the market—most of them were whole—and the result was superb.

A S T U C E . . . .

• *In the U.S., gizzards come already cleaned and free of grit. If for some reason you have gizzards that aren't cleaned, simply cut off the tough skin that holds the two gizzards together and scrape out any grit, then rinse them well.*

. . . .

2 pounds (1 kg) chicken gizzards,
    cleaned and well rinsed
¼ cup (50 g) coarse sea salt
10 sprigs fresh thyme, or ½ teaspoon
    dried
3 imported bay leaves
4 pounds (2 kg) pork fat, cut in 1-inch
    (2½ cm) pieces, or lard
2 small onions, each pierced with
    1 whole clove
1 teaspoon allspice berries

1. Place the gizzards in a large bowl. Add the salt, half the thyme, and one of the bay leaves, and mix until well combined and the salt is evenly distributed. Cover and refrigerate for 2 hours.

2. Rinse the gizzards well by placing them in a bowl and filling the bowl with water. Drain the gizzards, then repeat the procedure at least four times, to make sure you remove all the surface salt. Pat the gizzards dry.

3. Place the pork fat or lard in a large heavy saucepan over medium-high heat. When it is two-thirds melted, add the gizzards, onions, remaining herbs, and allspice berries, stirring and pushing them down into the fat. Lower the heat so the fat is simmering slowly. Cook, uncovered, until the gizzards are tender, about 2½ hours, stirring them occasionally and pushing any beneath the surface of the fat so they cook evenly, adjust-ing the heat if necessary (see Note).

4. When the gizzards are cooked, remove the pan from the heat and let them cool in the fat until it is nearly congealed. Transfer the gizzards and the fat to a bowl or an earthenware or glass container and let them cool completely. Either eat them imme-diately, or store in the refrigerator for up to 2 weeks, covered with the fat, and with alu-minum foil.

5. Remove the gizzards from the fat and warm them gently in a saucepan over low heat. Use a slotted spoon to remove them from the pan. Serve whole with toothpicks on the side.

About 24 gizzards

N O T E : Make sure the gizzards cook at a low simmer, for faster cooking will toughen them.

LA SOUPIERE
The Soup Terrine

On the French farm, soup is like blood in the veins—essential for life, and for happiness as well. On the one hand, it warms, comforts, soothes; on the other, it excites the appetite and paves the way for delights to come.

An old farm tradition called *faire chabrot* gives a flourish to the final sip of soup: A splash of red wine goes into the bowl and is swished gently around, then drunk with a satisfied "Mmm!" and a quick wipe to the lower lip with a napkin.

Faire chabrot dates to a time when there was just one shallow bowl for each person, and it needed rinsing between the soup and the main course. Now, of course, dishes are changed between courses, but many a farmer still practices *faire chabrot*, with the enjoyment of an old tradition.

Here you will find soups for all seasons and for all occasions. Most are intended to open a meal, although there are several that make a fine main course.

Whether or not you *faire chabrot*, you'll enjoy the essence of the French farm in a warming bowl of soup.

Seasonal Vegetable Soup
Le Potage

>···<

Potage is a mirror of the season, for its makeup relies completely on whatever vegetables are at their best in the garden. It can be thick or thin, deep green from Swiss chard, spinach, or other greens, or orangey from many carrots. Recipes for it are as numerous as the cooks in France, and it's a very personal dish. But in my years of eating and reading about it, I've discovered that there are certain givens, no matter who is at the stove. No mixed vegetable potage is really complete without carrots, leeks, turnips, and potatoes. Beyond that, it's up to the individual's whim and seasonal availability.

Although the ingredients vary according to what's available in the garden or market, the combination here—with Jerusalem artichokes, called *topinambours* in French—is my favorite.

Sometimes I throw in sprigs of fresh thyme, other times I add allspice berries. I always serve it with a small carafe of extra-virgin olive oil, and occasionally I sprinkle it with a *persillade*—garlic and parsley minced together.

1 large bunch Swiss chard
   (1 pound; 500 g), trimmed, carefully
   rinsed, and coarsely chopped
2 large carrots, peeled and cut into 1-inch
   (2½ cm) rounds
2 medium turnips, trimmed, peeled, and
   cut into quarters
2 large leeks, white and green parts trimmed,
   well rinsed, cut into 1-inch (2½ cm) lengths
1 medium onion, peeled and cut into quarters
1 medium waxy potato, peeled and cut
   into quarters
2 Jerusalem artichokes, peeled and cut into
   quarters (optional)
4 large cloves garlic, peeled and green
   germ removed
10 black peppercorns
2 imported bay leaves
1 teaspoon coarse sea salt

1. Place all of the ingredients through the garlic in a large heavy saucepan and add enough cold water to cover by 1 inch (2½ cm). Tie up the peppercorns in a square of cheesecloth and add them to the pan with the bay leaves and salt. Cover and bring to a boil over medium-high heat. Reduce the heat to medium and cook gently and slowly, covered, until the vegetables are completely tender, 25 to 30 minutes. Check them occasionally to be sure they are covered with plenty of water, adding some more if necessary.

2. When the vegetables are cooked through, remove the bay leaves and the peppercorns. Purée in a food processor or with a wand mixer. If the potage is very, very thick, add water to thin it to your taste. Adjust the seasonings and serve piping hot.

6 to 8 servings

Zucchini Soup
Soupe aux Courgettes

Zucchini has a wonderful fresh, clean taste that often gets lost when it is combined with other stronger flavored ingredients. In this simple soup its flavor comes through, clear and clean.

Inspired by Yvette Harel, whose husband, Jean, has little garden plots all over the village of Le Vaudreuil in Normandy, it is ideal for summer when zucchini are at their peak and their most abundant. You may do as I do and purée the soup so it has an even, bright green color with flecks of dark green, or just leave it as it is.

Try this hot the first day; then if there are leftovers, serve it cold the following day. I like to sprinkle a bit of finely snipped basil over it, hot or cold, just before serving. You'll find it simple, and simply divine.

1 tablespoon unsalted butter
1 medium onion, peeled and diced
2 pounds (1 kg) zucchini, grated
2 cups (500 ml) Chicken Stock
   (page 504)
2 cups (500 ml) water
Sea salt and freshly ground black pepper
½ cup (loosely packed) fresh basil leaves

1. In a large heavy saucepan, melt the butter over medium-high heat. Add the onion and cook, stirring frequently, until it

begins to turn translucent, about 5 minutes. Add the zucchini and stir to blend it with the onion. Then add the liquids.

2. Increase the heat just enough to bring the soup to a boil; then decrease it so the soup is simmering merrily. Cook, covered, until the zucchini is tender through, about 20 minutes. Season to taste with salt and pepper.

3. Purée the soup in a food processor or with a wand mixer, or leave it chunky if you like. Adjust the seasoning.

4. Just before serving, cut the basil into fine strips.

5. Divide the soup among six warmed shallow soup bowls, sprinkle with the basil, and serve immediately.

6 servings

Carrot Soup
Potage aux Carottes

After a trip through the austere, rugged mountains of the Doubs, we stopped in the hamlet of Bizot, where Mme. Colette Février has run a restaurant for more than sixty years. She cooks over the same woodstove her mother did, tends bar just as her father and later her husband did, and treats diners as though they were her own family.

We had this smooth, simple, but elegant potage to start our meal, followed by a delicious sauté of local ham and potatoes, salad, and finally the best rhubarb and red currant compote I've ever had.

I love this soup, which is pure and full flavored. I make it often, and each time I do, I think of Colette Février.

1 pound (500 g) organic carrots, peeled, trimmed, and cut into ½-inch (1¼ cm) rounds

1 medium potato, starchy such as russet, or all-purpose such as Yukon Gold, peeled and cut into quarters

5 cups (1¼ l) water

Sea salt

1 tablespoon unsalted butter

Freshly ground black pepper

1. Place the carrots, potato, water, and salt to taste in a large saucepan and bring to a boil over medium-high heat, covered. Reduce the heat to medium and cook until the carrots are tender, 25 to 30 minutes.

2. Transfer the vegetables and 1 cup (250 ml) of the cooking liquid to a food processor and purée. Return the purée to the pan and add the butter, stirring until it has melted. Season to taste with salt and pepper, and serve immediately.

4 servings

A Visit to Yesteryear

Colette Février grew up in the tiny village of Bizot, now about one hundred residents, and the house where she was born served as the local café and meeting place. Built in the 15th century, it was once, very long ago, the regional tribunal, where infractions were settled in front of a judge.

During Mme. Février's youth, her home and the café had the town's only telephone, so she and her parents never left—they had to be available in case any calls came in or needed to go out. It was quite a business: Residents would make appointments to make or receive calls, and while waiting, would order a coffee, a pastis, a glass of wine. If a family in the village had an occasion to celebrate, they did so at the Févriers, who catered everything from weddings to baptisms. Mme. Février continued the tradition after her father died. She and her husband ran their home as a café, and her five daughters grew up helping them out.

Now Mme. Février operates a restaurant by herself. The night we were there, she'd opened just for us—she doesn't require a group—and she prepared her own favorites. It was a bit odd at first to be ushered into an empty dining room right above the kitchen, and to hear the small sounds of one elderly woman preparing dinner. She wore slippers in the kitchen and changed into black pumps each time she entered the dining room, where she would casually ask how we were enjoying the meal. She was warm and attentive, funny and forthright, and we had a wonderful time.

After supper she invited us to join her for a glass of a local liqueur made from pine needles—it had a sharp resin flavor and was vivid green.

Time has always stood rather still in Bizot. "During the second war we heard a few things and saw a few troops go by, but really nothing changed," she said. She certainly doesn't seem to mind the slow pace. As long as she has some business, can work in the garden, and gets to see her five daughters on a regular basis, she's happy.

Wild Greens Soup
Soupe aux Herbes Sauvages

→ ··· ←

*H*erbes sauvages are wild greens that grow in the fields, often near a river, and they are a well-loved source of sustenance to French farm families. They are best in the spring-time, when they're full of sweet and tender flavor, and harvesting them is a pleasure, for it involves a pleasant, slow walk in the countryside.

Une Soupe aux Herbes Sauvages is the title of a book written by a memorable woman, Emilie Carles. She was a farmer at heart, and her poignant story, published in 1977, filled with joys and sorrows, is reminiscent of this simple country soup, where bitter and pungent flavors play off one another, with nothing to soften or hide them.

My version of this soup is one I found on a farm in Provence. With the appealing flavors of Swiss chard and tangy sorrel, it makes a full meal when served with croûtons (a must).

A S T U C E . . . .

• *If the sorrel you have is young, it will not be necessary to cut out the central stem of the leaf. If the leaves are large and older, however, the stem can be hard and stringy. To trim the stem, fold the leaf in half lengthwise and simply slice the stem away.*

. . . .

FOR THE SOUP
1 tablespoon olive oil

3 shallots, peeled and diced

8 ounces (250 g) potatoes, peeled and diced

1 pound (500 g) Swiss chard, well rinsed, trimmed, and coarsely chopped

1 bunch (about 4 cups, loosely packed) young sorrel leaves, rinsed and coarsely chopped

6 cups (1½ l) plus ½ cup (125 ml) water

Sea salt

Freshly ground black pepper

FOR THE CROUTONS
4 large slices bread

4 teaspoons extra-virgin olive oil

2 cloves garlic, peeled and left whole

1. To make the soup, heat the oil in a large heavy saucepan over medium-high heat. Add the shallots and the potatoes, stir so they are coated with the oil, and cook, stirring frequently, until the shallots begin to turn translucent, 2 to 3 minutes. Stir the Swiss chard and the sorrel into the potatoes. Then stir in the ½ cup (125 ml) water. Season with salt, cover, and cook until the greens have diminished in volume by half, about 4 minutes.

2. Add the 6 cups (1½ l) water, cover, and bring to a boil. Reduce the heat so the liquid is boiling gently, and cook until the potatoes are completely tender and the greens have "melted" and are olive green, about 25 minutes.

3. While the soup is cooking, make the croûtons: Preheat the oven to 300°F (150°C).

4. Toast the bread, either under a broiler or in a toaster. Brush the toast generously on each side with the olive oil, then rub each side with the garlic cloves. Cut the toast into small squares no larger than ½ inch (1¼ cm) and place them on a baking sheet or in a large baking dish, in one layer. Bake the croûtons until they are crisp through, about 15 minutes.

5. Purée the soup using a food processor or wand blender, and season to taste with salt and pepper. Divide the soup among six warmed soup bowls, sprinkle a handful of croûtons into each bowl, and serve immediately. Pass the additional croûtons.

6 generous servings

Winter Potage
Potage d'Hiver

>···<

This soup celebrates winter as surely as does Christmas or Three Kings' Day. A devotée of soup when the weather is chilly, I follow my instincts and the traditions of the French farmwife, who makes potage nearly every day. Sometimes the ingredients in potage are leftovers, though more often it is made with whatever is still growing in the garden or is at its best and most economical at the market.

I have only a tiny garden filled with herbs and lettuces, so my local markets serve as my garden, and the ingredients in this soup were what I found on a frigid Saturday just after Christmas.

Though wonderful for lunch, along with crisp salad and rustic bread, this soup can also serve as an elegant first course. Just add a dollop of crème fraîche—1 tablespoon per serving is a good amount—to dress it up.

Drink a nice lightly chilled red Chinon or Saumur-Champigny with this.

Wand Mixer

→·←

A wand mixer is a tool recently introduced to the U.S., but in use on the French farm for many years. It is, quite simply, a razor-sharp electric blade on a stick that you dip into soups and sauces to turn them into purées. With a wand mixer, no more pouring soup into a food processor and then back into the pan to heat it up—all is done while the soup is hot, on the stove. Wand mixers are easy to find and inexpensive. When next you have the chance, add one to your kitchen drawer.

1 small celery root, trimmed, peeled, and finely chopped

½ rutabaga, trimmed, peeled, and finely chopped

2 medium Jerusalem artichokes (see Note), peeled and finely chopped

3 small russet-type potatoes, peeled and finely chopped

5 medium leeks, white part and 1 inch (2½ cm) of green, well rinsed and finely chopped

1 bouquet garni (3 parsley stems, 2 imported bay leaves, 1 green leek leaf, 8 fresh thyme sprigs, tied in cheesecloth)

Sea salt

Freshly ground black pepper

6 to 8 tablespoons Crème Fraîche (page 520; optional)

1. Place all the vegetables in a large heavy stockpot and add enough water to cover by 1 inch (2½ cm); you will need approximately 7 cups (1¾ liters). Add the bouquet garni and 1 teaspoon salt, cover, and bring to a boil. Reduce the heat to medium and simmer until the vegetables are very soft, about 1½ hours.

2. Remove the bouquet garni and purée the soup in a food processor or with a wand mixer. Adjust the seasoning, adding pepper to taste, and add the crème fraîche if desired. Serve immediately.

4 to 6 servings

NOTE: In the U.S., Jerusalem artichokes are most commonly sold under the name "sunchoke."

Beauty Is in the Tasting

Jerusalem artichokes look as though they should be destined for the barnyard. Dark brown to purplish, they are small, knobby, and irregular. Inside, their flesh resembles a radish.

They appear at the market around October, a herald of winter, but they are best closer to December, after a frost or two, when their sugar content increases along with their digestibility (the carbohydrate that can cause gastric upset breaks down in cold temperatures). Ten minutes of boiling or steaming will complete the process, making them perfectly digestible.

A farmer at a nearby market reserves a kilo of Jerusalem artichokes for me each week, and when she hands them to me, she usually dispenses with a cooking tip or two. "Bake them first, then peel them. It's easier," she says. "Boil them with potatoes, they're better that way." "Use one or two in potage—you'll never taste anything better."

I've tried all her tricks, and found them generally true. Her advice to boil them with potatoes is inspired—the potatoes serve to smooth out the artichokes' powerful flavor. And, as she says, a dollop of cream won't do them any harm at all!

Jerusalem artichokes, like globe artichokes, tend to darken once peeled, which can be annoying but is an excellent sign, indicating the presence of iron. The Jerusalem artichoke contains three times the iron in a potato and an equivalent amount to that in meat.

To avoid darkening, pop them into acidulated water (water into which you've squeezed half a lemon) before cooking. Then, if you're boiling them and want them to stay white, cook them in a 50/50 blend of milk and water, which will preserve their color.

Unless I am making soup, I prefer to steam Jerusalem artichokes, however, for they retain their texture and flavor better that way, and do not become waterlogged. I don't mind that they turn a slight translucent gray in cooking. I never serve them plain, or in a dish where the color makes a difference.

Regarding peeling them, which at first may seem insurmountable: Just take a good, sturdy, garden-variety vegetable peeler and whale away. You may not be able to preserve all the bumps and knobs, but don't let that worry you!

Chestnut Soup
Soupe aux Châtaignes

→ ··· ←

This soup speaks of Gascony—its bucolic villages surrounded by golden fields of corn, its ducks and geese, its verdant forests that are alive, in the fall, with the sound of chestnuts hitting the ground.

The food of Gascony is hearty and rich, yet surprisingly subtle and sophisticated. Farm women have gardens full of the national standbys: leeks, carrots, Savoy cabbages, and the herbal trio of parsley, thyme, and bay laurel. And they have their *basse-cours* (farmyards), too, where chickens, ducks, and geese compete for food and space in a never-ending cycle.

They fatten their ducks and geese to produce that most unctuous of foods, foie gras. The succulent birds themselves are mostly conserved as confit. Certain pieces are reserved for soup, however, to give it depth and flavor. And this is where the Gascon magic comes into play, for these foods are cooked with a light hand unique to the region. Always, always, if there is any fat to be seen, it is skimmed off long before it can get to the table. The Gascon belief is that fat is for flavor, but it shouldn't be left in a dish.

Vegetables and herbs are used as seasonings, and the results are richly flavored yet light, so that you leave the table satisfied.

The basic flavoring in this soup, *anis étoilé* (star anise), is pure Gascon, too. Since Gascony was on the spice route between Bordeaux and Italy, many spices and herbs are strewn throughout the history of its cuisine, and star anise is one. In Gascony it is often combined with chestnuts, and here it lends its exotic aroma and flavor to bring out the sweetness of the chestnuts, the depth of the duck stock.

I recommend making this soup the day after a fine meal of roast duck. There is usually some meat left clinging to the bones, and they make a wonderful stock. There are a couple of things to remember: If your duck was stuffed, remove any remaining stuffing from the cavity. Then cut the duck carcass into four pieces if possible, so it cooks evenly. Add any giblets that didn't roast with the duck, or even those that did. Keep the cover mostly on the pot so the liquid doesn't evaporate during cooking. And if you can't wait to have a roast duck to make this, then buy a duck, remove the breasts to sauté or grill, and make the soup with what is left.

Another hint: If you don't want to peel chestnuts, which is a laborious, unenjoyable effort, peeled chestnuts are available, vacuum-packed or in jars, at most specialty shops.

Serve a white Côtes du Rhône with this.

FOR THE STOCK

*Carcass of 1 duck (original weight
    5 pounds; 2½ kg)*

*1 large carrot, peeled and cut into ½-inch
    (1¼ cm) rounds*

1 small onion, peeled and cut into quarters

*1 leek, white part and 1 inch (2½ cm) of
    green, well rinsed and cut into ½-inch
    (1¼ cm) chunks*

2 cloves garlic, peeled

*1 bouquet garni (3 parsley stems, 2 imported
    bay leaves, 1 green leek leaf, 8 fresh
    thyme sprigs, tied in cheesecloth)*

2 star anise

12 cups (3 l) water

FOR THE SOUP

*1 pound (500 g) chestnuts, peeled
    (page 45; weight after peeling 13 ounces;
    390 g)*

*Sea salt and freshly gound black
    pepper*

1. To make the stock, place the duck carcass in a large kettle with the remaining ingredients and bring to a boil over medium-high heat. Reduce the heat to medium and simmer, partially covered, until the vegetables are completely tender and the carcass is falling apart, 2 to 3 hours. Strain, discarding

the carcass and the vegetables. Skim the fat from the surface of the stock, or chill the stock overnight in the refrigerator and then scrape off the fat. Save the fat for another use (page 118).

2. To make the soup, place the chestnuts, the stock, and ½ teaspoon sea salt in a medium-size saucepan and bring to a boil over medium-high heat. Reduce the heat to medium, cover, and cook until the chestnuts are completely tender and falling apart, 20 to 25 minutes.

3. Remove one third of the chestnuts from the soup and reserve. Purée the remaining stock and chestnuts in a food processor or with a wand mixer. Add the reserved chestnut pieces and heat the soup until it is blistering hot but not boiling. Season to taste with salt and pepper.

4. Ladle the soup into four warmed soup bowls, season each with a quick shower of freshly ground black pepper, and serve immediately.

4 servings

Pumpkin and Chestnut Soup

Soupe au Potiron et aux Châtaignes

→···←

Pumpkin and chestnuts are a natural marriage, for they are fresh and sumptuous at the same time. They are both lightly sweet and they complement each other—whereas chestnuts are starchy, pumpkins are light and fresh.

This soup, really a simple potage, is hearty of flavor and color—the combination of chestnut and pumpkin gives it a gorgeous rust color. I prefer it on a windy, rainy night because it warms the palate, and the soul. It is also hearty enough that little else is required but a crisp endive salad and bread. I recommend making this with duck stock, but you can use chicken stock instead.

If your soup thickens more than you like (prolonged cooking or reheating may do this), add more stock or a bit of water.

2 medium onions, peeled and cut into eighths
1 whole clove
1½ tablespoons rendered duck fat (page 142) or olive oil
2½ pounds (1¼ kg) fresh pumpkin, peeled, seeded, and cut into 1-inch (2½ cm) squares
1 quart (1 l) chicken or duck stock
20 cooked chestnuts (about 5 ounces; 150 g), peeled (facing page)
1 bouquet garni (3 parsley stems, 2 imported bay leaves, 1 green leek leaf, 8 fresh thyme sprigs, tied in cheesecloth)
Sea salt and freshly ground black pepper

1. Pierce one section of onion with the whole clove.

2. Place all of the onions and the duck fat in a large saucepan over medium heat. As the fat heats up, stir the onions so they are thoroughly coated; then cook until they are just turning limp and translucent, about 5 minutes. Add the pumpkin, stock, chestnuts, bouquet garni, and salt and pepper to taste. Bring to a boil, lower the heat so the soup is simmering energetically, cover, and cook until the pumpkin is thoroughly softened and the chestnuts are falling apart, about 30 minutes.

3. Remove the bouquet garni and the clove (you may have to fish for the clove with a slotted spoon). Purée the soup in a food processor or with a wand mixer, and adjust the seasoning. Serve immediately.

6 servings

Peeling Chestnuts

Peeling chestnuts demands time and patience, but it's a job I enjoy. I cook chestnuts often, sometimes just roasting them for an afternoon snack but more often serving them as a side dish with dinner or adding them to a soup or stew. Though peeled chestnuts are readily available in cans or vacuum packs, and are of high quality, I prefer my own brand of relaxation, chestnut knife in hand!

Before peeling, there are a couple of things to understand. Some nuts just won't give up their inner skin. Local wisdom in chestnut regions says that chestnuts that are too fresh are hard to peel, that they must sit for a week or so before cooking. I wonder about that, for I'm sure that the chestnuts that come to market, even in France, are rarely too fresh, and they can still be hard to peel. Wisdom aside, if you've got a tough one, just carve the inner skin off, losing some of the nutmeat at the same time.

Also, a certain percentage of chestnuts will be spoiled once you get the peels off, no matter how well they've been cared for. Count on two out of each pound being throwaways and buy that many extra.

To peel chestnuts: Place them in a large saucepan, add water to cover, and bring to a boil. Boil for 5 minutes and then remove the pan from the heat. Remove the chestnuts from the water two or three at a time, and quickly peel them, using a knife, trying to remove the outer and inner skin at the same time. If they are too hot to handle, hold them with a tea towel. If the chestnuts become very difficult to peel after you've done a few, return the water to a boil. The chestnuts must be scorching hot—otherwise the skin won't come off easily. Once peeled, chestnuts will keep for several days in an airtight container in the refrigerator.

Pumpkin Soup
Potage au Potiron

I shop regularly at a farmers' market in Le Neubourg in Normandy (see page 136), and when I get there I head straight for a woman whose remarkable produce shines above all the others.

She doesn't have much—just a few bags of this and boxes of that, a handful of herbs, and a carton or two of eggs. She has an old-fashioned sense of both gardening and marketing, and she's willing to dispense cooking tips. After telling me how to make this pumpkin soup, she assured me that I would certainly have a *bon petit potage* if I followed her directions.

This potage resembles a thin purée, and although the flavor of pumpkin is subtle, the soup nonetheless has an intensity all its own. While I like it plain, I think a light sprinkling of Gruyère cheese enhances the flavor tremendously. Try it first without, however, to see what you prefer. The same goes for pepper—to me the soup is better without it, but try it first and make up your own mind.

Make this with a French "Cinderella" pumpkin, blue kabocha squash, or the pumpkin of your choice. The flavor will vary depending on what you use.

ASTUCE . . . .

• *What to do with those pumpkin seeds? I boil them quickly (about 5 minutes) in heavily salted water (1 tablespoon to 1 quart; 1 l), drain them, and toast them in a 350°F (175°C) oven until they are golden and crisp, about 15 minutes. They make a nice—and nutritious—snack.*

. . . .

1 tablespoon unsalted butter
1 small onion, peeled and diced
4¾ pounds (2½ kg) pumpkin, peeled, seeds
   removed, and diced
1 small potato, peeled and diced
5 cups (1¼ l) water
Sea salt
¾ cup (90 g) Gruyère or Comté cheese,
   grated

1. Melt the butter in a large heavy saucepan over medium-high heat. Add the onion and cook, stirring, until it begins to turn translucent, about 5 minutes.

2. Add the pumpkin, the potato, and the water; stir, and then season lightly with salt. Cover and bring to a boil. Reduce the heat to medium and cook, covered, until the potato is completely tender and the pumpkin is so soft that it comes apart, 25 minutes. Remove from the heat and purée the mixture in a food processor or with a wand mixer until smooth and uniformly blended.

3. Taste for seasoning, and serve with the cheese alongside.

4 to 6 servings

Green Cabbage Soup
Potage de Chou Vert (Garbure)

>···<

Another gem from Gasconne's, Denise Lascourrèges, this soup—also known as *garbure*—really should win the award of merit from the French government, for, with variations, it serves to sustain the country's citizens in wintertime. Made with Savoy cabbage (the one with the gorgeous wrinkled leaves), *garbure* is the centerpiece of the rural winter table.

When I sat with Mme. Lascourrèges in her parlor on a chilly fall day, she and her husband had just finished their lunch of *potage de chou vert.*

"Now, this is the real *garbure*," she said. "Others call a soup with lots of beans in it *garbure*, but for me, this clear soup with the chunks of cabbage in it is *garbure*, and it was for my mother and grandmother, too."

Her secrets? "Don't cook it too long, don't add any fat, and use the *gélée* from a good fat duck or chicken." As she put it, *"Le jus de canard est primordial pour moi"* ("Duck jelly [see page 48] is a basic for me"). An additional plus to this soup is its lack of fat. "Lots of people think fat is flavor, but it isn't," she said. "It carries flavor, but here you've got all the flavor in the *gélée* and the bones you put in the soup."

Each time I eat this, I think of Mme. Lascourrèges's ruddy face beaming as she watched me taste her soup.

"Je ne vis pas si je n'ai pas de potage" ("I can't live without soup"), she said. I know just what she means.

ASTUCES

• *When you buy a whole chicken, save the neck and freeze it for use in a soup like this, where you want the flavor but don't need the meat.*

• *What is chicken broth, and what is chicken stock? Chicken stock is a heartier, more flavorful version of chicken broth, usually made with a large quantity of bones. I prefer it because it adds a deeper flavor dimension than chicken broth. If you don't have the bones—or the time or the wherewithal—to make a true chicken stock, follow this simple recipe for an extra-flavorful broth: It begins with 6 cans (each 13¾ ounces; 415 ml) of low-salt chicken broth in a stockpot. Quarter 2 onions, stick a clove into one quarter, and add the onions to the pot along with 2 small carrots, a bouquet garni (3 parsley stems, 2 imported bay leaves, 1 green leek leaf, 8 fresh thyme sprigs, tied in cheesecloth) or a handful of parsley stems plus a sprinkling of thyme, and several peppercorns. Bring it all to a boil, reduce the heat, and simmer until it is reduced by one third, 10 to 15 minutes. Proceed with any recipe calling for chicken stock.*

Duck Jelly

→·←

Denise Lascourrèges adds two table-spoons of duck jelly to her **garbure**. Like concentrated stock, this jelly—the nat-ural juices that pool at the bottom of a cooked bird and jell as they cool—is full of rich poultry flavor. She uses it by the table-spoonful to flavor everything from soup to vegetables. I follow her lead, and whenever I find jelly left from a cooked chicken, I save it, freeze it in an ice cube tray, and use it to flavor dishes. It's amazing what it will do for a simple soup, a pasta sauce, even a plate of steamed vegetables. If I don't have any, I use stock, as in this recipe.

1 small Savoy cabbage (20 ounces; 600 g)

1 medium onion, peeled and diced

2 leeks, white part only, well rinsed and diced

1 medium white turnip, trimmed, peeled, and diced

2 medium potatoes, peeled and diced

1 pound (500 g) chicken pieces (optional)

2 cups (500 ml) Duck Stock (page 505) or Chicken Stock (page 504), or 1 cup (250 ml) poultry jelly plus 1 cup (250 ml) water

6 cups (1½ l) water

Sea salt and freshly ground black pepper

1 cup (loosely packed) flat-leaf parsley leaves

2 cloves garlic, peeled and green germ removed

1. When you've discarded any dark or damaged outer leaves of the cabbage, remove the remaining outer leaves, stack them, and slice them crosswise into very thin strips. Cut the tight cabbage head into six wedges and remove the core.

2. Place onion, leeks, turnip, and pota-toes in a large stockpot. Add the chicken (if using), the duck stock, and water, and bring to a boil over high heat. Reduce the heat to medium and simmer for 15 minutes. Season to taste with salt and pepper. Add the cab-bage and continue cooking until all the veg-etables are tender, 25 minutes (see Note).

3. Just before the soup has finished cooking make the *hachis*: Mince the parsley leaves together with the garlic.

4. When the vegetables are tender, remove the chicken pieces (if used) and save them for another purpose. Season the soup to taste with salt and pepper. Divide the soup among six warmed shallow soup bowls, giv-ing each person a wedge of cabbage, and sprinkle with the *hachis*. Serve immediately.

4 to 6 servings

N O T E : The cabbage in this soup is cooked through and tender, though not mushy. If you object to cabbage cooked that much, reduce the cooking time, but be forewarned that the soup won't have the same richness of flavor.

Herb and Pasta Soup
Soupe aux Crousets

>···<

This soup, traditionally served in Provence at Christmastime, has many variations. Sometimes fried salt cod and leeks are added. Most versions contain pasta. If hand-made lozenge-shaped noodles—thought to symbolize the blankets of the baby Jesus—are used, it is called *soupe aux louzans* or *soupe aux crousets*. Orzo, while a bit smaller than the traditional pasta, maintains the traditional lozenge shape.

The soup is garnished with olive oil and grated goat cheese.

1 recipe Herb Broth (page 508)
½ cup (60 g) orzo or other small pasta
1 teaspoon sea salt
4 teaspoons extra-virgin olive oil
⅓ cup (30 g) grated hard-aged
    goat cheese or Parmesan
    cheese

1. Bring the broth to a boil in a medium-size saucepan over medium-high heat. Add the pasta and salt to taste, stir, and cook until it is al dente, about 8 minutes.

2. Ladle the soup into warmed shallow soup bowls and drizzle each portion with a teaspoon olive oil. Serve the cheese alongside.

4 servings

Vegetable Soup with Basil and Garlic
Le Pistou

>···<

Like so many recipes, *pistou* is as individual as a person's name. It always contains green beans (and usually elbow pasta) and is always flavored with basil and garlic—the mixture that gives it its name. But from there it can contain any number of vegetables. This version, which is almost a stew, is light and fresh, and the basil and garlic pack a real wallop.

In this recipe I call for the bean called coco rouge, which is the bean traditionally used in Provence for *pistou*. Sweet, tender, and nutty, coco rouges can be added either fresh, as written in the recipe, or dried. Fresh borlotti or cranberry beans make a good substitute; in a pinch, you can use dried navy beans.

Some recipes for *pistou* say to remove the seeds from the green beans. Well, if you've got a day and a half, do it. I find it really doesn't make a great deal of difference to the soup.

We love this soup hot on the day it is made, but it is also delicious cold. Just be sure to make plenty of *pistou*, and to warn your guests that it is powerfully seasoned.

Try a lightly chilled Bandol Rosé along with this.

FOR THE SOUP

8 ounces (250 g) thin green beans, trimmed and cut into thin rounds

1 medium carrot, peeled and cut into small cubes

2 small potatoes, peeled and cut into small cubes

8 cups (2 l) water

Sea salt

1 large zucchini, cut into small cubes

1 leek, white part only, well rinsed, cut into lengthwise quarters, and then cut into small pieces

1 cup (140 g) fresh coco rouges, borlotti, or cranberry beans or ½ cup (90 g) dried (or dried navy beans), cooked until tender

½ cup (60 g) elbow pasta, cooked al dente

Freshly ground black pepper (optional)

FOR THE PISTOU

3 cloves garlic, peeled and green germ removed

1 cup (gently but firmly packed) fresh basil leaves

⅓ cup (80 ml) extra-virgin olive oil

1. Place the green beans, carrot, and potatoes in a large heavy saucepan. Add the water and ¼ teaspoon salt. Bring to a boil over high heat, cover, and cook until the carrot and potatoes are nearly tender through, about 12 minutes. Add the zucchini, leek, and fresh beans (if using) and cook until tender, about 15 minutes. Add the pasta (and cooked dried beans, if fresh weren't used), and cook until hot through, 5 to 8 minutes. Season with salt, and pepper if desired.

2. While the soup is cooking, make the *pistou*. Crush the garlic cloves in a mortar with a pestle or mince with a sharp knife; add the basil leaves and mince, then if using a mortar and a pestle, add the oil in a fine stream until the mixture is thick and pale green. If using a knife, transfer the basil and garlic to a small bowl and whisk in the oil, adding it in a fine stream, until the mixture is thick and pale green.

3. To serve, divide the soup among six warmed shallow soup bowls. Serve the *pistou* alongside.

6 servings

Pascale's Endive Soup
La Soupe à l'Endive de Pascale

→ • • • ←

From the north of France—endive country—this hearty soup has become a favorite of ours during fall and winter, when endives are abundant and the weather turns cold. It is revivifying, restorative, and simply delicious.

Endive is pleasantly bitter when raw. When cooked gently, as here, the bitterness mellows and a wonderful rich flavor emerges. I love this soup—it's chock-full of vegetables and rich chicken flavor, but never heavy.

Originally the recipe called for a great deal of crème fraîche, but I prefer it with a small dollop, or sometimes with none at all. As for the chicken, I always add it, for I always make a big pot of chicken stock from a fresh whole chicken for this soup, and I add just enough of the still-flavorful meat to make the soup hearty and not detract from the taste of the endive.

Try chilled beer with this.

1½ pounds (750 g) Belgian endive
2 tablespoons unsalted butter
1 large onion, peeled and thinly sliced
8 cups (2 l) Chicken Stock (page 504)
4 medium carrots, peeled and grated
Sea salt and freshly ground black pepper
1 tablespoon fresh thyme leaves, or
   1 teaspoon dried
2 cups (300 g) cooked chicken meat (optional)
Crème fraîche (optional)

1. Strip away any outside endive leaves that are discolored or very dark green. Trim the stem, and cut out about ½ inch (1¼ cm) of the core inside the stem end. Cut the endive into ¼-inch (½ cm) crosswise slices.

2. Melt the butter in a large saucepan over medium-high heat. Add the onion and cook, stirring occasionally, until it begins to turn translucent, about 5 minutes.

3. Add the chicken stock to the onion, stir, and bring to a boil. Reduce the heat to medium and add the carrots. Cook, covered, until the carrots are tender, about 10 minutes.

4. Stir in the endive and cook until it is just tender, about 10 minutes. Season to taste with salt and pepper. Add the thyme, and the chicken if desired. Stir and adjust the seasoning. Continue heating until the soup is steaming. Serve with the crème fraîche alongside, if desired.

6 to 8 servings

Aromatic Pork and Vegetable Stew
La Potée

→...←

In every region of France there is a *potée*, or aromatic pork stew, and for every *potée* there are a dozen recipes. But no matter how it is made, *potée* is hearty, substantial, redolent of herbs and garden-fresh vegetables.

This is a combination of *potée* recipes from Simone Lasseaux, who lives in the Champagne region, and from Monique Pelisse, in the Auvergne. For Mme. Lasseaux the secrets to a good *potée* include adding a handful of white beans and reserving half the potatoes until the end of the cooking so that some fall apart to thicken the soup and others retain their shape.

For Mme. Pelisse, a *potée* isn't a *potée* without her home-smoked sausages, a lively *sauce gribiche*, and hard-cooked eggs.

You will find the best of both here, a rich *potée*, which is nevertheless so light, you'll waltz out of your chair afterward.

I like to use a fresh ham hock, which lends the flavor of its meat and fat. In France, all would be enjoyed together. However, you may remove the fat. If you can't find a fresh ham hock, use the equivalent quantity of pork ribs or shoulder butt.

Pass the *sauce gribiche* along with the *potée*, and then the hard-cooked egg to sprinkle on top.

Serve a lightly chilled Sancerre Blanc or Rouge alongside.

FOR THE POTEE

1½ cups (270 g) dried white beans, such as navy beans

10 sprigs fresh thyme

2 imported bay leaves

2½ pounds (1¼ kg) fresh ham hock

10 black peppercorns

½ teaspoon sea salt

Juice of ½ lemon

2 pounds (1 kg) russet potatoes

4 small turnips, trimmed

4 medium carrots, peeled and cut diagonally into thin slices

4 leeks (white part and 1 inch; 2½ cm of green), trimmed, well rinsed, and cut into ½-inch (1¼ cm) chunks

6 smoked sausages, such as kielbasa

Freshly ground black pepper

1 large cabbage, preferably Savoy, trimmed, core removed, and cut into 2-inch-thick (5 cm) wedges

FOR THE GARNISH

3 hard-cooked eggs

Sauce gribiche (see Note)

1. Place the beans in a medium-size saucepan and cover with water. Bring to a boil over high heat, remove from the heat, and let sit for 1 hour. Drain the beans and reserve.

2. Tie the thyme and the bay leaves together with kitchen string. Place the ham hock in a large kettle with the herbs, the peppercorns, and the salt, and cover with water by 1 inch (2½ cm). Cover and bring to a boil over high heat. Reduce the heat to medium and cook at a rolling simmer for 30 minutes. Add the beans and cook for an additional 30 minutes.

3. Partially fill a large bowl with water and add the lemon juice. Peel and quarter the potatoes and turnips. Place half the potatoes in the bowl and reserve. Add the remaining potatoes to the kettle along with the turnips, carrots, leeks, and sausages. Cover and bring to a boil. Reduce the heat to medium and cook at a rolling boil, partially covered, until the vegetables are tender, about 30 minutes. Taste the *potée* for seasoning, adding salt and pepper if necessary.

4. Drain the remaining potatoes and add them, with the cabbage, to the kettle, pushing the vegetables down into the liquid. Cover and bring to a boil. Then reduce the heat and cook, uncovered, until the cabbage is tender but still has some crispness and deep green color, and the potatoes are tender through, about 30 minutes. Adjust the seasoning.

5. Just before serving, press the hard-cooked eggs through a fine sieve into a small serving bowl.

6. Ladle just the broth into warmed soup bowls and serve. When everyone has finished their soup, transfer the vegetables, ham hock, and sausages to a large warmed platter and serve with the *sauce gribiche* and the hard-cooked eggs alongside.

6 to 8 servings

N O T E : To make a *sauce gribiche*, prepare the Basic Vinaigrette on page 516, using 3 additional tablespoons red wine vinegar and ½ cup (125 ml) additional olive oil. Add 19 small dill pickles (cornichons), diced, 2 tablespoons drained tiny capers, freshly ground black pepper, and right before you plan to serve it, ½ cup loosely packed fresh tarragon leaves, minced.

LE SALADIER
The Salad Bowl

During a French farm meal, the green salad arrives at just the right moment. Served after the *entrée* (first course) and the *plat de résistance* (main course), it comes when you're not sure you can eat another bite. Whew. Thank goodness it's green salad. After you savor the lightness of the dressing and the fresh, flavorful lettuce, you find yourself not only ready but eager to continue with cheese, then dessert. Salads are, quite simply, miraculous.

Of course, salads come in many guises. There is the *salade verte* that is served after the meal—which can be a variety of greens, a bowlful of mâche (lamb's lettuce) or escarole, or another kind of lettuce, always simply dressed.

Then there is the *salade composée*, intended as a first course, where several ingredients are combined, like the hearty Warm Bacon and Lentil Salad; the luscious Dandelion, Apple, and Bacon Salad; the vivid Raw Beet Salad.

Whatever the salad, on the French farm it is always zingy and fresh, exciting and nourishing, full of flavor and often bursting with color.

Green Salad with Oil and Vinegar Dressing

Salade Verte à la Vinaigrette

>····←

This is a basic recipe, one that should be part of every culinary repertoire. On the farm it is an everyday salad that changes according to the season, depending on what greens are fresh in the garden.

In winter I am a slave to escarole, which I occasionally combine with Belgian endive. In spring and summer I mix greens, using green or red oak-leaf, mesclun (a fragrant mix of young greens), arugula, and fresh herbs.

2 teaspoons sherry vinegar
¼ teaspoon sea salt
Freshly ground black pepper
½ teaspoon Dijon mustard
1 small clove garlic, peeled, green germ removed, and minced
¼ cup (60 ml) extra-virgin olive oil
7 ounces (210 g) mixed salad greens (8 cups, loosely packed), such as escarole, oak-leaf, and romaine, rinsed, patted dry, and torn into bite-size pieces

1. Place the vinegar, salt, pepper, mustard, and garlic in a medium-size bowl and whisk together until blended. Slowly add the olive oil, whisking constantly, until the dressing is emulsified.

2. Add the greens and toss well until they are coated with the dressing. Season with pepper to taste and serve the salad immediately.

4 servings

Toss Till You Drop

>·←

Lettuce leaves, like most of us, like to be completely dressed before going out. Toss them in a large bowl until you see an even glint of vinaigrette on each leaf, then toss several times more. Your salad will have more depth of flavor, and your palate will thank you for the effort!

Lamb's Lettuce Salad
Salade de Mâche

>…←

Mâche heralds winter. With its meaty, tongue-shaped leaves and delicate violet flavor, it is, for me, one of the most seductive foods of the fall.

Called lamb's lettuce or corn salad in English, it gets the latter name from its proclivity for growing among the corn. There it grew wild, low to the ground, and farmers harvested it for its succulence and flavor. Now it is raised commercially, one of the more popular salad greens in France.

Mâche grows in a small rosette, with all of the leaves issuing directly from the root. Soil and sand collect in the hollow of each stem and lodge there with stubborn resolve.

When I was an apprentice at La Varenne Ecole de Cuisine in Paris, I received instructions from chef Fernand Chambrette on its cleaning.

"Seven times," he yelled (he never seemed to speak in any other tone of voice). "Rinse it seven times and not one time less, or it won't be clean." I can tell you that his rule is absolutely correct. Whenever I skimp on the washing, the result is an annoying bit of grit in the mâche.

Don't let that stop you from enjoying the gastronomic delights of mâche. In my market, where I get gorgeous little rosettes of organic mâche, it comes nearly clean. I go for the mâche that is deep green and vigorous, regardless of its state of cleanliness, and spend the time it takes to wash it.

Shallots are essential in a mâche salad. They enhance its delicacy as much as garlic snuffs it out. To me this salad is magic—it's so green, tender, and perfumed.

1 teaspoon sherry vinegar
Sea salt and freshly ground
*   black pepper*
2 tablespoons extra-virgin olive oil
1 small shallot, peeled and cut crosswise
*   into paper-thin slices*
4 ounces (125 g) mâche rosettes
*   (6 cups, loosely packed), roots snipped,*
*   carefully rinsed (do not separate the*
*   rosettes into leaves)*

Whisk the vinegar with salt and pepper to taste in a medium-size salad bowl. Then add the oil in a thin steam, whisking steadily. Stir in the shallot. Then add the mâche and toss so it is thoroughly coated with the dressing. Serve immediately.

4 servings

Of Baby, Icy, and Otherwise Unusual Greens

=

Mention Brittany and familiar images come to mind: briny oysters, trim sailors wearing blue-and-white striped shirts, colorful Quimper pottery, women whose hair is adorned with lacy white *coiffes*.

Behind the folk traditions in this verdant region lies a rich agriculture. Breton cauliflower, caressed by the maritime breezes and nourished by the rich black soil, and the round *camus* artichoke, which can often weigh more than a pound, are eagerly

looked for each year as they come to market. Breton tomatoes have worked their way up to the top of the class in flavor and quality, and pungently sweet *rose de Roscoff* onions are legendary.

It is also, although this is known to few, the only region in France to commercially produce, on a large scale, vegetables so tiny they look more like decorations than food, and unusual lettuces, one of which has leaves seemingly encased in ice.

One of the best places to see all of this splendor is in an unremarkable warehouse on the road between Morlaix and St. Pol de Léon. There a group of weary but enthusiastic people juggle phones and dollies stacked with crates, while welcoming growers and prospective clients.

The head of this enterprise, called HOTGAME, is a young man named François Lagadec. His father headed a growers' cooperative, and young François followed suit.

With the difficulties in agriculture that developed, however, the Lagadecs and a group of their growers decided they'd better think fast if they wanted to survive.

Their solution was to grow things no one else was growing, and to market them in places that no else had thought of. The result of the growers' efforts is a warehouse full of pincushion-size cabbages, cauliflowers, broccoli, and romanesco. In one crate rest bunches of tiny fennel, in another mini parsnips. Here there are eensy sprigs of spinach, there itty-bitty purple artichokes, and over in one corner is the strangest-looking green imaginable, the one encased in ice.

"It's *ficoïde glaciale*," said M. Lagadec. "It's an ancient plant we found." He handed me a fleshy leaf, and I expected it to be cold, but of course it wasn't. Native to South Africa, the *ficoïde* is a succulent, and the "ice" is actually miniscule sacs of water on the surface of the leaves that the plant develops to nourish itself during periods of drought. I bit into it. It was slightly juicy and almost tasteless.

"You're right, it doesn't have a lot of flavor. But you should see it on a plate!" said M. Lagadec.

INNOVATIVE GARDENING

The HOTGAME cooperative (the name is a play on words—*haute gamme* means "top-quality" in French) includes one hundred growers. "It's important to remember that our growers aren't farmers, though. They're *maraîchers*, closer to gardeners," M. Lagadec said. "The gardening tradition is based on innovation—the *maraîchers* are always open to new ideas. It's natural for them to experiment; it's part of the profession."

Competitiveness must also be part of the Breton nature, for at HOTGAME M. Lagadec doesn't want any of his growers to discuss what they do or to share information with outsiders.

Not all of his growers think he is right, but they all abide by his wishes. I did happen to meet a grower who agreed to show me his work on the condition that I not use his name. His father and mother were *maraîchers* who sold their vegetables at local markets, and he is steeped in the *maraîcher* tradition.

Most of his baby vegetables grow in well-worked fields around his home. His year-round production of flowers and lettuces comes from two hangar-size greenhouses within eyesight of his house. We stepped into one of them, and it was as warm, cozy, and dry inside as the weather was inclement outside.

(continued)

He looked around the greenhouse, which was pulsing with productivity. Rows of sunset-hued nasturtiums grew down one side, multicolored primroses grew on another, and just in front of us grew a lacy plant with tiny white flowers. He motioned to me to bend down and look.

"It's a *porte-bonheur*," he said, picking a leaf and flower for me to taste, "a member of the Oxalis family." I recognized its relationship to sorrel when I tasted it and instinctively puckered. "It brings happiness," he said, laughing. "But you don't want to eat too much of it."

After a long moment's reflection, he mentioned his astonishment at how different farming has become.

"It's so much harder," he said. "Now we work twice the land my father lived on, just to stay on top. And our prices haven't risen in ten years. Part of our difficulty is that when my father was growing, it was just the family who worked the land. Now I've got employees."

"These nasturtiums," he said, pointing to the long, straight rows, "they're an incredible *casse-tête* [headache]. They attract every kind of insect, so we do what we need to

do to keep them healthy, and that kind of care takes personnel."

He walked over to some *ficoïde glaciale* that was growing in abundant trailing rows. "This plant turns salty when it doesn't get enough water," he said, "so we keep it a bit stressed to give it some flavor."

I told him I'd heard it was an ancient plant that had been lost, then found. "Hardly ancient, but it did used to be common—it was in all the seed catalogs until the forties, but then it fell out of fashion. We went to the Belgians to get the seeds," he said.

Outside his greenhouse grew a lush stand of arugula, punctuated by several shoots of a slender green called stag's horn, both volunteers planted by the wind, which blew the seeds out of the greenhouse.

"These," he said, kneeling to pick a languid, dark green shoot of stag's horn, "are beautiful, and we grew them for a while. But they really don't keep, so we had to stop. It's too bad. They look so good on a plate."

He and his wife are completely enthralled with their crops. They are proud to know that flowers and vegetables from their farm are flown all over the globe and are eaten at the world's best tables.

Napa Cabbage Salad
Salade de Pet Sai

>···<

Because so many Asians have relocated to the Eure department of Normandy, where I live, the market stands often offer what are referred to here as "exotic" vegetables. Among them is creamy white napa cabbage, which the French call *pet sai* (pet-shee).

One day in midwinter I had my eye on some at the market, and the vendor asked me what I did with them. I explained, and he looked at me and said, "They're sublime in salad, that's how I prepare them. My son and I will sit down and eat a whole cabbage's worth in one sitting, no problem."

As he spoke, his clientele leaned toward him, listening, looking at the cabbages. One woman asked, "What do they taste like?" "Like cabbage but not like cabbage," he replied with a laugh. "It's excellent," piped up his wife.

I followed his directions, and this is the result. The cabbage may be of Asian influence, but the salad is undeniably French, with its smooth yet biting vinaigrette. I love its freshness, both right after it's made and up to several hours later, when the cabbage settles into the vinaigrette, "cooking" slightly under its influence.

I like to serve this as a first course, with plenty of bread alongside.

Try a Coteaux du Languedoc with the *pet sai*.

- *2 teaspoons best-quality red wine vinegar*
- *1 tablespoon Dijon mustard*
- *1 tablespoon grainy mustard*
- *1 clove garlic, peeled, green germ removed, and minced*
- *Salt and freshly ground black pepper*
- *3 tablespoons extra-virgin olive oil*
- *1 tablespoon hot water*
- *½ cup (loosely packed) flat-leaf parsley leaves*
- *1¼ pounds (625 g) napa cabbage, trimmed, cut into quarters lengthwise, and very finely sliced crosswise*

1. In a large bowl, whisk together the vinegar, both mustards, the garlic, and salt and pepper to taste. Slowly add the olive oil in a thin stream, whisking constantly until the dressing is emulsified. Whisk in the hot water.

2. Mince the parsley leaves.

3. Add the cabbage and the parsley to the dressing, and toss until all is thoroughly combined. Either serve the salad immediately, or let it sit for up to 2 hours before serving. If the salad sits, be sure to toss it again before serving.

4 generous servings

Dandelion Green Salad with Croûtons

Salade de Pissenlits aux Croûtons

This salad is spring on a plate, full of all the vitality that causes tulips to push up from the ground, birds to start singing, primroses to bloom.

It can really only be made in early spring, when dandelions have taken on a new, fresh green color before sending up their golden flowers. Once they've blossomed, the leaves lose sweetness, becoming overly bitter. So at the first hint of the season's change, run out and look for dandelion greens, or go to the market for the cultivated variety. Avoid any greens you suspect have been treated by herbicides or otherwise contaminated.

If you find dandelion greens too bitter, complement them, cup for cup, with young beet greens, arugula, or radicchio.

Homemade croûtons are infinitely better than any other. Make them from day-old baguette or from freshly made country bread (see Index).

A red Côtes du Rhône is ideal with this salad.

ASTUCES . . . .

• *When preparing the salad, give the croûtons added flavor by tossing them in the dressing and letting them sit for several minutes before you add the greens.*

• *When adding the dandelion greens to the salad, have scissors handy to snip any long leaves so they are more manageable. Also, if any dandelion plants are very large—that is, they consist of several plants growing together—separate the plants, keeping the individual root clumps in one piece.*

. . . .

FOR THE CROUTONS

½ baguette or 2 thick slices of bread

2 cloves garlic, peeled

FOR THE SALAD

*2 teaspoons best-quality red wine
    vinegar*

*Sea salt and freshly ground black
    pepper*

*3 cloves garlic, peeled, green germ
    removed, and minced*

⅓ cup (80 ml) walnut oil

*7 ounces (210 g) dandelion greens
    (8 cups, loosely packed), well
    trimmed, rinsed, and patted
    dry*

1. Preheat the broiler.

2. Make the croûtons: If you are using a baguette, slice it in half lengthwise. Place the bread on a baking sheet and toast it under the broiler until it is golden on both sides, 3 to 4 minutes. Immediately rub the toast generously on both sides with the whole garlic cloves—the toast should be redolent. Cut the toast into ½-inch (1¼ cm) cubes.

3. Make the salad: In a large bowl, whisk the vinegar together with salt and pepper to taste. Add the minced garlic and whisk to mix. Add the oil in a thin stream, whisking constantly until it is well combined. Add the croûtons and toss quickly. Snip any dandelion leaves that are very long into more manageable pieces; add the dandelion leaves to the bowl. Toss well, so the leaves are thoroughly coated with the dressing, and serve.

4 servings

The Germ of the Garlic

*W*hat, exactly, is the germ of garlic? It's the nascent garlic plant that sits at the heart of each garlic clove and begins to grow and turn green within weeks after the garlic is harvested. Opinions differ about how to slow the growth of the germ. In the Tarn, home of Rose de Lautrec garlic, farmers place garlic bulbs in a warm room to keep them from sprouting. In Gascony, local wisdom also calls for garlic to be stored in a warm, dry place. Others insist garlic be kept cool. Dryness is key, no matter what the temperature.

Gastronomically speaking, the germ does no harm, yet it can lend a subtle bitterness, detracting from the fine flavor of the garlic itself. Some say it can cause indigestion as well. I always remove the germ when I'm serving garlic raw, such as in a vinaigrette. I also remove it for cooking unless the recipe calls for the entire clove.

The Aroma of Garlic
L'Ail Rose de Lautrec

Every Friday morning from the end of July through March, station wagons and small trucks wind their way along country roads toward the medieval hill town of Lautrec, in the Tarn. Their trunks and back seats are piled high with rose-colored garlic, some of it tied into fat bunches, the rest packed into red net bags. All of it is the highly sought after garlic called *l'ail Rose de Lautrec,* and it is destined for the weekly wholesale garlic market.

Lautrec is crowned by a windmill, one among many in this warm, stony region where the wind blows 250 days a year. One wind called the *autan,* which can blow for three days or three weeks, is said to drive people in this raw and ancient region crazy no matter what its duration.

The air is calm today as vehicles line up on both sides of the road into town, open trunks to the center. A whistle blows at 9:30 A.M. and the market begins.

Farmers stand in hopeful clumps, smoking and gossiping. Two well-dressed gentlemen, both brokers, look over the garlic, taking notes on large pads. Haggling is jocular and sometimes loud as a broker teases a farmer, each of whom sets his own price for the garlic.

At the conclusion of a deal, the broker tears off a piece of paper and hands it to the farmer, who immediately closes the trunk of his car, signaling an end to the day's business. On a busy day, the farmer leaves the market immediately for the nearby cooperative, where his garlic is weighed and boxed. On a day like today, when mist hangs in the air and commerce is slow, farmers stay to pass the time.

Still, the market lasts only an hour. By 10:30 all of the garlic is sold.

"There's a huge demand for our garlic," says garlic farmer Jean-François Tournié, standing at the head of the market and looking down at the long line of cars. "In summer we'll sell eighty tons at each market."

Rose de Lautrec garlic is sought after for its rich, intense flavor, rosy hue, and keeping quality. It is recognized by the French government with a Label Rouge, a signal of quality granted only to garlic grown in a tight circle around the town, where the clay soil and warm spring air give it its unique characteristics.

Currently 205 farmers have the right to the Label Rouge, and they produce ten percent of France's garlic. M. Tournié is president of their union, a post he took on willingly when he feared the quality of the garlic was in question.

"We don't own the Label Rouge—the government can take it from us at any time," he says. "So I felt I needed to help keep things going, help keep the quality high."

Rose de Lautrec garlic is cultivated using time-proven methods. "We rotate our fields, planting garlic only one year out of five to keep down disease," M. Tournié says. "We're very careful because garlic has allowed Lautrec and its family farms to survive. We couldn't do all the work involved if we didn't have help from our families, and they wouldn't have work if it weren't for the garlic."

As in many agricultural families, every member is involved, sharing the work on each other's farms when they're needed. Often, parents and the children who take over the farm live in the same house.

"This was my grandfather's house, and my parents live downstairs," says M. Tournié as we walk up to the massive rectangular stone farmhouse, which is surrounded by tidy gardens and large open fields, and adjacent to an open barn full of garlic cloves that are this year's seeds. "We often eat together and we all work together, but we manage to be independent, too."

SOWING AND HARVESTING

M. Tournié plants about 3,000 pounds (1,350 kg) of garlic every year and harvests upwards of 24,000 pounds (10,800 kg). The plump cloves are sown in December, after the sun has shone on the soil for eight days, warming it up. In spring the garlic sends up a flower, which is cut so the plant can put its energy into the bulb. "That's when it really grows," he says. "It will go from the size of a golf ball to the size of a small orange in about two weeks."

He takes great pleasure in walking his fields, surveying the progress of his crops. He also considers it an indispensable part of the job. When he senses the garlic is ripe, he

(continued)

picks a bulb, and if the skin is a bit black, the harvest can begin.

Once ripe, the garlic must be harvested immediately, a job done by a combination of hand and mechanical labor. A tractor pulls a harvester which gently digs up the garlic, grabs it by the leaves, and gives it a hearty shake to loosen the clumps of soil clinging to the long roots. Workers sitting behind the tractor trim the stems by hand.

The garlic is immediately hung from wooden beams in open barns to dry in the hot summer wind.

"In July all you smell here is garlic," M. Tournié says with a laugh.

Once the garlic dries, the Tourniés go to work in the shade of the barn. M. Tournié's father cuts the roots flush with each bulb, and the rest of the family sorts them according to size. The largest, which are about 3 inches (7½ cm) across, are reserved for bunches. These are sorted again to remove any with imperfections, then all but one layer of their papery skin is peeled off to reveal the characteristic rosy garlic beneath.

"We have to be careful at this point not to make a mark on the cloves when we peel off the skin, or the garlic won't be up to quality standard," M. Tournié says.

Their garlic is the only variety with a rigid central stem, which makes it impossible to braid. Instead, farmers group stems and tie them to form stiff little bunches.

There is a certain quality M. Tournié is looking for in his bunches, and he does not allow anyone else to do the tying, for which they are all grateful. He carefully groups perfect bulbs, wraps their stems with orange string, and adds a red label that bears his name. He sells many of these bunches to visitors who stop by the farm.

What isn't sold by October undergoes a gentle heat treatment to prevent the germ inside the cloves from growing. This allows the garlic to keep without sprouting until May or June, one full year after it is taken from the ground.

Much of *l'ail Rose de Lautrec* goes to the country's largest wholesale market, Rungis, just outside of Paris. "Up there it's a known quantity," M. Tournié says with obvious pride. "They simply call it 'Lautrec.'"

Watercress, Beet, and Walnut Salad
Salade de Cresson et de Betteraves aux Noix

➔ ••• ◄

This salad celebrates the crossover of seasons, when winter segues into spring. Watercress is at its best at this time of year, it seems—gorgeously green, abundantly leafy. Beets are still sweet and luscious, and walnuts hardly have a season.

In France, beets are sold precooked. They appear in the market meltingly soft, leaving a little trail of crimson juice in the bottom of the market basket, on the merchant's hands, everywhere they touch something.

I love this salad for its crunch, its pepperiness, its sweetness. Serve this as a first course, before a roast chicken or Jacqueline Priaulet's Daube (see Index). A Saumur-Champigny is a fine accompaniment to the salad.

ASTUCES . . . .

• *If for some reason the beets aren't as sweet and flavorful as you'd like, increase the sherry vinegar by ¼ teaspoon and add a pinch of sugar to the dressing.*

• *Mix up the dressing and add the beets at least 30 minutes before you plan to serve the salad, so the flavors have a chance to meld.*

. . . .

---

1 large beet, trimmed

1 large bunch watercress

¼ teaspoon sherry vinegar

Sea salt and freshly ground black pepper

5 tablespoons walnut oil

1 shallot, peeled and very thinly sliced

½ cup (60 g) walnut meats, coarsely chopped

---

1. Bring 1 quart (1 l) water to a boil in the bottom of a vegetable steamer and steam the beet until it is tender, 30 to 45 minutes, depending on its size. When cool enough to handle, peel, dice, and set aside.

2. Before you unwrap the bunch of watercress, trim away any roots. Then unwrap the bunch and trim away any roots that remain. Taste the stems. If the flavor is very strong, trim them to right below the leaves. Otherwise, include them in the salad. You should have about 8 cups (210 g) of watercress. Rinse and pat dry.

3. In a large bowl combine the vinegar

with salt and pepper to taste. Whisking constantly, add the oil in a thin stream. Add the shallot and whisk quickly. Then add the diced beet and stir with a wooden spoon. (The dressing may be made to this point up to 30 minutes ahead.)

4. Add the watercress to the dressing

and toss well, so that it is well dressed with the oil and vinegar mixture. Add the walnuts, toss once more, and serve, being careful to scoop up some beets and walnuts as you do so.

4 servings

The Salt Raker's Salad

Salade à l'endive du Paludier

→ • • • ←

I think this simple salad is the perfect accompaniment to The Salt Raker's Fish (see Index). It is pure and clean-tasting like the fish, yet the slight bitterness adds an intriguing counterpoint. I also love the monochromatic combination—with perhaps a sprig or two of chervil.

1 pound (500 g) Belgian endive, trimmed,
*   rinsed, and patted dry*
2 tablespoons extra-virgin olive oil
Finely ground sea salt
Ground white pepper, if desired
Small handful of chervil for garnish
*   (optional)*

Just before serving, chop the endive into tiny dice. Place the endive in a bowl, drizzle with the olive oil, and toss until it is well coated. Season very lightly with salt, and white

pepper if desired. Toss and serve, garnished with chervil if you like.

4 to 6 servings

Endive and Walnut Salad

La Salade d'Endive aux Noix

This wonderfully refreshing salad is filled with different flavors and textures, and it brightens up a winter meal like nothing else. I got the recipe from Françoise Chevallier, who lives in Vinay, in Le Dauphiné, in the heart of walnut-growing country. She serves it often in winter when Belgian endive is fresh and crisp and her year's supply of walnuts are dry and sweet. It's quick and hearty, and can be served as a main course for lunch, with plenty of crusty bread and a good lightly chilled Maury or Rosé de Provence.

Sometimes Françoise dresses the salad with walnut oil, other times with olive oil. I prefer olive oil because it is a good contrast to the walnuts, allowing their flavor to emerge. To get the most from this salad, cut the ingredients into very small pieces. Cut the endives at the last minute, for they will turn an unattractive reddish color when exposed to the air. And use a good-quality Gruyère-type cheese, such as Comté or Beaufort.

FOR THE VINAIGRETTE

1 teaspoon Dijon mustard

2 tablespoons sherry vinegar

6 tablespoons extra-virgin olive oil

1 large shallot, peeled and cut into
    paper-thin rounds

1 clove garlic, peeled, green germ removed,
    and minced

Sea salt and freshly ground black pepper

FOR THE SALAD

4 large Belgian endive, trimmed

6 ounces (180 g) Gruyère-type cheese, cut
    into small cubes

1 cup (125 g) walnuts, finely chopped

1. In a large salad bowl, whisk together the mustard and the vinegar. Then add the olive oil in a fine stream, whisking constantly until the mixture is emulsified. Add the shallot and the garlic, whisk, and then season to taste with salt and a generous amount of black pepper.

2. Cut the endive into thin crosswise slices. Add the endive, the cheese, and the walnuts to the vinaigrette and toss thoroughly. Season to taste and serve immediately.

6 servings

Cornmeal Cake and Salad
Le Gâteau de Maïs et Sa Salade

This is an old-fashioned dish, a simple meal that Marie-Rose Sol makes often for herself and her husband, Gabriel. Farmers who have raised everything from foie gras geese to vegetables, they are semi-retired now and living by themselves, though not far from their children. For Marie-Rose that means cooking for two, something she's never quite gotten used to. "When I make this, I still make almost as much as I did when the family was here, and we eat it all, with salad!" she says.

This dish, which is like a crisp corn pancake, is wonderful in late winter when the weather's still cold but no longer biting. Marie-Rose makes it when she wants something delicious that takes little effort. "Besides, this is one of Gabriel's favorite things," she says.

It's simple and somewhat unusual, like a dessert but treated as a vegetable. There is very little batter to cover the apples, so the result is light and crisp. Don't be afraid to bake the cake until it is just this side of burned on the edges and golden in the center. Serve it immediately upon removing it from the oven. You'll see that it goes perfectly with a garlicky salad!

Try a simple Bergerac along with this.

1 tablespoon unsalted butter, melted
⅓ cup (80 ml) milk
1 large egg
2 tablespoons sugar
3 tablespoons coarse yellow cornmeal
2 teaspoons unbleached all-purpose
    flour
Pinch of sea salt
1 large apple, peeled, cored, and cut into
    thin slices
Green Salad with Oil and Vinegar
    Dressing (page 56)

1. Preheat the oven to 450°F (230°C). Pour the melted butter into a 10-inch (25 cm) tart pan and swirl it around so it evenly covers the bottom.

2. Heat the milk in a small saucepan

over low heat until it is hot but not boiling. Keep it hot over very low heat.

3. In a large bowl, whisk the egg with the sugar. Then whisk in the cornmeal, flour, and salt. Whisking vigorously, slowly add the hot milk, stirring until combined.

4. Strew the apple slices over the surface of the tart pan. Whisk the cornmeal mixture again and pour it over the apples, shaking the tart pan if necessary, so the batter evenly cov-

ers the surface. The apple slices will stick well above the batter. Bake in the center of the oven until the cake is deep golden on the edges and a lighter golden in the center, 15 to 20 minutes.

5. When the corn cake is cooked, remove it from the oven and serve it immediately, with the salad alongside.

2 to 4 servings

Fennel and Anchoïade Salad

Salade de Fenouil à l'Anchoïade

This salad is a variation on one of my favorite themes—fennel and anchovies. During the winter, when fennel is sweet and firm, I serve it as a first course. The anchovies excite the palate, the fennel lends an incredible sweetness, and together they wake up the taste buds to a new array of flavors.

Since it is best served at room temperature, remove the fennel from the refrigerator two hours in advance, so it has a chance to warm up; then toss it with the *anchoïade* about fifteen minutes before you serve it, so the flavors have a chance to blend.

Be sure to slice the fennel in very thin lengthwise slices, so it offers the maximum surface area for absorbing the *anchoïade*.

Serve as a first course, with a bottle of Côtes du Roussillon Rosé, before Jacqueline Priaulet's Daube (see Index).

ASTUCE . . . .

• *Trimming fennel bulbs can often involve removing most of the bulb and discarding it, for the outer layer can be tough and unappealing. Try to choose bulbs that are firm, white, and fresh looking. If you have one that's damaged on the outer layer from improper handling but otherwise fresh and crisp, peel it with a vegetable peeler, removing just the outer skin.*

The Power of Fennel

→·←

*T*he next time you need strength to, say, enter the ring and fight the lions, go to an important meeting or a half-price sale, or ride the subway, do as the gladiators did before they entered the ring, and chew on a piece of fennel.

You may not win the match, but you'll certainly exhibit great strength of body and brightness of spirit by doing so.

You may also want to keep bad luck at bay by hanging fennel near the chimney, a practice that is also believed, in some parts of France, to keep witches from entering the house.

2 large fennel bulbs, trimmed and very
    thinly sliced lengthwise, fronds
    (if available) reserved
3 tablespoons Monique's Anchoïade
    (page 2)
Freshly ground black pepper

1. Place the fennel in a large serving bowl. Whisk the *anchoïade* so it is well blended, then drizzle it over the fennel and toss until the fennel is thoroughly coated. Season generously with pepper, toss, and let sit for 10 to 15 minutes.

2. Mince the fronds, if they are available, sprinkle them over the salad, and serve.

4 to 6 servings

Grated Carrot Salad
Carottes Râpées

→···←

France should declare *carottes râpées* as its national salad, for one finds it as often in cafés throughout the country as at the farm table. Crisp and refreshing, it's a salad that wins every palate.

This version is particularly good because of the inclusion of fresh tarragon, whose anise-like flavor is an ideal complement to the carrots.

Serve it immediately for the best results!

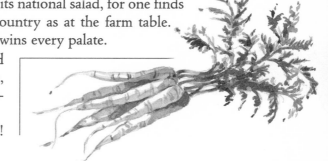

2 tablespoons freshly squeezed
   lemon juice
Sea salt and freshly ground
   black pepper
1 clove garlic, peeled, green germ removed,
   and minced
3 tablespoons extra-virgin olive oil
1½ pounds (750 g) carrots, peeled and
   grated (see Note)
⅓ cup (loosely packed) fresh tarragon
   leaves

1. In a large bowl, whisk together the lemon juice, salt and pepper to taste, and garlic. Slowly add the oil, whisking until the mixture emulsifies. Add the carrots and toss until they are thoroughly coated with the dressing.

2. Coarsely chop the tarragon and add it to the salad. Toss so it is thoroughly incorporated, adjust the seasoning, and serve.

4 to 6 servings

NOTE: The best grater for carrots is the Moulinex one that stands on three legs and has removable blades. The finest grating blade results in a nice crisp-textured grating.

Curried Cauliflower Salad
Salade de Chou-fleur au Curry

The cauliflower grown in Brittany tastes the way cauliflower should—subtle and nutty. It is never strong or biting, always smooth and crisp. Fields of cauliflower blanket Brittany's western coast, where it is bathed by the maritime breezes. It is the air, and the compost used to enrich the soil, that give Breton cauliflower its exceptional quality and renown.

I love seeing cauliflower at the market, still enrobed in its pale green leaves so that just the creamy white cloudlike crown shows through.

Cauliflower turns up in all sorts of dishes in France—gratins, soups, stews, even purées. I'm partial to it just about any way, though this lightly curried version is a favorite. Served on a colorful bed of winter lettuces such as *trévise* (radicchio), escarole, and mâche, it makes an easy first course.

FOR THE SALAD

1 small cauliflower, broken into florets
1 teaspoon best-quality red wine vinegar
¼ teaspoon best-quality curry powder
⅛ teaspoon cumin seeds
Sea salt and freshly ground black pepper
3 tablespoons extra-virgin olive oil
1 small shallot, peeled and cut into paper-
    thin rounds

FOR THE GARNISH

½ teaspoon best-quality red wine vinegar
Sea salt and freshly ground black pepper
1 tablespoon extra-virgin olive oil
1¾ ounces (55 g) mixed salad greens
    (2 cups loosely packed), such as
    radicchio, mâche, and escarole,
    rinsed and torn into bite-size pieces

1. Bring a large pot of salted water to a boil (2 tablespoons sea salt to 4 quarts; 4 l water) over high heat. Prepare a large bowl of ice water.

2. Add the cauliflower florets to the boiling water, return to a boil, and cook just until they are tender, 2 minutes. Drain the florets and plunge them into the bowl of ice water to stop the cooking. When the cauliflower is cool (after about 1 minute), drain and pat it dry.

3. In a large bowl, whisk together the vinegar, spices, and salt and pepper to taste. Slowly add the oil, whisking until the mixture is emulsified. Stir in the shallot. Then add the cauliflower and toss until coated with the dressing. Set aside at room temperature for at least 1 hour before serving.

4. Just before serving, prepare the garnish: In a medium-size bowl, whisk the vinegar with salt and pepper to taste. Then add the oil in a thin stream, whisking until the mixture is emulsified. Add the mixed greens, toss so they are coated with the dressing, and arrange them on a serving platter. Mound the cauliflower in the center and serve.

4 to 6 servings

Raw Beet Salad

Salade de Betteraves Crues

Although crisp, sweet, and juicy when raw, beets are rarely served that way in the U.S. I first ate them raw on a French farm, where they were finely grated and tossed in a simple vinaigrette. Immediately seduced, I have served them this way dozens of times since.

This salad is gorgeous as well as full of flavor and nutrition. The cumin seeds are the perfect seasoning for beets.

FOR THE BEETS
1 teaspoon balsamic vinegar
Sea salt and freshly ground black pepper
2 tablespoons extra-virgin olive oil
¼ teaspoon cumin seeds
1 shallot, peeled and cut into paper-thin slices
4 medium beets, trimmed, peeled, and finely grated

FOR THE GREENS
1 teaspoon balsamic vinegar
Sea salt and freshly ground black pepper
1 tablespoon extra-virgin olive oil
7 ounces (210 g) oak-leaf lettuce (8 cups, loosely packed), rinsed, patted dry, and torn into bite-size pieces

1. Whisk the vinegar with salt and pepper to taste in a large bowl. Add the olive oil in a thin stream, whisking constantly. Taste for seasoning; then stir in the cumin seeds and the shallot. Add the beets and toss so they are thoroughly coated with the dressing. Let the beets rest for at least 15 minutes before serving (see Note).

2. Prepare the greens: Right before serving, whisk the vinegar with salt and pepper to taste. Add the oil in a thin stream, whisking constantly. Add the lettuce leaves, toss so they are thoroughly coated with the dressing, and place them on a large serving platter. Toss the beets one more time and place them

atop the lettuce, leaving the lettuce showing around the edges. Serve immediately.

4 to 6 servings

NOTE: You may want to let the beets sit in the dressing for several hours before you serve the salad, to meld the flavors. This keeps well enough to be served the following day.

Be Careful How You Toss That Salad!

Before I was married, I often helped prepare meals on the Dubois farm in the Dordogne, where my intended was working. We had just a few weeks to wait until our wedding. It was late one night after a long day's work, and the dining room table was full of family members and workers. We were nearing the end of the meal and I went to get the salad, which I tossed at the table. The freshly picked leaves were unruly to the point of madness. Within the first toss, three had fallen to the table. In unison, Dany and Guy Dubois cried out, "You won't get married for three more years." Well, we were married on time, so I'm living proof that that particular adage, widely believed throughout the country, is as empty as our wine glasses were after eating that salad. But I'm sure I blanched, and maybe even gulped hard, before I laughed along with everyone else.

Zucchini Salad

Courgettes en Salade

→ ··· ←

Jean Gomis, a retired farmer near Poudenas, in Gascony, is not a fan of zucchini, a fairly recent addition to the Gascon garden. "It has no flavor," he says with disdain. "Why even eat it?"

His wife, Lina, defends the vegetable. She grows zucchini, picks them when they are young and tender, steams them just until they're hot through, and serves them with minced parsley and garlic.

I'm with Lina—I think their flavor is fresh and delicious. Be sure to use the best-quality extra-virgin olive oil you can find, and coarse sea salt if possible. If you are using fine sea salt, reduce the amount to your taste.

Serve this as a first course, or as a side dish with roast chicken or duck (see Index).

3 cups (750 ml) water
4 whole young zucchini, each no longer
  than 6 inches; 15 cm
1 teaspoon extra-virgin olive oil
½ teaspoon coarse sea salt
1 clove garlic, peeled, green germ removed,
  and minced
½ cup (loosely packed) flat-leaf parsley
  leaves

1. Bring the water to a boil in the bottom of a vegetable steamer. Add the zucchini (whole), and cook them, covered, until a skewer easily goes through them, about 9 minutes. Remove the zucchini from the steamer, let them cool until you can touch them, and then cut them in half lengthwise. Arrange them on a serving platter, drizzle them evenly with the olive oil, and sprinkle them with the sea salt. Set aside until they are cooled to room temperature.

2. Just before you are ready to serve the zucchini, mince the garlic and the parsley together, and sprinkle the mixture evenly over the zucchini. Serve immediately, while the parsley still has all its fresh flavor.

6 to 8 servings

Tomato Salad
Salade de Tomates

✦•••✦

O n the other hand, Lina Gomis's husband, Jean, does enjoy tomatoes, so she also gave me this recipe for her everyday fall salad. I love it because it combines late-season tomatoes, which are slightly underripe but full of flavor, and the first of the year's escarole, my favorite lettuce by far. She and her husband always eat it before a bowl of soup. Together the salad and soup make a fine and robust meal.

A S T U C E . . . .

• *If a hard-cooked egg is too fresh, or if it has been cooked too long, the shell will stick like glue. A simple way to solve the problem is to cut the egg in half lengthwise, shell and all. Using a tablespoon, just scoop each half egg from its shell. It works every time!*

. . . .

FOR THE VINAIGRETTE
1 teaspoon Dijon mustard
2 teaspoons best-quality red wine vinegar
¼ cup (60 ml) extra-virgin olive oil
1 shallot, minced
Sea salt and freshly ground black pepper

FOR THE SALAD
2 tablespoons flat-leaf parsley leaves
2 medium slightly underripe tomatoes,
*   cored and cut into eighths*
7 ounces (210 g) escarole leaves
*   (8 cups, loosely packed), rinsed, patted*
*   dry, and torn into small pieces*
2 large hard-cooked eggs, cut into quarters

1. In a large salad bowl, whisk together the mustard and vinegar. Add the olive oil in a thin stream, whisking until it is emulsified. Whisk in the shallot and season to taste with salt and pepper.

2. Coarsely chop the parsley leaves.

3. Add the tomatoes, escarole, and parsley to the salad bowl and toss until they are thoroughly coated with the dressing. Arrange the eggs on top, and serve (see Note).

6 servings

N O T E : For a more sophisticated presentation, mash the egg yolks into the vinaigrette to create a homogeneous mixture. Toss the escarole, parsley, and tomatoes in the vinaigrette, place in a serving bowl, and sprinkle with the egg white, diced.

Tomato and Sweet Pepper Salad

Salade de Tomates et de Piments Doux

→···←

Like the Basque flag, this salad is bright with the region's colors. Not-too-ripe tomatoes and curly Italian peppers are dressed with vinegar and oil to make a refreshing opener to a meal.

I discovered the salad high in the Pyrénées, at the *cayolar,* or mountain home, of François Poineau. He'd finished a day's worth of cheesemaking and when I prepared to take my leave, he said, "Of course you can't leave. You'll stay here and eat with me. We need to talk recipes, don't we?"

With that he set to, and before I knew it, this salad was in a bowl on the oilcloth-covered table, *pipérade* was simmering on the stove, and some of his own *confit de porc* was waiting to be sautéed. It was a memorable meal.

I made this salad as soon as I returned home, for I've rarely tasted anything more fresh and appealing. And each time I eat it, I return to the Pyrénées, feel the coolness of the breeze, and hear the tinkling of the sheep's bells.

> 2 teaspoons best-quality red wine
>   vinegar
> Sea salt and freshly ground black
>   pepper
> 1 tablespoon extra-virgin olive oil
> 1½ pounds (750 g) nearly ripe tomatoes,
>   cored and cut into eighths
> 2 medium Italian peppers (see Note),
>   trimmed, cut in half lengthwise, seeded,
>   and diced

In a medium-size bowl, whisk the vinegar with salt and pepper to taste. Then slowly add the olive oil, whisking until the mixture emulsifies. Add the tomatoes and the peppers, and toss. Adjust the seasoning and serve.

4 servings

NOTE: If you can't find Italian peppers, use bell peppers.

Tomato and Tapenade Salad
Salade de Tomates à la Tapenade

>···<

The robust flavors of Provence are the backbone of this summer salad. If you keep some tapenade on hand in your refrigerator, this will be simple to put together (particularly if you have a patch of basil in your garden).

ASTUCES . . . .

• *Be sure to use tomatoes that are just this side of pure ripeness, so they still have some firmness and that tart tomato tang. Don't be tempted to make this with winter tomatoes—it just won't have the right punch.*

• *Try tossing this salad with freshly cooked pasta. It makes a spectacular meal.*

. . . .

1½ pounds (750 g) almost-ripe garden tomatoes, cored and cut into eighths (see Note)
1 clove garlic, peeled, green germ removed, and minced
7 tablespoons Tapenade (page 4)
Sea salt and freshly ground black pepper
1 cup (loosely packed) fresh basil leaves

1. Place the tomatoes in a medium-size salad bowl. Add the garlic and toss. Then add the tapenade and toss until the tomatoes are thoroughly covered with it. Season to taste with salt and pepper.

2. Stack the basil leaves on top of one another and cut them into very fine slices (chiffonade). Add the basil to the salad. (Or use scissors and snip the basil leaves directly into the salad.) Toss, adjust the seasoning if necessary, and serve.

4 to 6 servings

NOTE: The tomatoes should be cut into even-size chunks for this salad. After coring, cut them in half vertically, then cut each half into four equal wedges.

Dandelion, Apple, and Bacon Salad

Salade de Pissenlits aux Pommes et aux Lardons

→···←

This recipe comes from Jean-Claude and Monique Martin, who sell their fresher-than-fresh produce at the Louviers market each Saturday. I willingly join the dozens of customers who line up around their crates and cartons filled with gorgeously fat carrots, wildly exuberant lettuces, tight-headed Brussels sprouts, rutabagas, potatoes, and the occasional pumpkin.

I like to watch the couple choose, weigh, and exchange snippets of conversation with their customers, who often will ask for advice about the appropriate vegetable for a specific recipe. In that case, Jean-Claude turns to his wife and they converse in a low tone, then he turns back, choosing just the right variety of potato for a gratin, the correct amount of leeks for soup, the right size rutabaga for potage. He usually adds *bon poids*—an extra handful of dandelion greens, several extra carrots, or two heads of lettuce for the price of one. That, and the quality of their produce, makes for a loyal clientele.

This recipe calls for cultivated dandelion greens, though those dug fresh from the garden would be excellent, too. Cultivated dandelion greens are tender, with a gentle bite, whereas those freshly dug are wild and woolly, with a snap to them.

This salad has a distinct Norman twist to it in the form of sweet/tart apple slices sautéed in, of course, fresh Normandy butter. Don't be alarmed by the blend of butter, oil, and bacon—the amounts are small, the combination sublime.

Try a lightly chilled Cassis Rosé with this, or go with the regional tradition of hard cider.

ASTUCE . . . .

• *When peeling apples, arm yourself with a European-style vegetable peeler (with a pointed end) and a melon-baller. Cut out the stem and the flower end of the apple with the vegetable peeler, peel the apple, then cut it in half. Using the melon-baller, scoop out the core with the seeds. You'll find yourself peeling and coring apples in half the time using this method.*

. . . .

FOR POACHING THE EGGS
3 tablespoons red wine vinegar
4 large eggs

FOR THE SALAD
7 ounces (210 g) dandelion
    greens (8 cups, loosely
    packed), white stems
    trimmed, well rinsed,
    and patted dry
7 ounces (210 g) slab bacon, rind
    removed, cut into 1 x ½ x ⅛ -inch
    (2½ x 1¼ x ¼ cm) pieces
2 tablespoons olive oil, if needed
1 tablespoon unsalted butter
1 large apple, such as Jonagold, McIntosh
    or Idared, cut into 16 thin, lengthwise
    slices
1 clove garlic, peeled, green germ removed,
    and diced
2 tablespoons best-quality red wine
    vinegar
Sea salt and freshly ground black pepper

1. Pour water to a depth of 3 inches
(7½ cm) in a large saucepan, add the vinegar,
and bring to a boil over medium-high heat.
Break one of the eggs into a small bowl.
Adjust the heat so the water is at a rolling
boil, and slide the egg into the spot in the
water where the bubbles emerge from the
bottom of the pan. (The swirling bubbles will
help wrap the egg white around the yolk, pro-
tecting it from direct heat.) If your pan is
large enough, add the remaining eggs (or as
many as will fit comfortably without crowd-
ing). Reduce the heat and simmer the eggs
until the whites are solid but the yolks are
soft, about 3 minutes. Remove the eggs, one
at a time, with a slotted spoon and transfer
them to a bowl of very warm salted water so
they will still be hot when you serve them.
Cook the remaining eggs and prepare the
salad. (For hot eggs, keep them no longer
than 15 minutes. You may poach them up to
an hour in advance and place them in a bowl
of room-temperature salted water, to serve
lukewarm on the salad.)

2. Tear the dandelion greens into bite-
size lengths and place them in a heatproof
bowl.

3. Place the bacon in a medium-size
heavy skillet over medium-high heat and
brown on all sides, stirring frequently, for
about 7 minutes. (If the bacon is dry and without much fat, add the olive oil at this point.)

4. While the bacon is browning, melt
the butter in a medium-size skillet over medium heat until sizzling hot. Be sure not to
brown the butter. Add the apple slices and
sauté until slightly golden and nearly soft
through, 3 to 4 minutes. Remove from the
heat and keep warm.

5. When the bacon is golden, drain off
all but 3 tablespoons fat. Add the garlic and
cook, stirring, just until it begins to turn
golden on the edges, about 1 minute. Then
stir in the vinegar, scraping up any browned
bits from the bottom of the skillet. Some of
the vinegar will evaporate, creating a cloud of
steam which may be irritating to your eyes, so
stand back as you stir.

6. Pour the bacon and its cooking juices
over the greens, and toss until all the ingredi-

ents are thoroughly combined. Add the apple slices and their cooking juices, and toss quickly. Then season with salt, if necessary, and a generous amount of pepper. (Taste the salad. If it doesn't have quite enough vinegar flavor, sprinkle a bit more on to satisfy your palate—vinegars vary greatly in their amount of acidity.)

7. Divide the salad among four warmed dinner plates. Drain the poached eggs and trim off any straggly egg white with kitchen shears. Top each salad with a poached egg, season the egg with a shower of pepper, and serve.

4 servings

Cooked Escarole and Bacon Salad
La Salade au Lard

→ ··· ←

This recipe comes from Simone Lasseaux, who has spent her life helping her husband, Jean, raise grapes and make Champagne in the Champagne region of France. While she has always worked alongside him in the vineyard, doing everything from trimming the vines to harvesting, she has also raised four children and fed them well.

All of their vegetables come from a garden behind their large, simple house in the village of La Neuville aux Larris. Driving down the town's main street, which was completely rebuilt along straight lines after World War II, one would never guess that behind each plain house lies a garden overflowing with bounty.

We experienced the bounty firsthand after a bone-chilling morning in the vineyard with the couple's eldest son, Philippe.

We were welcomed into Mme. Lasseaux's home, which was filled with the aroma of a famed regional specialty, *la potée* (see Index for Aromatic Pork and Vegetable Stew). This salad, another regional specialty and a favorite of the Lasseaux family, is comprised of fresh vegetables, cooked simply so that each bite is a celebration of their inherent flavors.

If the bacon you use doesn't give up much fat, add some olive oil to moisten the salad. It only adds to its rich, round flavor.

2 pounds (1 kg) russet potatoes, cut into quarters
1 tablespoon sea salt
6 ounces (180 g) slab bacon, rind removed, cut into 1 x ¼ x ¼-inch (2½ x ½ x ½ cm) pieces
2 shallots, peeled and minced
2 cloves garlic, peeled, green germ removed, and minced
2 tablespoons olive oil, if needed
1 pound (500 g) escarole or curly endive (about 16 cups leaves), rinsed and torn into large bite-size pieces
2 tablespoons sherry vinegar
Sea salt and freshly ground black pepper

1. Place the potatoes in a large saucepan and add enough water to cover them by 2 inches. Add the salt, cover, and bring to a boil over medium-high heat. Cook, partially covered, until the potatoes are tender through, about 20 minutes. Drain and keep warm.

2. While the potatoes are cooking, sauté the bacon over medium-high heat in a large skillet with 2-inch-high (5 cm) sides. When the bacon has begun to brown and has rendered some of its fat, add the shallots and garlic and cook, stirring constantly, until the shallots are translucent, about 10 minutes. If the bacon is very lean and does not give up enough fat, add the olive oil and stir so it coats all the ingredients. Reduce the heat to medium to keep the shallots and garlic from getting too brown.

3. Add the escarole and cook, turning frequently, until it is mostly limp but still slightly crisp and the green parts have turned a very dark green, 10 to 15 minutes. (You may need to add the lettuce in several batches. When the first has softened and reduced in volume, add the second, and continue until all of the lettuce is in the skillet.)

4. When the escarole is cooked, drizzle the vinegar over it and toss to incorporate it. Then season to taste with salt and plenty of black pepper.

5. To serve, place the potatoes in one warmed serving bowl, the lettuce mixture in another. To eat, place some warm potatoes on a plate, crush them gently with a fork, and top with the salad mixture. Enjoy!

4 to 6 servings

Curly Endive Salad with Hot Bacon Dressing and Goat Cheese

Salade Frisée aux Lardons et au Fromage de Chèvre

There is no salad more classic nor more delicious than *frisée aux lardons*, whether served on a farm, in a bistro, or at a fine restaurant. It requires nothing more than extra-fresh frisée, or curly endive, and flavorful slab bacon. In this case, the salad also includes a good-quality goat cheese, because its creamy texture and distinct flavor add a bright, satisfying touch.

Frisée is considered a winter green, and this boisterous salad is wonderful when the temperature drops because it is hearty and is served warm.

Try this with a lightly chilled Sancerre Blanc.

FOR THE GREENS

7 ounces (210 g) curly endive or escarole
  leaves (8 cups, loosely packed), rinsed,
  patted dry, and torn into small pieces
1 large shallot, peeled and cut into paper-
  thin rounds
1 clove garlic, peeled, green germ removed,
  and cut into tiny dice
8 small slices baguette or other fresh crusty
  bread
1 clove garlic, peeled
2 small goat cheeses (each 3½ ounces;
  105 g), such as Crottin de Chavignol,
  each cut into two horizontal rounds

TO SERVE

6 ounces (180 g) slab bacon, rind
  removed, cut into 1 x ¼ x ¼-inch
  (2½ x ½ x ½ cm) pieces
3 tablespoons olive oil, if needed
2 tablespoons best-quality red wine
  vinegar
Freshly ground black pepper
Sea salt (optional)

1. Preheat the broiler.

2. Place the curly endive, shallot, and diced garlic in a large heatproof salad bowl, and toss to mix.

3. Place the bread slices on a baking sheet and toast them on one side about 3 inches (7½ cm) from the heat element. Remove them from the broiler and rub on both sides with the whole garlic clove. Place one round of cheese on the *untoasted* side of

four toast slices and place them, along with the remaining pieces of bread (untoasted side up) under the broiler until the cheese is golden and bubbling, and the plain bread is toasted, 2 to 3 minutes.

4. Place the bacon in a large heavy skillet over medium-high heat and cook, stirring frequently, just until it is golden, about 5 minutes. Depending upon how much fat is rendered from the bacon, add up to 3 tablespoons oil. Add the vinegar, standing back as it gives off steam. Stir, scraping up all the browned bits from the bottom of the pan, then pour over the salad. Toss thoroughly, seasoning generously with pepper and salt if necessary, and toss again.

5. Divide the salad among four warmed salad plates. Place a cheese-topped toast atop each salad, and one piece of plain toast on the side of the plate. Serve immediately.

4 servings

Warm Lentil and Bacon Salad
Salade de Lentilles du Puy aux Lardons Chauds

This salad is ubiquitous in the Puy region, where France's best-known lentils are cultivated in rocky terrain that lends them an intriguing flinty flavor. The flavors in this salad—mustard, shallots, slab bacon—are big and gutsy. Combined with the lentils, they meld into a rich and delectable combination.

The recipe comes from the Paris restaurant Ambassade d'Auvergne, an unofficial tourist office for the Auvergne. Run by a delightful woman, Françoise Mouiller, who is a native of the Auvergne, one finds within its warm and cozy walls the best Auvergnat cooking this side of the Auvergne. I make this often, using an idea from Pierre Ambert, a lentil farmer in the Puy region (see page 261), who serves his version warm, with hard-cooked eggs and smoked trout alongside. I suggest you add at least the eggs—they are a wonderful accompaniment.

Try to get fresh, nutty walnut oil, for it makes a difference in this recipe. Otherwise, use the best-quality olive oil you can find. For the duck fat—use it if you can find it. If not, there's always good old olive oil!

Also, you may want to vary the garnish. Try adding chopped walnuts to the bacon while it cooks. If you'd like to omit either the chives or the scallions, do so. But don't forget, this is a hearty dish, served in a stony region where wind whips around corners, farmhouse walls are three feet thick, and appetites are demanding.

Serve this with a lightly chilled Beaujolais.

FOR THE LENTILS

3 tablespoons rendered duck fat
   (page 142) or olive oil
1 small onion, diced
2 ounces (60 g) thin-sliced ham, cut into
   tiny dice
1 pound (500 g) lentilles du Puy
1 bouquet garni (5 parsley stems,
   3 imported bay leaves, 2 green
   leek leaves, and 12 sprigs fresh thyme,
   tied in cheesecloth)
Sea salt and freshly ground black pepper

FOR THE VINAIGRETTE

1 tablespoon Dijon mustard
2 tablespoons best-quality red wine vinegar
Sea salt and freshly ground black pepper
⅔ cup (160 ml) walnut oil or extra-virgin
   olive oil

TO SERVE

4 ounces (125 g) lean slab bacon, rind
   removed, cut into 1 x ¼ x ¼-inch
   (2½ x ½ x ½ cm) pieces
1 bunch chives (¼ cup, minced)
2 scallions (green onions), trimmed and
   cut into paper-thin rounds
2 hard-cooked eggs, cut into quarters, for
   garnish (optional)

1. In a large heavy casserole, melt the duck fat over medium-high heat and sauté the onion and ham until the onion is translucent, about 5 minutes. Add the lentils and the bouquet garni, and cover with water. Bring to a boil. Then lower the heat and simmer, uncovered, until the lentils are crisp-tender, about 30 minutes. Season the lentils with salt and pepper to taste, let them cool slightly, and then drain.

2. While the lentils are cooking, prepare the vinaigrette: Whisk together the mustard, vinegar, and salt and pepper to taste. Then whisk in the walnut oil, adding it in a fine stream.

3. Place the slab bacon in a medium-size skillet over medium-high heat and sauté until golden brown, 5 to 6 minutes. Remove with a slotted spoon to a plate.

4. Mince the chives.

5. Remove the bouquet garni from the lentils. Add the lentils to the vinaigrette, mix well, and let sit until lukewarm, about 20 minutes.

6. Sprinkle the chives, scallions, and bacon over the lentils, and arrange the hard-cooked eggs around the salad. Serve immediately.

6 to 8 servings

Green Bean and Potato Salad

Salade d'Haricots Verts et de Pommes de Terre

>···<

There is something about the soil in France that brings out the best in green beans. Whatever the variety, *haricots verts* have a depth of flavor, a sweet and sophisticated nuttiness, that complements their inherent "green" flavor.

New potatoes are ready at the same time green beans come to market, and the combination is a natural—particularly in this salad, which is showered with shallots.

The salad is delicious served while it's still warm, or at room temperature.

ASTUCES . . . .

• *While steaming vegetables may be more nutritious, cooking them briefly in lightly salted water underlines their flavor and gives them depth. I recommend it here particularly, for the harmony of flavors.*

• *It may seem superfluous to call for "snipping," or "stringing" green beans, for it appears that contemporary varieties rarely have strings. But strings are often a function of maturity. The first couple of crops from a vine of "stringless" beans is usually just that—without strings. But subsequent crops often have strings. So don't be cavalier about stringing your beans. Always check them first.*

• *Green beans can have a tendency to turn yellow when left in contact with an acid. For that reason I don't add the beans until about 20 minutes before serving this salad. They have enough time to absorb the flavor of the dressing, yet retain their color.*

· · · · · · · · · · · · · · ·

3 tablespoons best-quality red wine vinegar
Sea salt and freshly ground black pepper
½ cup (125 ml) extra-virgin olive oil
3 shallots, peeled and cut into paper-thin horizontal slices
1½ pounds (750 g) green beans, snipped
2 pounds (1 kg) small new potatoes, scrubbed

1. In a large bowl, whisk the vinegar with salt and pepper to taste. Slowly add the oil, whisking until the dressing is emulsified. Add the shallots, whisk briskly, and set aside.

2. Bring a large pot of salted water to a boil (1 tablespoon sea salt per 2 quarts; 2 l water) over high heat. Prepare a large bowl of ice water.

3. Add the beans to the boiling water, return to a boil, and cook until the beans are tender but not mushy, 4 to 5 minutes. Using a slotted spoon, transfer the beans to the ice water and leave them there until they are chilled through. Drain the beans and spread them out on a tea towel to dry.

4. Bring the water back to a boil. Add

the potatoes, return to a boil, and cook until they are just tender, 12 to 15 minutes. Check the potatoes; depending on the variety and their freshness, they may take substantially longer to cook. Drain the potatoes and set them aside to cool slightly.

5. Whisk the dressing again to be sure all the ingredients are well blended.

6. As soon as you can handle the potatoes (they should still be quite hot), cut them into bite-size pieces, dropping them right into the dressing. Toss the potatoes and set them aside at room temperature. About 20 minutes before serving the salad, toss in the beans.

6 to 8 servings

Herring and Potato Salad
Salade de Hareng et de Pommes de Terre

P otato salad is a summer staple on the French farm, usually dressed with a simple, well-spiced vinaigrette. This version includes smoked herring, a natural complement, and a common staple, in the French farm kitchen.

Serve this salad before roast chicken or fish, with a Côtes du Rhône alongside.

4 pounds (2 kg) waxy potatoes, scrubbed
3 tablespoons best-quality red wine vinegar
Sea salt and freshly ground black pepper
½ cup (125 ml) extra-virgin olive oil
1 medium onion, cut in half lengthwise,
*   then cut crosswise into paper-thin slices*
⅓ cup (loosely packed) flat-leaf parsley leaves
4 small smoked herring fillets (12 ounces;
*   375 g), cut into 1-inch-long (2½ cm) pieces*

1. Bring a large kettle of salted water (1 tablespoon sea salt per 2 quarts; 2 l water) to a

boil, and cook the potatoes until they are just tender, but not mushy, 15 to 25 minutes. Drain them and set them aside to cool slightly.

2. In a large bowl, whisk the vinegar with salt and pepper to taste. Slowly add the oil, whisking until the mixture emulsifies. Add the onion slices, toss so they are thoroughly coated with the dressing, and set aside.

3. When the potatoes are just cool enough to handle but still hot, peel and cut them into bite-size chunks, dropping them directly into the onions and dressing. Toss so they are thoroughly coated with the dressing, and season to taste with additional salt and pepper.

4. If you are going to serve the salad immediately, coarsely chop the parsley. (If you are going to let the salad sit, wait until just before serving to chop it.)

5. Add the herring to the potatoes and toss gently. Garnish with the parsley, and serve immediately. (Or, let the potatoes cool to room temperature in the dressing. Just before serving, add the herring and garnish with the parsley.)

6 to 8 servings

Pork and Chard Salad
Caillettes en Salade

→···←

To me, *caillettes* (pork and Swiss chard sausages) conjure up the mystery of Provence because they're like the region itself: rustic, yet indefinably refined. I can just imagine a farmer tucking three or four in his *biasso*, or lunch bag, along with a slab of home-baked bread, a chunk of cheese, and a bottle of wine.

When that image fades and reality returns, I think about *caillettes* and salad. They make a terrific addition to a plate of crisp greens dressed with a nice vinaigrette.

Serve with a Coteaux d'Aix Rouge or Rosé.

1 recipe Pork and Chard Sausages (page 197)
2 teaspoons balsamic vinegar
1 teaspoon Dijon mustard
Sea salt and freshly ground black pepper
¼ cup (60 ml) extra-virgin olive oil
7 ounces (210 g) salad greens
    (8 cups, loosely packed), such as red or
    green oak-leaf, or a blend of arugula,
    oak-leaf, romaine, and lolla rossa
8 fresh sage leaves, for garnish (optional)

1. Preheat the oven to 350°F (175°C).

2. Put the sausages in a baking dish, cover, and bake until heated through, 25 to 30 minutes.

3. Just before serving, whisk together the vinegar, mustard, and salt and pepper to taste, in a large bowl. Add the oil in a thin stream, whisking constantly until the vinaigrette emulsifies. Tear the greens into large bite-size pieces and add them to the bowl. Toss the greens with the dressing, and divide them among four dinner plates. Top each salad with a hot *caillette*. Garnish with sage leaves if desired, and serve immediately.

4 servings

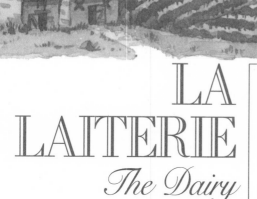

LA LAITERIE

The Dairy

Dairy products are basic to the French farm, today as always. The farm cook still uses fresh milk, and often someone—usually the grandmother, who has not only the time but also the skill—makes yogurt, butter, and cheeses.

Though France is generally divided into its butter and cream half (the north) and its olive oil half (the south), farm-fresh dairy products are ubiquitous. For traditionally, in Provence as well as in Normandy, every farm has at least one cow—and often a goat or two—to provide milk for the family and butter for the market. But even on farms where there are no longer any milk animals, the dairy products—purchased from a neighbor or from someone in the village—are as important as ever.

Every farm has its chickens, too, raised in the farmyard, not far from the milking barn. Their eggs go naturally with dairy products.

Within this chapter simple cheese dishes are matched up with recipes for luscious omelettes and other egg preparations, typical of the French family farm.

La Laiterie • The Dairy

Little Packets of Goat Cheese
Rissoles

→•••←

Nadine and Christian Devisme and their four children live on wooded acreage outside the town of Louviers in Normandy. There they raise pigeons, fruit, and vegetables, and occasionally bake their own bread in an ancient wood-burning oven that Christian restored.

Nadine, one of the more imaginative cooks I know, served these little packets as the cheese course one night while we were sitting near the huge fireplace in the dining room. I was intrigued by their shape, and even more intrigued by their flavor. I discovered that *rissoles* are prepared in many ways, including deep-fried in olive oil, but this remains my favorite. Be sure to let the *rissoles* cool slightly before serving them. The cheese is blisteringly hot when straight from the oven. I even like them the next day, gently warmed or at room temperature, too, for a picnic or a quick lunch.

Try these with a fruity Côtes du Rhône.

FOR THE RISSOLES
1 recipe Homemaker's Pastry (page 509)
¼ cup (loosely packed) flat-leaf parsley
*   leaves*
1 tablespoon fresh thyme leaves, or
*   1 teaspoon dried*
7 ounces (210 g) soft fresh goat cheese
½ teaspoon olive oil
Freshly ground black pepper

FOR THE EGG WASH
1 small egg
1 teaspoon water

1. Preheat the oven to 425°F (220°C). Line a baking sheet with parchment paper.

2. Roll out the pastry to form a 15-inch (38 cm) circle, and cut out six 5-inch (13 cm) rounds. Arrange the rounds on the prepared baking sheet.

3. Mince the parsley and the thyme together.

4. Divide the cheese among the pastry rounds, pressing it gently into a small mound in the center of each round. Drizzle the olive oil over the cheese, then sprinkle with the herbs. Grind black pepper to taste over the filling.

5. To form each packet, bring the pastry up around the cheese, gathering the edges together at the top. Pinch the pastry together gently but firmly just above the cheese, leaving the edges free in a little topknot.

6. Make the egg wash by whisking the egg and water together in a small bowl.

7. Brush each packet with egg wash, and bake in the center of the oven until the pastry is golden, about 30 minutes. Remove the packets from the oven and let them sit for 10 minutes before serving.

6 servings

Fromage Blanc

This is a mainstay of the French diet, sort of a cross between yogurt and cream cheese. Children love it as an afternoon snack or a simple dessert, particularly when it is mixed with a liberal amount of jam or honey. It also forms the basis for cheese tarts, for cheese spreads, for all number of cheese dishes. I like to use it for spreads and sweets because it has an intriguingly sweet/bitter flavor.

Making this very good facsimile of *fromage blanc* couldn't be simpler. It will keep for three to four days, tightly covered, in the refrigerator.

To cut calories, use low-fat versions of the ingredients. The *fromage blanc* will be slightly more acidic, but still delicious.

1¾ cups (435 ml) large- or small-curd cottage cheese
½ cup (125 ml) plain yogurt

1. Place both ingredients in a food processor and process until the mixture is entirely smooth, 3 to 5 minutes.

2. Line a sieve with a double layer of cheesecloth and place it over a bowl. Transfer the mixture to the sieve and refrigerate it. Leave it until most of the liquid has drained away and the *fromage blanc* has the consistency of loose cream cheese, at least 8 hours.

3. Either eat the *fromage blanc* as is or proceed with recipes that call for it.

1¾ cups (435 ml)

The Last Vintage

The music of bells from Montbéliard cattle sounded in the air as I drove up a winding dirt road between alpine meadows. Just outside the hamlet of Chapelle-les-Bois, in the Jura mountains, a sharp turn brought me to an old farmhouse where Bernard Vermot was making Morbier cheese. Known for its creamy texture and the thin line of black ash that runs through its center, Morbier is a favorite mountain cheese.

M. Vermot claims to be the only person who still makes Morbier in the old way, all by hand in a huge copper cauldron.

"It's a passion now," he said with a wry laugh. "It's got to be, otherwise I wouldn't be foolish enough to do it."

He'd already mixed the morning's milk with the milk from the night before, and had added a fermenting agent to it.

"I add about a fifth of what you're supposed to," he said. "The milk, which is forty percent fat and thirty percent protein, is such high quality that it doesn't need much help, really."

The fermenting agent helps the milk mature to the point where it will accept the rennet, which he now sprinkles in. Thirty minutes later, the cauldron contains what looks like an immense yogurt—the curd.

Taking a flexible metal band, M. Vermot cut the curd into small pieces. He then slid an electric blade into it to mix the curd and chase out the whey.

A compact man with the allure of an athlete, M. Vermot surveyed his cheese-in-the-making with intensity. He periodically touched the cheese and then stopped the mixer with a precise move.

"It's ready," he said.

He wrapped one end of a sheet-size piece of cheesecloth around a flexible metal blade that rested across the cauldron.

Moving quickly, he slid the metal blade and fabric under the curd, and swept all the curd out of the cauldron. He quickly gathered the four corners of the cloth in his hands and hefted it over to a sloped, stainless-steel table, whey gushing out as he went. He tied the corners together and left the fat bundle on the table to drain.

The whey continued to rush down a gutter alongside the table and into a drain, splashing the tile floor. When it slowed to a trickle, M. Vermot untied and cut the mass of curd apart, using a plastic scraper that resembled a dustpan. He shoved the pieces into fabric-lined wooden molds held together with rope, pushing hard to fit as much as possible in each. He weighted them briefly, then removed each cheese from its mold and sliced it in half horizontally, sprinkling one cut side with ash before reassembling it and returning it to its mold.

"The lady I learned from heated her cauldron over a wood fire, rubbed the bottom to get ash on her hands, then rubbed her hands on the cheese," he said.

Sanitation standards mean no more wood fires in cheesemaking facilities, so M. Vermot gets ash from the pharmacy. "It's used as a natural medicine," he said, laughing. "It's perfectly edible, but it doesn't add a thing to the cheese."

Why bother with it?

"Tradition," he said, surprised at being asked.

The origin of the ash goes back at least two hundred years. Then, during the summer when cows gave little milk, farmers would have only enough curd to fill a mold halfway.

They'd cover the top of the curd with ash to keep a skin from forming, and add the next day's curd to fill the mold up.

M. Vermot leaves the cheeses in the molds until the following morning, when he unmolds and sets them on the bench in the laboratory. When they are solid enough to be transported, he takes them to the ripening *cave*, down the hill by his house.

There they sit on spruce shelves for at least three months, gradually ripening to a creamy tang. His wife, Marie-Odile, salts them twice and rubs them regularly with a brine—a process that takes a good part of each morning, as the *cave* is filled with hundreds of cheeses in varying stages of ripeness.

M. Vermot doesn't seem to mind the killing labor that has him up at 5:00 A.M. to milk the cows, make cheese, and clean the *laboratoire* until just before noon, and then work the fields until nightfall.

Looking out the door at blue sky and flowering fields, he said, "Who could argue with this place, with this kind of work? I find that it is, quite simply, the most pleasant thing I've ever done."

Fromage Blanc with Herbs
Fromage Blanc aux Herbes

I first tasted this at Aux Pommiers de Livaye, a farm that has opened its doors and its heart to paying guests. There, the Lambert-Dutrait family raise poultry and dairy cattle and grow flower gardens so beautiful they make you weep. The cuisine they serve, prepared by M. and Mme. Lambert-Dutrait, is typical for Normandy, though with a slight difference. Their son, Emmanuel, plans to take over the farm and small restaurant, and to that end attended hotel management school. He returns to help them now and then, and he has brought some uptown ideas along with his expertise, particularly in the presentation.

Inspired by the Lambert-Dutraits, I serve this with thinly sliced crisp apples (such as Winesaps, Idareds, Granny Smiths, or Gravensteins), radish or carrot rounds, cucumber slices, and freshly baked bread. Use your imagination as you add herbs, too. I think that sorrel is an absolute, but beyond that, follow your own taste.

Fromage blanc is available at some specialty stores. If you can't find it, try the simple substitute on page 93.

A S T U C E . . . .

• *How does one measure chives? If you asked a farmwife, she would look perplexed, then respond, "Why would you want to measure them?" For the purposes of recipes, however, measurements are necessary. So when I call for a "bunch of chives," I mean a bunch that measures 1 inch in diameter. That said, use chives, and all herbs, generously to your taste!*

. . . .

2 cups (500 ml) fromage blanc,
   store-bought or homemade (page 93)
2 large sorrel leaves, ribs removed
1 bunch fresh chives, minced
   (a generous ½ cup)
Sea salt to taste
Freshly ground black pepper (optional)
1½ teaspoons Crème Fraîche (page 520)

1. The night before you plan to make this, place the *fromage blanc* in a stainless-steel strainer lined with a double layer of cheesecloth and set it over a bowl. Refrigerate and let drain for at least 8 hours, until the *fromage blanc* has the thickness of cottage cheese.

2. Combine the *fromage blanc* and the sorrel leaves in a food processor and purée until the sorrel is thoroughly combined and the *fromage blanc* has turned a pale green.

Add the chives and purée. Season to taste with salt (and pepper, if desired); then stir in the crème fraîche. Adjust the seasoning.

3. Mound the *fromage blanc* in a medi- um-size bowl and serve with the apples and vegetables of your choice alongside.

6 appetizer servings

Goat Cheese Tart

Tarte au Chèvre

>···←

This recipe comes from Monique Houssin, who works hard and diligently in her tidy, tiny *fromagerie* tucked into the hills of the Drôme, in northern Provence. She and her husband, Michel, bought their ancient farm—part of which dates from Roman times—in the 1970s, when there was a huge movement back to the land. Since then they have worked and cajoled it into a going concern.

They've never wavered from their faith in the land, despite its rocky unwillingness to produce. Instead, they've worked it until it has yielded enough grains and grasses for their goats. They rent some and own many acres, but most of these remain in wild, aromatic thyme and hard, lumpy rock with enough greenery to provide forage for the goats.

They both care for the goats, which includes letting them out to pasture twice a day in the summer, where they roam the rocky slopes in search of food. Either Monique or Michel accompanies them, a part of the job they love. "We walk, we take a book, we keep ourselves busy while they eat, then we bring them home," Monique says.

The downside is that they often don't get home until after dark, and then they're up before dawn to milk the goats and let them out again. "It only lasts for the summer—then we get our break," says Monique.

The goats produce rivers of sweet, rich milk from which Monique makes round disks of cheese. She uses old-fashioned methods, those she learned from neighboring farm women when she first moved onto the farm. She allows the milk to ferment, ladles it by hand into plastic molds, then ages it gently.

Monique's Cheeses—Aged for Flavor

→·←

Monique Houssin sells her cheeses at all stages of development. The freshest cheese, one day old, is soft and creamy. The next stage is ten days old, her most popular. It is just set, still creamy but beginning to develop the characteristically flavorful dryness of goat cheese.

"My favorite cheese is three weeks old," she said, holding one up to show. "It's firm and the flavor is developed. I like to tell my customers it's the best, but I'll sell them whatever age they want."

She keeps some cheeses for weeks, until they develop a natural blue mold similar to that in Roquefort. "I've got a few customers who love this," she said, showing me a round that was silvered from age and laced with mold. "Look at the veins right through it. It was an accident the first time, but it's so good that I leave a few purposely because we love it, too."

Monique seldom cooks with her cheeses, preferring to eat them as they are. This tart is an exception, however. "Most goat cheese recipes don't excite me," she says. "But we love this and it's easy, so I make it often."

I do, too, and we love it more each time. Serve this with a fruity Côtes du Rhône.

2 tablespoons unsalted butter

3 large leeks, white part only, well rinsed and cut into very thin rounds

Sea salt and freshly ground black pepper

3 large eggs

½ cup (125 ml) Crème Fraîche (page 520)

8 ounces (250 g) fresh goat cheese

½ teaspoon cumin seeds

One 10½-inch (26 ½ cm) tart shell, made using Homemaker's Pastry (page 509) and prebaked

1. Preheat the oven to 400°F (205°C).

2. Melt the butter in a large heavy skillet over medium-high heat. Add the leeks and sauté until they are translucent and softened, about 10 minutes. Season lightly with salt and pepper, and set aside.

3. In a medium-size bowl, whisk the eggs to break them up. Then add the crème fraîche and whisk until it is thoroughly combined with the eggs. Crumble the goat cheese into the mixture and whisk or stir it vigorously, so it breaks up and is incorporated. There may be some chunks of cheese, which is fine. Season lightly with salt and generously with pepper. Then whisk in the cumin.

4. Spread the leeks over the bottom of the prebaked pastry. Then pour in the filling, easing it over the leeks. Bake in the center of the oven until the filling is puffed and golden and a sharp knife inserted into it comes out clean, 25 to 30 minutes.

5. Remove the tart from the oven and bring it immediately to the table for your guests to admire. Wait about 5 minutes before serving, however, as it will be blisteringly hot.

One 10½-inch (26 ½ cm) tart; 6 to 8 appetizer servings

Warm Camembert Tart
Tarte au Camembert Chaude

I first tasted this at Le Loucel, a thriving *ferme-auberge* just steps from Omaha Beach, in Normandy. There, chef-owner Paulette Petit serves rustic cuisine made almost entirely with ingredients she raises on her farm. Her cooking, as a result, is rich with cream and butter, eggs, beef, and poultry.

Mme. Petit makes this cheese tart from *plein de petits bouts,* or lots of small leftover pieces. Leftover cheese is just one of the perks of having a restaurant in Normandy!

My slice of this tart came to the table hot and succulent, rich with cheese flavor, yet smooth, too. I was instantly won over, and made it as soon as we got home from our visit. Not having the luxury of leftovers, I used an entire Camembert. And mmm . . . is it delicious!

The shallots are my addition, and I think they add just the right amount of flavor, cutting and lightening the cheese just slightly.

For this dish use the best quality Camembert you can find—I suggest Vallée brand, which is French, but you may want to try a locally made Camembert-type cheese as well.

Be sure to present the tart at the table as soon as you take it from the oven, while it is still puffy, for even five minutes later it will have sunk slightly. Caution your guests, however, to wait a moment or two before tasting it, because the cheese will be tongue-searingly hot.

Serve this with a crisp green salad and perhaps Green Beans with Sage (see Index).

Try a red Bandol or a Côtes du Roussillon-Villages or chilled hard apple cider alongside.

4 large eggs
¾ cup (185 ml) milk
Sea salt and freshly ground black pepper
1 shallot, peeled and sliced into thin rounds
One 10½-inch (26 ½ cm) tart shell, made
    using Homemaker's Pastry (page 509)
    and prebaked
1 Camembert cheese (8 ounces; 250 g),
    chilled, rind removed, and cut into
    ¼-inch-thick (½ cm) slices

1. Preheat the oven to 450°F (230°C).

2. In a medium-size mixing bowl, whisk together the eggs and the milk. Season generously with salt and pepper.

3. Sprinkle the shallot slices all over the prebaked pastry, separating the rounds so they are well distributed. Cover with the slices of cheese, spreading them evenly over the pastry. Pour the egg mixture over the cheese, and bake in the center of the oven until golden and puffed, 25 to 30 minutes.

4. Remove from the oven, separate the tart from the mold, and transfer it to a serving platter. Serve immediately.

One 10½ -inch (26½ cm) tart; 6 to 8 servings

Well-Being

→·←

The French national consciousness and sense of bien-être, or well-being, is closely allied with the sound of clucking, a supply of fresh eggs, and the gutsy flavor and texture of free-range chickens.

Most farms in France would be soulless without their chickens pecking around the farmyard, and most farm cuisine would be bereft without the richesse contributed by chickens. Many a farm family may have sold away the bulk of its land to make way for industry, but they always retain enough land to raise chickens. And plenty of rural homes have installed a poulailler, or chicken house, on a corner of the property. Chickens are a basic comfort.

When chickens are in heavy laying season, which generally corresponds with good weather, they produce an average of two eggs a day. An average clutch of chickens numbers four, which makes eight warm brown eggs to gather.

What to do with them all?

Make omelettes, for one thing. There is nothing quite so wonderful as a simple, light omelette for lunch or supper, along with a green salad (from the potager, or kitchen garden, another essential to the rural French household) and a rousing bottle of red wine.

Cheese, Cheese, Cheese

Cheese in France remains deliciously overwhelming. Just when you think you have a good working knowledge of regional varieties, up comes another.

One of my favorite things about visiting different regions is sampling the cheeses made there, and on a farm the cheese course is never missing. It comes between salad and dessert, and acts as a regional fanfare.

In Alsace soft, fragrant Munster is always accompanied by a small mound of caraway seeds. In Provence goat cheese predominates, and in Normandy the aroma of the cheese platter precedes it, laden as it is with Camembert, Livarot, and Pont l'Evêque.

In the Pays Basque, sheep's-milk cheese is served—sometimes alone, sometimes with glass jars of homemade sheep's-milk yogurt. (Seasoned with a red-hot piece of cast iron that is plunged into the milk before it sets, the yogurt has a smoky flavor and is considered a real delicacy.)

Roquefort, or another blue like Fourme d'Ambert or Bleu d'Auvergne, is indispensable on a cheese platter, always accompanied by unsalted butter. Camembert, too, is a standard, though unless it is made in Normandy of good raw milk, it will be a shadow of itself.

The cheese course is a tradition worthy of emulating. When composing a farm cheese platter, turn to American farmstead cheeses, which are becoming increasingly abundant. Keep texture in mind, and have a good mix of soft and hard, creamy and distinctive. Look in your region for fresh goat, cow, or sheep's cheeses, aged Cheddars, flavorful jack or Swiss-type cheeses. Present three to five cheeses, always including a blue—Maytag and Oregon blue are both excellent—balancing it with French imports like Comté, Crottin de Chavignol (goat cheese), or a sharp Laguiole. When eating cheese, begin with the mild and creamy, and finish with the blue.

Serve plenty of bread and unsalted butter alongside. If you've sipped white wine throughout the meal, continue into the cheese course, preferably with a white that is light and fruity but full of body. If you've already moved to red wine, stay there. Either way, you'll enjoy the pause, the repose of a cheese course.

La Laiterie • The Dairy

The Delicious Omelette
L'Omelette Délicieuse

In the north of France, on a farm in a town called Doullens not far from Amiens, Miche Devisme was famous among her multitude of nieces and nephews for her omelettes. She always had a passel of chickens—up to twenty at a time, of every variety possible—for she loved chickens with soul and character. Her chickens ran free in the courtyard of the farm, occasionally mildly terrorized by her old dog, Ma Belle.

Miche, who had lived on the farm with her mother, lived on there alone for a time after her mother died, but her long, low farmhouse was never empty, for it was always full of children who loved a vacation with Miche—and that's where I first met her fifteen years ago.

"I remember when Miche made us omelettes," her niece, Edith, told me one day. "She'd melt so much butter you wouldn't believe it, until it was golden brown. Then she'd add the eggs and mix and stir until they were just set, then turn it out on a platter. Mmm. I can still taste it. It was incredible."

Miche is now a neighbor of mine, and one day, my curiosity having got the better of me, I asked her whether omelettes had been as significant to her as they were to her large family. "Oh," she said, blushing, "it was a ritual, for certain. The children would all go out and collect the eggs, bring them to me, and I'd make omelettes. Yes, omelettes were significant."

Raise a glass to Miche, creator of fine omelettes, and enjoy!

ASTUCES . . . .

• *A little water whisked into the eggs makes them lighter, fluffier.*

• *Whisk the eggs just enough to lightly blend them. You aren't looking for froth, but just to break them apart.*

• *A nonstick omelette pan makes cooking omelettes sinfully easy. You must still use butter, though—it is essential for flavor and texture. The trick is to keep the eggs moving across the hot surface of the pan. Use a fork or a wooden spatula to stir the eggs, bringing the outer edges into the center so that the uncooked egg can run out to the edges.*

. . . .

6 large eggs
2 tablespoons water
Sea salt and freshly ground black pepper
1½ tablespoons unsalted butter

1. Whisk together the eggs and the water in a medium-size bowl until just blended. Whisk in salt and pepper to taste.

2. Melt the butter in a 12-inch (30 cm) nonstick omelette pan over medium-high heat until it is hot and turning golden. Add the egg mixture and stir, bringing the cooked edges toward the center so the uncooked egg runs to the edges. When the omelette is generally set but still quite liquid, let it cook without stirring until it is nearly set through but still somewhat liquid, 1 to 2 minutes. (If you like your omelette cooked all the way through, adjust the time accordingly, but be sure it doesn't burn on the bottom. You may want to reduce the heat.)

3. When the omelette is cooked to your liking, turn it out onto a warmed serving platter. To do so, slide the omelette out of the pan until half of it is on the platter, then fold the remaining half over the first half. Serve immediately.

2 servings

Basque Pepper Omelette
Omelette Basque

Marie-Agnès Carricaburu, who runs a hotel in the small town of Esterençuby in the Pays Basque, told this story with a smile on her face:

"We had the shepherds here after market day in St.-Jean-Pied-de-Port, and they were at the bar drinking and singing until almost midnight. Then the heartiest among them said he was hungry and wanted a pepper omelette. 'Make it *piquant*,' he yelled back to the chef. 'Not one of those sissy omelettes.' So the chef, a boy with a good sense of humor, cut up three sweet peppers, and twice as many hot peppers, fried them, and put them in the omelette. The man took a bite, and another, and sweat beaded up on his forehead, but he said nothing. He ate the whole thing and said he wouldn't need to ask for it *piquant* next time."

Pepper omelettes are one of the most flavorful Basque gifts to the world of cuisine. I tasted one prepared by the same chef, though minus most of the hot peppers, and it ranks as one of the best things I've ever eaten. Stuffed with grilled Basque peppers, which turn sweet and toasty when cooked, it was toothsome and satisfying. I couldn't wait to get home and make it myself.

This is a simple dish, but the peppers must be cooked just right—so they're golden in spots—to give them a toasty flavor.

> 2 tablespoons olive oil
> 1 pound (500 g) Italian peppers (see
>   Note), cored, seeded, and cut into
>   2 x 1-inch (5 x 2½ cm) pieces
> 8 large eggs
> Sea salt and freshly ground black
>   pepper
> Cayenne pepper (optional)

1. Heat the olive oil in a large skillet (nonstick works well) over medium-high heat until it is hot but not smoking. Add the peppers (which should sizzle when they touch the pan) and toss so they are coated with the oil. Cook until the peppers are tender and

have turned a slightly pale green, about 10 minutes; toss the peppers occasionally as they cook, but let them rest in one place long enough to acquire a few gold spots. Remove the skillet from the heat, and transfer half the peppers to a plate.

2. Whisk 4 of the eggs in a large bowl just until they are broken up. Season them with salt and pepper, and cayenne if desired. Lightly season the peppers in the skillet as well. Return the skillet to medium heat and when the peppers are sizzling, add the eggs, rotating the skillet so the eggs cover the bottom. Cook, using a fork or spatula to pull the eggs from the edges and tipping the skillet so the uncooked egg goes toward the edge; move the peppers as necessary so they stay evenly distributed. If the eggs are not cooking, increase the heat slightly—but not too high or they will toughen.

3. When the eggs are nearly set (or, depending on your taste, completely set), fold one third of the omelette toward the center, and turn the omelette out onto a warmed platter so it folds over on itself, like a business letter. Keep that omelette warm while you repeat the process with the remaining peppers and eggs.

4. When both omelettes are cooked, serve immediately. Each omelette serves two.

4 servings

N O T E : You may want to substitute one hot pepper, such as an Anaheim, for one of the sweet peppers, just to give it that wonderful Basque bite.

La Rosière's Bacon and Potato Omelette

Omelette aux Lardons et aux Pommes de Terre La Rosière

>...<

Omelettes are to the French what macaroni and cheese is to Americans—homey, comforting. An omelette is a Sunday night supper, a quick midweek lunch, the kind of thing that is served when time is short, appetites are long, and the meal is casual. I've learned to love omelettes, and because I have the luxury of farm-fresh eggs and a garden that is generous with herbs, we eat them often. They are universally loved and simple to make.

This luscious omelette was served to us on the Normandy coast, not far from the D-day beaches of Omaha and Juno, by Brigitte Etienne. She and her husband run a *chambre-d'hôtes*, welcoming guests to their farm—La Rosière—to stay the night and to share the evening meal. Mme. Etienne loves to cook. Her specialties are simple, and what makes her food sing is the freshness of the ingredients and the light hand she applies to them. This omelette, made with eggs, bacon, and cream from the farm, is a perfect example. She served it with a crisp green salad, plenty of bread, and generous amounts of hard cider.

In a true French omelette, the eggs are not cooked all the way through. They are merely set around the ingredients, and then turned upside down onto a platter. The result is moist and luscious. If you prefer your eggs thoroughly cooked, adjust the timing—the result will still be tasty.

Try this omelette with a chilled hard cider.

6 ounces (180 g) small new potatoes, unpeeled

2 teaspoons sea salt

¼ cup (loosely packed) flat-leaf parsley leaves

4 large eggs

⅓ cup (80 ml) milk

Freshly ground black pepper

4 ounces (125 g) lean slab bacon, rind removed, cut into 1 x ¼ x ¼-inch (2½ x ½ x ½ cm) pieces

1 tablespoon unsalted butter, if needed

1 clove garlic, peeled, green germ removed, and minced

2 to 4 tablespoons Crème Fraîche (page 520)

La Laiterie • The Dairy

1. Place the potatoes in a small sauce-pan, cover them with water, and add the salt. Cover and bring to a boil over high heat. Cook, uncovered, until a knife pierces them easily, 15 to 20 minutes. Drain the potatoes and when they are cool enough to handle, peel them and cut them into ¼-inch (½ cm) slices. Set them aside.

2. Mince the parsley.

3. In a medium-size bowl, whisk togeth-er the eggs, milk, and parsley. Season gener-ously with salt and pepper, and whisk to blend.

4. Place the bacon in a 10-inch (25 cm) skillet and brown it over medium-high heat. If it is dry and does not give off much fat, add the butter.

5. When the bacon is browned, drain off any excess fat, leaving just enough to coat the bottom of the skillet. Stir in the garlic. Then add the potatoes and cook until they are hot through, 2 to 3 minutes. Pour the egg mix-ture over the potatoes and cook, using a fork

or spatula to pull the eggs back from the edges of the skillet as they solidify, allowing the uncooked egg from the center to run out to the edges. When the omelette is evenly set on the bottom but there is still a fair amount of uncooked egg on top, cover the pan and let it cook until the surface of the omelette is nearly cooked, about 4 minutes. The egg should still be slightly uncooked. (If you pre-fer your omelette entirely cooked, adjust the amount of time you leave it covered, being careful to check the omelette so it doesn't burn underneath.)

6. Invert a warmed serving platter over the skillet, then turn the skillet and platter over so the omelette falls onto the platter. Drizzle the omelette with the crème fraîche, and serve immediately.

2 servings

Dandelion Greens Omelette
Omelette aux Pissenlits

This is another treasure from the Dordogne, where in mid-February, as soon as spring announces itself, people set out to harvest dandelion greens. Stooping over, equipped with sharp knives, they comb the fields, gradually filling large bags with the pungent greens, which they then take home to use in everything from soups to salads.

Gathering dandelions is one of my favorite springtime jobs. Whether out in a field or in the garden, I find it a peaceful occupation, hunting for the dark green leaves pressed flat in the grass, knowing I'm going to revel in their flavor.

Serve a red Côtes du Rhône or Bergerac with this flavorful omelette.

ASTUCES . . . .

• *When trimming dandelion greens, it is very important to remember two things: First, do not detach the leaves from their central root; much of the charm of dandelion greens, besides their deep, rich flavor, is the crunch of the "heart," where the leaves join together at the base. Second, if there are any flower buds with the greens, leave them attached. They are tender, succulent morsels.*

• *Dandelions from your garden are the best and most flavorful you can find, provided they are not contaminated with chemicals that might be harmful. Arm yourself with a sharp knife (one that's not valuable, because the blade will be digging in mud and scraping against rocks) and go on a dandelion hunt. Begin looking for dandelion greens in early spring, when they are deep green and most succulent. They are best when small, about the size of your hand with the fingers stretched out, or roughly 5 inches (13 cm) across. Cut them from the ground right at the base of the root, and trim away any dead leaves and very dirty parts of the root right then and there.*

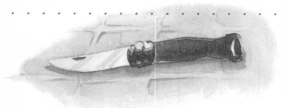

3½ ounces (105 g) dandelion greens
   (3 cups, loosely packed), rinsed, patted
   dry, and trimmed (see Note)
6 large eggs
2 tablespoons water
Sea salt and freshly ground black pepper
4 ounces (125 g) slab bacon, rind
   removed, cut into ¼-inch (½ cm) dice
1 tablespoon olive oil, if needed
1 clove garlic, peeled, green germ removed,
   and finely chopped

1. Cut the dandelion leaves if they are very long, but leave the base of each plant intact.

2. In a medium-size bowl, whisk together the eggs and the water just until blended. Season generously with salt and pepper, and set aside.

3. Sauté the bacon in a large shallow skillet or omelette pan over medium heat until it is cooked and tender but not too crisp, 4 to 5 minutes. If the bacon is very fatty, drain off the fat, leaving enough to coat the bottom of the skillet. If it is not fatty enough, add the olive oil.

4. Add the garlic to the skillet and cook, stirring, until it begins to turn translucent, about 2 minutes. Then add the dandelion greens and cook until they are wilted, about 3 minutes.

5. Pour the eggs over the dandelion greens and bacon. As the eggs cook, pull them from the edge of the skillet toward the center, allowing the uncooked egg from the center to run out to the edges. Rearrange the dandelion greens and bacon as necessary so

they stay evenly distributed throughout the omelette. Continue pulling the egg from the edges of the skillet and rearranging the dandelion greens until the omelette is nearly set (there will still be uncooked egg on the surface). Then cover the skillet with a large lid (such as that for a wok), and let the omelette cook until it is nearly solid on top, about 2 minutes. The top of the omelette should still be slightly runny; if you prefer yours entirely cooked, adjust the amount of time you leave it covered, being careful that it doesn't burn underneath.

6. Invert a warmed serving platter over the skillet and flip them together so the omelette falls, golden side up, onto the platter. Serve immediately.

2 to 4 servings

NOTE: To clean dandelions, first prepare a large bowl of cold water. Trim the root at the joint where the leaves join together, leaving the plant intact. Then scrape any brown parts off the root. Pull off any brown leaves, and toss the dandelions into the water. They will gradually form tight whorls—which is what you want, for they make a wonderful, unruly mouthful that way.

Soft-Boiled Eggs (Breakfast for Dinner)
Oeufs à la Coque (Le Petit Déjeuner au Soir)

On the farm, *oeufs à la coque* symbolize well-being, simplicity, and childhood. Eggs fresh from the henhouse and the sticks of toasted and buttered bread that are called *mouillettes* make a wonderful, nutritious, and always welcome meal.

Serving *oeufs à la coque* is one of the easier farm traditions to adapt, and I serve them regularly to my son for dinner. One summer, American friends were visiting

with their young daughter, and she and Joe were eating dinner together. I put the *oeufs à la coque*—each in a fanciful egg cup—and

a plate piled with *mouillettes* down in front of them, and the little girl cried, "Mom, we're having breakfast for dinner!"

Oeufs à la coque would never be served for breakfast on the farm (or anywhere else in France). It is strictly a lunch or dinner dish, sometimes accompanied by a salad. I like to make it after I've returned from the market with eggs I know were literally in their place of origin not two days before.

This recipe calls for a lot of bread for the number of eggs, but you'll find it won't be too much. Even if there are *mouillettes* left over, they won't be thrown away.

You may multiply the number of eggs to suit the number of people sitting down to eat. I find that two eggs per person (young or old) is the rule.

Everything Is Better with Butter

*I*n France, particularly in Normandy, it is still possible to buy small packets of fresh, creamy butter at a farmer's market. Sometimes oddly shaped, the butter varies in color from almost orange in the summer, when the amount of carotene in the grass is nearly double that of winter, to creamy pale yellow. It can be **doux** (without salt) or **demi-sel** (with), and it has a range of subtle flavors missing from pasteurized, commercially produced butters.

Normandy and Brittany remain the major butter regions in France, producing the bulk of the nation's annual production of 400,000 tons (363,000 metric tons). And in France, where the label **pur beurre** ("all butter") elevates a pastry to the height of its class, the national per capita consumption rests at about 17 pounds (8 kg) a year. Some of that is consumed in rich, smooth sauces, some in cakes and pastries.

But the greater part is spread fresh on toast or bread to make the ultimate **tartine**, or open-face sandwich, for dipping in a stout bowl of morning coffee.

Not all butter in France is created equal. There are several that have been awarded an Appellation d'Origine, or pedigree. Among those are Beurre Charentes-Poitou, Beurre des Charentes, and Beurre des Deux-Sèvres, all produced in the Loire region.

The other butter deemed worthy of an AOC is Beurre d'Isigny, from the maritime climate of Normandy. There is also Beurre d'Echiré, which is highly sought after for its clean pure flavor, a result of being washed in natural spring water.

Whether you choose to buy your French butter from its maker at the market, from the **fromagerie**, where you will find it in large **mottes**, or slabs, or simply from the supermarket, you will be seduced by its richness, its creaminess. In France, butter is not simply something used to moisten and enrich. It is a food, a flavor all its own.

ASTUCE . . . .

• *Eggs have a propensity for breaking while they're boiling. Place a folded tea towel or hot pad in the pan, then fill it with water and add the eggs. You'll find they'll stay in place and won't roll, bump, and break.*

. . . .

4 large eggs
8 slices bread such as Long Loaf
   (page 319)
Unsalted butter
Sea salt and freshly ground black pepper

1. Place a folded tea towel in the bottom of a medium-size saucepan, then fill the pan two-thirds with water. Add the eggs, place over medium-high heat, and bring to a boil.

2. While the water is heating, toast the bread, butter it generously, and cut it into long, thin sticks.

3. When the water has come to a boil, time the eggs for exactly 3 minutes, then remove them from the water, place them in egg cups, and quickly cut off the top end of each egg so the cooking will slow down. Serve instantly, with the toast and salt and pepper.

4. To eat, dip the toast sticks into the egg yolk. When all the yolk is gone, scoop out the whites with a small spoon. Go back for more.

2 to 4 servings

Fried Egg Crêpes
Crêpes aux Oeufs

→ ··· ←

If you're in Brittany, you are sure to eat crêpes, whether it is at a farm or the neighborhood *crêperie*. And this crêpe is sure to be on the menu. It is a nourishing and delicious stand-by, one I make often for an afternoon snack or light supper.

Lightly Salted Butter

➣·↢

*U*nsalted butter, or beurre salé, is the norm everywhere in France except Brittany, where salted butter reigns—spread on crêpes hot from the billig, or griddle, used in baking, cooking, anywhere butter is called for.

One customary use for salted butter is as an accompaniment for oysters, spread in a thin layer on slices of rye bread.

My favorite salted butter is studded with tiny chips of sel de Guérande (see page 119). I can't always find it, even here in France, so I decided to make my own. Now when I serve oysters, I serve this alongside for buttering the bread. It's also wonderful spread on crêpes or wherever you want fresh, lightly salted butter.

Use the best sea salt you can find—from Brittany, if possible, or "Celtic Sea Salt," which has a similar flavor and texture. Serve this any time you would normally serve butter. The little crunch of salt in the butter is irresistible.

> 16 tablespoons (2 sticks; 250 g)
>   unsalted butter, at room
>   temperature
> 1½ teaspoons good-quality
>   sea salt

In a medium-size bowl, whisk the butter until it is pale and fluffy. Whisk in the salt so it is thoroughly combined. Then pack the butter into a mold or a serving dish. Serve lightly chilled.

> 1 cup (250 g)

This is a simple dish, and it looks wonderful on the plate, with the yellow yolk placed right in the center of the crêpe, whose edges are folded right up to the egg as though to hold it in.

Serve this with chilled hard cider.

ASTUCE . . . .

• *Use the freshest eggs you can find, as they will hold together and stay on the crêpe as you fold up the sides.*

. . . .

> 1 recipe Buckwheat Crêpes (page 293),
>   see step 1, following page
> 6 large eggs
> Lightly salted butter, melted (optional)
> Sea salt and freshly ground black
>   pepper

1. Once the first side of the crêpe is cooked, flip it as per the directions in step 5 on page 294. When the second side is nearly cooked through, then break an egg in the center of it, and quickly fold up the sides of the crêpe so the edges leave the yolk and part of the white peeking through. This corrals the egg and makes for a nice presentation.

2. Cover the pan and let cook just until the yolk is set, about 1½ minutes.

3. With a pastry brush, brush the edges of the crêpe with melted butter, if desired, then season with salt and pepper and slide it onto a plate to serve immediately.

4. Prepare the remaining fried egg crêpes, and continue making crêpes until all the batter is used up. Serve the additional crêpes alongside, and spread with butter if desired.

6 egg crêpes; about 14 crêpes total

Eggs Fried in Walnut Oil
Oeufs sur le Plat à l'Huile de Noix

Historically in the Drôme, a hilly portion of Provence, the farmer returned home for breakfast around nine o'clock in the morning, after several hours work. Fresh eggs lightly fried in walnut oil and seasoned with a *filet* (drizzle) of vinegar were often his reward. Walnut oil was usually on hand in the Drôme, for each farm had its walnut trees, and most had a small mill, too, powered by a hardworking donkey, to grind their walnuts.

Some of the old mills are still standing, but they are rarely put to use. The production of walnuts has become more commercial, the mills larger. And although it is still used, walnut oil is no longer a standard farm product.

Eggs fried in walnut oil is still a well-loved dish, however. Robust and hearty, it is terrific fuel for a long morning spent in the fields.

Traditionally, the eggs are served with bread alongside. I like to rub a piece of toast with garlic and serve the eggs on top—the subtle flavors are wonderful in combination. When I want the undiluted flavor of walnut oil, however, I serve the toast alongside. And usually I serve this for lunch. Either way, and at whatever time, it is a sumptuous dish.

ASTUCE . . . .

• *Turning the eggs to finish the cooking time results in evenly cooked eggs that are just slightly more set than in the traditional French version. If you want to keep the yolk smiling up at you, cover the pan briefly, reduce the heat to low so the bottom of the egg doesn't overcook, and cook it to your liking.*

. . . .

4 slices bread, toasted
1 clove garlic, peeled
4 large eggs
3 tablespoons walnut oil
Sea salt and freshly ground black pepper
2 teaspoons best-quality red wine vinegar
Several sprigs fresh chervil or parsley, for
   garnish

1. Rub the toast with the garlic clove, and place two slices of toast on each of two warmed plates.

2. Break the eggs into a shallow soup plate or bowl.

3. Heat the oil in a skillet over medium-high heat until it shivers and sends a small wisp of smoke off the surface. Sprinkle the eggs generously with salt and pepper, and slide them into the pan. Reduce the heat to medium and fry, spooning the oil over the eggs, until the whites are nearly cooked, about 2 minutes. They will be bubbly and somewhat lacy at the edges. Drizzle the vinegar around the eggs, and carefully cut them apart. Shake the pan gently, to loosen the eggs if necessary and to allow the vinegar to cook and evaporate slightly. Then gently turn the eggs to finish cooking to your liking—for a soft yolk, that will be less than 1 minute.

4. Set each egg on a piece of toast and serve immediately, with the herbs garnishing the plate if desired.

2 servings

LA BASSE-COUR

The Farmyard

I have a tender feeling toward the *basse-cour*, or farmyard, of the French farm.

In the *basse-cour*, which may be a walled-in courtyard surrounded by farm buildings, a spot at the bottom of the vegetable garden, or simply the area right around the farmhouse, the farm wife raises chickens, rabbits, and ducks, and she often has a cow and a pig as well. There the children play when they're young, and work as they get older. They and their mother collect eggs and milk and care for the animals. The *richesse* they gather makes their lives more comfortable, more satisfying.

The dishes in this chapter represent some of the best cooking of the French farm, for they come from the heart of the French farm cook, and from the center of her existence. Prepared with care and pride, they are delicious, fresh, deeply satisfying.

I've gained tremendous respect for the French farm cook as I've visited farms and seen the variety and quality of work she performs. The *basse-cour* is but a part of her work, which encompasses fieldwork, raising children and tending to their many needs, often keeping the books and making sure a substantial meal is on the table at least twice and frequently three times a day. I've been humbled to witness the love with which the farm woman feeds her family, the strength she possesses to do everything required and do it well.

And I've eaten meal after sumptuous meal based on the products of the *basse-cour*. You'll enjoy them all as well, I'm certain.

Simple Roast Chicken
Poulet Rôti

→····←

Roast chicken may well be the most common dish on the French farm dinner table, because it's simple to make, crisp and delicious, and the raw ingredient is just a step away in the farmyard. It's also nourishing and goes a long way, characteristics appreciated on the farm.

I make roast chicken so often that I feel I've got it down to a science. Yet just when I think I've got temperature and time perfectly attuned, I have to readjust my thinking, for a roast chicken never emerges just like the one before it. It is always delicious, but the flavor, the texture, the juiciness, the crispness—they all vary just a bit. I've settled on this recipe, which I can guarantee will produce a bird so good it will make you sigh with pleasure.

The real work in roasting chicken comes before you ever put it in the oven. You must choose a good-quality chicken, one that has lived beyond the six or eight weeks of a battery-raised bird, one that has had a chance to move around during its life and has eaten good-quality food. Quality chickens are readily available now. They generally cost a little more, but the benefits extend from the moment you cook it and notice it doesn't shrink or melt into a pool of fat, to the flavor of the stock you make with the leftovers. Buy your chickens from a farm, if it's possible. If not, buy it from someone who bought it from a farm, the kind of farm where chickens have a life, not just a length of time in a dark box.

That's my chicken speech. Get the best bird you can, follow these directions, and you won't be disappointed. Serve a white Burgundy or a Chinon alongside, and perhaps some Seasoned Peaches, and *bon appétit!*

ASTUCE . . . .

• *This is truly a simple recipe. It can be varied in many ways. You might strew chopped onions around the chicken in the roasting pan (not piling them too high or they will prevent the chicken from browning). You can also strew cubed potatoes around the chicken after it has baked for 30 minutes, or minced celery root or rutabaga, or even chopped cabbage. If you add vegetables, you will not get cooking juices to pour over the chicken for they will be absorbed by the vegetables. Also, some vegetables will generate steam, which will not allow the chicken to brown quite as thoroughly.*

. . . .

Roasting and Resting

➣·➢

*T*o truss a chicken, place it on its back on a work surface. Take a 50-inch (125 cm) length of kitchen twine and slip it under the wings of the chicken, so you are holding two ends of equal length. Bring the ends together and cross them over the top of the breast, tightening the wings to the body. Bring each end around a leg just at the joint where it joins the thigh, slip them both under the chicken, and at the same time flip the chicken so it rests on its breast. Firmly tie the ends of the string together, and proceed with the recipe.

Resting, a trick as well known in the farm-house kitchen as it is in the three-star restaurant, is as important as the roasting. Resting allows the meat to relax and the juices to retreat back into all the meat, particularly the breast, making it moist.

How to solve the spattering problem? One way is to fit a thick strip of aluminum foil around the inside edge of the baking pan and bend it out and away from the chicken. The foil catches the spatters; the bird still gets brown. It doesn't get as brown as it does if the foil isn't there, but your kitchen doesn't fill with smoke either.

---

1 roasting chicken (3 to 4 pounds;
   1½ to 2 kg), with giblets
Sea salt and freshly ground black
   pepper
½ lemon
2 imported bay leaves (optional)
Seasoned Peaches (optional; recipe
   follows)

1. Preheat the oven to 450°F (230°C).

2. Pat the chicken dry all over with paper towels, if necessary. Remove the giblets from the cavity of the chicken, generously salt and pepper the cavity, and return the giblets. Squeeze the half lemon into the cavity, then add the lemon itself, pushing it in gently.

3. If you like, slip 1 bay leaf between the skin and the meat on each side of the breast, gradually working your fingers under the skin to gently loosen it so it doesn't tear.

4. Truss the chicken and place it breast side up, on a rack if you like, in a large baking pan. Roast in the center of the oven until the bird is golden on the outside and the leg joint moves easily when you rotate it, about 1 hour.

5. Remove the chicken from the oven, and salt and pepper it generously all over. Flip the bird onto the breast side and let it rest, uncovered, for at least 15 minutes and as long as 30.

6. Carve the chicken and arrange it on a warmed serving platter. Cut the giblets into thin slices and arrange them on the platter. If a substantial amount of cooking juices

remain in the baking pan, place it over medi-um heat and bring to a boil. Scrape up any browned bits from the bottom of the pan, and pour the juices over the chicken. If there are few juices but lots of browned bits, add ½ cup (125 ml) water, scrape up the bits, and pour the sauce over the chicken. (Alter-natively, you may present the bird whole for carving at the table, and serve the juices sep-arately.) Serve accompanied, if desired, by the Seasoned Peaches.

4 servings

SEASONED PEACHES
Les Pêches Assaisonnées

→···←

Try this in the summertime when you're preparing a roast chicken like the pre-ceding one, Steak in the Provençale Style (see Index), or simple grilled or baked fish. It makes a light, fresh, unexpected accompa-niment, a sort of French salsa.

Be sure to use ripe and aromatic peach-

Save That Fat

→·←

You know all those fine, golden layers of fat that are skimmed off chicken or duck stock or soup? Well, there's a good deal of flavor locked up within, so don't toss it. Instead, place the fat in a tightly sealed jar, refrigerate it, and the next time you want to sauté some vegetables and give them a little kick, pep up your mashed potatoes or parsnips, or add a tiny bit of spunk to a simple soup, add a couple of teaspoons. You'll be amazed . . .

---

es, and let the mixture sit for about 20 min-utes so the flavors have a chance to blend.

> 1½ pounds (750 g) fresh ripe peaches,
>   pitted, peeled, and cut into sections
> 1 large shallot, peeled and cut into
>   paper-thin crosswise slices
> 1 generous teaspoon fresh rosemary
>   leaves, minced, or ½ teaspoon
>   dried, minced
> Sea salt and freshly ground black pepper

Place the peaches in a medium-size mix-ing bowl, and toss with the shallot and rose-mary. Season to taste with salt and pepper. Let sit at room temperature for about 20 min-utes; then serve.

4 to 6 servings

Why Sea Salt?

You may think that calling for sea salt is gastronomic snobbery. Not at all. Sea salt is commonly used in France, and I began using it regularly when we moved here. It adds a saltiness that doesn't overpower other flavors.

Tasted alongside salt that comes from deep within the earth, there is a tremendous difference. Commercially mined salt is acrid, gives a sharp, aggressive saltiness to foods, and can even add bitterness.

The brand of sea salt I recommend comes from Guérande, a tiny area in the Morbihan section of southern Brittany. I recommend it quite simply because it is the best of French sea salts, though there are other brands of sea salt available.

It's odd looking, for it is not white but rather gray, and it is moist from the sea. Use it as you use regular salt, though you may find at first that you'll use a bit more. Then as your palate becomes accustomed to its flavor, you'll cut back down.

FLEUR DE SEL

Fleur de sel, the "flower of salt," is a layer of salt that occasionally forms right on the surface of the salt marsh, when sun and wind conditions are just right. As salt harvester François Lecallo says, "We know when there's *fleur de sel* in the water because it sparkles in the afternoon sun."

When they see it, the salt harvesters head for the dikes in the marsh. They carefully slide a special tool that resembles a rake without tines under the *fleur de sel*, which floats on top of the water. The *fleur de sel* is scooped up and swept into waiting wheelbarrows.

"You wouldn't believe it," said M. Lecall. "The smell of violets when we're working with *fleur de sel* is almost overwhelming."

That's what connoisseurs say about *fleur de sel:* it tastes like violets. I think you have to taste long and hard to get that flavor. Every now and then, though, I make a batch of french fries. We sprinkle them with *fleur de sel* and it's then that I get a little scent of violets and think of François Lecallo.

Chicken in a Bread Crust
Poulet Cuit Dans du Pain

This is a very impressive dish, which I got from Régine Sibelle, one of the best-known producers of *poulets de Bresse*. This dish is native to the Bresse area, generally considered a part of Burgundy, where the famous Bresse chickens, their white plumage shining in the sun, run, peck, and build up considerable flesh and flavor. This is a wonderful way to prepare a Bresse or any other kind of chicken, for it steams inside the dough, absorbing an herbal flavor which only enhances its own. It emerges from the oven looking like a big dumpling, golden, redolent of vegetables and herbs. Try to cut it at the table so that guests can share that magic moment when the steam curls forth and floods the room with aroma.

Serve a red Burgundy alongside.

FOR THE DOUGH AND THE EGG WASH
4 pounds (2 kg) Simple Bread
   (multiply the recipe on page 324 by 4)
1 large egg
2 teaspoons water

FOR THE CHICKEN
1 chicken (3½ to 4 pounds; 1¾ to 2 kg),
   with giblets
½ lemon
Sea salt and freshly ground
   black pepper
10 sprigs fresh thyme, or
   ½ teaspoon dried
2 imported bay leaves
1 to 2 tablespoons olive oil,
   more as needed

FOR THE VEGETABLES
8 ounces (250 g) carrots, peeled and cut
   into ¼-inch (½ cm) rounds
1 pound 10 ounces (800 g) leeks, white
   and pale green parts only, well rinsed
   and diced
2 small waxy potatoes, peeled and diced
2 cloves garlic, peeled, green germ
   removed, and minced
Sea salt and freshly ground black pepper
1 tablespoon fresh thyme leaves, or
   1½ teaspoons dried
1 cup (160 g) fresh green peas

1. Let the bread dough rise until not quite double, 1 hour. In a small bowl, whisk together the egg and the water.

2. Remove the giblets from the interior of the chicken. Squeeze the lemon half into the cavity and season the cavity with salt and pepper. Add the squeezed lemon half and the giblets to the cavity, along with the thyme and the bay leaves. Truss the chicken.

3. Heat the oil in a large heavy skillet or Dutch oven over medium-high heat until it is hot but not smoking. Add the chicken and brown on all sides, 2 to 3 minutes per side. Remove the chicken from the skillet, add more oil if necessary, and add the carrots, leeks, potatoes, and garlic. Reduce the heat to medium. Stir so the vegetables are coated with the oil and cook just until they wilt but are not cooked through, 8 to 10 minutes. Season to taste with salt and pepper, and add the thyme leaves. Transfer the vegetables to a large shallow dish, stir in the peas, and leave to cool to room temperature.

4. Preheat the over to 325°F (165°C). Lightly oil a 10½ x 14-inch (27 x 35 cm) baking pan.

5. Roll out the dough to form a 16-inch (40 cm) square, making it slightly thicker in the center. Place the cooled vegetables in the center of the dough, set the chicken atop the vegetables, and bring the dough up and around the chicken. To do this, bring three of the corners individually up and over the chicken, pressing them into each other. Bring the fourth corner up and over the others, pressing it down to lock them together.

6. Carefully lift the wrapped chicken

Poulet de Bresse

→•←

Poulets de Bresse, or Bresse chickens, are legendary for their quality and subtle, rich flavor. Not just any chicken, even if raised in the Bresse area which stretches over three regions—the Jura, the Aine, and the Saône-et-Loire—can qualify as a Bresse chicken. To carry the name, it must be of the species **Gallus** and have completely white feathers, blue feet, and a bright red crest. Each Bresse chicken is accorded 30 square feet all to itself, so that a field consecrated to Bresse chickens is hardly crowded. A farmer can raise only 500 each year, in two batches, with a hiatus between each batch so fields have a chance to regenerate and the farmer can clean and repair any farm buildings used in the production and preparation of **poulet de Bresse**.

A Bresse chicken must be at least four months old, and in the marketplace it sports three things: a special tag on its left leg with the name and address of the producer; a red, white, and blue seal around its neck with the name of the person who prepared the chicken (often the producer); and finally an **Appellation d'Origine Contrôlée** label, verifying its quality.

and place it in the prepared baking pan. Paint the bread with the egg wash, and place the pan in the center of the oven. Bake until the bread is cooked through and puffed and golden all over, about 2 hours.

7. Remove the pan from the oven and let sit for at least 20 minutes or as long as 1 hour. Use a serrated knife to cut the dough away from the chicken, and then carve the chicken as you usually do. Serve the pieces of bread along with the chicken and a spoonful of the vegetables.

6 to 8 servings

Chicken in the Pot
Poule au Pot

→ • • • ←

There isn't another dish, I don't think, that better represents French farmhouse cooking than this one. A chicken that has well served its owners by laying eggs for two to three years, has had free run of the farm, has pecked and scratched at will, reaches the end of its time. The lady of the farm dispatches it, perhaps with a bit of regret softened by anticipation of how it will perform in the pot. She places it in a pot, along with vegetables from her garden and some water, and proceeds to cook it gently on the back of the stove for two to three hours, until it is so succulent the meat almost falls from the bone. At least an hour before it is fully cooked, the aroma wafts through the house and out into the courtyard, causing nostrils to twitch in anticipation.

I've dressed up this recipe by stuffing the chicken, by cooking it in broth and water, rather than just water, and by replacing the vegetables near the end of the cooking time with new, flavorful ones for serving. Present the broth first, then the chicken, vegetables, and stuffing.

What you want for this dish is a stewing chicken, the most mature bird you can find. If you can't find one, use a large roaster and cook it no longer than two hours.

Serve a Buzet Rouge alongside.

ASTUCE . . . .

• *When preparing leeks that will be sliced, clean them by first peeling off any outer leaves that aren't fresh and firm. Then cut off the leaves at the point where the leek is tightly closed in on itself and the leaves are just a pale green. Trim off the root end. Carefully rinse the leek on the outside. Slice according to the recipe directions.*

. . . .

1 stewing chicken (3½ to 4½ pounds;
1¾ to 2¼ kg), with giblets
Sea salt and freshly ground black pepper

FOR THE STUFFING
6 ounces (180 g) salt pork, rinsed
(see Note)
6 ounces (180 g) ground veal
Giblets from chicken
1 teaspoon olive oil
1 small carrot, peeled and minced
½ small turnip, peeled and minced
4 ounces (125 g) celery root, trimmed,
peeled, and minced
1 small onion, peeled and minced
1 clove garlic, peeled and minced
2 large eggs, beaten
½ cup (30 g) fresh bread crumbs
2 tablespoons fresh thyme leaves, or
1½ teaspoons dried
Sea salt and freshly ground black pepper
2 imported bay leaves

FOR COOKING THE CHICKEN
2 good-size carrots, peeled
2 leeks (each about 4 ounces; 125 g),
white and pale green parts only,
well rinsed
Several sprigs fresh thyme
1 imported bay leaf
12 ounces (375 g) celery root (about half
a normal-size root), trimmed, peeled,
and cut into 2 pieces
2 cups (500 ml) Chicken Stock
(page 504)
5 black peppercorns
1 tablespoon sea salt

FOR SERVING
12 ounces (375 g) celery root, cut into
2 x ¼-inch (5 x ½ cm) sticks
1 pound (500 g) leeks, white part only,
well rinsed and cut into 2-inch (5 cm)
lengths
2 good-size carrots, peeled and cut into
2 x ¼-inch (5 x ½ cm) lengths
Several sprigs fresh thyme
1 cup (160 g) fresh green peas or fava
beans
Thyme sprigs, for garnish
Flat-leaf parsley leaves, for garnish

1. Remove the giblets from the chicken
and reserve them for the stuffing. Salt and
pepper the cavity of the bird.

2. Prepare the stuffing: Put the salt pork
and veal through the coarse blade of a meat
grinder, or you may finely chop it with a
knife or in a food processor. Transfer to a
large mixing bowl.

3. Process the giblets as for the meats.
Add to the ground meats and stir well.

4. Heat the oil in a medium-size skillet
over medium-high heat. Add the vegetables
and sauté just until the onions begin to turn
translucent and the other vegetables soften

slightly, about 5 minutes. Remove from the heat, let cool slightly, then add to the meat mixture.

5. Add the eggs and the bread crumbs to the meat and vegetables, and mix well. Then add the thyme, and season with salt and pepper. Pinch off a bit of the stuffing, brown it, and test for seasoning. It should be highly seasoned.

6. Stuff as much of the mixture into the cavity of the chicken as will fit easily without oozing out when you close the chicken. Slip a bay leaf inside on either side of the stuffing. Either sew or skewer the chicken closed; then truss it. Place it in a large kettle or stockpot. If there is extra stuffing, tie it in a square of cheesecloth and add it to the stockpot.

7. Cook the chicken: Tie the whole carrots and leeks, some of the thyme sprigs, and the bay leaf into a bundle, using kitchen twine. Add it to the stockpot along with the chunks of celery root. Add the chicken stock, then enough water to just cover the bird. A small part of the chicken will actually be sticking up above the water, but it will sink below the surface as the vegetables cook. Add the peppercorns and the salt, and bring to a boil over high heat. Reduce the heat so the liquid is boiling gently, above a simmer but not at a full boil, partially cover, and cook until the chicken is cooked through and the vegetables are tender, about 2 hours.

8. Remove and discard the bundle of vegetables. Discard the celery root as well. Add the remaining celery root, leeks, and carrots to the chicken, along with the fresh thyme sprigs, pushing them under the water.

Cook until they are nearly tender, about 25 minutes. Add the peas and cook until they are bright green and tender, about 5 minutes. Remove from the heat. Remove the bundle of stuffing from the pot, leaving it tied in the cheesecloth.

9. Ladle the broth into six warmed shallow soup bowls, and serve as a first course.

10. Cut open the chicken along the breastbone to reveal the stuffing, and transfer the stuffing to a cutting board. Untie the additional stuffing, if any, from the cheesecloth and place it on the cutting board. Cut the stuffing into medium-thick slices and arrange them down the center of a warmed serving platter. Remove the breast meat from the chicken, and cut it into 1-inch-thick (2½ cm) crosswise slices. Remove the meat from the legs, thighs, wings, and back, and arrange it nicely on the platter. Strew the vegetables over the meat and stuffing, and moisten with a bit of the remaining broth. Garnish with the herbs and serve.

6 servings

NOTE: To rinse salt pork, cut it in half and place the pieces in a medium-size saucepan. Cover with plenty of water, bring to a boil, drain, and rinse. Repeat the process. Pat the salt pork dry and proceed with the recipe.

Chicken with Lemon Thyme

Poulet au Thym Citronné

>···<

Another gem from Régine Sibelle, who raises the most gorgeous *poulets de Bresse* in the country. This one tops my list. The flavor of lemon thyme is at once intense and elegant, headily aromatic yet gentle. The chicken and onions and garlic all melt to a deep golden color, there are just enough juices to moisten the bottom of the pan and serve with the chicken, and while it is cooking, the entire kitchen smells heavenly.

Serve a lightly chilled Chablis or Meursault alongside.

2 tablespoons olive oil

1 chicken (3½ to 4 pounds; 1¾ to 2 kg),
*   cut into 8 pieces (2 breast pieces,*
*   2 wings with portion of breast attached,*
*   2 legs, 2 thighs), with giblets reserved*

Sea salt and freshly ground black pepper

2 large onions, peeled and diced

5 cloves garlic, peeled, cut in half,
*   and green germ removed*

1 large handful fresh lemon thyme
*   sprigs plus ⅓ cup (loosely packed)*
*   fresh lemon thyme leaves*

¼ cup (60 ml) freshly squeezed lemon juice

1. Heat the oil in a large heavy skillet over medium-high heat until it is hot but not smoking. Add the chicken, season it with salt and pepper, and brown it on both sides, about 5 minutes per side. The chicken should be deep golden.

2. Remove the chicken from the skillet and add the onions and garlic. Cook, stirring constantly, until the onions turn deep gold on the edges, about 5 minutes. Reduce the heat to medium, and return the chicken to the skillet. Add the lemon thyme sprigs and the lemon juice, and stir well, scraping the bottom of the pan. Add the giblets, cover, and cook until the chicken is nearly tender, about 20 minutes.

3. Stir 2 tablespoons of the lemon thyme leaves into the chicken, cover, and continue cooking until the chicken is cooked through, about 10 more minutes. Remove from the heat. Remove the lemon thyme sprigs, stir in the remaining lemon thyme leaves, and taste for seasoning. Let sit, covered, for about 10 minutes before serving.

4. Transfer the chicken pieces, all of the onion and garlic, and any cooking juices to a warmed platter, or simply divide them among four plates. Serve immediately.

4 servings

La Basse-Cour • The Farmyard

A Dream Business . . .

→·←

Pascale and François-Xavier Bouche and their three children live on Pascale's family farm. They took it over from her parents, gradually transforming it from a cattle farm into one that produces sturdy, flavorful birds, from chickens to guinea hens. Raising poultry was always a fantasy for François-Xavier, and returning home was a dream for Pascale, so they couldn't be happier.

Pascale and François-Xavier constructed a large hangar to house their birds in bad weather; they leave them outside to scratch when it's fine. One farm building behind the house was modernized to become a professional laboratory where they prepare the chickens. Another they turned into a pleasant little retail shop, where they sell the chickens and guinea hens, their fresh eggs, and honey and home-made jams produced nearby.

Raising chickens is untraditional in and around Aix-les-Orchies. Known as the cradle of endive production, it is also dairy and cattle country. The Bouches weren't interested in either of those, however, and their decision to produce chickens has been a good one.

"I have a steady clientele at the markets," François-Xavier told me when I paid them a recent visit. "We're the only ones around who produce them, and we sell nearly everything we raise."

François-Xavier looks forward to his two market days each week. "I love it," he said with a smile. "I get to meet the people of the community, hear about their lives and their problems. There's always something to talk about." Pascale prefers to stay home, take care of the children, and serve customers who stop at the store.

Business just gets better and better, though François-Xavier had a setback recently. "My customers told me my eggs weren't any good," he said. "I couldn't understand it. Then I realized what the problem was. I'm not going to tell you, though. Instead, I'll give you a test."

He asked me to describe what a farm-fresh egg looks like. "Well, it's firm, it sits up, and the yolk is a deep, almost red, orange," I said, noting that he and Pascale were exchanging a mirthful look.

"My customers think the same thing," he said. "But it's not true. The only reason the yolk is an intense color is because the chickens get a feed with a natural orange coloring in it, to give that color to the yolk. Without that feed, an egg yolk is pale yellow."

François-Xavier had run out of the colored feed and was giving his chickens a non-colored feed. The result? "Pale yellow egg yolks," he said. "I can't sell them. I've still got them."

He ran to get one of the eggs, cracked it open, and indeed, it was pale.

"There you have it," he said. "Perfectly good eggs. We're just eating them ourselves, and I've put an order in for the colored feed!"

Chicken Braised in Beer

Coq à la Bière

>···<

This recipe comes from Pascale Bouche, who raises poultry in the tiny village of Aix-les-Orchies, just a few kilometers from the Belgian border. Pascale grew up cooking with a Belgian accent. Instead of wine, she uses beer in savories and sweets, and instead of white sugar she often uses *cassonade*, a rich brown sugar processed in the north.

Pascale loves to cook, and chicken is often—understandably—on the menu. She likes to experiment with new ways of cooking it, but this recipe is a delicious variation on an old classic, a Belgian *coq au vin*. The beer reduces to a yeasty sweetness, enhancing the already delicious farm chicken. The garnish, too, is exceptionally flavorful. All the parts take a while to assemble, but the results are well worth the effort.

As the chicken actually improves overnight, you may want to cook it a day ahead, then prepare the garnishes just before serving. This also gives you a chance to skim any fat from the surface of the dish.

Traditionally the bacon and mushroom garnish, which is as classic as the French countryside, is prepared and stirred in at the last minute. This way it offsets the flavor of the dish rather than blending in with it, creating a counterpoint and allowing the bacon to remain crisp, adding textural interest.

Serve dark beer, just slightly cooler than room temperature, along with this *coq à la bière*.

2 tablespoons olive oil, more as needed
1 large chicken (3½ to 4 pounds; 1¾ to 2 kg),
    cut into 8 pieces (2 breast pieces, 2 wings
    with portion of breast attached, 2 legs,
    2 thighs), excess fat removed
Sea salt and freshly ground black pepper
1 large onion, cut in half, then in very
    thin crosswise slices
2 tablespoons unbleached all-purpose flour
4 cups (1 l) dark beer
1 bouquet garni (5 parsley stems, 3 imported
    bay leaves, 2 green leek leaves, 12 sprigs
    fresh thyme, tied in cheesecloth)

FOR THE GARNISHES
1 tablespoon unsalted butter
40 pearl onions, peeled
Sea salt and freshly ground black pepper
1 cup (250 ml) Chicken Stock (page 504)
10 ounces (300 g) slab bacon, rind removed
12 ounces (375 g) button mushrooms,
    brushed clean and cut into quarters
½ cup (loosely packed) curly parsley leaves,
    for garnish (optional)

1. Heat the oil in a large heavy skillet over medium-high heat until it is hot but not smoking. Add the chicken pieces, season them with salt and pepper, and cook on one side until the skin turns an even golden brown, about 5 minutes. (Do not crowd the pan; brown the chicken in several batches if necessary.) Carefully regulate the heat to avoid scorching the skin. Then turn the pieces, season again with salt and pepper, and brown on that side, 5 minutes.

2. Remove the chicken pieces from the skillet, reduce the heat to medium, and add the sliced onions (adding more oil if needed to keep them from sticking). Cook, stirring frequently, until the onions are translucent, about 8 minutes.

3. Sprinkle the flour over the onions and cook, stirring, until the flour has absorbed much of the cooking juices and has had a chance to cook, at least 2 minutes. Then return the chicken to the skillet, add the beer and the bouquet garni, stir, and bring to a boil. Reduce the heat and cook, partially covered, at a lively simmer until the chicken is cooked through, about 50 minutes. Remove the chicken from the sauce and return the sauce to a boil. Reduce it by half, until it has thickened to the consistency of thin gravy, 5 to 8 minutes. Return the chicken to the sauce, and remove the skillet from the heat; set it aside. (The chicken can be prepared up to this point a day ahead. Refrigerate it, covered. The following day, skim off any fat that has congealed on the surface, if desired. Reheat, covered, over medium-low heat.)

4. While the chicken is cooking, prepare the garnish: Melt the butter in a medium-size heavy skillet over medium-high heat. Add the pearl onions, season lightly with salt and pepper, and sauté until golden, about 10 minutes. Add the chicken stock, reduce the heat to medium, and cook at a lively simmer, shaking the pan occasionally so the onions cook evenly, until they are tender through and the stock has nearly evaporated, about 20 minutes. Remove from the heat and keep warm.

5. Cut the slab bacon into strips measuring 1 x 1 x ¼ inch (2½ x 2½ x ½ cm). Brown it in a medium-size heavy saucepan over medium-high heat. Remove the bacon from the pan with a slotted spoon or spatula and set it aside on a plate. Drain off all but 1 tablespoon of the fat. Add the mushrooms to the pan and cook, stirring constantly, until they begin to give up their liquid, are slightly golden, and are nearly tender through, about 5 minutes. Season generously with pepper, and remove from the heat.

6. Just before serving, mince the parsley, if using.

7. Add mushrooms, the bacon, and the pearl onions, along with any juices to the chicken, and gently mix them in. Either transfer to a large warmed serving platter (one with edges, so the juice won't run off) or serve directly from the cooking pot. Garnish with the parsley, if desired, and serve immediately.

4 to 6 servings

Chicken with Walnuts
Poulet aux Noix

→···←

This recipe comes from the heart of walnut-growing country, in the Rhône-Alpes near Grenoble. There Françoise Chevallier, whose husband, Jean, raises walnuts, adds them to all manner of dishes, constantly demonstrating their versatility. She has an unending supply of nuts, so she enjoys her experiments. Mme. Chevallier gave me this recipe, which I've adapted slightly, and I love it. Chicken and walnuts are an ideal combination—they set each other off—and the garlic smooths out the entire dish. Try to get a good farm-raised chicken and the sweetest walnuts you can find.

Though born on a farm in the French countryside, this recipe easily dresses up for dinner. For a perfect meal, put it on an elegant warmed platter, be sure to light plenty of candles, and serve a crisp escarole or Belgian endive salad afterward.

Try a nice, lightly chilled white Burgundy alongside.

2 tablespoons olive oil
1 chicken (3½ to 4 pounds; 1¾ to 2 kg),
  cut into 8 pieces (2 breast pieces,
  2 wings with portion of breast attached,
  2 legs, 2 thighs), giblets reserved
Sea salt and freshly ground black pepper
2 tablespoons freshly squeezed lemon juice
½ cup (125 ml) plus 2 tablespoons dry
  white wine, such as a Vouvray
12 cloves garlic, unpeeled
1¼ cups (140 g) walnut halves or large pieces

1. Heat the oil in a large heavy skillet over medium-high heat. When the oil is hot but not smoking, brown the chicken pieces, seasoning them liberally with salt and pepper, until they are golden, about 5 minutes per side.

2. Add the lemon juice, the 2 tablespoons wine, and the garlic cloves to the skillet. Reduce the heat to medium, cover, and cook until the chicken is nearly cooked through, about 15 minutes. Then stir the walnuts into the skillet, along with the giblets, cover, and continue cooking for about 8 minutes. Remove the cover from the skillet and continue cooking, stirring occasionally, until all the pan juices have evaporated and the chicken, walnuts, and garlic are golden, 5 to 8 minutes. Be sure to watch the walnuts, for they tend to brown easily. If they are getting too brown at any point in the cooking, remove and reserve them, returning them to the pan just before serving.

3. Transfer the chicken, garlic, and walnuts to a warmed serving platter and deglaze the skillet with the remaining ½ cup (125 ml) white wine, scraping the bottom to loosen any browned bits. Cook until the sauce is reduced by half, about 4 minutes. Then pour it over the chicken and serve immediately.

4 to 6 servings

Mme. Lascourrèges's Chicken with Shallots

Poulet aux Echalotes de Mme. Lascourrèges

This is an interpretation of a recipe given to me by Denise Lascourrèges, whom our son christened "Madame Châtaigne." It was she who revealed to us the marvelous Gascon woods, which were so full of chestnuts we had to dodge those falling from the trees (for more, see page 8).

Mme. Lascourrèges raises her own chickens and ducks, and they appear frequently on her table. At her house I found ways of preparing chicken that departed from the norm. This recipe, which relies on the sweet heat of shallots and the bite of vinegar, intrigued me most of all, and I've made it often since I returned from her farm. I use the oven most often, though occasionally I cook it on the grill, which is the way Mme. Lascourrèges usually makes it.

In general, French farm cooks use a lot of shallots, which here turn dark and caramelized—some turn almost black—but they don't get bitter. Instead, their flavor intensifies. The vinegar adds a pleasant tartness; the oil smooths all. At the last minute I like to add parsley, which scents the whole dish with its slight anise flavor. Consider it an option—it is my addition to Mme. Lascourrèges's recipe.

Try this with a lightly chilled dry red Bordeaux, or a Chinon.

3 tablespoons olive oil
1 chicken (3½ to 4 pounds; 1¾ to 2 kg),
    cut into 8 pieces (2 breast pieces,
    2 wings with portion of breast attached,
    2 legs, 2 thighs)
3 tablespoons red wine vinegar
4 large shallots, peeled and minced
Sea salt and freshly ground black pepper
1 cup (loosely packed) flat-leaf parsley
    leaves

1. Preheat the oven to 425°F (220°C).

2. Drizzle the oil into an ovenproof baking dish that is large enough to hold the chicken in one layer. Add the chicken pieces and turn them so they are thoroughly coated with oil. Drizzle the vinegar over the chicken, and sprinkle with the shallots. Turn the chicken so the shallots are evenly distributed over and under the pieces. With all the pieces skin side up, sprinkle generously with salt and pepper.

3. Place the dish in the center of the oven and roast until the chicken begins to turn golden, about 20 minutes. Remove the dish from the oven, turn the chicken pieces over, and season with salt and pepper. Return the dish to the oven and continue roasting until the chicken is thoroughly cooked (the juices should run clear when the flesh is pricked with the tip of a sharp knife), 17 to 20 minutes.

4. Mince the parsley.

5. Remove the chicken from the oven, sprinkle the parsley over it, and turn the pieces so the parsley is mixed evenly throughout. Let sit for 10 minutes, and then serve.

4 to 6 servings

Roast Chicken with Tarragon
Poulet Rôti à l'Estragon

This recipe comes from the Lange farm in Normandy, where black-eyed prize-winning cattle graze in complete luxury on the lush grass. The Langes' stark old farmhouse rises tall and serene in a farmyard that looks like a Norman farm museum. There are huge long brick barns scattered about the property, and there's a tall, graceful old carriage house that looks as though it should be on a movie set.

Mme. Françoise Lange cooks simple farm food, but with a touch of elegance. This recipe, made with chickens from her *basse-cour*, is a staple, a dish she makes nearly every time her grown children come to visit, for it is always requested.

I understood why the first time I made it. Tarragon is good in just about anything, but here it truly shines, its anise-like flavor gentled with cream and heightened with a bit of mustard. It's a simple, brilliant combination.

A S T U C E . . . .

• *On the farm a cut-up chicken is arranged as follows on the platter: The legs with thighs attached are placed on either side at the bottom of the platter, the wings on either side at the top. The breast meat is cut off, sliced into small crosswise pieces, and transferred, still in the shape of the breast, to the center of the platter between the wings. A one-dimensional re-creation of the chicken! The final touches are the giblets, which are scattered over the chicken, and the sauce, poured over all.*

. . . .

1 chicken (3½ to 4 pounds; 1¾ to 2 kg), with giblets
Sea salt and freshly ground black pepper
1 large handful fresh tarragon sprigs plus ⅓ cup (loosely packed) fresh tarragon leaves
½ cup (125 ml) dry white wine, such as a Sancerre or an Aligoté
⅓ cup (80 ml) Crème Fraîche (see page 520), or heavy (or whipping) cream
2 teaspoons Dijon mustard
Fresh tarragon or parsley leaves, for garnish

1. Preheat the oven to 450°F (230°C).

2. Remove the giblets from the cavity of the chicken. Season the cavity with salt and pepper, return the giblets, and stuff the tarragon sprigs into the cavity. Truss the chicken and place in a roasting pan. Roast until the skin is golden, puffed, and crisp, and the thigh joint moves easily in the socket, 1 hour to 1 hour and 20 minutes, depending on the size of the bird.

3. Remove the chicken from the oven. Season it all over with salt and pepper, transfer it to a cutting board, and let it rest, breast side down, for at least 20 minutes.

4. Meanwhile, make the sauce: Remove all but 1 tablespoon of the fat from the roasting pan, and place the pan over medium-high heat. Add the wine and deglaze the pan, scraping up any browned bits. Cook until the wine is reduced by one third, about 5 minutes. Then reduce the heat to medium, whisk in the crème fraîche and the mustard, and

cook until reduced by one third, about 4 minutes. Remove from the heat and set aside.

5. Cut the chicken into serving pieces and arrange them nicely on a warmed platter. Cut the giblets into small pieces and add them to the platter. Cover the chicken loosely with aluminum foil to keep it warm while you finish the sauce.

6. Mince the ⅓ cup tarragon leaves. Return the sauce to medium heat, and when it is hot but not boiling, stir in the tarragon. Adjust the seasoning, and pour the sauce over the chicken. Garnish with additional tarragon or parsley. Serve immediately.

4 servings

Roast Chicken with Garlic Croûtons
Poulet Rôti aux Croûtes d'Ail

This chicken incorporates one of the most useful foods on the farm: day-old bread. Crusty and full of flavor, the bread turns into a valued ingredient when rubbed with garlic and roasted. Remember, nothing on the farm is ever wasted.

Try this with a Bourgogne Blanc, a Chinon, or a hearty Cahors.

9 ounces (270 g) day-old French bread,
   cut into 1½-inch (4 cm) square chunks
3 large cloves garlic, peeled, cut in half,
   and green germ removed
1 chicken (3½ to 4 pounds; 1¾ to 2 kg),
   with giblets
Sea salt and freshly ground black pepper
½ lemon
1 large bunch fresh thyme, or ½ teaspoon dried
Fresh thyme sprigs, for garnish (optional)

1. Preheat the oven to 450°F (230°C).

2. Rub the chunks of bread on all sides with the garlic.

3. Pat the chicken dry all over with paper towels, if necessary. Remove the giblets from the cavity of the chicken, generously salt and pepper the cavity, and return the giblets. Squeeze the half lemon into the cavity, then add the lemon half, along with the bunch of thyme, pushing it in gently.

4. Truss the chicken and place it, breast side up, in a large baking dish. Roast the

chicken in the center of the oven until it is golden and nearly cooked through, about 50 minutes (see Note). Add the chunks of bread, arranging them around the chicken. Continue roasting until the leg joint moves easily when you rotate it, another 10 to 20 minutes, depending on the size of the bird.

5. Remove the chicken from the dish, and salt and pepper it generously all over. Place the bird on a warmed platter, breast side down, and let it rest for 15 minutes so the juices retreat back into the meat. Stir the croûtons in the dish so they are coated with the cooking juices, and return them to the oven. Roast until they are deep gold and very crisp, about 15 minutes. Then remove them from the oven.

6. Carve the chicken and arrange it on the platter. Thinly slice the giblets and add them to the platter. Then scatter the croûtons around and over the chicken. Pour any remaining cooking juices over the chicken and croûtons, garnish with thyme sprigs if desired, and serve.

4 to 6 servings

NOTE: The cooking time for the chicken depends on the size of the bird, so judge the cooking time for the croûtons accordingly.

Basque Chicken
Poulet Basquaise

>···≺

This is not the familiar *poulet basquaise* one sees on menus throughout that fertile region, where the chicken is braised on a bed of peppers, but rather one that is made on the Basque farm. This is simpler, and I think it is much more flavorful. It brings to mind the shepherds of the Pyrénées, the striking white houses with red shutters that dot the foothills, the gusto with which the Basque people enjoy their food.

While I was in the Pays Basque I spoke with farmwives and shepherds, and they all had a similar thing to say about cooking: "I want recipes to be quick, and I want them with plenty of flavor."

All the recipes I collected had the Basque edge—lots of onions, plenty of garlic, a touch of hot pepper, and good color. In the Pays Basque, a region of intensity on every level, flavor and presentation count equally, and a dish like this is good only if the chicken is golden, the onions nearly caramelized, the flavor rich and deep.

I like it with a peppery edge, so I season it well, and then I also put ground *piment d'Espelette* or a dish of cayenne pepper mixed with salt on the table so my guests can add seasoning if they like.

Serve an Irouléguy or a Coteaux du Lanquedoc Rosé alongside.

ASTUCE . . . .

• *In the Pays Basque the local pepper,* **piment d'Espelette** *(see Index), is dried, ground, and sprinkled on the chicken before baking. I've suggested using cayenne pepper, which has a much sharper heat and less flavor than the* **piment d'Espelette.** *The better substitute, if you can find it, is finely ground ancho chiles; you can grind your own if you find dried anchos.*

. . . .

1 tablespoon olive oil

1 chicken (3½ to 4 pounds; 1½ to 2 kg),
    cut into 8 pieces (2 breast pieces,
    2 wings with portion of breast attached,
    2 legs, 2 thighs)

Sea salt

1½ pounds (750 g) onions, peeled and
    thinly sliced

4 cloves garlic, peeled, green germ
    removed, and minced

¼ to ½ teaspoon cayenne pepper

¼ cup (loosely packed) flat-leaf parsley,
    minced for garnish (optional)

1. Preheat the oven to 400°F (205°C).

2. Heat the oil in a large heavy oven-proof skillet over medium-high heat. Brown the chicken on both sides, seasoning it with salt, 8 to 10 minutes. Remove the chicken from the skillet and set it aside. Reduce the heat to medium. Add the onions and garlic to the skillet. Cook, stirring frequently, until they are golden and softened but not completely cooked through, about 8 minutes. Season with salt.

3. Remove the skillet from the heat. Transfer the onions and garlic to a plate, and return the chicken to the skillet, arranging it in one layer. Sprinkle it with the cayenne. Then spoon the onions and garlic on top of the chicken. Bake in the center of the oven until the onions and the chicken are deep golden brown, about 1 hour.

4. Remove from the oven, garnish with the parsley if desired, and serve.

4 to 6 servings

Le Neubourg:
A Voyage Back in Time

The chicken squawks as the old lady pulls it from a cage and hands it across a table laden with fresh produce. The man on the other side takes the bird by its feet, weighs it first in one hand, then in the other, nods, and hands her some money. She glides the coins into the pocket of her apron and turns to the next customer. It's 8:45 A.M., and the Wednesday morning market in Le Neubourg has begun.

Le Neubourg is in Normandy, only an hour and a half from Paris. Every Wednesday, for hundreds of years, farmers have come to sell their live poultry and small farm animals, vegetables so recently pulled from the ground that the soil still clings to them, freshly churned butter, and cream still warm from the cow.

The town has been a commercial center since Roman times, a natural meeting place because of its location on a high plateau overlooking flat, fertile farmland. Its landmark is the church of St. Paul de Neubourg, a hulking 14th-century edifice that towers over the huge central square.

"The square is so large because Le Neubourg was once the largest and most important market in the region," says Henri Bonnel, now in his late eighties and honorary town mayor. "Wednesday was the vegetable market. Monday was the cattle market, and buyers came all the way from Paris.

"I remember it well," reminisces M. Bonnel. "Wednesdays were like Sundays for the farmers, who came to sell and to socialize. The square was as full as you saw it today, only there was hay and horse-drawn farm machinery." The machinery and hay are gone, replaced by clothing and notions, fishmongers, butchers, and cheese vendors.

The market wraps around the church and extends the length of the town center, which is divided into three different squares. Behind the church are the live chickens, geese, ducks, turkeys, guinea fowl, rabbits, and goats, and the *mémés* and *pépés* with their upturned crates stacked with beautiful bunches of produce. One woman has baskets of sweet and salted butter. Another waits expectantly with two fat chickens and bags of tender mâche. A young man sells pale green flageolets, crisp Normandy apples, gorgeous bunches of leeks, and mounds of potatoes.

The cramped aisles are crowded with buyers. "I drove for an hour this morning to buy a goose for my family," says a woman who has just picked out a lively gray bird. "I always come to Le Neubourg—where else do you find such a market?"

A FULL-SERVICE MARKET

In front of the church are the more commercial stalls: the butchers, cheese sellers, and fishmongers who work from trucks that open up to form market stands. Competition is friendly as one fishmonger hawks fresh clams, another tiny, firm mackerel called *lisettes*. The *charcutiers*, opposite the fishmongers, are no less competitive. "Guy-Guy" is one of the best, with his big pot of simmering *choucroute*, massive pâtés, and coils of freshly made *boudin noir*.

Past them are the clothing salesmen and the traveling fruit vendors, who offer juicy oranges and lemons, fresh walnuts, kiwis, and lychees. On the fringe of the hubbub in the Place du Château is the *frites* truck, where people wait for blistering country fries and *boudin* sandwiches.

For Boulangerie Ecalard on the rue de la République across from the square, the Wednesday market means selling their specialty, *pain chasseur*, a thin-crusted pizza loaded with crisp onions and bacon, from a sidewalk stand. For the Café de la Place it means endless orders of smooth cafés crèmes and croissants, *"vite, s'il vous plaît."*

The market begins to wind down at noon, just in time for the Hôtel Grand St. Martin to gear up for lunch service. Inside, shoppers, bags of produce beside them, relax over a traditional lunch of steamed mussels with *frites*, grilled steak with a big nugget of Normandy butter on top, or lamb knuckles. If they look out the big picture windows, they'll see the fishmongers hosing down their section of the street, the farmers packing up their wares, comparing notes before heading home from another fruitful market day in Le Neubourg.

Guinea Hen in Cider

Pintade au Cidre

Straight from Brittany, where the cider is lighter, fruitier, and just slightly finer than that of Normandy, this dish speaks of the farm. Guinea hens, often neighbors in the *basse-cour* with chickens and other fowl, are balls of fluff, their delicate deep gray feathers speckled with white. Their flavor is elegant, like a delicate game bird, and infinitely more complex than chicken. I tend to reserve it for special occasions. Here it is prepared simply, lightly simmered in cider with only apples, shallots, and herbs to enhance its flavor.

I like to serve this in the fall when the apples are crisp and flavorful and the cider is newly made. Serve chilled hard cider to drink, a big green salad, and plenty of bread alongside.

1 guinea hen (3½ to 4 pounds; 1¼ to
    2 kg), with giblets (see Note)
Sea salt and freshly ground black pepper
½ lemon
1 tablespoon olive oil
3 shallots, peeled and cut in half length-
    wise, then sliced paper-thin
3 large apples (such as Cox's Orange
    Pippin, Idared, Fuji, or Golden
    Delicious), peeled, cored, and cut into
    thick slices
1 cup (250 ml) hard cider
5 sprigs fresh thyme leaves, or
    ¾ teaspoon dried
1 imported bay leaf

1. Remove the giblets from the cavity of

Free-Spirited Guinea Hens

You will never find guinea hens packed into tiny cells, the way many commercially raised chickens are. The constitution of this bird with its delicate white-spotted gray feathers, does not allow it to survive in intensely crowded situations—it needs space to move and peck, which is why its meat has texture and flavor.

the guinea hen. Season the cavity with salt and pepper. Return the giblets to the cavity. Squeeze the lemon half into the cavity, then add it as well and truss the hen.

2. Heat the oil in a heavy flameproof casserole or Dutch oven over medium-high heat. Brown the guinea hen on all sides, about 10 minutes. Season it with salt and

pepper. Sprinkle the shallots around the guinea hen, tuck the apples around it, and then pour the cider over all. Add the herbs, pushing them under the cider. Cover the casserole and bring to a boil. Reduce the heat so the liquid is boiling gently, and cook until the guinea hen is tender and the meat is cooked through, about 45 minutes.

3. Remove the casserole from the heat, and carve the bird. Arrange the meat on a platter, and arrange the apples and shallots over and around it. Pour some of the cooking juices over all, and serve.

4 to 5 servings

N O T E : If you can't find a guinea hen, use two Cornish game hens or a small chicken. The flavor won't be quite the same, but it will still be a scrumptious dish.

Simple Roast Duck
Canard Rôti

Antoinette Dugord lives with her husband, Pierre, on the farm where she was born in Surtauville, a tiny village not far from Louviers. She is the third generation to raise poultry there, and her ducks and chickens are the most flavorful in the area. That's saying a lot in a region where poultry is king.

We are lucky to know Mme. Dugord, and we met her only by chance. Her daughter, Isabelle, is our favorite babysitter and a good cook in her own right. She told us about her mother, described the farm, and started taking our son, Joe, out there on Saturday mornings. Then I asked Isabelle to bring a chicken, and when we tasted it we were hooked. Now Mme. Dugord supplies us with all our poultry, from ducks to turkeys, and Joe goes out once a week to collect eggs. Occasionally Isabelle arrives with a bottle of her father's cider, a branch of rosemary or bay leaf (which the French call *laurier-sauce*), all of which are of extraordinary quality. Often, if Isabelle is at the house when I'm cooking, she'll offer a little tip or hint, picked up from the years she apprenticed to her mother in the kitchen.

Buy the best-quality duck you can find (try the local farmers' market) and follow these directions for sure succulence. If your duck is slightly larger (5 pounds; 2½ kg) or smaller (3 pounds; 1½ kg), adjust the timing a bit. You'll find there isn't a huge difference in cooking times between a 3½-pound (1¾ kg) duck and one that weighs 5 pounds (2½ kg).

Serve a hearty St.-Emilion or Buzet Rouge with this.

A S T U C E . . . .

• *Immediately after removing a roast fowl from the oven (and after presenting it, if desired), turn it on its breast side and let it sit for at least 15 minutes or as long as 45. The juices will drain into the breast meat, making it moist and succulent, and the meat will finish cooking evenly, all the way through. After 15 minutes, the meat will still be hot. After 45, it will be warm. Either way, it will be delicious.*

. . . .

1 duck (3½ to 5 pounds; 1¾ to 2½ kg),
wing tips trimmed, with giblets
Sea salt and freshly ground black pepper
2 cups (500 ml) water
2 tablespoons best-quality red wine vinegar

1. Preheat the oven to 450°F (230°C).
2. Remove the giblets from the duck and trim away any excess fat from the body cavity (see box, page 142). Rub the duck all over with 1 tablespoon salt, and pepper to taste. Season the cavity lightly with additional salt and pepper, and replace the giblets inside the duck. Place the duck, breast side up, in a roasting pan large enough to hold it with plenty of room, and pour 1 cup (250 ml) of the water around it. Place the pan in the center of the oven and cook until the duck is beginning to turn golden, 30 to 35 minutes. Remove the duck from the oven, closing the oven door to maintain the heat. Scrape the giblets into the roasting pan from the interior of the duck. Pour ½ cup (125 ml) of the water over the duck, and then turn the duck over onto its breast. Pour the remaining ½ cup (125 ml) water over it and return it to the oven. Roast for another 30 to 35 minutes.

3. Remove the duck from the oven, closing the oven door. Turn it so the breast side is up, sprinkle it with the vinegar, and return it to the oven until it is golden and the juices run clear when the thigh is pierced with a skewer, an additional 10 to 15 minutes.

4. To serve, remove the duck from the oven and season it again all over with salt and pepper. Present it on a serving platter so guests can admire it. Then return it to the kitchen, turn it on its breast side, and let stand for at least 15 minutes and up to 45 before carving.

5. Pour off any fat from the pan juices and bring the juices to a boil over medium-high heat, scraping up any browned bits from the bottom of the pan. Pour into a bowl and serve with the duck.

4 to 6 servings

Mme. Dugord's Roasting Tips

>·<

I spent a morning with Antoinette Dugord learning how she roasts duck, because her daughter, Isabelle, assured me that no one roasts a better bird. I'm inclined to agree. Whether it's duck or chicken, Mme. Dugord understands not only how to coax the best flavor from the bird, but also how to cook them through yet keep them moist and succulent.

Not all would agree with her methods, but no one would argue with the results. Her secrets include pouring water around and over the duck before cooking and again halfway through. "Water is necessary because it prevents the sugars in the juices from burning on the pan, and it keeps the meat moist," she told me.

About 20 minutes before pulling the duck from the oven, she sprinkles it with red wine vinegar. "We like the flavor vinegar gives the sauce, but I really do it because it makes the skin puff up and get crisp." (Try this on roast chicken, too, for moist meat and crispy skin.)

Mme. Dugord has several accompaniments for roast duck. In winter and early spring she favors turnips cooked long and slowly with garlic and shallots, plenty of bay leaf and thyme, and a good dose of white wine. In summer a typical accompaniment is a mixture of vegetables including peas, tiny carrots, thin green beans, and lightly sautéed radishes.

Duck with Fresh Herbs
Canard aux Herbes Fraîches

>···<

This recipe was suggested by Mark Meneau, chef and owner of L'Espérance in Joigny, Burgundy. He loves duck, which he buys in the Bresse area of Burgundy, and he prepares it in a wide variety of ways. He prefers the simple approach, particularly this one, which results in moist, herb-infused duck.

Grilling duck is tricky because the fat in the meat causes flare-ups, which can scorch the duck. Avoid that by preparing a hot, but not blazing, fire and by keeping the barbe-cue covered and the vents wide open; this allows the duck to grill and bake at the same time. The result is a lightly smoky flavor.

This duck is also wonderful baked in the oven, if you don't have a grill handy. Brown it and bake it slowly—it stays surprisingly moist. Serve this simply—with a large green salad and fresh bread, and a good bottle of lightly chilled Touraine Rosé or Rouge.

1 duck (3½ to 5 pounds; 1¾ to 2½ kg)
1 clove garlic, peeled, green germ removed, and minced
¼ cup (60 ml) olive oil
½ teaspoon sea salt
Freshly ground black pepper
20 sprigs fresh thyme
6 sprigs fresh rosemary
   (4 inches; 10 cm long)
6 fresh sage leaves, crushed
2 imported bay leaves, slightly broken

1. Cut the duck into quarters, leaving the breast meat on the bone, and trim away any excess fat. Rub each quarter with the garlic. Place the pieces in a nonreactive, flame-proof baking dish and drizzle with half the oil. Season with salt and pepper, and sprinkle with half the thyme and rosemary sprigs and half the sage. Turn each piece over, and repeat with the remaining oil, seasonings, and herbs. Tuck the bay leaves under the duck. Cover and marinate overnight, refrigerated, turning once to be sure the duck marinates evenly.

2. Build a medium-size fire in a barbecue (or preheat the oven to 400°F; 205°C). Meanwhile, bring the duck to room temperature (about 20 minutes).

Rendered Poultry Fat

→·←

You know all those pieces of fat that you remove from a chicken, duck, or other poultry, and the pieces of raw skin that fat still clings to? They can be rendered into a tasty fat, which will keep indefinitely and can be used to add a rich dimension of flavor to all of your meat and vegetable dishes.

To render the fat, coarsely chop the loose pieces of fat and skin and place them in a skillet over medium heat. Cook, stirring occasionally, until the fat has melted and the skin has turned golden, 20 to 30 minutes. Remove from the heat and strain the fat into a bowl or a wide-mouth jar. Cool to room temperature, cover tightly, and refrigerate.

3. When the coals are deep red and dusted with ash, place the grill rack on the barbecue. Let it heat up for 5 minutes. Then place the duck on the grill, skin side down. Leaving the grill open, let the duck pieces brown well, 3 to 5 minutes. Then cover the grill, open the air vents, and cook until the duck is medium-rare to medium-well, depending on your taste. Medium-rare breast meat will take 8 to 10 minutes, medium-well 12 to 15 minutes. Remove the breast meat and place it, skin side down, on a warmed plate. Cook the remaining duck until it is

medium-well, an additional 10 to 12 minutes.

Alternatively, if you have no grill, first brown the duck pieces, skin side down, in an ovenproof skillet over medium-high heat until golden, 5 to 8 minutes. Remove excess fat from the pan with a bulb baster or by carefully pouring it off. Place the skillet in the center of the oven and cook until the breast is medium-rare, 15 to 20 minutes. Remove the breast pieces from the oven and let them

sit, skin side down. Continue cooking the remaining duck until it is medium-well and tender, 12 to 15 minutes. Remove from the oven and let it sit for at least 8 minutes.

4. Cut the breast meat from the bone in one piece; then cut it into thin slices, across the grain of the meat. Cut and serve the other pieces alongside.

4 to 6 servings

Antoinette Dugord's Duck with Prunes

Canard aux Pruneaux d'Antoinette Dugord

➤ ••• ❖

"This isn't really a Normandy recipe," Antoinette Dugord said apologetically. "My daughter loves to make it—I think she got it from the south of France. But we all like it so much, we have it often."

Mme. Dugord, who raises some of the best, most beautiful ducks in the Eure section of Normandy, and who also gave me the duck recipe on page 139, has no need for apologies. Whatever the origin of this recipe, it is sublime. Duck, which already has rich, dark meat, opens up to the port and shallots like a flower. The prunes, which are added toward the end, practically melt into the sauce, making a rich and moist counterpoint. This is a lusty cold-weather dish, to be served along with steamed root vegetables and a big, green winter salad.

Prunes with pits are best for this recipe, as they keep their shape. Just remember to advise your guests about the pits.

Serve with a hearty Madiran or Cahors.

1 duck (3½ to 5 pounds; 1¾ to 2½ kg),
    wing tips trimmed, with giblets reserved
1½ *cups (375 ml) medium-dry port*
6 *shallots, peeled and cut in thin*
    crosswise slices
1 *teaspoon juniper berries*
6 *sprigs fresh thyme, or generous*
    ¼ *teaspoon dried*
2 *imported bay leaves*
Sea salt and freshly ground black pepper
1 *tablespoon olive oil*
1 *cup (250 ml) Duck Stock (page 505)*
1½ *cups (300 g) unpitted prunes*
⅓ *cup (loosely packed) flat-leaf parsley*
    leaves, for garnish

1. Cut the duck into quarters: two leg and thigh pieces and two breast pieces. Trim away any excess fat.

2. In a large saucepan, combine the port, shallots, juniper berries, thyme, and bay leaves and bring to a boil. Remove from the heat and let cool.

3. Place the duck pieces with the giblets in a nonreactive dish, and pour the port mixture over the pieces. Turn to coat with the marinade, then cover and marinate the duck, skin side down, in the refrigerator, turning the legs once, for at least 8 hours or overnight.

4. Preheat the oven to 400°F (205°C).

5. Remove the duck pieces from the marinade and pat dry. Season the pieces with salt and pepper. Heat the oil in a large heavy skillet over medium-high heat. Add the duck pieces, skin side down, and reduce the heat to medium. Brown the duck until the skin is crisp and mahogany colored, about 15 minutes. Turn the legs once during browning, and remove any excess fat as it is rendered with a bulb baster. Reduce the heat if necessary, if the skin begins to burn. Transfer the duck pieces, skin side up, to a shallow baking pan and roast in the middle of the oven 15 to 20 minutes for medium-rare, or to desired doneness.

6. Meanwhile, pour off any remaining fat from the skillet used to brown the duck. Add the marinade to the skillet, pouring it through a sieve. Add the stock and prunes and bring to a boil, scraping up any browned bits from the bottom of the skillet, and simmer, covered, until the prunes have plumped, 15 to 20 minutes. Uncover and simmer until the liquid has reduced by half. Season sauce with salt and pepper to taste.

7. Just before serving, mince the parsley.

8. Transfer the duck to a warmed platter. Pour the sauce and the prunes over and around the pieces. Sprinkle with the parsley and serve.

6 servings

Paulette Marie's Braised Duck
Canard Braisé de Paulette Marie

I tasted this duck at La Rivière, an ancient and lovely fortified farm right near the landing beaches of Normandy. There Paulette Marie turns out simply delicious and very traditional Norman food. This preparation makes the most of duck's flavor and texture. Simply stuffed with parsley, shallots, and the giblets, it is wonderfully succulent and tender. Be sure to brown the duck thoroughly before braising it, and garnish it liberally with fresh parsley when serving.

The cooking time for ducks varies greatly. Larger ducks don't necessarily take longer to cook—it is more a question of fat content and the way the duck was raised. The best way to judge whether or not a duck is fully cooked is to touch the breast—it should be tender-firm—and also to pierce the meat at the joint between the leg and the thigh. If the juices run clear, the duck is cooked through.

Try a Chinon Rouge or a lightly chilled Sancerre Blanc along with this.

1½ cups (loosely packed) flat-leaf parsley leaves
1 duck (3½ to 5 pounds; 1¼ to 2½ kg), wing tips trimmed, with giblets
2 shallots, peeled and minced
Sea salt and freshly ground black pepper
2 tablespoons rendered duck fat (page 142) or mild cooking oil
1 tablespoon unbleached all-purpose flour
2 cups (500 ml) dry white wine, such as a Sancerre
1 cup (250 ml) water
Additional ⅓ cup (loosely packed) flat-leaf parsley leaves, for garnish

1. Finely chop the 1½ cups parsley. Coarsely chop the duck giblets. Mix the parsley, half of the shallots, and the giblets in a small bowl.

2. Trim away any excess fat from the duck. Generously salt and pepper the cavity.

Stuff it with the parsley mixture. Truss the duck.

3. Melt 1 tablespoon of the fat in a 3-quart (3 l) heavy saucepan over medium-high heat. Add the duck and brown it on all sides, beginning with the breast, about 2 minutes per side. Remove the duck from the pan and pour off all but 1 tablespoon fat.

4. Add the remaining minced shallots to the pan and cook, stirring, until the shallots begin to turn translucent, about 3 minutes. Sprinkle the flour over the shallots and cook, stirring, until the flour and fat foam up and turn lightly golden, at least 2 minutes. Add ½ cup (125 ml) of the wine, stir, and season to taste with salt and pepper. Add the duck, breast side up. Pour in the remaining 1½ cups (375 ml) wine and the water and stir. Bring to a boil, reduce the heat so the liquid

is simmering merrily, cover, and cook until the duck is done to your liking. Thoroughly cooked duck, as is best in this recipe, will take 1 to 1¼ hours (a thermometer inserted into the fleshy part of the thigh should register 180°F; 82°C).

5. Remove the duck from the cooking liquid and let it sit, breast down, for at least 15 minutes. Reduce the cooking juices over high heat by one third, 10 to 15 minutes. Skim off any excess fat, if desired, and strain the cooking juices.

6. Mince the additional ⅓ cup parsley.

7. Carve the duck and transfer the pieces to a serving platter. Pour the cooking juices around the duck or serve them separately. Garnish with the parsley and serve.

4 servings

Marie-Claude Gracia's Roast Duck
Canard Rôti de Marie-Claude Gracia

Marie-Claude Gracia is the chef and owner of La Belle Gasconne, a sybaritic *auberge* in the tiny Gascon village of Poudenas. Mme. Gracia is considered by many to be one of the best chefs in France, an honor she regards with a certain insouciance. "I cook what I learned from my grandmother, changing things here and there, and I do it because I love it—it's that simple," she says with a smile.

I spent several days with her in the kitchen at La Belle Gasconne and came away with this method of roasting duck, which is unique to Gascony. It fits with Gascon cuisine, however, which is based on the notion that fat gives flavor to food, but shouldn't be a part of it. That is why, throughout the roasting, Mme. Gracia removes the fat that comes from the duck so that the roasting pan is nearly dry by the time the duck is cooked. The duck itself is tender and succulent.

The stuffing here is based on the one used by Mme. Gracia, though I have adapted it slightly.

If you can find only a 3- to 4-pound (1½ to 2 kg) duck, roast it for 10 minutes per side as described in step 8; then test it to see if it is cooked to your liking. Though ducks may differ in size by as much as a pound, surprisingly, the cooking time is often not that much different.

To test for doneness, press gently on the breast meat; it should spring back when touched. Also, pierce the leg and thigh joint with a sharp knife or skewer; the juices should run clear and golden (a thermometer inserted into the fleshy part of the thigh should register 180°F; 82°C). Try an excellent-quality red Burgundy with this dish.

1 duck (3½ to 5 pounds; 1¾ to 2½ kg),
    wing tips trimmed, with the liver
Sea salt and freshly ground black pepper
3 cups (180 g) fresh bread crumbs
1 tablespoon rendered duck fat
    (page 142) or olive oil
3 cloves garlic, peeled and minced
1 large shallot, peeled and minced
½ cup (loosely packed) flat-leaf parsley leaves
1 large egg
¼ cup (60 ml) Crème Fraîche (page 520),
    or heavy (or whipping) cream

1. Preheat the oven to 475°F (245°C). Measure out a piece of aluminum foil large enough to wrap around the duck, and set it aside.

2. Trim away any excess fat from the duck. Season the cavity of the duck with salt and pepper.

3. While the oven is preheating, place the bread crumbs on a baking sheet and toast them in the oven until golden, about 10 minutes, stirring them once or twice so they are evenly toasted. Remove from the oven and let cool to room temperature.

4. Melt the fat in a medium-size heavy saucepan and over medium heat. Add the garlic and shallot and cook, stirring, until they are softened and beginning to turn translucent, about 5 minutes. Remove from the heat.

5. Mince the parsley. Mince the duck liver.

6. In a medium-size bowl, whisk together the egg and the crème fraîche. Add the liver, the garlic and shallot, and the parsley. Using your hands, add the bread crumbs,

breaking up any clumps as you do; mix well. Season to taste with salt and pepper.

7. Place the stuffing in the cavity of the duck, gently pressing if necessary to fit it all in. Close the duck, skewering the flaps of skin over the opening. You may truss the duck if you like, though it is not necessary.

8. Place the duck, breast side down, in a roasting pan and roast just until golden on top, 10 to 12 minutes. Turn it on one side and roast for 10 minutes; then remove and discard any fat that has melted from the duck, using a bulb baster or a large spoon. Repeat on the other side, and then on the back, for 10 minutes per side, removing fat as necessary so the pan remains nearly dry. Turn the duck one final time, so it is resting on its back, and continue roasting until it is cooked to your liking, an additional 20 to 35 minutes. You can test the duck by pressing on the breast meat—if it is firm with just a bit of spring, it is cooked through. If it is still rather springy, it will be quite rare. If you like the breast meat rare, remove it from the oven immediately. If you like the meat more cooked but still pink, roast it an additional 10 minutes. The duck will take 1 to 1¼ hours to roast (a thermometer inserted into the fleshy part of the thigh should register 180°F; 82°C).

9. Transfer the duck to the reserved aluminum foil, back side down, and season it generously with salt and pepper. Turn it over and season the other side. Then enclose it loosely in the aluminum foil and let it rest for 10 to 15 minutes before serving.

10. To serve, carve the duck and transfer the pieces to a warmed serving platter. Scoop the stuffing from the cavity and arrange it nicely on the platter.

4 servings

Duck with Artichokes and Spring Onions

Canard aux Artichauts et Petits Oignons

Duck and artichokes are two of my favorite foods, and they share a common richness of flavor. I hit upon this recipe one day when spring was in full bloom and huge, fat artichokes from Brittany graced the market stands. What better, I thought, than to combine artichokes and duck, throw in some sweet spring onions, and cook them all together?

Preparing Artichoke Hearts

>•<

*U*sing your hands, pull off all the large outer leaves of the artichoke. Then, with a paring knife, cut off the stem and trim away any dark green parts that remain on the outside of the vegetable. Using a larger knife, slice off the cone of inner leaves. Prepare the artichoke heart according to the individual recipe. The hairy choke is easier to remove when the artichoke is cooked, so if you can get away with steaming it before proceeding with a recipe, do so. If not, scrape away the choke with a stainless-steel teaspoon. As you prepare them, squeeze fresh lemon juice over the uncooked artichokes, then place them in acidulated water as you finish preparing the remaining ones.

It turned out to be as sumptuous as I'd guessed, and it's a combination I go back to time and again. It's not an everyday dish, however, but rather one to serve for special occasions (or when you want an occasion to *be* special), for the flavors are deep and rich.

This recipe looks long, but it really isn't. There are several steps, but once those are completed, everything cooks together.

Serve this with a red Coteaux d'Aix-en-Provence or a Sang de Cailloux Vacqueras.

FOR THE VEGETABLES
2 tablespoons rendered duck fat
(page 142) or unsalted butter
4 large artichokes (each 1 pound; 500 g)
or 6 smaller ones, stem, leaves, choke
removed, and bottom cut into thin
vertical slices (see box, this page)
Sea salt and freshly ground black pepper
1 clove garlic, peeled, green germ removed,
and minced (not pressed)
2¼ cups (560 ml) Duck Stock (page 505)
or Chicken Stock (page 504)
40 small spring or pearl onions, peeled
and trimmed, an X cut into the stem
end of each

FOR THE DUCK
Sea salt and freshly ground black pepper
1 duck (3½ to 4 pounds; 1¾ to 2 kg),
cut into quarters, wishbone removed,
wing tips trimmed, with giblets
1 tablespoon rendered duck fat (page 142)
or mild cooking oil
2¼ cups (560 ml) Duck Stock (page 505)
or Chicken Stock (page 504)
Zest of 1 lemon, minced
1 large clove garlic, peeled and minced
8 sprigs fresh thyme, or ¼ teaspoon dried
2 imported bay leaves, crushed

1. Melt 1 tablespoon of the fat in a large nonstick skillet over medium-high heat. Add the artichokes, season them with salt and pepper to taste, and stir or shake the pan so they are lightly coated with the fat. Continue cooking, stirring or shaking the pan, until the artichokes are lightly browned on both sides, 6 to 8 minutes. Sprinkle the garlic over the artichokes, and pour 1 cup (250 ml) of the stock over them. Stir, cover, and cook until the artichokes are nearly tender through, 6 to 8 minutes. Check occasionally and add more stock if necessary to keep the artichokes moistened. Remove the cover and continue cooking, shaking the pan frequently so the artichokes cook evenly and don't stick, until the stock has reduced completely and the artichokes are tender through and golden, 5 to 6 minutes. Adjust the seasoning, remove from the heat, and keep warm.

2. While the artichokes are cooking, prepare the onions: Melt the remaining 1 tablespoon fat in a medium-size heavy skillet over medium-high heat, and add the onions. Season them with salt and pepper, and stir or shake the pan so they are lightly coated with the fat. Cook, stirring or shaking the pan frequently, until they are golden, about 2 minutes. Add the remaining 1¼ cups (310 ml) stock and cook, uncovered, until the stock has nearly evaporated and the onions are tender through, 20 to 25 minutes, occasionally shaking the pan to evenly distribute the onions. Adjust the seasoning, remove from the heat, and keep warm.

3. Preheat the oven to 400°F (205°C).

4. Prepare the duck: Salt and pepper the duck pieces on both sides. Heat the fat in a large heavy skillet over medium-high heat. When it is hot but not smoking, add the duck pieces, skin side down, and reduce the heat to medium. Cook the duck pieces until the skin is crisp and deep golden, about 40 minutes, removing any excess fat from the skillet as it is rendered with a bulb baster. Turn the legs once halfway through the cooking time. Transfer the duck pieces, skin side up, to a shallow baking pan and roast in the middle of the oven until cooked as desired, 10 to 15 minutes for medium rare. Transfer the pieces to a serving platter and keep warm in a low oven.

5. While the duck is roasting, pour off all the fat from the skillet and add the stock, giblets, zest, garlic, and herbs. Bring the mixture to a simmer over medium heat, scraping up any browned bits from the bottom of the skillet, then reduce to about 1¼ cups (310 ml).

6. To serve, cut the breast meat into thin slices and arrange them on a warmed platter, along with the remaining pieces of duck. Drizzle with some of the cooking juices. Surround the duck with the vegetables, or serve the vegetables separately. Serve the remaining cooking juices alongside.

4 generous servings

A Note About American Ducks

>·<

Several breeds of duck are raised in the U.S., including the Moulard, mallard, Muscovy, and the Pekin, which is the most common. Also referred to as the Long Island duck, the Pekin is valued for its fast growth, abundant meat, and mild flavor. When you buy a fresh duck, chances are it's a Pekin.

Muscovy ducks can be found as well, at a specialty butcher or through mail-order (see below). They are relatively lean, and their meat is more deeply flavored than the Pekin duck.

Pekin ducks are endowed with an enormous amount of fat. Before cooking a Pekin duck, remove as much fat as you can from the cavity, and while the duck is cooking, remove more fat as it renders from the bird. One suggestion is to plunge the duck (or duck pieces) into boiling water for 2 minutes, drain and pat it dry, then proceed with your recipe.

Any bits of fat that you pull from a duck can be rendered (see "Rendered Poultry Fat," page 142). You may freeze it until you have a large quantity to render, or render it bits at a time.

Muscovy, Pekin, and Moulard ducks are all available by mail-order from D'Artagnan, (800) 327-8246; (201) 792-0748.

Duck Pâté
Pâté de Canard

This recipe is a blend of a traditional Normandy duck pâté and my own flavorings. It is very, very simple and robust, yet delicate as well, thanks to the duck. Season it generously, always remembering that when the pâté is chilled, the seasonings tone down substantially.

Weighting and chilling the pâté is essential, for it makes it firm and easy to slice. Also, the flavors need time to mellow, so I always like to make pâté the day before I plan to serve it. Actually, the flavor of this pâté is at its peak *two* days after it is made.

Serve it with tiny cornichons (finely flavored dill pickles) and Dijon mustard, if desired.

1 duck (3½ to 4 pounds; 1¾ to 2 kg),
    preferably Muscovy (see "A Note
    About American Ducks," page 151),
    with liver
Sea salt and freshly ground black
    pepper
1 tablespoon unsalted butter
1 medium onion, peeled and finely
    chopped
1 clove garlic, peeled, green germ
    removed, and mashed
3 tablespoons Calvados (apple brandy) or
    brandy
1¼ pounds (625 g) lean boneless veal
1¼ pounds (625 g) medium-fatty boneless
    pork
2 large eggs, lightly beaten
¼ teaspoon ground allspice
12 sprigs fresh thyme, or
    a scant ½ teaspoon dried leaves
3 imported bay leaves

1. Using a sharp knife, cut around the duck breast so you can remove the skin (with any excess fat) covering the breast in one piece. Gently work your fingers between the breast skin and the meat, carefully pulling the skin from the meat. (You may need to use the knife to cut the connecting tissue, or to carefully cut any meat that won't easily separate from the skin.) Reserve the skin with the fat.

2. When the skin is removed, cut the breast fillets from the duck. Then cut the leg and thigh pieces, and the wings, from the duck. Remove the meat by cutting along the length of the bones, then scraping off the meat. Don't worry if you leave bits of meat on the bones. Discard the skin from the legs, thighs, and wings.

3. Cut one of the breast fillets into thin lengthwise strips. Cut the other breast fillet into chunks and set aside. Lightly salt and pepper the strips and wrap them in the piece of duck skin. If you weren't able to remove the skin in one piece and you have several small pieces, simply wrap the meat and skin in waxed paper and aluminum foil and refrigerate, along with the rest of the meat, either overnight or until you are ready to assemble the pâté.

4. To assemble the pâté, melt the butter in a medium-size saucepan over medium heat, add the onion and the garlic, and sauté just until the onion begins to turn translucent, about 7 minutes. Add 2 tablespoons of the Calvados and cook, stirring, until it has nearly evaporated, about 5 minutes. There should still be a bit of liquid clinging to the onion and garlic. Remove from the heat and let cool.

5. Cut the veal and the pork into chunks. Combine the veal, pork, duck chunks, and duck liver in a food processor, and coarsely chop. (You may need to do this in batches.) The chopped meat should be uneven, so that there are some larger pieces (about ¼ inch; ½ cm) and some finely ground, which will give texture to the pâté.

6. Transfer the chopped meat to a large mixing bowl, and add the onion and garlic mixture. Mix thoroughly, using your hands. In a small bowl, whisk the eggs, the remaining 1 tablespoon Calvados, the allspice, 2 teaspoons salt, and ¾ teaspoon pepper. Pour

this into the meat and onion mixture and combine, again using your hands, until thoroughly blended.

7. Test the seasoning by sautéing a tablespoonful of the mixture in a small pan over medium heat. Adjust the seasoning accordingly, remembering that when the pâté is chilled the seasonings will be more muted than when it is hot and freshly cooked.

8. Preheat the oven to 350°F (175°C).

9. Place half the thyme and 1 bay leaf on the bottom of an 8-cup (2 l) earthenware or glass baking dish. Add one third of the meat mixture, patting it firmly so there are no air holes. Unwrap the duck strips. Carefully lay half of them lengthwise over the meat. Cover with another third of the meat mixture, top with the remaining strips, and then cover them with the remaining meat mixture. Arrange the remaining thyme and bay leaves on top. Then cover the pâté mixture with the duck skin, fat side down, trimming it to fit with a generous overlap. Cover the dish with heavy-duty aluminum foil and bake in the center of the oven until cooked through, 1¾ hours (a meat thermometer inserted in the center should read 170°F; 77°C). Remove from the oven, leaving the foil in place. Place a flat board, one that just fits, right on top of the foil, and weight the pâté down with 5 pounds (2½ kg) of bricks or canned goods. Let cool.

10. When the pâté has cooled to room temperature, refrigerate it for at least 2 hours (ideally for 8) and up to 2 days, weights still in place. Before serving the pâté, you may want to drain off any excess liquid. Unmold the pâte onto a plate and serve.

8 to 10 servings

Herb-Brined Duck Breast
Petit Salé de Canette

This recipe comes from Claude Udron, who until recently was chef at Pile ou Face in Paris. Claude is a native of Normandy, from the area around Rennes, and he has many memories of eating duck as a child on his grandparents' farm. There it was most often roasted or braised. Here he takes a young duck, a *canette*, and gives it a contemporary twist, brining it in salt and herbs as is usually done with pork. He is right, as usual, about his flavor combinations and treatment, for this dish is simply sublime.

It is also a triumph of simplicity. Claude adds just enough herbs and brines the duck for just long enough to bring out its best and freshest flavor. And while you need to think about this recipe 24 hours in advance, then cook the duck for 2 hours, it's very easy to prepare. Another advantage is its gorgeous appeal—from first glance at the crisp brown duck to first bite.

Serve this along with a Bergerac Sec.

ASTUCE . . . .

• *Claude says, instead of using sea salt here, use kosher salt. Whereas sea salt may contribute its flavor, kosher salt is best for this preparation because it is mild and has a neutral flavor.*

. . . .

FOR THE BRINE
1½ cups (about 375 g) kosher salt
8 cups (2 l) cold water
6 imported bay leaves
12 sprigs fresh thyme, or ½ teaspoon dried leaves
8 sprigs flat-leaf parsley

FOR THE DUCK
1 duck (5 pounds; 2½ kg), wing tips
    trimmed, cut into quarters
2 medium carrots, cut into 2-inch (5 cm) lengths
1 medium onion stuck with 1 clove
4 shallots, peeled
2 leeks, white part only, well rinsed and
    cut into 2-inch (5 cm) lengths
1 bouquet garni (5 parsley stems, 3 imported
    bay leaves, 2 green leek leaves, 12 sprigs
    fresh thyme, tied in cheesecloth)
¼ teaspoon black peppercorns

FOR THE LENTILS
8 ounces (250 g) lentils
    (preferably lentilles de Puy)
3 carrots, peeled and cut into ¼-inch
    (½ cm) rounds
3 leeks, white part only, well rinsed
    and cut into ½-inch (1¼ cm) rounds
1 medium onion stuck with 2 cloves
4 ounces (125 g) slab bacon
1 teaspoon sea salt
Freshly ground black pepper
1 bouquet garni (5 parsley stems, 3 imported
    bay leaves, 2 green leek leaves, 12 sprigs
    fresh thyme, tied in cheesecloth)

FOR BROWNING THE DUCK
1 tablespoon unsalted butter, or
    2 tablespoons rendered duck fat
    (page 142)
1 tablespoon mild cooking oil,
    such as safflower

1. Prepare the brine: Combine the kosher salt, water, and herbs in a large saucepan. Cover and bring to a simmer over medium-high heat. Cook, stirring occasionally, just until the salt is dissolved, 10 to 15 minutes. Then remove from the heat and cool to room temperature.

2. Prepare the duck: Trim away any excess fat from the duck pieces. Place the duck, vegetables, bouquet garni, and peppercorns in a large saucepan and pour the brine and herbs over all. Refrigerate, covered, for at least 8 hours (see Note).

3. To cook the duck, remove it from the brine and quickly rinse it. Strain the brine, keeping the herbs and vegetables. Rinse the saucepan, and return the duck and the herbs and vegetables to it. Add water to cover by 1 inch (2½ cm), and bring to a boil over medium-high heat. Reduce the heat and cook, uncovered, at a steady simmer until the duck is cooked through (a knife should easily pierce it), about 1¾ hours. Check the duck occasionally to be sure it is submerged under the water and cooking evenly (see Note).

4. While the duck is cooking, prepare the lentils: Combine the lentils, vegetables, slab bacon, salt, pepper, and bouquet garni in a large saucepan. Add water to cover by 2 inches (5 cm) and bring to a boil. Reduce the heat and simmer, partially covered, until the lentils are just tender but still retain their texture, 35 to 40 minutes. Remove the lentils from the heat and reserve.

5. When the bacon is cool enough to handle but still hot, remove it from the lentils and cut it into thin slices. Then return it to the lentils so it will stay warm.

6. Brown the duck: Drain the duck pieces and discard the cooking liquid. Pat the duck dry. Heat the butter and the oil in a large skillet over medium-high heat. When the mixture is hot but not smoking, add the duck pieces, skin side down, to brown them. Turn them so they are evenly browned and hot through, about 5 minutes.

7. While you are browning the duck pieces, reheat the lentils over low heat. Remove the bouquet garni from the pan and transfer the lentils, using a slotted spoon, to a warmed serving platter. (You may reserve the lentil cooking liquid for a soup base or discard it.) Place the duck atop the lentils and garnish with the slices of slab bacon.

Alternatively, for a more formal dish, place one third of the lentils in a food processor and purée them. Add enough cooking liquid so the purée is quite thin. Transfer the purée to a small heavy saucepan and reduce it, over medium-high heat, until it is the thickness of heavy cream, 7 minutes. Watch it carefully so it doesn't burn. Adjust the seasoning, strain it through a fine-mesh sieve, and then divide the sauce among four warmed dinner plates. Place a piece of duck on the sauce, and serve the remaining lentils separately.

4 servings

NOTE: Once brined, the duck will keep for several days, drained, well wrapped and refrigerated.

• The duck can also be cooked in step 3 up to 24 hours in advance. When it is done, remove it from the cooking liquid, discarding the liquid, seasonings, and vegetables. Refrigerate the pieces covered.

Mme. Lascourrèges's Stuffed Rabbit

Lapin Farci de Mme. Lascourrèges

This recipe comes from Denise Lascourrèges, a delightful woman who lives just outside the village of Poudenas, in Gascony, where she and her husband, André, cultivate sixty-four acres of rich soil. They have an eighteen-acre vineyard which produces the regional Columba white wine, a distinctly dry and fruity wine that is served lightly chilled. It complements everything from foie gras to salad, and it is perfect on those sweltering summer days when heat shimmers off the cornfields and flies buzz languidly in the trees.

Mme. Lascourrèges insisted repeatedly while I was with her that she didn't know how to cook at all, and that I'd come to the wrong place for recipes or for any information about food.

This rabbit recipe, which she insists is nothing special, rolled off her tongue

along with dozens of others as we discussed food. The truth about Mme. Lascourrèges is that she has food and cooking, along with gardening and farming, in her bones. She also loves a good meal. So it follows, and I knew it would, that her recipes are luscious.

Regarding seasonings, Mme. Lascourrèges recommends seasoning *à bisto des naz*, Gascon for "according to instinct." Follow her advice, here and elsewhere!

Try a Sancerre Rouge with this.

ASTUCE . . . .

• *Bacon is much better diced by hand than in a machine, for the pieces keep their integrity and don't get mashed or ground. It's easier to do if the bacon is chilled first. You can even put it in the freezer for 10 to 15 minutes before dicing it.*

. . . .

FOR THE STUFFING

*1 slice (30 g) packaged white bread, such
    as Pepperidge Farm*

*⅓ cup (loosely packed) flat-leaf parsley
    leaves*

1 shallot, peeled and minced

*7 ounces (210 g) slab bacon, rind removed,
    cut into small dice*

Sea salt and freshly ground black pepper

FOR THE RABBIT

3 tablespoons olive oil

1 rabbit (3 pounds; 1½ kg)

Sea salt and freshly ground black pepper

3 tablespoons Dijon mustard

*3 medium onions, peeled and coarsely
    chopped*

*2 medium tomatoes, cored and thinly
    sliced*

*Flat-leaf parsley sprigs, for garnish
    (optional)*

1. Preheat the oven to 425°F (220°C).

2. Prepare the stuffing: Place the bread slice in a small bowl and add water to cover. Let it sit until it is thoroughly moist, then gently squeeze out the water until the bread is no longer dripping wet.

3. Mince the parsley.

4. Combine the bread, parsley, shallot, and bacon in a medium-size bowl. Season to taste with salt and pepper, and mix together with your hands until a homogeneous mixture is formed. To verify the seasoning, sauté a teaspoonful of the stuffing over medium heat until cooked through. Taste for seasoning and adjust accordingly.

5. Brush a 9 x 13-inch (22½ x 32½ cm) baking dish with 1 tablespoon of the olive oil.

6. Prepare the rabbit: Lay the rabbit on its back. Using a large sharp knife, cut the rabbit nearly in half at a place roughly in the middle of the rabbit's body, cutting through the backbone (at a spot between two vertebrae) but not through the meat behind it. This will enable you to fold the rabbit in half easily. Season the belly, the inside of the legs, and the chest cavity with salt and pepper. Pack the stuffing evenly into the body cavity of the rabbit and pull the belly flaps of skin around it, so the stuffing is completely enclosed. Skewer the flaps closed over the stuffing. Gently fold the rabbit in half, tucking the front legs inside the back legs (which will happen naturally). Truss the rabbit by tying it firmly, beginning at the back legs, then wrapping the twine several times around the body and front legs before tying the ends of the twine to one of the loops that goes around the body.

7. Brush the rabbit all over with the mustard.

8. Strew the onions and the tomatoes over the bottom of the baking dish, and set the rabbit on top. Drizzle all over with the remaining olive oil, then season the rabbit lightly with salt and pepper. Place in the center of the oven and bake for 30 minutes. Turn the rabbit, season it lightly with salt and pepper, and continue baking until the rabbit is cooked through and firm but not hard to the touch, about 1 hour. To test for doneness, prick the rabbit at the thickest part

(where the thigh joins the body), and look into the meat—if it is very pink, cook for an additional 5 to 10 minutes. If the juices are clear and the meat is ivory colored, remove the rabbit from the oven and transfer to a warmed serving platter to rest for 10 to 15 minutes, so the juices retreat back into the meat. Return the onions and tomatoes to the oven and continue cooking until the onions are tender and have caramelized slightly, about 10 minutes more.

9. Remove the twine from the rabbit, and cut it up into six serving pieces with poultry shears or a very large knife. To cut the rabbit up, first cut off each back leg, snipping up the backbone from the tail end. Then, cut two pieces from the stuffed center portion of the rabbit, then two shoulder and front leg portions. Gently scrape the stuffing from the rabbit and place each piece on a warmed dinner plate. Evenly divide the stuffing, and the onions and tomatoes, among the plates. (There will be a generous 2 tablespoons of stuffing per person.) Serve, garnished with parsley if desired.

6 servings

Rabbit with Sorrel
Lapin à l'Oseille

→…←

This recipe is a family favorite, and perfect in springtime when rabbits are young and tender and sorrel leaves are just developing their lemony tang. It is beautiful as well as delicious, worthy of a special occasion. It can be made the day before you plan to serve it and gently, *gently* reheated.

Try this with a Beaujolais Villages.

ASTUCE . . . .

• *The ideal weight for a rabbit is 3 to 3½ pounds (1½ to 1¾ kg). At that size it is tender and succulent, and not the least bit dry when cooked.*

. . . .

1 tablespoon olive oil

5 ounces (150 g) slab bacon, cut into
¼-inch (½ cm) dice

1 medium rabbit (3½ pounds; 1¾ kg),
cut into 6 pieces (2 back legs, 2 body
pieces, 2 shoulder and front leg pieces)

Sea salt and freshly ground black pepper

1 pound (500 g) onions, peeled, cut in
half, and sliced paper-thin

1 cup (250 ml) dry white wine, such as a
Sauvignon Blanc

2 imported bay leaves

4 cups (loosely packed) sorrel leaves,
rinsed and patted dry

1 cup (250 ml) Crème Fraîche
(page 520), or heavy (or whipping)
cream

1. Heat the oil in a large heavy skillet over medium-high heat. When it is hot, add the bacon and sauté until it is just golden on all sides but still tender and not too crisp, 3 to 5 minutes. Remove the bacon from the skillet with a slotted spoon and set it aside on a plate. Drain all but 1 tablespoon of the fat from the skillet.

2. Add as many pieces of the rabbit as will comfortably fit in the skillet without being overcrowded. Sprinkle them with salt and pepper and brown until golden, about 5 minutes. Turn, sprinkle with more salt and pepper, and brown the other side, 5 minutes. Repeat until all of the pieces are browned. Set the rabbit aside.

3. Add the onions to the skillet and cook, stirring, until they are softened, about 8 minutes. Then add the wine and scrape any browned bits from the bottom of the skillet. Return the rabbit to the skillet, along with the bay leaves, pushing the rabbit down among the onions. Bring to a boil, then reduce the heat to medium. Cover and cook at a gentle boil until the rabbit is tender and nearly cooked through, about 30 minutes.

4. While the rabbit is cooking, stack the sorrel leaves atop one another and cut them crosswise into very, very thin strips (chiffonnade).

5. Remove the rabbit from the skillet, place it on a serving platter, cover it loosely with aluminum foil, and keep it warm in a low oven. Add the bacon to the sauce, and stir in the crème fraîche. Raise the heat to medium-high and bring to a boil. Add the sorrel, stirring as it melts down into the sauce. Cook until the sorrel has wilted and turned an olive green, and the sauce has reduced by about one third, 5 to 7 minutes. Taste for seasoning.

6. Remove the rabbit from the oven, and pour the sauce over it. Serve immediately.

4 to 6 servings

LE PATURAGE
The Pasture

What would Burgundy be without its verdant pastures dotted with white Charolais cattle? Less charming, for certain. And the Pays Basque wouldn't be nearly as lovely without its woolly Têtes Rousses sheep grazing on steep mountain pastures.

Normandy would be poorer without its cattle, their big eyes ringed with black, their flanks as high as your shoulder. And France itself would cease to exist, I believe, without the humble hog, for it is transformed into so many wonderful, flavorful dishes.

Lamb and pork are the most common meats on the French farm. And what lamb! What pork! Sheep graze on wildflowers in spring, eat sweet hay in winter, grow to just the right size so their meat is tender, flavorful, succulent. Pigs are accorded a place of honor on the farm, where they can run and wallow at will. Fattened with corn, their meat is so full of flavor that at first one wonders, can pork really taste this good?

Beef is mostly a luxury, reserved for special occasions. When you sample Jacqueline Priaulet's Daube or Braised Beef with Onions, you will understand why it's special, for in the hands of a French farm cook, beef becomes uncommonly flavorful.

Meat is essential to French farm cooking. Herbs flavor it, slow cooking tenderizes it, oil and butter bathe it. Turn the pages of this chapter and your mouth will water. Then your feet will carry you into the kitchen to re-create these wonders from *le pâturage*—the pasture.

Jacqueline Priaulet's Daube
Boeuf en Daube de Jacqueline Priaulet

→···←

Jacqueline Priaulet remembers her mother's simple *daube* as the best she's ever eaten. That's saying something in Provence, where every other Sunday lunch is a pot of this fragrant and tender beef stew.

"My mother's was simple," Jacqueline said. "She made it her way, and our neighbor made it another. They both thought theirs was the best way."

I love the whole process of making *daube*: the marinating of the meat as it gradually turns a burgundy color, the tying of herbs into little bundles, the fragrance of the orange zest and fennel as it cooks. Then finally there is the thrill of serving the almost black, toothsome beef that literally glistens in the bowl. I can't think of a better dish for a winter day, when the sun might shine, but the chill goes right to your bones.

In Jacqueline's *daube*, the carrots are added toward the end so they retain their glorious orange color, and the subtle green olives give the stew its special flavor.

Naturally, a *daube* is more richly flavored when prepared the day before you plan to serve it. If you like, make it, let it cool, then refrigerate it. You can then remove the layer of surface fat.

You might serve this with a simple rice pilaf, as Jacqueline does occasionally; then it's called *boeuf gardian*.

Serve this with Hermitage Rouge or St. Joseph.

10 sprigs fresh thyme, or ½ teaspoon dried
6 imported bay leaves
4 strips (3 x ½ inch; 7½ x 1¼ cm) orange
  zest
4½ pounds (2¼ kg) stewing beef
  (round and chuck), cut into 2-inch
  (5 cm) pieces
2½ cups (625 ml) hearty red wine, such as
  a Côtes du Ventoux or a Vacqueyras
  (or any Côtes du Rhône)
2 tablespoons fennel seeds
9 ounces (270 g) slab bacon, cut into
  1 x ½ x ½-inch (2½ x 1¼ x 1¼ cm)
  pieces
2 tablespoons olive oil
3 medium onions, peeled and coarsely
  chopped
6 cloves garlic, peeled
Sea salt and freshly ground black pepper
3 large carrots, peeled and cut diagonally
  into thin rounds
1 cup (170 g) olives cassées (see Note)

1. Divide the fresh thyme, bay leaves, and orange zest into two lots, and tie each lot into a bundle with kitchen string. (If you are using dried thyme, tie it and the orange zest in two small squares of cheesecloth, leaving the bay leaves separate.)

2. Place the beef, wine, 1 bundle of herbs, and 1 tablespoon of the fennel seeds in a large nonreactive bowl. Mix well, and push the meat down so it is mostly covered with the wine. Cover and marinate at room temperature for 6 to 8 hours, turning the meat occasionally.

3. Drain the beef over a bowl, letting it sit for several minutes, and reserve the marinade. Discard the herb bundle.

4. Place the slab bacon and the olive oil in a large heavy stockpot over medium-high heat and sauté, stirring frequently, until the bacon is golden, about 5 minutes. Remove the bacon from the pot with a slotted spoon and set it aside on a plate. If there is an excess of fat, drain all but about 2 tablespoons from the pot. Add the beef, being sure not to crowd the pot, and thoroughly brown it on all sides. (If necessary, brown the beef in two batches.) The beef should be good and dark—far from scorched but solidly browned. It will take 10 to 15 minutes to brown the beef if you're doing it in one batch.

5. Add the reserved marinade, the onions, and the garlic cloves to the beef and stir, scraping up any browned bits from the bottom of the pot. Bring to a boil over medium-high heat. Then reduce the heat so the liquid is bubbling merrily, partially cover, and cook until the liquid has reduced and nearly evaporated, 30 to 40 minutes.

6. Add enough water to just cover the beef, along with the remaining bundle of herbs and the remaining 1 tablespoon fennel seeds. Season with salt and pepper to taste, partially cover, and cook until the beef is tender and has absorbed much of the cooking liquid, at least 2 hours. Check the *daube* occasionally, stirring to be sure it isn't sticking to the bottom of the pan.

7. Add the carrots, cover, and cook for 15 minutes. Then add the olives and continue to cook, covered, until the carrots are completely tender, another 15 minutes. Season carefully to taste.

8. To serve, remove the herb bundle and ladle the *daube* into warmed shallow soup bowls.

6 to 8 generous servings

N O T E : *Olives cassées* are brined with fennel and have a rich, aromatic flavor. If you can't find them, use ordinary (but unstuffed) green olives.

Eternal Olives

=

"The olive tree is eternal, you know," says Jacqueline Priaulet as we walk through one of her olive groves, stumbling over the rocky soil. It's hard to concentrate on what she's saying because of the breathtaking beauty that surrounds us. The gnarled, silvery green olive trees, which Jacqueline trims so they grow full and billowy, were set off by rusty red soil broken with sharp white rocks. Through the trees rose the jagged profile of Les Baux, bauxite hills topped by a medieval château. Though late fall, the air in Provence is warm and full of the green scent of ripening olives.

The town of Maussane and the Vallée des Baux has its roots in olives. "In the nineteenth century there were thirteen olive presses just in our town," says Jacqueline. "But then irrigation was put in and people ripped out olive trees to plant fruit trees." Fruit trees produce more quickly than olive trees, which meant easier, faster money for the growers. What they didn't know was that olive oil produced in the Vallée des Baux would become the luxury product it is today.

Like most growers in the Vallée des Baux, Jacqueline produces three varieties of olives, their names as poetic as the valley they grow in: Salonenque, Burruguette, and Grossane. The blend, along with the soil and the weather, is what gives character to the oil they produce. Fruity, flinty, with a wild edge, it is considered the best in France.

The Salonenques are the daintiest, and Jacqueline picks most of hers when they are still bitter and green, to be crushed and brined with fennel. Called *olives cassées* and wonderfully fragrant, they are served with an apéritif or tossed onto a roasting leg of lamb.

The Grossanes grow big and fat, like a date, and the Burruguettes are medium-size. Each starts out green and ripens to a purplish black.

Because Jacqueline sells an early crop of green olives for *olives cassées,* her harvest

season begins in September, when she and a hired hand literally comb the olives from the branches with a plastic tool that looks like a child's sand rake. Most growers lay a fine net around the trunk of the tree to catch the olives. Jacqueline designed a contraption based around a wheelbarrow frame hung with netting, which she calls the *hirondelle* because it looks like a swallow in flight. It catches the olives and funnels them gently into a box.

Jacqueline picks a big Grossane, squeezes it, and oil oozes out. She smiles. "The longer olives stay on the tree, the more oil they have," she says. She usually doesn't rush to harvest them, but a sharp wind had come through and blown many to the ground.

"Watch out, don't step on any," she says, deftly tiptoeing over the ground. "I'll use every one of these."

The olives go to the nearby Coopérative Oléicole de la Vallée des Baux to be pressed into extra-virgin olive oil.

The olive harvest lasts until the first of the year, and its speed depends on the mill. The olives can be picked only a few days before pressing, so growers wait for the phone to ring with the news that it's time to pick.

Once picked, they must be cleaned of leaves and small branches before being delivered to the coop. They are stored in big piles in an airy attic for three days so they can develop what Jacqueline calls "sec-

ondary aromas." They must be pressed at the exact moment their flavor is fullest, yet before they begin to develop acidity. In a process unchanged since the mill was built in the fifteenth century, the olives are crushed between huge, round granite millstones.

Once crushed, the olives and pits, together called *la pâte*, are layered between rush mats called *scourtins* and pressed at a cool temperature. This *pression à froid* guarantees the purity of the oil, which is put into a centrifuge to rid it of water. It is then stored in metal vats for at least three months to settle.

Settling is an integral step in the production process, giving the oil its smooth richness. But according to Jacqueline, some people just can't wait the three months. "If they've run out of our oil, they come here as soon as they find out we're pressing," she says, laughing.

So they should. She's got the best in France.

Huile d'Olive Vierge de la Vallée des Baux can be mail-ordered (internationally) from Coopérative Oléicole de la Vallée des Baux, 13520 Maussane-les-Alpilles, France. Tel.: (011-33) 90-54-32-37.

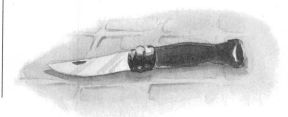

Braised Beef with Onions

Le Boeuf Braisé aux Oignons

Everything about this dish evokes farm cooking: quality ingredients, the time to cook them, rich and simple flavors. The beef here emerges from the herbal broth with a wonderfully fresh flavor, sweetened by the lightly browned onions.

Though at first glance this appears to be a winter dish, I serve it year-round, particularly on cool spring and summer evenings when I can get fresh-from-the-ground onions the size of golf balls.

Be sure to make this when you have the time to keep an eye on it. It takes little effort, but the meat does require basting so it stays moist and tender. This dish is sublime the day it is made, sumptuous the day after.

Try a Bandol alongside.

ASTUCES . . . .

• *It is essential to skim off the fat from the cooking juices before serving this dish. Either use a special pitcher designed to separate fat from juices, or make the dish in advance and chill the cooking juices (in the refrigerator), then scrape off the layer of fat that forms on top.*

• *Choose onions that are uniform in size so they cook evenly. And time the cooking according to their size, for you want them to hold their shape.*

. . . .

*1 beef top or bottom round roast
(3 pounds; 1½ kg); (see Note)*

9 cloves garlic, peeled

6 ounces (180 g) slab bacon, rind removed, cut into 1 x ¼ x ¼-inch (2½ x ½ x ½ cm) pieces

1 to 2 tablespoons olive oil or rendered goose fat (page 142), as needed

1½ to 2 cups (375 to 500 ml) dry white wine, such as an Aligoté

¼ cup (60 ml) eau-de-vie, such as Calvados, brandy, or Armagnac

1 to 1½ cups (250 to 375 ml) Beef Stock (page 506)

1 large bouquet garni (5 parsley stems, 3 imported bay leaves, 2 green leek leaves, 12 sprigs fresh thyme, tied in cheesecloth)

Sea salt and freshly ground black pepper

35 pearl onions, peeled

Fresh thyme sprigs, for garnish

Fresh parsley sprigs, for garnish

1. Pat the beef dry. If it has not been tied, secure it in several places along its length. Cut 5 of the garlic cloves in half lengthwise, removing the green germ. Make ten slits in the beef, and fit the garlic halves into the slits.

2. In a heavy saucepan or flameproof casserole just large enough to hold the meat, liquids, and onions, lightly brown the bacon. If it doesn't give up enough fat to keep it from sticking, add a bit of the oil to the pan. If there is a great deal of fat in the pan once the bacon is browned, drain all but about 2 teaspoons.

3. Add the beef and brown it gently on all sides over medium-high heat, about 7 minutes total.

4. Add the wine, eau-de-vie, and enough stock to bring the liquid about one third of the way up the meat. Add the bouquet garni and the remaining 4 garlic cloves. Turn the meat, cover the pan, and bring to a boil. Reduce the heat to medium and simmer, basting frequently, for 1 hour. Season the beef with salt and pepper, turn it, cover the pan, and cook, basting, for another 2½ hours.

5. Meanwhile, heat 1 tablespoon of the remaining oil in a medium-size skillet, and brown the onions for 4 to 5 minutes on all sides over medium-high heat, stirring or flipping them in the pan so they brown to a golden turn without burning. Remove from the heat.

6. Thirty minutes to 1 hour before the beef is done, add the onions, pushing them under the meat. (The cooking time for the onions will vary according to their size. If they are the size of a large marble, they will require about 30 minutes. If they are larger, approaching golf-ball size, they will require 1 hour.)

7. When the beef and onions are tender, transfer the meat to a cutting board that will catch the juices. Using a slotted spoon, transfer the onions to a warmed serving platter. Discard the bouquet garni. Skim the fat from the surface of the cooking juices (see Astuce), then taste. If they are richly flavored, simply adjust the seasoning as necessary. If the flavor seems thin, bring the juices to a boil and reduce by up to half; you should have at least 2 cups of juices to serve with the beef. Adjust the seasoning.

8. Remove the string from as much of the beef as you plan to slice, and cut it into ½-inch (1¼ cm) slices. Overlap the slices on the warmed platter, surrounding them with the onions. Arrange some of the onions on top of the meat, drizzle with some of the cooking juices, and garnish the platter with the herbs. Serve the remaining cooking juices separately.

6 to 8 servings

NOTE: While top or bottom round is ideal for this dish because it holds together well, you may also use boneless chuck shoulder or a chuck eye roast. These are closest to what is used on the farm, which is a mix of lean and fat.

Le Pâturage • The Pasture

Steak in the Provençal Style
Steak Provençale

→····←

Steak is steak, you say? Not if you prepare it this way, as Provençal farmers do. Summer in Provence means that life, including cooking, moves outdoors. Herbs are gathered from the hills and the garden, minced with garlic, and sprinkled atop a steak that is grilled just until it is dark on the outside, blood-red on the inside.

Even if you prefer your steak well done, you will find it is succulent prepared *à la provençale*.

Try it with a Sablet from Domaine des Gouberts.

4 porterhouse or T-bone steaks
   (each about 8 ounces; 250 g),
   trimmed of fat if desired
   (see Note)
2 tablespoons olive oil
½ cup (loosely packed) mixed fresh
   herbs, such as summer savory,
   thyme, and rosemary
2 cloves garlic, peeled, green germ
   removed, and minced
1 teaspoon sea salt
Freshly ground black pepper

1. Prepare a medium-size fire in a barbecue grill. When the fire has burned long enough that the coals are glowing red and dusted with ash, place the grill rack over the fire.

2. Brush the steaks on both sides with 1 tablespoon of the olive oil. Place the steaks on the rack and cook them to your liking, 4 to 5 minutes per side for medium-rare.

3. While the steaks are cooking, finely mince the herbs with the garlic. Combine this mixture with the salt in a small bowl, and stir in the remaining 1 tablespoon oil.

4. When the steaks are done, remove them from the grill and season them with pepper. Spread the herb mixture over the steaks, and serve immediately.

4 servings

NOTE: I've suggested porterhouse or T-bone steaks, but you may want to try tri-tip steaks or rib steaks. Tri-tip steaks are steaks cut from the bottom part of the sirloin. They are lean and tender, and much less expensive than sirloin, and are becoming more popular because of these qualities. If you choose rib steaks, be forewarned that they have wonderful flavor but are a bit tougher than the others.

Veal Stew

Fricassée de Veau

I first had *fricassée de veau* in Alsace, when we were visiting the Riehls, a farming family who live in and around the small town of Dauendorf. It came to the table rich, creamy, the sauce chockful of mushrooms and flavor. I've re-created it here, with the addition of some carrots for color. You may serve either pasta or rice as an accompaniment, or simply plenty of crusty bread.

Serve a lightly chilled Riesling alongside.

ASTUCES . . . .

• *Veal dries out if it is cooked too long—be sure to respect the cooking time listed here. If you want your sauce thicker than indicated in the recipe, remove the veal from the sauce and reduce it to the thickness you like, then either return the veal to the sauce for serving, or pour the sauce over the veal as indicated in the recipe.*

• *When using flour in a recipe like this, be sure to cook it (once sprinkled on the meat and vegetables) for at least 2 minutes, which will cook out its floury taste.*

2 tablespoons unsalted butter

2 large onions, peeled and thinly sliced

2½ pounds (1¼ kg) veal shoulder, boned, cut into 3½ x 2-inch (9 x 5 cm) chunks

Sea salt and freshly ground black pepper

4 teaspoons unbleached all-purpose flour

1 cup (250 ml) dry white wine, such as a Riesling or Sylvaner

1 cup (250 ml) Beef Stock (page 506)

3 large carrots, peeled, trimmed, and cut into thin rounds

1 bouquet garni (5 parsley stems, 3 imported bay leaves, 2 green leek leaves, 12 sprigs fresh thyme, tied in cheesecloth)

1 pound (500 g) button mushrooms, stems trimmed and brushed clean

6 tablespoons Crème Fraîche (page 520) or heavy (or whipping) cream

1 tablespoon freshly squeezed lemon juice

1. Melt 1 tablespoon of the butter in a large heavy skillet over medium-high heat. Add the onions and cook until they are tender and golden, about 20 minutes, stirring frequently and lowering the heat if necessary to keep the butter from smoking. Add the veal, season it lightly with salt and pepper, and sauté, turning it so it begins to turn an ivory color all over, but doesn't brown, about 5 minutes.

2. Sprinkle the flour over the meat and onions, stirring so the flour becomes absorbed into the butter and any cooking liquids, and cook, stirring constantly, for at least 2 minutes, until you see no more flour.

3. Pour the wine and the stock over the meat; stir, then add the carrots and the bouquet garni and season with salt and pepper. Cover and bring to a gentle boil.

4. Reduce the heat so the liquids are simmering gently and cook, covered, for 1 hour 15 minutes. The meat will not yet be tender, but the sauce will be slightly thickened.

5. While the meat is cooking, melt the remaining 1 tablespoon butter in a medium-size heavy skillet over medium-high heat. Add the mushrooms and cook, stirring constantly, until they have softened, given up their liquid, and become tender and golden, about 15 minutes. Remove from the heat and reserve.

6. When the meat has cooked, add the mushrooms and any cooking juices to the skillet. Season with salt and pepper and continue cooking, uncovered, until the meat is tender and the sauce is reduced by about one fourth and has thickened to the consistency of light cream, another 15 minutes and *no longer*. (Longer cooking will dry out the veal.)

7. Transfer the veal to a warmed serving dish and cover loosely with aluminum foil to keep it warm. Whisk together the crème fraîche and lemon juice in a small bowl, then whisk the mixture into the cooking juices in the skillet until combined. Let the sauce come to a simmer over medium-low heat and cook until it has reduced and thickened slightly, about 5 minutes more; it should coat the back of a spoon. Adjust the seasoning, being generous with the black pepper, and pour the sauce over the veal. Serve immediately.

8 servings

Save That Jelly
⇢•⇠

*T*he juices that cooked meats exude, if left to cool, coagulate into a wonderfully flavorful jelly. This jelly, when separated from fat, can be used as an intense flavoring for soups, stews, and sauces. So be mindful of the juices produced by your next roast or baked chicken or duck (see page 48), or roast beef or leg of lamb. It's a powerhouse of flavor and should be collected and stored in a covered container in the refrigerator. It should be used within one week. If frozen, it keeps indefinitely.

Alsatian Meat Stew

Baekeoffe

>···<

Though *baekeoffe* is as Alsatian as its name, I got this recipe in the Pays Basque, at the table of Valerie and Manex Lanatua. Honey producers, they are both possessed of fine palates and hearty appetites, and this is a dish that Mme. Lanatua's mother—who often cooks dinner for the Lanatuas—makes often. It was odd finding it in the Pays Basque, but on the other hand, it made some sense—the Têtes Rousses lambs that graze outside the house, and whose milk goes into the *ardi gasna* cheese that M. Lanatua makes for his family, have wonderful, tender meat. Beef isn't lacking, nor is pork. And Basque pork is unparalleled for flavor.

You can mix and match the meats in this dish—lamb is essential, to my palate, and pork plays a big part as well. But you may want to substitute veal for the beef, or use just pork and lamb.

The condiment of choice for this dish in the Pays Basque is ground *piment d'Espelette*, or spicy peppers. If you were in Alsace, it would be mustard.

Try a lightly chilled Riesling or Pinot Blanc alongside.

1 pound (500 g) beef shoulder, boned, trimmed of fat and cut into 2-inch (5 cm) squares

1 pound (500 g) lamb shoulder, boned, trimmed of fat, and cut into 2-inch (5 cm) squares

1 pound (500 g) pork shoulder or blade end, boned, trimmed of fat, and cut into 2-inch (5 cm) squares

4 medium onions, very thinly sliced

4 medium carrots, peeled, trimmed, and cut into thin rounds

2 leeks, white part only, well rinsed and cut into thin rounds

1 bouquet garni (5 parsley stems, 3 imported bay leaves, 2 green leek leaves, 4 whole cloves, 12 sprigs fresh thyme, tied in cheesecloth)

2 cloves garlic, peeled, cut in half, and green germ removed

Sea salt and freshly ground black pepper

2 cups (500 ml) Alsatian white wine, such as Riesling or Pinot Blanc

2½ pounds (1¼ kg) waxy potatoes, peeled and cut into large chunks

1. Place the meats in a large nonreactive bowl with the onions, carrots, leeks, bouquet

garni, and garlic. Season with salt and pepper, toss, and pour the wine over all. Toss again, cover, and refrigerate for 24 hours.

2. The following day, preheat the oven to 375°F (190°C).

3. Butter a baking dish large enough to hold all the ingredients. Place one third of the potatoes on the bottom of the dish and lightly salt them, top with half the meat and vegetables, add another third of the potatoes, the rest of the meat, and finally the rest of the potatoes. Pour the marinade over the potatoes, lightly salt and pepper them, cover the dish, and bake in the center of the oven until the meat is tender and cooked through, about 3 hours (see Note).

4. Remove the dish from the oven. Remove the bouquet garni and serve immediately, as is, right from the oven.

8 to 10 servings

N O T E : You may cook it up to 30 minutes longer with no evil results.

Mme. Fautrel's Shoulder of Lamb
Epaule d'Agneau de Mme. Fautrel

Mme. Fautrel and her son, Michel, eat a great deal of lamb, naturally. Michel prefers his roasted or, if chops, grilled in the fireplace.

"You've got to keep it simple," he says. "This is fine-flavored lamb, and you don't want to do too much to it." In fact, by American standards they don't even cook it very much. The French prefer lamb that's still purplish—closer to raw than this recipe indicates.

Meantime, for this recipe choose the smallest lamb shoulder you can find. It will be from a very young lamb, and the meat will require longer cooking per pound than a larger shoulder would (unless you agree with the Fautrels and like your lamb nearly raw).

A Hint of Progress

>•<

Mme. Fautrel, who is well into her eighties and has a back bent double from hard work, has the youngest, most sparkling eyes I've ever seen. She and her son, Michel, live in a hulking stone farmhouse that dates back at least to the fourteenth century. Its walls are thick enough to harbor a two-foot-wide sink, which they uncovered recently when working on the house.

I visited with the Fautrels on a blustery midwinter day. The sky was patched with fluffy clouds and the rain came down infrequently, but in torrents. Mme. Fautrel sat near, practically in, the huge old fireplace reading the paper, keeping warm in the only heated spot in the house.

"Oh, we had a furnace once," she said, nodding at her son. "Do you remember?" He nodded back. "But it was expensive, and besides, we only needed heat in here and we've got the fireplace."

As we sat and talked at the rough wood table where the Fautrels and their workers eat, I looked around the room, which hadn't changed much since it was built. The stone sink was worn with time, as were the dark beams. The tiny, deeply set windows let in a minimum of light. How odd, then, to see a microwave oven in one corner of the kitchen, a giant freezer in the other, a drip coffee machine on the counter.

"Well," Mme. Fautrel said, noticing my roving eye, "we can't entirely ignore progress, can we? We couldn't live without the freezer—that's where our garden produce and our lambs go."

Why? As my butcher explained, the meat on a very young shoulder is slightly gelatinous, and longer cooking tenderizes it, allowing the flavor to come through. His rule is 15 minutes per pound, which I find just right. Try it and see what you like; then adjust the cooking time accordingly. Don't stint on the rest time, for resting has a great deal to do with evenness of texture, tenderness, and juiciness.

Drink an Hermitage Rouge alongside, and enjoy!

2½ pounds (1¼ kg) bone-in lamb shoulder
  (see Note)
3 cloves garlic, peeled, green germ
  removed, and minced
Sea salt and freshly ground black pepper
1½ pounds (750 g) onions, peeled and
  diced
Fresh sage leaves, parsley leaves, or
  rosemary leaves, for garnish (optional)

1. Preheat the oven to 450°F (230°C).

2. Using a very sharp knife, cut between the fat and the meat on the top of the shoulder, making a sort of pocket (do not remove the fat). You may have to do this in several places, depending on how the fat is distributed on the shoulder. When you have several "pockets," stuff the minced garlic into them, spreading it evenly over the meat; then cover it with the fat. You want as even as possible a distribution of garlic between the meat and the fat. If there are places on the shoulder not covered by fat, spread these areas with some of the garlic as well.

3. Generously rub the shoulder with salt and pepper.

4. Place the onions in a 12 x 8-inch (30 x 20 cm) baking dish, and season them with salt and pepper. Then set a roasting rack among the onions and place the shoulder on the rack. Roast in the center of the oven until the meat is golden on the outside and cooked to your liking inside. A cooking time of 40 to 50 minutes results in meat that is medium at the surface and quite rare near the bone; adjust the timing to your own taste.

5. When the shoulder is cooked, remove it from the oven but leave the oven on. Sprinkle it a second time with salt and pepper, and let it rest in the baking dish for at least 10 minutes (preferably 20 to 30). Most of the juices will retreat back into the meat, but some will drip down on the onions, giving them an incomparable flavor.

6. Ten minutes before serving, or after the lamb has rested for 10 to 20 minutes, transfer the lamb to a cutting board and return the onions to the oven. Bake until they are hot through, 10 minutes. Meanwhile, carve the lamb into thin slices.

7. Transfer the onions to a warmed serving platter. Arrange the lamb atop the onions, letting the onions show just slightly around the edges of the meat. Garnish with the herbs if desired, and serve immediately.

4 to 6 servings

NOTE: Use American-raised lamb. Raised according to very high standards, it is tender and flavorful, without the gamey muttony taste of some imported lamb. It is generally not previously frozen, either, as is the case with much imported lamb. Ask your butcher for the youngest American-raised lamb available.

Roast Lamb with Sage

Gigot à la Sauge

›•••‹

Basting lamb with a big sage branch dipped in oil and vinegar is rustic, earthy, and oh-so-delicious. The flavor reminds me of the dry and aromatic hills of the Vallée des Baux, the backdrop of Jacqueline Priaulet's olive groves (see page 164). It was from her that I got this idea. Nothing could be simpler; nothing could be better.

Choose a nice big sage branch for basting, then use it as a garnish on the platter. If that's not possible, add a handful of fresh sage leaves to the oil several hours before using it to baste the lamb—that way the oil will absorb the flavor of the leaves. Don't, however, expect the sage flavor to bowl you over. It is intended as a subtle aromatic undercurrent.

Try this with a hearty Côtes du Rhône.

6 tablespoons extra-virgin olive oil
1½ tablespoons good-quality red wine
vinegar
1 large sage branch, preferably with a long
stem, or a large handful (24 or so)
fresh leaves, or 1 tablespoon dried
1 leg of lamb (4 to 5 pounds; 2 to 2½ kg),
bone in, fat trimmed if desired
17 cloves garlic, 16 unpeeled, 1 peeled,
green germ removed, and minced
Sea salt and freshly ground black pepper
2 pounds (1 kg) small new potatoes
(about the size of a large marble),
scrubbed

1. Whisk together 5 tablespoons of the olive oil and the vinegar in a small bowl. Crush the sage leaves (even those on the branch, but leaving them still attached) and place them in the oil mixture, gently pushing them down so they are completely submerged in the oil. Set the oil and sage aside to infuse for up to 8 hours.

2. When you are ready to cook the lamb, preheat the over to 400°F (205°C).

3. Rub the leg of lamb all over with the remaining 1 tablespoon olive oil, then rub it with the minced garlic. Season it generously with salt and pepper. Place the leg of lamb, fattiest side up, on a rack in a roasting pan, and set it in the lower third of the oven. Roast the lamb for 30 minutes, basting it twice (if you used a sage branch, use it as your basting brush). Turn the lamb so the fattiest side is down and continue roasting, basting every 15 minutes, until it reaches an internal temperature of 125°F (52°C), for rare meat, 45 minutes.

4. Fifteen minutes before the lamb is

cooked, add the 16 whole garlic cloves and the potatoes to the pan. Stir as best you can so they are coated with the drippings, and roast until they are golden and the potatoes are cooked through, 30 to 35 minutes.

5. Remove the leg of lamb when it is cooked to your liking, leaving the potatoes and garlic to continue roasting. Set the lamb on a warmed serving platter to rest.

6. When the potatoes and garlic are

cooked through, arrange them around the leg of lamb. Pour any cooking juices over all and serve immediately, garnished with the sage branch if desired.

6 to 8 servings

Lamb Stew with Spring Vegetables
Blanquette d'Agneau

*B*lanquette d'agneau is a hearty yet elegant farm dish, and this version comes straight from Provence. Light and fragrant, it speaks of freshness and late spring, which is when it is best. There are several steps, but it is very simple to make.

And for those of you who are tempted to omit the cream and egg yolks in the interest of reducing calories, *Halt!* A *blanquette* won't live up to its name if its sauce isn't thickened with their subtlety. When you do some arithmetic, you'll find that each diner gets approximately 1½ tablespoons of cream and a third of an egg yolk—hardly a sinful amount.

Serve with a lightly chilled Sauvignon Blanc or Aligoté.

ASTUCES . . . .

• *Carrots are the color in this dish, so when you serve it, be sure to have several slices in view. If I have some fresh chervil, I sprinkle it over as a garnish; its lacy leaf and delicate flavor add the final touch of springtime.*

• *Try preparing the vegetables the morning before you plan to serve the stew, so you can take your time. Once they are cooled, place them in one layer on a work surface or in dishes, and leave them in a cool spot, covered with a lightly dampened tea towel; or refrigerate them, tightly covered.*

. . . .

FOR BLANCHING THE LAMB

2 pounds (1 kg) lamb shoulder, boned, cut
    into 4 x 4 x 1-inch (10 x 10 x 2½ cm)
    pieces (see Note)
1 tablespoon sea salt

FOR BLANCHING THE VEGETABLES

1 recipe Herb Broth (page 508), strained,
    herbs discarded
4 teaspoons sea salt
20 pearl onions, peeled
4 smallish carrots, peeled, trimmed, and
    cut diagonally into medium-size slices
7 small young turnips, peeled (see Note)
1 pound (500 g) waxy new potatoes,
    peeled and cut into quarters
    lengthwise

FOR COOKING THE BLANQUETTE

1 tablespoon olive oil
Sea salt
1 tablespoon unbleached all-purpose flour
1 cup (250 ml) dry white wine, such as a
    Sauvignon Blanc or an Aligoté
1 large bouquet garni (5 parsley stems,
    3 imported bay leaves, 2 green leek
    leaves, 12 sprigs fresh thyme, tied in
    cheesecloth)
1 medium onion, peeled and stuck with
    2 whole cloves
1 small carrot, peeled, trimmed, and cut
    into quarters lengthwise
½ cup (125 ml) Crème Fraîche (page 520)
    or heavy (or whipping) cream
2 large egg yolks
1 small bunch fresh chervil, for garnish
    (optional)

1. Blanch the lamb: Place the lamb in a stock pot, cover it with plenty of water, and add the salt. Bring to a boil over medium-high heat, boil for 2 minutes, then drain. Set the lamb aside.

2. Fill a large bowl with ice water.

3. Blanch the vegetables: Combine the herb broth and 2 teaspoons of the salt in a large saucepan, and bring to a boil over medium-high heat. Add the onions, cover partially, and cook until they are tender but not soft, 7 to 8 minutes. Using a slotted spoon, transfer the onions to the ice water to cool. When they are completely cooled, transfer them to a cotton tea towel and pat dry. Set them aside.

4. Return the broth to a boil and add the carrots. Cover, bring back to a boil, and cook just until they are tender but not soft, about 7 minutes. Using a slotted spoon, transfer the carrots to the ice water; let them cool; then transfer them to a tea towel. Prepare a new bowl of ice water if necessary.

5. Return the broth to a boil and add the turnips. Cover, bring back to a boil, and cook until they are tender but not soft, 8 to 10 minutes. Transfer the turnips to the ice water, repeating the procedure of cooling and transferring to a tea towel. Remove the herb broth from the heat and set it aside.

6. Place the potatoes in a medium-size saucepan, cover them generously with fresh water, and add the remaining 2 teaspoons salt. Bring to a boil over medium-high heat, and cook, partially covered, until the potatoes are just tender through, 15 minutes. Drain and set aside.

7. When you are ready to cook the stew, heat the oil in a large heavy skillet over medium-high heat. Add the lamb, season it lightly with salt, and stir so it is coated with the oil. Brown the lamb very lightly, stirring it constantly, 1 to 2 minutes. Then sprinkle it evenly with the flour, stir, and continue cooking, stirring constantly, until the flour has cooked through, 2 minutes. (You do not want the flour to brown, but just to cook enough so it loses its floury taste.) Slowly add the reserved herb broth and stir, scraping up any browned bits from the bottom of the skillet. Add the wine, the bouquet garni, the onion with cloves, and the quartered carrot. Bring the liquid to a boil, then reduce the heat so that it is simmering evenly. Cover and simmer gently until the lamb is tender, 45 minutes.

8. In a small bowl, whisk together the crème fraîche and the egg yolks.

9. When the lamb is tender, remove the bouquet garni, the onion, and the carrot. Stir the crème fraîche mixture into the lamb. Then add the blanched vegetables, gently pushing them down under the cooking liquid. Raise the heat to medium-low, and stir constantly until the sauce has thickened slightly, to the consistency of light cream, and the vegetables are hot through, about 10 minutes.

10. Serve the *blanquette* in warmed shallow soup bowls or rimmed plates, garnished with small sprigs of chervil if you like.

6 servings

NOTES: The pieces of lamb should not be bite-size! If they are smaller than suggested, they will cook too quickly and turn insipid. For this dish, the lamb must have good, rich, sophisticated (yet delicate) flavor.

• The recipe calls for small spring turnips. If you can't find them, use larger ones and cut them in half, or in quarters if they are very large. Watch the cooking time carefully.

Grilled Lamb with Rosemary
L'Agneau Grillé au Romarin

→•••←

Summer surrounds us with its heat, its pervasive sense of freedom from the usual rituals and roles. In France that means everything is a bit more relaxed, and while meals are still copious, well planned, and well prepared, they take on a more casual air.

Here, thinly sliced lamb shoulder fits the summer season with its vivid flavor and appealing texture (and simplicity of preparation). It is marinated briefly, then grilled just until golden on the outside and still rare inside, and served alongside or atop a lively green salad.

Try a Gigondas with this.

A S T U C E S . . . .

• *Lightly oil a clean grill rack with mild vegetable oil to prevent foods from sticking.*

• *Mince fresh herbs right before you use them, as they lose their fresh flavor quickly after being minced.*

• *You may want to skewer the meat to make for easier cooking. Just weave a metal skewer through the slices before placing them on the grill.*

. . . .

1¾ pounds (875 g) good-quality boneless
   lamb shoulder, in one piece (see Note)
2 tablespoons olive oil
¼ cup fresh rosemary leaves, or 2 teaspoons
   dried
2 cloves garlic, peeled, green germ
   removed, and minced
Branches of fresh rosemary, for the fire
   (optional)
Sea salt and freshly ground black pepper
Double recipe Green Salad with Oil and
   Vinegar Dressing (page 56)

1. Cut the lamb against the grain into thin slices. Place the lamb slices in a nonreactive dish and drizzle with the oil. Turn the meat so it is evenly coated with the oil.

2. Mince the rosemary leaves. Sprinkle the rosemary and the garlic over the meat, turning the meat so it is sprinkled evenly on each side. Let the meat sit, covered, at room temperature for at least 30 minutes, or up to several hours in a cool spot or in the refrigerator.

3. Build a medium-size fire in a barbecue grill. When the coals are glowing red and dusted with ash, place the rosemary branches on the coals. Lightly oil the rack and place it on the grill. Season the meat lightly with salt and pepper, and grill it until golden on both sides but still rosy in the middle, about 5 minutes total (the cooking time will depend upon how thick your slices are, and how hot the fire). Remove the lamb from the heat and season it again with salt and pepper. Serve immediately, on top of the salad or alongside.

6 servings

N O T E : Be sure to get very good quality American-grown lamb for this recipe.

On the Norman Salt Marsh

═

From Michel Fautrel's farmhouse in Normandy, one can see across the salt marsh, or *pré-salé*, to Mont St. Michel, rising massively above the water, its spire reaching to the sky.

It is said that France's best lamb is raised on these salt marshes. Certainly the animals that graze here are endowed with a magic combination of muscle tone from bounding over the rocks and rivulets, and flavor from feeding on the hardy, salt-washed grasses. The result is lamb with texture, yet indescribable tenderness, and an ethereal, distinct flavor.

These *pré-salé* lambs, which graze around the clock in summer and in the early mornings in winter, are so highly valued they are protected by an Appellation d'Origine, a standard that limits how many can be raised and where, the amount of land each lamb must have for grazing, and their size. Several hundred farmers are entitled to produce these lambs, and they are required to let them out on the marsh every single day of their ninety-day lives.

The tides around Mont St. Michel are the highest in France, rising up to 45 feet (13½ m) in a matter of hours, sweeping in as far as 9 miles (15 km).

"We have major tides once a month, and they last for two days," M. Fautrel told me the day I visited his farm. "We bring the lambs in then, of course, then take them out as soon as the tides recede."

We drove down a rutted road to the salt marsh, a broad expanse of hillocky field. "We can't fence the marsh in," M. Fautrel said. "This is a tourist area, and the government doesn't want anything to disturb the view."

Though the Fautrel family has leased a portion of the salt marsh for generations, M. Fautrel must reapply for the lease each year. "It's a little unsure," he said, shrugging.

"This mayor is in favor of lambs on the marsh, the next one might not be."

We stepped onto the marsh. "I love it here," M. Fautrel said. "If I couldn't get out here every day, I'm not sure what I'd do."

As it is, his job requires at least a daily visit to the marsh. "Sometimes a lamb will fall in a rivulet or get stuck in a bend in one of the streams that runs through the marsh. And tourists bring dogs that love to chase after them. We've got to check them at least once a day," he said.

I kicked a tuft of the tough grass. "That right there is too long for the lambs," M. Fautrel said, smiling. "They want grass moistened with dew, so it isn't too salty, and they won't touch it if it gets too long or too tough."

BARN PHILOSOPHY

We returned to the Fautrel farm, where we escaped the biting wind by ducking into a barn that made up one side of a large courtyard. It was warmer inside, but still breezy.

"The barns have to be open so the differ- ence in temperature isn't so striking to the lambs," M. Fautrel said. "If it were warmer in here, they'd get sick when we let them out."

We walked through the feeding area of the barn, where bunches of dried and faded holly hung from the rafters.

"Those? We hang them up each year before Christmas," M. Fautrel said. "It's a superstition, I guess you'd say. We think it keeps illness away from the animals."

We turned into another part of the barn, where his lambs, which he'd just brought in a couple of hours before, were snuggled in clumps. The newest, about the size of lapdogs, huddled against the older lambs to keep warm. The barn was fresh smelling, the straw golden.

"We change the straw every day, and keep the barn clean for them, so they're comfortable, and so we meet the standards of the Appellation d'Origine," M. Fautrel said. "But we've always raised our lambs this way, so it doesn't feel like any extra work or care."

His reward, aside from contented lambs, is twice the price for their meat.

"I'd raise them this way any- way, but I don't mind the pay!" he said.

Le Pâturage • The Pasture

Shepherdess's Lamb
Agneau à la Bergère

→····←

This recipe comes from Jeanine Ouret, who, with her husband, cares for a flock of more than four hundred sheep in the heights of the Pyrénées mountains.

In May, the Ourets, their two children, and their sheep move to the mountains, where the family lives in a *cayolar*, a shepherd's cabin. The Ourets' *cayolar* is a flower-bedecked, welcoming place with chickens in the front courtyard and pigs rooting around alongside the sheep, who languidly munch the mountain grasses. Out behind the one-story cabin is a handful of ducks, and to one side there is a thriving vegetable garden.

Just down the mountain from the *cayolar* is another structure, which is part cheese-making studio, part guest house. The cheese-making room looks like a small laboratory: walls and floor completely tiled in white, the equipment (a press for the cheeses, a great vat for heating the milk) all stainless steel, the windows neatly screened. Its modernity—dictated by new laws that conform to European Economic Community norms—is a real contrast to the surrounding simplicity and wildness. Rather than jarring, however, it is impressive, and it is one of the reasons the Ourets' cheese is sought after from as far away as Biarritz.

Mme. Ouret, whose strong arms and lithe form are testament to a working outdoor life, loves to cook in her small but well-equipped kitchen. She cooks from the garden and makes good use of all the animals they raise. Her one rule is simplicity, for they have many visitors and she works full-time making cheese for more than half the period they're in the mountains, so time in the kitchen is kept to a minimum.

This dish is a good example of an Ouret *cayolar* main course. It cooks on its own in the oven, and the one thing Mme. Ouret insists on is that it must be golden brown. "It's a brown, brown dish," she said. "It has to be, to be good."

She adds a bit of ground Espelette peppers, which are hot and flavorful, and puts the jar on the table for her husband, who can never get enough. With a fresh garden salad and a bottle of the local Irouléguy red, this makes a full and satisfying meal.

Serve with Irouléguy, or with a deep, red Cahors.

1 tablespoon olive oil

2 pounds (1 kg) boneless lamb shoulder,
cut into 2-inch (5 cm) cubes
(see Note)

Salt and freshly ground black pepper

1½ pounds (750 g) onions, peeled and
sliced paper-thin

4 cloves garlic, peeled, green germ
removed, and chopped

¼ teaspoon piment d'Espelette, or a pinch
of cayenne pepper (see Note)

1 tablespoon best-quality red wine vinegar

1. Preheat the oven to 400°F (205°C).

2. Heat the oil in a large heavy oven-proof skillet over medium-high heat. Add the lamb and brown it on all sides, seasoning it with salt and pepper as it cooks, about 5 minutes.

3. Remove the lamb from the skillet and add the onions and garlic. Cook, stirring, until they are deep golden, 5 to 8 minutes.

Season with salt and pepper. Return the lamb to the skillet, stir to loosen the onions and garlic, sprinkle with the Espelette or cayenne pepper, and cover. Transfer the skillet to the center of the oven and bake until the lamb is tender and just slightly pink in the center, about 40 minutes.

4. Remove the skillet from the oven, and drizzle the vinegar over the lamb. Stir lightly, adjust the seasoning if necessary, and serve immediately.

4 to 6 servings

NOTES: If you can't find a whole good-quality (American-grown, nonfrozen) lamb shoulder, buy thick-cut blade chops and cut the meat from them.

• If you do substitute cayenne pepper for the local *piment d'Espelette*, do so gingerly, as cayenne's heat is much more fiery than the Basque pepper.

Provençal Pork and Vegetable Stew
La Baiana

>•••<

*L*a baiana is a year-round dish that reflects the seasons with the vegetables it contains. In winter, it is rich with cabbage and root vegetables; in summer, it contains the panoply I've included here.

This is a perfect summertime dish because it takes little time to prepare and can be made in advance. It reminds me of Provence, from whence it comes, when the sun sets slowly over the gray-green hills and the ground reverberates with the day's heat while the cooling evening air licks around the trees.

Roundly flavored with herbs, *la baiana* is two meals in one—a broth and a main course. Meat is nearly always a part of this dish, but if you care to make it an all-vegetable meal, just omit the pork. Note that fresh herbs (except dried bay leaves) are essential here. While summer savory (called *poivre d'âne* in Provence, *sarriette* elsewhere) is typically used in many Provençal dishes, it is not an absolute necessity. Plenty of thyme and bay leaves are a must, however.

I have suggested certain vegetables that are traditionally part of *la baiana*, but use what is best and freshest, and grown most locally. As always, think of good color and texture balance.

This is fresh and delicious the day it is made. The following day, when the vegetables have soaked up the vinaigrette, it takes on an added dimension. If you have leftovers, dice the pork, toss it with the vegetables, and serve, adding additional vinaigrette if necessary.

Serve with a lightly chilled Bandol Rosé or a red Côtes du Rhône.

ASTUCES . . . .

• *Don't use potatoes that are too small (that is, the size of a large marble) because you want to leave them whole, and they need to withstand up to 35 minutes of cooking time. A fresh, waxy new potato is what you want. Leave the skin on the potatoes. If guests object, they may do as the French do and peel them at the table.*

• *I like to dress the vegetables with the vinaigrette so they can absorb some of its flavor while they cool. But you may also serve them hot from the pot, with pitchers of oil and vinegar, and a small dish of minced garlic on the side so guests can dress their own vegetables and meat. The meat must rest before you cut into it so it has a chance to relax and retain its juices.*

. . . .

FOR THE PORK
10 sprigs fresh thyme
10 bushy sprigs fresh summer savory (optional)
2 imported bay leaves
2 pounds (1 kg) blade end or shoulder of pork, or bone-in pork loin
1 teaspoon sea salt, or more to taste
10 black peppercorns

FOR THE VEGETABLES

2 pounds (1 kg) fresh beans
  (such as limas) in the pod
10 sprigs fresh thyme
5 bushy sprigs fresh summer savory
  (optional)
2 imported bay leaves
1 pound (500 g) waxy new potatoes
3 medium carrots, peeled and cut into
  medium-size dice
4 cloves garlic, peeled
10 black peppercorns
12 cups (3 l) water
1 tablespoon sea salt, or to taste
36 pearl onions, peeled
1 pound (500 g) Swiss chard, trimmed,
  well rinsed, stems and leaves coarsely
  chopped

FOR THE VINAIGRETTE

⅔ cup (160 ml) best-quality red wine
  vinegar
Sea salt and freshly ground
  black pepper
4 cloves garlic, peeled, green germ
  removed, and minced
1 cup (250 ml) extra-virgin olive oil
1 tablespoon mixed fresh thyme and
  summer savory leaves, or fresh thyme
  leaves alone

FOR SERVING THE BROTH

1 large clove garlic, peeled
6 to 8 slices day-old country-style
  bread
Fresh summer savory and/or thyme leaves,
  for garnish

1. Cook the pork: Tie the herb sprigs and bay leaves together with kitchen twine. Place the pork in a large heavy saucepan with the herb bundle, the salt, and the peppercorns. Cover with water and bring to a boil over medium-high heat. Reduce the heat so the water is boiling merrily and cook, partially covered, until the meat is cooked through, about 1 hour.

2. Meanwhile, cook the vegetables: Pod the fresh beans. Tie the herb sprigs and bay leaves together with kitchen twine. Place the beans, potatoes, carrots, garlic, peppercorns, and the herb bundle in a large kettle or stockpot, and add the water. Season with the salt, cover, and bring to a boil over medium-high heat. Reduce the heat to low and cook until the carrots are partially tender, about 10 minutes. Add the onions and Swiss chard, and cook until the vegetables are tender but not soft or mushy, about 25 minutes (see Note).

3. While the vegetables are cooking, prepare the vinaigrette: In a medium-size bowl, whisk together the vinegar, salt and pepper to taste, and the garlic. Slowly add the oil, whisking all the while, until the mixture emulsifies. Whisk in the fresh herbs if desired. Pour half the vinaigrette into a large serving bowl. Reserve the other half.

4. When the meat is cooked, transfer it to a cutting board or platter and let rest at least 15 minutes.

5. When the vegetables are cooked, use a slotted spoon to transfer them to the serving bowl containing the vinaigrette. Toss, and let them cool to room temperature.

6. Serve the broth: Rub the garlic over both sides of the bread slices. Place a slice in each shallow soup bowl. Pour the broth from the cooked vegetables over the bread, and serve immediately.

7. When the pork has rested for at least 15 minutes, cut it into thick slices, cutting around the bone, and arrange the slices on a serving platter. Drizzle with most (or all) of the remaining vinaigrette. If you use only part of the vinaigrette, place the rest in a serving bowl or pitcher, to pass separately.

8. Toss the vegetables once more, and garnish with the additional fresh herbs. Serve the vegetables and the pork together after everyone has finished their broth.

6 to 8 servings

NOTE: The cooking time will vary depending on the vegetables you choose.

Hearty Pork and Vegetable Stew with Buckwheat Dumplings
Kig ha Farz

→ ··· ←

K*ig ha farz* takes me right back to the landscape of Brittany, with its tidy stone houses, its gorgeous rocky coast, and the mist that gives richness and flavor to everything that grows there, from artichokes to potatoes. I was lucky enough to sample this stew at the home of François and Marceline Grall, who raise artichokes and cauliflower in the Nord Finistère area of Brittany.

When we arrived at the farm, Mme. Grall was at the door to greet us. I knew instantly that this was a place where I'd like to spend some time. She showed us our rooms, which were more luxurious than usual for a farm, and so tidy they gleamed. Luscious aromas wafted throughout the house; dinner would be ready in fifteen minutes.

We sat down to a simple meal of chicken with mushrooms and a huge platter of fresh-from-the-field steamed artichokes. Though she didn't eat with us, Mme. Grall couldn't stay away from the table, and soon she and her husband had joined us. We talked of farming and traveling, of their lives and the pleasure they get from having guests on their farm.

"Tomorrow I will make you a *farz*," she announced. "I think we'll have a party!"

The next evening the whole family was there, and an air of celebration permeated the house. After apéritifs, Mme. Grall brought in the *kig ha farz* as though she were presenting us with the king's treasure. Indeed it looked like the crown jewels, a huge platter laden with bright vegetables, chunks of pork, bacon, and a mound of *farz*—buckwheat cooked in a cotton sleeve right with the meat and vegetables, then rolled until it is fluffy like couscous.

I'd heard about *kig ha farz* before, but always in the most disparaging terms. I had a feeling I'd like it, however, since earthy flavors, lots of vegetables, a seasoning of meat is one of my favorite combinations. I was right. It was sumptuous.

Kig ha farz is the simplest of farm meals, yet because it's so copious and colorful, it puts people into a party frame of mind. We certainly were—we sat around the table until well into the morning, enjoying a crisp escarole salad after the stew, then a fluffy *far breton* (a dessert similar to the Clafoutis on page 363). The cheerful evening finally closed with an accordion concert by Ann-Hélène, the couple's eldest daughter.

Hard apple cider is the best drink choice here.

FOR THE FARZ

2 large eggs

½ cup (125 ml) milk

4 tablespoons (½ stick; 60 g) unsalted butter, melted

Scant 1¾ cups (250 g) buckwheat flour

1 teaspoon sea salt

FOR THE STEW

4 medium carrots, peeled, cut in half lengthwise, then cut into medium-size half moons

3 leeks, white part only, well rinsed

3 small potatoes, peeled and cut into quarters

1 bouquet garni (5 parsley stems, 3 imported bay leaves, 2 green leek leaves, 12 sprigs fresh thyme, tied in cheesecloth)

1 fresh (not smoked) pork hock (about 3 pounds; 1½ kg)

1 pound (500 g) slab bacon, cut in half

Sea salt and freshly ground black pepper

2 kielbasa sausages (each about 8 ounces; 250 g)

3 large artichokes prepared as directed in "Preparing Artichoke Hearts" (page 149)

1. Prepare the *farz*: Whisk together the eggs, milk, and melted butter in a medium-size bowl. Using a wooden spoon, slowly add the flour and the salt, stirring until thoroughly combined. Place the mixture in the center of a clean, dampened piece of cotton cloth

Le Pâturage • The Pasture

The Farz

→·←

Marceline Grall brought out a long, thin, heavy-duty cotton bag, which she uses to contain the farz in the stewpot. "Sometimes a woman used the sleeve from a cotton shirt, which she'd tie at both ends," she said, laughing. "Whatever she used, it was in use for a long time. She would bequeath her farz bag to her daughter. I only just got this new one. I'd had my other one for I don't know how many years, but it got too old and thin to use."

The farz (also spelled fars or far) comes in many forms in Brittany. The dumpling can be sweet or savory, made with white or buckwheat flour, and baked, poached, or steamed.

Kig ha farz means farz with pork. There are as many variations as there are cooks, and the stew often includes whatever is available the day it is made. Sometimes a kig ha farz includes beef in the broth, and raisins and/or prunes in the farz. For my taste, this version is simply the best.

Mme. Grall varies her kig ha farz by adding artichoke bottoms—a luxury for some, a fact of life for her. "We all love artichokes," she said, "so I just go out and pick a few. We eat them nearly every day."

that measures at least 24 inches (60 cm) square. Gather the corners of the cloth together and secure them tightly with kitchen string, leaving room for the *farz* to expand by about one third. Set it aside.

2. Make the stew: Combine the carrots, leeks, potatoes, bouquet garni, pork hock, bacon, and salt and pepper to taste in a large stock pot. Add water to cover by 2 inches (5 cm). Add the *farz* bundle, gently pushing it under the surface so it is moist all over.

3. Cover the pot and bring to a boil over medium-high heat. Then remove the cover, reduce the heat to medium so the liquid is simmering merrily, and cook the stew until the *farz* is nearly firm to the touch, and the

vegetables are tender but still have some texture, about 1 hour. The *farz* will tend to float in the liquid as the stew cooks, which is fine. Occasionally turn the bundle so it cooks evenly, and skim off any fat that rises to the surface of the stew.

4. While the farz is cooking, cook the kielbasa: Place the sausages in a medium-size saucepan, cover them with water, and bring

to a boil over high heat. Reduce the heat so the water is boiling gently and cook, partially covered, until the sausages are done, 30 to 40 minutes. Remove from the heat, leaving the kielbasa in the water to stay warm.

5. When the *farz* is cooked (after about an hour), remove the bundle from the stew and set it, still in its cotton bag, in a sieve placed over a shallow bowl. Let it drain for 15 minutes. Meanwhile, add the artichoke hearts to the simmering soup and cook until they and the other vegetables are completely tender.

6. Transfer the *farz*, still in its cotton bag, to a work surface and roll it back and forth, applying pressure gently but firmly. At first the *farz* will feel hard and rubbery, but it will gradually crumble into small bits. Keep rolling the bundle until most of the *farz* is in small bits (it should resemble couscous). Some stubborn pieces will remain large and

somewhat hard, but don't be concerned— they are delicious, too!

7. Carefully open the cotton bag and pour the *farz* onto a large warmed serving platter. Remove the artichokes from the cooking liquid and cut them into quarters. Slice the meat from the pork hock, and cut or slice the slab bacon into serving-size pieces. Do the same with the kielbasa. Arrange the vegetables and the meats over and around the *farz*. Fill a warmed pitcher with the cooking juices, and serve it separately to drizzle (not pour) over the *farz* (see Note).

6 servings

NOTE: If the *farz* seems a bit dry, do as the Bretons do and drizzle it with a bit of the cooking juices—not too much or it will turn to mush. You can also dab it with butter, if you like.

Pork Confit
Confit de Porc

>...<

Just the aroma of this simmering gently on the stove takes me to the Dordogne and the kitchen of Dany Dubois. *Confit* is traditional in the Dordogne, and hers is surely among the best.

Dany grew up making *confit*, as most farm women did in the southwest. It was the best way, before refrigeration, to preserve pork and duck for the entire year. Cooked in fat, completely covered in fat, and then stored in the *cave*, where the temperature stays cool and constant, the *confit* not only improved as it aged, but was there to provide a quick, satisfying meal.

Confit is simple, but it takes some time and a little twist of attitude. For to properly "confit" something, you must cook it, very gently, completely covered in fat, a notion Americans are not used to. The result is not fatty, it is simply rich in flavor, so tender and moist the *confit* melts in the mouth.

This is Dany's recipe for *confit*, one she generously gave me over a decade ago, and which I have continued to make when seized with the desire for *confit*. Of course, once seized I must wait a good two weeks to taste it, but the seizure is never, fortunately, a passing one.

You need a good, solid piece of pork, preferably from a pig that has lived a bit longer than the ordinary. Common southwestern wisdom holds that a more mature pig gives better *confit*.

Serve *confit* with a *pipérade* or simply with potatoes sautéed in, of course, the fat from the *confit*.

Try a Languedoc Rouge alongside.

A S T U C E S . . . .

• *Heat the fat very slowly, until it sends some bubbles to the surface in a slow, restful boil. Adjust the heat so the fat is simmering gently, and cook the pork until it is done all the way through—trust the 3½-hour time given for the 2 pounds (1 kg) meat.*

• *Slow cooling is essential to the confit as well. Don't do anything to hurry it up.*

. . . .

FOR MARINATING THE PORK

2 pounds (1 kg) pork shoulder meat, bone in

3 cloves garlic, cut in half and green germ removed

2 tablespoons coarse sea salt

20 sprigs fresh thyme, or 1 teaspoon dried leaves

6 imported bay leaves

FOR COOKING THE PORK

4 pounds (2 kg) pork fat, cut in 1-inch (2½ cm) cubes, or an equivalent amount of lard (see Note)

8 sprigs fresh thyme, or scant ½ teaspoon dried leaves

2 imported bay leaves

1. Marinate the pork: Make 6 incisions in the pork, spacing them evenly around the meat, and stick a half clove of garlic in each incision. Rub the pork with 1 tablespoon of the salt. Sprinkle half the remaining salt and half the thyme and bay leaves in the bottom of a glass or other nonreactive bowl or dish. Set the pork on top, then cover with the remaining salt and herbs. Cover the dish and refrigerate for 48 hours.

2. Render the pork fat: Place the pork fat in a heavy pot or saucepan with ½ cup (125 ml) water. Turn on the heat to medium. Cook, without boiling, until the fat is melted, about 1 hour. There will be bits of skin or meat, which, if they continue to cook, will turn into cracklings—a tidy snack in themselves. When all of the fat has been rendered, strain it and reserve for the *confit*.

3. Cook the pork: Remove the pork from the refrigerator and brush off any excess salt. Discard the herbs. Pat dry.

4. Truss the pork with kitchen string, being careful not to truss it too tightly—it will shrink some as it cooks some, but will also tend to tense up at the beginning if it is tied too tightly, thus poking too far out of the fat.

5. Place the pork in a pot or Dutch oven large enough to hold both it and the rendered fat. Pour in the rendered pork fat, adding more rendered fat or lard if necessary to completely cover the pork (see Note).

6. Add the thyme and bay leaves to the pot, and bring the fat to a gentle boil over medium heat. Reduce the heat so the fat is barely simmering and cook the pork, uncovered, further reducing the heat if necessary to keep the fat at a simmer, until the meat is tender and the bone is loose, about 3½ hours. The meat may poke up above the fat; turn it once or twice if necessary so it cooks evenly.

7. Remove the pork from the heat and let it cool in the fat.

8. When the pork is cooled, but the fat is not quite congealed, remove the pork. Cut the trussing string from the meat, transfer the meat to an earthenware crock, bowl, or dish, and pour the fat over it. If the fat has congealed, heat it gently just to melt it enough so it can be poured over the pork. The pork should be entirely obscured by the fat. Cover and refrigerate for at least 2 weeks before eating. The longer the meat mellows in the fat, the better its flavor will be.

9. Serve the *confit*. Warm it just enough so you can remove the meat from the fat. Scrape as much fat from it as possible, then cut the meat into thin slices, working around the bone. Sauté it in a skillet over medium to medium-high heat until it is golden around the edges, and serve. If you don't want to prepare all the *confit* at once, return what you don't use to the crock, cover it with fat, and refrigerate, covered, until you are ready to use it.

4 to 6 servings

NOTE: Have extra pork fat or lard on hand, to be sure you have enough to completely cover the pork. The amount you'll need depends on the size of the pot you choose. A pot that is too big will cook the pork too quickly, so choose one that holds the pork and the fat without much excess space.

The Tale of the Boudin Blanc

=

In our neighboring village, Le Vaudreuil, Saturday evening heralds fresh *boudin blanc* at Marcel and Francine Leborgne's charcuterie. From late morning until the supply is gone, village residents stream out the door, packets of *boudin blanc* in hand. I am almost sure of being correct when I say that each person will go home and prepare them in the same way—carefully sautéed in sweet butter and served with golden apple compote.

M. Leborgne also makes *boudin* midweek, and one morning after a run I stopped in to see if, by chance, I could buy some for lunch. Three hung from a hook, and I took them. Mme. Leborgne motioned me behind the counter. "Marcel is about to mix up more. Why don't you stay and watch?"

I was delighted, and she opened the door to the kitchen. "Marcel, Susan is here, and she wants to put her hand on your back," she said, referring to an expression, *main dans le dos,* that means "to flatter."

M. Leborgne slowly walked out, rubbing his hands clean on his long white apron. "All right," he said. "We'll start mixing up the *boudin* in fifteen minutes. You're welcome to come look."

The Leborgnes and I share a special connection. They used to have Sunday lunch at the home of a friend who lived across the street from where I stayed on weekends, first when I was a student, and later when I was cooking at a restaurant in Paris. The Leborgnes always brought lunch, and they insisted I try their delicacies. While they had their Calvados and coffee, I sampled country pâté, a slice of smoked ham, Marcel's famed rabbit terrine, Francine's tender *gésiers,* a crisp, brown morsel of pork, or even a bit of *boudin.*

We had many good tastes and good times, and when I returned to live in the village, we were all thrilled. But when it came time for me to watch the assemblage of *boudin,* M. Leborgne was unexpectedly shy. He wasn't sure why I'd want to watch him do something he's done twice a week, six months a year (*boudin* is seasonal, made only in the winter months), for the past forty years.

THE SECRET TO HIS SUCCESS

"It's so simple, there are no secrets in this *boudin,*" M. Leborgne said as he showed me the bottle of Madeira he uses before he drizzled it over the lean, ground pork in its huge mixing bowl.

He put a mound of flour on one side of the pork, a handful of sea salt and pepper on the other. On the counter stood a saucepan full of steaming milk with an onion and some carrots bobbing in it. "I get the milk right from the farm, it isn't even pasteurized, and I infuse it until it picks up the flavors of the vegetables," he said.

An assistant mixed the huge quantity of *boudin* by hand, reaching up to his elbows into a large bowl set on the floor. M. Leborgne slowly strained the milk into the mixture as the young man stirred, gradually incorporating all the ingredients, working his entire arm right from the shoulder in broad, round sweeps. M. Leborgne slowly poured in more milk, then finally added a bowlful of lightly beaten fresh farm eggs all at once, and the assistant mixed until they disappeared into the mixture.

"That's enough," M. Leborgne said. "Some places mix it by machine, but then it has no texture. Even doing it by hand, you have to watch so it doesn't get mixed too much."

Now it was time to stuff the casings, and another assistant fit one onto a hand-cranked machine attached to a table. As the casing filled, it fell gently to the table in a coil, until a three-foot length was filled. Then we all pitched in to twist it into long sausages.

We continued working until a huge bowl was filled with links, which were lowered into a sink-sized vat of gently boiling water, where they cooked for fifteen minutes. Once cooled, they went on hooks in the shop until purchased.

I watched and wrote, bought all the ingredients, and went home to make my own (see page 194). Surprisingly, they were a success the first time, and I even took one in to the Leborgnes to taste. They laughed, tasted, and pronounced my version just fine.

Le Pâturage • The Pasture

Marcel Leborgne's Boudin Blanc

Le Boudin Blanc de Marcel Leborgne

I call this *boudin blanc* the "Saturday night special," because Marcel Leborgne makes it every Saturday in winter at his village charcuterie in Le Vaudrevil, using pork raised on a nearby farm. A simple Norman tradition, its flavor is rich and sophisticated, set off perfectly with lightly sautéed apples. Try this with chilled hard cider.

2 cups (500 ml) milk

1 medium carrot, peeled and cut into medium-size rounds

4 to 6 sprigs fresh thyme, or ¼ teaspoon dried leaves

1 imported bay leaf

1 vanilla bean

1 medium onion, cut in half

1 whole clove

1¾ pounds (875 g) lean pork (such as shoulder), coarsely ground

1 tablespoon fine sea salt

1½ teaspoons freshly ground black pepper

⅓ cup (45 g) unbleached all-purpose flour

8 large eggs

2 tablespoons port or Madeira

3 yards (3 m) sausage casing, natural if possible, well rinsed under cool running water and cut into 3 equal lengths

1 tablespoon unsalted butter, or more as needed

1. Place the milk, carrot, thyme, bay leaf, and vanilla bean in a medium-size saucepan.

Pierce one half of the onion with the clove and add it, with the other onion half, to the milk. Heat the milk over medium heat until steaming and small bubbles form around the edges. Remove from the heat, cover, and let sit for 30 minutes.

2. Place the ground pork in a large bowl and, using your hands, thoroughly mix in the salt and pepper. Sprinkle half the flour over the meat and blend until it is incorporated, then repeat with the remaining flour. Strain the milk into the meat mixture and gently mix it into the pork, using your hands, until the blend is homogeneous. Add the eggs, one at a time, mixing slowly and thoroughly until they are combined. Mix in the port until blended. The mixture will be very loose.

3. To test the flavor of the mixture, sauté 1 tablespoon in a small amount of butter in a small skillet over medium heat. Adjust the seasoning, if necessary.

4. Fit a pastry bag with a ½-inch (1¼ cm) tip. Fill the bag half full of the pork mixture. Fit one end of one length of sausage casing

snugly over the end of the pastry tip and squeeze the bag gently so the pork mixture goes into the casing, leaving about 2 inches (5 cm) at the other end. Tie a secure knot in that end, and continue filling the casing until it is firmly packed, though not so tight it will burst during cooking. Remove the casing from the pastry tip and tie that end securely so you have a tube of sausage. Measure a 6-inch (15 cm) length and twist the tube several times to form an individual sausage. Measure another length and twist the tube the opposite way, to form another sausage. Continue making sausages until you reach the end of the tube, adjusting the lengths of the sausages so they are more or less equal. (You may make the sausages any length you like, though the suggested length is traditional). Repeat with the remaining mixture and sausage casings (see Note).

5. Prick the *boudins* all over with a sharp skewer, so they won't burst during cooking.

6. Bring a large kettle of water to a simmer, and gently add the *boudins*. The water should barely move once the boudins are in it; cook them until they turn pale and firm, 25 to 30 minutes. Remove the *boudins* carefully from the water, and let cool to room temperature. Separate the boudens by cutting between the links.

7. To serve the *boudins*, melt 1 tablespoon butter in a nonstick skillet. Add the

> *Palpating, cracking, splitting on the grill, Boudins whistle louder than blackbirds in April.*
>
> —Paul Harel

boudins in batches, being careful not to crowd the pan, and sauté until they are golden on all sides and hot through, which will take about 7 minutes total if the *boudins* are at room temperature, and 10 to 12 minutes if they have been refrigerated. Depending on how many *boudins* you are sautéing, you may have to add more butter. If you don't plan to use all the *boudins*, you may freeze them, tightly wrapped, for up to 2 months.

8. Once steaming hot and golden, serve the *boudins* immediately.

About eighteen 6-inch (15 cm) sausages

NOTE: If you have too much *boudin* mixture for the amount of sausage casing, simply pour what remains into a buttered mold. Bake in a hot-water bath at 350°F (175°C) until it is firm and a knife inserted in the center comes out clean (about 40 minutes).

Roast Pork with Potatoes and Onions

Rôti de Porc aux Pommes de Terre et aux Oignons

→...←

Marie-Thérèse Maho is an energetic woman who, along with her husband, Gabriel, has transformed a large barn that adjoins their farmhouse into a six-room guest house. A serious cook, she recently purchased a huge oven that she uses to cook the main course and the dessert at the same time when she has a full house. "I hesitated over it a long time, but then when I thought about all the people I have here, I figured I needed an oven where I could roast at least three chickens and bake a tart at once," she says.

This dish, called *forn* in Breton, is traditional in the Morbihan area of Brittany, on the southern coast, where the Mahos farm. According to Mme. Maho, when she was growing up, the *forn* was often taken to the nearest bread oven in operation and slid inside after the bread was baked, to cook in the residual heat.

"We had an oven, and I think my parents fired it up once a month to bake bread," she remembers. "We'd bake other people's bread, too, and that's how it worked around here. One week our oven was fired up, the next week a neighbor's. That way we could all bake bread somewhere once a week."

The pork in this dish resonates with garlic, which is raised in the area. Seasoned with the local sea salt, the meat is succulent and moist, with a wonderful golden crust. The potatoes emerge tender on the inside, with a crust of their own, and the onions melt to a marmalade, blending with the cooking juices to add a wonderful sweetness.

The pork seems to cook forever here, which goes against the grain for me since I like pork with a pink tinge in the center. However, you'll see that the long, slow cooking results in tenderness and flavor.

Be sure to use a bone-in pork roast, for it will have twice the flavor of a boneless loin. Get the butcher to just cut through the bone for you, so that you can easily slice the roast into portions once it is cooked.

Serve a chilled hard cider, as the Mahos do, or a Rully Blanc or a Côtes du Rhône Rouge.

2 cloves garlic, peeled, halved, and green
germ removed
1 bone-in pork sirloin or blade roast
(about 3½ pounds; 1½ kg)
¼ cup (60 ml) olive oil
Sea salt and freshly ground black pepper
2 medium onions, peeled and coarsely chopped
2 pounds (1 kg) all-purpose potatoes, such
as Yukon Gold, peeled and cut into
large chunks

1. Preheat the oven to 350°F (175°C).

2. Cut the garlic cloves into very thin lengthwise slices. Make slits in the pork roast and insert the slices of garlic, distributing them as evenly as possible throughout the roast.

3. Spread the oil generously over the roast, and then rub in 2 teaspoons salt (or to taste) and a generous amount of pepper.

4. Place the onions in a 13 x 11-inch (32½ x 27½ cm) baking dish. Set the pork roast on top of the onions, and surround it with the potatoes, tucking them in and around it, even under it if necessary. Season the potatoes with salt and pepper, and place the dish on the center rack of the oven. Roast until the pork is cooked through and golden, about 2½ hours (a meat thermometer inserted in the thickest part of the roast, away from the bone, should read about 165°F; 74°C).

5. Remove the roast from the oven and let it sit for 15 minutes. Either slice the meat and serve it on a platter, along with the potatoes, onions, and cooking juices, or serve the roast whole, in the baking dish, and slice it at the table.

6 servings

Pork and Chard
Sausages
Les Caillettes

>···←

In the old days, before cars and other timesaving devices, if a farmer didn't have time to go home for lunch, he took it with him to the fields in a *biasso*, a long sack with a pocket at either end that he slung over his shoulder. *Caillettes*, a transportable meat and vegetable course rolled into one, were usually somewhere in that *biasso*.

Also in the *biasso* was plenty of crusty bread and some fruity red wine, made on the farm, to revive the spirits after a hot morning in the fields. The farmer sat in a shady spot to eat, took a short *sieste*, or nap, and then returned to work, making sure he left a chunk of bread in the *biasso* for the long walk home.

These *caillettes* are loaded with ground pork and Swiss chard, and aromatic with garlic and onions. They are easy to make and nice to have on hand for a light lunch, atop a salad.

Crépine is caul fat—difficult but not impossible to find. It adds a lot to *caillettes*, helping to maintain their form and keeping them moist as they cook. If you can't find it, don't be concerned, but do lower the oven temperature by about 25 degrees and increase the cooking time by 5 to 10 minutes (check them occasionally to see if they are cooked through) so the *caillettes* cook more slowly and don't dry out.

Try your best to find fresh sage for garnishing each *caillette*. The leaves are lovely, hidden slightly under the caul fat, which cooks to a shiny gold, and they add a high point of flavor, too.

Try a Rully Blanc or a Côtes du Rhône Rouge alongside.

ASTUCES . . . .

• *As soon as you remove the* caillettes *from the oven, drain as much fat as possible from them; then transfer them to a plate or tray lined with several thicknesses of paper towels.*

• *Caul fat—fat from the abdomen of a pig—can be found at a butcher shop, or ask at the supermarket—you never know! To use caul fat, cut it into squares large enough to wrap tightly around the* caillettes. *You will be surprised at how far a bit of caul fat goes. Like the delicate lace it resembles, it looks like nothing until you unfold it, when it stretches into an almost impossible thinness. Rinse the caul fat under warm (not hot) running water for at least 5 minutes, until the water running off it is fresh and clear. Gently pat it dry before using it.*

. . . .

Sea salt

2 pounds (1 kg) Swiss chard, well rinsed

2 pounds (1 kg) unseasoned ground pork

2 medium onions, peeled and diced

3 cloves garlic, peeled, green germ removed, and minced

2 tablespoons fresh thyme leaves, or 2 teaspoons dried

Freshly ground black pepper to taste

18 to 20 fresh sage leaves, or 1 tablespoon dried

5 ounces (150 g) caul fat (optional)

1. Preheat the oven to 400°F (205°C).

2. Bring a large pot of salted water to a boil (2 tablespoons sea salt to 4 quarts; 4 l water) to a boil. Cook the Swiss chard, in several batches if necessary, until the stems are tender, about 4 minutes. Drain the cooked chard, and when it is cool enough to handle, wrap it in a large tea towel and gently squeeze out as much liquid as possible without turning it to mush. Finely chop the chard.

3. Combine all the ingredients except the sage and the caul fat in a large bowl, using 1 teaspoon sea salt, or to taste. Using your hands, blend thoroughly. Pinch off about 1 tablespoon of the mixture and sauté it in a small pan over medium heat until it is cooked through; taste for seasoning, and adjust if necessary.

4. Divide the mixture into 18 to 20 portions (each about 3 ounces; 90 g). Set a fresh sage leaf (or a small pinch of dried sage) atop each sausage, with the inside of the leaf toward the sausage.

5. If you are using caul fat, cut it into roughly 4-inch (10 cm) squares, and wrap each sausage firmly in a square. You may need to do a bit of patchwork if the squares don't all quite stretch to cover the sausage. Alternatively, if you have a good-size piece of caul fat, lay it out on a work surface and set the sausage portions on the fat, leaving a 2-inch (5 cm) border of fat around each sausage. Cut around the sausages and proceed with the recipe.

6. Arrange the sausages in two large (12 x 8-inch; 30 x 20 cm) baking dishes, placing them about ¼ inch (½ cm) apart. Bake in the center of the oven for 35 minutes. Turn the sausages over and continue baking until they are firm (though not rubbery) and cooked through, an additional 10 to 15 minutes.

7. Remove the *caillettes* from the oven and drain off any excess fat. Serve immediately, as part of a salad (see page 89), or let cool and serve at room temperature. The *caillettes* will keep for up to 3 days, refrigerated.

18 to 20 caillettes

Rillettes Baked in Brioche
Gâteau de Viande

Not at all a *gâteau*, or cake, this bread, with its flat layer of *rillettes* tucked inside, is a specialty of Peyrenègre, in the Dordogne, where Madeleine Dubois has always made it for her family. She guarded the recipe carefully for many, many years, refusing to give it to anyone, including her daughter-in-law Dany. Then one summer day I asked her about it, and she invited me to come watch her make it.

Astonished, I walked down the road to her farmhouse and into the dark, cool kitchen. Though sun bounced off the stone exterior, inside the house a small fire burned in the huge fireplace. Madeleine began making the *gâteau de viande* with slow, sure movements on a long, low table in the center of the kitchen. "You must use good flour, for it will rise better," she said as she stirred up the starter and set it aside. "Leave it just long enough for the yeast to begin working, about the time it takes you to make the filling."

She mixed up the filling with her hands, using *rillettes* that Dany had made. Finished, she poured flour into a large mixing bowl, made a well in the center, and broke the eggs into it. This she mixed with her hands. Then she slowly poured in the melted butter, followed by the starter, which was frothing lightly. She worked the flour gradually into the dough, then beat it vigorously with a wooden spoon until she was red in the face. I took over.

"You've got to work your dough so it has plenty of air in it," Madeleine said, wiping her forehead.

When it came time to roll out the dough, she generously floured her table—which also serves as the dining table—cut the dough into several pieces, and went to work.

"You must roll it thin, so that it hangs over the edge of the bread pan," she said, flipping the dough over on itself and transferring it to the baking pan, then easing it in just as you would a piece of fabric.

Within minutes she'd assembled the two *gâteaux*, patting each of them firmly into its pan, and tucked them into a niche in the fireplace to rise.

"That's it. Now you'll come back this evening and try it," she said, dismissing me.

I did, and it was as good as any I'd ever had, with its soft, buttery *brioche* and gently spiced *rillettes*.

The intervening years have mellowed Madeleine, and when I returned recently to Peyrenègre, I discovered that not long ago she had given her recipe to Dany—who already had it from me!

I like to serve the *gâteau* for lunch along with a variety of salads, as a first course for dinner, even for breakfast. It's ideal for a picnic, as well.

Try a red Burgundy or an Alsace Pinot Noir alongside.

ASTUCE . . . .

• *When letting bread dough rise, place it in a warm spot (68° to 70°F; 20° to 21°C), away from air currents (which would cause it to rise unevenly).*

. . . .

FOR THE BRIOCHE
1 teaspoon active dry yeast
½ cup (125 ml) lukewarm water
1 tablespoons sugar
4 cups (540 g) unbleached all-purpose flour
12 tablespoon (1½ sticks; 180 g) unsalted butter
2 tablespoons milk
1 teaspoon sea salt
4 large eggs, lightly beaten

FOR THE FILLING
¼ cup (60 ml) milk
¾ cup (45 g) fresh bread crumbs
2 large eggs, lightly beaten
1¾ cups (1 pound; 500 g) Pork and Duck
   Rillettes (page 21)

FOR THE EGG WASH
1 large egg
2 teaspoons water

1. Prepare the *brioche* dough: Combine the yeast, lukewarm water, sugar, and ¼ cup (35 g) of the flour in a small bowl. Mix well and let sit, covered loosely with a towel, in a warm spot until bubbles begin to form on top, about 20 minutes.

2. Place the butter and the milk in a small pan over low heat, and heat just until the butter is melted (be very careful not to let the mixture boil). Remove from the heat and let cool to room temperature.

3. Stir the remaining 3¾ cups (500 g) flour and the salt together in a mixing bowl (or in the bowl of an electric mixer). Make a well in the center and add the eggs. Whisk the butter mixture, then the starter mixture, into the eggs in the well. Using a wooden spoon, or the mixer on low speed, slowly incorporate the flour into the liquids to make a soft dough.

4. Vigorously knead the dough to incorporate as much air into it as possible, until the dough comes away from the sides of the bowl and from your hands; this will take about 10 minutes by hand, about 5 minutes in a heavy-duty electric mixer. If it remains very sticky, sticking to your hands, add a bit more flour. But do so judiciously, for you don't want to add too much flour—the dough should be very soft.

5. Place the dough in a bowl, cover with a damp towel, and let rise in a warm spot until doubled in bulk, about 1½ hours.

6. To make the filling, combine all the ingredients in a medium-size bowl and mix well. Taste for seasoning (it should be highly seasoned). Set the filling aside.

7. Generously butter two 8½ x 4-inch (22 x 10 cm) loaf pans. Make the egg wash by whisking together the egg and the water in a small bowl. Cover and set aside until needed.

8. Punch down the dough and divide it in half. Take one of the halves, cut off one fourth of it, and set aside the small portion. Roll the remaining piece out to form an 18 x 14-inch (45 x 35 cm) rectangle, and carefully transfer it to one of the prepared loaf pans,

easing it down inside so the dough fits the loaf pan. Leave the edges hanging over the outside of the pan (there should be about ½ inch [1¼ cm] of dough hanging over the edge of the loaf pan on all sides).

9. Spoon half the filling mixture into the prepared pan, gently pressing it down onto the dough. Roll out the reserved quarter of the dough to form an 8½ x 4-inch (22 x 10 cm) rectangle, and lay this over the filling. Bring the overhanging ends of the bottom piece of dough up and over the top piece. Then bring the sides over, overlapping them neatly so the filling is entirely enclosed. Press gently but firmly on the dough so the dough and filling are firmly compacted into the loaf pan. The loaf will be very flat, and there will be several seams in the dough, but don't be concerned, for the dough will rise and the seams will bake away. Repeat with the remaining dough and filling, using the second pan.

10. Set both loaves, covered with a tea towel, in a warm spot (68° to 70°F; 20° to 21°C) to rise, until they are puffed up to the edges of the pans, 2½ to 3 hours.

11. Meanwhile, preheat the oven to 400°F (205°C).

12. Brush each loaf with the egg wash. Bake the loaves in the center of the oven until they are golden and puffed, and sound hollow when tapped, about 30 minutes.

13. Remove the pans from the oven and turn the loaves out onto wire racks. Let them cool completely before serving. To serve, cut the bread into thick (½-inch; 1¼ cm) slices and arrange them in a basket, on a platter, or on individual plates.

2 loaves; 16 servings

Pork Braised in Milk

Porc Cuit au Lait

→ • • • ←

Josiane Duedal ambled around the kitchen in her brother's farmhouse, preparing lunch. She doesn't like to cook, preferring instead to eat her sister-in-law's cooking. But today Corinne was at her job as a rural social worker and would only have time to eat lunch; Josiane was filling in, following instructions Corinne had left for her.

"I know Corinne makes this all the time, and she told me exactly what to do, but I really don't have any idea what I'm doing," she said, laughing as she awkwardly sliced onions and put them in a pan to sauté.

We worked together, sautéing the onions, browning the pork, and trying to figure out Corinne's brand-new electronic oven. Fortunately, Corinne arrived just in time to set us straight.

I've tasted this dish on several farms, too, and I preferred it at the Duedals', for there it was light, the meat cooked to a moist tenderness. It was exceptionally flavorful as well, due to the quality of pork they raise.

I've adapted the recipe slightly, even taken it back in time, for traditionally, it was cooked on the stovetop. It's easier to control that way, and the results are moist and delicious—the pork absorbs the milk and emerges so tender and flavorful, you can cut it with a spoon.

I turn the cooking juices into an elegant soup that captures all the robust flavors. It is perfect for starting the meal, and a reflection of Norman cuisine in its creamy blend of onions and milk.

I do as Josiane did the day of my visit: I serve cooked apples alongside, for a tart balance to the tender pork. I don't sweeten the apples, but you may if you like.

Serve with chilled hard cider, a Côtes de Brouilly, or a Beaujolais Villages.

FOR THE PORK
2 teaspoons unsalted butter
2 teaspoons olive oil
1 boneless pork loin (about 3 pounds;
1½ kg)
1 pound (500 g) onions, peeled and thinly
sliced
4 cups (1 l) whole milk
4 imported bay leaves
1 generous tablespoon fresh thyme leaves,
or 1 teaspoon dried
1 clove garlic, peeled, cut in half, and
green germ removed
Sea salt and freshly ground black pepper

FOR THE APPLES
2 pounds (1 kg) tart cooking apples, such
as Stayman, McIntosh, or Gravenstein,
peeled, quartered, and cored
2 to 4 tablespoons water
Sugar to taste (optional)

FOR SERVING
1 good-size bunch watercress

1. Heat the butter and the oil in a large heavy saucepan or flameproof baking dish

over medium-high heat until it is hot but not smoking. Add the pork loin and brown it on all sides, about 2 minutes per side. Remove the pork from the pan and reduce the heat to medium. Add the onions and cook, stirring frequently, until they are golden and softened, 10 to 12 minutes.

2. Heat the milk with 2 of the bay leaves in a medium-size saucepan over medium heat until it is steaming and small bubbles have formed around the edges. Be careful not to boil the milk. Cover and keep hot over low heat.

3. On a cutting board, mince the thyme and the garlic together so they are well combined.

4. When the pork is cool enough to touch, rub it all over with the garlic and thyme mixture. Season it generously with salt and pepper, and return it to the pan with the onions. Remove the bay leaves from the hot milk, and pour the milk over the pork. Add the remaining 2 bay leaves to the pan, cover, and bring to a simmer over medium heat. Reduce the heat to low and cook at a slow simmer until the pork is tender but still slightly pink in the center (on a meat thermometer, 145° to 150°F; 63° to 66°C),

about 1 hour. Turn it occasionally to be sure it cooks evenly.

5. While the pork is cooking, place the apples in a pan with 2 tablespoons water, cover, and bring to a boil over medium-high heat. Reduce the heat to medium and cook, stirring occasionally, until the apples are tender but still have some texture, about 20 minutes. Add 2 tablespoons or so additional water if necessary to keep the apples from sticking. They should be cooked to a chunky purée. Season with sugar, if desired, and keep warm over low heat.

6. Transfer the pork to a warmed platter, leaving behind the onions and the cooking liquid. Cover the pork loosely with aluminum foil to keep it warm. Discard the bay leaves, and purée the onions and liquid in a food processor or blender to make a soup. Taste for seasoning, reheat quickly, and serve as the first course.

7. To serve the pork, cut it into thick slices. Line a warmed serving platter with the watercress, arrange the pork slices on top, and surround them with the apples. Serve immediately.

6 to 8 servings

Going Home

Josiane Duedal and her brother, Didier, realized a rare dream. After leaving the farm where they grew up, they both returned.

I was spending a day at the farm, and Josiane, her cheeks rosy from working in an unheated barn-turned-laboratory where she makes cheese and yogurt, described to me how they were able to do so.

"It was simple, really. I was working as a secretary, but what I really wanted was to work on the farm," she said. "Didier was teaching, and he felt the same way. Our parents were willing for us to return, so there were no real obstacles."

Josiane and Didier bought their parents' dairy herd. "All the farmers around here laughed. Everyone had sold their herds because there was no money in milk, and they were planting wheat because the wheat market was good. Now it's not, and dairy is better, so we're happy we made the choice," she said.

Josiane and Didier added hogs to their farm, because they wanted to make and sell charcuterie: pâtés, *rillettes*, sausages, hams. Business was all right, but after several years of being pulled in too many directions, they decided to concentrate on raising hogs and the dairy herd. When they're more established, they'll pick up charcuterie again. For now, this young team has narrowed its focus, intent on success.

What's helping them is a government-sponsored quality program referred to as Label Rouge, which they adhere to for their hogs. Under the program, the animals live outdoors, have room to wallow and snuffle, eat rich food that Didier raises with a minimum of synthetic chemicals, and sleep in small Quonset huts.

For the hogs, it's a comfortable, healthy life. For Didier and Josiane, it's more francs per hoof. For the consumer, it's better-quality pork.

Didier and Josiane are aiming toward organic farming, and being part of the Label Rouge program imposes a discipline they feel will help them make the leap. For now, they are intent on making enough from the farm to support their two households with a modicum of comfort. From the looks of it, the Duedal family farm will be in business for generations to come. (Enjoy the recipe for Pork Braised in Milk, page 202, that Josiane shared with me.)

Le Pâturage • The Pasture

Goat with Almonds
Chevreau aux Amandes

In Provence, this dish is traditionally made with *chevreau*, or baby goat, and it is always served at Easter. It is the centerpiece of the meal that follows the traditional Provençal Easter egg hunt celebrated by those farmers with young children and/or grandchildren.

The children come back from the hunt just in time for lunch, a huge platter of *chevreau aux amandes* and a big platter of fresh spring vegetables.

Try this with goat, if you can get it (goat has a flavor similar to, though milder than, young lamb). If not, buy the youngest lamb you can find—it is equally delicious.

Serve a hearty Beaune Blanc with this dish.

2 tablespoons olive oil
2 pounds (1 kg) goat ribs and shoulder
    (or lamb shoulder), cut into 2-inch
    (5 cm) cubes
½ cup (60 g) almonds
2 small onions, peeled, cut in half, then
    cut crosswise into paper-thin half-moons
4 cloves garlic, peeled, cut in half, and
    green germ removed
¾ cup (loosely packed) flat-leaf parsley
    leaves
Sea salt and freshly ground black pepper
1¼ to 1½ cups (310 to 375 ml) Herb
    Broth (page 508)

1. Heat 1 tablespoon of the oil in a large heavy skillet over medium-high heat. Add just enough pieces of goat to fit easily into the skillet without overcrowding, and brown them on all sides until they are golden, about 8 minutes. Remove the meat from the skillet and brown any additional pieces. If the meat gives up a great deal of liquid, drain it after you've browned the meat. Reduce the heat to medium and add the remaining 1 tablespoon oil. Add the almonds and cook until they are toasted, stirring frequently, about 4 minutes. Remove the almonds from the skillet, keeping them separate from the meat. Add the onions to the skillet and cook, stirring constantly, just until they begin to soften slightly, about 2 minutes.

2. Mince the garlic and the parsley together.

3. Return the meat, and any juices it has given up, to the onions in the skillet. Stir, season with salt and pepper to taste, and add 1 cup (250 ml) of the herb broth. Stir, scraping up any browned bits from the bottom of

the skillet. Add the parsley mixture, stirring so it is incorporated into the liquid. Cover and simmer until the meat is nearly cooked through and tender, about 30 minutes, stirring occasionally so it doesn't stick.

4. While the meat is cooking, combine the almonds with 2 to 3 tablespoons of the remaining broth in a food processor, and grind until they form a thick paste.

5. Check the meat. If it is dry, add up to ⅓ cup (80 ml) additional broth. Stir the almond paste into the meat, cover, and continue cooking until the sauce has thickened slightly, 10 minutes.

6. Remove the skillet from the heat and either transfer the meat to a warmed serving dish or divide it among four warmed dinner plates. Serve immediately.

4 servings

Easter in Provence

➤•◄

*I*n Provence, a farmer always makes sure he has a white **lapin**, or rabbit for Eastertime among his collection. The adults in the family make tiny nests, each filled with a single egg, which they hide throughout the garden before the children get up on Easter morning.

Then, when the children are assembled, the farmer ties a gaily colored ribbon around the rabbit's neck and sends it out into the garden. After it has run around for a while, the children follow it outside, hunting throughout the garden for the nests that the **lapin** has filled.

In some families, the Easter **lapin** also puts a honey cake or a slice of **pain d'épices** (see Index for Babette's Spice Bread) in the basket. In others, the nests might be filled with small chocolate eggs.

LA MER
The Sea

Seafood recipes may seem surprising in a farmhouse cookbook. But France is a seafood-eating country, and that goes for its farmers as much as anyone. French coastlines, from Normandy and Brittany to the Pays Basque and the Mediterranean, are rich with farms, and seafood easily makes its way to the farm table. Many farmers cultivate the sea as well, and they enjoy, and are dependent on, its fruits.

Historically, salt cod was the most common fish on the farm because it made its way throughout the country well before the advent of the refrigerated vehicles we see here now. Every farm had a salt cod or two hanging in a cool, dry place that would serve as the basis for one delicious meal or another. In Brittany, the variety of seafood that turns up on farms seems virtually endless, from fresh, meaty tuna to brilliant white squid. But no wonder—one has simply to look out the window to see the rolling surf, and the Breton air intoxicates one with its briny tang.

The Pays Basque puts its peppers and tomatoes to use in hearty fish dishes, and its tiny eels, *pibales*, are renowned. Anchovies, sardines, mackerel, and a host of reef fishes are most likely to appear in Provence and along the Mediterranean, where farmers make a weekly trek to their nearest market to satisfy their urge for fresh seafood.

The handful of seafood dishes here are full of flavor, and easy to make, and representational of farm cooking.

Salt Cod with Tomato Sauce
Morue Sauce Tomate

>···←

This dish is one of the keystones of a traditional *veille de Noël*, or Christmas Eve dinner, in Provence. Made with tomatoes picked at their height of freshness and conserved in jars, it is richly aromatic, colorful, full of flavor and substance. I love to make it, though I use fresh tomatoes when I can find them—either plum tomatoes fresh from the farm or the ones that come from Italy or Spain, still on their vines.

Serve a Coteaux d'Aix-en-Provence Rosé with the salt cod.

ASTUCE . . . .

• *When buying salt cod, look for the whole fillet. It should be an even white to cream color, with just a bit of skin on it. It will be covered with rock salt, and will require soaking to make it edible. If all you can find is the salt cod that comes in a small wooden box, go ahead and use that.*

. . . .

2 pounds (1 kg) salt cod, well rinsed

FOR THE TOMATO SAUCE
2 teaspoons olive oil
2 medium onions, peeled, cut in half, and
    thinly sliced
3 pounds (1½ kg) tomatoes, cored and
    diced, or 2 cans (each 28 ounces; 840 g)
    plum tomatoes, drained
10 sprigs fresh thyme, or ½ teaspoon dried
½ cup (loosely packed) flat-leaf parsley
    leaves
3 imported bay leaves
Sea salt (see Note) and freshly ground
    black pepper

FOR COOKING THE SALT COD
1 cup (135 g) all-purpose flour
Freshly ground black pepper
3 tablespoons olive oil
12 cloves garlic, unpeeled
1 small bunch flat-leaf parsley, for garnish
    (optional)

Boning Salt Cod

> ·←

*S*alt cod has some skin and a normal amount of bones in it. Try to remove as much skin and bone as you can after desalting the fish. To remove the bones, some of which are in an even line just off the center of the fillet, cut close to the bones on either side, using a very sharp knife, and lift them out. Other bones are less regularly spaced. Hunt for and remove as many as you can, using a strawberry huller or needle-nose pliers, and then remind your guests that there may still be bones.

1. The day before you plan to serve the dish, remove as many bones as possible from the salt cod (see box, this page), and if you have an entire fillet, cut it crosswise into several large pieces. Place the salt cod in a bowl or a bucket and cover it with plenty of cold water. Let it soak for 24 hours, changing the water a minimum of four times to remove as much salt as possible.

2. Drain the cod, pat it dry, and refrigerate it, covered, until right before using.

3. Prepare the tomato sauce: Heat the oil in a large heavy skillet over medium-high heat. Add the onions and stir so they are coated with the oil. Cover, reduce the heat to medium, and cook just until they are limp and turning translucent, 4 to 5 minutes. Check the onions once or twice to be sure they don't stick. Add the tomatoes and the

herbs, and season to taste with salt and pepper. Stir and cook, covered, until the tomatoes are tender through and have melted into a sauce, about 35 minutes. The sauce will be chunky. Taste for seasonings and keep warm.

4. To cook the cod, first season the flour with pepper and mix well. Dredge as many pieces of cod as will fit easily into a nonstick skillet.

5. Heat 1½ tablespoons of the oil in the skillet over medium heat. Add the garlic cloves and stir so they are coated with oil. When the oil is hot enough that it shimmers and sends a wisp of smoke off the surface, and the garlic cloves are sizzling merrily, add the cod. Cook until it is golden on one side, 5 to 7 minutes. Turn and continue cooking until it is cooked through, an additional 5 to 7 minutes. Shake the pan occasionally to detach the cod from the bottom and to stir the garlic cloves. If some of the pieces of cod are very thin, they will cook more quickly, so check them often. To tell if the cod is cooked, lift it with a spatula: If the flakes separate easily, it is cooked. If they stay tightly together and the cod feels somewhat rubbery, it needs additional cooking.

6. Transfer the cod from the skillet to a plate lined with an unprinted brown paper sack or a double thickness of paper towels. Place in a low oven to keep warm. Add the remaining 1½ tablespoons oil to the pan and turn the garlic cloves so they continue to cook evenly. Dredge the remaining cod and add to the pan when the oil is hot. Cook as for the first batch.

7. To serve, arrange the fish and the gar-

lic cloves on a warmed serving platter. Remove and discard any herb stems and the bay leaves from the tomato sauce, and transfer it to a warmed serving bowl to serve alongside the cod. Garnish with parsley, if desired.

6 to 8 servings

N O T E : Don't be afraid of seasoning with salt in this dish. Just because the fish was salt-ed doesn't mean the dish automatically has enough salt in it. Taste both the sauce and the fish before serving, for proper seasoning.

Salt Cod and Mashed Potatoes
Morue et Sa Purée

Dany Dubois remembers her grandmother, Noémie Sol, preparing this meal over the woodstove in the cozy kitchen of their farmhouse perched at the edge of the road between Chavagnac and La Dornac, in the heart of the Périgord. Fish wasn't an every-day occurrence in the Périgord, land of truffles, foie gras, and *confit d'oie*, so when it was on the menu it was a considerable treat. Often the fish that was served was salt cod. "We loved it," remembers Dany. "I still serve salt cod to my family, even though we can get just about any kind of fish we want in town."

Salt cod has many advantages, not the least among them its keeping quality. That, and the fast day once a week when no meat is allowed, accounts for the *morue* that has infiltrated French farm cooking. Preserved by salt, it can be kept in a cool cupboard for months, with no fear of spoilage.

There are two categories of salt cod available in France—cod from the French fishery, which is trimmed into tidy fillets and freshly salted so it is soft and wet, and

La Mer • The Sea

cod from Spain or Portugal, which is often butterflied, the bones removed, and dry-salted so it is stiff as a board. I love watching people at the market walking away from the Portuguese merchant with their salt cod balanced on their shoulder and bobbing through the crowd like a sail.

I've always loved salt cod, and this ranks as my favorite preparation so far. Like a *brandade* with pizzazz, it comes to the table looking like the Matterhorn showered with green, and the aroma of sizzling parsley and garlic is irresistible.

Serve this with a simple green salad, seasoned with shallots instead of garlic, and a lightly chilled rosé, such as Haut Poitou, a Coteaux d'Aix-en-Provence or a Sauvignon Blanc.

ASTUCE . . . .

• *To tell when fish is cooked, lift it with a spatula. If it flakes, it is done. If it holds together or only partially flakes, it requires further cooking. If it flakes easily, it is ready to serve.*

. . . .

2½ pounds (1¼ kg) salt cod

6 cups (1½ l) water

3 pounds (1½ kg) starchy potatoes, such as russets, peeled

3 cups (750 ml) dry white wine, such as a Sauvignon Blanc

2 imported bay leaves

5 sprigs fresh thyme, or ¼ teaspoon dried

5 black peppercorns

2 tablespoons unsalted butter, at room temperature, cut into 4 pieces

Sea salt and freshly ground black pepper

3 cloves garlic, peeled, green germ removed, and coarsely chopped

2 cups (loosely packed) flat-leaf parsley leaves

⅓ cup (80 ml) olive oil

1. Cut the cod into several large pieces. Soak the cod in plenty of cold water in a large nonreactive bowl or kettle for 24 hours, changing the water at least four times.

2. The next day, drain the cod and pat it dry. Trim off as much skin as possible, and cut out any bones that are easy to remove (see "Boning Salt Cod," page 211).

3. Pour 3 cups (750 ml) of the water into a vegetable steamer, and place the potatoes on the steamer rack. Cover, bring the water to a boil, and steam the potatoes until they are soft through, 20 to 25 minutes.

4. While the potatoes are steaming, poach the cod: Pour the wine and the remaining 3 cups (750 ml) water into a nonreactive wide saucepan or a skillet with sides at least 4 inches (10 cm) high. Add the bay leaves, thyme, peppercorns, and cod. Bring to a boil

over medium-high heat. Reduce the heat to medium so the liquid is simmering, and cook until the cod flakes but isn't soft, 15 to 20 minutes. (To test a fish for doneness, see the Astuce on page 213.)

5. Drain the potatoes, and then, using a heavy-duty whisk, a food mill, a potato masher, or the mixing attachment of an electric mixer, mash with the butter until smooth. Season to taste with salt and plenty of pepper.

6. Mince the coarsely chopped garlic and the parsley together.

7. Place the mashed potatoes in a warmed large shallow serving bowl. Flake the fish on top of the potatoes, discarding any remaining bits of skin and any bones that are easily removed, keeping the flakes fairly large. Sprinkle with the garlic-parsley mixture.

8. Heat the oil in a small pan over medium heat until it is very hot and a wisp of smoke comes off the surface. Pour the oil over the parsley and garlic, which will sizzle and steam. Serve immediately.

4 to 6 servings

Poached Fish with Aïoli

La Bourrido, La Bourride

Call it *la bourrido*, its Provençal name, or *la bourride*, its French name—it's the same dish. Redolent of garlic, smooth with olive oil, this elegant but hearty combination is for real *gourmands*, those who love the intense pleasures in life.

The basis of *bourride* is aïoli thinned with a fragrant court bouillon. The resulting sauce, here more of a soup, is traditionally poured over hake, a soft-fleshed fish that is extraordinarily tender. Hake is looked at with some disdain in the U.S., but it shouldn't be, for it is, quite simply, elegant. It cooks in an instant and yields itself willingly to the pale yellow sauce here.

This dish is monochromatic, which is part of its charm. To give it a lift, I sometimes garnish it with brilliant blue borage flowers or orange calendula petals.

1 recipe Court Bouillon (page 507)
2 pounds (1 kg) hake, cut into 1½-inch-
    thick (4 cm) steaks (see Note)
1 recipe Aïoli: The Sauce (page 235)
6 slices good-quality white bread, toasted
Borage flowers or calendula petals (or
    any edible flower), for garnish
    (optional)

1. Bring the court bouillon to a boil in a large skillet with sides at least 3 inches (7½ cm) high. Add the fish and return to a boil. Then reduce the heat to medium and simmer gently until the fish is nearly opaque through, 5 to 8 minutes.

2. Remove the fish from the court bouillon and keep it warm, covered, in a low oven. Strain the court bouillon, reserving 1½ cups (375 ml).

3. Place the aïoli in a medium-size heavy saucepan over medium heat. Whisk in the reserved court bouillon and cook, whisking constantly and moving the pan on and off the heat if necessary, until the sauce has thickened somewhat, about 7 minutes. It should be about the consistency of light cream. Be careful not to boil the sauce, or it will curdle. When it has thickened, immediately remove the pan from the heat.

Buying Fish

→·←

When buying whole fish, check the gills to be sure they are red and healthy looking. Then get your fish merchant to snip them out and to clean the fish as well. To finish the job and completely remove all the blood from the fish, use a sharp knife to cut down the length of the backbone inside the fish, releasing the membrane that covers the bone. Place the fish under running water and brush the blood from the bone with your fingers or with a toothbrush reserved for the purpose. Trim off any bits of torn belly flap, and trim the tail if necessary to make the fish fit in the pan. Rinse the fish one more time under cool running water, and pat it dry.

4. To serve, place a piece of toast in each of six warmed shallow soup bowls. Top the toast with the fish, and ladle the sauce over it. Garnish with the flower blossoms or petals if desired, and serve immediately.

6 servings

NOTE: Any white fish will do for this dish—ranging from hake to cod, monkfish, halibut, lingcod, or petrale sole. Or you can use a mixture of fishes. If you can't get steaks, use fillets and adjust the cooking time (they will cook much faster).

The Salt Raker

=

François Lecallo was describing his first taste of table salt. "I felt I had to taste it if I was going to be well rounded and know just what it was," said the youngish professional sea salt harvester.

Screwing his face up at the memory, he said, "It was awful, bitter, acidic. I wouldn't want to eat it on any *frites* of mine."

There aren't many people who concern themselves with the flavor of salt, surely one of the intangibles in this world. But M. Lecallo does. He spends his life outdoors in the salt marshes of Brittany, near the small town of Guérande, coaxing salt water through a complex series of channels and pools until it finally, almost magically, crystallizes into salt.

There are a handful of artisanal sea salt producers, known as *paludiers*, in France, but M. Lecallo and others like him in and around Guérande produce what is considered the country's best.

At first glance, the job he loves appears simple: Corral sea water, let the sun and wind evaporate it, rake in the results. However, during a day of clambering down grassy banks, balancing on clay dikes, and walking through warehouses filled with salt,

I came to understand the skill, finesse, and patience required to produce what we so easily sprinkle on our food.

"It's hard work, the kind that uses up your body, nets you little money, puts you at the mercy of the weather," M. Lecallo said frankly. "But when you're outside every day, you fish for the sea bass that come and spawn in the marshes, see the birds, feel the wind and salt on your face—well, there isn't anything that could be better than that."

It's hard to imagine a more archaic profession than that of *paludier*. Indeed, M. Lecallo acknowledges that neither the tools nor the simple technology he uses has changed much since the time of the Romans, when the harvesting of salt was first recorded in Guérande.

M. Lecallo was showing me his terrain, measured in number of *oeillets*, the finishing ponds where the salt is actually extracted. Being a full-timer, he harvests from sixty *oeillets*. Part-timers can handle only fifteen to twenty.

He pointed out his brother's ponds, which, like his, were neat and tidy, well trimmed and finished. Gesturing to a disheveled section nearby, he said with a laugh, "Those are my uncle's. He's always been sloppy. He just doesn't have the *paludier*'s touch."

THE ART OF THE *PALUDIER*

Tidiness is not just a mania, it's a necessity to the paludier. Everything about the pools and channels he leases from the state (or from private owners) must be so clean, so firmly packed, that salt water can glide over it without a hitch.

M. Lecallo explained how during the highest tides of the month, which occur every fifteen days, salt water comes into the marsh. During the summer, the *paludier* lets some of that water into a holding pool by raising a wooden door across a channel that funnels it in. The wind and the sun immediately begin evaporating and warming the water, raising its concentration of salt.

Then the water slowly follows a circuitous route through graded channels and basins, all carved out of the clay soil. "The idea is to make the water travel as long a distance as possible. It's the movement that warms, evaporates, and cleans it," M. Lecallo explained.

The art of being a *paludier* lies in controlling the water, for it must be kept moving constantly, not too fast, not too deep. He must watch the weather, being poised at all times to let more water in if necessary.

"It's all in the *fee-ling*," M. Lecallo said, using an English word to describe intuition and experience.

The water's final destination is the *oeillets*, which are about an inch deep. This is where the *paludier* rakes, slowly and carefully, his translucent gray harvest.

Balancing on dikes around the *oeillets*, often in bare feet, the *paludier* brings in the big gray crystals with a tool that looks like a rake with no teeth. M. Lecallo skillfully scoops the salt out of the water and deposits it in a mound on the dike, where it drains overnight.

The following day, the *paludier* will transport the salt by wheelbarrow, often thirty to forty loads a day, to a designated spot where it will be stored until it can be sorted. At this time of year the *paludier* fears one thing, and one thing only: rain, the specter of failure.

"Fortunately, we don't have much rain in summer. In fact, we have less than the Mediterranean," M. Lecallo said.

Traditionally, salt was stored in thick-walled, buttressed stone buildings. Without buttressing, the force of the salt settling would have pushed the walls apart. Now large hangars called *salorges* stand high and dark in the marsh, their wood walls angled slightly to resist the pressure. In some spots, the salt is simply mounded and covered with black plastic. "As long as it's dry, it will keep forever," M. Lecallo said.

La Mer • The Sea

The Salt Raker's Fish

Le Poisson du Paludier

Just outside Guérande, a tiny fishing village in Brittany which is now more tourist than fish, the salt rakers, or *paludiers,* pursue their craft.

Since the Romans first began harvesting the salt marshes, food in Guérande has been seasoned with the local sea salt, *sel de Guérande.* In fact, residents in and around Guérande don't even known what any other salt tastes like. If they have occasion to taste ordinary table salt, they wrinkle their nose at its bitter tartness.

For François Lecallo, a *paludier* for seventeen years, salt is not only a seasoning but a cooking vehicle and a condiment as well. Among his specialty dishes is this fish, which is completely buried in salt as it bakes. When it's buried in *sel de Guérande,* eating it is a near-holy experience.

Of course fish and sea salt are an obvious, natural combination. Each leans into the other as they almost trade molecules, and all the while, the fish retains every ounce of moisture it ever had. The flavor in each cell is trapped, to burst forth only when your fork touches the meat.

You can bake any whole fish in salt, as long as you've got a pan large enough to hold and completely bury it. Resist the temptation to add a lot of additional seasoning to the fish—imported bay leaves are fantastic, but a lot of spices would be overpowering. What you want is to taste the flavor of the fish as encouraged by the salt. You'll see, after you've carefully knocked the salt from the fish, that it is one of the purest flavors you've ever enjoyed.

Serve this with The Salt Raker's Salad alongside. For wine, try an Aurey Duresses Blanc or a Bergerac Blanc.

ASTUCES . . . .

• *Don't ever present fish on a hot dinner plate—it may overcook as you take it to the table.*

• *If your fish is slightly undercooked when you check it (the meat is not quite opaque, still a bit translucent), just leave it where it is, in the pan and on the bone, for 5 to 10 minutes. It will continue to cook in the residual heat.*

. . . .

2 whole fish (each 1 pound; 500 g),
    such as trout, tilapia, or sea bass, gills
    removed, head on, completely cleaned
    (see "Buying Fish," page 215)
Freshly ground white pepper
8½ cups (3½ pounds; 1¼ kg) coarse sea
    salt or kosher salt (see Note)
16 imported bay leaves
The Salt Raker's Salad (optional; page 68)
Chervil sprigs, for garnish

1. Preheat the oven to 400°F (205°C).

2. Season the inside of fish with a gentle grinding of white pepper.

3. Cover the bottom of a large enameled baking dish with one third to one half the salt. With one short side of the dish facing you, arrange 4 of the bay leaves crosswise down one side of the dish, on the salt. Lay one fish atop the bay leaves. If the tail hangs over slightly, don't be concerned—you can trim it if that helps, or just leave it alone. Arrange another 4 bay leaves atop the fish, spacing them at regular intervals. Repeat the procedure with the remaining 8 bay leaves and fish, positioning this fish head to tail with the first fish.

Why Is Sel de Guérande Gray?

>·<

*A*t first look, sel de Guérande is off-putting for those accustomed to pure white salt. A luminous gray to ivory, it is sodden. The color comes from the clay marsh bottoms, which also contribute healthful minerals. The moisture is sea water (about six percent remains in the salt). Rather than being a detriment, its color is an attribute, a sign of the real thing—the best quality label there could be.

4. Cover the fish with the remaining salt, making sure they are completely concealed (except the tail if it's overhanging). It should look as though your baking dish is filled with nothing but salt.

5. Bake in the center of the oven until the fish are cooked through, about 20 minutes. Of course you can't check, but read on; there is a way to control the doneness.

6. Remove the dish from the oven and place it on a solid, unencumbered work surface. Tap firmly on the salt. It will have hardened during baking and will come off the fish in chunks, often taking the skin with it. Working carefully so the salt doesn't fall back on the fish, remove the top layer. Check the fish for doneness by inserting the blade of a sharp knife right behind the head, at the thickest part of the body, and gently pulling

back so you can see the bone. If it is still a bit translucent and not to your liking, leave it on the bone (out of the oven) for 5 to 10 minutes, and it will continue to cook.

7. Lift both fish from the bed of salt and place them on a clean surface where you can continue to remove all the skin. Brush off any salt crystals that may cling to the fish. This step is important but, you will see, not onerous.

8. Lift the fillet from the top of each fish and place it in the center of a lightly warmed (*not* hot) dinner plate. Place a touch of the salad, if using, and a sprig or two of chervil at the side of the fish. Then to get the other fillet, lift the bone carefully from each fish, check the fillets quickly for salt, and transfer to dinner plates. Serve immediately.

4 servings

NOTE: It is not recommended to reuse the salt for another cooking adventure.

Mme. Maho's Tuna
Le Thon de Mme. Maho

The ports around Locoal-Mendon, near Lorient on the southern coast of Brittany, were once home to a good-size tuna fleet. The local farmers, whose fields practically run into the sea, were as attuned to the fleet's progress as the fishermen were, and they would often be at the dock to greet the returning boats. As they waited for their fish to be cut, they traded news and, sometimes, recipes. The fleet is small now, but tuna is still a major part of farm cooking in and around Locoal-Mendon.

This recipe comes from a farm near the coast, and according to Marie-Thérèse Maho, who gave it to me, it has been in her family for a long time. It is more Provençal than Breton, however, so perhaps it came from a sailor with origins in the south. Whatever its source, it is a luscious dish, one that fills the kitchen with tempting aromas.

Tuna is surprisingly forgiving, particu-

larly when oven-braised, as it is here. Try to time it carefully, but if you let it cook a bit longer, it will still be moist and tender.

Serve this with a white Graves or with hard cider.

1¾ pounds (875 g) fresh tuna steaks,
    cut ¾ inch (2 cm) thick, skin
    removed
2 tablespoons olive oil
1½ pounds (750 g) onions, peeled,
    cut in half lengthwise, then cut
    into very thin half-moons
3 cloves garlic, peeled, green germ
    removed, and thinly sliced crosswise
1½ pounds (750 g) just-ripe tomatoes,
    cored and cut into eighths
Sea salt and freshly ground black
    pepper
½ cup (125 ml) dry white wine, such as a
    Sauvignon Blanc or an Aligoté
45 sprigs fresh thyme, or 2¼ teaspoons
    dried leaves
1 imported bay leaf

1. Rinse the tuna steaks and pat them dry. Refrigerate, covered, until right before cooking.

2. Preheat the oven to 325°F (165°C).

3. Place 1 tablespoon of the oil in a heavy nonreactive heatproof baking dish that is large enough to hold the fish steaks in one layer. Heat the oil over medium-high heat. Add the onions and garlic, and stir so they are coated with the oil. Cook, stirring frequently, until they are limp and beginning to turn translucent, 10 to 12 minutes. (Adjust the heat if necessary so the onions don't burn.)

4. Stir in the tomatoes, and season with salt and pepper to taste. Cook, still over medium-high heat, until the tomatoes soften and give up about half their liquid but still retain most of their shape, about 10 minutes.

5. Add the wine, 5 thyme sprigs (or ¼ teaspoon dried thyme), and the bay leaf, pressing the herbs down into the vegetables. Arrange the tuna steaks on top of the vegetables (they may completely cover them). Drizzle the tuna with the remaining 1 tablespoon oil. Then sprinkle the steaks lightly with salt and generously with pepper.

6. Remove the leaves from the remaining 40 thyme sprigs and sprinkle them (or the remaining 2 teaspoons dried thyme) over the tuna.

7. Place the baking dish in the oven and bake, uncovered, until the tuna is cooked through, 20 to 25 minutes. (At 20 minutes the tuna will probably be just this side of perfectly cooked. Remove it from the oven and let it finish cooking in its residual heat, or leave it in for up to 5 more minutes. If you leave it in for the full 5 minutes, it will be cooked through entirely, though still very moist and flavorful.)

8. Remove the dish from the oven and serve the tuna with the vegetables alongside. (Just warn your guests about the bay leaf and the thyme sprigs; it's not worth fishing around in the soupy vegetables to find them before serving.)

6 servings

Basque-Style Cod
Morue Basquaise

→ ··· ←

This dish speaks of the Pays Basque, from which it comes. Simple and robust, it goes together quickly and makes for a cheerful presentation. You may use any meaty variety of white fish you like.

Serve with a Cahors, a Côtes du Rhône, or a Buzet.

2 pounds (1 kg) firm white fish fillets, such as Atlantic cod, lingcod, halibut, or tilapia, bones removed
2 tablespoons olive oil
4 red bell peppers, cored, seeded, and cut into large dice
2 leeks, white part and 2 inches (5 cm) of green, rinsed well and diced
2 medium onions, peeled and diced
2 cloves garlic, peeled, green germ removed, and coarsely chopped
Sea salt and freshly ground black pepper
3 medium fresh plum tomatoes, cored and coarsely chopped
Cayenne pepper

1. Rinse the fish and pat it dry. Cut it into large chunks. Refrigerate until just before cooking.

2. Heat the oil in a large skillet over medium heat. Add the peppers, leeks, onions, and garlic. Season with salt and pepper to taste, and cook until the onions begin to soften, about 20 minutes, stirring occasionally. Stir in the tomatoes, cover, and cook until all the vegetables are thoroughly cooked and almost dissolved. This will take about 30 minutes.

3. Purée the vegetables in a food processor. Return them to the skillet, and season with salt and cayenne pepper to taste. The mixture should have a slight bite, but shouldn't be so hot it burns.

4. Lightly salt the fish and add it to the sauce, pushing the pieces down into the sauce so they are at least half covered with it. Cover and cook just until the fish is opaque and cooked through, about 15 minutes depending on the thickness of the fillets. Thin fillets will cook in a shorter amount of time.

5. Taste the sauce for seasoning and adjust if necessary. Serve immediately.

4 to 6 servings

Pickled Mackerel

Maquereaux en Marinade

⇥•••⇤

Here, mackerel are salted and pickled to emerge firm and tangy (see Note). They resemble pickled herring, and are wonderful served with buttered bread, or on or alongside a salad, such as Watercress, Beet, and Walnut Salad (see Index).

8 mackerel fillets (each about 2 ounces;
   60 g), trimmed, bones removed (see Note)
2 teaspoons fine sea salt
12 sprigs fresh thyme
6 imported bay leaves
2 cups (500 ml) white vinegar
1 cup (250 ml) water
½ cup (100 g) sugar
2 whole cloves
1 teaspoon green peppercorns
10 black peppercorns
6 allspice berries
6 shallots, peeled and cut crosswise into
   thin slices

1. Sprinkle the mackerel fillets evenly on both sides with the salt. Place 4 thyme sprigs and 2 bay leaves in the bottom of a shallow bowl, top with the fillets, and cover with another 4 thyme sprigs and 2 bay leaves. Cover and refrigerate overnight.

2. Place the vinegar, water, and sugar in a medium-size saucepan. Cover and bring to a boil over medium-high heat. Stir to dissolve the sugar, then add the cloves, green peppercorns, black peppercorns, and allspice berries. Remove from the heat and let cool to room temperature.

3. Remove the salted fillets from the refrigerator and drain them. Discard the herbs, rinse the fillets, and pat them dry.

4. Arrange the fillets in a nonreactive dish, scatter the shallots on top, and pour the marinade over. The fillets and the shallots will tend to float, which is fine. Add the remaining 2 bay leaves and 4 thyme sprigs, cover, and refrigerate for 24 to 36 hours.

5. To serve, remove the fillets from the marinade and arrange on a serving dish. Let them sit at room temperature for about 15 minutes before serving so they are slightly chilled but not ice cold.

8 to 10 servings

N O T E : Since the fish in this recipe is not cooked, buy only very fresh mackerel and freeze it for 48 hours before thawing and pickling it. The freezing will kill any bacteria.

There's a Future in Growing Mussels

=

Here, off the coast of La Rochelle, in the Poitou-Charentes, it is inky black and pouring rain, and the sea laps at our boots. We are waiting on the dock for Bernard Bouyé's crew, his *matelots*, to turn up for work. When the two young men arrive, we pile into a small motorboat and speed to his mussel boat, the *Tamaris*.

There M. Bouyé and the crew unload plastic baskets, which they will fill with cultivated mussels before the day is over. We crowd into the *Tamaris*'s spotless cabin, have a cup of lemon tea, and slowly steer out to M. Bouyé's "fields."

The sun rises to reveal a bay surrounded on three sides by sloping white beaches and low, scrubby dunes.

A native of the area, M. Bouyé is a mytiliculturist, a mussel farmer. His father was before him, and he hopes his children will follow. "The future is good," he says firmly. "We have a tough time supplying the market now, which means there's room for growth."

He noses the long, flat boat out from the Bay of Charron, known nationwide for

the quality of its mussels. The tide is almost out, and rows of oak pilings stick up evenly above the water. "This is my farm," M. Bouyé says, sweeping his hand toward the pilings. "They're my *bouchots*, the home for my mussels."

There are hundreds, maybe thousands, of pilings in the water, belonging to the sixty mussel farmers who cultivate the area. Other boats nose out now, and each heads to its own spot.

We come close to M. Bouyé's pilings, where we can see the blue-black clumps of mussels, festooned with algae and little white barnacles. To harvest them, he hooks up a hydraulic claw that swings out over the water, closes down on a piling, and comes up scraping it clean of mussels, which it deposits on the boat.

We head out to open water, where M. Bouyé has more mussels growing, this time on ropes that hang from a long line held up by buoys. "This is a technique we copied from the Japanese," he says. "It took us two years to get it in place."

M. Bouyé was one of the growers responsible for introducing the new system, and he's pleased with the results. "I can't believe how quickly the larvae grow in the open water," he says.

A DECADE OF CHANGE

Introducing a new system to a region that has cultivated mussels since the 12th century wasn't easy. "It was hard for people to adapt to this system," he explains. "Everything about cultivating mussels here has changed dramatically."

As proof, he shows romantic black-and-white photos of his father leisurely heading a sailboat out to the mussel beds to harvest them the old-fashioned way. "That wasn't so long ago—about ten years," he says. "People around here don't like change, though if you can prove that it will help them, they'll do it overnight."

That's how Charron mussel boats came to have enclosed cabins. "Traditionally, mussel farmers worked out in the open on the boats, with no shelter. Then some outsider who married a local girl got into mussels, and was so cold on his boat that he built a cabin. At first people thought he was lazy and stupid. Then they realized he harvested more mussels than they did, and he could stay warm at the same time, so everyone put cabins on their boats," says M. Bouyé, laughing at the memory.

"We got special loans to purchase these boats, which are extremely expensive," he says. "But that's about all the help we get from the government."

His face clouds over slightly as he talks about the industry as a whole. "We had a sickness among our mussels in the sixties, which forced all of us to go elsewhere to find work," he says. "There's more interest in finding the *Titanic* than there is in discovering and curing the problem with our mussels."

The mussels are fine now, however, and young people clamor to get into raising them, a sure thing in a region where unemployment is high.

Harvesting done and the morning coming to a close, M. Bouyé heads the boat back to shore. Crewman Ludovic Brunet, who, along with Denis Gaudin, spends any leisure time tidying the boat, turns on an automated cleaning machine for the mussels. The shellfish go in muddy and clumped on one side, and emerge brushed clean on the other. "All the buyer has to do is rinse them, pull out the beards, and cook them," M. Bouyé says.

The mussels are bagged in 30-pound sacks, which M. Bouyé sprinkles with a handful of sea salt before he ties them up.

"If the mussels open, they taste the salt and close immediately," he says. "It helps them keep longer."

Some mussels go into plastic mesh bags, others into natural jute bags. "Parisians prefer the jute bags." M. Bouyé laughs. "They're more aesthetic."

La Mer • The Sea

Mussels Cooked in Cider
Moules au Cidre

>···←

When Mathilde Durand served these mussels at her dairy farm in the south Finistère, Brittany, I was delighted. It was the first time I'd been served shellfish on a farm, and I mentioned my pleasure.

"We live so near the beach that these mussels are as local to us as the butter I make myself. I like to give people an idea of what we eat in the region, so I serve seafood as often as I can," Mme. Durand said.

"We make our own cider," she continued, "so it seems to me the right way to cook them." She liberally seasoned the mussels with garlic, shallots, and pepper, which was also the right thing to do. They were luscious—three of us ate them all, with gusto.

The waters off the Breton coast are cold. Even in summer they rarely get warm enough for any but the hardiest of bathers. What is tough for swimmers is ideal for seafood, however, for cold waters mean plump, sweet, firm shellfish and delicate, flavorful fish.

A couple of times a week, the Durands go meet the fishing boats in the evening—a beautiful sight as they roll in on the surf—and buy right from the captain. Seafood doesn't come much fresher than that.

Breton mussels are generally tiny, like those I had at the Durands'. To me, tiny is best, for they are firm, and rich with flavor. Flavor, of course, depends on where mussels are raised or harvested. Those from southern Brittany live a wild life in the surf and are succulent, pure-tasting morsels. Comparable mussels in the U.S. can be had from the West Coast, particularly the Pacific Northwest, where water temperatures are similar.

Make this dish with the best mussels you can find, and drink hard cider or a white Burgundy along with it. Also, serve lots of bread for sopping up the juices.

Debearding Mussels

>·<

*T*he tufts of tough filaments by which mussels attach themselves to pilings or other solid objects in the water are called byssuses, or "beards," and they must be removed from the mussels before cooking.

Never debeard mussels too far in advance, for it causes them to die. The best advice is to debeard them right before cooking. Some producers in the U.S. offer mussels already debearded, but they aren't really, technically debearded, though you won't find a beard hanging from them. The visible part of the beard is snipped off, but the root inside the mussel meat is usually left. Sometimes you'll notice it (it's chewy). I prefer to debeard my own mussels. Then I know the beard is truly gone.

If the mussels are small, the only tool you need is your fingers. Grab the small beard hanging from the mussel and give it a quick tug. It should come off easily. If the mussels are bigger, you may have to fight for the beard, using pliers in extreme cases. While you're at it, scrape any barnacles off the mussels, too, or any other flora on the shells that could result in grit at the bottom of your bowl.

A S T U C E . . . .

• When eating mussels, take a tip from the experts, those who have grown up raising and eating them. Eat the first one with a fork (or your fingers), then use the shell as a utensil to capture the others. Proper mussel etiquette calls for the shells, once empty, to be neatly stacked inside each other and set around the rim of the plate.

. . . .

3½ pounds (1¼ kg) mussels
1 cup (250 ml) hard cider
3 cloves garlic, peeled, green
　　germ removed, and coarsely
　　chopped
1 large shallot, peeled and cut
　　crosswise into thin slices
Freshly ground black pepper

1. Rinse and debeard the mussels (see box, this page) not more than 1 hour before you plan to cook them.

2. Place the mussels in a large heavy stockpot, pour the cider over them, and shower them with the garlic and shallot. Shake the pan to mix the ingredients, cover, and bring to a boil over medium-high heat. Cook, shaking the pan occasionally, until the mussels open, which will take anywhere from 3 to 10 minutes, depending on their size. Discard any that don't open.

3. When the mussels are cooked, sprinkle them with a generous amount of freshly ground black pepper. Serve them in shallow soup bowls.

4 generous servings

Oysters for Your Health

→•←

According to an article in Madame Figaro magazine, the French medical profession says oysters can and should be eaten with abandon. One dozen oysters contain as much protein as an average-size steak, and ten times less fat. They are loaded with zinc, too, which regenerates cells, synthesizes proteins, and helps the body rid itself of alcohol. Oysters are good for the skin, reinforce the immune system, and sharpen the palate. And all of this might mean nothing without citing what is, perhaps, the most important element of the oyster, an amino acid that fights fatigue and stress by helping fix magnesium in cells, and that contributes to fertility in males. In case all this is true, what are you waiting for? Run right down to the nearest oyster bar and down a dozen, tout de suite!

Provençal Clams with Spinach
Palourdes aux Épinards

→•••←

I was standing in a Provence cherry orchard when Monique Tourrette told me about this recipe. I was intrigued—it sounded delicious. Though she lives far from a coastline—Marseilles is a good three-hour drive—Monique loves fish and shellfish. She goes into the nearby Carpentras market each week to satisfy her craving with the fresh catch from Marseilles.

Though she likes just about any kind of seafood, from mackerel to salt cod, Monique particularly favors this dish because of the *palourdes*, a sweet, nutty-flavored clam that is about the size of a steamer. "This is often a part of our Christmas Eve meal," said Monique. "We can't eat meat that day, so we make up for it by eating lots of seafood."

I couldn't wait to try this, and it proved to be as luscious as it sounded. Simple yet surprising, it is a wonderful combination of subtle flavors. This is clearly a late-autumn, early winter dish, when both spinach and clams are at their sweetest.

The best U.S. substitute for *palourdes* is

either steamers—the smallest member of the East Coast quahog family—or Manila clams, which are abundant on the West Coast.

Serve this with a dry white wine, such as a Cassis or a Sauvignon Blanc.

2 pounds (1 kg) small clams, such as Manila or steamers, rinsed and purged (see box, this page)

¼ cup (60 ml) dry white wine, such as a Sauvignon Blanc

1 shallot, peeled and cut crosswise into very thin slices

5 sprigs fresh thyme, or ¼ teaspoon dried leaves

1 imported bay leaf

Freshly ground black pepper

Sea salt

2 pounds (1 kg) fresh young spinach, trimmed and carefully rinsed

1 cup (loosely packed) flat-leaf parsley leaves

1 tablespoon olive oil

3 cloves garlic, peeled, green germ removed, and minced

1. Place the clams, wine, shallot, thyme, bay leaf, and a generous grinding of black pepper in a medium-size heavy saucepan. Toss the pan to mix the ingredients, and place over medium-high heat. Cover and cook, shaking the pan and checking the clams frequently. Remove the clams as soon as they open, 3 to 5 minutes. Remove the meat from the shells. Discard the shells and any clams that haven't opened. Reserve the clam meat and the cooking liquid.

2. Strain the clam cooking liquid through two thicknesses of cheesecloth to remove any remaining grit or pieces of shell.

3. Bring a large stockpot of salted water to a boil (2 tablespoons salt to 4 quarts; 4 l water). When the water is boiling, add the spinach, pushing it down so it is submerged. When the water returns to the boil, remove the spinach from the stockpot, transferring it to a colander to drain. Press on it gently to help squeeze out some of the liquid. It shouldn't be dry, but not dripping wet, either. (You may want to save the blanching liquid for soup—it will be lightly flavored by the spinach.)

Purging Clams

➤•◄

Purging clams, or cleaning them of sand and grit, is a simple matter. Check with your fish merchant to see if the clams have already been purged before you buy them. If they haven't, rinse and scrub them well to remove any grit on the outside of their shells. Blend ⅓ cup (90 g) sea salt with 1 gallon (4 l) water in a large pot or bucket. Add a handful of cornmeal (it expedites the purging), stir, and then add the clams. Keep them in the water for about 2 hours, in a cool spot or in the refrigerator. Drain and rinse. The clams are now ready to prepare.

4. Mince the parsley.

5. Heat the oil with the garlic in a large heavy skillet over medium heat. Cook the garlic, stirring constantly, until it begins to turn translucent, 3 to 4 minutes. Add the spinach to the skillet and cook, stirring and turning it so all the ingredients in the pan are well combined. Add the clam cooking liquid, stir, and increase the heat, if necessary, to bring to a simmer. Add the parsley. Reduce the heat to medium and simmer, stirring occasionally, until the liquid has reduced by half, 4 to 5 minutes.

6. Add the clams to the spinach, toss, and cook just until they are hot through, about 3 minutes. Season to taste with salt and pepper, remove from the heat, and serve immediately.

4 servings

Breton-Style Clams
Coques Breton

→•••←

This recipe comes from Marie-Thérèse Maho, a farmer who takes in paying guests and feeds them royally. Her farm is right near the Brittany coast, so in her family, as in the farm families all through the southern Brittany region, there has always been a strong tradition of eating seafood. "We just used to go down to the shore and get our own clams," she said. "Now we buy them, but they're just as good."

The clams Mme. Maho finds most easily are actually cockles, closest in size to the Manila clam that is cultivated on the West Coast of the U.S. You can also use this preparation for quahogs, or even mussels.

I've collected cockles on the Breton shore, and this dish reminds me of the first time I did. My son was tiny, and he sat on my back bundled in a hundred layers of cotton and wool, for it was windy and rainy. As he chortled into the wind, I raked until we finally had enough to feed six hungry people. The result was a feast, as you'll find this dish to be. It is simple and wonderful, taking advantage of the aromatic onion and garlic, major seasonings in southern Brittany.

Serve this as a first course, or as a main course along with Pain au Levain (see Index). A dry hard cider, a white Saumur Sec, or a chilled Sauvignon Blanc makes an ideal complement.

ASTUCE . . . .

• *If some clams are stubborn and won't open, continue cooking them for an additional 3 to 5 minutes, vigorously shaking the pan. If they still refuse to open, discard them.*

. . . .

4¼ pounds (2¼ kg) clams, purged
  (see "Purging Clams," page 229,
  and Note)
2 cloves garlic, peeled, green germ
  removed, and finely diced
2 small onions, peeled and diced
2 imported bay leaves
15 sprigs fresh thyme, or ¾ teaspoon
  dried leaves
½ cup (125 ml) dry white wine,
  such as a Sauvignon Blanc or an
  Aligoté
Freshly ground black pepper

1. Place all the ingredients except the pepper in a large heavy saucepan, and bring to a boil over high heat. Reduce the heat to medium and cook, frequently shaking the pan, until the clams open, 5 to 10 minutes. Transfer the clams to a warmed serving bowl as soon as they open so they don't overcook (see Astuce).

2. Pour the cooking juices over the clams, season with a generous amount of pepper, and serve.

4 to 6 servings

NOTE: *Coques* (cockles) are very tiny, about the size of a quarter, but their shells are rounded, their meat plump. Thus this recipe makes 6 ample appetizer servings. If you are using Manila clams or quahogs such as littlenecks, the yield may be a bit different—you'll have to judge for yourself.

Lina Gomis's Prawns
Les Gambas de Lina Gomis

This is a rather surprising dish to find on a farm in the heart of southwestern France, but Lina Gomis has a son in the grocery business, and through him she gets top-quality frozen shrimp. Her natural inclination for garlic and parsley, and a ready supply of Armagnac (made by her husband, Jean, from their own Columba grapes), account for the evolution of this sophisticated, light yet gutsy Gascon dish.

Mme. Gomis doesn't peel her shrimp, and neither do I, which means that the diner uses his or her fingers to peel and then eat the shrimp. Shrimp cooked in their shells have more flavor than those that are peeled.

The recipe serves four as a first course, or two as a main course (follow it with a salad). Serve the *gambas* with plenty of crusty bread and a lightly chilled Chablis *premier cru* or a Muscadet.

ASTUCES . . . .

• *Honestly, if the vein in a shrimp is not huge and dark—which it won't be in the size called for in this recipe—there is no real reason to devein the shrimp. If your sense of aesthetics requires it, however, peel each shrimp and make a shallow slit down its back with a sharp knife. Remove the vein by lifting it out. If you want to leave the peel on, you can cut through the peel and remove the vein.*

• *To thaw frozen shrimp, place them in the refrigerator for at least 24 hours, and more likely 36. Then rinse them quickly under cold water, pat them dry, and cook immediately.*

. . . .

1½ teaspoons unsalted butter
1½ teaspoons olive oil
1 pound (500 g) medium
    (30 count) shrimp
Sea salt
Cayenne pepper
1 clove garlic, peeled, green germ removed,
    and minced
1 cup (loosely packed) flat-leaf parsley
    leaves
3 tablespoons Armagnac or brandy

Flambéeing

→•←

When flambéeing—that is, sprinkling a dish with brandy or other alcohol, then igniting it with a match to burn the alcohol off—follow these safety precautions:

• **Tie back your hair.**
• **Work off the heat and away from obstructions.**
• **Stand back from the pan and avert your face.**
• **Use a long kitchen match.**

1. Place the butter and the oil in a large heavy skillet over medium-high heat. When the butter is almost melted, add the shrimp and cook until they are pink on one side and beginning to curl, 2 to 3 minutes. Turn the shrimp and cook them on the other side for 1 minute. Then season them with salt and cayenne pepper to taste, add the garlic and the parsley, and mix well.

2. Remove the pan from the heat. Standing back, slowly and carefully pour in the Armagnac, preferably using a long-handled ladle. The pan is so hot, the Armagnac should ignite. Let the flames burn until they die out. If the Armagnac doesn't flame, light it with a long match—standing back and averting your face.

3. Serve the shrimp as soon as the flames have died down.

4 appetizer or 2 main-course servings

LE CHAMP ET LE JARDIN

The Field and the Garden

The French farm cook revels in vegetables, serving them as first courses, main courses, accompaniments. As each new season arrives, out come tried-and-true recipes.

There are the tiny radishes, turnips, and onions of spring, and the firm and flavorful zucchinis, gorgeous tomatoes, incredible green beans of summer. As fall approaches, out come the cauliflowers, their white heads protected from the sun by leaves the farmer carefully wraps around them, every type of potato you can imagine, fresh shell beans, those first wrinkled Savoy cabbages, and bunches of sweet, aromatic leeks.

Winter is a wonderful time, too—there are turnips and Jerusalem artichokes, huge green artichokes, sweet and snappy carrots, celery root, fennel, fat round purple cabbages, and tiny Brussels sprouts.

Whatever the season may be, fresh and luscious vegetables are always at the fingertips of the French farm cook, and they emerge from the kitchen well seasoned and succulent.

Leaf through these pages, purchase the freshest vegetables you can find, and revel in the pleasures of the French field and garden.

Aïoli: The Dish
Aïoli: Le Plat

→···←

Aïoli. The very word brings to mind warm evening temperatures, with family and friends gathered under an ancient oak tree, where the table is set with a platter of fresh vegetables, bowls of the garlicky aïoli, and plenty of lightly chilled rosé to wash it all down.

Aïoli is the kind of dish that creates a fête, even if it's just being served to the family, as it was at least once a week on Paula Roux's farm in the Toulourenc valley of the Drôme, on the border of the Vaucluse. She made the sauce, then harvested vegetables from her garden, a short walk from her farmhouse on the road from Montbrun-les-Bains to Brantes. When her husband came in from the fields, her children arrived home from school, a relative or two showed up from a neighboring farm, what greeted them on the table was aïoli.

For me, aïoli is a tonic, a blend of my favorite flavors, ripe with the aromas of summer. It makes for a simple, relaxed meal to serve to a group.

Use this recipe simply as a guide, remembering to serve fresh seasonal vegetables. (I blanch most of the vegetables in order to soften them slightly and bring out the best of their flavor and color.) I always serve some fresh bread alongside, too, for dipping along with the vegetables. Though this is traditionally a summer dish, it lifts the spirits in winter, too, when the choice runs to rutabagas, winter turnips, Brussels sprouts, broccoli, and cauliflower.

Try a Côtes de Provence alongside.

ASTUCES . . . .

• *Use whatever is local and seasonal. Try green beans, edible pea pods, fava beans, fennel. A mix of raw and blanched vegetables gives the dish some complexity because of the texture contrasts. And present the vegetables in as natural a state as possible, leaving the leaves on the radishes, the stems on the onions, and so on.*

• *When blanching a variety of vegetables, you do not necessarily need to change the water. Begin with the mildest tasting and end with the strongest, such as any* **brassica** *(broccoli, cauliflower) or root vegetable (turnips, rutabagas).*

. . . .

Sea salt

8 ounces (250 g) carrots, peeled and cut
   in half crosswise, then in quarters
   lengthwise

10 ounces (300 g) spring turnips, peeled
   and cut in half

1 pound (500 g) small white (boiling)
   onions

1 pound (500 g) small new potatoes,
   scrubbed

1 head lettuce, such as green leaf, red or
   green oak leaf, or romaine, trimmed,
   rinsed, and patted dry

10 ounces (300 g) tomatoes, cored and cut
   into quarters

1 bunch (about 12) radishes, with leaves,
   root end trimmed

Aïoli Sauce (recipe follows)

1. Fill a large bowl with ice water, and spread several tea towels out on a work surface.

2. Bring a large pot of salted water to a boil (2 tablespoons salt for 4 quarts; 4 l water).

3. Cook the carrots in the boiling water until they are tender but still have some crunch, about 4 minutes. Using a slotted spoon, remove them from the water and plunge them directly into the bowl of ice water. When they are cooled through, remove and pat dry with a tea towel.

4. Return the same water to a boil, and cook the turnips until they are tender with some crunch, 4 to 5 minutes. Transfer them to the ice water, let cool, and pat dry.

5. Bring a new potful of salted water to a boil, and cook the onions until they are just tender through, 3 to 4 minutes, depending on their size. Transfer them to the ice water, let cool, and pat dry. Return the same water to a boil, and cook the potatoes until they are tender through, about 15 minutes, depending on their size. Drain, let cool in the ice water, and pat dry.

6. To serve, line a basket or a platter with the lettuce leaves, and arrange the vegetables on the leaves. Place half the aïoli in a small bowl and set it in the center of the basket. Place the remaining aïoli in another small bowl to serve separately.

8 appetizer servings, 4 main-course servings

AÏOLI: THE SAUCE
Aïoli: La Sauce

→...←

When making aïoli (or any mayonnaise-like sauce), think *slow, slow, slow*. Even if your arm feels as if it might fall off from

all the whisking, keep adding the oil in a thin stream. It is your surest guarantee of success. Don't make this in a food processor, as the results will be heavier, and less enjoyable.

Be sure that all your ingredients, and the mortar or bowl you are working with, are at room temperature. Differing temperatures can cause the aïoli to separate.

ASTUCE . . . .

• *There is a simple remedy for separated aïoli: Put a fresh egg yolk in another bowl, and slowly whisk the separated aïoli into it.*

. . . .

> 12 cloves garlic, peeled, cut in half, and
>   green germ removed
> 1 teaspoon sea salt
> 1 large egg yolk (see Note)
> 1½ cups (375 ml) light, fruity olive oil
> 4½ teaspoons freshly squeezed lemon
>   juice
> 1 tablespoon warm water, or more
>   as needed

1. Make a paste of the garlic and salt by working the pestle around slowly in the mortar, always in the same direction. If you don't have a mortar and pestle, you can finely mince the garlic with the salt, transfer it to a medium-size bowl, and press on it with a wooden spoon until it makes a rough paste; or simply mince the garlic and salt together in a food processor, and transfer the mixture to a medium-size bowl.

2. Whisk in the egg yolk until it is blended with the garlic and salt. Then, *very slowly*, add ¼ cup (60 ml) of the oil in a fine, fine stream, stirring with the pestle or a whisk until the mixture is very thick. If you add the oil too quickly, the mixture will not emulsify.

3. Add the lemon juice and the warm water. Then add the remaining 1¼ cups (315 ml) oil, very, very slowly, whisking or turning the pestle constantly. The aïoli will gradually thicken to the consistency of a light mayonnaise. If it becomes very thick, like a commercial mayonnaise, add some more warm water, a teaspoon at a time, until it is the consistency you like. Generally, however, you shouldn't need any additional water.

4. Taste for seasoning, and add more salt if necessary. Aïoli will keep for several days in an airtight container in the refrigerator, but it is best served within 24 hours of being made.

About 2 cups (500 ml)

NOTE: This sauce includes an egg yolk that remains uncooked once the recipe is completed. Like me, you should use only the best-quality, farm-fresh egg to make the aïoli. If you are unsure of the quality of the eggs available to you, it is best to avoid recipes that include them uncooked.

Asparagus with Two Sauces
Asperges aux Deux Sauces

As a French person might say, *"Il n'y a pas trente-six façons"* (there aren't thirty-six ways) to serve asparagus—meaning that there are actually very few ways! Here, I offer two different sauces to serve with blanched white asparagus, which has a delicate flavor edged with a slight bitterness. Both will work very well with green asparagus, too. You may choose to serve just one sauce at a time, or serve them both for a nice contrast.

ASTUCE . . . .

• *White asparagus must be peeled, for its skin is so fibrous it is impossible to bite through. Use a European-style vegetable peeler that takes off a good thickness of skin, and peel each spear right up to the base of the tip; leave the tip untouched. Using kitchen string, tie the asparagus into two fat bundles which will help it cook evenly and make it easier to retrieve from the pot.*

. . . .

FOR THE ASPARAGUS
Sea salt
2½ pounds (1¼ kg) white asparagus,
   peeled

FOR THE CREAM SAUCE
½ cup (125 ml) Crème Fraîche
   (page 520), or heavy (or whipping)
   cream
1 tablespoon Herb Vinegar (page 428)
1 bunch fresh chives, minced
Sea salt and freshly ground black pepper

FOR THE MAYONNAISE
1 large egg yolk (see Note)
¼ teaspoon Dijon mustard
½ teaspoon white wine vinegar
½ teaspoon freshly squeezed lemon juice
6 tablespoons extra-virgin olive oil
2 tablespoons Crème Fraîche (page 520),
   or heavy (or whipping) cream
½ teaspoon minced lemon zest
Sea salt and freshly ground white pepper

1. Fill a bowl with ice water, and spread several tea towels out on a work surface.

2. Bring a large pot of salted water to a boil (2 tablespoons salt for 4 quarts; 4 l water). Add the asparagus, setting the stalks horizontally into the water, and cook until it is tender and soft, but not mushy or so limp the stalks flop when you lift them, about 12 minutes. Transfer the asparagus to the ice water. As soon as it has cooled, remove from the water, and drain on tea towels.

3. While the asparagus is cooking and cooling, make the sauces.

4. Prepare the cream sauce: In a small bowl, whisk the crème fraîche and the vinegar together, then stir in the chives and season to taste with salt and pepper.

5. Prepare the mayonnaise: In a second small bowl, whisk the egg yolk, mustard, vinegar, and lemon juice together until blended. Slowly whisk in the oil, in a fine stream, until the mixture emulsifies. Whisk in the crème fraîche, lemon zest, and salt and pepper to taste. Set the mayonnaise aside.

6. To serve the asparagus, arrange the spears on a plate or platter in layers so all the tips are visible. Serve at room temperature, with the two sauces alongside.

8 servings

NOTE: This delicious mayonnaise includes an egg yolk that remains uncooked once the recipe is completed. Like me, you should use only the best-quality, farm-fresh egg to make the mayonnaise. If you are unsure of the quality of the eggs available to you, it is best to avoid recipes that include them uncooked.

Broccoli Purée
Purée de Brocoli

→•••←

Bright green, rich, and nutty tasting, broccoli purée is simple to make and an ideal accompaniment to roast chicken or duck. Don't be surprised if you find yourself making it to eat all on its own, too, for it is almost irresistibly delicious!

ASTUCE . . . .
• *Once the purée is made and seasoned, keep it warm for 10 minutes before serving, to allow the flavors to mellow slightly. It will be worth the wait.*
. . . .

2 pounds (1 kg) broccoli
Sea salt
¼ cup (60 ml) Crème Fraîche (page 520), or heavy (or whipping) cream
Freshly ground black pepper

1. Preheat the oven to 200°F (about 95°C).

2. Separate the florets from the broccoli stems, and cut the florets into large bite-size pieces. Trim and peel the stems and cut into bite-size pieces.

3. Bring a large pot of salted water to a boil (2 tablespoons salt to 4 quarts; 4 l water). Add the broccoli stems and cook

until they begin to turn tender, 2 to 2½ minutes. Add the florets and cook until they and the stems are tender, 6 to 7 minutes.

4. Drain the broccoli, purée it in a food processor, and add the crème fraîche. Mix well, then season to taste with salt and pepper.

5. Transfer the purée to an ovenproof serving dish, cover with aluminum foil, and let sit in the preheated oven for 10 to 20 minutes before serving.

6 to 8 servings

Broccoli with Snail Butter
Brocolis au Beurre d'Escargots

Broccoli and snails have nothing in common, except that they both go uncommonly well with the compound butter flavored with parsley, shallots, and garlic. Monique Martin of Criqueboeuf-sur-Seine gave me this recipe and it has become a favorite.

1¼ pounds (625 g) broccoli, florets separated, stems peeled and cut into bite-size pieces
Sea salt
4 tablespoons (½ stick; 60 g) unsalted butter, softened
1 small shallot, peeled and minced
½ clove garlic, peeled, green germ removed, and minced
¼ cup (loosely packed) flat-leaf parsley leaves, minced
Freshly ground black pepper

1. Separate the florets from the broccoli stems, and cut the florets into large but bite-size pieces. Trim and peel the stems and cut into bite-size pieces.

2. Bring a large pot of salted water to a boil (2 tablespoons salt to 4 quarts; 4 l water). Add the broccoli stems and cook for 2 to 2½ minutes. Add the florets and cook until they and the stems are tender, 6 to 7 minutes.

3. While the broccoli is cooking, mix the butter, shallot, garlic, and parsley together in a small bowl. Season to taste with salt and pepper.

4. Drain the broccoli and transfer it to a warmed serving bowl. Dot it with as much of the butter mixture as you like. Toss, and serve immediately.

4 side-dish servings

The Maraîchers of Cr_queboeuf

I've gotten to know Jean-Claude and Monique Martin simply through buying lush produce from them every Saturday morning at the Louviers market. I'm drawn not only to the quality of their produce but also to their rapport with the customers who form a small crowd around their ancient scales and stacks of crates.

The Martins work efficiently, choosing and weighing, always adding *bon poids*, a little something extra, always smiling, chatting, joking. As the season gets warmer, they get tanner, their hair color lightens. They don't just look healthy—they look strong, vital, serious.

I went to visit their farm in Criqueboeuf-sur-Seine, a lovely old town on the banks of the Seine. When I arrived, I entered through the huge wooden doors in the wall that surrounds the family compound: the old farmhouse where the Martins live, and two newer houses where her parents and their eldest son and his family live.

"I grew up here and we lease my father's land," Monique said. "It works out all right."

Monique didn't dream of taking over the family farm, but when she married Jean-

Claude, who was a truck driver, he wanted to give farming a try. She'd always worked alongside her parents, so she slipped into it naturally, and now the two of them work together with remarkable harmony and expertise. Over the past twenty-two years they've developed extremely high standards, which show in the way their fields are planted and in the produce they bring to the market.

She wanted me to see their land, so we drove through town and over a bridge onto a five-mile-long island between the Seine and the Eure rivers, past fields of broccoli, cauliflower, and cabbage.

We walked through the fields and came upon a row of zucchini, one of melons, and a patch of kohlrabi.

"We always try new things, and I planted these for a customer who gave me the seeds," she said, bending down to show me a cool green kohlrabi. "I don't really know what it is or when to harvest it."

She pulled one out of the ground and gave it to me, then went over to cut me a cauliflower. A cloud of white butterflies flew up as she moved.

"I suppose you think those butterflies are pretty," Monique said with disgust. "Well, they aren't. They lay eggs on the vegetables, and I have to throw them out. I'm not going to sell wormy plants to my customers. For health reasons, Jean-Claude won't spray them. I agree with him, but what are we supposed to do?"

She posed the question, then forgot it. It's just one of the issues *maraîchers*—truck farmers—like the Martins have to consider. They rotate crops, use compost to fertilize, spray only when necessary, do everything they can, naturally, to keep their sandy soil productive. But still, nature has her way.

Of more importance to them than butterflies is how they can continue the backbreaking work.

"What we'd like to do is to reduce our acreage and sell at more markets," she said. "We live from the money we make at the Louviers market."

She explained their financial position to me, so I would understand.

What they don't sell at the market in Louviers they deliver to a local cooperative.

"You'll think I'm a thief when I tell you this, but in Louviers I sell you a head of lettuce for three and half francs [about 70 cents]. I take that same lettuce to the cooperative and get paid fourteen francs [about $2.80] for fourteen heads. The cooperative keeps eight percent of that, and we pay them for the crates that they want us to deliver them in."

She looked at me with a sideways glance, to see my reaction.

I was stunned, naturally, and it made me even more willing to pay that seventy cents for a head of lettuce, which is what I would pay if I bought it at the supermarket, where the cooperative delivers.

Neither of the Martins let the way things are going affect the quality of their work or their sunny natures. They take things as they come. They are usually among the first to arrive at the Louviers market and the first to leave, their crates empty, their purse full. And recently they told me they've begun selling at another nearby market, a step closer to their goal.

Normandy Brussels Sprouts
Choux de Bruxelles à la Normande

→···←

When fall arrives in Normandy, my local Saturday market turns magical. The chill air means that soon I'll be able to buy freshly made butter, back after the cows' summer hiatus. And the vegetable stands are filled with all of my favorite foods: celery root, Brussels sprouts, turnips, gorgeous carrots with their leafy tops, beets (precooked, as is the French fashion). There's a hint of smoke in the crisp air—throughout the surrounding countryside, gardeners and farmers are burning their leaves.

On a drizzly November morning, I couldn't wait to purchase the year's first Brussels sprouts, tiny and perfect, like miniature cabbages. I asked for a generous kilo. As I took the bag from the farm woman, I asked her how she prepared them. "Don't ask me," she said with a sheepish grin. "I don't do any of the cooking at home."

A small woman next to me timidly touched my elbow. "Well," she said, "you want to steam them and cook them with a little cream—not too much—and some *lardons* [bacon], and you'll see, they're excellent. That's how we do it here, anyway."

By "here" she meant Normandy, by "cream" she meant the fresh-from-the-cow crème fraîche available at the adjoining stand. I followed her advice—and went straight to heaven. I love Brussels sprouts anyway, but these were sublime. Lightly steamed, then sautéed with a touch of crème fraîche and bacon, they exude a delicate nutmeg-like flavor that I find astonishing. I sea-

son them lightly with salt and pepper, and leave their own flavor to complete the seasoning.

ASTUCE . . . .

• *When preparing Brussels sprouts, cut an X in the base of each one with a sharp knife. This prevents the sprout from falling apart during cooking.*

. . . .

1 pound (500 g) Brussels sprouts, trimmed
3 ounces (90 g) slab bacon, rind
    removed, cut into 1 x ¼ x ¼-inch
    (2½ x ½ x ½ cm) pieces
¼ cup (60 ml) Crème Fraîche (page 520)
    or heavy (or whipping) cream
Sea salt and freshly ground black pepper

1. Bring water to boil in the bottom of a vegetable steamer, and steam the Brussels sprouts until they have gone just beyond their brightest green color, and a sharp knife

goes through them with just the slightest resistance, about 9 minutes.

2. While the sprouts are steaming, sauté the bacon in a large heavy skillet over medium heat until it is limp and slightly golden, about 10 minutes. It shouldn't brown, so watch the heat and adjust it accordingly. Drain off the fat if desired. Add the crème fraîche, stir, and remove from the heat.

3. When the sprouts are cooked, add them directly to the bacon and crème fraîche,

season with salt and pepper to taste, and bring to a simmer over medium-high heat. Reduce the heat to medium and stir the sprouts until they are coated with crème fraîche and all the ingredients are hot through, 2 to 3 minutes. Adjust the seasoning, if necessary.

4. Remove from the heat, transfer to a warmed serving dish, and serve immediately.

4 servings

Cardoons for Christmas Eve
Les Cardons du Gros Souper

This dish is a once-a-year event in Provence, where it is essential for *le gros souper*, Christmas Eve supper. As one man told me, "This is one of my favorite things to eat, but we make it once a year only, because it wouldn't be appropriate at any other time." The sentiment is understandable, but this dish is so full of dusky flavor that it's almost addictive, and I find myself tempted to make it throughout winter, when cardoons are in season.

The cardoon, a relative of the artichoke, with a similar though milder flavor, has long leaves with a wide, crisp, pale ivory central stem. In the garden, they resemble the artichoke plant, for the stem is bordered at its narrow end by spiky, silver-green artichoke-like leaves. Cardoons are uncommon in the U.S., though they are sometimes available in supermarkets and often available at farmers' markets, particularly those that serve a French or Italian clientele.

Everyone has their own way of cooking cardoons. This version comes from Monique Tourrette of Venasque, in the Vaucluse.

ASTUCES . . . .

• *Don't omit the chunk of bread in this recipe, for it magically absorbs bitterness from the cardoons. Without it, they are so bitter as to be inedible. There are other methods for removing bitterness, but none is as simple as this one.*

• *The best tool for stringing either cardoons or celery is a vegetable peeler that is calibrated so it takes a decent thickness of peel off the vegetable. Those that remove a very fine layer of peel won't do the trick because the strings are slightly buried under the skin.*

• *Whenever you are making a flour-based sauce or using flour to thicken, always let the flour cook for at least 2 minutes to allow the flour flavor to cook away.*

. . . .

Acidulated Water

*A*cidulated water prevents the darkening of vegetables such as potatoes, Jerusalem artichokes, cardoons, and artichokes. To make acidulated water, squeeze half a lemon into a large bowl of water (about 3 quarts; 3 l), stir, and there you have it. I leave the lemon half in the water as well. You can make acidulated water with vinegar, but it is not as effective as lemon juice.

As a point of interest, the darkening of vegetables is a good sign, for it means they contain prodigious amounts of iron. They can, however, look unappealing.

½ lemon
1 bunch cardoons (about 3½ pounds; 1¾ kg; see Note)
10 cups (2½ l) plus ⅔ cup (160 ml) water
Sea salt
1 square chunk (3 inches; 7½ cm) of slightly stale country bread
4 anchovy fillets
2 tablespoons milk
2 tablespoons olive oil
2 shallots, peeled and diced
4 cloves garlic, peeled, green germ removed, and minced
1 tablespoon all-purpose flour
2 imported bay leaves
Freshly ground black pepper

1. Using the half lemon, prepare a bowl of acidulated water (see box).

2. Peel the cardoon stalks, making sure you remove all of the strings. Immediately place the stringless stalks into the bowl of acidulated water to prevent them from discoloring.

3. Cut the cardoon stalks into small (1 inch; 2½ cm) pieces. Place with the 10 cups water, 1 tablespoon salt, and the bread in a large heavy saucepan and bring to a boil over high heat. Reduce the heat to medium-high and cook, partially covered, at a rolling boil until the cardoons are tender but still have plenty of texture, about 40 minutes. Drain the cardoons, pat them dry, and set them aside. Discard the bread.

4. Place the anchovies in a small bowl and cover with the milk. Let sit for 10 min-

utes. Then drain, rinse under cold water, and pat dry.

5. Heat the oil in a medium-size heavy skillet over medium-high heat. Add the shallots and cook, stirring, until they turn golden at the edges, 3 to 4 minutes. Add the garlic and stir. Then sprinkle with the flour, stir, and let the flour cook and bubble for 2 minutes. Stir in the ⅔ cup (160 ml) water. Then add the cardoons, bay leaves, anchovies, and plenty of pepper. Stir, and cover the pan. Reduce the heat to medium and cook, checking frequently to stir and be sure nothing is sticking to the bottom of the pan, until the cardoons are tender through and the flavors are well blended, about 30 minutes. Adjust the seasoning and serve.

4 to 6 servings

N O T E : If you can't find cardoons, try this with celery ribs. Instead of the precooking in Step 3, simply blanch the celery for 2 to 3 minutes, just until tender-crisp.

Carrots with Juniper Berries
Les Carrottes aux Baies de Genièvres

This gem comes from Patrick Jeffroy, a young chef whose restaurant is tucked into a fold of the Breton countryside, in a tiny town called Plounérin. A bright, ambitious person with his feet firmly rooted in the agricultural and culinary traditions of Brittany, he works small miracles with humble ingredients.

These carrots are a good example of his thoughtful preparations. The juniper berries highlight the earthy sweetness of the carrots, the touch of honey softens their flavor, and the butter rounds it all out. I, who don't exactly leap into the air at the thought of cooked carrots, love them this way. And they make an easy, elegant side dish.

Cooking time will depend on the carrots' freshness, so check them as they cook, particularly during the first round. If you feel they are cooking too quickly, remove the cover so the water can evaporate more quickly. The texture should be tender but not mushy.

1½ pounds (750 g) carrots, peeled,
    trimmed, and cut into thin rounds
1 teaspoon sea salt
1½ teaspoons wildflower honey
2 cups (500 ml) water
1½ tablespoons unsalted butter
Generous 1½ teaspoons juniper berries,
    finely ground

1. Place the carrots, salt, honey, and water in a medium-size saucepan over medium-high heat, cover, and bring to a boil. Cook at a good rolling boil until the carrots are nearly soft through, about 15 minutes. Remove the cover and adjust the heat so the water is boiling vigorously. Continue cooking the carrots, shaking the pan frequently so they cook evenly and don't stick to the pan, until all but about 2 tablespoons of the water has evaporated, about 10 minutes.

2. Stir in the butter and the juniper berries and toss. Add more salt, if needed, and serve.

4 to 6 servings

Cauliflower and Celery Root Gratin
Gratin de Chou-fleur et de Céleri-rave

This is a simple winter dish that will seduce you with its gentle sweetness. You'll find yourself making it over and over again, for its flavor, its simplicity, its charm.

1 smallish cauliflower (1½ pounds; 750 g),
    trimmed, cored, and broken into florets
1¼ pounds (625 g) celery root (celeriac),
    peeled and cut into very thin slices
2 cups (500 ml) Crème Fraîche (page 520),
    or heavy (or whipping) cream
¼ teaspoon freshly grated nutmeg
Sea salt and freshly ground black pepper
¾ cup (60 g) finely grated Gruyère cheese

1. Preheat the oven to 400°F (205°C).
2. Bring water to a boil in the bottom of a vegetable steamer, and steam the cauliflower florets until they are just tender through, about 6 minutes. Transfer them to a medium-size baking dish. Add the celery root slices to the steamer, cover, and steam until they are nearly tender through, about 5

minutes. Transfer them to the baking dish.

3. Dollop the vegetables with the crème fraîche, and season with nutmeg and salt and pepper to taste. Using a spatula or wooden spoon, carefully stir the cream and seasonings into the vegetables, making sure they are thoroughly combined.

4. Place the dish in the oven and bake until the vegetables are golden on top, 35 minutes. Remove from the oven and sprinkle with the cheese.

5. Preheat the broiler.

6. Place the baking dish under the broiler until the cheese is melted and slightly golden, 3 to 5 minutes. Serve immediately.

6 to 8 servings

Cauliflower and Cream
Chou-fleur à la Crème

I'm always tempted, and often persuaded, to make this in spring when the tarragon is pushing itself up out of the ground after a winter slumber and the cauliflower is still sweet and firm. The tarragon echoes the sweetness in the cauliflower, and crème fraîche softens it all.

Make this as an accompaniment to Simple Roast Duck or The Salt Raker's Fish (see Index). Or do as I occasionally do, and serve it as a main course with salad, cheese, and bread.

Try a Mâcon-Villages alongside.

1 large cauliflower (2½ pounds;
    1¼ kg), trimmed, cored, and
    broken into florets
¾ cup (185 ml) Crème Fraîche (page 520),
    or heavy (or whipping) cream
1 tablespoon freshly squeezed
    lemon juice
½ teaspoon sea salt
2 tablespoons fresh tarragon leaves, or
    ¾ teaspoon dried
Freshly ground black pepper
3 tablespoons fresh bread crumbs
1 tablespoon unsalted butter, melted

1. Preheat the oven to 400°F (200°C).

2. Bring water to a boil in the bottom of a vegetable steamer. Steam the cauliflower florets until they are tender but not soft, 9 to 11 minutes. Remove from the heat.

3. While the florets are steaming, whisk together the crème fraîche, lemon juice, and salt in a small bowl. Mince the tarragon, and whisk it into the crème fraîche. Taste for seasoning, and add salt and pepper as needed.

4. Place the cauliflower in a medium-size baking dish. Pour the cream mixture over the cauliflower, and carefully stir the florets so they are coated with cream. Sprinkle the bread crumbs evenly over the cauliflower, and drizzle them as evenly as possible with the melted butter. Bake in the center of the oven until the cauliflower is completely hot through and the crumbs are lightly golden, about 20 minutes. Remove the dish from the oven.

5. Preheat the boiler.

6. Place the baking dish about 3 inches (7½ cm) from the broiler and toast the bread crumbs until they are golden, 4 to 5 minutes. Remove from the oven and serve immediately.

6 to 8 servings

Celery Root, Jerusalem Artichoke, and Potato Gratin

Gratin de Céleri-rave, de Topinambour, et de Pommes de Terre

This most incredible gratin—golden and bubbly on top, lusciously smooth inside—is a variation on a theme that usually involves only potatoes. In it, my three favorite root vegetables are combined to bring out the best in each other.

In order for the gratin to be truly smooth and lush, both the celery root and the Jerusalem artichokes must be slightly precooked. They don't have the same absorption potential as potatoes, and if not precooked, they retain a certain crispness that is not appropriate.

When it comes to Jerusalem artichokes, the precooking time will vary. If your artichokes are fresh and crisply firm, they will cook more quickly than if they're a bit soft. In fact, they will take almost twice as long to cook when they're slightly aged. Treat them gently, for they are fragile. Surprisingly, however, although fragile to the touch, they hold up perfectly in the gratin, keeping their shape throughout the long, slow cooking.

Stirring the gratin is essential for evenness of cooking. Other than that, the oven and the vegetables do the rest of the work.

I like to serve this as a main course with a crisp escarole salad and bread for sopping up the gratin's glorious sauce.

Serve this with a nice Saumur Champigny or a Pinot Noir.

½ lemon
1½ pounds (750 g) russet potatoes
4 ounces (125 g) Jerusalem artichokes
1 cup (250 ml) milk
2 cups (500 ml) Crème Fraîche
    (page 520), or heavy (or whipping)
    cream
9 ounces (280 g) celery root (celeriac),
    trimmed
Sea salt
Freshly ground black pepper
2 shallots, peeled and minced

1. Preheat the oven to 375°F (190°C).

2. Fill a large bowl with water, squeeze the half lemon into it, and then add the lemon half itself. Peel the potatoes and the Jerusalem artichokes, placing them in the acidulated water as you do so.

3. In a medium-size bowl, whisk the milk and crème fraîche together to blend.

4. Cut the Jerusalem artichokes and the celery root into very thin slices.

5. Fill two medium-size saucepans two-thirds full with water, and bring to a boil. Add 1 tablespoon salt to each saucepan. Place the Jerusalem artichoke slices in one saucepan, the celery root slices in the other. Cook the Jerusalem artichokes until they are nearly tender through but still have plenty of texture, 3 to 5 minutes. Cook the celery root slices until they are nearly tender through, about 4 minutes. Drain the vegetables separately, and quickly rinse with cold water.

6. Cut the potatoes into very thin slices. Arrange half the potatoes in an even layer on the bottom of a medium-size baking dish. Season with salt and pepper and sprinkle one third of the shallots evenly over them. Top with an even layer of the celery root and Jerusalem artichoke slices. Season that with salt and pepper, and sprinkle with one third of the shallots. Top with a layer of the remaining potatoes. Season well with salt and pepper, and sprinkle with the remaining shallots. Pour the crème fraîche mixture over the vegetables, lifting and adjusting as necessary so they are thoroughly coated with the liquid and submerged in it.

7. Bake in the center of the oven for 15 minutes. Stir the vegetables gently in the

baking dish, and bake for an additional 20 minutes. Stir the vegetables again, and bake until the vegetables are tender through and the gratin is bubbling and golden on top, another 20 to 35 minutes.

8. Remove from the oven and serve immediately.

4 to 6 servings

Eggplant with Tomato Coulis
La Bohémienne

→···←

*L*a bohémienne is a style of dish that is made principally with eggplant and tomatoes. Traditionally the eggplant is fried, but I find it absorbs too much oil that way. Here it is baked with just a hint of oil on it to amplify its flavor and texture. When the tomato coulis is poured over it, the eggplant is free to absorb its fresh flavor, too.

Try a Bandol Rosé with this.

FOR THE TOMATO COULIS
1 tablespoon olive oil
2 medium onions, peeled and diced
4 pounds (2 kg) tomatoes, peeled and
*   diced*
3 large cloves garlic, peeled, green germ
*   removed, and minced*
1 bouquet garni (5 parsley stems,
*   3 imported bay leaves, 2 green leek*
*   leaves, 12 sprigs fresh thyme,*
*   tied in cheesecloth)*
Sea salt and freshly ground
*   black pepper*

FOR THE EGGPLANT
2 medium eggplants (each 12 ounces;
*   375 g), cut into thin slices*
1 tablespoon sea salt
1 tablespoon olive oil

1. Preheat the oven to 425°F (220°C). Line 2 baking sheets with parchment paper.

2. Prepare the tomato coulis: Heat the oil in a medium-size heavy saucepan over medium-high heat, and add the onions. Reduce the heat to medium, stir so the onions are coated with oil, cover, and cook until the onions are translucent and tender, about 20 minutes.

3. Stir the tomatoes into the onions, and

then add the garlic and the bouquet garni. Season lightly with salt and pepper. Cook, covered, until the tomatoes are tender and juicy and beginning to lose their shape, 20 minutes. Remove the cover and cook until most of the juice has evaporated and the tomatoes are cooked through, another 10 minutes. They will still retain some of their shape, making the coulis somewhat chunky. Season to taste with salt and pepper, and set aside.

4. Prepare the eggplant: Place the eggplant slices on a cotton tea towel or a stainless-steel rack and sprinkle lightly on both sides with the salt. Let them rest for 30 minutes; then brush off as much salt as you can

and pat the slices dry. Paint each slice lightly on both sides with the oil, and place on the prepared baking sheets. Bake in the center of the oven until the slices are golden on top, about 12 minutes. Turn and bake until the slices are golden on the other side and tender through, another 12 minutes.

5. Meanwhile, reheat the coulis over low heat. Remove the eggplant from the oven and transfer to a warmed serving platter. Top with the sauce, and serve immediately.

6 to 8 servings

Roast Eggplant
Aubergines Rôties

>···<

When I see eggplants in the marketplace, I rarely resist buying them. I love them just about any way, but particularly prepared according to this recipe. Sublime, gutsy, simply delicious, it takes one by surprise with its combination of flavors and textures. It is inspired by a small book called *L'Alimentation provençale et la Santé*, published by a group of Provençal growers intent on sharing not only the agricultural wealth of Provence but also the tricks with which to turn them into mouthwatering delicacies.

Prepared this way, the eggplant melts to a fine texture, keeping its integrity completely while absorbing the fresh flavors of the tomatoes, garlic, and parsley.

This dish is a juicy one, so serve plenty of fresh crusty bread to sop up the juices—you won't want to leave any on the plate!

Try a simple and hearty Côtes du Rhône alongside.

ASTUCES . . . .

• *To peel tomatoes, use a well-sharpened vegetable peeler rather than dip them in boiling water. It's faster, less messy, and more efficient.*

• *Salting eggplant is generally necessary, for it removes any nascent bitterness. It is a simple, effective process, so unless you have fresh-from-the-garden eggplants, don't omit this step.*

. . . .

4 medium eggplants (each 10 ounces;
   300 g), trimmed and cut in half
   lengthwise
Sea salt
4 cloves garlic, peeled, halved, and
   green germ removed
1 cup (loosely packed) flat-leaf parsley
   leaves
Freshly ground black pepper
4 thick slices slab bacon
   (each 1½ ounces; 45 g), rind removed
2 tablespoons olive oil
2½ pounds (1¼ kg) slightly underripe fresh
   tomatoes, peeled and cut into quarters
1 bouquet garni (5 parsley stems,
   3 imported bay leaves, 2 green leek
   leaves, 12 sprigs fresh thyme, tied in
   cheesecloth)

1. Sprinkle the cut sides of each piece of eggplant with the salt, and let sit for at least 30 minutes in a colander so the eggplant can give up some of its liquid and bitterness. Then rinse the pieces quickly under cold running water and immediately pat dry.

2. Mince the garlic and parsley together.

3. Season the cut sides of the eggplants with pepper. Divide the parsley and garlic into four portions. Press one portion onto one cut side of an eggplant, spreading it entirely over that side. Top with the matching half of the eggplant. Wrap a piece of bacon around the middle of the eggplant, and tie it with kitchen string to secure it in place. (Or secure with a small metal skewer by inserting it into the eggplant to hold it closed and keep the bacon in place.) Repeat with the remaining eggplants and garlic and parsley mixture.

4. Heat the oil in a large stockpot or Dutch oven over medium-high heat until it is hot but not smoking. Add the eggplants and brown them on all sides, watching them carefully. They should get very brown without burning, which will take 10 to 13 minutes. Add the tomatoes, pushing them down and around the eggplant. Add the bouquet garni, and season to taste with salt and pepper. Reduce the heat to medium and cook, covered, until the eggplants are tender through and the tomatoes are very soft but still hold their shape, 40 to 45 minutes. Check the eggplants and tomatoes occasionally to be sure they aren't sticking to the bottom of the pot, and turn them if necessary.

5. Remove the pot from the heat, and adjust the seasoning. Remove and discard the bouquet garni. Transfer one eggplant to each of four warmed dinner plates. Then, using a slotted spoon, divide the tomatoes among the four plates, arranging them around the eggplant. Drizzle any remaining cooking juices around the eggplant, and serve immediately.

4 servings

Nadine's Braised Endive

L'Endive Braisée de Nadine

Belgian endive is a gutsy vegetable that requires a certain understanding. When raw it is crisp and succulent, perfectly set off by a highly spiced vinaigrette. Cooked, it becomes another creature, melting to a juicy tenderness with an appealing bitter edge. In this recipe first prepared for me by my friend, Nadine Devisme, the bitterness is mellowed with crème fraîche, the endive's flavor heightened with a generous sprinkling of nutty cheese.

Here the endives become brown and slightly caramelized with the long, slow cooking. Don't be tempted to cut back on the time. It is essential that the endives be soft and tender, and the darker and more caramelized they are, the better.

Serve this as a side dish with Simple Roast Chicken or Simple Roast Duck (see Index).

2 pounds (1 kg) Belgian endive, stems
*   trimmed*
2 tablespoons olive oil
Sea salt and freshly ground black pepper
3 tablespoons Crème Fraîche (page 520)
*   or heavy (or whipping) cream*
1½ cups (125 g) finely grated Gruyère
*   cheese*

1. Place the endives (whole) in a large heavy ovenproof saucepan. They should be in one layer, but don't be concerned if they are crowded, because they will shrink in the cooking. Drizzle with the oil, season gener-ously with salt and pepper, and turn so they are coated. Cover and cook over medium-low heat, turning occasionally, until they are soft and tender through and well browned, about 1 hour.

2. Preheat the broiler.

3. When the endives are cooked, dot them with the crème fraîche and sprinkle with the grated cheese. Place them about 3 inches (7½ cm) from the broiler, and broil them until the cheese is melted and golden, 4 to 5 minutes. Serve immediately.

4 servings

The Pearl of the North

Wet road and gray sky were nearly indistinguishable as I traveled northeast from Rouen to the north, and endive country.

After several wrong turns, past Lille I finally found the village I was looking for, Aix-les-Orchies, a wide spot in the road. I pulled up at a contemporary house in front of a cluster of charming, much older farm buildings. It was the home of François-Xavier and Pascale Bouche, poultry farmers and endive aficionados. They were taking me out on the endive trail.

Cultivating endive is hardly new in *le nord*. Farmwives traditionally put buckets filled with soil under the kitchen table and, there in the dark, forced enough endive for their families.

Commercial production didn't begin until the 1930s, however. The endive flourished with the aid of heating pipes laid under the soil to keep it at a constant temperature, the same system used today. An increasing number of farmers turned to its cultivation.

Botanists discovered that the endive adapted easily to hydroponic growing systems as well. Since hydroponics aren't dependent on climate and soil, endive production sprouted up all over France, flooding the market and leaving traditional growers scratching their heads. That is the endive industry I walked into in the winter of my visit, at the height of the season.

Our first stop was the Rollier farm, where endive is cultivated the old way—in the soil, completely obscured from daylight.

The endive year begins in early spring with careful cultivation, so as not to disturb the underground network of pipes. Seeds are sown in April, and in October leafy green plants are harvested, roots and all. The leaves are cut off right at the crown of the root and used as animal feed. The roots are the jewel of the endive; they will give birth to the pearly white, missile-shaped vegetable we know.

Called *carrottes*, the roots are planted in rows and covered with long, low, corrugated metal tunnels. The tunnels are each covered with a tarp, straw, then another tarp, to provide insulation.

This stage is called *forçage*, when the roots are forced to produce the endive.

If it's a very cold season, the endive will grow in four long weeks (thirty days).

In a normal wet year, they take four short weeks (twenty-five days). During that time, the Rolliers must coddle the endives, checking the temperature of the tunnels and the humidity of the soil, making sure the roots thrive without actually looking at them.

At harvest time, the Rolliers pull off the layers of insulation and dig the endives up. In a barn at the back of the house, a small assembly line is set up for the crew of women who cut the endive from the root—which is discarded or used for feed—and peel away the outer leaves. Each endive, referred to as a *chicon*, is calibrated, then carefully packed in crates lined with light-reflective purple paper.

"The endive shouldn't be too pointed nor too rounded, and it can't have any green leaves on it," M. Rollier said.

Such care in both cultivation and packing distinguishes *endive de terre*, or endives grown in the soil, as does their firm texture and distinctive bitterness.

Growers in the north have formed a union to promote the soil-grown crop, which they call *la perle du nord* (the pearl of the north). They have applied for a quality label, which would limit production and ensure them a higher price, so they can continue its cultivation.

"Right now it costs us two francs [about 38 cents] a pound to produce, and that's about what we sell it for," M. Rollier said. "We're hoping to change that."

A HYDROPONIC FARM

We stopped next at the farm of Michel Verbeke, where a huge hangar in the farmyard shelters a hydroponic production.

There are three stages of hydroponic production. The first is refrigeration or freezing of the *carrottes* so there is a constant supply. The *carrottes* are then put into mildly fertilized water, which is gradually beefed up with chemicals until the third stage, when it is loaded with nutrients to make the plants fat and full.

Hydroponic production like that at the Verbekes' is quantity-driven. There they raise ten times the amount raised at the Rolliers', and they do it more easily and at less cost.

While hydroponics does nothing more than chemically reconstitute the soil, the endive it produces differs greatly from the *endive de terre*. It is fat, lacks bitterness, and when cooked releases a great deal of liquid.

For now, both types fetch the same price at the market. But growers like M. Rollier are determined to fight for more recognition and better prices. Chances are good that the *perle du nord* will soon have its quality label, nudging it into the specialty-product category. Its price will rise, but there's no doubt consumers will pay it to get that firm, bitter endive. The side effect will be keeping the Rolliers on the farm.

Green Beans, Breton Style
Haricots Verts Breton

→···←

Green beans are sublime in the summer, when they're just picked from the vine. Blanching brings out their full flavor and softens their green, somewhat "grassy" taste. This preparation is typically Breton—the garlic's the giveaway.

ASTUCE . . . .

• *The verb* **sauter** *means "to jump." In cooking, "sauté" means to keep the food moving across the surface of the pan so it is heated evenly without being burned. The best way to do this is to hold the handle of the skillet and jerk it toward you while you raise the edge of the pan farthest from you. This causes the vegetables to literally jump off the surface.*

. . . .

Sea salt
2 pounds (1 kg) green beans, trimmed and checked for strings
1 cup (loosely packed) flat-leaf parsley leaves
1 clove garlic, peeled, cut in half, and green germ removed
1 tablespoon fresh summer savory leaves (optional)
2 tablespoons lightly salted butter
Freshly ground black pepper

1. Bring a large pot of salted water to a boil (2 tablespoons salt for 4 quarts; 4 l water.) Fill a large bowl with ice water.

2. Add the beans to the boiling water, return to a boil, and cook until they are tender but not soft, about 5 minutes. Transfer the beans to the ice water with a slotted spoon. When they are thoroughly cool, drain and pat dry.

3. Mince the parsley and the garlic (and the savory if you are using it) together.

4. In a large skillet, melt the butter over medium-high heat. Add the beans and sauté until they are hot through, 3 to 4 minutes. Stir in the garlic mixture and continue sautéing just until you can smell the garlic cooking, 1 to 2 minutes. Season to taste with salt and pepper, toss, and transfer to a warmed serving bowl. Serve immediately.

6 servings

Green Beans with Onions

Haricots Verts aux Oignons

In July and August, green beans flood the marketplace, and they are snapped up as fast as they appear. They go into soups, into salads, and are simply sautéed—as in this recipe, which I overheard at my local market.

I like to combine green and yellow string beans, which makes for a showy dish. The yellow beans have a different flavor and are less tender than the green, but they make a nice color contrast.

ASTUCE . . . .

• *Always trim beans and check for strings, for even if they're advertised as "stringless," they may have the vestige of strings still on them.*

. . . .

Sea salt
1½ pounds (750 g) green beans
   (or a mix of green and wax beans),
   trimmed and checked for strings
2 tablespoons unsalted butter
1 medium onion, peeled, cut in half lengthwise
   and then crosswise into paper-thin slices
1 cup (loosely packed) flat-leaf parsley leaves
Freshly ground black pepper

1. Bring a large kettle of salted water to a boil (2 tablespoons salt for 4 quarts; 4 l water). Fill a large bowl with ice water.

2. Add the beans to the boiling water and cook them until they are tender-crisp, 3 to 4 minutes after they have returned to the boil. Transfer the beans to the ice water with a slotted spoon. When they are thoroughly cool, drain and pat dry.

3. Melt the butter in a large heavy skillet until it bubbles. Add the onion slices and cook, stirring constantly, until they just begin to turn translucent but are still crisp, about 4 minutes. Add the green beans, toss so they are coated with the butter, and cook until they are nearly tender through but still have some crispness, about 7 minutes.

4. Meanwhile, mince the parsley.

5. Add the parsley to the green beans, toss so it is well mixed, season to taste with salt and pepper, and serve.

6 servings

Warm Green Beans
in Walnut Oil
Haricots Verts à l'Huile de Noix

→•••←

This is a simple, and simply delicious, recipe for garden-fresh green beans. The beans are tossed into the dressing warm, which brings out full, round flavors from all of the ingredients.

Buy the best possible quality walnut oil, and check it for freshness. Store what you don't use in the refrigerator, as it is delicate and will spoil easily.

I like to serve this as a first course, to whet the appetite.

1 tablespoon red wine vinegar

2 cloves garlic, peeled, green germ removed, and minced

Sea salt and freshly ground black pepper

3 tablespoons best-quality walnut oil

1 pound (500 g) green beans, trimmed and checked for strings

⅓ cup (30 g) walnut pieces

1. In a large bowl, whisk together the vinegar, garlic, salt, and pepper. Add the oil in a thin stream, whisking constantly, and set the dressing aside.

2. Bring a large pot of salted water to a boil (2 tablespoons salt for 4 quarts; 4 l water). Add the beans, return to a boil, and cook until crisp-tender, about 5 minutes. Drain.

3. Quickly whisk the dressing once more, and add the hot beans to it, along with the walnut pieces. Toss thoroughly and serve immediately.

6 servings

Noémie's Leeks in Red Wine

Poireaux, Sauce Vin de Noémie

>...<

This rich and beguiling dish is as much a part of the history of the Périgord as are the caves of Lascaux or the walnut trees that dot the landscape. Simple, made with the most basic of farm ingredients, it forms part of the gastronomic memory of every Périgord farm family.

Traditionally in farm families, where work was onerous and children were abundant, the grandmother, or *mamie*, did the cooking. Such was the case with Noémie Sol, a Périgord *mamie* revered by her grandchildren, particularly by my friend Dany Dubois, the eldest of the family—the one who would step into her grandmother's shoes as soon as education and level of skill permitted.

Until the age of fourteen, the eldest granddaughter went to school like all the rest of the family. But then the farm called and she stopped, staying home instead to learn alongside her grandmother just how to nourish a family of nine, all of whom came to the table with yawning hunger.

Today that granddaughter runs a farm and a restaurant where she feeds another kind of hunger, that of tourists eager to taste the local fare. She prepares dishes she learned from her grandmother, because they are the simplest and the ones she prefers. This dish she often reserves for her own family because, as she once told me, it's almost too personal to serve to guests. What she meant was that she feared it was too humble. But she knows it is sustaining, and it requires little attention. She puts it all together in a moment, makes sure the fire underneath the pan is low and steady, and returns to it when she can, swiftly breaking the eggs into it moments before serving.

It's not only a simple way to satisfy the appetites of a group of hardworking farmhands but also an economical one. And all that is said without even mentioning the rich and dusky flavor of this simple farm dish.

Serve a salad, and a Bergerac or Côtes du Rhône, with the leeks.

6 ounces (180 g) slab bacon, rind
   removed, cut into 1 x ¼ x ¼-inch
   (2½ x ½ x ½ cm) pieces
1 tablespoon rendered goose or duck fat
   (page 142), or olive oil
5 large leeks (1¼ pounds; 625 g total),
   white part only, well rinsed and cut
   into ¼-inch (½ cm) rounds
2 small onions, peeled, cut in half
   lengthwise and then crosswise into
   thin slices
Sea salt and freshly ground black
   pepper
2 tablespoons all-purpose flour
3 cups (750 ml) simple, hearty red
   wine, such as a Bergerac or
   Côtes du Rhône
1 imported bay leaf
4 large eggs
½ cup (loosely packed) flat-leaf parsley
   leaves (optional)

1. Sauté the bacon in a large, deep, heavy sauté pan over medium-high heat until it is lightly golden. Remove the bacon from the pan with a slotted spoon and set it aside on unprinted brown paper bags to drain. Drain any fat that remains in the pan and add the goose fat. Add the leeks and the onions, season with salt and pepper to taste, and cook, stirring occasionally, until the vegetables soften and turn limp, 5 to 7 minutes.

2. Before you start this step, review "Flambéeing," on page 232. Sprinkle the flour over the vegetables and stir so they are coated with it as evenly as possible. Then continue to cook, stirring, for at least 2 min-

utes, until the flour is cooked and begins to turn golden. Stir in the wine and the bay leaf and bring to a boil, then remove from the heat. Flame the wine to remove any alcohol by lighting a long kitchen match and passing it over the surface (be prepared to quickly pull back your hand). The flame will die down quickly. Return the skillet to medium heat, and simmer gently, stirring occasionally, until the leeks are tender and the sauce has thickened slightly, 45 minutes.

3. Stir the cooked bacon into the leeks, and adjust the seasoning. Make 4 individual wells in the leeks (which will be slightly soupy but not really runny). Break an egg into each well. Cover, and cook until the eggs are done to your liking: after 5 minutes the yolks will be soft; after 8 minutes they will be nearly hard through.

4. Meanwhile, mince the parsley if you are using it.

5. When the eggs are cooked, season them sparingly with salt and pepper, garnish with the parsley if desired, and serve.

4 servings

NOTE: While the recipe calls for 4 eggs and makes 4 ample servings, I sometimes add 2 eggs and stretch it to 6 appetizer servings.

Not Your Ordinary Lentil

The lentils from the volcanic plateau around Le Puy, France's best-known lentil-growing region, have an Appellation d'Origine, a quality standard recognized by the French government. It is based on their flavor and appearance (they are small and delicate looking, and a rich gray-green color). These lentils are the only ones in the country to bear the city's name.

What lentil farmers in and around Le Puy dread is the *folie de la moisson*, harvest fever. It can happen to anyone who's waited through a long and difficult growing season, who's short on cash, who can't wait to get their hands on the crop. The fever causes a farmer to harvest his lentils too early.

Pierre Ambert, whose family has raised Le Puy lentils in the ruggedly spectacular Auvergne region around Le Puy for three generations, has never succumbed to the fever, but he's seen plenty of farmers who have. "Growing lentils is more stressful than other types of farming," he says. "You've got to have know-how, *savoir-faire*."

"You watch the plants," he says, fingering a dry frond he'd saved from last year's harvest. "When they're brown and dry and the little seedpods are violet, you test them. If you can break the lentil with your fingernail, it's immature. If you need to use your teeth, it's ready."

Lentil seeds are planted at the end of February in fields previously sown with barley or corn. The plants prosper in the shallow red volcanic soil, which is where the lentils pick up the distinctive and delicate flinty flavor that sets them apart from other lentils. By August they're approaching maturity, and that's when things can turn ugly in this rough, hilly region.

"We can get the *vent du Midi*, a hot wind that will completely dry out the plants so we lose half the harvest," says M. Ambert. They can get rain, too.

"Lentils like some rain, and the volcanic soil drains well, but they don't want too much," he adds. "We hope for rain on July 14—Bastille Day—but not after that."

He's happy, looking back at a good year, warm and secure inside the three-foot-thick walls of the old farmhouse inherited from his wife's family. "Everything hit it right this year," he says. "We'll have plenty of lentils to go around."

Simple Country Lentils
Lentilles Vertes du Puy au Naturel

→•••←

Monique Pelisse, who with her husband, Marcel, runs a *ferme-auberge* in the Auvergne, near Le Puy, also raises dairy cattle, lentils, and all the vegetables she uses in her hearty farm cooking. Because they are situated in the heart of France's famed Le Puy lentil region, and because they both are indefatigable promoters of regional products, Mme. Pelisse serves their home-grown lentils to guests at least once a week.

The Pelisses have retired from full-time farming, leaving the bulk of the work to their eldest son. They are nonetheless occupied full time welcoming guests to the farm, cultivating a large garden outside the kitchen window, feeding the farm animals, and preparing three meals a day for guests. All the food they serve is raised on the farm, so guests enjoy home-churned butter, yogurt, fresh milk, homemade sausages, and home-dried lentils.

The Pelisses are lucky—their son and his wife are ready to take over the *ferme-auberge* when the elder Pelisses retire in earnest, so they have no worries.

When I stayed the night in their comfortable house, Mme. Pelisse served this dish for supper, along with their garlicky homemade pork sausages. I love lentils just about any way, but when I tasted these it was as though I'd never tasted them before—they were so fresh, peppery, almost flinty. My relish was obvious, for Mme. Pelisse passed me the platter several times.

At the end of the meal, she handed me a sprig of delicate dry lentil stems, their pods rattling with hard green lentils. "Someone who enjoys lentils so much should have this bouquet," she said with a smile.

These lentils make a full and satisfying main dish with nothing more than a green salad alongside. I use them as a base for other dishes as well—sometimes I place grilled salmon atop them, or I add spicy pork sausages midway through cooking. If I have leftovers, I add some chicken stock or water and cook the lentils until they are soft, for a warming soup.

You may use regular brown lentils if you can't find green ones. They won't give quite the depth of flavor, but the dish will still be delicious. The cooking time varies, depending on the variety of lentils you use, so check them after 30 minutes and frequently thereafter. They should retain their shape and texture without remaining tough or hard. To be sure they cook evenly and stay in one piece, shake the pan rather than stir the lentils with a utensil, which can break them up.

  1 pound small green lentils
    (preferably from Le Puy)
  1 tablespoon olive oil
  1 medium carrot, peeled and diced
  1 rib celery, diced
  1 small onion, peeled and diced
  4 ounces (125 g) slab bacon, rind
    removed, cut into ¼-inch (½ cm)
    squares
  2 cups (500 ml) dry white wine, such as a
    Vouvray
  2 imported bay leaves
  4 to 5 sprigs fresh thyme, or ¼ teaspoon
    dried leaves
  2 cups (500 ml) water
  Sea salt and freshly ground black pepper

1. Rinse the lentils under cold running water, and set them aside to drain.

2. Combine the oil, carrot, celery, onion, and slab bacon in a large heavy skillet. Stir so the oil thoroughly coats the ingredients, and cook over medium-high heat, stirring frequently, until the onions begin to turn translucent and the bacon is browned, 5 to 7 minutes. Add the wine and the herbs, and cook until the wine is reduced by half, 5 to 8 minutes.

3. Add the lentils and the water. Stir, cover, reduce the heat so the lentils are boiling gently, and cook for 20 minutes. Season with salt and pepper to taste, and continue cooking, shaking the skillet occasionally so the lentils cook evenly and testing them for doneness, until they are tender but still have plenty of texture, 10 to 20 minutes. Serve immediately.

6 servings

Sautéed Wild Mushrooms
Sauté de Champignons Sauvages

➤•••❖

During a good fall with intermittent rains and patches of dry weather, mushrooms abound in the woods of France, and after an afternoon mushroom hunt (see page 302), sautéed mushrooms are a natural reward.

At the Sol household in the Dordogne, Marie-Rose pulls out her slightly battered skillet, places it on the burner, and adds a nugget of goose fat. When the fat is hot, she adds the cleaned mushrooms and sautés them over a vibrant flame. A touch of *hachis*, and this is the result. You'll find it goes well with just about anything, including an omelette, roast poultry, or a slab of country bread. Drink a hearty Bergerac or Cahors alongside.

1 tablespoon rendered goose or duck fat
   (page 142), or olive oil
1½ pounds (750 g) wild mushrooms (or a
   mix of wild and cultivated mushrooms),
   brushed clean, stems trimmed, and cut
   into large pieces
1 tablespoon Dordogne Hachis
   (page 517)
Sea salt and freshly ground black
   pepper

1. Heat the fat in a large skillet over medium-high heat. When the fat is hot, add the mushrooms and sauté them until they begin to soften and "melt," losing their shape, about 2½ minutes.

2. Continue cooking, stirring occasionally, until the mushrooms are tender and golden and have given up most of their liquid, another 5 minutes or so.

3. Reduce heat to medium, add the *hachis* and stir until it has melted into the mushrooms. Season generously with salt and pepper and serve.

4 servings

Pasta with Onion Confit
Pâtes aux Oignons Confits

→ • • • ←

What to do when an unexpected guest stops in just around dinnertime, with no hotel reservation, starved from a day on the road, begging for warmth and hospitality? Offer a hearty welcome in the form of a smooth glass of port or a rousing glass of Côtes du Rhône, and this simple pasta dish.

The focus of this dish is an onion marmalade, blended with crème fraîche and tossed into pasta. From start to finish it takes about fifteen minutes, and the result is elegant, flavorful, and robust. I serve it with a fresh endive salad, dressed with a simple vinaigrette, and a Côtes du Rhône.

3 imported bay leaves
12 sprigs fresh thyme, or generous
1½ teaspoons dried leaves
1 tablespoon sea salt
10 ounces (300 g) dried fettuccine
Generous ½ cup (125 ml) Rich Onion
Marmalade (page 412)
2 tablespoons Crème Fraîche
(page 520), or heavy (or whipping)
cream
Salt and freshly ground black pepper

1. Bring a large pot of water to a boil. Add the bay leaves, thyme, and salt. Cover, and boil for 5 minutes. Add the pasta and cook until it is *al dente*, or tender to the bite, 8 to 10 minutes.

2. While the pasta is cooking, heat the onion marmalade with 1 tablespoon of the pasta cooking liquid in a small pan over medium heat. Stir in the crème fraîche, and season with salt and pepper to taste.

3. Drain the pasta, reserving the cooking liquid and removing the bay leaves and thyme sprigs. Transfer the pasta to a warmed serving bowl, add the onion mixture and ½ cup (125 ml) of the cooking liquid, and toss thoroughly. Adjust the seasoning and serve immediately.

4 servings

Fresh Green Peas
Petits Pois Frais

This recipe comes direct from the kitchen of Mme. Mireille Cartier, who along with her husband, Jean-Pierre, makes rich, sumptuous wines near Gigondas, in the Côtes du Rhône.

The Cartiers are exceptional among their colleagues in and around Gigondas for several reasons. They have a highly sharpened notion of quality, which leads M.

Cartier to make wine that stands out among that of his colleagues. Even his "table wine" from his vineyards at Sablet, a tiny town

Long Live the Pea

→ • ←

Catherine de' Medici brought the first peas to France, tucked into her baggage along with fennel and artichokes, and with them a whole new way of cooking. Louis XIV became such a fanatic about the tiny green vegetable that he directed his gardeners to produce it year-round, a feat they accomplished thanks to greenhouses. And peas became such a fad in Paris that women of the court—who dined sumptuously each night—would return to their suites and enjoy a nightcap of freshly cooked and buttered peas.

Peas gradually faded as a fad, although they remained well loved and were cultivated on the outskirts of Paris, in the Clamart and Saint-Germain neighborhoods.

France is still a country of pea eaters— the French like them fresh, frozen, or canned. The north of France has become pea country, producing most of the annual production of 400,000 tons (363,000 metric tons), an astonishing ninety percent of which are either frozen or canned.

near Gigondas, is notable for its rich, slightly peppery, yet almost flowery taste.

Mme. Cartier is involved in every aspect of the vineyard, though her primary job is selling the wine and keeping the books. She loves to cook but finds herself with such limited time that she has evolved a style of cooking based primarily on vegetables, which she

steams or lightly boils. And rather than water, she prefers to use wine as a cooking medium—which makes sense, since she has an abundance at her disposal.

Mme. Cartier has a weakness for peas, and this is her favorite way to prepare them. When she is pressed for time, this dish becomes a main course, along with salad and bread.

ASTUCE . . . .

• *Fresh-from-the-garden peas are best here, of course, though even in France it's tough to find peas at their perfect ripeness. If all I see in the market are green bullets—that is, peas past their moment—I go ahead and use the frozen kind with no shame. Good-quality frozen vegetables retain all their flavor and, like seafood, can often be better than what is called "fresh" but has been off the vine longer than necessary.*

. . . .

1 tablespoon olive oil, or rendered goose or
    duck fat (page 142)
5 ounces (150 g) slab bacon, rind
    removed, cut into 1 x ¼ x ¼-inch
    (2½ x ½ x ½ cm) pieces
1 pound (500 g) onions, peeled and
    thinly sliced
2 cups (500 ml) dry white wine, such as a
    Sauvignon Blanc
5 cups (750 g) peas, fresh or frozen
    (see Note)
Sea salt and freshly ground black pepper

1. Place the oil and the bacon in a large heavy saucepan over medium-high heat, and

cook until the bacon is golden on all sides but still nice and tender, about 5 minutes. Remove the bacon from the pan with a slotted spoon and set it aside on a plate. Drain all but 1 tablespoon fat from the pan.

2. Add the onions to the pan and cook until they are tender, limp, and nearly translucent but still have some crispness, 8 to 10 minutes. Add the wine, stir, and bring to a boil. Boil for 2 to 3 minutes. Then add the peas, season with salt and pepper to taste, cover, and return to a boil. Cook until the peas are done to your liking. If you're a fan of bright green, barely cooked peas, that will be 5 to 8 minutes. If you like your peas on the olive green side (*à la française*), cook them for up to 15 minutes. If the peas were frozen, they may take slightly longer to cook.

3. Adjust the seasoning, and stir the bacon into the peas. Using a slotted spoon, transfer the peas, onions, and bacon to a warmed serving dish, and serve.

6 to 8 servings

NOTE: When using frozen peas, do not thaw them first—just put them straight into the pot. They will take slightly longer to cook than fresh peas.

Slow-Cooked Red Peppers and Tomatoes with Garlic
Confit de Poivrons Doux à l'Ail

I found this dish on a farm deep in the heart of the Dordogne, on the table of a *ferme-auberge*. The woman of the house admitted it was hardly a regional specialty, but rather one a guest from Provence had given her. It suits the Dordogne well, however, for the hot summer sun there ripens peppers to a turn and produces sweet onions, bay leaves, and pungent thyme in abundance.

On the farm, this was served in different ways—as an appetizer with freshly baked bread, alongside roasted pork or chicken, and also for a simple Sunday night supper with French Fries (see Index). It keeps well, and I like to have it on hand in summer for all the above uses, as well as a few of my own.

It makes a lively pasta sauce, is sublime on a cheese sandwich, and as for a pizza topping, well, in my opinion, there isn't anything much better.

I don't add salt or pepper to this dish— the flavor is pure, bright, and simple without seasonings. However, you may wish to add some.

4 large red bell peppers (total 2 pounds; 1 kg)
1 pound (500 g) Roma or other garden-fresh tomatoes, cored and cut into eighths
2 medium onions, peeled and diced
1 imported bay leaf
4 to 6 sprigs fresh thyme, or generous ¼ teaspoon dried leaves
2 large cloves garlic, peeled, green germ removed, and minced
1 tablespoon olive oil
Sea salt and freshly ground black pepper (optional)

1. Core and seed the peppers (see Astuce, page 269). Cut them into quarters lengthwise, and cut the quarters crosswise into ¼-inch (½ cm) strips.

2. Place all the ingredients except the salt and pepper in a medium-size heavy saucepan. Stir so the oil coats the ingredients and cook uncovered, over medium-low heat, stirring occasionally, until the peppers, onions, and tomatoes have melted down to complete tenderness, about 1 hour. Check the vegetables occasionally, and stir to be sure they are cooking evenly.

3. When the vegetables are cooked, season with salt and pepper if you like. Remove the bay leaf and the thyme sprigs, and let cool to room temperature. Serve chilled. This will keep in the refrigerator for 1 week, tightly covered.

1 quart (1 l); 6 to 8 servings

Pipérade I

→•••←

Pipérade evokes the Basque country not only with its vivid red and green colors but also with its vibrancy of flavor. It is the national dish, for which there are dozens of different styles and recipes and uses.

Basque Ham
Jambon de Bayonne

→·←

Lightly sweet with a hint of spice, the flavor of jambon de Bayonne goes as well with fresh wedges of melon as it does with peppers and eggs.

To what does this incomparably flavorful ham owe its seductive flavor? In part, to the salts from the nearby Salies-de-Béarn and the gray crystals of sel de Bayonne, a sea salt, which are rubbed into the fresh ham. Also to the ground piments d'Espelette, peppers from the tiny Basque town of Espelette, which are rubbed on the surface. Along with the salts, they season and preserve.

More important than any seasoning, however, is the rich diet of sweet chestnuts and hickory nuts on which the pink-and-black Basque pig feeds. The meat, marbled with fat, is sweet, flavorful, and moist.

At one time the very quality that gave it its distinction nearly caused the extinction of the Basque pig, for farmers found it way too fat. But it was brought back in the mid-1980s, and by the end of the decade it was reestablished, running (or waddling) free in many a chestnut and hickory woods.

The town of Aldudes, in the heart of the verdant Pyrénées, is known for the quality of its hams, which are seasoned and then dried for eighteen months.

What was once a product with more cachet than substance has once again become the pride of the Pays Basque.

Typically a *pipérade* is thickened with beaten eggs for a full, hearty dish. Or it can be left thin and used as a sauce for meat, as in Pork Confit (see Index).

This version of *pipérade* is heavy on sweet, thinly sliced, green Italian peppers. With its tiny pieces of ham and the sweetness of the onions, it makes a beguiling dish on its own. I don't add beaten eggs, but I do occasionally break whole eggs into it, cooking them just until they are set. Served with plenty of crusty bread, it makes a fine supper.

ASTUCES . . . .

• *To seed tomatoes, remove the cores, then cut the tomatoes in half horizontally. Gently squeeze and shake the tomatoes, and most of the seeds will fall out. Scoop out any remaining seeds.*

• *To seed peppers, cut around the stem end of the pepper, leaving just a bit of it intact, and pull out the stem. The bulk of the core and seeds will come with it. To remove additional seeds clinging to the pith, cut the peppers in half lengthwise and rinse them briefly under cold running water. Remove the pith by shaving it off with a sharp knife.*

. . . .

1 tablespoon olive oil

1 large onion, peeled and cut into very
   thin slices

2 cloves garlic, peeled, green germ
   removed, and minced

3 ounces (90 g) very thinly sliced air-
   cured ham, such as jambon de Bayonne
   or Parma ham

2 pounds (1 kg) tomatoes, cored and
   seeded

1½ pounds (750 g) sweet green Italian
   peppers, cored, seeded, and cut crosswise
   into very thin slices

Sea salt

Cayenne pepper, or freshly ground black
   pepper

1. Place the oil, onion slices, and garlic in a large heavy skillet over medium-high heat. Stir so the vegetables are coated with the oil and cook, stirring frequently, until the onions are golden, about 10 minutes. Reduce the heat if the onions are browning too quickly.

2. While the onions are cooking, cut the ham into small pieces.

3. Stir the ham into the onions. Then stir in the tomatoes and peppers. Cook, covered, until the tomatoes and peppers have melted into a tender mixture, at least 35 minutes. The vegetables will keep their shape but they will be mouthwateringly tender.

4. Season to taste with salt and cayenne or black pepper, and serve.

4 to 6 servings

Pipérade II

O ne *pipérade* is as good as—or better than—another. I wasn't able to choose just one from among the many recipes I obtained, so here is number two for you to experiment with. It's very different from Pipérade I, because it's made with more tomatoes and fewer peppers, which gives it a lighter flavor and more liquid texture. But you'll find it equally delicious.

ASTUCE . . . .

• *To turn this into a main course, break as many as 6 eggs into the sauce about 3 minutes before serving, cover the pan, and cook them until set. Season the eggs with salt and either cayenne or black pepper, and serve. Or whisk together 4 eggs and add them to the hot* **pipérade***, stirring evenly and quickly so the eggs blend smoothly into the sauce.*

. . . .

1 tablespoon olive oil

1 large onion, peeled and thinly sliced

6 large sweet Italian peppers, cored, seeded, and cut crosswise into very thin slices

2 cloves garlic, peeled, green germ removed, and minced

4 ounces (125 g) very thinly sliced air-cured ham, such as jambon de Bayonne or Parma ham

4 pounds (2 kg) tomatoes, peeled, cored, and seeded

Sea salt

Cayenne pepper, or freshly ground black pepper

1. Place the oil and the onion slices in a large heavy skillet over medium heat and cook, stirring occasionally, until the onions soften and begin to turn translucent, about 5 minutes. Add the peppers and the garlic and cook, stirring occasionally, until the peppers have softened but aren't completely limp, 5 to 7 minutes.

2. While the peppers are cooking, cut the ham into small pieces.

3. Stir the ham into the peppers. Then add the tomatoes. Increase the heat if necessary to bring the mixture to a boil, then decrease it so it is simmering steadily. Season lightly with salt, cover, and cook until the ingredients have formed a soupy mixture and are tender, about 1 hour. Check and stir from time to time to be sure nothing is sticking to the bottom of the pan.

4. Add cayenne or black pepper to taste. Cook an additional 5 minutes, adjust the seasoning, and serve.

4 to 6 servings

Dany's Potato Cake
Galette de Pommes de Terre Façon Dany

Dany Dubois, who has a *table d'hôte* (small restaurant) on her farm in the Dordogne, offers this *galette* year-round, as part of a traditional menu. Long before it became a favorite of clients at the restaurant, it was a family favorite, and one that can be found in many homes in the Dordogne. Once you've tasted this, you'll understand its appeal—it's the ideal mix of crisp and soft, bold and comforting.

A S T U C E S . . . .

• *To cut the potatoes just the right thickness, use a European vegetable peeler, with wide blade and a plastic handle. It cuts a thicker slice than an American vegetable peeler, just right for the galette.*

• *The ideal galette is a lovely golden color on both sides. If you're in a hurry, however, follow Dany's lead and brown it on one side, then present it with that side showing. Don't be concerned—the potatoes are cooked through.*

. . . .

2 tablespoons rendered goose or duck fat
    (page 142) or olive oil
3½ pounds (1¼ kg) waxy potatoes
Sea salt and freshly ground black pepper
¼ cup (60 g) Dordogne Hachis
    (page 517)

1. Melt the fat in a large nonstick skillet with about 3-inch-high (7½ cm) sides over medium to medium-high heat.

2. You will need paper-thin potato slices for this *galette*. Slice or, if using a vegetable peeler (see Astuce, this page), "peel" the potatoes into the hot fat, stirring them occasionally so they don't stick, and seasoning them regularly as they are added to the pan. This whole process will take about 20 minutes (the potatoes will cook evenly as they fall into the pan as long as you stir them; if they become golden on the bottom, that's all right). If they stick together somewhat, break them up gently as you stir.

3. When all of the potatoes have been sliced into the pan, season them generously with salt and pepper, and mix so they are coated with fat. Add the *hachis*, stirring so it melts evenly throughout the potatoes, and cook until the potatoes are evenly golden on the underside, about 10 minutes. You may want to lower the heat slightly so they brown evenly and don't burn.

4. When the underside is golden, carefully invert the *galette* onto a plate large enough to hold it, and slide it back into the pan to cook the other side until golden, about 10 minutes.

5. To serve, place a serving platter on top of the skillet and invert so the *galette* falls onto the platter. Serve immediately.

4 to 6 servings

The Potato

>·<

*T*he French consume 100 pounds (50 kg) of potatoes per capita per year, thanks to Antoine-Augustin Parmentier, who took it upon himself, out of altruism, to publicize the tuber.

He began around 1789, first by convincing Louis XVI to wear potato flowers in his buttonhole for a reception at Versailles, which started a fad in the capital.

Then Parmentier planted some potatoes on what is now the Avenue de la Grande Armée in Paris and had them guarded by soldiers dur-ing the day. Such heavy security excited the interest of the city's peasants, which is exactly what Parmentier intended. The plants were left unguarded at night, peasants stole and cooked them, and the underground telephone worked its miracle.

Finally, Parmentier hosted a dinner for celebrities in Paris, where everything from appetizers to dessert was made of potatoes. It was a smash. By the 19th century, potatoes were a staple on the French table.

Potato Tart from the Auvergne
Pastis I Tartifle (Auvergno)

>···<

*B*asking in the Provençal sun near her home in Venasque, Monique Tourrette talked of food, flavor, and cooking. A native of the Auvergne, her food reflects her heritage as well as her life in Provence, where she's spent the past thirty-some years. She loves to cook, loves to research the cooking of her native region and that of Provence, and loves to have people come taste what she's made. She gave me this recipe as one of her favorites, using the Provençal name, though it is a recipe from the Auvergne.

Though hearty and filling, this potato tart manages to be elegant as well. I find myself making it for guests, too, and serving it along with Andrée Le Saint's Zucchini Gratin with Tapenade with Tuna as a first course (see Index).

Serve a simple country red wine with this country dish.

FOR THE PASTRY
Double-Crust Pâte Brisée (page 511)
1 small egg
1 teaspoon water

FOR THE TART
1½ pounds (750 g) waxy potatoes, peeled
    and cut into very thin slices
2 tablespoons fresh thyme leaves, or
    ½ teaspoon dried
1 clove garlic, peeled, halved, green germ
    removed, and cut into very thin slices
¼ cup (60 ml) Crème Fraîche (page 520),
    or heavy (or whipping) cream
Sea salt and freshly ground black pepper
1 tablespoon unsalted butter, cut into
    quarters

1. Roll out one half of the pastry dough on a lightly floured work surface to form a 11½-inch (29 cm) round to fit a 10½-inch (26½ cm) tart pan with removable bottom. Transfer the dough to the pan, fitting it against the bottom and sides, and form a lip around the edge. Roll out the second half of the dough to form an 11½-inch (29 cm) round. Place the remaining round on a baking sheet and place both the baking sheet and the tart pan in the refrigerator for 1 hour.

2. Preheat the oven to 425°F (220°C).

3. Prick the pastry in the tart pan all over with the tines of a fork or a sharp knife. Line the pastry with aluminum foil, and fill the foil with pastry weights or dried beans. Bake in the center of the oven just until the pastry is golden at the edges, about 15 minutes. Remove the pan from the oven and remove the foil and pastry weights. Let the pastry cool.

4. In a small bowl, whisk together the egg and the water for an egg wash. Set it aside.

5. In a large bowl, combine the potatoes, thyme, garlic, and crème fraîche, tossing the ingredients with your hands until they are combined. Season with salt and pepper to taste, and toss again. Transfer the potato mixture to the baked pastry shell, spreading it out as evenly as possible.

6. Brush the edges of the pastry shell with the egg wash, and fit the top crust over the tart, being careful not to stretch it tightly across the potatoes; let it fall gently over them. Press the top crust gently onto the edges of the bottom crust. Brush the egg wash over the crust, and cut a ½-inch-diameter (1¼ cm) hole in the center. Bake in the center of the oven until the pastry begins to turn golden and the potatoes are nearly tender, 30 minutes.

7. Remove the tart from the oven, and gently push the nuggets of butter into the center hole. Return the tart to the oven (if the butter hasn't entirely melted, it will as the tart finishes baking), and bake until the pastry is pale and golden and the potatoes are tender through, 10 minutes.

8. Remove the tart from the oven, remove the sides of the pan, and let it cool for 5 minutes before serving.

One 10½-inch (26½ cm) tart; 6 to 8 servings

Potato Ragout with Green Olives
Ragoût de Pommes de Terre aux Olives Vertes

→•••←

I was sitting in the kitchen at Jacqueline Priaulet's home, enjoying a snack of her home-cured *olives cassées* and some *oreillons*, tender sweet pastries she'd made the day before. We'd spent the day in her olive groves and were having a coffee with her father, Louis. Afternoon light cut through the window into the cozy room, the aroma of fresh fennel in the *olives cassées* mingling with that of strong coffee. It was an oddly delightful combination.

We were talking recipes, with Jacqueline and her father discussing their favorites. This ragout topped their list.

It couldn't be more basic, nor more delicious. First there is the secret to much good food: slow, slow cooking. Then there is the bright addition of cloves, which lend a sweet softness. Finally there are the olives, which make it elegant, different, delightful.

The dish speaks of the multilayered landscape and atmosphere of Provence, which never ceases to surprise and astonish with its sun, its heat, and its aromas.

Try a light Bandol Rosé with the ragout.

ASTUCE . . . .

• Cut the vegetables thin and small so they yield the most possible flavor: the onions in paper-thin slices, the tomatoes and potatoes in ½-inch cubes. Cook the ragout until some of the potatoes are so soft they fall apart and thicken the dish. This should be hearty and thick, not soupy.

. . . .

4 ounces (125 g) salt pork
2 tablespoons olive oil
1 large onion, peeled and very thinly sliced
4 medium tomatoes, cored, seeded, and
    coarsely chopped
3 imported bay leaves
12 sprigs fresh thyme, or generous
    ½ teaspoon dried leaves
2 whole cloves
3 cloves garlic, peeled and crushed
2 pounds (1 kg) russet potatoes, peeled
    and cut into small cubes
Salt and freshly ground black pepper
½ cup (85 g) olives cassées
    (see Note, page 163), or green olives

1. Place the salt pork in a small saucepan and cover it with water. Bring to a boil, drain, rinse under cool running water, and cut into 1 x ¼ x ¼-inch (2½ x ½ x ½ cm) pieces.

2. Place the oil, the onion slices, and the salt pork in a large heavy saucepan, and cook over medium-high heat, stirring frequently,

until the onions have softened and are golden at the edges, about 10 minutes.

3. Add the tomatoes and cook, stirring frequently, until they have softened and most of their liquid has evaporated, 10 to 15 minutes.

4. Wrap the bay leaf, thyme, and cloves loosely in a cheesecloth bag. Add it to the mixture, along with the garlic and the potatoes. Then add enough water to cover, about 1½ cups (375 ml). Stir, scraping up any browned bits on the bottom of the saucepan, and season generously with salt and pepper. Cover and bring to a boil. Reduce the heat to medium so the mixture is

simmering, and cook until the potatoes are soft through and beginning to crumble, about 45 minutes. Remove the cover and continue cooking until the liquid has evaporated and the mixture has become quite thick, another 15 minutes. Stir the ragout occasionally to prevent it from sticking to the bottom of the pan.

5. Five minutes before removing the ragout from the heat, stir in the olives. When they are heated through, remove the pan from the heat and adjust the seasonings. Remove the herbs and serve.

6 to 8 servings

Angèle Riehl's
Crisp Potato Pancakes
Galettes de Pommes de Terre d'Angèle Riehl

Angèle Riehl made these crisp mouthfuls for us one hot summer day when she and her family were entertaining us for lunch. Referred to in Alsace as *Grumbeereknepfl*, they are luscious potato pancakes, prepared and made in an instant. They are generally served with a crisp, garlicky green salad, sliced fresh tomatoes drizzled with oil and vinegar, and tiny dill pickles (cornichons). Angèle grows her own vegetables and makes her own cornichons. Everything she served tasted so good and so fresh, we kept going back for more. Serve these the way Angèle did—with plenty of chilled beer.

2 pounds (1 kg) russet potatoes, peeled
1 medium onion
2 large eggs
¾ cup (loosely packed) flat-leaf parsley
   leaves
¼ teaspoon freshly grated nutmeg
Sea salt and freshly ground black pepper
½ to ¾ cup (125 to 185 ml) mild cooking
   oil, for frying

1. Cover a plate or baking sheet with an unprinted brown paper bag, and set it aside.

2. Using the grater blade, grate the potatoes and onion together in a food processor. Transfer them to a colander and gently press on them to remove some, but not all, of the liquid. The vegetables should be moist but not dripping wet.

3. Mince the parsley.

4. In a medium-size bowl, whisk together the eggs, parsley, nutmeg, and salt and pepper to taste. Add the potatoes and onion, and stir well so all the ingredients are thoroughly combined.

5. In a large heavy skillet, heat ½ cup (125 ml) of the oil over medium-high heat until it is hot but not smoking. Spoon the potato pancake mixture by heaping tablespoonfuls into the hot oil, gently pressing them out flat. Cook until the pancakes turn deep golden brown on one side, 3 to 4 minutes. Then flip them and cook until they turn deep golden brown on the other, another 4 minutes. You may need to adjust the heat to keep them cooking evenly and to keep them from browning too much. Transfer the pancakes to the paper-covered plate and keep warm in a low oven.

6. Repeat with the remaining mixture, stirring it well between batches and waiting a minute or so for the oil to heat up again; add more oil as necessary. Serve immediately.

38 pancakes; 4 to 6 servings

Potatoes and Cream
Pommes de Terre à la Crème

>···<

What could be simpler—or better—than boiled potatoes and cream? It may sound banal, but they are absolutely sumptuous, particularly when a good-quality potato is the subject. Good homemade crème fraîche is essential, too.

Subscription Gardening

>·<

Subscription gardening is a strange idea in France, where farmers' markets are held in nearly every village and town at least once a week.

But five years ago the idea came to France, by way of Japan and Switzerland, and there are now sixteen functioning subscription gardens throughout the country, supplying more than 1,600 individuals with fresh organic produce.

The French organization of subscription gardening, which is called Cultivons la Solidarité (We Cultivate Solidarity), has a twofold purpose. Consumers who invest in the gardens each year receive a weekly supply of produce. Instead of farmers tilling the soil, however, it is people who have fallen on hard times and are out of work. A professional gardener supervises each garden, but it is the unemployed who do the work.

According to an organizer of the project, "We get people who are incapable of working for health or other reasons, and we help them become capable."

The program has been wildly successful, and there are more than three hundred new gardens in the planning stages. Supported by a variety of sources, including subscriptions and local communities and industries, it links two novel ideas—organic farming and helping the unemployed—in a country where there aren't many alternatives for those who have fallen on hard times.

Few of the workers actually take up farming after leaving the program, but they have a high insertion rate into the workforce. Time spent in the program helps them establish a regular routine and develop a commitment to work. And it puts more organic produce into the marketplace.

Subscription gardening in France is, apparently, a program where no one loses.

This recipe comes from Paulette Marie of La Rivière, an ancient fortified farm in Normandy, just a few kilometers from the coast and not even a kilometer from the town of Isigny, known throughout France for its butter and cream. The dish speaks eloquently of the quality of Mme. Marie's local ingredients. She gets cream from a neighbor's cows, potatoes and parsley from her own garden.

There are many possibilities for this recipe. Try infusing the cream with some bay leaves, a handful of fresh thyme, or a garlic clove cut in half. If you like, choose smallish potatoes so they can be cooked whole; then cut them into small pieces before serving.

Serve this alongside Simple Roast Chicken, Simple Roast Duck (see Index), or by itself with a big green salad.

1½ pounds (750 g) all-purpose potatoes,
    such as Yukon Gold, peeled
Scant 1 tablespoon sea salt
1 cup (250 ml) Crème Fraîche (page
    520), or heavy (or whipping) cream
Sea salt and freshly ground black pepper
½ cup (loosely packed) flat-leaf parsley leaves

1. Place the potatoes in a large saucepan, add the salt, and pour in enough water to cover. Bring to a boil and cook until the potatoes are tender through but not mushy, 15 to 20 minutes. Drain.

2. While the potatoes are cooking, bring the crème fraîche to a simmer in a medium-size saucepan over medium heat. Season it to taste with salt and pepper, and cook just until it is slightly thickened, by about one third, 5 to 8 minutes. (If you'd like to add herbs or garlic as suggested in the headnote, now is the time.)

3. Finely mince the parsley leaves.

4. Place the potatoes in a warmed serving dish and sprinkle them with parsley. Serve the cream sauce separately (removing any seasoning herbs you may have added).

4 servings

Potato, Celery Root, and Jerusalem Artichoke Purée

Purée de Pommes de Terre, de Topinambours, et de Céleri-rave

At the market in Le Neubourg, not far from where I live in Normandy, each Wednesday farmers bring out their produce in a panoply that directly mirrors the seasons. This dish, which I make with vegetables from that market, is a celebration of fall.

Farmers in Le Neubourg are really mostly market gardeners or truck farmers, or *maraîchers*. They and others like them are the backbone of the French agricultural system, providing from their small plots the best and the freshest produce in the country. Because they are small and sell direct,

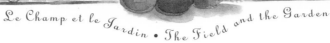
they can grow a wide variety of vegetables, which is why I can find Jerusalem artichokes alongside potatoes and celery root, dandelion greens, and wild mushrooms gathered in the surrounding woods.

Though the vegetables in this dish are unglamorous, the balance here is luscious, rich, and satisfying.

½ lemon
2 pounds (1 kg) russet potatoes, peeled
    and cut into quarters
12 ounces (375 g) Jerusalem artichokes,
    peeled
1 medium celery root (celeriac),
    peeled, cut in half, then cut into
    thick slices
3 tablespoons unsalted butter, at room
    temperature
Sea salt and freshly ground black pepper

1. Fill a large bowl with water, squeeze the half lemon into it, and then add the lemon half as well. Peel the potatoes and the Jerusalem artichokes, placing them directly in the acidulated water.

2. Bring plain water to a boil in the bottom of a vegetable steamer. Place the celery root in the top and cook until it begins to turn tender, 10 minutes. Add the potatoes and cook until the celery root is nearly tender through, 10 minutes. Then add the Jerusalem artichokes and cook until they are tender through, about 10 minutes.

3. Transfer the vegetables to a large bowl, or to the bowl of an electric mixer fitted with the dough blade, and blend to a consistent but slightly chunky purée (do not purée them in a food processor or they will turn to glue). Add the butter and continue mixing until it is incorporated. Season to taste with salt and pepper, and serve piping hot.

6 servings

Rosemary Baked Potatoes
Pommes de Terre au Romarin Cuites au Four

Potatoes cooked in the oven are very common on the French farm, but what makes this dish different is the addition of rosemary.

Aromatic Alarm
➣·<

Instead of installing an expensive alarm system to keep thieves away from your property, find the thieves and wash their feet with rosemary oil—they'll lose all their thieving desires. At least, some people in France believe this to be true.

M. and Mme. Jacques Tanguy, who raise twenty-five varieties of herbs on their small farm on the Bay of Morlaix, in Brittany, created this recipe. Rather unusual to find on a farm, the herbs fit their philosophy: If they haven't tried it, they should—it might be good.

A couple with an eye toward the future, the Tanguys realized they were having an increasingly difficult time making a living from artichokes and cauliflower, the traditional crops in their area. Their alternative was culinary herbs, and with those they've experienced tremendous success.

Their major market is the Saturday morning one in Morlaix. On any given market day the Tanguys' herb basket will include flat-leaf parsley, lovage, thyme, tarragon, edible flowers like pansies, chives, dill, savory, coriander gone to seed, and oregano. Within hours of the market opening, their basket is empty.

M. Tanguy also experiments with vegetables, and he's currently excited about golden carrots and yellow plum tomatoes, novelties for him and his customers. And when the artichoke season has ended, he sells big bouquets of artichokes gone to seed, their brilliant blue flowers accenting his herbs.

The Tanguys are potato lovers, and rosemary does well in the maritime climate of Brittany, where the bushes grow huge and tall, and productive. You'll enjoy the crispness of the potatoes and rosemary (which is good to nibble), and the pungent flavor.

ASTUCES . . . .

• *Potatoes have a way of cooking forever and still tasting wonderful. This recipe is flexible in that way. Ideal after about an hour in the oven, the potatoes will still taste incredible after an hour and a half.*
• *The trick to perfect-tasting oven-roasted potatoes is to serve them directly out of the oven and not let them sit, for they deflate rather quickly. If guests are late, leave the potatoes in the oven.*

. . . .

3 long branches (about 12 inches;
     30 cm) fresh rosemary, or ¼ cup dried
     leaves
2 pounds (1 kg) new potatoes, scrubbed
     clean
3 tablespoons olive oil
½ teaspoon sea salt, or more
     to taste
Freshly ground black pepper

1. Preheat the oven to 450°F (230°C).
2. Arrange the rosemary in a large bak-

ing dish. Set the potatoes on top of the rose-mary, drizzle the oil over them, and turn each potato so it is coated in oil. Sprinkle the pota-toes with salt and pepper, and bake in the cen-ter of the oven until they are crisp and cooked through, 1 hour to 1 hour 10 minutes.

3. Remove from the oven and serve immediately.

4 to 6 servings

French Fries

Frites

→•••←

In France *frites*, or French fries, are more than just a well-loved snack. They're an essential memory of childhood, as indispensable as the soil that clings, metaphorically at least, to each French person's shoes. For *frites* are a food of the farm, made better by "Mamie," or Grandma, than by anyone else.

On French farms there is often an extra stove placed in an outbuilding or workshop adjacent to the house. This is the *frites* stove, clear of the kitchen so the smell of frying won't permeate the house. From there issue *frites*, always golden, usually crisp, sprinkled lightly with salt.

My favorite *frite* memories are linked with Georgette Dancerne, a wonderful, energetic farm woman. She did everything in her life, from working a farm to owning a restaurant. I knew her for over a decade, and she was my first stop on every visit back to France. Mme. Dancerne is gone now, but not from my memory. I learned a great deal about cooking from her—she was a real

old-fashioned cook and a good teacher. Every time I pass her house, which still has vestiges of her tidy but profuse garden, I remember her words and her cheerful face.

A big treat for me, and for friends we had in common, came when Mme. Dancerne invited us over for *frites*. It wasn't often that she'd get out the *frites* pot, but when she did, she'd peel and cut pounds of potatoes, buy thinly cut steaks, and we'd have a real French country meal on our hands.

Frites don't necessarily mean fat. If the oil is at the right temperature, the *frites* will absorb little. They will be crisp and golden, and richly tasting of potatoes rather than of the fat they were fried in (though immersing them in hot goose fat does give them a spectacular edge).

One tip for making good *frites:* Don't rush them, or they will burn on the outside without cooking inside. Another tip: For extra-special results, sprinkle them with *fleur de sel.* As you carry them to the table, your nostrils will twitch as they trap the aroma, not only of freshly fried potatoes but also of the light hint of violets that comes from the salt.

ASTUCES . . . .

• *Rinse the potatoes and pat them dry to give them a crisp, clean flavor. A potato that combines starchy and waxy characteristics, such as a Yukon Gold, works best, though even a russet will perform well.*

• *There is a 25-degree leeway in the temperature of fat for frying. Try to be exact and keep the temperature constant, but don't be too concerned if it varies a little. More variation than that, however, isn't good. The operative word here is* patience.

• *Turn the* frites *out on an unprinted brown paper grocery bag rather than on paper towels. The brown paper will absorb the fat without softening the* frites, *as paper towels tend to do.*

. . . .

2 pounds (1 kg) potatoes, peeled if desired
    (if you don't want to peel them, choose
    organically raised potatoes and scrub
    the skin well)
8 cups (2 l) oil, preferably peanut oil,
    or a mix of peanut oil and melted
    rendered goose or duck fat (page 142)
Sea salt
Freshly ground black pepper (optional)

1. Cut the potatoes into thin (¼-inch; ½ cm) sticks (see Note). Rinse them under cool running water, and pat them dry with a tea towel.

2. Heat the oil in a deep-fryer (or a deep saucepan reserved for frying) over medium-high heat until it shimmers. The oil should register 330°F (166°C) on a frying thermometer. Place two handfuls of potatoes into a frying basket if you have one, and lower them carefully into the oil. The oil will hesitate, then boil up in clear, pale bubbles. Give the potatoes a quick stir so they do not stick together, and cook them until they turn whitish on the outside and are soft but not entirely cooked through, about 1½ minutes. You don't want them to turn golden at this stage—this is the precooking.

3. Remove the potatoes from the oil with a slotted spoon or by pulling out the basket, and transfer them to a tray lined with an unprinted brown paper bag. Repeat with the remaining potatoes, placing them in a single layer on the paper. Let them cool.

4. Turn up the heat under the oil slightly, so it reaches 375°F (190°C). Return two small handfuls of potatoes to the oil (or the

frying basket), and fry them until they turn an even golden color, about 3 minutes. Remove from the oil, and transfer them to a tray lined with a clean unprinted brown paper bag. Sprinkle with salt to taste, and pepper if desired. Repeat with the remaining potatoes, serving them directly as they come out of the oil if possible, so they don't have a chance to wilt.

2 to 6 servings, depending on appetites!

NOTE: The crispness and cooking times depend a great deal on the size of your *frites*. Thinner *frites* are easier to control, emerging golden, light, and crisp without fail. Fat *frites* need more cooking time, and they have a tendency to burn before they are fully cooked.

Potatoes Roasted in Duck Fat
Pommes de Terre Rôties à la Graisse de Canard

Something larger than myself takes hold when I have duck or goose fat on hand. I can't help it—I have to roast some potatoes in it until they are crisp on the outside, tender on the inside, and so addictive that two pounds barely feeds two people.

This is the recipe I always use, one I came up with as I looked at the fat rendered from a foie gras I cooked for Claude Udron's Foie Gras Terrine (see Index). You can vary it to your heart's content. I usually add garlic, but every now and then I leave it out and instead shower the potatoes with freshly ground black pepper and sea salt.

If you don't happen to have duck fat on hand, use olive oil. The flavor will be different, of course, but the crisp, golden effect is the same.

2 pounds (1 kg) all-purpose potatoes, such as Yukon Gold, peeled and cut into small cubes
¼ cup (60 ml) rendered duck fat (page 142), melted, or olive oil
Sea salt and freshly ground black pepper
2 cloves garlic, peeled, green germ removed, and minced

1. Preheat the oven to 500°F (260°C).
2. Pat the potato cubes dry and place

them, with the duck fat, in a large baking dish. Toss the potatoes with the fat so they are thoroughly coated. Sprinkle generously with salt and pepper, and roast in the center of the oven for 20 minutes.

3. Then add the garlic, stirring it into the potatoes. Shift the potatoes so they will get evenly browned, and continue baking until they are golden and crisp, 15 minutes.

4. Remove from the oven and serve immediately.

2 to 4 servings

Potatoes with Bay Leaves
Pommes de Terre au Feuille de Laurier

➤ ··· ◄

Nicole Vallortigara, who I was visiting in her hilltop village in Provence, remembered this recipe as she was talking to me. Her face lit up and her words fell all over themselves as she explained the procedure.

"Oh, you've got to make this one. Everyone here makes this, it's the best, it doesn't cost a thing, you'll love it." She was right, it is, and I do.

Use a baking potato or a potato that combines both starchy and waxy qualities, like an Urgenta. Look for organically raised potatoes and scrub them thoroughly, because you want to leave the skin on so you can savor its crispness right along with the potato.

Serve these alongside Mme. Fautrel's Shoulder of Lamb or as an accompaniment to The Salt Raker's Fish or even Simple Roast Chicken (see Index). They dress up a meal immeasurably, and nothing could be simpler.

These need no garnish, and no embellishment. The potatoes emerge moist and well seasoned, a perfect dish unto itself.

ASTUCE . . . .

• *Serve these potatoes **directly from the** **oven**, for the moment they are removed from the heat, they lose their crispness. Like most baked potato dishes, the cooking time has some flexibility. You may cook them for up to 15 minutes more than the indicated time, and they will be fine.*

. . . .

8 large potatoes (3 pounds; 1½ kg total),
   scrubbed clean
Sea salt
8 imported bay leaves
1 tablespoon olive oil
Freshly ground black pepper

1. Preheat the oven to 450°F (230°C).
2. Cut a potato in half lengthwise, stopping just before you separate the halves so the potato stays intact. Gently open the potato and sprinkle salt on each half, as well as possible. Slip a bay leaf into the cut, press the halves back together, and place the potato in a medium-size baking dish, or one that will easily hold the potatoes in one layer. Repeat with the remaining potatoes.

3. Drizzle the potatoes with the olive oil; then roll them so they are covered with oil. Season them with a bit more salt, and generously with pepper. Bake in the center of the oven until they are puffed and tender through, about 1 hour. To test for doneness, pierce them through with a skewer or a sharp knife. Remove from the oven and serve immediately, with a mention to guests not to eat the bay leaves.

8 servings

Crêpes with Potatoes and Cabbage
Galettes de Morvan

The Morvan is a wildly beautiful region of France, officially considered a sub-region of Burgundy. But while Burgundy undulates with pastures, vineyards, and wealth, the Morvan is *rude*, sometimes so austere and poor as to be desperate.

In history, citizens of the Morvan were looked down upon by their Burgundian cousins for being *mangeurs de mouton*, or lamb eaters—that is, the poorest of the poor. But while they looked down at their neighbors, Burgundian landowners hired them by the hundreds to work their land. They knew that no one would work better, longer, or harder than a Morvandais.

The Morvan was a haven in the 1960s for young French people, called *soixante-*

huitards ("sixty-eighters," or people who wanted to return to the land). They purchased or leased the hard land, and have since settled there. Because of their enterprise, the Morvan is now dotted with cottage industry farms that produce everything from fragrant honey to rich-tasting jams. It is also, with the help of the French government, becoming a tourist haven renowned for its walking trails and unforgettable scenery.

This homey dish represents the cuisine of the Morvan—it is very basic and without pretension. Like comfort food, it satisfies and nourishes, and I find it simply delicious. I've adapted it by adding garlic and lots of black pepper and parsley. You may think of other ways to embellish it as well.

Eat this with a simple, hearty Beaujolais, such as one from Duboeuf.

FOR THE CREPES
4 large eggs
1¾ cups (435 ml) milk
1 cup (135 g) all-purpose flour
1 cup (135 g) whole-wheat flour
½ teaspoon salt

FOR THE VEGETABLES
12 ounces (375 g) potatoes, either waxy or
  starchy, peeled and cut into quarters
½ medium Savoy cabbage (1½ pounds;
  750 g), cored and cut into large dice

FOR FINISHING THE DISH
6 ounces (180 g) slab bacon, rind
  removed, and minced
1 clove garlic, peeled
½ cup (loosely packed) flat-leaf parsley
  leaves
1 tablespoon unsalted butter
Sea salt and freshly ground black pepper

1. Prepare the crêpe batter: Break the eggs into a large bowl and whisk until they are thoroughly blended. Whisk in the milk until combined. Sift both flours and the salt into the egg mixture, and whisk just until combined. Let the batter sit, covered, for 1 hour at room temperature, or overnight, refrigerated. (If you make the batter the night before, you will need to stir in at least 6 tablespoons additional milk to thin it before cooking the crêpes.)

2. Prepare the vegetables: Bring water to a boil in the bottom of a vegetable steamer over high heat. Add the potatoes to the steamer top, then the cabbage, and cook until the potatoes are tender through and the cabbage is tender but still has some texture, about 15 minutes.

3. Meanwhile, preheat the oven to 200° to 225°F (95° to 110°C).

4. Cook the crêpes: Place 1 tablespoon of the minced slab bacon in a medium-size nonstick skillet, or a cast-iron crêpe pan or skillet with low sides, and cook over medium-high heat until just golden, about 1 minute. Pour in ¼ cup (60 ml) of the crêpe batter and swirl it around in the pan so it covers the bottom, incorporating the bacon.

5. Cook the crêpe just until it is golden and has nearly cooked through, about 2 minutes. Flip it and cook an additional 10 seconds. Transfer the crêpe to a plate in the warm oven, and repeat with the remaining bacon and batter. (Alternatively, you may serve the crêpes immediately, as long as you don't mind staying at the stove while others eat.) If the bacon gives off too much fat, wipe the pan lightly with a paper towel after every 2 or 3 crêpes. Continue until all the crêpes are made.

6. Mince the garlic with the parsley.

7. When the vegetables are cooked, transfer them to a warmed serving bowl. Add the butter, season with salt and pepper to taste, and toss to mix well. Add the parsley and garlic, toss again, and serve with the crêpes alongside. If you haven't made all the crêpes yet, keep the vegetables warm in the oven while you finish using up the batter.

4 to 6 servings

Monique's Ratatouille
La Ratatouille de Monique

→•••←

Perhaps no dish is so classically Provençal as ratatouille, though like many classic dishes, each cook has his or her own ideas about how to make it. This ratatouille is based on a recipe I got from Monique Tourrette, who prefers to cut her vegetables in very small pieces. She also adds a bit of bacon, which is delicious but, to my taste, not necessary. If you want to try it, just cook 4 ounces (125 g) of good-quality slab bacon, cut into small pieces, along with the onions.

The final touches of parsley and vinegar are optional, but they add a little spice which I find welcome, particularly when the ratatouille is first made. Incidentally, ratatouille is like a good stew—it gets better and is actually at its height of flavor on the third day.

We love ratatouille, and sometimes it is our main course, along with bread and a salad. It is delicious as a sandwich filling, by itself or with cheese or ham, and it is also wonderful spread on fresh bread dough and baked, as for a pizza.

Try a Coteaux du Languedoc Rosé or a Coteaux d'Aix-en-Provence Rosé with this.

FOR THE RATATOUILLE

1 large eggplant, cut into medium cubes
Sea salt
5 tablespoons olive oil
3 onions, peeled and cut into small
    cubes
Freshly ground black pepper (optional)
2 large green bell peppers, cored, seeded,
    and cut into small dice
1 large zucchini, cut into small cubes
1 pound (500 g) plum tomatoes, peeled
    and diced
2 cloves garlic, peeled, green germ
    removed, and minced
1 imported bay leaf
1 tablespoon fresh thyme leaves or
    1 teaspoon dried

GARNISHES

1 cup (loosely packed) flat-leaf parsley
    leaves (optional)
¼ cup (60 ml) best-quality red wine
    vinegar (optional)
1 lemon, cut into eighths

1. Place the eggplant in a colander, sprinkle it with 1 tablespoon salt, toss, and let sit for 1 hour.

2. Meanwhile, preheat the oven to 425°F (220°C).

3. After an hour, rinse the eggplant quickly and pat dry. Place the eggplant and 2 tablespoons of the oil in a bowl. Toss so the eggplant is as evenly coated with the oil as possible; then spread the eggplant in a single layer on a baking sheet. Bake in the center of the oven, stirring occasionally, until the eggplant is soft and golden, about 40 minutes.

4. During the time the eggplant is salted or baking, prepare the rest of the dish: In a large heavy skillet, combine 1 tablespoon of the oil with the onions. Stir, cover, and cook over medium heat until the onions begin to turn golden and are very soft, 20 to 25 minutes.

5. When the onions are cooked, season lightly with salt, and pepper if desired. Transfer the onions to a bowl and set them aside. In the same skillet, combine 1 tablespoon of the oil and the green peppers. Cook, covered, stirring occasionally, until the peppers are olive green and tender, about 15 minutes. Remove the peppers to the bowl with the onions.

6. Add the remaining 1 tablespoon oil to the skillet. Add the zucchini, toss so it is coated with oil, cover, and cook until it is tender through, about 15 minutes. The zucchini will lose some of its shape and texture.

7. Meanwhile, combine the tomatoes, garlic, bay leaf, and thyme in a medium-size saucepan and bring to a boil over medium-high heat. Cook until the tomatoes are softened and tender through but still have some shape, 8 to 10 minutes. Remove from the heat.

8. To finish the ratatouille, combine the eggplant and all the other ingredients in the skillet with the zucchini.

Stir to combine, and season to taste. Let cook just long enough so that the ingredients are hot through, about 5 minutes. Adjust the seasoning.

9. Mince the parsley leaves and place them in a small serving bowl. Place the vinegar in a small pitcher.

10. Transfer the ratatouille to a warmed serving platter, garnish it with the lemon wedges, and serve the parsley and vinegar alongside.

8 to 10 servings

Buttery Rice
Riz Gras

This rice should really be called *poivre au riz*, or pepper with rice, for it is an astonishing platform for the goodness of freshly ground black Tellicherry peppercorns.

The recipe comes from Marie-Thérèse Maho, who also provided her recipe for Breton-Style Clams (see Index). I follow her example and serve it alongside the clams—it's great for absorbing their juices.

Over the years, I've gotten out of the habit of buttering rice, preferring instead to drizzle it with olive oil. But when I tasted this, the flavor catapulted me back to childhood, and I remembered how much I loved white rice with a little pool of butter on the top. It's wonderful.

I like to use Asian long-grain rice because it has a slight perfume of its own. You can also use basmati, or just try plain long-grain white rice.

Note that the recipe indicates a "gener-ous sprinkling" of freshly ground pepper. I grind until the surface of the rice is almost black, then fold the pepper into the rice.

ASTUCES . . . .

• *Common wisdom in France says that by using the method discribed here, rice should cook in no more than 18 minutes. I've always found it just the right amount of time, when combined with a substantial resting period afterward to fluff up and tenderize the rice. Resist the temptation to look at the rice as it's cooking. After it has rested for 10 minutes, check it for doneness. It will be ready to serve.*

• *Rice will be most tender when it's cooked at a gentle, rather than a violent, boil.*

. . . .

3 tablespoons unsalted butter

2 cups (405 g) long-grain white rice,
    rinsed and drained

2½ cups (625 ml) water

¾ teaspoon sea salt

2 imported bay leaves

Generous sprinkling of freshly ground
    black pepper

1. Melt 1 tablespoon of the butter in a large heavy skillet over medium-high heat. When it is bubbling, add the rice and stir until it is lightly coated with the butter. Continue stirring until you can smell a toasty aroma, 2 to 3 minutes. Add the water, salt, and bay leaves. Stir, cover, and bring to a boil.

2. Reduce the heat so the liquid is just above a simmer, and cook until the rice has absorbed the liquid and is nearly tender, 18 minutes. Remove the pan from the heat (leave the cover on), and don't touch the rice for at least another 10 minutes, and up to 20. The rest time is essential for the rice, which will absorb any remaining liquid, puff just slightly, and become even more tender.

3. Transfer the rice to a warmed serving bowl, discarding the bay leaves. Cut the remaining 2 tablespoons butter into small cubes and add them to the rice, tossing until the butter is blended in. Sprinkle generously with pepper, fold it into the rice, and serve.

6 servings

Braised Shallots
Echalotes Braisées

>···<

Shallots are a luxury, it's true, but they're well worth what it takes to procure them, for they offer the sweetness of onions combined with the depth of garlic. Here they braise gently, absorbing moisture and flavor yet retaining their own special taste. When finished they glisten, as pretty to serve as they are delicious to eat. The butter adds to their shine and flavor. These are excellent as an accompaniment to roast poultry, meat, or fish.

1 pound (500 g) shallots, peeled

1 cup (250 ml) white wine, such as Sauvignon
    Blanc or a Burgundy Aligoté

1 cup (250 ml) Chicken Stock (page 504)

4 sprigs fresh thyme, or scant ¼ teaspoon
    dried leaves

2 imported bay leaves

Sea salt and freshly ground black pepper

2 tablespoons unsalted butter (optional)

1. Cut a shallow X in the stem end of each shallot.

2. Combine the wine, stock, thyme, bay leaves, and shallots in a medium-size saucepan over medium-high heat and bring to a boil. Reduce the heat and cook at a gentle boil, shaking the pan once in a while so the shallots cook evenly, until the liquid has reduced to about 2 tablespoons and the shallots are tender, about 25 minutes. The remaining liquid will be quite thick; shake the shallots frequently so they become evenly glazed.

3. Remove the thyme sprigs and bay leaves and season to taste with salt and pepper. If you like, add the butter and swirl and shake the shallots so they are all covered with melted butter. Remove the pan from the heat, transfer the shallots to a warmed serving dish, and serve immediately.

4 to 6 servings

Crêpes with Shallots
Crêpes aux Echalotes

>···<

I had crêpes served this way in Brittany, in a tiny restaurant right in Cancale, a touristy town filled with quaint little restaurants. This one was extraordinary in that it was authentic, down-to-earth, and extremely simple, and it was also very crowded. We went often during our visit because we found the crêpes to be of unusually high quality—and a quick and easy meal to satisfy our hungry child. Not only that, but as in most crêperies, you could watch the crêpes being made, so entertainment was provided as well.

This combination is starkly simple, requiring nothing but fresh butter and crunchy sea salt. It was a revelation, and it has turned into one of our favorite ways to eat crêpes.

A white Sancerre is a fine accompaniment.

1 recipe Buckwheat Crêpes (recipe follows)
3½ tablespoons unsalted butter, melted
Fine sea salt, preferably fleur de sel
5 shallots, peeled and minced

Make the crêpes, brushing them liberally with the melted butter (which works out to about 1 teaspoon per crêpe). Sprinkle each crêpe with salt to taste and 1 teaspoon of the shallots, roll up or fold the crêpe in quarters, and serve immediately, while hot.

4 to 5 servings

Buckwheat Crêpes
Galettes au Sarrasin

The buckwheat *galette*, or crêpe, is the true crêpe of Brittany, the one that is still a staple on some farms. In the old days, every farmwife had her *billig*, a three-legged crêpe pan that stood right over the fire. She would spend all day Friday—a meatless day in the Catholic church—making *galettes* on the *billig* and mounding them on the table as she deftly scooped them off. After every third crêpe or so, she would take a rag that sat in a pot of lard and egg yolks and run it over the *billig*, to oil it for the following *galettes*. Many crêperies in Brittany use the same antiquated, though efficient, system.

Lacy, toasty, tender, these are generally served with a pat of butter, and nothing is better straight from the griddle.

Now crêperies offer *galettes*, which are savory and can be filled with everything, from a fried egg to ham and cheese to

vegetables. White-flour crêpes (see Index) are lightly sweetened and served as dessert.

I love these crêpes, which are both lacy and substantial, nutty tasting and nourishing. It isn't the easiest batter to work with, and as they say in Brittany, it takes a *tour de main,* or some experience, to get the crepes just right. Do not despair if they are irregular in any way. They are delicious, no matter what they look like.

ASTUCES . . . .

• *The crêpe batter should be thinly spread—just thicker than a veil—on the bottom of the skillet. It will have holes in it, and it will be thinner at the edges than in the center (the thinner spots cook to a wonderful crisp toastiness). I use a nonstick crêpe pan or a nonstick skillet and brush it with clarified butter every third crêpe or so. The best technique for spreading the batter is to pour it in the center of the pan with one hand, and with the other rotate and shake the pan so the batter runs and jiggles over the bottom, creating a thin layer. You can encourage the batter with a spatula if you like, though I've found that it tends to gum up the crêpe.*

• *Steady, relatively high heat is the trick for crêpes. The pan should be hot enough that the batter sizzles when it hits, but not so hot that it bounces and bubbles and won't affix enough to make a flat crêpe. There will be small holes in the batter.*

. . . .

1¾ cups plus 1 tablespoon (240 g)
   buckwheat flour
2¼ cups (560 ml) water
2 large eggs
½ teaspoon sea salt
1 tablespoon Clarified Butter
   (page 519)

1. Place the flour in a medium-size bowl. Slowly whisk in the water to form a smooth batter. Then whisk in the eggs and the salt. Whisk vigorously for several minutes, until the batter is smooth and the ingredients are thoroughly combined. The batter will be quite thin but elastic; when you lift the whisk, the batter will drop off in "ropes." You may use it immediately or let it sit for up to 2 hours, loosely covered. If it sits, whisk it to blend the ingredients before using.

2. Heat a 10½-inch (26½ cm) nonstick or cast-iron skillet or crêpe pan over medium-high heat. Brush it lightly with clarified butter.

3. Whisk the batter quickly to mix it.

4. Pour ⅓ cup (80 ml) of the batter in the center of the skillet and quickly rotate the skillet to spread the batter as evenly as possible across the bottom. It is fine if the batter is thicker in the center than at the edges.

5. Cook the crêpe until it begins to curl up on the edges, about 1½ minutes. If it is browning too quickly, reduce the heat slightly. Using your fingers, carefully pick up the edge and gently pull the crêpe from the skillet, flip it over, and continue cooking just until it is set on the other side, about 30 seconds. As the crêpes are done, stack them on a baking sheet and keep, covered with a tea towel, in a low oven as you continue with the recipe.

About 10 crêpes

At Day's End

Picture a farmhouse, empty most of the day because the farmers—the husband and his wife, and perhaps the older children—are all in the fields. Go into the kitchen, lit only by a window near the door. There, near or even in the fireplace, hang ham, sausages, slab bacon—whatever is left of the most recently killed pig. Just outside the door, somewhere off to the left between the house and the nearby forest, is the vegetable garden.

Though the onset of winter has declared itself, the garden is still green with leeks and Savoy cabbages. There are carrots and turnips, too, covered with straw to keep them from freezing when the weather turns very cold. The potatoes are in a part of the barn where they stay cold, but are kept from freezing by the warmth of the animals.

The day ends at dusk, and the farmers return. The wife goes into the kitchen for a knife, then back into the garden to cut a cabbage. Into the barn for potatoes, back to the kitchen with her harvest.

After a quick hand washing, she starts to prepare the meal. She has already collected the day's eggs and milk; her supply of flour is good. She grabs a hunk of slab bacon and slices off a good-size piece. She mixes up some batter for crêpes, then removes the skin of the bacon and minces the bacon fine. She dices the cabbage, peels the potatoes, brings a big pot of water to a boil.

While the vegetables are boiling she makes the crêpes, which are dotted with pieces of bacon, what the French call *lardons*. She works with the economy of movement born of many years' experience, turning and flipping crêpes quickly.

Though the meal is basic and plain, the kitchen is filled with wonderful aromas. The cabbage, picked so fresh, is incredibly sweet and green tasting, its aroma mouthwatering as it mingles with that of the bacon.

Perhaps it is nostalgia to yearn for such food. I know perfectly well the work required to create it is far from romantic, as is the life that can surround it. Still, I've met many farm families who do appreciate their food, who are proud of its quality. They work hard and they eat well, and they know that because it's simple and the result of their labor, they're getting the best possible food there is. Who wouldn't be proud?

Shell Beans in Walnut Oil

Cocos à l'Huile de Noix

→•••←

There is just a small window each year, at the end of summer into fall, that lets in that most flavorful of beans, the shell bean. There are many varieties, but in French markets, they are all referred to as *haricots à écosser*, beans to be shelled.

These tender, succulent beans are so nutty and flavorful, their tender texture so satisfyingly substantial, that I can sit down and eat practically the whole bowl single-handedly. They cook in minutes, and they get better as they sit, being best about an hour after they're blended with the oil.

This is my favorite way to prepare them. I vary the herbs, and I sometimes use olive oil. Fresh summer savory or rosemary are naturals, and sea salt is essential.

4 pounds (2 kg) fresh shell beans, such as
*   cranberry beans or Jacob's cattle, shelled,*
*   to give 6 cups (700 g) shelled beans*
Sea salt
1 tablespoon fresh summer savory leaves or
*   fresh rosemary leaves, or 1 teaspoon*
*   dried (optional)*
3 tablespoons walnut oil
1 large clove garlic, peeled, green germ
*   removed, and minced*
Freshly ground black pepper

1. Place the beans in a large heavy saucepan and cover with water. Add about 2 teaspoons sea salt, cover, and bring to a boil. Reduce the heat so the beans are boiling gently, and cook until they are tender, about 13 minutes.

2. While the beans are cooking, mince the herbs if you are using them.

3. Blend the walnut oil, garlic, and herbs in a large serving bowl. Drain the beans and add them, tossing so they are thoroughly coated, and season to taste with salt and pepper. Either serve the beans immediately or let them cool to room temperature. The flavor will improve as the beans sit.

6 generous servings

Savory— an Herbal Wake-up Call

Savory is a popular herb in France, particularly throughout the Mediterranean area, where it is sprinkled in one heady dish after another. Medieval Provençal texts tout its tonic effects, claiming that it wakes up even the most somnolent lust. During the same time, certain religious orders even prohibited its use in cooking so it wouldn't trouble the serenity of the community. During pagan rituals then, students and clerics elected a "bishop" for the day, who was crowned with a ring of savory, then paraded through throngs of revelers heady from drinking a liqueur in which were macerated fistfuls of . . . savory. Shocked and affronted, the church put a stop to such wanton lack of decorum by prohibiting the ritual. Today the ways of savory are more acceptable—it brightens up dishes of tender-cooked beans, livens soups and stews, brings sunshine to grilled meat.

Spelt with Bacon
Epeautre au Lardons

Spelt is an ancient grain, perhaps the oldest form of wheat ever cultivated. It is reputedly from Egypt, where it was considered of such value that it was placed in tombs alongside jewels and other treasures intended for comfort in the next life. It was rediscovered in a tomb, and the grains that had sat there for eons sprouted and multiplied.

Spelt has long been grown in Provence, high in the hills that support little other than goats in search of forage. It shows up in old Provençal texts, prepared in a variety of ways. Because the grain is encased in a rather thick shell that must be discarded before it can be cooked—an operation that was always performed by hand—its cultivation largely disappeared. With the invention of automatic shelling methods, however, its cultivation is now expanding, again in the hills where little else will grow. Farmers in and around the picturesque town of Sault grow spelt, and the local pâtisserie offers pastries made with spelt flour. They are light, buttery, and delicious.

Spelt, *épeautre* in French and *espeute* in Provençal, is filled with vitamins and minerals, and it has gentle nutty flavor and a wonderful, almost chewy texture. It is used in soups and stews, or served simply like this. It is available in the U.S. in health-food stores, but if you can't find it, you can substitute wheat berries.

Serve this as a main course, along with a hearty salad and a bottle of Coteaux d'Aix-en-Provence Rouge. Use it as a basic recipe and vary it according to your taste. Try adding roasted bell peppers, or mince some fresh basil along with a clove or two of garlic to add right before you serve it.

10 ounces (300 g) slab bacon, rind
    removed, cut into 1 x ¼ x ¼-inch
    (2½ x ½ x ½ cm) pieces
1 large onion, peeled and diced
2 cloves garlic, peeled, green germ
    removed, and minced
2½ cups (575 g) spelt, rinsed well
1 teaspoon sea salt
Freshly ground black pepper
2 cups (500 ml) Chicken Stock (page 504)
2½ cups (625 ml) water
1 bouquet garni (5 parsley stems,
    3 imported bay leaves, 2 green leek
    leaves, 12 sprigs fresh thyme, tied in
    cheesecloth)
3 whole cloves

1. Brown the slab bacon in a large heavy saucepan over medium-high heat, stirring frequently, until golden on all sides, about 7 minutes. Remove the bacon with a slotted spoon and set it aside on a plate. Discard all but 2 tablespoons of the bacon fat in the pan.

2. Add the onion and garlic to the pan and cook, stirring frequently, until the onion softens and begin to turn translucent, about 5 minutes. Add the spelt and cook, stirring frequently, until it begins to turn slightly golden and gives off a toasty aroma, about 5 minutes.

3. Add the salt (see Note) and pepper to taste, the stock, water, bouquet garni, and cloves. Stir, cover, and bring to a boil. Reduce the heat to medium and boil gently, partially covered, until the spelt is tender and has absorbed much of the liquid, 25 to 35 minutes (the cooking time will vary, depending on the age of the grain). There will still be some liquid in the spelt. The spelt should be tender but somewhat chewy.

4. Remove the pan from the heat, cover it completely, and let it sit for 10 minutes. Then drain the spelt, discarding any cooking liquid. Discard the bouquet garni and the cloves (you'll have to fish a bit for them). Correct the seasoning, stir in the bacon, and serve.

6 to 8 main-course servings; 10 to 12 side-dish servings

NOTE: If the bacon you use is very salty, wait to season with salt until just before the spelt has finished cooking.

Spring Vegetables
Légumes Printanières

➤•••◄

This recipe came to me on the wings of an angel, I'm certain. One day at the market, I was standing in line at my favorite stand, list in hand. When my turn came, I asked for two pounds of carrots, and the farmer looked at me, stricken. "We only have these left—we've run out," he said pointing to a little bunch at the bottom of a crate. "How could I have forgotten to bring more carrots? How stupid. I've got peas this week."

Seeing my confusion, his wife soon helped me out: "We always cook peas and carrots together, with a little butter, some new onions, and a head of lettuce, just until everything is tender."

She rattled off her recipe and technique, looking at her other regular customers for approval. The recipe sounded so simple that I took the rest of their carrots, and everything else I needed, and went right home and made it.

It was so good I felt I'd never eaten a fresh pea or carrot before. Get the best vegetables you can and try it. It's elegant to eat, and to look at.

1½ tablespoons unsalted butter

1¾ pounds (875 g) carrots, peeled and cut into thin rounds

10 ounces (300 g) pearl onions, peeled and very thinly sliced

3 shallots, peeled, cut in half lengthwise, then into thin half-moon slices

Sea salt

1 cup (250 ml) water

Freshly ground black pepper

4 pounds (2 kg) fresh peas in their pods, to give 4 cups (600 g) shelled peas

1 head (1 pound; 500 g) butter lettuce, leaves separated, heart left intact, and rinsed

1. Melt the butter in a large heavy saucepan over medium heat. Add the carrots, onions, and shallots, stirring so they are coated with the butter. Season lightly with salt. Cover and cook, stirring occasionally, until the carrots are softened but still have plenty of texture, about 8 minutes.

2. Stir in the water, season with salt and pepper, and continue cooking, covered, until the carrots are nearly tender, an additional 8 minutes. Add the peas and stir. Then lay the lettuce heart and leaves over the vegetables. Cover, and cook until the lettuce leaves are wilted and the peas are done to your liking (I like them bright green and just cooked through to a juicy tenderness), 10 to 15 minutes.

3. Adjust the seasonings and serve.

4 to 6 servings

Swiss Chard and Artichoke Gratin
Gratin de Blette et de Fonds d'Artichauts

I n Provence, this gratin was traditionally baked in the wood-burning bread oven for Christmas Eve supper. Substantial and deeply flavored, it is still a favorite on the Provençal Christmas Eve table.

I don't necessarily reserve this for Christmas, however—it's just too good. With its overflow of rich green flavor, its vitamins, its haunting touch of anchovies, it is the first dish I think of when I see Swiss chard and artichokes at the market.

Serve it as a main lunch course, with a salad and plenty of bread. Try a Côtes de Roussillon alongside.

FOR THE VEGETABLES
2½ pounds (1¼ kg) Swiss chard, rinsed
4 large artichokes, prepared as directed in "Preparing Artichoke Hearts" (page 149)
12 anchovy fillets
½ cup (125 ml) milk

FOR THE BECHAMEL
1 cup (250 ml) milk, or more as needed
1 imported bay leaf
1½ tablespoons unsalted butter
1½ tablespoons unbleached all-purpose flour
2 cloves garlic, peeled, green germ removed and minced
Sea salt and freshly ground black pepper

1 tablespoon olive oil, for garnish

1. Bring a large pot of salted water to a boil (2 tablespoons salt for 4 quarts; 4 l

water) and add the artichoke hearts. Cook until they are tender through but not mushy, 35 to 40 minutes. Drain, and as soon as they are cool enough to handle, scrape out the choke with a stainless-steel spoon (or your fingers). Cut the artichoke hearts into very thin slices and set aside.

2. Bring another large pot of salted water to a boil. Fill a separate large bowl with ice water, and spread several tea towels out on a work surface.

3. Trim the stem ends, then cut the stems from the chard leaves. Add the chard stems to the boiling water, return to a boil, and cook until they are tender and almost translucent, 8 to 10 minutes. Using a slotted spoon, transfer the stems to the bowl of ice water. When they are chilled through, transfer them to tea towels to drain.

4. Add the Swiss chard leaves to the boiling water. Bring to a boil and cook until they are tender, 4 to 5 minutes. Transfer the leaves to the ice water, and when they are chilled through, drain them.

5. Place the anchovy fillets in a shallow bowl and cover them with the milk. Let soak for 20 minutes (this removes the salt). Drain, rinse lightly, and pat dry.

6. Preheat the oven to 400°F (200°C).

7. Prepare the béchamel: Combine the milk and the bay leaf in a small saucepan over medium-high heat. When tiny bubbles form around the edge of

the pan, remove it from the heat, cover, and let infuse for 10 minutes.

8. Melt the butter in a medium-size heavy saucepan over medium heat. Whisk in the flour, and after the mixture begins to bubble, cook it for 2 minutes (this removes the flour taste). Strain the hot milk into the mixture and cook, stirring constantly, until the sauce thickens to the consistency of heavy cream. If the sauce becomes too thick, stir in up to 2 tablespoons additional milk. Stir the garlic into the béchamel, and season to taste with salt and pepper.

9. Coarsely chop the Swiss chard stems and leaves. Place half of the Swiss chard in a medium-size baking dish, and season lightly with salt. Top with two thirds of the sliced artichoke hearts, and season them lightly with salt. Arrange the remaining Swiss chard over the artichokes and season lightly with salt; top with the remaining artichoke slices, again seasoning with salt. Then pour the béchamel over the top, nudging the vegetables so it runs down into them. Arrange the anchovies in pairs forming six X's on top of the gratin. Cover with aluminum foil and bake in the center of the oven until the gratin is hot and bubbling, 25 minutes.

10. Remove from the oven, drizzle with the olive oil, and serve.

6 to 8 servings

Wild Mushrooms in the Dordogne

=

66 *V*oilà, here's my Mercedes. We're bound for the *autoroute*," cried Gabriel Sol as he rolled a vintage 2CV (France's version of the VW Beetle) out of the stone garage and drove along a narrow dirt road. "I call this the *autoroute*," he said as he veered off the track, across a field, and nearly bumped into a chestnut tree. He parked the car and we got out.

I was on a mushroom hunt near the tiny hamlet of Sagournat, in the Dordogne, with Gabriel and his wife, Marie-Rose. "If we don't find any mushrooms," Marie-Rose said, donning a crumpled cap and grabbing a basket from the car, "we can always harvest chestnuts."

The Sols headed straight to the woods, much of which they own, navigating it familiarly—they go out almost every fall day looking for mushrooms. Their favorites are cèpes and chanterelles, and as their guides, they use animal tracks and landmark trees and shrubs.

"We're looking for the *fleur de champignons*," said Marie-Rose as she walked, eyes to the ground. "It looks like a cloudy white flower on the ground, and it signals that cèpes are nearby."

Now in her seventies, Marie-Rose has lived in the stone farmhouse she shares with Gabriel all her life. She had hoped to do something besides farming—in fact, her dream was to be a seamstress—but when her elder brother was killed in World War II, the farm came to her, so she stayed on with her parents. She met Gabriel after he'd done a short stint in the seminary, and he joined her on the farm. Together they've cultivated everything from beans to corn, hunted everything from mushrooms to wild game, and now they help their daughter, my friend Dany Dubois, raise geese for foie gras.

Marie-Rose and Gabriel both love to get out and walk in the woods, and hunting for mushrooms gives them a reason to go. What they don't eat, they give to Dany, who runs a small restaurant at her nearby farm.

The Sols separated when they got deep into the woods, heading for their own spots.

"This year has been odd," Marie-Rose said. "We've found mushrooms in spots we never expected to, and have found none in spots that were always productive."

We heard a hoot from a nearby clump of trees. It was Gabriel, and he'd found a ring of *pieds de moutons*, or sheep's feet, a small, mild-flavored golden mushroom.

"They always grow in a ring, and I just knew if I looked carefully, I'd find some," he said. "If you girls would quit talking and start looking, you'd find some, too."

Marie-Rose looked at him, her eyes twinkling, and went back on her way. We came to a dirt track that wound among the trees. "This is the *chemin de Califours*," she said. "I remember playing here when I was a girl. The Romans used this road to hook our village up with Sarlat."

FOLLOW THOSE SLUGS

We kept our eyes down, looking under ferns and near tree roots for the telltale firm, dark brown cap of the cèpe. "Sometimes the slugs eat the brown skin off, and it makes them hard to find," she said.

"I like to follow the slugs," Gabriel piped up from behind us. "I figure if I follow them, eventually I'll come upon a mushroom."

Marie-Rose and I stumbled into a *tapis*, or rug, of golden chanterelles in a soft bed of leaves. Gabriel came to help, pulling out his well-worn mushroom knife to cut them right at the base. "This is the only way to pick mushrooms," he said, scornfully watching us pick them by hand.

"He says it's better that way. I don't see the difference," Marie-Rose said, laughing.

While they are generous about taking friends mushrooming, the Sols nonetheless guard their spots carefully. "Once we were hunting and I found some mushrooms and called Marie-Rose," Gabriel said. "She didn't answer, and I got worried because I was afraid something had happened to her. I finally found her in a huge patch of chanterelles. She hadn't wanted to answer me because she was afraid the other people in the woods would hear her and come find her mushrooms."

The Sols take their mushrooms home, and Marie-Rose carefully trims them, washes them, and then sautés them with some garlic in goose fat until they're tender. If there are many of one variety, she keeps them separate; otherwise she cooks them together. The rich and flavorful result is a simple feast, the reward of an afternoon walk in the woods.

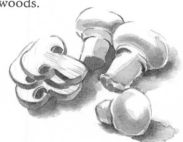

Melted Tomatoes
Confit de Tomates

When summer yields its abundance of tomatoes, this is a favorite way to prepare them on the farm. It takes practically no time to put together, and demands only fresh herbs and a modicum of patience.

Pearl onions add a great deal, but if you don't have them, don't deny yourself tomatoes cooked this way—they melt, turning sweet and delicious.

These are wonderful served as a first course (they will serve about 4), or alongside roasted poultry, and grilled meats and fish.

ASTUCES . . . .

• *Make this with good, ripe tomatoes—the cardboard variety from the supermarket will not provide good results.*

• *You may sprinkle a teaspoon of sugar over the tomatoes if you want to remove the slight acidic edge tomatoes develop as they cook. I like the edge—it provides great balance—but do as you prefer. Most farm cooks add the sugar.*

8 medium tomatoes, cored and
    cut crosswise in half
16 pearl onions, peeled
8 whole cloves garlic, unpeeled
2 tablespoons olive oil
Sea salt and freshly ground black pepper
1 teaspoon sugar (optional)
4 small sprigs fresh rosemary, or
    ½ teaspoon dried, crushed leaves
8 sprigs fresh thyme, or scant
    ½ teaspoon dried leaves
1 sprig fresh summer savory, or ¼ teaspoon
    dried leaves

1. Preheat the oven to 350°F (175°C).

2. Place the tomatoes, cut side down, in a nonreactive baking dish large enough to hold them in a single layer. (If they are slightly crowded at first, don't be concerned—they reduce in volume as they cook.)

3. Place the onions and garlic among the tomatoes, and drizzle the oil overall. Season generously with salt and pepper (and sugar, if you are using it), and lay the herbs atop the tomatoes.

4. Place the tomatoes in the bottom third of the oven and bake until they are melted and turning slightly golden on top, about 1 hour. Remove from the oven and let cool for at least 10 minutes before serving. You can make these several hours before you plan to eat, and serve them at room temperature.

4 to 6 servings

Baked Pasta with Caramelized Tomatoes
Gratin de Nouilles

Denise Lascourrèges was out in the vineyards, harvesting grapes as fast as she could when she looked at her watch and shrieked. She had twenty harvesters coming to lunch in an hour. She tipped her grapes into a waiting container, ran to the house, and produced this dish.

"I had no idea what I was going to cook, but you know," she said, laughing, "it was simply delicious. I surprised myself."

It *is* simply delicious, and what makes it so are the tomato halves, which are lightly cooked in olive oil so their skins turn a golden color, their cut sides become lusciously seared. They produce a wonderful tart and caramel-like sauce which is sumptuous over pasta. Mme. Lascourrèges served this dish with Gruyère cheese. I prefer it with Parmesan.

Serve with a Buzet or Sancerre Rouge.

5 good-size, slightly underripe tomatoes (see Note), cored

¼ cup (60 ml) olive oil

3 cloves garlic, peeled, halved, and green germ removed

1 cup (loosely packed) flat-leaf parsley leaves

Sea salt and freshly ground black pepper

10 ounces (300 g) dried pasta, such as fettuccine

½ cup (60 g) finely grated Parmesan cheese (optional)

1. Cut the tomatoes in half horizontally.

2. Place the oil in a large skillet over medium-high heat. When it is hot but not smoking (when small ripples move over its surface), add the tomatoes, cut side up. Cook, shifting them slightly in the pan to avoid scorching, until their skin is slightly bubbled on the bottom and has a golden spot on it, about 4 minutes. Turn the tomatoes over and continue cooking until the cut side is golden, about 6 minutes. Shake the pan two or three times to move the tomatoes around so they don't burn.

3. While the tomatoes are cooking, finely mince the garlic and parsley together.

4. Turn the tomatoes again, so the cut side is up. Working around the tomatoes, scrape up any browned bits from the bottom of the skillet. Sprinkle the tomatoes with the garlic and parsley, and season them generously with salt and pepper. Reduce the heat to medium and cover the skillet. Cook the tomatoes until they are tender through and the garlic is tender, about 10 minutes, shaking the pan occasionally to prevent the tomatoes from sticking. The juice from the tomatoes will turn a deep caramel color but it shouldn't burn.

5. While the tomatoes finish cooking, fill a large pot two-thirds full with salted water and bring it to a boil (2 tablespoons salt for 4 quarts; 4 l water). Add the pasta, stir, and cook just until it is al dente, about 10 minutes. Drain, reserving 1 cup (250 ml) of the pasta cooking liquid. Return the pasta to the pot, pour half the reserved cooking liquid over it, and toss so the pasta is thoroughly moistened.

6. Arrange the tomatoes around the edges of a large warmed platter. Deglaze the skillet with the remaining pasta cooking liquid, scraping up any browned bits, and pour that over the pasta as well. Toss so the liquid is well blended with the pasta. Transfer the pasta to the center of the serving platter, so it is surrounded with the tomatoes. Serve immediately, with the Parmesan cheese alongside.

4 to 6 servings

NOTE: If the usual globe variety isn't at its peak, use plum tomatoes, cutting them in half lengthwise. If you do have fresh garden tomatoes, pick them just before they turn ripe—their flavor and texture are best then, particularly for a dish like this.

Andrée Le Saint's Zucchini Gratin

Courgettes Gratinées d'Andrée Le Saint

→ ··· ←

The idea for this recipe comes from Pierre Le Saint, a *maraîcher* on the northern coast of Brittany, where he and his wife, Andrée Le Saint, cultivate baby vegetables and edible flowers on seventeen acres, working long days year-round. Mme. Le Saint used to keep house—and the farm books—while the couple's two sons were growing up, but now that they're on their own, she works on the farm. "I'd much rather do that than be at home," she says, laughing. "And you know what my favorite thing to do is after a long day at work? Put my feet under the table of a restaurant, where someone else has done the cooking!"

Mme. Le Saint was the first French woman I'd ever heard say that, and after I got over my culturally ingrained shock, I listened on. "Oh, I'll cook, and when I do I'm good at it," she said. "But I'd much rather be outside all day or in the greenhouses, busy and active and working." I understood her well, as I sat in her lovely living room, which was furnished with heavy, highly polished Breton furniture and so tidy, I hesitated to move. "I did my work in the house. Now it's time for me to be on the farm," she added.

"Still, she makes the best *courgettes gratinées* of anyone I know," M. Le Saint said. "Mmm. Just thinking about it, I get hungry."

Mme. Le Saint uses the zucchini that grow too large for them to sell as "babies." They're still tiny, tender, and succulent. I've tried this gratin with larger zucchini, too, and found it luscious. Just be sure the zucchini you get are firm and unblemished. They'll give you that wonderfully elusive, nutty flavor, which is so often overlooked in this most abundant of vegetables.

*1 cup (250 ml) Crème Fraîche (page 520),
    or heavy (or whipping) cream*
*3 cloves garlic, peeled, green germ
    removed, and minced*
*1 large shallot, peeled and minced
    (to give 2 generous tablespoons)*
2 teaspoons sea salt
Freshly ground black pepper
¼ teaspoon freshly grated nutmeg
*3 pounds (1½ kg) zucchini, trimmed and cut
    in very fine, almost paper-thin rounds*
1½ cups (125 g) grated Gruyère or Comté cheese

1. Preheat the oven to 375°F (190°C). Lightly butter a medium-size baking dish.

2. In a large bowl, whisk together the

crème fraîche, garlic, shallot, salt, pepper to taste, and nutmeg. Add the zucchini rounds and mix, using your hands or a very large rubber scraper, until the zucchini is thoroughly covered with crème fraîche. Transfer the zucchini to the prepared baking dish, pressing it gently into the pan so it forms an even layer. Then sprinkle with the cheese.

3. Bake in the center of the oven until the zucchini is tender through and the cheese is deep golden brown, about 45 minutes. Serve immediately.

6 to 8 servings

Sautéed Zucchini

Courgettes Sautées

The best zucchini tumble into the market all at once, but at least in the French marketplace, they are picked at the right moment. Never too large or too small, they are fresh and crisp, rich with nutty flavor.

This is one of my favorite ways to prepare zucchini, a vegetable my family thoroughly enjoys. I like to serve it with roast meats or fish, or with several other summer vegetable dishes like Tomato and Sweet Pepper Salad, either of the Pipérade recipes, and Grated Carrot Salad (see Index).

1 tablespoon olive oil

1 large shallot, peeled and cut crosswise into thin slices

4 or 5 medium zucchini (1¾ pounds/875 g total), cut into thin rounds

Sea salt and freshly ground black pepper

1 cup (loosely packed) fresh basil leaves

1. Place the oil and the shallot in a large skillet (preferably nonstick) over medium-high heat. Stir so the shallot is coated with the oil, and add the zucchini slices. Season with salt and pepper to taste, and cook, tossing or stirring frequently, until the zucchini are tender but not mushy, 5 to 7 minutes. Their flavor is wonderful if they are allowed to become slightly golden on each side.

2. While the zucchini are cooking, mince the basil leaves.

3. Transfer the zucchini to a shallow serving dish, add the basil, toss, and serve immediately or later, at room temperature.

6 servings

A Garden's Worth of Vegetables
Jardinière de Légumes

A *jardinière de légumes* is like an ode to spring, for it contains the first, the sweetest, perhaps the best vegetables of the year. It can be any mix you like, whatever is available. This recipe includes green asparagus, a relative novelty in France, regarded as a completely different vegetable from the traditional fat white variety. Green is preferable in this dish, because it adapts well to the preparation.

You may want to add a sprinkling of fresh thyme, which is sweet and gentle in spring, or even some of the year's first tarragon. My favorite way to serve it, however, is plain, seasoned with nothing but salt, pepper, and a touch of butter or oil. This can make a meal in itself, with a crisp white Riesling or a Bourgueil and some fresh homemade bread.

ASTUCES . . . .

• *Refreshing vegetables in ice water immediately stops the cooking, so they maintain the desired texture and color. Leave them in the water just long enough to cool—any longer and they may become waterlogged.*

• *All the vegetables in this mixture are cooked in the same water, beginning with the lightest flavored (potatoes and carrots) and ending with the more strongly flavored (garlic and turnips). The resulting cooking water makes a wonderful vegetable broth.*

8 ounces (250 g) small new potatoes,
　peeled
Sea salt
3 small carrots, peeled, cut in half
　lengthwise, and then into thin
　half-rounds
1 pound (500 g) green asparagus,
　trimmed
8 ounces (250 g) green beans, trimmed
　and cut on the diagonal into 1½-inch
　(4 cm) lengths
1 pound (500 g) small white (boiling)
　onions, trimmed and peeled
12 cloves garlic, peeled, halved, and green
　germ removed
10 ounces (300 g) small spring turnips,
　trimmed, peeled, and cut into thin
　vertical slices
2 tablespoons olive oil, or unsalted
　butter
1 pound (500 g) fresh peas in the
　pod (to give ¾ to 1 cup shelled),
　or ¾ to 1 cup frozen peas
Freshly ground black pepper
Several sprigs fresh thyme, for garnish

1. Fill a large bowl with ice water, and spread several tea towels out on your work surface.

2. If the potatoes are the size of large marbles, leave them whole. If they are the size of golf balls, cut them in half or in quarters. Bring a good-size saucepan of salted water (1 tablespoon salt for 2 quarts; 2 l water) to a boil over high heat. Add the potatoes, cover, and return to a boil. Then reduce the heat to medium so the potatoes are boiling gently,

and cook until they are just tender through, 10 to 15 minutes. Using a slotted spoon, remove them from the water and set them aside.

3. Return the water to a boil and add the carrots. Cover, return to a boil, and cook until they are tender but still slightly crisp, 3 minutes. Remove the carrots with a slotted spoon and plunge them into the ice water. When the carrots are cool, remove them from the ice water and place on a tea towel to drain. Gently pat them dry.

4. Cut the asparagus stems on the diagonal into 1½-inch (4 cm) lengths, leaving the tips intact.

5. Return the cooking water to a boil and add the asparagus stems (leave the tips uncooked). Cook for 2 minutes, and transfer them to the ice water with a slotted spoon. When the asparagus is cool, transfer it to a tea towel to drain. Gently pat dry.

6. Repeat this process with the remaining vegetables (except the peas) in the given order, changing the refreshing water when necessary to keep it ice cold. Cook the green beans for 3 minutes, the onions for 2 minutes, the garlic cloves for 5 to 7 minutes, the turnips for 3 minutes. (The vegetables can be prepared to this point up to 8 hours in advance: If you are holding them briefly, cover them with another tea towel to keep them fresh and slightly moist. Or roll them up gently in the towels, place the bundles in plastic bags, and refrigerate. Refrigerate the asparagus tips and the peas as well.) Reserve the vegetable cooking liquid for another use.

7. Just before serving the vegetables, heat the oil in a large nonstick skillet over medium heat. Add the peas and the asparagus tips first, tossing them in the pan so they are coated with the oil. Season them with salt and pepper to taste, and then add the remaining vegetables. Toss the vegetables so they are all lightly coated with oil. Cook, tossing frequently, until they are sizzling hot, about 10 minutes. If you like your vegetables slightly golden, toss them less frequently. They are best, however, if they are just heated through rather than seared. Adjust the seasoning and transfer to a warmed serving bowl. Garnish with the fresh thyme, if desired, and serve immediately.

Serves 6 to 8

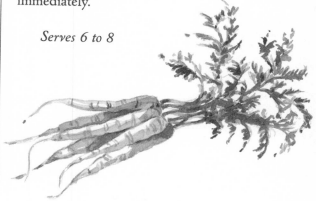

LE FOUR À PAIN

The Bread Oven

There was a time when most farms in France had their own bread ovens, and farmers would rotate the task of firing up the oven for everyone in the neighborhood to bake their bread. When the bread-baking was done, the farmwives came laden with gratins and pizzas, *cakes* (sweet or savory baking-powder breads) and tarts, and put them in the oven to bake in the residual heat.

Ovens still exist on farms, but are put to use infrequently, brought back to life mostly on special occasions. Then, following the farm tradition, bread is baked first and other dishes baked afterward.

Even when a wood-burning oven no longer exists on the farm, the dishes that were baked within do, and they make up a good part of the soul of French farm cooking. You'll find many examples here in the form of crisp-crusted breads and pizza, bubbling savory tarts, rich brioche. Mouthwatering, hearty, flavorful, they capture the essence of the French *le four à pain*.

The Starter
Le Levain

→•←

*T*he following takes you through the care and feeding of le levain, *the bread starter used in the Sourdough Bread recipe that follows, and other recipes in this chapter. Creating the starter is part of the Sourdough Bread recipe. While starter is hardy and tough, it is nonetheless a living thing. It needs nourishment, which it gets if bread is made every three or four days. If not, then it needs to be fed, and certain minimum and maximum temperatures should be respected.*

CARING FOR YOUR STARTER

To keep the starter going, you must always remember to cut out ¾ cup (185 ml) worth of dough from the loaf you are making, right before you form the loaf. Place the starter in an earthenware bowl, and cover it loosely with a towel if you plan to use it soon. The ideal temperature for a frequently used starter is between 68° and 70°F (20° and 21°C). If you aren't going to use it within a week, allow it to go dormant by covering and refrigerating it.

If you want to leave your starter out of the refrigerator so it is ready to use at a moment's notice, you will need to "feed" it every 4 days to keep it active. To feed it, blend 1 tablespoon flour and about 2 tablespoons water into the starter. Judge the amount of water by the consistency of the starter—it should be neither too runny nor too stiff, but about the consistency of heavy cake batter. Remember to cover it loosely after each feeding.

REVIVING THE STARTER IF YOU FORGET IT

If you forget about your unrefrigerated starter for a week or so, it is probably fine, though weak. Feed it, cover it loosely, and let it become active again—you'll know by the bubbles on the surface and its general air of liveliness.

USING A REFRIGERATED STARTER

Remove the starter from the refrigerator at least 8 hours before you plan to make bread, and feed it. Cover it loosely and when bubbles form on top and the starter is active, it is ready.

FREEZING YOUR STARTER

I always keep a "reserve" starter in the freezer, in case of emergencies. To freeze a starter, place it in a plastic bag filled with flour, burying it in the flour to protect it from any air that might seep into the container. Remove it from the freezer the day before you plan to use it, dust it off, place it in a bowl, and loosely cover it. When it has thawed, feed it and loosely cover. When bubbles have formed on top and it is active, it is ready to use.

YOUR RISING BASKET AND CLOTH

Rising baskets called bannetons, *lined with linen and specially made for bakeries, are available from La Vannerie de Villaines-les-Rochers, 37190 Azay-le-Rideau (011.33.47.45.43.03). You can order just about any dimension you'd like, and they will send it to you. They like to be paid by check or cash, not credit cards.*

If you don't have a special basket, you may use any basket you have, or even a metal colander. Line it with a cotton or linen towel or cloth and sprinkle heavily with flour. Dust the loaf all over with flour, set it in the receptacle, and dust it again on top so that all surfaces of the bread are well floured. The loaf will likely stick at first, but as the towel "ages," it will develop a layer of flour on it that will help protect from stickiness. (The floury residue that stays on the towel may turn black, but this is what you want. It is not necessary to wash the towel between bakings. Many bakers treasure their blackened ban-netons, for the black is a sign that wild yeasts are present, working to make the bread light and flavorful.) You must continue to dust loaves with flour when you put them in the receptacle, no matter how black the towel gets, but not quite as much as those first few times.

TIRED STARTER

If your bread lacks air holes and seems heavier than it should be, try adding ¼ teaspoon active dry yeast when you blend the starter with water. It gives the wild yeasts a kick, and results in lighter bread. It may have the undesired effect of reducing the sour flavor, but this is temporary. Don't add yeast each time, but just now and then, if you sense the starter is tired and needs some energy.

KNEAD OR NOT

When working with a dough like the one for any of the pains au levain, *you are technically beating it, scooping one hand under the dough mass, then bringing that hand toward you and up through the dough as you rotate the bowl clockwise with your other hand. Dough for* pain au levain *is not like regular bread dough, because it is loose and soft. It firms up as you add flour and work it, but it will never be firm enough to knead on a work surface like regular bread dough. The easiest way to make a loaf is to work the dough in the bowl until the very end, when you turn it out on a well-floured surface and quickly form a loaf, as directed in the recipe, which will hold the loaf together long enough to get it into the prepared rising basket.*

NOTE: *When you are adding ingredients like raisins, seeds, or oatmeal or other grains, to* pain au levain, *they stay in the starter and become part of subsequent loaves of bread. If you don't want them to be part of the starter, remove the starter before you add such ingredients to the bread.*

Sourdough Bread

Pain au Levain

→···←

This is the basic bread dough that was made on the farm. It requires nothing but flour, water, salt, and the wild yeasts that roam in the air. Today, bread like this can still be found in country bakeries and in some specialized bakeries in cities and towns as well (such as Lionel Poilâne, Max Poilâne, or Poujauran in Paris), where it is becoming more and more popular. It's no secret that the French love bread, and increasingly they are returning to country bread, with its ivory-colored crumb, its hearty texture, its crackling crust. In our town of Louviers alone, there are three bakers within a few blocks who make bread similar to this—and they always run out before the day is over.

You won't need to buy bread again if you get into the rhythm of making this loaf. You may use an electric mixer, but if you want the real thing, with lots of big holes in a tender, moist interior, and a rich and crunchy crust that tastes almost like molasses, do as the farmwife did and make it by hand.

My husband has baked our bread for the past twelve years, and he has taught many of his friends this simple art. He loves to make it, and most men who have learned from him continue to do so as well.

I love to make it, too, however, and we occasionally have competitions to see whose bread is lightest, most flavorful, most active. There is never a surplus, no matter who is making it, for the bread disappears about as quickly as it can be sliced.

The first time you do this, the entire process will take about a week. The first

three or four loaves are likely to be flat, but don't be discouraged. The starter just needs to find its equilibrium. If you keep at it, it won't be long until your loaves are mounded and wonderful. They will never rise as high as a yeast loaf, though, so keep your expectations within the realm of reality. Once you have a good starter established, you'll be able to skip to step 5 and prepare the dough just one day ahead.

ASTUCES . . . .

• *Before proceeding with the recipe, be sure you read "The Starter," on page 314.*

• *Be sure the basket you use for the long rising isn't too high for the loaf, or when you turn it into the baking pan, the loaf will fall and deflate. The loaf should rise just about to the edge of the basket.*

. . . .

> 5 to 6 cups (670 to 800 g) unbleached
>   all-purpose flour (see Note)
> 2½ cups (625 ml) lukewarm water
>   (see Note)
> 1 tablespoon sea salt

1. Place 1 cup (135 g) of the flour and ½ cup (125 ml) of the water in a medium-size bowl and whisk together. The mixture will be the consistency of thick pancake batter.

2. Cover the bowl with a kitchen towel and leave it in a warm place until the mixture has a slight sour smell and has puffed up and is bubbling, about 3 days. Don't even look at it the first 2 days; just leave it to attract the wild yeasts that are floating in the air. On the third day, check it. It should be lively, with bubbles in it and possibly a slightly dark surface; this means the yeasts are doing their work.

3. Add an additional 1 cup (135 g) flour and ½ cup (125 ml) water to the mixture, and mix well. Cover the bowl with the towel and let it sit in a warm place for an additional 24 to 48 hours, until the mixture has bubbles and emits a nice sour smell. The surface may have turned slightly dark.

4. Now you have a lively starter and are

>···<

"Never put bread

on its back,

because you don't earn

bread on your back."

—Breton incantation
against laziness

>···<

ready to make your first loaf of bread. Place a clean cotton tea towel in a basket or a colander, and dust it heavily with flour.

5. Transfer the starter to a large mixing bowl and add the remaining 1½ cups (375 ml) lukewarm water. Stir in the salt. Then gradually add the remaining 3 to 4 cups (405 to 540 g) flour, about 1 cup at a time, mixing all the while. If you are using your hands, make wide, open movements to incorporate as much air as possible into the dough. Mix until the dough is thick, but still very soft (too soft to knead easily on a board like you would other dough) and no longer sticks to your hands or the sides of the bowl. This will take about 15 minutes (see Note). To test the consistency of the dough, touch it quickly with a clean finger. If some dough sticks to your finger, add flour in small amounts until the dough is the proper consistency.

The Bread Cage

→·←

On the farm, in days past, the month's bread was stored in special wooden bread cages, which were hung from the ceiling so the rats wouldn't decimate the supply. By month's end, that bread was hard. Often the farm family would have to soak it in water or milk so they could eat it. Though bread cages are mostly relegated to museums now, many homes have an **hûche à pain,** *a tall wooden bread box, or a bread bag hanging on a hook, somewhere in the kitchen.*

6. Cut out ¾ cup (185 ml) of starter for your next loaf. Turn the remaining dough out onto a well-floured work surface. Form a round loaf by bringing the edges of the dough on three sides into the center, pushing each edge into the dough so it sticks. Bring the fourth edge of the dough all the way over to the opposite side of the loaf (bypassing the center, where the other edges adhere to the loaf) and press it gently but firmly into the dough. This fourth edge is the "key" that holds the entire loaf together.

7. Quickly scoop up the loaf and place it, "key" side down, in the prepared basket. Let it rise, uncovered, in a warm spot (68° to 70°F; 20° to 21°C) until the dough has puffed and risen by about one third and is looking stretched, at least 8 hours.

8. Preheat the oven to 500°F (260°C).

9. Heavily dust the top of the loaf with flour, covering the entire surface. Set a 10-to-12-inch (25 to 30 cm) round pan with 2-inch (5 cm) sides over the loaf in the basket. Holding the pan and the basket firmly, flip them over so the loaf lands in the pan. Slash the top of the loaf three or four times, making a crosshatch pattern, and place on the center rack of the oven. Bake for 20 minutes. Then reduce the temperature to 450°F (230°C) and continue baking until the loaf sounds hollow when tapped and the crust is golden and hard, about 40 minutes.

10. Remove the pan from the oven and turn the loaf out onto a wire rack. Let it cool completely before slicing.

1 loaf (nearly 2 pounds; 1 kg) and ¾ cup (185 ml) starter

NOTES: To make whole wheat Pain au Levain, simply substitute 2 cups (270 g) whole wheat flour for 2 cups (270 g) unbleached all-purpose flour.

• If using already prepared starter, you will need only 3 to 4 cups (405 to 540 g) flour and 1½ cups (375 ml) water.

• You may do the mixing in the electric mixer, beating at the lowest speed for about 10 minutes, until the dough is ropy.

Long Loaf
Pain Long

>·····<

This loaf reminds me of the three-foot-long (1 m) loaves René Neuville, a farmer and baker, pulls out of the oven on his farm, high on a hill in the Dordogne. Though more modest in size, this one has the gutsy quality and hard crust of a true country bread.

The preparation here is slightly different than for other sourdough breads in this book. Because of the addition of yeast, it rises for a shorter time, gets turned out and worked into a shape, then is left again to rise for a relatively short time. Long bread like this has a great percentage of crust to crumb—ideal for people who love crust.

The wheat germ adds nuttiness and, I believe, encourages additional lightness. You may also add raisins, flax seed, sesame seeds, or as I have here, rolled oats.

¾ cup (185 ml) sourdough starter
   (see recipe for Sourdough Bread on
   page 317, steps 1 to 3))
3 cups (750 ml) lukewarm water
¼ teaspoon active dry yeast
½ cup (60 g) untoasted wheat germ
1 tablespoon sea salt
About 6¾ cups (910 g) unbleached
   all-purpose flour
1 cup (105 g) rolled oats

1. In a large mixing bowl whisk together the starter, water, and yeast. Add the wheat germ and salt and mix well. Gradually add 4 cups (540 g) of the flour, 1 cup (135 g) at a time, and mix it with your hand until the dough begins to stiffen. Add the rolled oats, mix well, and continue to add the flour, working the dough vigorously, until it no longer sticks to your hands. This is a firmer dough than most *pains au levain*, so it will feel more like regular bread dough, but still soft and somewhat limp. Working in the flour should take 10 to 15 minutes. If you've added all the flour and your hands still stick to the dough, clean your hands well, then touch the dough quickly with a finger. It will probably come away completely clean. If it doesn't, add more flour in small amounts until your hand comes away clean.

2. Cover the mixing bowl and let the dough rest in a warm spot (68° to 70°F; 20° to 21°C) until it has risen slightly (less than one third, but with a definite lightness), about 4 hours.

3. Turn out the dough onto a floured work surface and knead it for about 3 minutes. Shape the dough by patting it flat, then

folding or rolling it to make a 20-inch-long (50 cm) oval. It will be floppy and limp.

4. Thickly dust a baking sheet (or two baking sheets without raised edges if needed to get the desired length) with flour. Transfer the loaf quickly to the baking sheet and dust the top with flour. Let the bread rest, uncovered, for about 1½ hours—it will rise perceptibly, but not a great deal.

5. Preheat the oven to 500°F (260°C).

6. Using a very sharp knife or a razor blade, make ¼-inch (½ cm) criss-cross slashes along the top of the loaf. Bake for 20 minutes. Reduce the heat to 450°F (230°C) and continue baking until the loaf is a deep golden brown and sounds hollow when tapped, about 1 hour.

Close to the Heart
>·←

In the Dordogne, women traditionally cut the bread by holding the loaf to their chest and cutting toward themselves with a large serrated knife. Men didn't practice this seemingly dangerous operation because their lives were considered too valuable. To this day, a woman on a farm in the Dordogne cuts the bread toward her chest.

7. Remove the bread from the oven and let it cool on a wire rack before slicing.

One 19-inch (48 cm) loaf

Sourdough Corn Bread
Pain de Maïs, au Levain

>···←

This bread is so toothsome and hearty, it almost makes a meal in itself. Because of the cornmeal, the interior of the bread, or *mie* as it's called in France, will have few large holes, and it will not rise as high as its white-flour cousin. Don't be concerned—bake it, let it cool, and enjoy it.

ASTUCE . . . .
• *Before proceeding with the recipe, be sure you read "The Starter," on page 314.*

¾ cup (185 ml) sourdough starter
  (see recipe for Sourdough Bread on
  page 317, steps 1 to 3)
3 cups (750 ml) water
1 tablespoon coarse sea salt
6½ cups (880 g) unbleached
  all-purpose flour
2 cups (280 g) coarse yellow cornmeal

1. Place the starter in a large mixing bowl, and using a whisk, incorporate the water to form a relatively smooth paste. Don't worry if there are some lumps—they will gradually disappear.

2. Whisk in the salt. Then add 1 cup (135 g) of the flour and whisk until smooth. Whisk in the cornmeal. Then continue whisking in flour until the dough becomes too stiff to whisk; this will be after about 3 cups (405 g) flour.

3. Retire the whisk and use your hands to add the remaining flour, 1 cup (135 g) at a time, using wide movements to incorporate as much air as you can. Continue mixing the dough until it is elastic and comes away from the sides of the bowl, leaving them almost clean, about 15 minutes. It should no longer stick to your hands.

4. Line a basket or a colander with a tea towel, and sprinkle the towel generously with flour. Heavily flour a work surface, and turn the dough out onto it. Cut out ¾ cup (185 ml) of starter for your next loaf (see Note). Turn the remaining dough out onto a well-floured work surface. Form a round loaf by bringing the edges of the dough on three sides into the center, pushing each edge into the dough so it

sticks. Bring the fourth edge of the dough all the way over to the opposite side of the loaf (bypassing the center, where the other edges adhere to the loaf) and press it gently but firmly into the dough. This fourth edge is the "key" that holds the entire loaf together.

5. Quickly pick up the loaf and deposit it in the prepared basket, "key" side down. Leave the dough in a warm spot (68° to 70°F; 20° to 21°C) until it has risen appreciably and is beginning to look stretched, at least 8 hours, and depending on the temperature and humidity, up to 12 hours.

6. Preheat the oven to 500°F (260°C).

7. Heavily dust the top of the loaf with flour, covering the entire surface. Set a 10- to 12-inch (25 to 30 cm) round pan with 2-inch (5 cm) sides over the loaf in the basket. Holding the pan and the basket firmly, flip them over so the loaf lands in the pan. Quickly slash the top several times with a sharp knife, and immediately place the loaf in the center of the oven. After 20 minutes, turn the oven temperature down to 450°F (230°C) and continue baking until the loaf is a good golden brown and sounds hollow when tapped, 40 to 50 minutes.

8. Turn out the loaf onto a wire cooling rack and let it cool thoroughly before slicing.

1 loaf (nearly 2 pounds; 1 kg)

NOTE: After you've made this dough, your starter will have cornmeal in it, which will lightly flavor future loaves. If you are a purist, you may want to have a separate, "pure" starter on hand.

Raisin Sourdough Bread

Pain au Levain et aux Raisins

This may be my favorite sourdough bread, and it is certainly one of the most sought after in bakeries where it is made. It is studded with sweet, rich-tasting raisins, whose flavor plays off the almost caramel flavor of the crisp, darkened crust. It is wonderful as toast, simply eaten as is, or topped with cheese.

I add the raisins after the fourth cup of flour, because I don't mind that they become part of my starter, and they are easier to add at that point. However, you may want to remove the starter after you've added all the flour, then incorporate the raisins.

ASTUCE . . . .
• *Before proceeding with the recipe, be sure you read "The Starter," on page 314.*

. . . .

¾ cup (185 ml) sourdough starter
    (see recipe for Sourdough Bread on
    page 317, steps 1 to 3)
3 cups (750 ml) lukewarm water
¼ teaspoon active dry yeast
1 tablespoon sea salt
4⅔ cups (630 g) unbleached all-purpose flour
    (see Note)
3 cups (405 g) whole-wheat flour (see Note)
1½ cups (250 g) raisins

1. Line a basket or a colander with a cot-
ton or linen tea towel, and heavily dust the towel with flour.

2. In a large mixing bowl, whisk together the starter, water, and yeast. Add the salt, then gradually add the flour, 1 cup (135 g) at a time, blending it in with your hand. Mix vigorously for at least 10 minutes, until the dough has thickened, but is still quite soft, and does not stick to your hands or to the sides of the bowl. To test if it is at the right stage, touch the dough with a clean finger. If the finger comes away clean, the dough is just fine.

3. Cut out ¾ cup (185 ml) of starter for your next loaf. Mix in the raisins until they are evenly dispersed throughout the bread. Turn the dough out onto a well-floured work surface. Form a round loaf by bringing the edges of the dough on three sides into the center, pushing each edge into the dough so it sticks. Bring the fourth edge of the dough all the way over to the opposite side of the loaf (bypassing the center, where the other edges adhere to the loaf) and press it gently but

firmly into the dough. This fourth edge is the "key" which holds the entire loaf together.

4. Quickly pick up the loaf and deposit in the prepared basket, "key" side down, and dust lightly with flour. Let rise in a warm spot (68° to 70°F; 20° to 21°C) for at least 8 hours and as long as 12.

5. Preheat the oven to 500°F (260°C).

6. Heavily dust the top of the loaf with flour, covering the entire surface. Set a 10- to 12-inch (25 to 30 cm) round pan with 2-inch (5 cm) sides over the loaf in the basket. Holding the pan and the basket firmly, flip them over so the loaf lands in the pan. Slash the top several times with a sharp knife, and bake it in the center of the oven for 20 min-

Breakfast on the Farm

>·<

*T*he farmer gets up and out by dawn to milk the cows, feed the geese, begin his day in the fields. His fuel? A quick cup of warmed-over coffee loaded with sugar.

By 8:30 A.M., he's back and ready to eat, and by that time, the household is awake and the day is well on its way. Breakfast is set on the table—big bowls mark each place. A huge basket of fresh breads sits in the center of the table, flanked by a slab of pale yellow butter, an array of homemade jams, and a pitcher of warmed milk. If children will be eating, a tray holds hot chocolate or a pitcher of herb tea and a variety of cereals (they've invaded the French morning table, too).

Whoever made breakfast—usually the lady of the house, although if a fieldworker comes in early, chances are he'll get at it—brings in the coffee, steaming and stout.

If the farm is in Brittany, there is likely a stackful of crêpes, some leftover far breton, or a simple, light breakfast cake.

If the farm is in the Dordogne, fresh cheeses have their place, along with leftover foie gras or a pot of rillettes, walnut bread, and of course a bottle of red wine.

In Provence the farm table is likely to offer goat cheeses and honey; in Alsace, a kugelhopf and sausages. Normandy farmers like their compote de pommes, crème fraîche, and raisin bread.

Breakfast etiquette never varies: You fill your bowl with coffee, and add hot milk and sugar to taste. Then you slather your bread with your choice of topping. If it's butter and jam, the tartine is dipped in the coffee as is cake, if that's your choice.

Breakfast is sociable, and substantial after a French fashion. It's also matter-of-fact. A brief half an hour after it's begun, the table is empty, the crumbs swept away. Another farm day is well into its rhythm.

utes. Reduce the heat to 450°F (230°C) and continue baking until the loaf is a good golden brown and sounds hollow when tapped, about 1 hour.

7. Turn out the loaf onto a wire cooling rack and let it cool thoroughly before slicing.

1 loaf (1½ pounds; 750 g)

N O T E : The amount of flours called for in this and all sourdough breads may vary, depending on everything from the brand of flour to the humidity in the air. You will have to observe and learn exact amounts through making the bread over and over (which, you'll see, will become a pleasure).

Simple Bread
Pâte à Pain

>•••<

This no-fail recipe makes a tender, light loaf of bread. I use it as a base for just about all my recipes that call for bread dough, varying it occasionally by adding herbs or nuts or any number of things. You can make wonderful rolls with it, too, by breaking off little pieces, rolling them into balls, and baking them for a mere 12 minutes. The beauty of this bread is that it can go into the oven 1½ hours after you start to assemble it, making it an almost instant recipe.

A S T U C E . . . .
• *There isn't really any reason to oil the bowl in which this dough rises. If the bowl is covered with a damp cloth, the dough doesn't form any kind of crust as it rises, and it doesn't stick to the bowl when you remove it. Save yourself the effort and mess.*

. . . .

1½ teaspoons active dry yeast
2 cups plus 2 to 3 tablespoons
(265 to 280 g) unbleached
all-purpose flour
¾ cup (185 ml) lukewarm water
¼ to ½ teaspoon salt

FOR THE EGG WASH
1 large egg
1 teaspoon water

1. In a large mixing bowl, whisk the yeast and ½ cup (70 g) of the flour into the lukewarm water. Add the salt. Using a wooden spoon, mix in the remaining flour, ½ cup (70 g) at a time, until the dough is too hard to mix with the spoon. Dust a work surface with any remaining flour and knead it into the dough. Continue kneading until the dough is smooth and satiny, about 10 minutes.

2. Place the dough in a bowl, cover it with a dampened tea towel, and let it rise in a warm spot (68° to 70°F; 20° to 21°C) until doubled in bulk, about 1 hour. Punch down the dough and shape it into a round loaf 5 inches (13 cm) in diameter, or into an oblong loaf 9 inches (23 cm) long, and set it on a lightly floured baking sheet. Alternatively, lightly oil a 9 x 5 x 3-inch (23 x 13 x 7½ cm) loaf pan and place the dough in it to rise. Let it rise, covered with the tea towel, until almost doubled in bulk, about 30 minutes.

3. Preheat the oven to 400°F (205°C).

4. Prepare the egg wash: Whisk the egg and the water together in a small bowl until thoroughly combined.

5. Paint the top of the loaf with the egg glaze, slash it several times with a sharp knife, and place it in the center of the oven. Bake until it is golden and sounds hollow when tapped, about 30 minutes.

6. Turn out the loaf onto a wire cooling rack and let it cool thoroughly before slicing.

1 loaf (about 1 pound; 500 g)

Quick Brioche
Brioche Rapide

➤•••◄

I tasted this brioche in the tiny hilltop town of Flavigny, in Burgundy, at a long table where red-cheeked farmers and their wives were eating, talking, and laughing their way through a warm fall afternoon. The occasion was simply Sunday, the setting, a *ferme-auberge* unlike any other in France.

Les Granges des Quatres Heures Soupatoires is run exclusively by farm women, who raise the food that they cook and serve. The diners come from all over the world.

The food these women serve is not sophisticated, but it's stunning in its own way and exactly what you hope to find in farm country—solid, simple, delicious, rich with the flavors of ingredients fresh from the farm. The carrots are sweet and heady, the potatoes earthy, the rutabagas tender and full. The pork is round and satisfying, the broth an elixir. The brioche was so light it might have floated off the plate, and the *crème renversée*, that most classic of desserts, was eggy, creamy, satisfying.

As we ate the last of the brioche and *crème renversée*, the room broke into a rousing song led by one of the farm women, who was standing on a chair at the head of the room, a huge smile on her face.

"Oh, I know we're all tired—but what's a meal and a celebration without some singing?" she said, pausing in mid-song. We agreed, sang a few bars, and then went out into the fall sunshine.

The ingredients for this brioche—made by Marie-Françoise Couthier, who is considered the brioche specialist of the group—all go into a bowl together, are unceremoniously blended, and produce a loaf that is redolent of butter and eggs. It's not a true brioche, but it's a quick version that is nonetheless delicious.

Use it for Brioche French Toast with Caramelized Apples (see Index), for breakfast with fresh cheese and preserves, or for a mid-morning snack. Do try it toasted, too, with honey and a bowl of strong coffee.

Flour Makes the Bread
>·<

*U*se unbleached flour for bread—it has undergone less refining than bleached flour, and will not only give better flavor, but more body and substance as well. It also lends what the French value so highly, an ivory color to the interior of the bread, rather than a sickly refined white.

Even better than unbleached white flour is a blend of flours—whole wheat, corn, spelt, rye, buckwheat (go easy on the last two, adding no more than ¼ to ½ cup (35 to 70 g) of either to a loaf).

I recommend King Arthur and Stonebuhr brands for all flours.

3 cups (405 g) unbleached all-purpose
   flour
¼ cup (50 g) sugar
1½ teaspoons sea salt
3 tablespoons warm water
1 teaspoon active dry yeast
4 large eggs, beaten
8 tablespoons (1 stick; 125 g) unsalted
   butter, melted

FOR THE EGG WASH
1 egg
2 teaspoons water

1. Stir the flour, sugar, and salt together in a large bowl, or in the bowl of a heavy-duty electric mixer. Make a well in the center, and

pour the warm water into the well. Sprinkle the yeast over the water and stir it in. Add the eggs to the well, and combine with the water. Gradually stir the dry ingredients into the wet to form a firm dough. Continue beating by hand for 5 minutes or in the mixer for 3 minutes until the dough is elastic. It will be somewhat sticky, but it shouldn't stick to your hands.

2. Add the melted butter and mix just until it is incorporated. Now the dough will be more like a batter—sticky (it may stick to your fingers) but not wet.

3. Cover the bowl with a tea towel and leave it in a warm spot (68° to 70F°; 20° to 21°C) until the dough has risen slightly (almost imperceptibly), about 1 hour.

4. Generously butter an 8½ x 4½ x 2½-inch (21 x 11½ x 6½ cm) loaf pan.

5. Punch down the dough and place it in the prepared loaf pan, spreading it as evenly as possible so it fills the pan. Cover with a damp towel and let rise in a warm spot (68° to 70F°; 20° to 21°C) until it has increased by about one third (the change in size is not dramatic), about 1½ hours.

6. Preheat the oven to 375°F (190°C).

7. Prepare the egg wash: Whisk the egg and water together in a small bowl, and paint the loaf with the mixture. To help it rise evenly, slash the top of the loaf in several places (or snip it with a pair of kitchen shears). Bake in the center of the oven until the brioche is puffed and golden, 35 to 40 minutes.

8. Remove the pan from the oven and turn the brioche out onto a wire rack to cool.

1 loaf (about 1 pound; 500 g)

Ham and Parsley Bread

Cake au Jambon et Persil

Savory *cakes,* or breads, are a country trend, and I've found recipes for them on farms throughout France. Sometimes they're studded with olives and peppers, other times with ham and cheese. They're almost always served as an appetizer, cut into small cubes or thin slices. (There are also sweet *cakes*—see pages 380 to 384.)

Boulangerie, Pâtisserie

>·<

One wonders, when walking the streets of any village, town, or city in France, what is the real difference between a boulangerie and a pâtisserie. Well, at times the distinction is subtle.

A boulangerie is a bakery where the main offering is breads of just about every variety. Long baguettes fill one case, oval pains aux céréales fill another. There are round pains de campagne, which are lightly whole wheat; delicate ficelles, which are simply skinny baguettes; graceful épis, long loaves cut to look like a sheaf of wheat; and depending on the region, there may be dozens of other varieties. Boulangeries always offer pains au chocolat, croissants, and the panoply of yeasted pastries for breakfast and goûter. But bread is the focus.

A pâtisserie, on the other hand, offers delicate and sophisticated (usually) pastries, homemade candies, the myriad and delicate creations that cause the mouth to water. In a pâtisserie window one sees tarts festooned with buttercream rosettes and ribbons, topped with shimmering fruit glazes, filled with pastry creams of every flavor. Multilayered cakes show stripes of red fruit filling, and there are fanciful individual pastries of every shape and color. In one of our neighborhood pâtisseries (we are blessed with three within short walking distance), meringue tennis balls dusted with flaked coconut share shelf space with chocolate hedgehogs and caramelized choux pastries that look like ermine-ringed hats for royalty. Inside, a few specialty breads fill a basket, next to kugelhopfs and madeleines. But achingly sweet pastries are the focal point.

As a rule, which has many exceptions, the best breads are found at the boulangerie, the best pastries at the pâtisserie.

This *cake* (pronounced "kek") comes from Héloïse Tuyeras, a native of the Limousin, the area west of the Massif Centrale. She grew up there, and her palate was formed on a hearty cuisine replete with herbs, wild mushrooms, garlic, and savory braised ham. When I tasted this, I had to have the recipe, for it is light, fresh, herbal, and looks gorgeous on the plate.

Serve this as an appetizer, cut into slices, cubes, even triangles! Or serve it slightly warm with a vegetable soup, spread with *fromage blanc,* or even for breakfast. (This is also a hit with children, and it makes a wonderful afternoon snack.)

The amount of salt you use will depend on the saltiness of the ham. I always recommend adding at least a pinch to any batter or dough, but you may want to reduce the amount here if your ham is very salty.

Serve a lightly chilled Rosé d'Anjou or Champagne alongside.

1½ cups (200 g) unbleached
   all-purpose flour
1 tablespoon baking powder
½ teaspoon sea salt
1½ cups (firmly packed) flat-leaf parsley
   leaves
6 large eggs
3 tablespoons Dijon mustard
1 small shallot, peeled and minced
Freshly ground black pepper
8 tablespoons (1 stick; 125 g) unsalted
   butter, melted and cooled
6 ounces (180 g) boiled ham, fat removed,
   cut into ¼-inch (½ cm) squares
2 cups (180 g) grated Gruyère cheese

1. Preheat the oven to 425°F (220°C). Butter an 8½ x 4½ x 2½-inch (21 x 11½ x 6½ cm) loaf pan. Line it with parchment paper, and butter the parchment. Dust it lightly with flour.

2. Sift the flour, baking powder, and salt together onto a piece of waxed paper. Mince the parsley.

3. In a large bowl, whisk together the eggs and the mustard. Add the parsley, shallot, and a generous amount of pepper. Then quickly whisk in the flour. Whisk in the melted butter until it is thoroughly combined. Then fold in the ham, followed by the cheese, making sure they are well distributed throughout the batter.

4. Pour the batter into the prepared loaf pan, rap it sharply on a work surface to release any air bubbles, and bake in the center of the oven until the top of the bread is golden and a sharp knife stuck in the center comes out clean, 40 to 45 minutes.

5. Remove the bread from the oven and turn it out onto a wire cooling rack. After about 5 minutes, peel off the parchment paper. Let it cool, and serve.

1 loaf; 10 to 12 appetizer servings

Olive Bread
Cake aux Olives

This version of *cake* originated in Provence, where olives, basil, and garlic create a harmonious triumvirate. Here they combine with roasted red bell peppers and Parmesan cheese to create a bread that is gutsy, aromatic, and lovely to look at. Serve this along with a glass of Orange Wine (see Index), as an appetizer, in tandem with fresh goat's- or cow's-milk cheese, or even lightly toasted with a poached egg on top.

1½ cups (200 g) unbleached all-purpose
flour

½ teaspoon sea salt

2 teaspoons baking powder

1 very large red bell pepper, roasted
(see box, below)

1 cup (155 g) Greek-style black olives,
pitted

4 cups (loosely packed) fresh basil
leaves

6 large eggs

¼ cup (60 ml) olive oil

1 clove garlic, peeled, green germ
removed, and minced

Freshly ground black pepper

½ cup (60 g) finely grated Parmesan
cheese

1. Preheat the oven to 400°F (205°C). Butter an 8½ x 4½ x 2½-inch (21 x 11½ x 6½ cm) loaf pan. Line it with parchment paper, lightly butter the paper, and dust it with flour.

2. Sift the flour, salt, and baking powder together onto a piece of waxed paper.

3. Coasely chop the roasted pepper and the olives.

4. Mince the basil leaves.

5. In a large bowl, whisk the eggs. Then add the oil and the basil, and whisk until combined. Add the garlic. Then whisk in the flour mixture just until combined. Grind black pepper to taste over the batter and whisk it in. Then whisk in the cheese. Fold in the olives and the roasted pepper.

Roasting Peppers

There are several ways to roast a bell pepper. My preference is directly over the flame of a gas burner. Just turn on a burner (preferably a smallish one with a small center piece so the flame will evenly roast the pepper), and place the pepper right on the flame. When the skin on that side is completely black, rotate the pepper. Keep watch over the pepper at all times. Continue until the entire pepper is black on the surface. The skin will be charred, and will crackle, and bits will fall off. When it is completely charred, wrap it in a tea towel, a piece of aluminum foil, or a plain brown bag, and let it sit for at least 15 minutes. It will steam slightly, which will make the skin easier to remove. The pepper will be very soft. When it has cooled, rub off the skin (easiest to do under running water). Core and seed the pepper, pat it dry, and proceed with the recipe.

If you don't have a gas stove, place the pepper on a large piece of aluminum foil and roast it under a preheated broiler, turning it until it is completely charred all over. Remove the pepper from the broiler, wrap it as described, and proceed with the instructions.

6. Pour the batter into the prepared loaf pan and rap the pan once, hard, on a work surface to release any air bubbles. Bake the *cake* in the center of the oven until the top is golden and springs back when touched, about 45 minutes.

1 loaf; 10 to 12 appetizer servings

Jacqueline Priaulet's Pizza Tart
La Pizza de Jacqueline Priaulet

>···<

This recipe depends for its goodness on the generous bounty of the summer sun. It is lush and juicy with vine-ripened tomatoes, which are heightened with mustard and a layer of cheese. Sounds almost too simple, but some magic occurs as it bakes, for it emerges from the oven steaming with flavor. The drizzle of oil tops off a perfect dish.

I follow the lead of Jacqueline Priaulet, whose recipe this is, and add no salt or pepper—it doesn't need it. Sometimes I add garlic, sometimes I don't, and I love it either way. The essence of this pizza is the ingredients, which play off the crisp and buttery crust. Make this when you want to celebrate, when you want a taste of Provence, when you're so hungry you could eat it all. And if you're that hungry, make two, because you *will* eat it all!

2 tablespoons Dijon mustard
One 10½-inch (26½ cm) tart shell, made using Homemaker's Pastry (page 509) and prebaked
6 ounces (180 g) Gruyère cheese, cut into very thin slices
1 large clove garlic, peeled, green germ removed, and finely minced (optional)
2 large, very ripe tomatoes cored and cut into thick slices
2 tablespoons extra-virgin olive oil

1. Preheat the oven to 425°F (220°C).
2. Spread the mustard evenly over the bottom of the prebaked pastry shell. Top it with the cheese slices, then sprinkle with the minced garlic if you are using it. Arrange the

tomato slices evenly over the cheese. Place the tart pan on a baking sheet and bake in the center of the oven until the cheese is thoroughly melted and bubbling and the tomatoes are cooked through and thoroughly tender, about 40 minutes.

3. Remove the tart from the oven and drizzle the olive oil over it. Remove the sides of the pan and serve immediately.

One 10½-inch (26½ cm) tart; 6 to 8 appetizer servings, 4 to 6 main-course servings

Tomato, Olive, and Anchovy Tart
Pissaladière

*P*issaladière lilts with the accent of the south of France, with its anchovies and cured black olives. It's a real classic, and can be found in dozens of guises. Here, tender onions are thickly spread on crisp pastry and garnished with tomatoes, olives, and anchovies. I've found that even those who think they don't like anchovies eat this tart with abandon.

ASTUCE . . . .
• *Check the onions often as they cook, allowing the condensation on the lid of the pan to drip right back into the onions when you lift it off. This keeps them moist and helps them cook to buttery tenderness.*

. . . .

2 pounds (1 kg) onions, peeled and thinly sliced
¼ cup (60 ml) olive oil
Sea salt and freshly ground black pepper
One 10½-inch (26½ cm) tart shell, made using Homemaker's Pastry (page 509) and prebaked
3 slightly underripe medium tomatoes, cored and cut into thin slices
18 anchovy fillets
20 cured black olives, with pits

1. Place the onions and oil in a large

heavy skillet over medium heat. Toss so the onions are coated with the oil and cook, covered, stirring occasionally, until the onions are completely tender and sweet, about 40 minutes. Season with salt and pepper.

2. Preheat the oven to 425°F (220°C).

3. Place the prebaked pastry shell, still in its pan, on a baking sheet. Transfer the onions to the shell, spreading evenly.

4. Arrange the tomato slices in slightly overlapping concentric circles over the onions. Arrange the anchovy fillets atop the tomatoes, making 9 crosses with them. Evenly distribute the olives on the top of the *pissaladière*, pressing them gently into the tart so they don't roll off. Carefully place the baking sheet in the center of the oven and bake until the tart is hot through and slightly golden on top and the tomatoes are tender, about 35 minutes.

5. Remove the tart from the oven and remove the sides of the pan. Let the tart cool for about 10 minutes before serving. Remind diners that the olives in the tart have pits in them.

One 10½-inch (26½ cm) tart; 6 to 8 appetizer servings, 4 to 6 main-course servings

Gruyère and Sorrel Tart

Tarte à l'Oseille et au Gruyère

This recipe comes from the Daneyrolles' farm in Saignon, a town in the Lubéron part of Provence, not far from Apt. There Jean-Luc Daneyrolles tends a tidy, impeccably arranged vegetable and herb farm, selling his produce at the Apt market.

He also caters to passersby, though his farm is located on a narrow, winding road that even in the best situations is not easy to find. Nonetheless, in summer he is inundated by people who come to buy everything he can harvest. He calls his farm *le potager d'un curieux* ("the garden of a curious man"), and he is known in gardening circles throughout France.

Sorrel is a favorite crop for M. Daneyrolles—and for his wife, Joëlle. In addition to looking after their four children, she is a schoolteacher and the chief cook in the household, though it is difficult to see where she finds the time.

This tart is a fine example of her cooking. Light yet robust, it's tangy with sorrel

Sorrel

>·<

*S*orrel is the lemon of the vegetable garden, a plant with so much acid that it causes instant puckering. It brightens everything it touches, adding an edge, a counterpoint, a little spark. Try it snipped and sprinkled over pasta, added to soup at the last minute, folded into an omelette.

Sorrel resembles spinach, though its leaves are a paler green and slightly less fleshy. A huge quantity of leaves—enough to feed the neighborhood, it seems—will melt down into nearly nothing in the saucepan, forming a purée all on its own. Soften it with butter and cream and serve it alongside fish. Traditional, yes, and inspired as well.

To have sorrel all year round, try freezing the leaves: Place the fresh leaves in a heavy self-seal plastic bag, pushing out all the air as you close it. Freeze, and use as you like. Or try this method: Steam the leaves in a skillet until they are melted to a purée, transfer the purée to a jar, cover it with a thin (¼-inch; ½ cm) layer of olive oil, and seal the jar. Stored in the refrigerator, the purée will keep for several months.

To trim sorrel leaves: Snip out the central stem of each leaf with a pair of scissors.

and mellowed by the richness of eggs and cheese. It's an ideal dish for summertime, when sorrel is producing as fast as it can be cut. Eat it at room temperature—that's when it is at its best.

Serve this as a main course at lunch, with a salad, or as a first course for supper, with a light Gamay de Touraine alongside.

ASTUCE . . . .

• The stems of large sorrel leaves can be stringy. Fold the leaf in half lengthwise and, with kitchen shears, cut away the stem to the point where it becomes very fine at the tip of the leaf. If you are using very small tender leaves, stemming is not necessary.

. . . .

9 ounces (270 g) sorrel (see Note), rinsed
  and trimmed of stems
¾ cup (185 ml) milk
¼ cup (60 ml) Crème Fraîche (page 520),
  or heavy (or whipping) cream
2 large eggs
2 large egg yolks
¼ teaspoon sea salt
Freshly ground black pepper
One 10½-inch (26½ cm) tart shell, made
  using Homemaker's Pastry (page 509)
  and prebaked; see also Note opposite
1½ cups (120 g) grated Gruyère or Comté
  cheese

1. Preheat the oven to 425°F (220°C).
2. Place the rinsed sorrel, with the water

still clinging to it, in a medium-size heavy pan over medium heat. Cook, covered, until the sorrel "melts" and turns an olive green, about 5 minutes. Stir it occasionally so it cooks evenly, and continue cooking until it gives up most of its liquid and turns to a thick purée, another 2 to 3 minutes. Remove the pan from the heat and set it aside.

3. In a medium-size bowl, whisk together the milk and the crème fraîche. Add the whole eggs, one at a time, whisking until thoroughly blended. Then whisk in the egg yolks, one at a time. Season with the salt and pepper to taste.

4. Place the prebaked pastry shell, still in its pan, on a baking sheet. Spread the sorrel in the pastry shell, and top it with the cheese. Then pour in the egg mixture. Carefully place the baking sheet in the center of the oven and bake until the tart is puffed and golden, 25 to 30 minutes.

5. Remove the tart from the oven, and remove the sides of the pan. Serve hot or at room temperature.

One 10½-inch (26½ cm) tart; 6 to 8 appetizer servings, 4 to 6 main-course servings

NOTES: If sorrel is hard to find, use 1 pound (500 g) fresh spinach, trimmed and thoroughly rinsed. Steam it until it is completely tender (8 minutes), drain and mince it, then season it with ¾ teaspoon freshly squeezed lemon juice and sea salt and freshly ground black pepper to taste.
• Prebake the pastry for this tart at 400°F (205°C). It should be a *pale* golden color when it is finished prebaking.

Mme. Sibelle's Mushroom Tart
Tarte aux Champignons de Mme. Sibelle

>···<

Mme. Régine Sibelle is a powerhouse. On her Burgundy farm, south of Dijon, she raises more than five hundred prized *poulets de Bresse,* caring for them like house pets, coddling them to maturity, and preparing them with such care that each looks like a personally wrapped Christmas gift when it's ready for market.

She loves to cook, and always has. She raised three children, and one son and his wife still live in the house with her and her husband. She cooks for them, cooks for her two daughters when they come home with their families, and cooks for the joy of cooking. Her cooking is traditional, naturally born of her region, and rich in cream and butter. This mushroom tart is a luscious example. It takes simple white button mushrooms, called *champignons de Paris*, to new heights, making the most of their flavor.

I like to serve this as a first course, along with a glass of port or a lightly chilled Beaune Blanc.

> *1½ pounds (750 g) fresh button*
>   *mushrooms, brushed clean*
> *2 tablespoons unsalted butter*
> *1 shallot, peeled and minced*
> *¼ cup (60 ml) port*
> *¼ cup (60 ml) Crème Fraîche (page 520),*
>   *or heavy (or whipping) cream*
> *Sea salt and freshly ground black pepper*
> *¼ teaspoon freshly grated nutmeg, or to*
>   *taste*
> *One 10½-inch (26½ cm) tart shell, made*
>   *using Homemaker's Pastry (page*
>   *509) and prebaked*

1. Preheat the oven to 425°F (220°C).

2. Trim off just the very end of the mushroom stems, leaving most of the stem intact. Then cut the mushrooms into ¼-inch-thick (½ cm) slices.

3. Melt the butter in a large heavy skillet over medium-high heat. Stir in the shallot, and cook just until it begins to turn translucent, 2 to 3 minutes. Add the mushrooms and sauté until they begin to give up their liquid and start to darken at the edges, about 5 minutes. Add the port and the crème fraîche. Continue cooking until the mushrooms are nearly tender through, and the cream and port have thickened and reduced, 8 to 10 minutes. The mushrooms should still have texture though they will be soft, and while there should be some liquid left in the pan, the mushrooms shouldn't be juicy. Season with salt and pepper to taste, and the nutmeg.

4. Transfer the mushroom mixture, with the liquid, to the prebaked pastry shell. Place the tart pan on a baking sheet and bake in the center of the oven until the filling is hot through, 5 to 7 minutes.

5. Remove the tart from the oven and remove the sides of the pan. Let cool slightly before serving.

One 10½-inch (26½ cm) tart; 6 to 8 appetizer servings

Breton Onion Tart

Tarte Bretonne à l'Oignon

>···<

Brittany—land of onions, shallots, cream, and simple hearty food—is the birthplace of this recipe. This tart is something of an exception, for it has a sophisticated look to it. It emerges golden and sweet-smelling from the oven, so tempting you can hardly resist it.

Serve this as an appetizer, along with a sweetish white wine such as a white Burgundy. Alternatively, serve it for lunch with Watercress, Beet, and Walnut Salad (see Index).

ASTUCE . . . .

• *When baking tarts, place the tart pan on a baking sheet so it is easy to remove from the oven—and so you won't pick up the tart from the bottom, forgetting that it's removable!*

• *Remove the onion marmalade from the refrigerator at least 30 minutes before you plan to make the tart, so it has a chance to come to room temperature. If it is very cold, it will be difficult to blend it into the egg mixture.*

. . . .

One-quarter recipe Puff Pastry (page 512), chilled

2 large eggs

1 cup (250 ml) Crème Fraîche (page 520), or heavy (or whipping) cream

1 recipe Rich Onion Marmalade (page 412)

½ teaspoon sea salt

Freshly ground black pepper

1. Roll out the puff pastry on a lightly floured work surface to form a round 11½ inches (29 cm) to fit a 10½-inch (26½ cm) tart pan with removable bottom. Transfer the pastry to the pan, fitting it against the bottom and sides. Refrigerate the pastry shell for 1 hour.

2. Preheat the oven to 425°F (220°C).

3. Remove the pastry shell from the refrigerator. Prick it all over with the tines of a fork and line it with aluminum foil. Fill the foil with pie weights or dried beans and bake in the center of the oven until the edges of the pastry begin to turn golden, 10 to 15 minutes. Remove the foil and the weights, and continue baking until the pastry is cooked through and pale golden, another 10 to 15 minutes. Remove the tart shell from the oven and let it cool slightly. Leave the oven on.

4. In a medium-size bowl, whisk together the eggs and the crème fraîche. Add the onion marmalade and whisk until thoroughly blended. Season with the salt and pepper to taste.

5. Place the prebaked pastry shell, still in its pan, on a baking sheet. Pour the filling

mixture into the pastry shell, and bake in the center of the oven until the tart is golden and slightly puffed, 25 to 30 minutes. To test for doneness, shake the tart. If it is loose in the center, bake it for an additional 5 minutes or until it is set.

6. Remove the tart from the oven, and remove the sides of the pan. Let the tart cool for 5 minutes before serving.

One 10½ inch (26½ cm) tart; 6 to 8 appetizer servings, 4 to 6 main-course servings

Spinach, Ham, and Cheese Turnover
Chausson aux Epinards

→•••←

This recipe comes right from the garden of my neighbor Edith Leroy, whose property in the small village of Le Vaudreuil is cultivated by a local farmer, Jean Harel. It's an excellent arrangement. M. Harel is officially retired, but he loves nothing more than cultivating the soil, and he has just a small bit of property himself. Edith loves fresh vegetables, but has no time to take care of them. So they share: he cultivates her land and gives her half the vegetables.

Now Edith can run out to the garden year-round to pick the fresh vegetables she loves, and M. Harel can do the same. He has turned a half-acre into a perfectly tidy little farm, complete with a cold frame for growing Belgian endive in the winter, patches of early strawberries, a corner for parsley, chervil, basil, and chives. Depending on the season, the garden is full of carrots, turnips, spinach, or young cabbages. Recently he even built a chicken run, at Edith's request.

One spring when the spinach was young and abundant, we harvested bags full and used it to make this *chausson*, which was Edith's inspired idea. It couldn't be more classic, with its mix of nutmeg-scented béchamel, spinach, ham, and cheese, though Edith adds her own touch of fresh garlic. The puff pastry brings it up a notch, makes it special, turns it into a Sunday lunch dish.

I love to make this because it's elegant yet simple, and there are enough elements in it to satisfy everyone. Try it using your own homemade puff pastry (see Index), or buy good-quality frozen puff pastry made with butter.

If you are using frozen puff pastry, remove it from the freezer 2 hours before you plan to roll it out. For the ham, use the best-quality cooked-on-the-bone ham you can find, such as a good baked Virginia ham.

Drink a Graves along with this.

One-half recipe Puff Pastry (page 512), chilled

FOR THE BECHAMEL

1 cup (250 ml) milk
2 imported bay leaves
1½ tablespoons unsalted butter
1½ tablespoons unbleached all-purpose flour
Sea salt and freshly ground black pepper
½ teaspoon freshly grated nutmeg, or to taste

FOR THE EGG WASH

1 large egg
1 tablespoon water
Pinch of sea salt

FOR THE TART

1¼ pounds (625 g) fresh spinach, trimmed and carefully rinsed
4 ounces (125 g) best-quality baked ham, cut into very thin slices
Sea salt and freshly ground black pepper
½ teaspoon freshly grated nutmeg, or to taste
1½ cups (125 g) grated Gruyère cheese
1 large clove garlic, peeled, green germ removed, and minced

1. Roll out the puff pastry on a lightly floured work surface to form an 11½-inch (29 cm) round. Line a baking sheet with parchment paper and transfer the pastry to the baking sheet. Refrigerate for 1 hour.

2. Meanwhile, prepare the béchamel: Heat the milk with the bay leaves in a medium-size saucepan over medium-high heat just until steaming and tiny bubbles form around the edges. Immediately remove the pan from the heat, cover it, and let sit for 10 minutes; then remove the bay leaves.

3. Melt the butter in a medium-size saucepan over medium heat. Whisk in the flour and cook until the butter and flour foam. Continue cooking, whisking occasionally, for 2 minutes, adjusting the heat if necessary so the butter and flour don't brown. Whisk in the warm milk, and cook, whisking constantly, until the sauce thickens, 2 minutes. Season to taste with salt, pepper, and the nutmeg. Cook for an additional 10 minutes so the sauce becomes smooth; then remove it from the heat and let it cool. (If you want to avoid a skin forming on the béchamel, spread

the surface with a bit of butter.)

4. Preheat the oven to 425°F (220°C).

5. Prepare the egg wash: Whisk together the egg, water, and salt in a small bowl until thoroughly combined.

6. Place the spinach, with the water still clinging to the leaves, in a large saucepan and cook, covered, over medium heat just until it wilts but is still bright green, about 5 minutes. Remove from the heat and transfer to a colander to drain. Gently squeeze the spinach so it gives up most of its liquid. It should be slightly moist, however.

7. Remove the baking sheet with the pastry round from the refrigerator. Brush around the outer edge of the round with some of the egg wash. Lay half the ham on the lower half of the pastry, leaving a 1-inch (2½ cm) border. Coarsely chop the spinach and lay half of it on top of the ham. Season

lightly with salt, pepper, and nutmeg. Pour half the béchamel over the spinach, directing it so it seeps into the spinach. It has a tendency to run, so work quickly. Top with half of the cheese, then sprinkle with the garlic. Repeat with the remaining ingredients. Quickly fold the top half of the pastry over the filling to form a half-moon shape, firmly pressing the edges together. Slip the *chausson* onto the baking sheet and paint it with egg wash. Make several shallow ½-inch (1¼ cm) slits in the top of the *chausson*, and bake in the center of the oven until it is golden brown, puffed, and cooked through, about 40 minutes.

8. Remove from the heat and let cool for 10 minutes before serving.

4 main-course servings or 6 appetizer servings

Asparagus Tart

Tourte aux Asperges

→ • • • ←

This simple *tourte* comes directly from Provence, where green asparagus thrives. An old-fashioned farm *tourte*, it is rich with simple flavor, filled with homey ingredients. But don't be fooled: It is elegant to look at and sophisticated of flavor.

This can easily serve as a main course, along with a salad. Or serve it as a first course before fish or roasted poultry.

Try Muscat d'Alsace Sec alongside.

ASTUCE . . . .

• To trim green asparagus, hold a stalk with the forefinger and thumb of one hand below the tip, the other at the base, and bend. The stalk will snap naturally at the spot on the stem where tenderness gives way to toughness. Discard whatever breaks off at the root end.

. . . .

1 recipe Double-Crust Pâte Brisée (page 511)
Sea salt
2 pounds (1 kg) asparagus, trimmed
1 tablespoon olive oil
6 ounces (180 g) salt pork, refreshed
    (see Note) and cut into 1 x ¼ x ¼-inch
    (2½ x ½ x ½ cm) pieces
1 medium onion, peeled, cut in half, and
    thinly sliced
1 tablespoon unbleached all-purpose flour
Freshly ground black pepper
1 egg
2 teaspoons water
Zest of 1 lemon, minced
1¼ heaped cups (150 g) grated Gruyère or
    Comté cheese

1. Roll out one half of the pastry on a lightly floured work surface to form a 13-inch (32½ cm) round to fit a 10½-inch (26½ cm) tart pan with removable bottom. Transfer the pastry to the pan, fitting it against the bottom and sides. Leave plenty of pastry hanging

What Is Zest?

>•<

It is just the colored part of citrus peel (lemon, for this recipe). It is easily removed from the fruit with a special tool called a zester or with a traditional vegetable peeler. If any pith (the white substance next to the zest) remains on zest you've removed with a vegetable peeler, trim it away, for it has a bitter flavor.

over the edges. Roll out the second half of the pastry to form an 11½-inch (29 cm) round. Place the remaining round on a baking sheet and place both the tart shell and the pastry round in the refrigerator for 1 hour.

2. Meanwhile, fill a large bowl with ice water, and spread several tea towels out on your work surface. Bring a large pot of salted water to a boil (2 tablespoons salt for 4 quarts; 4 l water) over high heat. Add the asparagus, return to a boil, and cook just until it is tender and turns bright green, 1 to 4 minutes, depending on the thickness of the asparagus. Transfer the asparagus to the ice water, reserving 1 cup (250 ml) of the cook-

ing liquid. As soon as the asparagus is cool, remove it from the water and pat it dry.

3. Heat the oil in a large heavy saucepan over medium-high heat, and add the salt pork. Cook just until it is golden, 3 to 4 minutes. Reduce the heat to medium, add the onions, stir, and cook just until they are beginning to turn translucent, about 5 minutes. Sprinkle the flour over the salt pork and onions, and stir. Stir in ¼ cup (60 ml) of the reserved asparagus cooking liquid. Cook, stirring constantly, until the liquid thickens and the flour is cooked, at least 2 minutes. Add the remaining ¾ cup (185 ml) cooking liquid, stirring and scraping up any brown bits from the bottom of the pan. Cook until the mixture has thickened to the consistency of mayonnaise, about 5 minutes. Season to taste with salt and pepper. Remove the pan from the heat and let the mixture cool to lukewarm. (The recipe can be made up to this point several hours in advance.)

4. Preheat the oven to 400°F (205°C). Whisk together the egg and the water to make an egg wash.

5. Cut the tips from the asparagus stalks; then cut the rest of the stalks into 2-inch (5 cm) lengths. Stir the zest into the salt pork mixture.

6. Remove the tart pan from the refrigerator and place on a baking sheet. Spread half the salt pork mixture as evenly as possible in the pastry shell. Top with half the asparagus, and sprinkle with half the cheese. Dot the remaining salt pork mixture over the cheese, and top it with the remaining asparagus. Sprinkle the remaining cheese evenly over the asparagus.

7. Paint the edges of the pastry with some of the egg wash. Place the top pastry round over the filling, easing it so it fits loosely (any wrinkles or imperfections will disappear in the baking). Trim the edges of the pastry, and crimp the top and bottom edges together. Paint the top crust with the egg wash and pierce it at least 8 times with a sharp knife to allow steam to escape. (If you like, cut out several asparagus-shaped pieces

Sweet Scraps

>·<

*A*fter you've put the **tourte** in the oven, you'll have lots of pastry scraps left over. I gather them up and transfer them to a baking sheet, leaving them curled as they fell when I trimmed them from the **tourte**. I lightly dust them with sugar and heavily dust them with cinnamon, refrigerate them, and then bake them for 8 to 10 minutes after the **tourte** has come out of the oven. They make a nice little snack with coffee, or they can even be served with fruit for dessert.

of extra pastry and arrange them attractively on top of the *tourte;* pressing gently to adhere; brush with egg wash.) Bake the *tourte* in the center of the oven until the crust is golden on top, about 30 minutes.

8. Remove the *tourte* from the oven and remove the sides of the pan. Let the *tourte* cool for 10 to 20 minutes before serving.

NOTE: To refresh salt pork, place it in a saucepan and cover it with cold water. Bring to a boil, drain, and repeat. Pat dry and cut as directed for the recipe.

Leek and Mushroom Tart
Tourte aux Poireaux et aux Champignons

This *tourte* has been on the menu at La Belle Gasconne (in Poudenas, Gascony) for more than fifteen years, ever since M. and Mme. Gracia opened the restaurant. Mme. Gracia remembers both her mother and her grandmother making it, and she continues the tradition. Mme. Gracia comes from a farm family, and all of her food is a reflection of the region's farm cooking, taken up a step in sophistication.

The *tourte* couldn't be simpler to make, but its goodness depends on fresh ingredients—and on rolling the pastry so thin you can nearly see through it. (Roll it until you think you can't roll it anymore and then slip your hand under it, knuckles up, and slightly bend your fingers. If you can see your knuckles, the pastry is the right thickness.)

The leeks are wilted just slightly before they're added to the *tourte,* so they give up some of their liquid. Nonetheless, they give up more while baking in the pastry. Letting the *tourte* sit for at least 10 minutes after removing it from the oven and before serving it reduces the amount of liquid that drains out when you cut into it—and leaves more of the flavor to be savored.

Try a white Burgundy or Bergerac alongside.

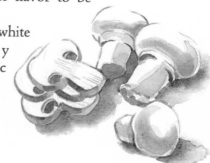

ASTUCES . . . .

• *To wash leeks that will be diced, first cut off the dark green leaves, the best of which you can save for soup or stock. Then trim the root end from the leek. Cut the leek in quarters lengthwise, leaving the bottom ½ inch (1¼ cm) intact. Hold the leek under briskly running water to remove any bits of sand or dirt that are lodged deep inside, then pat it dry on a cotton towel and dice it.*

• *Leeks vary in size, of course. Here I call for 2 pounds (1 kg), about 5 leeks. If you're not quite sure you have the right amount, weigh them after you've removed the green leaves. You need 1 pound (500 g) of fat white parts. Use half that weight in mushrooms, and your tart will be sublime.*

. . . .

1 recipe Double-Crust Pâte Brisée
   (page 511)
1 egg
½ teaspoon water
5 large leeks (2 pounds; 1 kg), white part
   only, cut into quarters lengthwise and
   well rinsed, then finely chopped
1 cup (250 ml) Crème Fraîche (page 520),
   or heavy (or whipping) cream
Sea salt and freshly ground white pepper
8 ounces (250 g) button mushrooms,
   brushed clean, trimmed, and sliced as
   thin as possible

1. Roll out one half of the pastry on a lightly floured work surface to form a 13-inch (32½ cm) round to fit a 10½-inch (26½ cm) tart pan with removable bottom. Transfer the pastry to the pan, fitting it against the bottom and sides. Leave plenty of pastry hanging over the edges. Roll out the second half of the pastry to form an 11½-inch (29 cm) round. Place the remaining round on a baking sheet and place both the tart shell and the pastry round in the refrigerator for 1 hour.

2. Preheat the oven to 425°F (220°C).

3. In a small bowl, whisk together the egg and the water for an egg wash.

4. Place the leeks, with the rinse water still clinging to them, in a heavy saucepan over medium-high heat. Cook, stirring, just until they wilt very slightly and turn bright green, about 3 minutes. Remove the pan from the heat and transfer the leeks to a large platter or baking dish, spreading them out in a thin layer so they will cool quickly.

5. Place the crème fraîche in a small bowl, and add salt and white pepper to taste. Whisk, and adjust the seasoning if necessary.

6. When the leeks are cool, transfer them to a large mixing bowl. Add the mushrooms and the seasoned crème fraîche. Toss the ingredients with your hands until the vegetables are coated with the crème fraîche.

7. Remove the tart pan from the refrigerator and place on a baking sheet. Spread out the vegetables in an even layer in the pastry shell, pressing them gently. They should be just about even with the edge of the tart pan, not mounded above it.

8. Paint the edges of the bottom pastry with some of the egg wash. Place the top pastry round over the filling, easing it so it fits loosely (any wrinkles or imperfections will disappear in the baking). Trim the edges of the pastry, and crimp the top and bottom edges together.

9. Paint the top crust with egg wash and pierce it at least 8 times with a sharp knife to allow steam to escape. Bake it in the center of the oven until the crust is golden on top, about 30 minutes.

10. Remove the *tourte* from the oven and remove the sides of the pan. Let cool for 10 to 25 minutes, to allow the juices to be absorbed back into the vegetables.

11. To serve, place the *tourte* on a platter, preferably with a rim because some juice will run from it. Cut it into wedges and serve.

One 10½-inch (26½ cm) tourte; 6 to 8 appetizer servings, 4 to 6 main-course servings

Mme. Sibelle's Onion Tart
Tarte à l'Oignon de Mme. Sibelle

This recipe is an old-family favorite and a regional specialty. Mme. Régine Sibelle's father always made bread on their Burgundy farm when she was growing up, and with some of the dough, he made this onion tart, which is a specialty of Burgundy. Mme. Sibelle makes it often, sometimes making the bread dough herself, sometimes running down to the local bakery to buy some. The vinegar and the long, slow cooking give the onions a caramel color and a slight edge; the crème fraîche rounds it out. For a variation, try sprinkling the tart with a generous amount of fresh thyme leaves.

I make the bread dough, which is a simple affair, and pop this in the oven so it is hot and ready as a first course. This also makes a great lunch dish, served with a big green salad or a plate of crudités. Sometimes I double the bread recipe to make the Cinnamon Cream Bread Tart (see Index) for dessert. That makes two tarts in the same meal, but I've not yet had any objections.

Serve this with a Bourgeuil alongside.

1 tablespoon unsalted butter
3 large onions, peeled and thinly sliced
1 tablespoon best-quality red wine vinegar
¼ cup (60 ml) Crème Fraîche (page 520), or heavy (or whipping) cream
Sea salt and freshly ground black pepper
1 recipe Simple Bread (page 324)

1. Preheat the oven to 425°F (220°C). Liberally dust a baking sheet with flour or cornmeal.

2. In a large heavy skillet, melt the butter over medium heat. Stir in the onions, cover, and cook, stirring occasionally, until the onions are translucent and soft, about 20 minutes. Add the vinegar and cook, stirring until it has evaporated, 2 minutes. Then stir in the crème fraîche. Season with salt and pepper to taste and remove from the heat.

3. Roll out the dough on a lightly floured work surface to form a 14 x 11-inch (36 x 28 cm) rectangle. Dust the dough lightly with flour, roll it loosely around the rolling pin, and unroll it on the prepared baking sheet. Spread the onion mixture over the dough, leaving a ¼-inch (½ cm) margin at the edges. Bake in the center of the oven until the tart is golden and puffed around the edges, about 20 minutes.

4. Remove the tart from the oven, cut it into serving-size pieces, and serve immediately.

One 14 x 11-inch tart (36 x 28 cm); 6 to 8 servings

Tomato and Sweet Pepper Pizza

Pizza aux Tomates et Poivrons Doux

This dish was inspired by Marie-Agnès Carricaburu, who sat with me one cool morning in the foyer of her mountain hotel and talked to me about her family's cooking. It was midsummer, right before the rush of tourists would descend on her tiny town of Esterençuby, near St. Jean-Pied-de-Port, and she had some free time.

Marie-Agnès got a faraway look in her eyes as she remembered her grandmothers' soups, her mother's stews, the *taluas* (yeasty Basque crêpes) they make as a family. Pizza made with bread dough was anoth-

er favorite she mentioned, and because she didn't dwell on her favorite topping, I created this one.

It's a natural, and made with typical

Basque ingredients. It looks gorgeous before it goes into the oven, completely different but just as lovely when it comes out.

If you can't find slim and snaky Italian peppers, use green bell peppers cut very thin.

ASTUCE . . . .

• If you're nervous about transferring the rolled dough from the work surface to the baking sheet, just roll it out right on the baking sheet!

. . . .

1 recipe Simple Bread (page 324)
1 pound (500 g) tomatoes, cored and
    thinly sliced
1 pound (500 g) sweet Italian peppers,
    cored, seeded and thinly sliced crosswise
Sea salt and freshly ground black pepper
1¾ heaped cups (150 g) grated sheep's-
    milk cheese, such as Ossau-Iraty or
    Gruyère
1 tablespoon olive oil (optional)

1. Preheat the oven to 425°F (220°C). Dust a baking sheet liberally with flour or cornmeal.

2. Roll out the dough to form a 14 x 11-inch (36 x 28 cm) rectangle. Dust it lightly with flour, roll it loosely around the rolling pin, and unroll it on the prepared baking sheet. Top with the tomatoes and the pep-

What Is Gruyère Cheese?

>·<

Gruyère, an elegant, slightly sweet, Swiss-type cheese, is almost universal in French cooking. In some regions where other similar cheeses are made, cooks will naturally use the local variety, but in most places that I visited, and in most of the recipes I obtained that called for cheese, the cheese was Gruyère.

I personally prefer to use Comté, a nuttier, less sweet, richer, and more complex-tasting cheese. If you can get Comté, try it. If, on the other hand, your cheese options are limited, buy the best-quality, not-too-sweet, Swiss-type cheese you can find.

pers, spreading them evenly over the surface. Season to taste with salt and pepper, then sprinkle evenly with the cheese.

3. Bake in the center of the oven until the edges of the dough are puffed and golden, the vegetables are cooked through, and the cheese is melted, 25 to 30 minutes.

4. Remove the pizza from the oven, drizzle it with the oil if desired, and serve.

One 14 x 11-inch (36 x 28 cm) tart; 6 to 8 servings

LE GOÛTER
Time for a Snack

As 4:00 P.M. approaches, the French stomach gives a collective rumble. Adults dash to the nearest *boulangerie*, make a quick *tartine* of butter and jam, or nibble on a piece of cake. Children, just out of school and ravenous, are taken home by way of the nearest pâtisserie for a *pain au chocolat* or *croissant aux amandes*.

It's time for *le goûter,* the snack, a French institution indulged in by adults and children alike. Sometimes referred to as *le quatre heures,* "the four o'clock," it can occur anywhere between 4:00 and 5:30, depending primarily on after-school schedules.

On the farm, the *goûter* is ready when the children arrive home from school. It might be freshly made strawberry jam poured, still warm, over buttered bread, a stick of chocolate sandwiched in a baguette, a pile of cookies, a fruit salad, or a yogurt sweetened with sugar.

It is not negligible, the *quatre heures,* but rather a substantial part of the French diet, a well-guarded habit nurtured since infancy. As integral to the country as the Eiffel Tower or the cave paintings of Lascaux, it feeds the body and nurtures the soul, taking everyone back, for just a moment, to the comfort of home.

The recipes here are taken directly from *goûters* I have been part of on the farm, but they can as easily be served as dessert, or even for breakfast. Use them to create your own tradition of *goûter,* with its sense of warmth and history.

Le Goûter • Time for a Snack

Butter Cookies from Normandy
Sablés de Caumont-l'Éventé

→•••←

The *sablé*, a simple butter cookie, graces the shelves of every pastry shop and many *boulangeries* in France. They are never the same from one spot to another. Some are as small as silver dollars, plain or dusted with sugar. Others are as large as a coffee can lid, shiny with egg glaze and marked with a crosshatch design. The *sablé* can range as much in quality, too.

A perfect *sablé* should be tender and thin, with a clear taste of butter and a touch of vanilla. These *sablés* are just what they should be—only a touch better. M. Gérard Pupin, who sells them by the dozen, says the secret is not to work them too much. "These are quickly made," he said. "In fact you shouldn't spend too much time on them."

These are truly quick to make, and you can use either confectioners' sugar or regular sugar, according to M. Pupin. I've tried them both ways and much prefer the confectioners' sugar, for then the *sablés* most closely resemble those from Pâtisserie Pupin.

In France, *sablés* are generally eaten for *quatre heures*, the afternoon snacktime. On the farm, everyone stops for a quick bite and sip around then, and we've adopted the habit at home, too. It's my favorite time for a *sablé* and coffee or tea.

This dough is so tender that it doesn't take well to being rolled out more than once. After rolling it out initially, cut out the *sablés* as carefully as possible. Then reserve the scraps, roll them into a cylinder, and refrigerate them (see step 7). You can also freeze the dough scraps for up to one month. Let them thaw somewhat before cutting them into disks.

13 ounces (3¼ sticks; 400 g)
  unsalted butter, at room temperature
1 cup plus 2 tablespoons (140 g)
  confectioners' sugar
1 large egg, lightly beaten
½ teaspoon vanilla extract
3¾ cups (500 g) unbleached all-purpose flour
Pinch of sea salt
½ teaspoon baking powder

1. In a large bowl, or in the bowl of an electric mixer, mix the butter until it is soft and pale yellow. Add the confectioners' sugar and mix well. Then add the egg and mix just until it is blended. Stir in the vanilla.

2. Sift the flour, salt, and baking powder together onto a piece of waxed paper.

3. Add the dry ingredients to the butter mixture and mix well. Cover with aluminum foil and refrigerate for at least 2 hours, and overnight if the dough is still too soft to roll out.

4. Preheat the oven to 425°F (220°C). Line two baking sheets with parchment paper.

5. On a very lightly floured work surface, roll out one fourth of the dough to a thickness of ¼ inch (½ cm). Cut out the *sablés* with a 2-inch (5 cm) round cookie cutter or a glass of the same diameter, and place them ½ inch (1¼ cm) apart on the prepared baking sheets. The dough is somewhat fragile, so work as quickly as you can. Assemble the scraps and set them aside.

6. Bake the *sablés* in the center of the oven until they are golden at the edges, 7 to 8 minutes. Remove from the oven and transfer them to wire racks to cool. Repeat with the remaining dough.

7. Form the scraps into a log with a diameter of 2 inches (5 cm). Wrap, first in parchment paper, then in aluminum foil, and refrigerate overnight, or freeze, until firm. (If frozen, remove from the freezer 30 minutes before slicing.) Slice the log into ¼-inch-thick (½ cm) rounds, arrange them on parchment-lined baking sheets, and bake until golden at the edges, 7 to 8 minutes.

About 60 cookies

The Sablé Expert

→•←

I got my sablé *recipe from Gérard Pupin over the phone, after an afternoon visit to his spotless pâtisserie in the farming community of Caumont-l'Eventé. I spoke with Mme. Pupin when I called to get the recipe, and I could tell she was reluctant to give it to me. She put her hand over the phone to talk to her husband, and he was equally reserved. I explained that I could come back to the pâtisserie, that it would be no trouble even though I lived two hours away. When she heard that, she said, "Oh no, that's way too far," and her hand went over the phone again.*

She got back on and we chatted a bit . . . but no recipe. So I said thank you, that I'd make a trip out and looked forward to it, when suddenly from the background I heard M. Pupin yell, "Eight hundred grams of flour!"

"He wants to give it to you," Mme. Pupin said, laughing, "but he's got his hands in chocolate and can't take the phone." I'm not sure what convinced M. Pupin to part with his recipe—he'd been worried that I was a competitor—but he let it go with abandon, shouting out ingredients and little tricks and hints. Mme. Pupin interpreted, sometimes shouting back with her hand over the phone. By the end of it, we were all laughing. Mme. Pupin made me promise to call her back and tell her the results, which I did. They were remarkable.

Golden Walnuts

=

Jean Chevallier pours two glasses of deep red wine. "To your health," he says as he hands me one. It's sweet, and rich with the taste of walnuts. "My father makes it," he says. "He's known for his walnut wine."

We are in Jean's office in the town hall of Vinay, the heart of France's walnut country. Jean is one of the largest walnut growers there, and he's also the assistant mayor.

"If you're born in Vinay, you're in walnuts. Everybody has walnut trees on their property, and we all work in the nuts somehow."

There are many fewer walnut growers in and around Vinay than there once were, but there is more acreage than ever. "It's not possible to survive with just a few hectares now," Jean says. "We've all gotten bigger, more efficient."

You won't find him complaining about the size of his fields or the amount of work he does. A man who has trouble sitting still, he's an incurable *bricoleur* ("do-it-yourselfer"), building and adapting machinery to make the job easier, constantly on the run among his walnuts, his politics, and his family. His father, Emile, now retired, still

works with him full-time, and his mother and his wife, Françoise, are the designated walnut crackers, bakers, cooks, and promoters.

"We cultivate the same trees my grandfather did," Jean says. "Walnut trees last a long time, more than sixty years." The trees also take a long time to come into production, so walnut growers know the meaning of patience. A walnut tree planted at the birth of a child will mature when the child does, at fifteen to twenty years old.

The Chevallier walnut trees are scattered throughout the town, which is nestled in the Isère Valley at the foot of the Alps, not far from Grenoble. Some grow around the tall, wide stone farmhouse where Jean grew up, and where he and his family live. The house was built to accommodate more than one family, and his parents live downstairs. It's a cozy arrangement, but you'd never know there were two families in the same house—the walls are so thick, the entrances so discreetly separate.

The old farmhouse is situated at the back of a courtyard, and to gain access you must drive between two huge, airy barns. Off to one side of the courtyard and beyond a wall are the trees, spreading and regal against the sky.

A FALL HARVEST

Walnuts are harvested in September. A pre-harvest begins on September 20 for *noix fraîches*, fresh walnuts, which are a delicacy, and the real harvest begins a week later. Jean and his father take a *secoueur*, or shaker, into the groves. Fitted with a long arm, it has a big metal "hand" at the end that closes around the trunk of a tree and gently but firmly shakes it so the nuts tumble to the ground. Jean salutes the Californians who invented the machine. "Thank you, Americans," he says. "It's helped us a lot."

Back at the farm the nuts are put in a tub full of water, where any debris sinks to the bottom. "We wash and sort them according to size," says Françoise, who supervises this step.

They keep the small nuts for themselves. Beautiful large ones they send to the town's cooperative, which is the biggest in the country. There the nuts are mechanically dried, bagged, and sold. The bulk of the market is for walnuts in the shell, though cracked walnuts are increasingly sought after. A noisy machine at the cooperative obliges, spitting the shells out one side, the nutmeats out the other.

Jean and Emile pile some of the nuts they'll keep for themselves on the top floor of one barn, which has slatted floors so the air can circulate and dry them.

"This is how we used to dry all our nuts," Jean says. "These barns were built for that purpose." They also have a small gas dryer in another barn, to give the nuts a final, complete drying.

Emile picks up four nuts in his large, knobby hand and rubs them together. "When they rattle, you know they're dry enough to use," he says. "These are ready."

Françoise spends winter nights cracking walnuts and classifying their meats according to size and color. She likes to experiment with them and puts them into everything from salad to dessert. Like others in Vinay, she also serves them as an apéritif, along with a glass of walnut wine. Broken or small nuts are ground into oil.

"We don't make our own oil—we've got some elderly neighbors who make it for us," Jean said. Once, nearly every farm had a stone mill somewhere on the property. Now just the older farmers have the time and patience to keep the mills running. They gently toast the nutmeats and grind them, still hot, until the oil runs golden and clear.

In France, and throughout Europe, walnuts are a luxury product in high demand. That keeps the Chevallier family busy, and it ensures a future for all the families in and around Vinay who owe their prosperity to the golden walnut.

Walnut Butter Cookies

Sablés aux Noix

→····←

This recipe comes from Françoise Chevallier, who with her husband, Jean, raises *noix de Grenoble*, France's famed sweet walnuts. Since 1938 their walnuts—and all of those grown in a small region around Grenoble, at the foot of the French Alps—have had an Appellation d'Origine Contrôlée, allowing them their label Noix de Grenoble. Noted for their light honey color, their size, and their incomparable flavor, these walnuts are highly sought after and are generally more expensive than other walnuts.

One evening as I sat at the Chevalliers' table, Françoise served freshly cracked walnut halves along with her father-in-law's award-winning walnut wine as an apéritif. She was surrounded by small boxes of nuts. "These are the whole halves, which I'll use for decorations," she said, sweeping her hand over a stack of boxes. "These are the broken pieces that go into pastries."

Broken walnuts go into these *sablés*, a tried-and-true recipe that Françoise makes often. Simple and quick to make, they are wonderful with a glass of wine or with a small cup of coffee after a meal.

Be sure to buy the best possible walnuts before you make the *sablés*. The oil in walnuts is volatile and it won't take long for a fresh, sweet nut to become bitter, so sample the walnuts if possible. Once you get them home, keep them in a very cold place, such as the freezer.

ASTUCE . . . .

• *When grinding up to 2 cups walnuts in a food processor, add 1 tablespoon granulated sugar. This will prevent the nuts from being overground and turning oily.*

. . . .

¾ cup (90 g) walnut pieces

½ cup (100 g) sugar

7 tablespoons (105 g) unsalted butter, at
    room temperature

1½ cups (200 g) unbleached all-purpose
    flour

1 large egg

1. Preheat the oven to 400°F (205°C). Line two baking sheets with parchment paper.

2. Place the walnuts in a food processor, add 1 tablespoon of the sugar, and process, pulsing, until they are finely ground. Transfer them to a small bowl and set aside.

3. Place the butter, the remaining sugar, and the flour in a food processor and process, pulsing, until the mixture has the consistency of sand.

4. Add the egg and process just until it is incorporated and the dough is beginning to hold together, 2 to 3 minutes. Transfer the dough to a smooth, lightly floured work surface, and quickly but thoroughly knead in the reserved ground nuts.

5. Divide the dough in half. Roll the first half out to form a 7½-inch (19 cm) square, ¼ inch (½ cm) thick. Cut it into 1½-inch (4 cm) squares. Repeat with the second half. Place the *sablés* on the prepared baking sheets, leaving about ¼ inch (½ cm) between them, and bake in the center of the oven until the cookies are golden at the edges, about 11 minutes.

6. Remove from the oven and transfer the *sablés* to wire racks and let cool to room temperature. Then store them in an airtight container. They will keep for about 4 days.

50 cookies

Almond Crisps
Croquants d'Amandes

These hard almond- and honey-scented cookies offer a sweet, nutty taste of Provence. I first discovered them in the charming hilltop village of Sault, near Jean Giono (the seminal Provençal writer) country in Provence, at the wood-fronted *confiserie/pâtisserie* André Boyer. There, the thin *croquants* are carefully packed in cellophane bags and tied with a glittering gold tie, so they look like packages of jewels on the shelf.

I searched long and far for a good *croquant* recipe, and finally found this, given to me by Brigitte Emeric of Montbrun-les-Bains, near Sault. They are my favorites still, rich with toasty almond flavor, and totally satisfying. They go as well with a glass of Gigondas as they do with a mid-morning cup of coffee, and will keep for several weeks in an airtight container.

A S T U C E . . . .

• *You may twice-bake these cookies, as indicated in the recipe, or simply bake them once, cut, cool, and serve. They are less toasty when baked once, and slightly softer, though still pleasantly crunchy. It will depend on your time and your taste.*

. . . .

> 2¼ cups (300 g) unbleached all-purpose
>   flour
> Pinch of sea salt
> 3 large eggs, lightly beaten
> 1½ cups (300 g) Vanilla Sugar
>   (page 521)
> 1 tablespoon honey, preferably lavender,
>   lightly warmed (softened)
> 2¼ cups (300 g) whole almonds

1. Preheat the oven to 450°F (230°C). Line one or two large baking sheets with parchment paper.

2. Sift the flour and the salt into a large mixing bowl. Make a well in the center and add the eggs, then slowly whisk in the sugar, gradually incorporating the flour as well, until you have a smooth, thick dough. Stir in the honey, then add the almonds and stir until they are well distributed throughout the dough.

3. Turn the dough out onto a lightly floured surface and dust it with flour. Divide it into thirds, and form three thick, flat ovals, placing them at least 2 inches (5 cm) apart on one of the prepared baking sheets. You may

Flouring a Work Surface

→•←

U *nless otherwise specified, always light-ly flour your work surface before rolling out pastries or doughs.*

To lightly and evenly flour the work surface, use the classic French technique I learned from Albert Jorant, the delightful and enlightening pastry chef at La Varenne Ecole de Cuisine. Grab a large pinch of flour with your fingers and strew it, with a sharp snap of the wrist, over your work surface. You will see that the flour falls in a light and even veil. Repeat if necessary as you work.

need to lightly flour your hands as you work, as the dough tends to be quite sticky.

4. Bake in the center of the oven until the ovals are golden and feel firm, though not hard, when you touch them, about 23 minutes. Remove the baking sheet from the oven and transfer the ovals to your work surface.

(If you are going to bake them again, leave the oven on.) Cut them, crosswise, into about 18 slices. If you don't plan to bake them again, leave the slices to cool completely on wire cooling racks. Or to bake a second time, lay the slices, cut side down, on the baking sheet or sheets, leaving just a bit of space between each slice. Bake just until they begin to turn golden, about 4 minutes. Turn the slices and bake an additional 4 minutes. Remove from the oven and let cool on wire racks.

About 54 cookies

Macaroons

Macarons

>····<

These delicate little cookies come from Marie-France Goussard, who lives on a farm in the Beauce, just an hour south of Paris. Since Roman times, the Beauce has been the heart of wheat country, and it is still referred to as the *grenier de France*, the granary of France, although wheat is now grown in many other regions.

Mme. Goussard has always lived in the Beauce, and always on a wheat farm—first her parents', now the one she shares with her husband and their three children. She claims there is no regional cuisine in the Beauce, something I heard repeatedly while I was in that golden region. I believe it is true. It is a small area that has borrowed recipes from throughout the country, and feels itself no poorer for it.

On the day I visited at the farm, Mme. Goussard insisted that she wasn't much of a cook, but that her mother, who is a very good cook, wanted me to have the following recipe as one that was representative of a family favorite.

"We eat meat and vegetables here, nothing much special," she told me apologetically. "But these *macarons*, you'll see, are delicious."

She's right. Tiny and most delicate, these very, very sweet little cookies, which don't resemble standard macaroons, are crisp little mouthfuls, unusually flavored with cinnamon.

You'll question the simplicity of the ingredients—how could they possibly turn out anything tasty? Try the recipe and see.

You'll find these macaroons irresistible.

The dough for the macaroons can be prepared well in advance, stored in the freezer, and baked on the spot.

1½ cups (180 g) cake flour
1 teaspoon baking powder
1 teaspoon ground cinnamon
Pinch of sea salt
3 tablespoons unsalted butter,
*   at room temperature*
1 cup (200 g) sugar
1 large egg

1. Sift the cake flour, baking powder, cinnamon, and salt together onto a piece of waxed or parchment paper.

Room-Temperature Eggs
→•←

Current wisdom in the U.S. calls for the refrigeration of eggs so they don't develop unhealthy bacteria at room temperature. On the French farm, refrigerating eggs is akin to boiling a crème anglaise. In other words, it's considered a grave error that ruins flavor and texture.

Practically speaking, a cold egg won't blend or cook properly, and eggs should always be at room temperature before being added to sauces, batters, or doughs. So if your eggs are refrigerated, remember to remove them from the refrigerator at least 30 minutes before you plan to use them.

2. In a medium-size bowl, cream the butter and sugar until the mixture is well blended and light. Add the egg and mix well. Then add the dry ingredients and mix just until blended.

3. Form the dough into three logs that measure about 12 inches (30 cm) long and ½ inch (1¼ cm) in diameter (they should be almost like short ropes). Wrap them individually in waxed paper, then in aluminum foil, and refrigerate for at least 2 hours, and preferably overnight.

4. Preheat the oven to 400°F (205°C). Line two baking sheets with parchment paper.

5. Cut the logs into ¼-inch-thick (½ cm) rounds, and place them ¾ inch (2 cm) apart on the baking sheets. Bake in the center of the oven until they begin to turn golden at the edges, 6 to 8 minutes. Remove the baking sheets from the oven. Pull the parchment paper off the baking sheets and let the macaroons sit for 2 minutes. Then remove the macaroons from the parchment and let them cool on a wire rack.

About 12 dozen macaroons

Nicole's "Lost Bread" Cake
Pain Perdu de Nicole

➔•••◄

Nicole Vallortigara's father was a *métayer*, or tenant farmer, who had a sense of wanderlust. Though he never strayed from Provence, he had many jobs on many different farms. According to Nicole, who is one of seven children, moving wasn't an unpleasant experience, but it meant they never owned a thing of their own. They lived in houses provided by the owners of the farms, which were usually furnished, and they took little with them when they moved.

Nicole was the only person I met in my travels around the French countryside who had had such a peripatetic childhood. She has vivid memories and a profound understanding of how to make the best of very little. Her stories, which she tells with verve, are rife with little observations about farm life. For instance, when she was telling me about this recipe, she said, "There was no thought about giving stale bread to animals, the way people do now. We *ate* that stale bread. Nothing went to waste—we didn't have the means to waste things."

Her family was very poor, her mother thrifty in the way of all farm women forty years ago. She was always inventing ways to use stale bread, and this was the family's favorite. Though Nicole, her husband, Germain, and their daughter, Elodie, are much less restricted, Nicole loves this sweet, citrus-y pudding so much that she still saves her bread to make it.

"Germain can eat the whole thing," she said, looking at him and laughing.

I love this recipe, not only because it makes good use of dry bread (after you've ground as much as you'll need for a year's worth of bread crumbs) but also because it's comforting, like a rich and homey pudding, perfect for dessert or *goûter*. Traditionally laced with orange-flower water, it can also be studded with candied fruit (if you're tempted to do this, use the best quality you can find), raisins, apples, or pears. I like it best this way, simply flavored with vanilla, orange, and lemon.

It is best served warm, so time the cooking so it is steaming when you bring it to the table, seducing your guests with its sweet aroma. It is not the loveliest dessert, so you may want to present individual portions, garnished with whipped crème fraîche and mint leaves.

A S T U C E . . . .

• *Don't be tempted to avoid the water bath. It is essential for the texture of this pudding. If it cooks without it, it develops a tough, unappealing crust.*

. . . .

8 ounces (250 g) stale white bread,
    cut into 1½-inch-thick (4 cm) slices
    or chunks
4 cups (1 l) whole milk
3 large eggs, beaten
⅔ cup (135 g) sugar
1 teaspoon vanilla extract
Zest of 1 orange, minced
Zest of 1 lemon, minced
1 tablespoon unsalted butter
1 tablespoon mild honey
Fresh mint leaves, for garnish (optional)
1 cup (250 ml) Crème Fraîche
    (page 520), or heavy (or whipping)
    cream, whipped, for garnish
    (optional)

1. Place the bread in a large mixing bowl and pour the milk over it. Stir the bread so it is completely covered with milk, and let it sit at room temperature until it has absorbed the milk, about 2 hours. Turn the bread occasionally so it absorbs the milk evenly.

2. Preheat the oven to 400°F (205°C).

3. When the bread has absorbed all the milk, purée the mixture in a food processor. Return the purée, which will have the consistency of thick whipping cream, to the mixing bowl. Whisk in the eggs until thoroughly incorporated. Then add the sugar, vanilla extract, and citrus zests.

4. Place the butter in a 3-quart (3 l) baking dish, and place it in the oven to melt, 4 minutes. Remove the baking dish from the oven and paint the bottom and sides with the melted butter. Drizzle the honey over the butter on the bottom and blend it in.

5. Turn the batter into the baking dish, and place the dish in a large baking pan with sides that are at least 2 inches (5 cm) high. Pour boiling water into the large pan until it is half full, and place it in the middle of the oven to bake.

6. Bake until the *pain perdu* is slightly puffed, golden on top, and a deeper golden just around the edges, about 1 hour. (The *pain perdu* doesn't puff dramatically—just slightly.) To test it for doneness, stick a knife into the center. If it comes out clean, the *pain perdu* is cooked through.

7. Remove the dish from the oven and from the water bath, and let it cool for at least 10 minutes before serving. The *pain perdu* will settle, falling slightly. Serve with the mint leaves as garnish and the whipped crème fraîche alongside, if desired.

6 to 8 servings

Crêpes with Sugar
Crêpes au Sucre

>···<

*C*rêpes de froment are the traditional crêpes found in Brittany, the kind you buy in packages from the *crêperie*, set on the car seat beside you, and munch on through the long miles!

The *crêpe de froment* is served as a dessert crêpe and can be filled with anything from melted chocolate to applesauce to vanilla ice cream with both applesauce and melted chocolate. It is tender, slightly sweet, and scented with vanilla.

A typical way to serve *crêpes de froment* is simply to slather them with butter (preferably lightly salted) and sprinkle them with sugar. I like that, but I like this way even more. Suggested by a friend who is known for her crêpes, I think it is the perfect crêpe dessert—fresh, light, and simple.

I've given exact measurements for the lemon juice and sugar so that you can assemble all the ingredients in advance. But really, the best thing to do is to set a bowl of lemon wedges and one of sugar—either white or brown—on the table and serve the crêpes warm, already brushed with melted butter.

This is also a delicious way to serve Buckwheat Crêpes (see Index).

*1 recipe Sweet White-Flour Crêpes
(recipe follows)*
*5 tablespoons (about ⅔ stick; 75 g) lightly
salted butter, melted*
⅓ cup (65 g) granulated or brown sugar
*⅓ cup (80 ml) freshly squeezed
lemon juice*

Make each crêpe, brushing it liberally with melted butter (it works out to 1 teaspoon per crêpe), then sprinkle it with 1 teaspoon sugar and 1 teaspoon lemon juice. (Or serve the crêpes directly from the pan, after brushing them with butter, and let the diners garnish their own.)

6 to 8 servings

Sweet White-Flour Crêpes
Crêpes de Froment

→····←

It was Germaine Plassart who headed me on my way to crêpe appreciation, for when I stayed with her and her husband, Jean, in their Brittany home, she got out her electric *billig*, or griddle for making crêpes, and presided over a *crêpe soirée*. Standing over the *billig*, she spread batter and quickly flipped the crêpes like an expert, getting enough ahead that she could sit down and eat with us.

Spreading that batter over the griddle is no mean trick, for the batter cooks as soon as it hits the surface, meaning the crêpe maker has to move fast and gracefully. Germaine invited me to try my hand, and after turning out several doilies, I finally made a reasonable crêpe.

Crêpes de froment are generally sweetened with vanilla sugar, but if you'd like to use a savory filling, just leave out the sugar. Also, if you don't have milk on hand, use water. You'll be surprised at the results—they're very, very delicate and delicious.

This batter is very easy to work with—it spreads neatly across the pan. But pull it from the pan with care, for the cooked crêpe has a tendency to tear.

Typically, a crêpe like this is spread with butter and sprinkled with sugar (see previous recipe). They make a fine *goûter* or dessert after a light meal.

1¾ cups (230 g) unbleached all-purpose flour
¾ teaspoon sea salt
2½ cups (625 ml) milk
1 tablespoon Vanilla Sugar (page 521; optional)
3 large eggs
1 tablespoon Clarified Butter (page 519)

1. Sift the flour and salt together into a bowl, and make a well in the center. Add 1¼ cups (310 ml) of the milk and all the vanilla sugar, and gradually whisk the flour into it. Add in the eggs one at a time, whisking just until they are blended. Then whisk in the remaining milk. Let sit for 30 minutes.

2. Heat a 10½-inch (26½ cm) crêpe pan

over medium-high heat. Brush the pan with some of the clarified butter, and using a ¼-cup (60 ml) measure, pour the batter into the center of the pan. Quickly turn and shake the pan until the batter coats the bottom. Let cook until the crêpe is golden and beginning to curl at the edges, about 1½ minutes. If the crêpe is cooking too quickly and getting close to burned on the bottom, reduce the heat slightly. Take the edge of the crêpe in your fingers, or lift it using a wooden or plastic spatula, and gently pull the crêpe up. Turn it over and continue cooking until the other side is slightly gold-

en, 30 seconds. Repeat with the remaining butter and batter.

3. Place the crêpes on a plate and keep them warm in a very low oven, covered with a cotton tea towel. Or serve them as you take them from the pan.

14 crêpes

Clafoutis

→•••←

Clafoutis (CLA-foo-tea), a custardy, fruit-studded cake, is the dessert that all French farm women have at their fingertips. They can make it, using no recipe, for an impromptu afternoon *goûter* or for a more formal occasion, whenever a pleasant and satisfying dessert is called for.

There isn't a standard recipe for *clafoutis*. In fact, the number of versions are head-spinning, and trying to sort them out is like documenting the family tree. Little threads get lost because no one quite agrees on proportions or method.

This, however, was presented to me in written form. It comes from a friend who

lives in rural Normandy, on farmland that she and her husband use for horses and for a huge vegetable garden. I think it is the best *clafoutis* I've ever tasted, for it is light, shy on flour, big on custardy fruit flavor.

I like to make *clafoutis* with cherries or apricots, but it is common, particularly where I live, to use apples or pears, which are delicious variations. Whatever fruit you choose, use the same quantity as given here for apricots.

ASTUCE . . . .

• *The tricks to a good* clafoutis: *a minimum of flour to custard, a hot oven and quick cooking, and nuggets of butter on top just before baking.*

. . . .

*12 ounces (375 g) fresh apricots, pitted
   and cut in half
1 cup minus 2 tablespoons (125 g) sifted
   unbleached all-purpose flour (see Note)
Heaping ¼ teaspoon sea salt
2 cups (500 ml) milk
3 large eggs
⅓ cup (70 g) Vanilla Sugar (page 521)
½ teaspoon vanilla extract
1 tablespoon unsalted butter, cut into
   6 pieces*

1. Preheat the oven to 450°F (230°C). Butter and lightly flour a 9½-inch (24 cm) nonreactive round tart pan or baking dish.

2. Place the apricots, cut side down, in the tart pan.

3. Combine the flour and the salt in a large bowl and mix with your hands. Whisk in 1 cup of the milk until smooth. Then add the eggs one by one, whisking briefly after each addition. Whisk in the vanilla sugar, the remaining 1 cup milk, and the vanilla extract.

4. Pour the batter over the apricots. Dot it with the butter, place it on the center rack of the oven, and bake until it is golden and puffed, about 25 minutes. Remove it from the oven and let it cool thoroughly before serving.

6 to 8 servings

NOTE: Sift the flour before measuring, which will result in a lighter batter.

Sugar Tart
Tarte au Sucre

→ • • • ←

This tart comes from the north of France, where sugar is a specialty. There one finds sugar in every shape and color imaginable, from tiny white pearls to small, creamy ivory blocks. There is also *sucre vergeoise,* a slightly moist, very fine sugar that comes in pale or dark brown and is a sort of by-product of white sugar. It has an arresting flavor, a hint of the sugar beet from which it is produced. It is the sugar most commonly used in pastries in the north, and it's the sugar I prefer for this tart. The U.S. equivalent is dark brown sugar.

Not a tart in the strict sense of the word, this is more of a pizza, though made with a light brioche-like dough. Simple, rich with the golden flavor of butter, crisp and sweet, it goes as well after supper as it does in the morning with coffee. In fact, take a hint from the north and dip your *tarte au sucre* into a steaming bowl of coffee. You'll be tempted to murmur, as friends of ours did, "*Le petit Jésu en culottes de velour*" ("Little Jesus in velvet pants"), which expresses the notion of ultimate goodness.

Tarte au sucre can be made in an hour. The dough, called *pâte briochée*, is simple to put together and as light as a feather when baked. It requires ingredients that are usually on hand, so you can put it together at a moment's notice. Try adding lemon zest to the dough, or a hint of allspice to the sugar, for a variation.

In winter I like to serve this with Apple Compote (see Index). In summer I occasionally make it on cool evenings and serve it with fresh sliced peaches or a mixture of berries.

ASTUCE . . . .

• *If you want to serve this for breakfast, make the dough and refrigerate it, covered with aluminum foil or a plastic lid, overnight. In the morning, punch it down, roll it out, and proceed with step 3 of the recipe.*

. . . .

FOR THE PATE BRIOCHEE
2 cups plus 2 tablespoons (290 g) unbleached all-purpose flour
¾ teaspoon sea salt
⅓ cup (80 ml) warm milk
1 tablespoon sugar
1 teaspoon active dry yeast
2 large eggs
6 tablespoons (¾ stick; 90 g) unsalted butter, at room temperature

FOR THE TOPPING
2 tablespoons unsalted butter
¼ cup (50 g) loosely packed dark brown sugar

1. Butter a 16 x 12-inch (40 x 30 cm) baking sheet.

2. Prepare the dough: Place the flour and the salt in a large bowl, or in the bowl of an electric mixer, and mix to blend. Make a well in the center, and add the milk mixture and the sugar, stirring. Sprinkle the yeast over the liquid and mix it in. Let sit just long enough for the yeast to dissolve and begin to bubble, about 5 minutes. Add the eggs one at a time, mixing after each addition. Gradually incorporate the flour, beating about 7 minutes by hand, 3 to 4 in a mixer, until the

dough readily detaches from the sides of the bowl. It will be firm yet soft, and it should not stick to your hands. Add the butter in small portions, mixing just until it is blended into the dough. The dough will be pale yellow and almost fluffy. It should be easy to handle—soft but not sticky.

3. Roll out the dough on a lightly floured work surface to form a 15 x 11-inch (38 x 28 cm) rectangle, and transfer it to the prepared baking sheet. (An easy way to do this is to fold the dough in half, quickly place it at one end of the baking sheet, and unfold it. Alternatively, you can roll it out on parchment or waxed paper, place it on the baking sheet with the dough side down, and peel off the paper.)

4. Let the dough rise, uncovered, in a warm spot (68° to 70°F; 20° to 21°C) until nearly doubled in bulk, about 30 minutes.

5. Meanwhile, preheat the oven to 400°F (205°C).

6. Just before baking, prepare the topping: Cut the butter into small chunks. Sprinkle the brown sugar evenly over the dough, and scatter the butter over the sugar.

7. Bake the tart in the center of the oven until it is puffed and golden on top and the sugar has caramelized slightly, about 20 minutes.

8. Remove the tart from the oven and transfer it to a warmed platter to serve immediately, or to a wire rack if you'll be serving it at room temperature.

6 to 8 servings

Honey Tart
Tarte au Miel

This is a version of the tart—really more of a sweet pizza—that was made and put in children's Easter baskets in Provence, according to Nicole Vallortigara, who remembers from her childhood. You may make individual tarts, or do as I do and press the dough out on a baking sheet, then cut it into squares to serve.

This is sumptuous for dessert, particularly accompanied by Peaches in Red Wine (see Index). It is also delicious for breakfast, quickly dunked in nice, strong coffee or tea.

ASTUCE . . . .

• In this recipe, softened butter means butter that is so soft it has the consistency of mayonnaise. To make it this way, cut the butter in pieces and let them warm in the oven, just long enough so that the edges begin to melt. Then, using a firm whisk, whisk until the butter is the desired consistency.

. . . .

2 cups (210 g) almonds
½ cup (125 ml) honey
2 cups (285 g) unbleached all-purpose
  flour
1 teaspoon sea salt
3 tablespoons sugar
2 tablespoons lukewarm water
1 tablespoon active dry yeast
3 large eggs, lightly beaten
6 tablespoons (¾ stick; 90 g) unsalted
  butter, softened

1. Preheat the oven to 350°F (175°C).

2. Place the almonds on a baking sheet and toast them in the oven just until they begin to turn golden, about 10 minutes. Remove from the oven and set aside. When the almonds have cooled, coarsely chop them.

3. In a small saucepan, heat the honey very gently over low heat, just until it melts; don't let it boil, or even simmer. Remove from the heat and let cool. The honey will stay soft enough to spread.

4. Place the flour and the salt in a large bowl, or the bowl of an electric mixer. Stir to mix, and make a well in the center. Place the sugar, the water, and the yeast in the well and mix together, then add the eggs. Gradually incorporate the flour to form a soft dough (see Note). Continue beating by hand for 5 minutes, or by machine for about 3 minutes, until the dough is elastic. It will be somewhat sticky, but shouldn't stick to your hands.

5. Work in the butter and mix just until it is incorporated. At this point the dough is almost more of a batter than a dough—it is sticky, and though it isn't wet, may stick to your fingers.

6. Cover the bowl with a tea towel and let the dough rise in a warm spot (68° to 70°F; 20° to 21°C) until it is nearly a third larger, about 45 minutes.

7. Preheat the oven to 350°F (175°C). Generously butter a baking sheet.

8. Punch down the dough and gently spread it out with your fingers on the prepared baking sheet to form a 12½-inch (32 cm) square. Make a slightly raised border all around the edges of the dough.

9. Spread the honey over the dough, and sprinkle with the reserved almonds. Bake in the center of the oven until the dough is golden and the honey is bubbling, about 45 minutes.

10. Remove from the oven and let sit for at least 10 minutes before serving, as the honey is blistering hot right from the oven. You may also serve this at room temperature.

8 to 10 servings

NOTE: In an electric mixer, all will come together very quickly, as the well one forms is small, so it is hard to contain the liquids in it. Don't be concerned.

Le Goûter • Time for a Snack

Breakfast Cake
Le Gâteau du Petit Déjeuner

→···←

Until I stayed on farms in Brittany, I didn't realize that cake was ever served for breakfast in France. Undoubtedly reserved for special company, cake nonetheless appeared at breakfast on every farm I visited. Always light and simple, it accompanied the usual offerings of crêpes and the *clafoutis*-like *far breton*.

I feel that if they serve cake in Brittany, then surely it is a custom worth repeating, and this is the recipe to use. Ideally suited for breakfast, it is not too sweet, and its texture is on the coarse side, ideal for dipping in a bowl of coffee. It is also perfect for *le goûter* for all the same reasons.

The nutmeg is my addition, but the cake is also good the way they serve it in Brittany, simply flavored with vanilla.

ASTUCE . . . .

• *When baking a cake, line the bottom of the pan with parchment paper, then butter and flour the paper. The layer of paper between the cake and the pan not only makes it easy to unmold but also keeps any metallic flavor out of the cake.*

. . . .

1½ cups (200 g) unbleached all-purpose
    flour
2 teaspoons baking powder
½ teaspoon freshly grated nutmeg
    (optional)
¼ teaspoon sea salt
14 tablespoons (1¾ sticks; 210 g) unsalted
    butter, at room temperature
⅔ cup (135 g) Vanilla Sugar (page 521)
3 large eggs

1. Preheat the oven to 350°F (175°C). Butter and flour a 9-inch (23 cm) round cake pan. Then line the bottom of the pan with parchment paper, and butter and flour the paper.

2. Sift the flour, baking powder, nutmeg (if using), and salt onto a piece of waxed paper.

3. In a large bowl, or in the bowl of an electric mixer, cream the butter until it is pale yellow and light. Then add the vanilla sugar and continue beating until the mixture is fluffy. Beat in the eggs, one at a time, until well mixed. Then fold in the flour mixture in three separate batches.

4. Turn the batter into the prepared pan, and tap it on the counter once or twice to remove any air bubbles. Bake in the center of the oven until the cake is golden and a cake tester inserted in the center comes out clean, 25 to 30 minutes.

5. Let the cake cool on a wire rack for about 10 minutes, then unmold it. Let it cool thoroughly before serving.

8 to 10 servings

NOTE: This cake keeps well, if tightly wrapped, for 2 to 3 days.

Alsatian Coffee Bread
Kugelhopf

→•••←

This sweet vanilla-laced, raisin-studded bread is the signature pastry of Alsace, and every pâtisserie in the region displays them in the front window. It is generally served for a late-afternoon snack along with a steaming cup of black coffee, or for breakfast.

Kugelhopf molds are treasured in Alsace, where years of use mellow them to the point that butter isn't needed to keep the dough from sticking. Bakers insist that the older and more used the mold—some are nearly black with use—the better and more flavorful the kugelhopf.

Kugelhopf is best baked the day before it is to be served, so the flavors have a chance to ripen.

¾ cup (125 g) golden raisins

2 tablespoons kirsch, or other fruit-based liqueur

1 cup (250 ml) milk, heated to lukewarm

1 scant tablespoon (1 package) active dry yeast

¾ cup (150 g) Vanilla Sugar (page 521)

2 eggs

3¾ cups (500 g) unbleached all-purpose flour

1 teaspoon salt

12 tablespoons (1½ sticks; 180 g) unsalted butter, cut into small pieces, at room temperature

17 whole almonds (see Note)

1. About 1 hour before you plan to bake the kugelhopf, combine the raisins and kirsch in a small bowl. Stir, and set aside.

2. In a large mixing bowl, combine the lukewarm milk and the yeast. Stir, then add the vanilla sugar and stir well. Let sit for 5 minutes, until the yeast begins to foam. Whisk in the eggs, one at a time, until thoroughly combined. Then gradually add the flour and salt, mixing well with a wooden spoon. The dough will be quite sticky. Continue mixing the dough, using a wooden spoon or your hands, by slapping it against the side of the bowl until it is quite elastic, about 10 minutes (5 minutes in an electric mixer).

3. Gradually add the butter piece by piece, kneading until it is incorporated and the dough is smooth and elastic, and comes cleanly off the sides of the bowl, about 5 minutes (2 to 3 minutes in an electric mixer).

Mix in the raisins until they are distributed throughout the dough. Leave the dough in the bowl, cover it with a tea towel, and let it rise in a warm spot (68° to 70°F; 20° to 21°C) until it has nearly doubled in bulk, about 1½ hours.

4. Punch down the dough and knead it briefly to remove all of the air. Then let it rise again until nearly doubled in bulk, about 1½ hours.

5. Heavily butter a 6-cup (1½ l) kugelhopf mold, and place the almonds in the indentations in the bottom of the mold. Punch down the dough and place it in the mold as

Vanilla Sugar

→•←

*Y*ou'll notice vanilla sugar appears in many sweet recipes in this book. Why? Because a touch of vanilla softens and rounds out the flavor of sweet baked goods.

In France, little packets of intensely flavored vanilla sugar are readily available at supermarkets and groceries, and many sweet recipes call for a packet or two. In the U.S., those little packets aren't easily available, nor are they necessary when one has sugar flavored with a couple of whole vanilla beans (see Index for the recipe). In recipes calling for vanilla sugar, you may always use plain white sugar and it will turn out fine, though it will lack that wonderful roundness that vanilla gives.

In a Warm Spot

>·<

Yeast doughs need several things to help them work, and one is a reasonably warm atmosphere. I find room temperature—generally 68° to 70°F (20° to 21°C)—ideal. This encourages the yeast without pushing it, allowing it to work in optimal conditions.

evenly as possible, then let it rise until it reaches the top, about 1 hour. (If you don't have a kugelhopf mold, use a 6-cup (1½ l) soufflé dish. Place the dough in the soufflé dish, and arrange the almonds on top of the dough.)

6. Preheat the oven to 350°F (175°C).

7. Bake the kugelhopf in the center of the oven until it is golden and sounds hollow when the mold is tapped, 1 hour.

8. Remove the mold from the oven and let it sit for 5 minutes. Unmold the kugelhopf and let it cool on a wire rack. Dust it with confectioners' sugar before serving, if desired. (If you used a soufflé dish, cool the kugelhopf almond side up on a wire rack, and serve it so the almonds are showing.)

About 8 servings

N O T E : The 17 almonds correspond to the number of indentations in a kugelhopf mold. If you are using a soufflé dish, you can use more or less according to your taste.

Isabelle's Semolina Cake
Gâteau de Semoule d'Isabelle

>···<

A favorite on the Dugord farm in Normandy, this cake (which is really more of a pudding) wins with everyone. According to Isabelle Dugord, who convinced her grandmother to share the recipe, her family ate this all the time when she was growing up, and it's still her preferred sweet. Isabelle works part-time at a day-care center and always has the children make this at least once while they're with her. "It's easy to make, healthy, and they all, down to the last child, just love it," she said.

It can be served hot, lukewarm, or chilled, and is best the day it is made.

Raisins are traditional, though dates or figs are luscious, too.

ASTUCES . . . .

• *The operative words when making caramel are "shake" and "swirl," for once the sugar begins to caramelize, you must periodically remove the pan from the heat and swirl it so the sugar caramelizes evenly. Shake when the sugar begins to melt so that it is always evenly distributed across the bottom of the pan; swirl when there are slightly darker streaks in it; swirl right toward the end of the process if there is a spot of finely layered sugar just on the top. Finally, when the sugar is a light caramel color, remove it from the heat and tip the pan so most of the caramel runs to one side. Then pour it into the mold, swirling the mold as you pour so it will evenly cover the bottom. If there are holes, just move the caramel pan over them so drips of caramel will fall in and fill them.*

• *To clean the caramel pan, simply fill it with water and bring to a boil. This works as well for any utensils that have caramel welded onto them.*

• *Don't worry about testing this cake for doneness— just trust the time and the cooking temperature. You would have to cook it until it had the consistency of cement to get a knife to come clean from it.*

. . . .

¾ cup (150 g) plus 6 tablespoons sugar
1 teaspoon unsalted butter, melted
3 large eggs
4 cups (1 l) milk
1 vanilla bean, split down its length
Pinch of sea salt
¾ cup plus 1 tablespoon (120 g) semolina
¼ teaspoon freshly grated nutmeg
½ cup (75 g) raisins

1. Preheat the oven to 400°F (200°C). Have ready a 6-cup (1½ l) soufflé dish or charlotte mold.

2. Make the caramel: Place the 6 tablespoons sugar in a small heavy saucepan over medium heat. It will gradually dissolve, and as it does so, swirl it around in the pan. When it is a pale caramel color, after 4 to 5 minutes, quickly pour it into the mold, swirling the mold so the caramel completely covers the bottom. Use a pastry brush to brush the sides of the mold with the melted butter.

3. Whisk the eggs in a small bowl until they are blended and set aside.

4. Place the milk, ¾ cup (150 g) sugar, and vanilla bean in a medium-size heavy saucepan. Stir, and heat over medium heat until the milk is steaming and small bubbles have formed around the edges. Immediately remove from the heat, cover, and let infuse for 10 minutes. Then remove the vanilla bean, rinse it well, and reserve it for another use.

5. Return the milk to medium heat, and when small bubbles have formed around the edges, add the salt and the semolina, lightly sprinkling the semolina over the milk (see

Note) and stirring constantly. Continue to stir constantly as the semolina cooks (it will thicken dramatically), until it has become like a paste, at least 10 minutes.

6. Remove the semolina from the heat and whisk in the eggs until they are thoroughly combined. Then whisk in the nutmeg and stir in the raisins.

7. Pour the mixture into the prepared mold and bake in the center of the oven until

the cake is puffed and golden, 45 minutes.

8. Remove the mold from the oven and let it cool for 10 minutes. Then unmold the cake onto a serving platter.

6 to 8 servings

N O T E : When adding the semolina, do as Isabelle advised me: Add it *en fine pluie,* in a fine rain, to avoid lumps.

Pound Cake
Quatre Quarts

>•••<

One of the more common cakes on the French farm, *quatre quarts* is made with ingredients at hand: fresh farm butter, eggs still warm from the chicken, and store-bought flour and sugar. The beauty of this cake is that it can be varied in a million ways. I've been served *quatre quarts* with tiny cubes of apple in it, flavored with hazelnuts, zingy with lemon, or simply flavored, as it is here, with vanilla sugar.

This is an easy cake to make, but it must be baked slowly, at a low temperature, to emerge tender and moist from the oven.

1½ cups (200 g) unbleached all-purpose
    flour
Sea salt
4 large eggs, at room temperature,
    separated
1 cup (200 g) Vanilla Sugar (page 521)
2 teaspoons vanilla extract
14 tablespoons (1¾ sticks; 210 g) unsalted
    butter, at room temperature

Whisking Egg Whites

→·←

*W*hen whisking egg whites, remember the following tricks:

• *The egg whites should be at room temperature so they will take on volume more easily.*

• *Always add a pinch of salt to help break up the whites.*

• *It is vital not to stop whisking once you've begun, for if you do, the whites will fall as flat as pancakes, and you will never be able to revive them.*

• *Before adding sugar, beat the whites just until they are foamy and white, but are still liquid and "plop" when you lift up the whisk. Add the sugar, then beat just until the whites whiten and thicken slightly. They will be just this side of holding soft peaks.*

1. Preheat the oven to 325°F (165°C). Thoroughly butter and flour a 9-inch (23 cm) springform pan. Cut a piece of parchment paper to fit the bottom of the pan, place it inside, and butter and flour it as well.

2. Sift the flour with a pinch of salt onto a piece of parchment paper.

3. If using an electric mixer, use the whisk attachment if you have one. In the bowl of the mixer, or in another large bowl, whisk the egg yolks with all but 1 tablespoon of the sugar until they are foamy and pale yellow, and have at least doubled in volume. Whisk in the vanilla extract. Sprinkle the flour over the egg yolk mixture and whisk it in quickly, just so it is mixed. Don't be concerned if some flour still clings to the sides of the bowl; you'll get that later.

4. Add the butter in thirds, whisking continuously. Scrape down the sides of the bowl, and whisk the batter once more, forcefully, so all is combined. Finally, gently stir the batter several times in a folding motion, as a last assurance that all the ingredients are mixed together.

5. In a medium-size bowl, whisk the egg whites with a pinch of salt until they are white and foamy but still quite liquid. Gradually sprinkle the reserved 1 tablespoon sugar into the egg whites whisking constantly until they are whiter and slightly firmer, but still this side of forming soft peaks.

6. Fold one fourth of the egg whites into the batter. Then add the remaining whites and gently fold them in until they are fully incorporated.

7. Turn the batter into the prepared pan and bake in the center of the oven until the cake springs back when touched, or until a cake tester inserted into the center comes out clean, 25 to 35 minutes. Remove from the oven and let it cool for 5 minutes; then loosen the edge of the mold. After 15 minutes' cooling, remove the cake from the pan and let it cool thoroughly on a wire rack.

6 to 8 servings

Hazelnut Pound Cake
Quatre Quarts aux Noisettes

>···<

The subtle, toasty flavor of hazelnuts is perfect in this rich cake. Serve this piled with whipped cream or lightly dusted with confectioners' sugar.

1 cup (200 g) Vanilla Sugar (page 521)
⅓ cup (50 g) hazelnuts, toasted
    (see Note)
1½ cups (200 g) unbleached all-purpose
    flour
Sea salt
14 tablespoons (1¾ sticks; 210 g) unsalted
    butter, at room temperature
4 large eggs, at room temperature,
    separated
2 teaspoons vanilla extract

Hazelnut Portents
>·<

When the hazelnuts hang heavy on the tree, French country folk say the year will bring many children. And hazelnut cake is often served at weddings to ensure a fruitful union.

1. Preheat the oven to 325°F (165°C). Thoroughly butter and flour a 9-inch (23 cm) springform pan. Cut a piece of parchment paper to fit the bottom of the pan, place it inside, and butter and flour it as well.

2. Divide the sugar into three separate amounts: 2 teaspoons for grinding with the hazelnuts, 2 teaspoons for whisking into the egg whites, and the remaining sugar for creaming with the butter.

3. Combine the cooled toasted hazelnuts with 2 teaspoons sugar in a food processor, and process until finely ground.

4. Sift the flour with ¼ teaspoon salt onto a piece of parchment paper.

5. If using an electric mixer, use the whisk attachment if you have one. In the bowl of the mixer, or in another large bowl, whisk the egg yolks with the sugar until they are foamy and pale yellow, and have at least doubled in volume. Whisk in the vanilla extract. Sprinkle the flour over the egg yolk mixture and whisk it in quickly, just so it is mixed. Don't be concerned if some flour still clings to the sides of the bowl; you'll get that later.

6. Add the butter in thirds, whisking

continuously. Scrape down the sides of the bowl, and whisk the batter once more, forcefully, so all is combined. Finally, gently stir the batter several times in a folding motion, as a last assurance that all is mixed together. Fold in the ground hazelnuts.

7. In a medium-size bowl, whisk the egg whites with a pinch of salt until they are white and foamy but still quite liquid. Gradually sprinkle the remaining 2 teaspoons sugar into the egg whites, whisking constantly until they are whiter and slightly firmer, but still this side of forming soft peaks.

8. Fold one fourth of the egg whites into the batter. Then add the remaining whites and gently fold them in until they are fully incorporated.

9. Turn the batter into the prepared pan, and bake in the center of the oven until the cake springs back when touched, or until a cake tester inserted into the center comes out clean, 25 to 35 minutes. Remove from the oven and let it cool for 5 minutes; then loosen the edge of the mold. After 15 minutes' cooling, remove the cake from the pan and let it cool thoroughly on a wire rack.

6 to 8 servings

NOTE: To toast hazelnuts, place them on a baking sheet and bake in the middle of a preheated 325°F (165°C) oven until they are deep golden, about 15 minutes. Remove them from the oven and immediately rub them in a cotton tea towel to remove as much of the skin as possible. Let them cool.

Marbled Pound Cake
Quatre Quarts Marbre

→···←

At our house we prefer this version of pound cake over all others because it's so beautiful to cut into. It reminds me of the famed pottery from the Atelier Bernard in Apt, whose designs go all the way through the clay in some mysterious way, just the way the chocolate does in this cake.

FOR THE WHITE CAKE BATTER

¾ cup (100 g) unbleached all-purpose flour

Sea salt

2 large eggs, separated

½ cup (100 g) Vanilla Sugar (page 521)

1 teaspoon vanilla extract

7 tablespoons (105 g) unsalted butter,
   at room temperature

FOR THE CHOCOLATE CAKE BATTER

¼ cup (22 g) unsweetened cocoa powder

½ cup (70 g) unbleached all-purpose flour

Sea salt

2 large eggs, separated

½ cup (100 g) Vanilla Sugar (page 521)

7 tablespoons (105 g) unsalted butter, at
   room temperature

1. Preheat the oven to 325°F (165°C). Thoroughly butter and flour a 9-inch (23 cm) springform pan. Cut a piece of parchment paper to fit the bottom of the pan, place it inside, and butter and flour it as well.

2. Prepare the white cake batter: Sift the flour with ¼ teaspoon salt onto a piece of parchment paper.

3. If using an electric mixer, use the whisk attachment if you have one. In the bowl of the mixer, or in another large bowl, whisk the egg yolks with all but 2 teaspoons of the sugar until they are foamy and pale yellow, and have at least doubled in volume. Whisk in the vanilla extract. Sprinkle the flour over the egg yolk mixture and whisk it in quickly, just so it is mixed. Don't be concerned if some flour still clings to the sides of the bowl;

you'll get that mixed in later.

4. Add the butter in thirds, whisking continuously. Scrape down the sides of the bowl, and whisk the batter once more, forcefully, so all is combined. Finally, gently stir the batter several times in a folding motion, as a last assurance that all is mixed together.

5. In a medium-size bowl, whisk the egg whites with a pinch of salt until they are white and foamy but still quite liquid. Gradually sprinkle the reserved 2 teaspoons sugar into the egg whites, whisking constantly until they are whiter and slightly firmer, but still this side of forming soft peaks. Fold half of the egg whites into the batter. Then add the remaining egg whites and fold them in until they are fully incorporated.

6. Prepare the chocolate cake batter as you prepared the white batter in steps 2 to 5, sifting the cocoa powder onto a sheet of parchment along with the flour and salt and then proceeding as directed in those steps.

7. When the two batters are made, quickly add the chocolate batter to the vanilla batter, stirring it just enough so that it marbles. Do not fully mix them together.

8. Turn the batter into the prepared pan, and bake in the center of the oven until the cake springs back when touched, or until a cake tester inserted into the center comes out clean, about 25 minutes. Remove from the oven and let it cool for 5 minutes; then loosen the edge of the mold. After 15 minutes' cooling, remove the cake from the pan and let it cool thoroughly on a wire rack.

6 to 8 servings

Chocolate Pound Cake

Quatre Quarts au Chocolat

→•••←

I thought I'd found the best-ever chocolate cake, but thank goodness, a basic rule of life held true: Just when you think you've tasted the best there is, something better comes along. And this chocolate pound cake is it!

This is moist, dense, satisfying, and very chocolatey. I like to serve it with a simple Chocolate Cream Icing (opposite) or even dusted with confectioners' sugar. If you want to truly impress your guests, make a double batch, bake it in two layers, spread red currant jelly between the layers, and frost it with the icing.

> *1 cup (135 g) unbleached all-purpose*
> *flour*
> *½ cup (55 g) unsweetened cocoa powder*
> *Pinch of sea salt*
> *4 large eggs, at room temperature,*
> *separated*
> *1 cup (200 g) Vanilla Sugar (page 521)*
> *2 teaspoons vanilla extract*
> *14 tablespoons (1¾ sticks; 210 g) unsalted*
> *butter, at room temperature*

1. Preheat the oven to 325°F (165°C). Thoroughly butter and flour a 9-inch (23 cm) springform pan. Cut a piece of parchment paper to fit the bottom of the pan, place it inside, and butter and flour it as well.

2. Sift the flour, cocoa powder, and salt onto a piece of parchment paper.

3. If using an electric mixer, use the whisk attachment if you have one. In the bowl of the mixer, or in another large bowl, whisk the egg yolks with all but 1 tablespoon of the sugar until they are foamy and pale yellow, and have at least doubled in volume. Whisk in the vanilla extract. Sprinkle the flour over the egg yolk mixture and whisk it in quickly, just so it is mixed. Don't be concerned if some flour still clings to the sides of the bowl; you'll get that later.

4. Add the butter in thirds, whisking continuously. Scrape down the sides of the bowl, and whisk the batter once more, forcefully, so all is combined. Finally, gently stir the batter several times in a folding motion, as a last assurance that all is mixed together.

5. In a medium-size bowl, whisk the egg whites with a pinch of salt until they are white and foamy but still quite liquid. Gradually sprinkle the reserved 1

tablespoon sugar into the egg whites, whisking constantly until they are whiter and slightly firmer, but still this side of forming soft peaks.

6. Fold one fourth of the egg whites into the batter. Then add the remaining whites and gently fold them in until they are fully incorporated.

7. Turn the batter into the prepared pan, and bake in the center of the oven until the cake springs back when touched, or until a cake tester inserted into the center comes out clean, about 25 minutes. Remove from the oven and let it cool for 5 minutes; then loosen the edge of the mold. After 15 minutes' cooling, remove the cake from the pan and let it cool thoroughly on a wire rack.

6 to 8 servings

Chocolate Cream Icing
Glaçage au Chocolat

>···<

This is actually a *ganache*, one of the pillars of French pastry making. Simply crème fraîche heated with bitter chocolate added, it makes a wonderfully versatile frosting, filling, or snack right from the spoon! Make it, let it cool until it is firm, then use it as you wish. Try this as a frosting for any of the pound cakes.

ASTUCE . . . .

• *You may make this several days ahead and refrigerate it. Remember to remove it from the refrigerator to soften before using—you may need to heat it gently.*

. . . .

2 cups (500 ml) Crème Fraîche
　(page 520), or heavy (or whipping)
　cream
15 ounces (450 g) bittersweet chocolate,
　such as Lindt or Tobler, broken into
　pieces

Heat the crème fraîche in a medium-size saucepan over medium-high heat to just below a simmer, or until it steams and tiny bubbles begin to form around the edges. Remove from the heat, and add the chocolate piece by piece, stirring as it melts, until blended. Let the mixture cool until it is the consistency of a thick but easily spreadable frosting. This should take just a few minutes.

About 1¼ cups (310 ml)

Mamie's Sweet Bread from the Farm at Bout du Prés

Cake de Mamie du Bout du Prés

*C*ake is a cornerstone of French farm cuisine. In fact, it is a part of all French cooking, for as soon as girls are old enough to be at ease in the kitchen, they learn to make *cake* at school. The recipe, which results in a fruit-filled pound cake-like loaf, is basically the same throughout the country, with only slight variations. (For some savory versions, see pages 327 and 329.)

I have tasted many a *cake*—and rejected most of them because they were too dry, too wet, too sweet. This one is perfect: It is not too sweet, it crumbs easily but isn't dry, and it can be varied in a thousand ways. It comes from a farm called Bout du Prés, where Miche Devisme and her mother, simply referred to as Mamie ("Grandma"), kept an active farmyard, a huge vegetable garden, and a herd of cows. They both cooked all the time, for with their large extended family there were always mouths to feed.

I got this recipe from one of Miche's nieces, and after testing it, I passed it along to my friend Edith, another of Miche's nieces, who made it for a family gathering. Miche tasted the *cake*, turned to Edith, and said, "You've got to give me this recipe. It's the best *cake* I've ever had."

Edith dissolved in laughter. "But, Miche, it's your recipe—Susan gave it to me just the other day."

We all had a good laugh over that one, particularly Miche.

Cake is quick to put together, and it keeps a long while. When I'm visiting someone, I always know I'm going to be served *cake* if I hear the familiar sound that announces it: the scrape of the lid being removed from the tin where it is invariably stored.

This is the most typical version of *cake*, with raisins macerated in alcohol; the alcohol is traditional but always optional.

Make several of these at once, wrap them in waxed paper and then in aluminum foil, and put them in a cake tin or other airtight container if you've got one. They will keep well for up to 2 weeks, if you can keep them around that long!

1 cup (150 g) raisins

1 tablespoon rum, Calvados, or Armagnac (optional)

1¾ cups (230 g) unbleached all-purpose flour

1 teaspoon baking powder

¾ teaspoon sea salt

11½ tablespoons (about 1½ sticks; 170 g) unsalted butter, at room temperature

⅓ cup (135 g) Vanilla Sugar (page 521)

3 large eggs

1 teaspoon vanilla extract

1. Preheat the oven to 375°F (190°C). Butter and flour a 9 x 5 x 3-inch (23 x 13 x 7½ cm) loaf pan.

2. Place the raisins in a small bowl and cover them with boiling water. Let sit for 10 minutes; then drain and pat dry. Return the raisins to the bowl, add the rum (if using), stir, cover, and let sit for at least 30 minutes and as long as 1 hour. (You can prepare the raisins the night before you plan to make the *cake*.)

3. Sift the flour, baking powder, and salt together onto a piece of waxed paper.

4. Just before making the *cake*, drain the raisins, reserving any rum that they haven't absorbed. Add 2 tablespoons of the flour mixture to the raisins and toss so they are evenly coated. (This will keep the raisins from sinking to the bottom of the *cake*.)

5. In a large bowl, or in the bowl of an electric mixer, blend the butter and sugar until the mixture is light and pale yellow. Add the eggs, one at a time, beating after each addition. Beat in the vanilla. Then add the remaining flour mixture and mix just until it is combined. Add the raisins and any remaining rum, and mix just so they are evenly incorporated into the batter.

6. Turn the batter into the prepared loaf pan, and rap the pan sharply on a hard surface to release any air bubbles in the batter. Bake in the center of the oven until the *cake* has puffed and a knife inserted into the center comes out clean, about 50 minutes.

7. Remove the pan from the oven and immediately remove the *cake* from the pan. Let it cool on a wire rack.

8 servings

NOTE: The batter for *cake* is stiff, as for a quick bread, and will need to be spooned into the pan.

Date and Hazelnut Bread
Cake aux Dattes et aux Noisettes

→•••←

A sophisticated variation on *cake*, this is wonderful served with tea or coffee in mid-morning, late in the afternoon, or whenever you need a nourishing pick-me-up.

Be sure to make this a day before you plan to serve it, for it improves a great deal with age. It will keep very well for at least 1 week, and up to 2 if it is well wrapped.

1¾ cups (230 g) unbleached all-purpose
    flour
1 teaspoon baking powder
¾ teaspoon sea salt
11½ tablespoons (170 g) unsalted butter,
    at room temperature
⅓ cup (135 g) sugar
3 large eggs
1 teaspoon vanilla extract
½ cup (75 g) hazelnuts, toasted, skinned, and
    coarsely chopped (see Note, page 376)
1 cup (195 g) dates, pitted and coarsely
    chopped

1. Preheat the oven to 375°F (190°C). Butter and flour a 9 x 5 x 3-inch (23 x13 x 7½ cm) loaf pan.

2. Sift the flour, baking powder, and salt together onto a piece of waxed paper.

3. In a large bowl, or in the bowl of an electric mixer, blend the butter and sugar until the mixture is light and pale yellow. Add the eggs, one at a time, beating after each addition. Beat in the vanilla extract. Then add the flour mixture and mix just until it is combined. Add the hazelnuts and dates, and mix just until they are evenly incorporated into the batter.

4. Turn the batter into the prepared loaf pan, and rap the pan sharply on a hard surface to release any air bubbles in the batter. Bake in the center of the oven until the *cake* has puffed and a knife inserted into the center comes out clean, about 50 minutes. (Because the dates are soft and sticky, they may leave a sticky trail on the knife, so it won't be truly "clean" when it emerges; but you will be able to tell whether the batter is completely baked.)

5. Remove the pan from the oven and immediately remove the *cake* from the pan. Let it cool on a wire rack.

8 servings

Candied Fruit Bread
Cake aux Fruits Confits

>···<

O f all the candied fruit made in France, the fruit from Apt, in Provence, is the best. There, in several shops that line the quay, candied fruit is mounded like jewels that shine in the city's intense dry light. I am partial to candied clementines, which glisten like stars, though I am awed by whole candied melons, candied oranges, perfect candied figs. I've tried just about every candied fruit in Apt to see if its flavor equals its beauty, and I can say unequivocally that they all do. What a joy to bite into candied fruit that tastes of fruit rather than of the sugar that preserves it.

This version of *cake* must be made with candied fruit that retains a semblance of its original flavor. If you can't find that, then use dried fruit or freshly candied citrus peel (see Index for Candied Lemon Zest).

You'll find this *cake* light and delicate. In France, it is made year-round, not just at holiday time. It offers a simple variation, however, on holiday fruitcake, and it's much more edible.

1¾ cups (230 g) unbleached all-purpose
    flour
1 teaspoon baking powder
¾ teaspoon sea salt
11½ tablespoons (170 g) unsalted butter,
    at room temperature
⅓ cup (135 g) sugar
3 large eggs
1 teaspoon vanilla extract
½ cup (75 g) candied fruit, coarsely
    chopped

1. Preheat the oven to 375°F (190°C). Butter and flour a 9 x 5 x 3-inch (23 x 13 x 7½ cm) loaf pan.

2. Sift the flour, baking powder, and salt together onto a piece of waxed paper.

3. In a large bowl, or in the bowl of an electric mixer, blend the butter and sugar until the mixture is light and pale yellow.

Add the eggs, one at a time, beating after each addition. Then add the vanilla extract. Stir the candied fruit into the flour mixture so the pieces are thoroughly coated. Then add the flour/fruit mixture to the butter mixture, and stir, just until combined.

4. Turn the batter into the prepared loaf pan, and rap it sharply on a hard surface to release any air bubbles in the batter. Bake in the center of the oven until the *cake* has puffed and a knife inserted into the center comes out clean, about 50 minutes. (Because the fruits are soft and sticky, they may leave a sticky trail on the knife, so it won't be truly "clean" when it emerges; but you will be able to tell whether the batter is completely baked.)

5. Remove the pan from the oven and immediately remove the *cake* from the pan. Let it cool on a wire rack.

8 servings

Apricot and Lemon Zest Bread

Cake aux Abricots et au Zeste de Citron

This is one of my favorite versions of *cake*, for it is bright with tart dried apricots and lemon zest. It is ideal with tea around four in the afternoon.

This cooks more quickly than some *cakes* because it contains a minimal amount of fruit. Be sure to check it carefully, however. (Do as a friend's grandmother used to do: Stick a wooden knitting needle in, and if it comes out clean, the cake is baked through.)

Make several of these *cakes* at once, wrap them in waxed paper and then in aluminum foil, and put them in cake tins or other airtight containers if you have any. They will keep well for up to 2 weeks.

ASTUCE . . . .

• *Apricots are often treated with sulfur to keep them from turning rust-colored as they dry. It reduces their flavor as well, and I much prefer naturally dried apricots.*

. . . .

1¾ cups (230 g) unbleached all-purpose
    flour
1 teaspoon baking powder
¾ teaspoon sea salt
11½ tablespoons (170 g) unsalted butter,
    at room temperature
⅓ cup (135 g) sugar
3 large eggs
1 teaspoon vanilla extract
½ cup (75 g) dried apricots (unsulfured if
    possible), coarsely chopped
Zest of 1 lemon, minced

1. Preheat the oven to 375°F (190°C). Butter and flour a 9 x 5 x 3-inch (23 x 13 x 7½ cm) loaf pan.

2. Sift the flour, baking powder, and salt together onto a piece of waxed paper.

3. In a large bowl, or in the bowl of an electric mixer, blend the butter and sugar until the mixture is light and pale yellow. Add the eggs, one at a time, beating after each addition. Beat in the vanilla extract. Stir the apricots into the flour mixture so the pieces are thoroughly coated. Then add the flour and apricots to the butter mixture and stir just until it is combined. Add the lemon zest, and mix just until combined.

4. Turn the batter into the prepared loaf pan, and rap the pan sharply on a hard surface to release any air bubbles in the batter. Bake in the center of the oven until the *cake* has puffed and a knife inserted into the center comes out clean, 35 to 45 minutes.

5. Remove the pan from the oven and immediately remove the *cake* from the pan. Let it cool on a wire rack.

8 servings

Three Kings Cake
Galette des Rois

→ • • • ←

Delicately flavored, almond cream makes its way into tarts and cakes, and is the filling for the *galettes des rois* that show up not too long after Christmas, in January, to celebrate Three Kings Day.

The Three Kings Cake
La Galette des Rois

→·←

*H*istory has it that the cardinals of Besançon, near Dijon, originated the tradition of galette de rois *in the 14th century. To choose a chapter head, they held a sort of lottery at Epiphany—the feast of the Magi—which consisted of hiding a coin in a loaf of bread. Whoever got the coin was awarded the post. Over the years, the bread evolved into brioche, the coin became a* fève *(bean), and the custom spread throughout the land.*

Today, the Fête des Rois, or Feast of the Magi, begins shortly after Christmas. Pâtisserie and boulangerie *shelves fill with* galettes, *which differ according to geography. In the north of France, the* galette *is a flat, shiny round of puff pastry usually filled with* frangipane, *or almond cream. In the south of France, the* galette *is made of brioche, usually flavored with lemon zest. In Brittany,* galettes *resemble Breton Cake (see Index) studded with candied fruit. All contain a* fève.

Fèves have become highly collectible, and boulangers *and* pâtissiers *compete to see who can come up with the cleverest* fève. *This competition results in prodigious sales, as I witnessed the first year I returned to live in France.*

The best baker in our town makes several types of galette des rois, *all luscious, including one with a thin layer of raspberry jam and almond cream inside and a layer of meringue on top. Between us, a friend and I must have purchased twenty* galettes *over the course of a month to share with friends and family. Our real goal, however, was to collect the tiny cobalt-blue and gold cups and saucers, tea and coffee pots, inside.*

Other fèves *depict figures from history, characters from television serials, different saints, or sports figures.*

FOR THE ALMOND CREAM
½ cup (75 g) whole almonds
⅓ cup (65 g) sugar
4 tablespoons (½ stick; 60 g) unsalted butter, at room temperature
1 large egg, at room temperature
1 tablespoon unbleached all-purpose flour
1 teaspoon vanilla extract

FOR THE CAKE
Puff Pastry (page 512), chilled
1 large egg, at room temperature
2 teaspoons water

1. Prepare the almond cream: Grind the almonds in a food processor with 1 tablespoon of the sugar until finely ground.

2. In a medium-size bowl, whisk the but-

ter with the remaining sugar until it is soft and well combined. Whisk in the egg until the mixture is light, then whisk in the flour and vanilla extract until thoroughly combined.

3. Stir in the ground almonds until combined. Then cover the bowl with aluminum foil and chill until the mixture is solid but not too hard, about 30 minutes. Shape the cream into a flat round no more than 5 inches (13 cm) in diameter and chill for at least 1 hour before using (see Note).

4. Roll out the puff pastry to a very thin (⅛ inch; ¼ cm) rectangle. Cut out two 10-inch (25 cm) circles, place them on a baking sheet, and refrigerate for 30 minutes. Reserve the scraps for another use.

5. Whisk together the egg and water for an egg wash.

6. Assemble the *galette:* Remove the pastry rounds and cream from the refrigerator. Place the cream in the center of one of the pastry rounds. There should be a pastry border of at least 2½ inches (6½ cm) all around the cream. (If you want to place a *fève* in the *galette*, now is the time. Gently press one into the almond cream.) Lightly brush the pastry border with egg wash, being sure not to let any drip over the edges of the pastry. Then top with the second pastry round. Press this gently onto the bottom round, and brush the entire top of the *galette* with egg wash. Refrigerate the *galette* for at least 30 minutes.

7. Preheat the oven to 425°F (220°C).

8. Remove the *galette* from the refrigerator and brush it once again with egg wash. Using a sharp knife and beginning in the center of the *galette*, make long curved cuts into the pastry but not all the way through it, right to the edge of the *galette*, leaving about ½ inch (1¼ cm) between each cut. Using the back of the knife blade (the dull edge), press it into the edges of the *galette* at regular intervals to make a scalloped effect. This is decorative, and it also helps the pastry rise evenly.

9. Bake in the center of the oven until the *galette* is puffed and deep golden on top, about 28 minutes.

10. Remove the baking sheet from the oven and transfer the *galette* to a wire rack to cool for about 20 minutes. The *galette* should be served warm, but not blistering hot.

8 to 10 servings

N O T E : The almond cream will keep for several days in the refrigerator, tightly wrapped, and can be frozen as well, for up to several weeks.

Pain d'Epices

→•←

Today, Burgundy claims **pain d'épices** *as its own, but in fact its origins are ancient and complex.*

The first recorded honey-and-spice bread served as rations for Genghis Khan and his army. Crusaders brought it to Europe by way of northern Africa, and its dense spiciness quickly seduced the population, from nobles to peasants.

In the 14th century, Henry IV created a corporation called Le Pain d'Epiciers (Shopkeepers'

Bread), and there is some argument that this was the origin of its name, rather than the spices (épices) that give it flavor.

In France, it was first made in the northeastern parts of the country, what is now Alsace, and down into the Champagne region, where it can still be found. Some time later, it was adopted by Burgundy, and Dijon is now noted throughout the country for its fine artisanally made **pain d'épices**.

Babette's Spice Bread
Pain d'Epices de Babette

→···←

Few *cakes* evoke more memories than *pain d'épices*. It has long been a common *goûter*, or after-school snack, and one taste can bring an otherwise reasonable French adult to tears.

Always made with honey, *pain d'épices* sometimes includes a mix of white and rye flours. The spices vary depending on the recipe, as do the amounts and proportions.

I searched and searched for a good recipe, rejecting many because they were too dry or too heavy or too sweet. When I tasted this, given to me by my friend Babette, I knew I was home, for it is the most delicate *and* the most intensely flavored of them all.

It looks dense and somewhat dry, but actually the bread is quite moist and very finecrumbed, an oddly addictive blend of bread and cake.

It makes a wonderful *goûter*, a fine breakfast along with coffee, even an excellent dessert when paired with fresh fruit or a preserved fruit like Bachelor's Confiture (see Index). Kept cool and wrapped airtight, it will keep for at least 2 weeks and as long as a month. It can be frozen, though it will emerge from the freezer slightly dry.

ASTUCES . . . .

• *Heat the honey just until it melts. Don't let it boil, which would destroy some of its more subtle aromas.*
• *The cooking time can vary widely, depending on the moistness of the jam. Check it often after 1¼ hours (quickly so the oven temperature doesn't fall).*

. . . .

2 cups (500 ml) milk
2 tablespoons ground cinnamon
1 teaspoon ground cloves
1 teaspoon ground cardamom
2 tablespoons whole anise seeds
2¼ cups (685 ml) mild, flowery honey
7⅓ cups (2 pounds; 1 kg) unbleached all-purpose flour
¾ cup (185 ml) orange marmalade or red currant jelly, homemade if desired (see pages 406 and 399)
2 teaspoons baking soda
2 tablespoons warm water

1. Preheat the oven to 325°F (165°C). Butter and flour two 9 x 5 x 3-inch (23 x 13 x 7½ cm) loaf pans.

2. Combine the milk and the spices in a medium-size saucepan over medium-high heat, and whisk gently. As soon as bubbles have formed around the edges of the milk, remove it from the heat, cover, and let the spices infuse for 10 minutes.

3. Heat the honey in a saucepan just until it is liquid. Transfer it to a large mixing bowl or the bowl of an electric mixer, add the spiced milk, and mix well. Add 2 cups (270 g) of the flour and mix well. Then add the marmalade. Slowly add the rest of the flour, stirring until the mixture is thoroughly combined.

4. In a small bowl mix together the baking soda and the warm water; the mixture will fizz and bubble. Stir this into the batter and continue mixing (at medium speed if using a mixer) until the dough is satiny, at least 10 minutes (5 minutes in a mixer).

5. Divide the batter between the two prepared loaf pans (the batter will come very close to the top of the pans). Place them in the center of the oven, leaving room between the pans so the heat can circulate. Bake until the loaves are puffed and golden and spring back when touched, 1 hour and 20 to 40 minutes.

6. Remove the pans from the oven, then remove the loaves from the pans and let them cool on wire racks. When cool, wrap the loaves in waxed paper, then aluminum foil, and wait at least 24 hours before tasting, as the flavors need a chance to mature. The *pains d'épices* will keep well, wrapped and stored in an airtight container in a cool spot for at least 2 weeks. They can also be refrigerated for up to 1 month and frozen for up to 2 months, though they lose their most subtle aroma in the freezer.

16 servings

Juliette's Caramels
Les Caramels de Juliette

→ • • • ←

I first tasted these caramels at my friend Edith Leroy's house. One afternoon her teenage daughter, Juliette, took it into her head to make them, and when I walked into the kitchen I saw a mound of small foil-wrapped packets on the kitchen counter—and Edith standing behind it, chewing happily. She handed me one, which I unwrapped to reveal a dark-brown caramel. Mmm! It was instant passion.

I do love these caramels. They're unusual—perfumed with honey, rich with chocolate. "We had these growing up," said Edith. "I remember taking a box of them back to school with me after a weekend at home. My best friend would wait for me and pounce on the box as soon as I got there, and we'd finish the whole box in one day."

This recipe makes a very typical country caramel—easy to make, easier to eat. Here I've measured and calculated to make them more or less uniform, but normally the mixture is poured out onto a slab of marble or another smooth work surface, left to harden, and then cut into shapes *au hasard*, or at will. The real work comes in wrapping the caramels individually in foil. The result is a huge mound of irregular packets that are, quite simply, irresistible. They look as if they're made with love, and indeed that's the best way to make them.

Follow my directions to the letter and make nice little uniform caramels, or just let them flow across the work surface—the

caramel stops and hardens fairly quickly. The result will be thinner, but just cut the caramels larger.

ASTUCE . . . .

• *When cooking caramels, test them by drizzling a ribbon of caramel on a plate and placing it in the freezer for several minutes; the mixture should quickly turn solid. This way you can quickly see the results and avoid overcooking.*

. . . .

16 tablespoons (2 sticks; 250 g) unsalted butter, cut into tablespoon-size pieces
1¼ cups (250 g) sugar
8 ounces (250 g) bittersweet chocolate, such as Lindt, cut into 1-inch (2½ cm) squares
¾ cup (185 ml) lavender honey (see Note)

1. Prepare a baking sheet, a piece of marble, or another smooth surface by rubbing it

lightly but thoroughly with mild cooking oil, such as safflower, in a roughly 11 x 7-inch (28 x 18 cm) rectangle.

2. Place the butter in a medium-size heavy saucepan over medium heat and let it melt about halfway. Add the sugar, stir to blend, and then add the chocolate and the honey. Stir. Let the ingredients melt together, swirling the pan occasionally to be sure they aren't sticking, stirring with a wooden spoon if necessary.

3. When the ingredients are blended and the mixture comes to a boil, cook it, stirring frequently to be sure it doesn't stick to the pan, until it achieves the consistency you like. (To test the consistency, see Astuce.) If you like your caramels to hold their shape but be quite chewy, cook the mixture 10 to 12 minutes. If you prefer them hard, so they chip into bits in your mouth (then melt quickly into a wonderful chewiness), try 20 minutes. Don't be too nervous about the cooking time—you will love these caramels whether they turn out in the end to be soft or hard.

4. When the caramel has reached the desired consistency, pour it out on the prepared surface, quickly scraping as much caramel from the pan as you can. You need to move quickly at this point, corralling the caramel so it doesn't spread too thin.

I like my caramels thick, so I've devised two corralling methods: First I bully the caramel into shape by pushing it back onto itself with a dough scraper. It doesn't take long, for the caramel hardens quickly. Once the caramel has quit flowing rapidly and just sort of oozes, I turn two rectangular Pyrex baking dishes upside down and push them up against the longer sides of the caramel to hold it in place until it completely hardens. The shorter sides don't need corralling. Call it artisanal, but it works just fine. Don't think you can beat this by pouring the caramels into a Pyrex dish—they are literally impossible to remove, even if the dish is oiled. I've tried it.

Here's another solution: Oil the rim of a springform mold and set it, closed, on an oiled baking sheet or smooth work surface. Pour the caramel into it to cool. When the caramel is cool, just loosen the mold to remove it. The caramels will be thicker, the yield about 20 fewer, but they are slightly easier to deal with this way.

5. When the caramels have hardened enough so they are not sticky but are still a bit soft (and so they won't stick to your knife blade), 15 to 20 minutes, cut them into ¾-inch (2 cm) squares. Wrap each square in aluminum foil. They will keep no longer than 1 day, because they will all be eaten. If you manage to squirrel some away, they will keep well for at least 2 weeks, stored in a cool place.

About 13 dozen caramels

NOTE: I recommend using lavender honey, which is traditional in this recipe. If you can't find it, use a good-quality, mildly aromatic, mixed-flower honey. Generally, the lighter honey is in color, the milder it will be in flavor.

LA CAVE ET L'ARMOIRE
The Cellar and the Pantry

I always love being shown the *cave* on a French farm, for it's like entering Ali Baba's treasure house. The cellar floor is usually hard-packed soil or concrete, and the walls are always thick, both of which help to keep the temperature constant.

Barrels filled with everything from table wine (often made on the farm) to homemade liqueurs sit along one wall. The vinegar is usually in a corner, and there are jars of home-canned *rillettes*, *confits*, and pâtés stacked on shelves. One shelf is reserved for cornichons, miniature pickles pungent with tarragon, and perhaps there are cherries in liqueur, *confiture de vieux garçon*, or jars of homemade tomato sauce waiting to be poured over pasta.

The other spot I love is the part of the pantry where the jams and bottled liqueurs are hidden, which is usually a gorgeous old armoire. There sit jars of jellies and jams, their colors deep, their flavors rich. There is also an assortment of bottles, many old and mis-shapen, tied with ribbon or raffia, which hold the house liqueurs.

Whatever they contain, the French farm cellar and pantry are storehouses of culinary riches. And one rule generally holds true: Only the farmer and his wife, and maybe the *grandmère*, have the keys, which they are loath to relinquish!

Bachelor's Confiture
Confiture de Vieux Garçon

→···←

From the Périgord, this mixture of marinated fruits was once felt to be suitable only for single male diners *(vieux garçons)*—hence its charming name. Times have changed, however, and today it is served to everyone at the table—though it does remain a special favorite at fall hunting dinners, which tend to be a male province.

This needs to mellow for at least two months, which is why, though full of spring and summer fruits, it is a fall specialty. Be sure to cover the jar *loosely.* I covered a jar tightly one year and was surprised one fine fall day by a loud explosion in the kitchen, where I found a wonderful aroma and a terrific mess. The alcohol had built up heat and caused the jar to explode, sending *confiture de vieux garçon* everywhere!

The quantities given are enough to get your *confiture* started. As the season progresses, add more fruits, vodka, and sugar.

Confiture de vieux garçon is wonderful over ice cream, along with cake or with Walnut Butter Cookies (see Index).

2 pounds (1 kg) fresh peaches, plums, apricots, pears, apples, figs, strawberries, raspberries, cherries, grapes, or currants
3 cups (750 ml) vodka, or more if needed
2 pounds (1 kg) sugar, or more if needed
1 large lemon, preferably organic (see "Organic Citrus," page 407), well scrubbed and cut into very thin rounds

1. Prepare your chosen fruits: Peel and pit the peaches, and cut them into eighths. Pit the plums and apricots, and cut them into sixths. Peel, halve, and core the pears and apples, and cut them into eighths. Halve the figs. Leave the remaining fruits whole.

2. Pour the vodka into a large glass bowl. Add the sugar, and stir to dissolve it. Place the fruits, including the lemon slices, in a large wide-mouth jar, and pour the vodka mixture over it. Add more sugar and vodka (at a ration of ⅓ cup; 65 g sugar to every 3 tablespoons vodka) if necessary to completely cover the fruits.

3. Cover loosely with a cork stopper, if the jar has one, or aluminum foil, and place in a dark, cool place to mature, at least 2 months. Add more fruits as they ripen and come into season, with equivalent amounts of sugar and vodka to cover.

10 to 12 servings

Simple Apricot Jam

Confiture d'Abricots

>···<

This method for making apricot jam, as traditionally French as the "Marseillaise," is magical. The apricots macerate with the sugar overnight, releasing much of their liquid to make a thick juice. No water is added, so what you get after slowly cooking it to a rich, rusty color is pure apricot flavor.

*5 pounds (2½ kg) apricots, pitted
  (see Note)*
8¼ cups (3½ pounds; 1¼ kg) sugar

1. Place the apricots and the sugar in a large stockpot. Stir, cover, and let sit for 12 hours. The apricots will soften and give up some of their liquid. Stir them once or twice if you like, but it isn't necessary.

2. When ready to make the jam, prepare eight 8-ounce (250 ml) canning jars and lids by sterilizing them in boiling water according to the manufacturer's instructions.

3. Place the stockpot with the fruit and sugar over medium-high heat, stir, and bring to a boil. As the mixture boils, a pale orange foam will form on top. Continue to cook the jam for 10 minutes before you begin to skim off the orange foam, then skim away and discard until there is almost no foam. Watch the mixture carefully, as it can easily boil over the edges of the pot, depending on its size. If it does get close to boiling over, quickly blow on it and stir as fast as you can; the foam will

recede. Continue cooking and skimming until the mixture has thickened and turned a rust color, about 1 hour. To test for consistency (which will be determined by your preference), see "Is It Jelly?," page 403. If it is very runny after testing, the jam should be cooked longer.

4. Remove the stockpot from the heat. Ladle the jam into the sterilized canning jars, leaving ¼ inch (½ cm) headroom. Seal according to the jar manufacturer's instructions.

About eight 8-ounce (250 ml) jars

N O T E : Inside the pit of an apricot is a bitter "almond." Crack the pits and divide the "almonds" among the jars of jam. They offer a satisfying, almond-y crunch.

Apricot and Red Currant Jam
Confiture d'Abricots et Groseilles

→···←

Apricots and red currants appear at the market side-by-side, the red blush on the apricots echoing the ruby red of the currants. I couldn't resist combining them—they fit so naturally together. This bright and flavorful jam is the result.

ASTUCE . . . .

• *Red currants give off a great deal of pink foam if they are cooked over very high heat, so keep the heat low and even. There will always be some foam—skim it off and spread on bread for hungry children (and adults). Make sure it has cooled, however, for it can be blisteringly hot.*

. . . .

2 pounds (1 kg) apricots, pitted and cut
    into quarters
6 cups (2½ pounds; 1¼ kg) sugar
2 pounds (1 kg) red currants, rinsed

1. Place the apricots in a large nonreactive stockpot or saucepan. Cover with half the sugar. Add the currants, and cover with the remaining sugar. Stir gently so the sugar is evenly blended with the fruit. Cover and let sit for 12 hours.

2. When ready to make the jam, prepare eight 8-ounce (250 ml) canning jars and lids by sterilizing them in boiling water according to the manufacturer's instructions.

3. Place the stockpot over medium-high heat and bring to a boil, stirring occasionally so the sugar doesn't stick to the pan. Skim off any pink foam from the surface of the jam while it cooks, but don't be concerned if you can't get it all. Let the mixture boil gently for about 25 minutes, and test for consistency (see "Is It Jelly?," page 403). The jam shouldn't be too stiff or too liquid. Your own preference is the best judge.

4. When the jam is cooked to your liking, ladle it into the sterilized canning jars, leaving ¼ inch (½ cm) headroom, and seal according to the jar manufacturer's instructions.

*About eight 8-ounce
(250 ml) jars*

Plum and Vanilla Jam
Confiture de Prunes à la Vanille

>•••⮜

Late in the afternoon in the Pays Basque, in a dark farmhouse kitchen that is closed against the midsummer sun, out comes the *ardi gasna*, a sharp, yet creamy sheep's-milk cheese, the homemade plum jam, and bread. The cheese is so thinly sliced that it almost floats down onto the plate. A dab of jam is set alongside, and one of the rare and wonderful Basque flavor combinations is made.

Eating jam with cheese is a ritual in one of the few regions in France where sweet and sour together is not only tolerated but sought after. Some say the tradition comes from the flavor of the cheese, which becomes increasingly sharp and pungent as it ripens. Jam softens the sharpness, providing a satisfying foil.

In Itxassou, near the colorful village of Espelette, every farmhouse has a black cherry tree planted by the front door: Its fruit goes into a sweet cherry jam, the village choice for eating with *ardi gasna*.

But away from Itxassou the jam choice is plum, and once you taste this you'll see why. Fresh and bright, softened with vanilla, it is wonderful with any sharp cheese. And don't miss trying it on toast in the morning, with Breakfast Cake (see Index), or anywhere jam is called for.

5 pounds (2½ kg) Italian prune plums,
  pitted (see Note)
7 cups (3 pounds; 1½ kg) sugar
1 vanilla bean

1. Place the plums and the sugar in a large nonreactive kettle or stockpot. Mix gently, cover, and let sit for 12 hours.

2. When ready to make the jam, prepare ten 8-ounce (250 ml) canning jars and lids by sterilizing them in boiling water according to the manufacturer's instructions.

3. Add the vanilla bean to the plum mixture, and bring to a boil over medium-high heat. Reduce the heat so the mixture is bubbling merrily but not furiously. Skim off any foam that rises to the top (depending on the ripeness of the plums, there may be a substantial quantity). Cook the jam until it has thickened to the desired consistency, which will be about 18 minutes for a thick, though not firm, jam. (To test for consistency, see "Is It Jelly?," page 403.)

4. Remove the vanilla bean from the jam and set it aside.

5. Ladle the jam into the sterilized canning jars, leaving ¼ inch (½ cm) headroom. Cut the vanilla bean into as many pieces as there are jars, and push a piece down into each jar. Seal according to the jar manufacturer's instructions.

About ten 8-ounce (250 ml) jars

N O T E : Italian prune plums are notoriously good producers. If you can't handle the whole crop, or don't have time to make the jam when the prunes are ripe, don't hesitate to freeze them.

Raspberry Rhubarb Jam
Confiture aux Framboises et à la Rhubarbe

→ ··· ←

This jam will tease you with its sparkling raspberry flavor and gorgeous rosy color. I say "tease" because it's really rhubarb jam. The handful of raspberries lend their incomparable flavor, making it seem almost more raspberry than rhubarb.

Raspberries are at much more of a premium than rhubarb, which is exceedingly generous in its spring and summer abundance. Here you get the best of both: The rhubarb provides the background, the raspberry the punch and verve.

If you can't get fresh raspberries at the time that you've got piles of rhubarb, use unsweetened frozen berries. Berries are one type of fruit that freezes extremely well. Let them cook an additional five minutes so they soften and have a chance to spread their flavor throughout the jam.

2 pounds (1 kg) rhubarb, leaves trimmed away, stalks peeled and cut into ½-inch (1¼ cm) chunks
1¾ cups (435 ml) water
3⅓ cups (770 g) sugar
⅔ cup (90 g) fresh raspberries

1. Prepare five 8-ounce (250 ml) canning jars and lids by sterilizing them in boiling water according to the manufacturer's instructions.

2. Place the rhubarb and water in a large

heavy saucepan and bring to a boil over medium-high heat. Reduce the heat, cover, and simmer until most of the rhubarb is soft, with some pieces still holding their shape, about 15 minutes.

3. Stir in the sugar and continue cooking, uncovered, at a rolling boil until the mixture begins to thicken, about 40 minutes. Add the raspberries and cook until the mixture thickens enough to jell (see "Is It Jelly?," page 403), about 10 minutes. Remove from the heat. Ladle the jam into the sterilized canning jars, leaving ¼ inch (½ cm) of headroom, and seal according to the jar manufacturer's instructions.

Four to five 8-ounce (250 ml) jars

Red Currant Jelly
Gelée de Groseilles

In France, summer is ushered in by an abundance of berries, among them jewel-like, nearly transparent, bright crimson *groseilles,* or red currants. They appear at the market mounded in plastic *barquettes* (small boat-shaped containers), cascading from wooden crates, piled with abandon on tables. They're succulent, if puckery, eaten out of hand, and they have a pleasant little crunch, thanks to their tiny seeds. When pressed, they give juice of an uncommon translucence, which makes for the most gorgeous of jellies.

Gelée de groseilles sparkles in the jar and on the palate. It is a national obsession, as becomes obvious during the season when the fever sets in, and women who don't have their own bushes rush to reserve kilos of berries at the market. You'll understand after you've dipped *tartine*—a slab of bread slathered with butter and *gelée*—into a steaming bowl of coffee. It is surely what the gods eat for breakfast.

It's virtually impossible to fail when

making *gelée de groseilles*. The berry juice contains so much natural pectin that it thickens easily.

Red currant jelly can be used as a filling or topping for cake, in a tart (see Index for Rhubarb and Red Currant Jelly Tart), in a sauce or marinade for lamb, game, or poultry—anywhere you need a touch of tartness. But it's best on a thick piece of buttered bread.

ASTUCES . . . .

• *When you are pressing on the currants as they cook, press gently so that you are just urging the juice out instead of literally pressing it out. The juice will be more clear. The same holds true when you are straining the juice from the berries. If you let the juice drain out naturally, without pressing on it, it will be more clear.*

• *The recipe says to cook the jelly for 3 minutes after it has come to a full boil. That 3 minutes must be respected. If the jelly is cooked any longer, it will harden too much and lose its pure flavor—unless it's a low-pectin year. If so, your **gelée** may take a bit longer to jell—but such a year is rare.*

• *If you find white currants, include them with the red ones, for a rounder, slightly less tart **gelée**.*

. . . .

   8 pounds (4 kg) red currants (see Note),
      rinsed
   7 cups (3 pounds; 1½ kg) sugar

1. Prepare fourteen 8-ounce (250 ml) canning jars and lids by sterilizing them in boiling water according to the manufacturer's instructions.

2. Place the berries, with the rinse water still clinging to them, in a large heavy stockpot over medium-high heat. When the berries are hot, stir and press on them gently so they release their juices.

3. When the berries have released their juices, strain the berries and juices through a fine-mesh strainer into a large bowl. Rinse the stockpot, pour in the strained juice, and return it to a boil over medium-high heat. Stir in the sugar, and continue stirring until it is dissolved. When the liquid comes to a full boil—so that bubbles are erupting all over the surface—set the timer for exactly 3 minutes. Skim off any pink foam from the surface of the jam while it cooks, but don't be concerned if you can't get it all. As soon as the timer goes off, remove the jelly from the heat. Ladle it into the sterilized canning jars, leaving ¼ inch (½ cm) headroom, and seal according to the jar manufacturer's instructions.

About fourteen 8-ounce (250 ml) jars

What to Do with Your Jelly if It Doesn't Jell

Do as the French do, and use it to glaze tarts, breads, and cakes after they've baked. It works perfectly. As for putting it on toast, why not? It's no messier than honey!

The Goose Feather and the Red Currant

>·<

Come July in the 14th century, many young French women had their hands full . . . of goose feathers.

July is currant season, and the women had a very painstaking job to do. They used the end of a goose feather, cut on the diagonal, to pick out the six to eight seeds from each currant before the fruit was turned into jelly.

If you're familiar with currants, which are roughly the size of large peas, you are right to shake your head in awe—at both the patience of the women and the demand for quality that created their job.

Today, the typical way to remove seeds from red currants is either to cook the currants and squeeze them in a cloth sack, in itself a painstaking occupation, or simply to put the raw berries through a food mill or a fine-mesh sieve, and strain out the seeds.

Some say the modern techniques result in poorer-quality jelly. I say, if you have a goose feather and wish to use it to remove the seeds, it would certainly help pass the time on those long, hot July days. But if you're content to leave such pursuits to the past, then turn to page 399 for Red Currant Jelly.

Quince Jelly
Gelée de Coings

>···<

If you mention quince jelly in France, a certain hush settles. People get a dreamy look in their eyes, their mouths form a small "O," soon followed by "Mmm." Then out comes a memory, usually involving a grandmother or a great-aunt, vats of boiling liquid, and slabs of bread with a thin, thin layer of butter and a thick drizzle of homemade *gelée de coings*. Quinces are a rather magical fruit. They're odd, like fragrant apples with a taste that evokes pears, apples, bananas, and strawberries.

Quinces are hard as stone, and stay that way until they've been cooked for at least twenty-five minutes, when they become soft without losing a bit of their shape or character. Cook them much beyond that and they'll begin to crumble, but they never turn mushy.

In France quinces are most often turned into jelly, though they are also cooked with lamb and with apples, and are used to make eau-de-vie. In other countries, Italy for instance, and in the Middle East, where they are thought to have originated, quinces are combined with raisins and fragrant spices and turned into chutneys and jams, or cooked and served either as dessert or as a side dish.

Here is a simple recipe for the quince jelly that I see at the market each fall, always in funny little jars, always gorgeously sunset-hued, always sitting near huge piles of the golden lumpy fruit. I enjoy making it for its beauty and for the elegance of its flavor. I always fill one of my antique jelly jars, which has little bubbles and whorls in the glass, and set the jelly on the windowsill to admire for a while before we eat it. The jelly is crystal clear, and it's almost impossible to tell where the glass ends and it begins.

Some years quinces have less pectin than other years, which causes those who are making jelly to fret (see "Quinces, Fabulous Quinces," page 404). There is a simple solution if the pectin doesn't take as strongly as it should: Add a tablespoon of freshly squeezed lemon juice, which activates the solidifying process. Your jelly won't be firm, but as long as it holds together—enough to spread on bread—it's just fine!

A S T U C E . . . .

• *Cook quince jelly in a large pot so it offers an expansive surface to the air. This helps it to cook quickly and thoroughly.*

. . . .

*5 large (each 10 ounces; 300 g)
    quinces
8½ cups (3¾ pounds; 1¼ kg) sugar
1 tablespoon freshly squeezed lemon
    juice (if necessary)*

1. Prepare six 8-ounce (250 ml) canning jars and lids by sterilizing them in boiling water according to the manufacturer's instructions.

2. Working with quinces takes some muscle. First, rub them briskly with a towel to remove any fuzz (you won't find any on cultivated quinces, only on the wild variety).

The skin is thought to be essential for making jelly, so don't peel them. Cut them in half horizontally. Then use a melon baller to scoop out the seeds and the hard white case that surrounds them. (Alternatively, cut the quinces lengthwise in quarters, and using a very sharp paring knife, cut out the seeds and their cases.) Tie the seeds and the white cases in a double thickness of cheesecloth.

3. Place the fruit and the seed bundle in a large heavy stockpot. Add water to cover by about 1 inch (2½ cm), so the quinces are floating slightly but not wallowing. Cover, bring to a boil over medium-high heat, then reduce the heat so the liquid is simmering merrily.

4. Cook, partially covered so very little liquid evaporates, until the quinces can be pierced easily with a metal skewer, about 25 to 40 minutes (the time varies greatly depending on the quality and age of the fruit). While the quinces are cooking, press on the seed bundle often to extract the pectin. Drain, reserving the liquid and the seed bundle.

5. Measure out 6¼ cups (about 3 l) liquid and return it and the seed bundle to the same stockpot. Add the sugar, stir, and bring to a boil over medium-high heat. Reduce the heat so the liquid is boiling steadily but not wildly, and cook, stirring and pressing on the bag of seeds, until the liquid thickens, anywhere from 10 to 25 minutes. (To test for consistency, see box, below). If the liquid has not jelled after 30 minutes, stir in the lemon juice and cook until it jells sufficiently, 5 to 10 minutes.

6. Remove the jelly from the heat and strain it, if necessary, to remove any bits so it is perfectly clear. Then proceed to ladle it into the sterilized canning jars, leaving ¼ inch (½ cm) of headroom. Seal according to the jar manufacturer's instructions.

About six 8-ounce (250 ml) jars

Is It Jelly?

➤•◄

*H*ow can you tell if your jelly is ready? Drizzle some of the jelly liquid on a cold plate, place it in the refrigerator for 1 to 2 minutes, and then check to see if it has thickened enough that it won't run all over the plate. If it is still very runny, continue cooking until it thickens to your liking. (Another test is to drizzle the liquid into a glass of ice water. If it disappears into the water, continue to cook. If it forms soft little lumps, or a single soft lump, it is ready.)

Quinces, Fabulous Quinces

Quinces are the fruit of nostalgia. Golden and knobby, they belong to an era when women had more time in the kitchen, and when every garden had a *cognassier*, or quince tree. The quince was commonplace then, and its unusual subtle aroma filled the house with an incredible perfume.

In France the quince is becoming increasingly rare, now the issue of an occasional backyard or garden rather than of orchards devoted to its production. Yet emotion about and interest in them remains high. Few fruits are as well loved or as little understood.

Though I remember quinces from my girlhood, when my grandmother often cooked a few slices with applesauce to give it a gorgeous rosy hue, I'd never worked with them until I moved to Normandy. There, the moment quinces form on the tree they are picked, and soon jars of crystal-clear, golden to rosy to rust-colored jelly begin appearing on windowsills and at the market.

My own experience began when I walked into my friend Edith's house one early fall day and was struck by the most luscious aroma. She had put two quinces on her kitchen radiator "just to make the house smell good."

I went to the market, and there were quinces, heaps of them, their aroma wafting all around. The woman who was selling them, and her own jelly, shouted the cooking instructions over the din of the marketplace. I noted it all down and returned home eager to begin.

First I read through my cookbooks about quinces, then called friends who I thought might have some information. What I learned from both sources was all quite uniform, and had a lot to do with sugar.

I began full of confidence, convinced that, as one friend had put it, *"La gelée de coings est inrattable"*—it is impossible to fail with quince jelly.

I cored the quinces, put them in a huge pot, added water and the seeds, which I had carefully tied into a small square of cotton, and cooked them until they were tender. Then I mixed the cooking liquid with sugar and cooked that, along with the seeds, waiting for the moment of truth, the moment when the liquid would turn to jelly. I cooked and stirred, well beyond the twenty minutes I had been told it would take. It got a bit thicker, then thinned out again. Its color became increasingly pink. I tested it after an hour and it still seemed loose to me, but I removed it from the heat, convinced it wouldn't thicken any more.

I called a friend who has made quince jelly all her life, and she exclaimed to me over the phone that for the first time *her* quince jelly hadn't jelled. "I don't know why. I usually only cook it ten minutes and this time, can you imagine, I cooked it more than twenty and it still didn't jell." I recounted my experience. "You cooked yours too long. Never cook quince jelly more than forty-five minutes," she said sternly.

So I went back to the market and got more quinces to try again. The woman who'd sold them to me raised her eyebrows. "Making more?" I told her of my failure. "I had trouble this year, too," she said. "Apparently there's not much pectin in the quinces."

I tried four more times and finally had success, but only after adding a secret ingredient—a tablespoon of lemon juice. Then I got on the phone, found other quince experts, and we all agreed on one thing: No one really knows much about quinces. Everyone agrees the pectin is contained in the seeds, though some think it is also in the skin, in the pulp, and even concentrated in the hard white substance that forms the hollow where the seeds sit.

I finally spoke with a research scientist, a man who has made quince jelly for fifteen years from fruit that grows in his backyard. He is passionate about quinces and had posed many of the questions I was asking. He agreed that no one seemed to know much, but he gave me his empirical information: "Don't cook more than four pounds at once, and don't worry about overcooking it. I cooked a batch for an hour and a half before it jelled this year." I was encouraged. I talked with a friend, Monique Tourrette, who makes quince jelly at her home in Provence every year, and learned she has had the opposite problem: "Sometimes mine seizes up so fast, I end up making caramels." She laughed. "It's okay. Sometimes I let it happen on purpose—my grandkids love them."

For the final effort, I scooped out the seeds and all of the white substance that surrounds them, put that in a cotton square, and cooked it right along with the fruit, then with the juice. Miracle of miracles, my jelly jelled within minutes.

All of this experimentation helped me establish one rule about quinces: Prepare for the unexpected. Whether it be syrup or jelly, you'll not be disappointed.

Orange Marmalade
Confiture d'Oranges

→···←

This marmalade is so simple to make, you'll be amazed. In the south of France, where bitter oranges are available, it is made with their skins and yields a jam with a bitter edge. In the rest of France, however, bitter oranges are close to impossible to find, so farmwives make it with the oranges at hand. While I love bitter orange jam, I love this, too, for it brings a sweet summery flavor to the table. We slather it on bread spread with fresh goat cheese or lightly salted butter—sublime. Also try it as a cake filling or in a tart shell.

3 pounds (1½ kg) oranges, preferably organic (see box, opposite), or more if needed, well scrubbed

2½ quarts (2½ l) water

2 or more large lemons, preferably organic, well scrubbed

13 cups (5½ pounds; 2¾ kg) sugar

1. Halve and juice the oranges. You should have 2 cups (500 ml) juice. If you don't, squeeze enough extra oranges to give that much juice. Reserve the skins from the original 3 pounds (1½ kg) of oranges, and discard any remaining orange skins.

2. Cut the orange skins, which will still have some pulp clinging to them, into very thin strips. Then cut the strips into tiny dice. (You may do this in a food processor, but the results won't be as nice or as professional.) Place the orange peels, the juice, and the water in a large nonreactive stockpot. Cover and let sit overnight.

3. When ready to make the marmalade, prepare fourteen 8-ounce (250 ml) canning jars and lids by sterilizing them in boiling water according to the manufacturer's instructions.

4. Halve and squeeze the lemons. You should have ½ cup (125 ml) juice. Squeeze additional lemons if necessary to get that amount of juice. Discard the peel and the

pulp. Stir the lemon juice into the orange mixture.

5. Stir the sugar into the orange mixture, and bring to a boil over medium-high heat. Reduce the heat so the mixture is bubbling seriously and cook, stirring occasionally, until it is thick enough to make a marmalade that will sit up on a spoon but will not be too solid, 1½ to 1¾ hours. As the marmalade gets close to the correct consistency, the bubbles will get bigger and will almost pop. You can check the consistency by following the instructions in the box called "Is It Jelly?," on page 403.

6. When the jam is cooked to your liking, remove it from the heat and ladle it into the sterilized canning jars, leaving ¼ inch (½ cm) headroom. Seal according to the jar manufacturer's instructions.

Fourteen 8-ounce (250 ml) jars

N O T E : The yield will vary by as much as 8 ounces (250 ml), depending on how long you cook the marmalade. The less you cook it, the greater the yield.

Organic Citrus

→•←

Organically raised oranges and lemons are preferred in recipes where the peel is used. If you can't find them, use fruit that has not been treated after harvest with a fungicide wax. (In any case, be sure to scrub the fruit well with soap and water before proceeding.)

Generally, you can identify treated fruit by its unnatural shine; labeling identifying post-harvest treatment is also required. If in doubt, ask the manager in the produce department of your grocery store.

Orange and Lemon Marmalade
Confiture d'Oranges et de Citrons

Like the plain orange marmalade, this jam brings the sun right onto the breakfast table. I love it, and can't decide which of the two I prefer. This is less sweet, more like a traditional marmalade. Try them both—they are so luscious, you won't be left with any of either one on your hands.

3 pounds (1½ kg) oranges, preferably organic
  (see "Organic Citrus," page 407), or more
  if needed, well scrubbed
2 or more large lemons, preferably organic,
  well scrubbed
2½ quarts (2½ l) water
7 cups (3 pounds; 1½ kg) sugar

1. Halve and juice the oranges. You should have 2 cups (500 ml) juice. If you don't, squeeze enough extra oranges to give that much juice.

2. Halve and juice the lemons. You should have ½ cup (125 ml) juice. Squeeze additional lemons if necessary to get that amount of juice.

3. Reserve the skins from the 3 pounds of oranges and the 2 lemons, and discard any additional skins. Cut the orange and lemon skins, both of which will still have some pulp clinging to them, into thin strips (⅛ inch; ¼ cm), and then into small dice. (You may do this in a food processor, but the results won't be as nice or as professional.) Place the peels, the juices, and the water in a large nonreactive kettle or stockpot. Cover and let the mixture sit overnight.

4. When ready to make the marmalade, prepare eight 8-ounce (250 ml) canning jars and lids by sterilizing them in boiling water according to the manufacturer's instructions.

5. Add the sugar to the fruit mixture, stir, and bring to a boil over high heat. Reduce the heat to medium or medium-low to keep the mixture at a healthy rolling boil. Cook, stirring occasionally, until the marmalade thickens to your liking, 1 to 1¾ hours. (To test for consistency, see "Is It Jelly?" page 403.) Toward the end of the cooking time, you will need to stir the mixture more frequently because the fruit peels tend to bunch up.

6. When the marmalade is cooked to your liking, remove it from the heat and pour it into sterilized jars. Seal according to the jar manufacturer's instructions, and store.

Eight 8-ounce (250 ml) jars

Candied Lemon Zest
Confit de Zeste de Citron

→ • • • ←

I like to have candied lemon zest on hand—it brightens everything from a dish of rice to a dessert like Goat Cheese in Red Wine (see Index). You can mince it and add it to a cake batter (instead of candied fruit, for instance) or use it in your favorite fruitcake recipe.

You'll find many ways to use it once you've got it in your pantry (try it sprinkled on spinach).

I store my candied zest on a shelf in a cool room. If any mold forms on the top of the syrup, just scrape it off—it has no effect on the flavor of the zest. If you prefer to seal it, follow the jar manufacturer's instructions for sealing jam.

> 2 large lemons, preferably organic (see
>   "Organic Citrus," page 407), well scrubbed
> 1½ cups (250 g) sugar
> 1½ cups (375 ml) water

1. Halve and juice the lemons. Reserve the juice for another use.

2. Place the juiced lemon halves in a medium-size nonreactive saucepan and cover with water. Bring to a boil over high heat, then reduce the heat to medium-high so the water is boiling gently, and boil until you can easily scrape the pulp and pith (the white part of the peel) from the zest (the yellow part of the peel), about 15 minutes. Drain, and when the lemon halves are cool enough to handle, cut each again in half lengthwise, and using a small stainless-steel spoon, carefully scrape away the pulp and all of the pith, so what you have left are pieces of pure yellow zest. (This takes a bit of time and finesse—don't scrape too hard or the zest will break. You'll get the trick quickly.)

3. Rinse out the saucepan. Place the sugar and the 1½ cups (375 ml) water in it, whisk, and bring to a boil over medium-high heat. Reduce the heat so the mixture is simmering, then cook, covered, until all the sugar has dissolved, about 7 minutes, uncovering to whisk occasionally.

4. Add the lemon zest to the sugar syrup, pushing it under the surface. Cover and simmer until the zest is transparent, about 20 minutes. Check the zest occasionally to be sure the pieces are not cooking too quickly—the syrup should not turn golden, an indication it is caramelizing and getting bitter.

5. Remove the pan from the heat and let the zest cool in the syrup.

6. Place the zest, still in the syrup, in a jar that holds at least 3 cups, and cover tightly, or seal as for jam. Drain before using.

Candied zests of 2 lemons

"Johnny Onions"
"Les Johnnies"

=

In northern Brittany, the town of Roscoff is noted for its lacy Renaissance church spire, its active port, its abundance of fresh and sparkling seafood, and its onions. Called *rose de Roscoff*, the round, hard, reddish-skinned onion grows abundantly in the fertile soil and gentle coastal air.

Rose de Roscoff is an onion the likes of which is seldom found anymore. Its flavor is full, intense, and pungent, yet it cooks down quickly to a mouth-melting sweetness. Noted for its keeping qualities, a characteristic developed for sailors who used it aboard ship, it has become a specialty onion, sold in braids from the shelves of high-quality groceries.

As early as the 1400s, ships set sail from Roscoff to Plymouth, their holds full of goods from sea salt to onions, which the plucky Bretons then sold door-to-door. The way was paved for commerce between Roscoff and England.

Much later, English cooks who tasted the *rose de Roscoff* clamored for more, and in the early 1800s an enterprising Breton, Henry Ollivier, took a wagonful to England and, following the lead of his forebears, sold them door-to-door. He made a fortune, and an industry was born.

For more than a century after that, boats left Roscoff for Plymouth loaded with onions and men, some as young as eight years old. The men would lodge wherever they could, and stay until their onions were sold, usually all winter.

They were all called "Johnny" by their customers, who couldn't pronounce their Breton names. Each staked out his territory, some going as far north as Wales.

The "Johnnies," or "Johnny onions," often worked in pairs, which helped relieve the tedium. Evenings were reserved for a quick trip to the local pub, a simple dinner, and braiding onions. By daybreak the "Johnnies" were on the road, strings of onions hanging from a stick balanced across their shoulders, a familiar and welcome sight.

In 1929 more than 1,500 "Johnnies" made the trip to England, worked hard, lived simply and frugally, and returned to Brittany rich as kings.

The last "Johnny" was still selling onions in Plymouth and Swansea in the 1980s. By then the job was simplified. He traveled by car, and only to clients who ordered onions in advance. When he ran out he called his wife at home, and within days a new load of onions had arrived in Plymouth.

A LOOK TO THE FUTURE

Pierre Jezekel, a young farmer outside of Roscoff whose soil is black and rich, is one of few growers who still cultivates the *rose de Roscoff*, though he doesn't go to Britain to sell them. The competition of inexpensive onions from Spain and Eastern Europe has all but wiped out the market for specialty varieties, but M. Jezekel believes *rose de Roscoff* and its history is too good to lose.

Obtaining a quality label, or Appellation d'Origine Contrôllée, for the onions would ensure their survival. M. Jezekel helped document the onion's history and qualities, and along with other growers, presented a huge file to the government. They await a reply.

"It's our best hope," he said, worriedly. "We think we'll get it. There's not another onion like it."

M. Jezekel treats his onions with care, cultivating them carefully, laying them gently in baskets right out of the soil as if they might break. He braids and sells them to small shopkeepers and to wholesalers who supply specialty markets.

His commercially successful crops are shallots and potatoes, but it's the *rose de Roscoff* and its rich and vital history that keeps him going.

Thanks to M. Jezekel and his colleagues, it looks as if "Johnny's" onions will survive.

Rich Onion Marmalade
Lipig

→ ··· ←

In northern Brittany, where the flavorful *rose de Roscoff* onion grows, *lipig* is commonly served as a condiment for *kig har farz* (see Index for Hearty Pork and Vegetable Stew), the lush and warming Breton stew that stars a tender buckwheat dumpling. It sets that dish off in much the same way a chutney might another. In the south, where the flat, pungent *jaune paille* ("yellow straw") onion grows, the same preparation is used as the base of a *tarte* (see Index for Breton Onion Tart).

A really rich onion marmalade, *lipig* has dozens of uses. The onions must cook long and slowly so their flavor and sugar develop. Don't try to hurry this along, for the onions may burn, giving them an acrid flavor. The onions begin to turn color during the last 15 minutes of cooking, which is when they will bear careful watching and stirring.

This will keep for several weeks in the refrigerator. Reheat it slightly before serving to melt the butter. Once made and chilled, *lipig* is not a lovely sight to behold. Warm it up, however, and it takes on its original glistening hue.

> 1½ tablespoons unsalted butter
> 2 pounds (1 kg) onions, peeled and very thinly sliced
> Sea salt and freshly ground black pepper (optional)

1. Melt the butter in a large heavy skillet over medium heat. Add the onions, stir so they are coated with butter, and reduce the heat to medium-low. Cover the skillet and cook, stirring occasionally to be sure the onions aren't sticking, until they are reduced in volume by two thirds and are a pale golden color, 1½ hours. Continue cooking, stirring often, until they melt by another one third and turn a deeper golden, 10 to 15 minutes.

2. Remove the skillet from the heat, season the onions with salt and pepper if desired, and let cool. Store in an airtight container in the refrigerator.

About 1 cup (250 ml)

Honey and Hazelnut Spread
Confit de Miel et Noisettes

>···<

This sublime combination is Valerie and Manex Lanatua's answer to Nutella, an almost sickeningly sweet chocolate and hazelnut spread commonly used throughout Europe. I much prefer this for spreading on toast in the morning because it is full of subtle, rich flavor. And it doesn't make your teeth feel as though they want to fall out with its sweetness.

The Lanatuas produce honey in Axaha, near St. Jean-Pied-de-Port in the Pays Basque. They like their food fresh and natural, and this *confit* fills the bill. I think you'll agree.

1 cup (150 g) hazelnuts
½ cup (125 ml) honey

1. Preheat the oven to 350°F (175°C).
2. Spread the hazelnuts on a baking sheet and toast them in the oven until they are deep golden, 10 to 12 minutes. Remove them from the oven and transfer them immediately to a tea towel. Rub the hazelnuts in the towel to remove their skin (which lends a bitter taste).
3. Place the hazelnuts in a food processor and purée them. When the purée is smooth and almost oily, add the honey and pulse until thoroughly combined. Use immediately or store in an airtight jar, refrigerated, indefinitely.

1 generous cup (250 ml)

Honey and Walnuts
Miel aux Noix

>···<

I was at the market in the lovely little medieval town of Terrasson, in the Dordogne, strolling along the line of vendors set up on the quay of the Vézère River. Just about to turn and cross the Roman bridge, I noticed a man with a small table on which sat jars of

The French Farm Pantry

➤·◄

The French farm cook always has eggs and butter on hand, often from her own animals. She is also sure to have the following ingredients so that a meal is never far away. Follow her example and you'll be prepared for all occasions.

- Onions
- Potatoes
- Shallots
- Garlic
- Dijon mustard
- Parmesan cheese
- Bay leaves
- Nutmeg
- Couscous
- Raisins
- Lentils
- Bacon, salt pork, or pancetta
- Rice, white and brown
- Pasta
- Olive oil, preferably extra-virgin
- Red wine vinegar
- Sea salt
- Black peppercorns
- A pot of chives
- Unbleached all-purpose flour
- Whole-wheat flour
- Cornmeal
- Sugar, white and brown
- Lemons

Place onions and potatoes in separate baskets and keep them in a cool, dark place. Cover the potatoes with a tea towel if they are exposed to light, so they won't develop green areas on the skin. Shallots should be placed in a basket and kept in a cool place or, if you must, in the door of the refrigerator. Don't place them in the refrigerator itself—they'll just lose flavor and get soggy. Garlic should be in a basket—small wire baskets are made expressly for the purpose.

Mustard will keep well, refrigerated, for about 1 month. It tends to lose its bite, however, so buy small jars that you will use up.

Fresh Parmesan cheese will keep almost indefinitely if wrapped in parchment or waxed paper, then in aluminum foil.

Buy dried imported bay leaves, rather than fresh ones. Fresh bay leaves, from the variety of bay tree most commonly grown in the U.S., are acrid and unpleasant. The imported dried variety is sweet and subtle, and keeps its flavor for a long, long time if kept airtight. As with all herbs, keep them out of direct light and buy small quantities.

Fresh nutmegs are easy to find, and a sprinkling on a cake, an omelette, in a cream sauce, will always be welcome.

Couscous plumps up in moments, and you can add any kind of vegetable you like to it for a quick salad. Or blend in some raisins or prunes, season it with curry, and serve it as a side dish.

Lentils, seasoned with a chunk of bacon, salt pork (refreshed), or pancetta, will provide you with a hearty main course. White or brown rice, seasoned with garlic and drizzled with olive oil, makes a savory side dish.

Pasta is self-explanatory. On the French farm it is most often tossed with unsalted butter and topped with grated Gruyère cheese. Mmm.

And so on down the list. Do as the farm cook does: Have a well-stocked pantry and you will never be caught unawares.

honey and bags of walnuts. In among it all was one small jar filled with amber honey and walnuts. I bought it, and tried it later over some of the fresh *cabécou* goat cheese that I had purchased elsewhere in the market. It was heaven.

I now always have honey and walnuts on hand, because it's like an instant dessert in a jar. I pour it over goat cheese and serve it along with fruit (a mix that goes well for breakfast, too), and it's good over ice cream or even over a simple cake. It also makes a wonderful, and unusual, gift.

1½ cups (375 ml) best-quality wildflower honey
1 cup (120 g) walnut halves

1. In a small pan over very low heat, melt the honey if it is hardened, being very careful not to let it come to a boil. Let it cool.
2. Place the walnuts in a 2-cup (500 ml) jar, and pour the lukewarm honey over them. Let cool completely before using or storing, airtight, in the refrigerator.

About 2 cups (500 ml)

Orange Wine
Vin d'Orange

→···←

Imagine making your own richly flavored orange wine. With this recipe, it's as simple as peeling a batch of oranges and having the patience to wait a week for the wine to mature.

This is one of the liqueurs commonly found in the farm liqueur cabinet (usually an armoire that also contains the family's linens). It is considered a hot-weather apéritif, but I love it in winter, when the sky is leaden and a breath of orange flavor is like a taste of summer. In winter, serve it at room temperature. On a fine summer day, lightly chilled is best.

I have a friend who takes all the ingredients for this wine on her ski vacations. The first thing she and her friends do when they get to their chalet is to make the wine. They have two weeks to ski, and by the end of the first week the wine is ready to drink. "I smell this wine and I think of the slopes," she said.

For skiing, sunning, or just as a palate opener, try this. You'll be thrilled to have it in your liquor cabinet.

ASTUCES . . . .

• Straining the ingredients through fine cheesecloth is important, because otherwise the wine will have particles floating in it. They don't affect the flavor, just the aesthetics. Occasionally, even after careful straining, sediment will form; ignore it, pouring carefully.

• If you can't get to the wine after 48 hours, leave it for as long as another 24. It will be slightly bitter at first, but it will mellow within a week or so. Though it can be enjoyed after 1 week, it improves with age; I like to wait 4 weeks before uncorking a bottle.

. . . .

10 good-size oranges, preferably organic
   (see "Organic Citrus," page 407),
   well scrubbed
8 cups (2 l) dry white wine, such as Sancerre
2 cups (500 ml) vodka
1 tablespoon dried chamomile flowers
   (as sold for tea)
2 cups minus 2 tablespoons (375 g) sugar

1. Peel the oranges right down to the fruit, including the pith. Put the fruit aside for another use.

2. Place the skins with the pith in a large nonreactive pot or bowl. Add the wine, vodka, chamomile flowers, and half the sugar. Stir.

3. Caramelize the remaining sugar: Place the sugar in a small heavy saucepan over medium-high heat. The sugar will melt and begin to bubble, then gradually liquefy, turning a golden color. This will take about 7 minutes. Continue cooking, swirling the pan occasionally if it colors unevenly, until the sugar is a deep golden color, like light molasses, about 5 minutes.

4. Remove the pan from the heat and pour the caramelized sugar into the orange mixture, scraping as much of the sugar as possible from the pan with a wooden spoon. The caramel will sizzle and send up steam, and it will instantly harden. Don't be concerned—it will gradually dissolve.

5. Stir the orange mixture again, cover the container with a lid, or waxed paper and aluminum foil, or parchment paper and aluminum foil, and let sit for 48 hours. Stir it once to be sure all the caramelized sugar is mixed with the other ingredients.

6. Strain the mixture through a sieve lined with dampened cheesecloth or a dampened cotton tea towel. Discard the orange skins and decant the liquid into sterilized bottles. Seal with corks. Let sit for at least 1 week before drinking.

About 2½ quarts (2½ l)

Apéritif
→·←

U ntil the end of the 18th century, the word *apéritif* was used as an adjective to describe a dish that "opens the appetite for the rest of the meal." Today *apéritif* most commonly refers to a drink served before the meal.

Quality First

====

Jean-Pierre and Mireille Cartier exude an expert, highly refined presence as they lean against the tasting counter at their vineyard, Domaine Les Gouberts. Just outside the town of Gigondas, in the Côtes-du-Rhône appellation, the Cartiers are well placed to make fine wines, for they have ideal soil and climatic conditions. Their house, where M. Cartier was born in the late 1940s, and the winery are built on some of the area's most historic land.

"The first building ever constructed outside the town of Gigondas was on our land," says Mme. Cartier. "It was most likely a stable constructed for peasants, and it dates to 1636."

M. Cartier's mother's family, the Gouberts, long ago received the land from the lord who owned it, a thank-you gift for services rendered. Like many landowners in France, they lost most of it during the Revolution, and the rest of it sometime later, through marriage.

"They were obliged to buy it back," says Mme. Cartier, shaking her head as though the tragedy was recent.

The land was doled out to succeeding generations, and when it came time for Jean-Pierre to inherit, there were just twelve acres to divide between two children. Mme. Cartier brought four acres with her when the couple married, and in 1970 they bought more.

They now have forty-six acres, a medium-size vineyard for the area, which produces from 150,000 to 225,000 gallons (563,000 to 844,000 l) of wine a year.

The land around Gigondas that now bristles with gnarled grapevines was once covered with olive trees. A freeze in 1929 killed most of them, and growers who didn't want to wait the fifteen years for young olive trees to mature planted grapevines instead. Another freeze in 1956 was the death knell for the remaining olive trees, and growers replaced all the trees with vines.

"The soil is poor," Mme. Cartier says. "It's perfect for vines."

(continued)

By the 1940s the area was known for its wine, though it wasn't until after World War II that Gigondas, the wine of the area, received its Appellation d'Origine Contrôlée, or pedigree.

The Cartiers' vines are scattered among several tiny sun-baked villages, including Sablet, Seguret, Gigondas, Beaumes-de-Venise, and Lafare. The soil is unique in each area, giving the grapes their own distinctive flavor.

Planted among the vineyards are nearly a dozen grape varieties, which M. Cartier blends to create his different wines.

In order for a wine to receive an appellation, rules for certain quantities and varieties of grapes must be respected. But within the rules there is great flexibility. To be called Gigondas, a wine can have a maximum eighty percent Grenache Noir and a minimum fifteen percent of either Syrah or Mourvèdre. M. Cartier uses sixty-two percent Grenache Noir and twenty-five percent Syrah, along with Mourvèdre and touches of Cinsault and Clairette, in his Gigondas.

His Sablet Rouge Côtes du Rhône-Villages is based on Grenache Noir, with an equal amount of Syrah and Mourvèdre and a good dose of Cinsault. He also makes an elegant Viognier from one hundred percent Viognier grapes.

Just recently M. Cartier planted some "antique" grape varieties—Picpoul, Terret Noire, and Vaquerez. "For fun, to see what I can make with them," he explains.

"Remember, it isn't just the grapes that make for good wine," he says almost admonishingly. "They play a role, combined with the soil and the method in which the wine is made. I know how to make my wines because I know what varieties I planted in which soil."

M. Cartier's father made wine and was his first teacher. "I learned from my father, it's true," says M. Cartier. "But I started working on my own at age fourteen, and I'm about to do my thirty-fifth harvest, so I feel as though I've taught myself a great deal."

Though he recognizes the science of making wine, he feels it must adapt to the conditions. "There's a side to being a winemaker that is artistic and inventive," he says.

When asked why he ages his Cuvée Florence—a sumptuous Gigondas named after the couple's daughter—in young oak barrels from the Vosges mountains, a practice that is unheard of for Gigondas, he says, "Because it pleases me to do so, and the results please me very much."

Most of the wines made in Gigondas are aged in old oak barrels previously used to age beer. M. Cartier feels that practice removes the delicacy from most Gigondas wines, making them deep-flavored, chewy.

"Old oak, particularly those beer barrels, gives the wines heaviness," he says. "I don't feel I can tell my colleagues how to make their wine, but I certainly don't want my wines to touch that old oak."

He got the idea for using young oak from tasting fine Burgundies. They pleased his palate. Why not, he reasoned, transfer one of their techniques south?

M. Cartier differs from his neighbors in other ways as well. While they do everything to increase production, M. Cartier does exactly the opposite.

"I don't fertilize, nor do I irrigate," he says. "I don't want to push my vines to produce more. I want them to produce the best they can. And a small year can be a great year, while a year when the harvest is good can be a bad year."

If his vines are heavily laden, M. Cartier trims them so the grapes that remain are rich in flavor. He lets weeds grow between the vines, then turns them into the soil to enrich it.

"My vineyards may not be pretty, but I think it's important to do it that way," he says.

Normally a young vine produces the most grapes in its second and third years, and many growers make wines from those first harvests. Not M. Cartier. He wants his vines strong and well established, and doesn't harvest until the fifth or sixth year.

"A vine will produce for forty to fifty years," he says. "I'm not in a hurry. I'm looking for quality. I produce a wine I like to drink, and I want to continue to do so."

All his principles aside, M. Cartier is quick to point out that the grower's control is extremely limited. "September makes the wine," he says. "You must never forget that. We can control it just so much."

A freeze after the vines produce leaves and rain in September are the two things a grower fears most, though M. Cartier is philosophical. "Even if it rains, we can salvage some of the grapes and try through vinification techniques to make a good wine. Often it will rain in one parcel and not another, so the whole crop won't be lost."

When the wine is ready for bottling, M. Cartier does so without filtering. "Filtering removes more than just deposits from a wine," he says. "It also removes nuances."

The Cartiers have the self-assurance of people who truly enjoy and reflect on what they do, and who know they produce something desirable. Yet their pride is a quiet one.

"Our *métier* is the school of modesty," M. Cartier says. "But we feel there is a place for people who produce quality wines."

Vovo's Peach Wine

Vin de Pêche de Vovo

→···←

Vovo lives in Peyrenègre, the village where our friends Dany and Guy Dubois have their farm and restaurant. I got to know Vovo years ago when I'd visit the farm and help Dany put up her foie gras and *rillettes*. Vovo would come to help, too, and we'd all work together in the old farm kitchen.

Whenever we return to Peyrenègre, we always stop by to see Vovo and her husband, Pierrot. They love to sit over a glass of peach wine and tell village stories that spin long and lively. When I don't get a chance to visit for a while, I'm sure to send Vovo an occasional note. "Vovo" is a nickname that comes from the word *voisine*, or neighbor. When I write I simply address the letter "Vovo, Peyrenègre" because the postman, Hubert, knows exactly who I mean.

This is Vovo's recipe for peach wine. One would never believe, when macerating a handful of leaves in alcohol and wine, that anything delicious would be the result, but here it is! Leaves from a peach tree lend this a soft fruit flavor that soothes and satisfies.

As she says, "Make it in good health, and drink it likewise." It will only improve as it ages, so don't feel obliged to drink it all right away! Or make a larger recipe, so you have some to save.

ASTUCE . . . .

• *Season with nutmeg according to your taste, or as Vovo says, "Au petit bonheur la chance!" ("A bit for luck and happiness!")*

. . . .

> 1 bottle (750 ml) hearty red wine, such as
> a Côtes du Rhône or a Bergerac
> 1 cup (250 ml) vodka
> ½ cup (100 g) sugar
> ¼ teaspoon freshly grated nutmeg
> 30 peach leaves, well rinsed and patted dry

1. Blend the wine, vodka, and sugar in a large mason jar or other glass container with an airtight seal. Either close the jar and shake it or stir until most of the sugar is dissolved, then add the nutmeg, shake to mix, and add

the leaves, pushing them right down into the liquid so they are covered. Seal the jar and let macerate for 8 days, shaking gently each day if necessary to dissolve any remaining sugar.

2. Strain the wine, discarding the leaves, into sterilized bottles. Seal them with corks. Let rest before drinking for at least 1 month, in a cool, dark spot.

About 5 cups (1¼ l)

Cherry Wine
Vin de Cerises

This recipe is a bit hard to believe, but it works and the results are astonishing. Take beautiful, unblemished cherry leaves, which you've picked on a morning toward the end of June, if possible, so they are still nice and fresh. Macerate them for at least 2 days, then strain. Bottle the wine and forget about it for three months. When you remember it then, open it and taste it. You won't believe the delicate, rich, almond flavor of cherries that meets your palate.

This is a very common apéritif in the countryside throughout France. This recipe comes from Annie Grodent, a friend in Normandy who has an enormous cherry tree and makes the wine once a year. She serves it, at room temperature, before a meal. I like it best in wintertime, when the wine echoes the memories of a cherry-filled spring.

1 bottle (1 l) hearty red wine, such as a
*   Côtes du Rhône*
1 cup (250 ml) vodka
1 cup (200 g) sugar
75 fresh cherry leaves

1. Whisk the wine, vodka, and sugar together in a large mixing bowl until the sugar is nearly dissolved. Add the cherry leaves, pushing them gently down into the liquid. Cover and let sit for 48 to 72 hours.

2. Strain the wine, discarding the leaves, into sterilized bottles. Seal them with corks. Let it sit in a cool, dark spot for 3 months, until the wine has had a chance to mature and any sediments have completely settled.

About 5 cups (1¼ l)

Quince Liqueur
Ratafia de Coings

→•••←

Quinces intrigue me, and an eau-de-vie made from them that is the color of sunset intrigued me more. So, I couldn't resist making it during quince season. I'm glad I did, for its delicate flavor is surprising and soothing after a hearty supper.

The only trick here is to work quickly so the quince is buried in alcohol before it has a chance to turn dark brown, which it will begin to do as soon as it is exposed to the air.

2 large quinces
1 cup (200 g) sugar
2 cups (250 ml) vodka

1. Cut the quinces lengthwise in quarters, then mince or grate them (skins and seeds included) in a food processor. Place them in a jar with at least a 2½-quart (2½ l) capacity—you need room for shaking. Add the vodka, then the sugar, and shake vigorously. Keep the jar in a cool, shadowed place.

2. Shake the contents of the jar every other day for 10 days, then when you think of it after that, about once a week for at least 4 additional weeks. Strain the eau-de-vie through a sieve lined with a double thickness of dampened cheesecloth, into a sterilized bottle. Seal it with a cork.

3. The *ratafia de coings* will keep indefi-

nitely. A sediment will form on the bottom of the bottle over time. Don't be concerned, just pour carefully so it doesn't cloud the individual glasses of eau-de-vie.

About 3½ cups (875 ml)

Ratafia

→•←

Apparently the Romans ended their business deals with a drink, or **rata fiat**, which in Latin means roughly "deal concluded." Thus the current name for many an after-dinner liqueur: ratafia.

Liqueur 44

>···<

In every farmhouse across France, there is at least one cupboard consecrated to liqueurs of every sort. While they change slightly from region to region—for instance, in Provence one is likely to find made-on-the-farm pastis, whereas in the Dordogne the staple is *vin de noix*—they are all made with seasonal fruits and/or herbs, in small batches.

This is a typical farm recipe with a twist. It comes from Claude Udron, a former restaurateur with one foot in Marseillan and one in the soil of his native Normandy, who makes it every year. The "44" refers to the number of coffee beans, the number of times each ingredient is pierced, the number of days the liqueur is left, and the number of sugar cubes. The amount of sugar listed here is the equivalent of 44 French sugar cubes. While most recipes for "44" consist simply of an orange, a vanilla bean, coffee, and sugar, Claude adds a banana for its softening effect. "The banana will turn black, but don't worry," he said, laughing. "It doesn't mean a thing."

I loved having this "working" in my cupboard, where I would check it once a day just to be sure it wasn't boiling over or emitting any strange essences. Indeed, it made itself, and it turned out to be as smooth and revivifying as Claude had promised.

We sampled it immediately on the forty-fifth day, then left it to rest for another several weeks—which is the right thing to do, for it continues to mellow.

1 large orange, preferably organic (see "Organic Citrus," page 407), well scrubbed

1 banana, peeled

1 vanilla bean

1⅓ cups (270 g) sugar

44 coffee beans

1 quart (1 l) vodka

1. Using a sharp knife, pierce the skin of the orange all over 44 times, going right through the peel but not into the fruit. Pierce the banana all over 44 times, and also the vanilla bean.

2. Place the sugar, coffee beans, orange, banana, and vanilla bean in a nonreactive container large enough to hold all the ingredients with some room to spare. Pour the vodka over all, seal the container airtight, and place it in a dark place for 44 days. Each day for the first week, gently shake the container to help dissolve the sugar.

3. Strain the liqueur and bottle into a sterilized bottle. Seal it with a cork. It will be very drinkable now, but it will improve with age.

About 4½ cups (1⅛ l)

Thyme Liqueur

Liqueur de Thym

→···←

Germain Vallortigara works at an essence factory in the small Provençal hilltop town of Montbrun-les-Bains, near Sault. He has worked there for more than twenty years, surveying the vats, pipes, and cauldrons that are filled with simmering herbs and plants.

One building is used exclusively for a specific type of moss collected from around oak trees that gives a soft and refreshing perfume used in men's colognes. The night I visited Germain at work, peppermint was simmering in one huge stainless-steel vat while lavender simmered in another, sending out opposing aromas that seared the throat.

Some of the essences are blended right at the factory according to very specific recipes provided by well-known perfume manufacturers from around the world. Others are shipped to pharmacies and laboratories.

Germain has a highly developed sense of smell and taste. While he is used to the intense aromas that fly around the factory, at the table he tastes the nuances of everything put before him.

This liqueur is his recipe, and it is redolent of the thyme that grows in the hills around Montbrun-les-Bains. He encouraged me to make it, insisting that I make it strong enough to bend a nail—in other words, with 90-proof alcohol. But he was

joking, and he called me back later to tell me that 45 proof would do. As it is, this liqueur sends a pleasant thyme-infused burning sensation down the throat. If I want to bend nails, I guess I'll have to get out a pair of pliers.

Serve this as a digestive after a hearty meal of Provençal Pork and Vegetable Stew followed by Goat Cheese in Red Wine (see Index).

3 ounces (90 g) fresh thyme leaves
1 quart (1 l) vodka
1 quart (1 l) water
¾ cup (150 g) sugar

1. Place the thyme and the vodka in a 1-quart (1 l) jar that will close airtight. Shake it slightly; then let it sit in a dark place for 30 days.

2. Strain the mixture, discarding the thyme.

3. Bring the water and sugar to a boil in a large saucepan over medium-high heat. Reduce the heat so the mixture is simmer-

ing, and stir until the sugar is completely dissolved. Remove from the heat and let cool.

4. Blend the thyme essence and the sugar syrup together, and pour into a 2-quart (2 l) jar that will close airtight. Let it sit for 1 month before drinking. This will get gentler and better with age.

About 2 quarts (2 l)

Lemon Verbena Liqueur
Eau-de-Vie de Verveine

→ ··· ←

If you have a lemon verbena bush in your garden, you'll find yourself wanting to eat, sleep, and bathe with it. Its perfume is so heady, so intensely yet softly lemony, that it begs to be steeped for tea, used to flavor a cake or a custard, or macerated in alcohol for a revivifying after-dinner drink.

I've given exact measures for this liqueur, but basically you blend the vodka and sugar, then stuff as many fresh lemon verbena branches into it as will fit—the more the merrier. Cover and wait patiently for at least 2 months and up to 6 before you break the seal. Strain the liqueur and sip slowly—you'll find the wait will have been worthwhile.

⅔ cup (135 g) sugar
1 quart (1 l) vodka
8 good-size branches (each about 16 inches; 40 cm) fresh lemon verbena, cut in half, plus 1 fresh branch, for bottling

1. Place the sugar and vodka in a large canning jar or bottle that can be sealed. Shake, then let sit until most of the sugar has almost entirely dissolved, which may take a couple of hours. Push in the verbena branches, without being concerned if several leaves stick above the alcohol—they will still lend their flavor.

2. Close the jar or cork the bottle. Place in a dark place, such as a closet. Shake daily until the sugar has completely dissolved, then let rest for 2 to 6 months before opening.

3. Strain the liqueur into a sterilized bottle. Push the fresh whole verbena branch into the bottle and seal the bottle with a cork. The liqueur will keep indefinitely.

1 quart (1 l)

The Vinegar Pot
Le Vinaigrier

I learned the secret of making vinegar at the Dubois farm, in the Dordogne. The first salad I ate there drew me to it. Sharp fresh dandelion leaves topped with succulent preserved goose gizzards, it was nutty with the farm's walnut oil, perfectly balanced with rich, lightly acidic vinegar.

Like nearly everything on the farm, the vinegar was homemade. When I asked to see where, Dany Dubois led me to her cellar. There on a shelf sat an innocuous brown pot with an ill-fitting lid and a crooked spigot. Dany removed the lid, dipped in her hand, and pulled out a strange-looking ruby red, gelatinous mass—what she called the *mère du vinaigre,* or mother of vinegar.

It was this amoeba-like mass, according to Dany, that made the vinegar. All she did was pour in wine and wait.

The *mère,* I later discovered, is a film of bacteria that floats on the surface of the wine and works with oxygen to transform alcohol into acetic acid, or vinegar. Any wine, red or white, pasteurized or unpasteurized, can be made into vinegar, though it must be at least eight percent (and preferably no more than eleven percent) alcohol to give the right degree of acidity.

Dany gave me some *mère,* and I've made vinegar ever since. I love having the *vinaigrier,* or vinegar pot, at hand so I can pour the remains of bottles and even glasses into it at will. I have a ready supply of deep, richly flavored vinegar to use wherever quality vinegar is called for. It's simple and satisfying to make (see opposite), makes use of what otherwise might be wasted, and is necessary because I've become addicted to its flavor.

Red Wine Vinegar
Vinaigre de Vin Rouge

>···<

Make your own vinegar? Why not? In every French farm kitchen there's a crock of rich, deep-flavored vinegar working away somewhere, which the cook dips into for use in salad dressings, to deglaze a pan after browning chicken, for marinades. It's indispensable, and once you've made your own, you'll see how simply delicious it can be.

Wine turns to vinegar with the help of a *mère de vinaigre,* or mother of vinegar (see "Making Your Own Vinegar," page 429). Simply put, the *mère* is a blanket of bacteria that transforms wine into vinegar. The *mère* needs oxygen to live, so when you add wine to your pot, add it gently, for you don't want to submerge the *mère*.

ASTUCES . . . .

• *Use wine that is low in alcohol, no higher than eleven percent. That implies an imported red wine, and I recommend a country red from the Loire. Once your vinegar is working, go ahead and add any kind of wine you like.*

• *Don't use any metal when making vinegar, as it can give the vinegar an unpleasant metallic taste. Use either glass or crockery.*

• *Changes in temperature are good for vinegar making. Some people have their vinegar works outside.*

. . . .

1½ cups (375 ml) unpasteurized
   red wine vinegar
4½ cups (1⅛ l) red wine

1. Place the vinegar and the wine in a crock or jar, such as a large canning jar. It should hold at least 1 gallon (4 l), with enough extra space to allow for plenty of air circulation. Cover the opening with a cotton tea towel or a piece of muslin, secure it with a rubber band, and place it in a warm spot (68° to 70°F; 20° to 21°C) for 1 to 2 months. Check it occasionally, and sniff it. It will gradually assume a distinct vinegar aroma, and you will notice a slight film, or *voile,* appearing on the top. Don't move the jar, for it might disrupt the film, which is the beginning development of the bacteria that will eventually create a blanket on top of the vinegar, and will turn any wine you add to it into vinegar.

2. When the mixture has a distinct smell of vinegar (after at least 1 month), transfer it to a crock with a spigot, or to a small barrel with a spigot and a bunghole, by pouring as much of the vinegar as possible into the new container, then carefully transferring the *mère* by hand. Draw off one third of the vinegar and bottle it for use. Replace that with an equal amount of wine. From then on, add ends of bottles and glasses of wine to the vinegar crock, making sure you never submerge the *mère* and that you don't add too much all at once, which may also cause the *mère* to expire.

3. After adding wine, wait at least 2 weeks to draw off additional vinegar.

Unlimited

Herb Vinegar
Vinaigre Aux Aromates

→•••←

This recipe comes from Dany Dubois, who makes her own vinegar on the farm at Peyrenègre, in the Dordogne, then reserves some to turn into this fine herb vinegar. It is wonderful in a vinaigrette, or drizzled over grilled meat or poultry. This vinegar keeps indefinitely.

ASTUCE . . . .

• *Store the vinegar in a dark-colored container to protect the herbs from the light.*

. . . .

2 cups (500 ml) best-quality red wine vinegar
6 branches fresh thyme
Two 6-inch-long (15 cm) branches fresh
    rosemary

1. Place the herbs in a container that will hold at least 2 cups (500 ml) of liquid (I use an empty half wine bottle.)

2. Pour in the vinegar, seal the container, and let sit for at least 2 weeks before using. You may replenish the vinegar at least once before replacing the herbs.

2 cups (500 ml)

Making Your Own Vinegar

>•<

I was given a mère de vinaigre, but it is easy enough to make one. You need unpasteurized vinegar, such as certain top-quality imported brands, particularly aged vinegar from France, Italy, or Greece, or vinegar from certain U.S. producers, particularly in California. Regular supermarket vinegar won't do.

• *Before you purchase it, check the vinegar bottle to see if there is a sediment at the bottom. If there is, chances are good that it will produce a mère.*

• *After your vinegar mixture has rested for 2 weeks, peek into the pot to see if you see a voile, a whitish-gray veil on the surface, which will become the thicker mère de vinaigre and to smell the liquid for acidity. If there's a tangy aroma and the voile is there, you're on the way. If not, leave the mixture for another week. It is rare that the process doesn't work, but if after a month you detect nothing but flat wine, start with another batch.*

• *Over time—6 months or a year—the mère can expand to a surprising volume. It grows in layers, which can practically fill the pot. When it gets too cumbersome, peel off and discard (or give away) about two thirds of the layers, and return the rest to the pot. According to Charles Divies, microbiologist at the University of Bordeaux in Dijon, the highest-quality mère is the voile that rests on the surface. The lower-quality mère sinks to the bottom of the pot.*

Both supply essential bacteria, however, so don't be tempted to throw out the mère that falls to the bottom. Keep some of it, and some of what floats on top.

• *A potential, though rare, inconvenience is finding tiny vinegar eels in the pot. They are the unwelcome gift of flies, which are attracted to vinegar and can contaminate it with whatever they carry. Keep them at bay by covering the openings with tightly woven cheesecloth or a loosely woven cotton tea towel.*

• *If you do find vinegar eels, don't panic. Strain all of the vinegar through a fine-mesh sieve, gently rinse the mère, and thoroughly scrub the pot with boiling water. Replace the vinegar and the mère and proceed. Vinegar eels are harmless and will not affect the quality of the vinegar.*

• *The flavor and quality of vinegar, which is directly affected by the flavor and quality of the wine you make it with, improves with aging, particularly if it is in an oak barrel. Even in a bottle, vinegar will mellow slightly with age. If it becomes cloudy, filter it several times through fine-mesh cheesecloth.*

• *Pasteurization will stabilize the vinegar: Heat it to 150°F (66°C) and seal it in hot sterilized bottles or jars. It will keep indefinitely.*

• *Don't use your homemade vinegar for pickling foods, for its degree of acidity may not be sufficient to preserve them over a period of time.*

TOUS CE QUI EST SUCRE

Everything Sweet

On the farm, cakes and tarts are as common as potage and *poulet*, for no self-respecting farm meal would be complete without its sweet finale. And not one farm dessert is ordinary. They're all simply luscious—so fresh and full of flavor, you wonder how it's done.

It's simple, really. Fresh seasonal fruits play a big part in these desserts, and they're usually used without the addition of anything but sugar, so you taste their essence.

Light and tender cakes are a French specialty. I believe French cooks are born with a certain gene that makes them all good bakers. No matter how often I heard a French farm cook say her desserts were nothing special and she didn't know how to bake, I always found it to be false modesty. "False" may not be the right word—perhaps when you're born with a gift, you overlook it.

But it would be impossible to overlook the goodness of its results, for French farm desserts are divine.

All you need to know to re-create them is within the pages of this chapter. Just remember one simple thing: Use fresh, fresh ingredients, and you'll not be disappointed.

Alsatian Apple Tart
Tarte aux Pommes Alsacienne

>···<

This is a traditional Alsatian apple tart like the one I tasted at the home of Malou Luck, who lives in Dauendorf, just east of Strasbourg. Rich and creamy, it is her specialty and she serves it proudly. It is simple to make—just remember to prepare the pastry at least an hour in advance so it has a chance to relax before being rolled out.

FOR THE PASTRY

1 cup plus 6 tablespoons (190 g)
unbleached all-purpose flour

¼ teaspoon sea salt

1 tablespoon sugar

8 tablespoons (1 stick; 125 g) unsalted butter,
cut into pieces, at room temperature

⅓ cup (80 ml) ice water

FOR THE TART

2 large eggs

1 cup (250 ml) Crème Fraîche (page 520),
or sour cream

½ cup (100 g) Vanilla Sugar (page 521)

2 sweet, firm medium apples, such as
Golden Delicious, Jonagold, or
Cortland, peeled, cored, and cut into
paper-thin slices

¼ teaspoon ground cinnamon

⅓ cup (40 g) walnuts, grated or finely
chopped

1. Prepare the pastry: Combine the flour, salt, and sugar in a food processor and process once or twice to mix. Add the butter and process until the mixture resembles coarse meal. Then slowly pour in the water, pulsing until the pastry just holds together but does not form a ball, about nine times. Turn the pastry out onto a lightly floured work surface, gather it together, and pat it into a flat round about 6 inches (15 cm) across. Cover and let sit unrefrigerated, 1 hour.

2. Roll out the pastry on a lightly floured work surface to form an 11½-inch (29 cm) round to fit a 10½-inch (26½ cm) tart pan with removable bottom. Transfer the pastry to the pan, fitting it against the sides and bottom. Refrigerate the pastry for 1 hour.

3. Preheat the oven to 400°F (205°C).

4. Prick the pastry shell all over with the tines of a fork, and line it with aluminum foil. Fill the foil with pie weights or dried beans, and bake in the center of the oven until the edges of the pastry begin to turn golden, 10 to 15 minutes. Remove the foil and the weights, and continue baking until

the pastry is cooked through and golden, another 10 to 15 minutes. Remove the pastry shell from the oven and let cool slightly. Leave the oven on.

5. Prepare the tart: In a medium-size bowl, whisk together the eggs, crème fraîche, and vanilla sugar until thoroughly combined and frothy.

6. Line the cooled pastry shell with the apples. It is not necessary to do so in any pattern, though you can if you like. Pour the crème fraîche mixture over the apples and sprinkle it evenly with the cinnamon, then with the walnuts. Place the tart pan on a baking sheet and bake in the center of the oven until the filling is set and the nuts and the pastry are golden, about 25 minutes.

7. Remove the tart from the oven, and remove the sides of the pan. Place the tart on a wire rack and let it cool. Serve it just barely warm or at room temperature.

One 10½-inch (26½ cm) tart; 6 to 8 servings

Upside-Down Caramelized Apple Tart
Tarte Tatin

>···<

Could this be the best loved tart in France? I think so. Throughout France *tarte Tatin* is greeted with joy and appreciation, eaten with gusto, much discussed afterward. It takes guts for an American to make *tarte Tatin* for the French, who consider it *their* dessert. But since I live on rue Tatin, and because I love this tart, I felt a responsibility to produce the best possible *tarte Tatin*. I've served this to many a *tarte Tatin* chauvinist, and I can humbly say it has passed the test.

Some rules have sprung up around the making and serving of this popular dessert. Rule 1: Leave the apples in halves and fit as many into the pan as possible. Rule 2: The caramel must be good, rich, and dark, which will only happen through long, slow cooking. Rule 3: The tart must be served warm, otherwise it is considered inedible.

The preferred apple for *tarte Tatin* is Boscop, which is similar to a Cox's Orange Pippin (also excellent in *tarte Tatin*), only larger. The Boscop has the necessary tartness and a wonderful, floral flavor.

I've experimented with many different kinds of apples to make *tarte Tatin*, and have always had the best results with Boscops, but only those I purchased from one particular farmer. If I got them at the supermarket, or at a local *épicerie*, the apples turned to purée before the sugar turned to caramel.

I was discussing this baffling situation with a friend, and she said, "If the Boscops have been refrigerated, they turn to purée when they're cooked. If they haven't, they'll keep their shape." Sure enough, when I investigated my sources, I found that the stores refrigerated their apples, while the farmer didn't. She kept hers cold in the barn.

I am now rigid about storing my apples when they're destined for *tarte Tatin*. I buy them from the farmer, and they go right to the cellar, or to the coldest spot in the house, and there they stay until I cook them.

Serve this accompanied by crème fraîche.

ASTUCES . . . .

• *You can make an excellent* **tarte Tatin** *with Fujis, Criterions, Winesaps, or Northern Spies. Jonagolds or Golden Delicious will work, too, though with these the dessert will lack a fine edge of acidity, so I recommend sprinkling the apples with a couple of teaspoons of lemon juice right before you place the pastry over them.*

• *If you make the tart in advance (no longer than a few hours, or it won't taste good and fresh), gently reheat it before serving. Don't serve it piping hot because the caramel can inflict a bad burn.*

. . . .

One 10½-inch (26½ cm) tart shell, made
  using Homemaker's Pastry (page 509)
  and prebaked
1½ cups (300 g) Vanilla Sugar (page 521)
10 tablespoons (1¼ sticks; 150 g) unsalted
  butter, cut into thin slices
4½ pounds (2¼ kg) apples (see Astuce),
  peeled, halved, and cored

1. Line a baking sheet with parchment paper or lightly flour it.

2. Roll out the pastry on a lightly floured work surface to form an 11½-inch (29 cm) round. Transfer the pastry to the prepared baking sheet and refrigerate for at least 1 hour.

3. Spread the sugar evenly over the bottom of a very heavy 10- to 10½-inch (25 to 26½ cm) ovenproof skillet; a simple cast-iron skillet is perfect. Place the butter slices evenly over the sugar, then arrange the apple halves on top of the butter. Begin at the outside edge and stand the halves on their sides, facing in one direction with stem ends toward the center. Pack the apples as close together as possible, gently pushing them together so they are held standing by pressure. Make a second circle of apple halves inside the first, packing them in on their edges as well. Place one apple half right in the center of the second circle to fill in the small space that remains. The idea is to get as many apples into the pan as possible, while keeping them nicely arranged.

4. Place the skillet over medium-low heat and cook the apples in the butter and sugar, uncovered, until the sugar turns golden brown; this will take at least 1 hour. Watch the apples closely to be sure they don't stick; you may want to adjust the heat now and then, to slow down or speed up the cooking. As the sugar and butter melt and the apples give up some of their juices, baste the apples occasionally with a turkey baster. Gradually, the sugar will caramelize the apples nearly all the way through, though they will remain uncooked on top.

5. Preheat the oven to 425°F (220°C).

6. When the cooking juices are deep golden and the apples are nearly cooked through, remove the pastry from the refrigerator and quickly and carefully place it over the apples, gently pushing it down around them, simultaneously easing it toward the center so that if it shrinks on the sides there will still be enough of it to cover the apples.

Using a sharp knife, trim off and discard any extra pastry.

7. Place the skillet on a baking sheet. Bake in the center of the oven until the pastry is golden, 25 to 30 minutes. Don't be concerned if the juices bubble over; the tart will be more or less juicy, depending on the variety of apple you've used.

8. Remove the skillet from the oven. Immediately invert a serving platter with a slight lip over the skillet. Quickly but carefully invert the two so the crust is on the bottom, the apples are on top, and the juices don't run off onto the floor. Remove the skillet. Should any apples stick to it, gently remove them and reinsert them into their rightful place in the tart.

9. Serve generous slices as soon as the tart has cooled slightly, but is still very warm through.

One 10-inch (25 cm) tart; 6 to 8 servings

Apple Tart with Apricot Preserves
Tarte aux Pommes à la Confiture d'Abricots

This is another gem from Jacqueline Priaulet, the olive farmer in Maussane-les-Alpilles. She also raises sweet, succulent apricots and makes her own chunky jam. One of her standard desserts is this tart, which is so delicious that, though the recipe officially feeds six to eight, I've known a group of four to consume the entire thing.

You'll see why. The combination of sweet/tart jam, tartish apples, and cream is sublime, and it has a lightness to it, too. I love to serve this after a meal, but it's also wonderful for an afternon snack, or *goûter*, in the French manner.

1 large egg
¼ cup (50 g) sugar
⅓ cup (80 ml) Crème Fraîche
    (page 520), or heavy (or whipping)
    cream
1 teaspoon vanilla extract
⅓ cup (80 ml) apricot jam, homemade
    if desired (page 395)
One 10½-inch (26½ cm) tart shell,
    made using Homemaker's Pastry
    (page 509) and prebaked
2 medium-sweet to sweet-tart apples,
    such as Jonagold, Golden
    Delicious, Cortland, or
    Gravenstein, cored, peeled,
    and cut into ⅛-inch-thick
    (¼ cm) slices

1. Preheat the oven to 375°F (190°C).

2. In a small bowl, whisk together the egg, sugar, crème fraîche, and vanilla.

3. If there are large pieces of apricot in the jam, coarsely chop them. Spread the jam evenly over the bottom of the prebaked pastry shell. Then top the jam with the apple slices, attractively arranged in concentric circles, overlapping the slices. Pour the cream mixture over the apples. (There is not a lot of the cream mixture—just enough to moisten the tart—so don't be concerned if it seems skimpy.) Place the tart pan on a baking sheet and bake in the center of the oven until the apples are golden and the cream is firm, 35 to 40 minutes.

4. Remove the tart from the oven, and remove the sides of the pan. Place the tart on a wire rack and let it cool to room temperature before serving.

One 10½ inch (26½ cm) tart; 6 to 8 servings

Normandy Apple Tart
Tarte Normande aux Pommes

→•••←

Everywhere you go in Normandy, apple trees decorate the landscape. I say decorate, because there is something delicate, lovely, and poetic about a Norman apple tree. Part of it has to do with tradition—apple trees have grown in Normandy for centuries, and cultivation methods have been refined for as long. So they are placed in the best possible spot, usually on a slope so their roots can reach down, their branches take advantage of the temperate, soft air that sweeps through.

The fruit these trees give will never win a beauty contest. Among the best is the tart/sweet Boscop, a homely apple covered in greenish red skin spotted with rust. No one cares what it looks like, however, for it is so flavorful in the hand, or baked in a tart, that looks count for nothing.

I tasted this tart, which is really more of a *clafoutis*, or custardy pie, at La Rivière, an ancient and lovely fortified farm right near the landing beaches of Normandy. There, Paulette Marie turns out very traditional and simply delicious Norman food.

I must admit that while I love apples, I've tasted my share of Normandy apple desserts that left me wishing for a good bar of chocolate. But this was different. It came to the table golden and crisp, almost caramelized, and it was moist and full of delicious, flavorful apples perfumed with just the right amount of vanilla. I loved it.

It's a simple recipe, but it takes some time and attention. It is, in fact, the kind of recipe that reminds me how a little care and

time yield results that are astonishing instead of just good. The sugar, butter, eggs, and flour must be beaten long enough to make them light and airy, the apples must be chosen carefully for their flavor, and a butter and egg mixture must be spread over the tart halfway through the cooking. Find the best possible apples and make it—what results will become a family favorite.

FOR THE TART
6 tablespoons Vanilla Sugar (page 521)
2 tablespoons unsalted butter, at room
temperature
2 large eggs
¾ cup (100 g) unbleached all-purpose flour
¾ cup (185 ml) milk
1 teaspoon baking power
2 pounds (1 kg) tart cooking apples, such
as Winesap, peeled, cored, and cut into
½-inch (1¼ cm) slices

FOR THE TOPPING
⅓ cup (65 g) Vanilla Sugar (page 521)
4 tablespoons (½ stick; 60 g) unsalted
butter, at room temperature
1 large egg

1. Preheat the oven to 400°F (205°C). Thoroughly butter and flour a 12½ x 7½-inch (32 x 19 cm) baking pan or a 2-quart (2 l) round baking dish about 4 inches (10 cm) deep.

2. Prepare the tart: In a large bowl, whisk together the vanilla sugar and the butter until the mixture is pale yellow and fluffy, 3 to 5 minutes. Add the eggs and whisk until they are thoroughly incorporated. Then

whisk in the flour. Continue whisking vigorously until the mixture is smooth and pale, about 5 minutes. Slowly whisk in the milk. Then sift in the baking powder and whisk to incorporate it. Fold in the apples, and pour the mixture into the prepared baking pan. Bake in the center of the oven until it begins to puff and look golden, 30 minutes.

3. While the tart is baking, prepare the topping: Whisk together the vanilla sugar and the butter until light and fluffy. Then whisk in the egg to combine.

4. Remove the tart from the oven (leave the oven on and close the oven door to maintain the temperature), and quickly spread the topping evenly over it. Return it to the oven and cook until the topping is a deep golden color, another 25 to 30 minutes.

5. Remove the tart from the oven and let it cool for 5 minutes before serving. Or let it cool to room temperature and then serve right from the pan.

6 to 8 servings

Christmas Eve Tart
Tarte de la Veille

→ • • • ←

This tart is reserved for Christmas Eve *(la veille de Noël)* in Provence, a special treat on a day when hard work and privation are forgotten. There is nothing luxurious about it except its flavor.

Use the most flavorful pears you can, and add sugar to your taste. I find that just a touch of brown sugar magnifies the floral flavor of the pears.

FOR THE BREAD DOUGH
1 teaspoon active dry yeast
1¼ to 1½ cups (175 to 200 g) unbleached all-purpose flour
½ cup (125 ml) lukewarm water
¼ teaspoon fine sea salt

FOR THE FILLING
1½ pounds (750 g) firm, ripe pears, such as Bartlett, peeled, cored, and diced
2 tablespoons dark brown sugar
¼ cup (60 ml) water
¼ teaspoon anise seeds

FOR THE EGG WASH
1 large egg
1 teaspoon water

Les Treize Desserts

>·<

The crowning moment of Christmas eve dinner (le gros souper) is dessert, which isn't touched until after midnight mass. Called **les treize desserts**, it includes thirteen different foods, each with a specific symbolism.

Though no one really seems to agree on why thirteen is the magic number—and indeed, in certain areas it can swell to fifteen or more—it is generally thought to relate to Christ and his twelve apostles.

Whatever the number, the idea is simple and sweet. *Les treize desserts* consist mostly of fresh and dried fruits, including grapes that are carefully harvested, still attached to the branch, in late November and hung in a cool spot to keep.

Almonds, figs, raisins, and walnuts, called **mendiants**, represent the colors of monks' robes. Nougat (a confection made of almonds and honey), mandarin oranges, apples and pears, in some areas simple fruit tarts, in others calissons, or almond candies, sweet breads made with olive oil and flavored with anise and orange-flower water (which according to tradition must be broken, not cut, to ensure successful harvests), dried golden prunes, and apple doughnuts can all figure in the selection.

1. Prepare the dough: Combine the yeast, ½ cup (70 g) of the flour, and the lukewarm water in a medium-size mixing bowl. Stir to dissolve, and let sit until the yeast bubbles, about 5 minutes. Add the remaining flour, ¼ cup (35 g) at a time and the salt, and continue mixing until the dough is quite stiff. Dust a work surface with flour, turn the dough out onto the surface, and knead the dough until it is firm and satiny but not dry, about 5 minutes, adding the extra flour if necessary. Place the dough in a bowl, cover with a damp tea towel, and let rise in a warm spot (68° to 70°F; 20° to 21°C) until doubled in bulk, about 1 hour.

2. Meanwhile, make the filling: Place the pears in a medium-size saucepan over medium-high heat, and add the brown sugar and the water. Cover, bring to a boil, and reduce the heat to medium. Cook, covered, until the pears are completely soft through, about 30 minutes. Purée in a food processor. Return the purée to the pan, stirring occasionally,

and cook, uncovered, over medium heat until any liquid has evaporated and the purée has thickened slightly, which can take 15 to 20 minutes, depending on the quality of the pears. It should have the consistency of smooth applesauce. Add the anise seeds, stir, and let cool.

3. Preheat the oven to 400°F (205°C). Stir together the egg and water for the egg wash.

4. Punch down the dough. Roll out two thirds of the dough on a lightly floured work surface to form an 11½ inch (29 cm) round to fit a 10½-inch (26½ cm) tart pan with removable bottom. Transfer the dough to the pan, fitting it against the bottom and sides. Some excess dough should hang slightly over the edges. Roll out the remaining dough to a 10½ x 4-inch (26½ x 10 cm) rectangle and cut it into sixteen ¼-inch-wide (½ cm) strips.

5. Spread the pear purée in the shell. Paint one side of the dough strips with the egg wash, and lay 8 of them, painted side up, diagonally across the purée, pressing the ends into the edges of the dough. (The strips are a bit difficult to work with because they stretch, so work quickly, easing them back to their original length as you set them onto the purée.) Repeat with the remaining strips, painting them, then laying them atop the first batch of strips so they create a crisscross pattern.

6. Roll the excess dough over the ends of the strips as neatly as possible, to make a sort of ragged rim, and paint it with egg wash. (Don't be too concerned about the tidiness of the tart before it goes into the oven. Tidiness is not the result you are looking for.

And What About the Partridges?

→ • ←

*O*ne day, a priest who wanted to be very modern had the stone statues in his church replaced with statues sculpted from pear wood. His parishioners were unhappy with the choice, and when he asked why, one responded: "How do you expect me to pray in front of these? I knew them when they were pear trees."

You will see that it bakes to a rustic, golden perfection.) Place the tart pan on a baking sheet and bake in the center of the oven until the dough is slightly puffed and golden, 25 to 30 minutes.

7. Remove the tart from the oven and remove the sides of the pan from the tart. Let it cool on a wire rack, to either lukewarm or room temperature before serving. (Don't eat it straight from the oven, as the purée is hot enough to seriously burn.) This tart can be made up to 2 hours in advance.

One 10½-inch (26½ cm) tart; 6 to 8 servings

Christmas Eve in Provence
La Veille de Noël et le Gros Souper

═

When Germaine Giniès Grosjean talks of *la veille de Noël,* or Christmas Eve, she recalls the aroma of leeks sizzling on the woodstove, the ritual of soaking salt cod, the fruit tarts, golden and crisp from the bread oven on her family's farm.

In Provence when Mme. Grosjean was a child, more than eighty years ago, *la veille de Noël* was the most important day of the year and its focus, *le gros souper,* the most important meal. For her family and for all Provençal farming or fishing families, it honored the past year's arduous labor and augured hope for the next.

Though *la veille de Noël* revolves around the Nativity, it is also a fête of the soil and the sea, the seasons and the crops— a blend of religion and mysticism. Each detail that makes up *le gros souper* has a significance that reaches beyond the food that is being eaten.

Provence stretches roughly from Valence south to Marseilles, and within its boundaries are many smaller areas called *départements.* Each *département* has its own celebration, with its distinct dishes, methods of preparation, and symbolism. Around Marseilles, seafood figures prominently, and the rituals have much to do with fishing. Inland, in the Toulourenc valley of the Drôme, where Mme. Grosjean lives, all relates to farming.

No matter what the location, the *veille de Noël* is always a *jour maigre,* or fast day, with no meat eaten all day.

In farming communities, preparations begin well before Christmas. On December fourth, the feast of Saint Barbara, three shallow dishes are filled with lentils or wheat berries, moistened, and placed in a warm spot to grow thickets of lush green "grass" by Christmas.

Closer to the big day, the family takes down a box from the attic or armoire and opens it to reveal the figures of the crêche. Called *santons* and made of clay, they represent a mix of holy figures and familiar personages, including the mayor, the fish merchant, the shepherd, the cobbler.

(continued)

Children are sent out into the hills to gather wild thyme and savory, mosses, pieces of bark, pebbles, and small branches, all used in the crèche to re-create the local landscape.

To prepare the dining room, three white cloths are placed on the table to signify the Holy Trinity. A trio of candles is set on the table or the mantel, along with the three dishes of sprouted seeds. Mandarin oranges are scooped out to make lanterns, the central core soaked in paraffin to make a wick. Their spicy aroma is an indelible part of *la veille de Noël*.

Nicole Vallortigara, who lives near Mme. Grosjean, remembers the extra place set at the table: "It's for the lonely or poor person who might stop by," she said. "Of course no one ever stopped by, but we always hoped!"

ON THE DAY

Aromas from *le gros souper* waft through the house all day. In the Drôme, the air is aromatic as thyme, bay, sage, and laurel are simmered in water to make a broth for *soupe aux crousets*, which calls for pasta, a grating of dried goat cheese, and olive oil.

When night falls, the family members arrive for *le gros souper*. Before anyone can sit down, however, a solemn ritual is observed. The eldest and the youngest males in the family together bring a log—always from a fruit tree—to the fireplace and set it on the fire. The eldest sprinkles it with a glass of sweet wine and recites a blessing for the coming year. That done, appetites roused, everyone takes his or her place.

Eating is accompanied by a great deal of comment and critique, and the noise level mounts as the meal progresses. The salad course—served at the end of the meal, contrary to the usual Provençal treatment of salad as an opener—signals a winding down. Appetites sated, it is story time.

Church bells interrupt the stories to signal midnight mass, and everyone, from sleepy toddlers to the very oldest, bundles up to go. Mass over, they return home for the *treize desserts* served with sweet walnut wine. Before the children go to bed, the baby Jesus is placed in the manger. Afterward, the slippers are filled. Mme. Grosjean remembers surreptitiously watching her mother collect the children's slippers late at night to fill with goodies for the morning. "The adults always told us it was Jesus who filled them," she says wickedly, "but I knew better!"

When the holidays are over, farmers carefully divide those sprouted seeds into four separate bunches and plant one at each corner of a newly tilled field. Fishermen take a handful of ashes from the Christmas Eve log to sprinkle over the water. Final gestures to nature, final nods to the mystical, they ensure a good harvest for the coming year.

Prune Cream Tart
Tarte à la Crème de Pruneaux

>···<

I have the best memories of this tart. Our friend Dany Dubois, who has a farm in the heart of the Dordogne where she raises geese for foie gras, made it all the time, and we never tired of it. It was particularly called into play when unexpected guests came, or when the wind was howling outside and everyone needed warmth and cheering. In short, it was a favorite at the farm, and it has become a favorite at our table, too.

This prune tart is quick and simple to make, since the filling is put together in under 10 minutes and doesn't require any further baking after it's spread in the tart shell. You can cut down the time on the pastry, too, if you omit the folding procedure in step 3 of the pastry recipe. Be sure to buy good-quality prunes, for the flavor of the tart is dependent on them.

Dany flavors her prune purée with rum. I prefer brandy, but of course you may use what you like. You'll find the results luscious and full of deep flavor.

8 ounces (250 g) good-quality pitted prunes
Boiling water
2 tablespoons water
2 tablespoons brandy or rum
2 tablespoons sugar
One 10½-inch (26½ cm) tart shell, made using Homemaker's Pastry (page 509) and prebaked
2 tablespoons Crème Fraîche (page 520), or heavy (or whipping) cream

1. Cover the prunes with boiling water and let stand 5 minutes. Drain well. In a food processor, purée the prunes with the 2 tablespoons each water, brandy, and sugar.

2. Spread the prune mixture in the prebaked pastry shell and drizzle the crème fraîche in a spiral pattern over the tart. Remove the sides of the pan from the tart and serve at room temperature.

One 10½-inch (26½ cm) tart; 6 to 8 servings

Tous ce qui est Sucré • Everything Sweet

Mme. Roulleau's Rhubarb Tart

Tarte à la Rhubarbe de Mme. Roulleau

→•••←

This tart has a historic origin, at least for me. I first tasted it on Bastille Day 1994, in Michel Devisme's back garden in Louviers. It was a gorgeous day, thankfully, for M. Devisme had invited all of his children and their families, as well as assorted cousins, to the celebration.

I've known the Devismes for years, but hadn't seen them all together in a decade, and hadn't met many of the cousins. It was a happy, sunny reunion.

We had all brought dishes to the party, and two long tables were laden with pork pâté and sausages, cheeses, breads, and salmon terrine. What drew me to the dessert table was the most beautiful tart I'd ever seen. Huge, round, and golden, it was both delicate and rustic. I knew without asking who had made it: Mme. Roulleau.

Mme. Roulleau has been a part of my life for as long as I've known the Devismes. She was their surrogate mother, as well as the cook and housekeeper, when they were growing up, there to help out and listen to confidences. A tiny woman whose mouth turns up in a perpetual smile, she has always accepted me as one of the family. I know, both from tasting and from the multitude of stories I've heard from my friend Edith Devisme, that she is a cook without peer.

Mme. Roulleau was happy to give me the recipe, and I wasted no time making it.

I like to think it's as good as hers—it has passed the test of the Devisme sisters, Edith and Hélène, who found it luscious.

Try this with other fruits as well, such as blueberries, apricots, plums, even apples.

¼ cup (53 g) sliced almonds
½ cup (100 g) Vanilla Sugar (page 521)
3 large eggs
3 tablespoons Crème Fraîche (page 520),
    and heavy (or whipping) cream
3 tablespoons cornstarch
1 pound (500 g) rhubarb, trimmed,
    peeled, and cut into ¼-inch (½ cm) dice
One 10½-inch (26½ cm) tart shell, made
    using Homemaker's Pastry (page 509)
    and prebaked

1. Preheat the oven to 425°F (220°C).

2. Place the almonds and 1 tablespoon of the vanilla sugar in a food processor, and process until the almonds are finely ground.

3. In a medium-size bowl, whisk together the eggs and the remaining vanilla sugar

until the mixture is pale yellow. Whisk in the crème fraîche. Sift in the cornstarch and whisk it. Then, finally, whisk in half the ground almonds.

4. Arrange the rhubarb in an even layer in the prebaked pastry shell. Pour the egg mixture over the rhubarb, shaking the tart pan so the cream is evenly distributed over the fruit. Sprinkle the remaining ground almonds over the tart, place it on a

baking sheet, and bake in the center of the oven until it is golden and puffed, about 30 minutes.

5. Remove the tart from the oven, and remove the sides of the pan. Place the tart on a wire rack and let it cool for 10 minutes before serving.

One 10½-inch (26½ cm) tart; 6 to 8 servings

Rhubarb and Red Currant Jelly Tart
Tarte à la Rhubarbe et à la Gelée de Groseilles

The idea for this tart comes from Colette Février, who runs an astonishing little restaurant in the Doubs, a mountainous region that abuts the Jura. This woman, who can't be younger than seventy, cooks meals on a lumbering wood stove tucked into what was once a glorious fireplace with a mantel of carved stone. Mme. Février's cuisine is ultra-simple, and she tries to tailor her food to her guests. When I called and told her what I was doing for this book, she said, "I know what I'll make you—a mushroom toast." She also made a perfectly simple, deliciously fresh carrot potage, local ham and fried potatoes, salad, and a wonderful rhubarb and red currant compote.

"I sweeten the rhubarb with my red currant jelly, and we love the combination," she said, referring to herself and her daughters, all of whom live nearby. "I'm so glad you like it."

I took her compote idea and turned it into a tart. You'll find it leaps from the plate with flavor. I use a sweet pastry to offset the tartness of the rhubarb, and not too much sugar—you want the flavor of the rhubarb and the jelly to come through.

Try to find green rhubarb, a slightly different and much more flavorful variety than the red. Like Mme. Février, I peel rhubarb with an ordinary vegetable peeler, so it is tender and succulent. It means you need a bit more, but who ever suffered, in summer, from a lack of rhubarb?

¼ cup (60 ml) red currant jelly, homemade if desired (page 399) warmed

One 10½-inch (26½ cm) tart shell, made using Sweet Pastry (page 514) and prebaked

2 pounds (1 kg) rhubarb, trimmed, peeled, and cut into very thin crosswise slices

½ cup (100 g) Vanilla Sugar (page 521)

1. Preheat the oven to 400°F (205°C).

2. Spread the warmed jelly over the bottom of the pastry shell. Arrange the rhubarb in the shell in as even a layer as possible, gently pressing on it. (Don't press too hard or the pastry will crack.) Sprinkle the vanilla sugar over the rhubarb. Place the pan on a baking sheet and bake in the center of the oven until the rhubarb is tender and juicy, about 30 minutes. Remove the tart from the oven, remove the sides of the pan, and serve immediately.

One 10½-inch (26½ cm) tart; 6 to 8 servings

Rhubarb

A Zoroastrian text says that the first man and woman appeared on earth as two rhubarb plants. When they matured, they fell in love and multiplied.

The story is thought to signify the medicinal importance ascribed to rhubarb many years ago. Rhubarb appeared in the first European garden in the 17th century, apparently a gift of the Crusaders. It wasn't until two hundred years later, however, that the British moved it from the pharmacy to the table. They used it in desserts and went to work improving it, making it less acidic.

By the late 1800s, rhubarb finally came to France, and the French quickly made up for lost time, adopting it in their gardens, using it in tarts, jams, cakes, and sauces for everything from meat to fish.

One finds two varieties at the market from spring through fall: the type with thin green stalks, and the one with fat red stalks. Although the red is sweeter, the green is sought after because it's more flavorful, and aficionados mix the two.

The next time you have occasion to pick a fresh stalk of rhubarb, cut off the leaf (which is poisonous), dip the end of the stalk into sugar, and take a bite. Your mouth will be flooded with sensations and flavor! When you've had enough, turn to the rhubarb recipes here.

Biodynamic Farming

Biodynamic farmers follow principles outlined in 1924 by Rudolf Steiner, a German scientist and reputed clairvoyant. The term "biodynamic" comes from the Greek *bios*, which means "life," and *dynamis*, which means "energy." Steiner believed in a "farm organism," the farm as an entity in itself. He felt that everything the crops need, in terms of fertilizers and soil nutrients, should be generated on the farm through natural methods.

Steiner developed several preparations that he felt would regenerate nutrients, minerals, enzymes, and natural growth hormones in the soil, to create and maintain its fertility and health.

These preparations remain highly suspect to those who practice "conventional" farming based on synthetic soil additives. Indeed, they do at first sound bizarre. One calls for stuffing cow manure into a cow's horn, burying it on September 24, and digging it up six months later. The manure transforms into a remarkably sweet-smelling soil, tiny portions of which are hand blended into water, following a very specific method. The "tea" which results is sprayed on fields to help regenerate them.

There are many such preparations in biodynamic farming, each of them assigned a number, such as 500 or 501. As explained to me, they were assigned numbers to appear more scientific, and to be more acceptable to skeptics.

I have visited with biodynamic farmers in the U.S. and in France, and I've been struck by their assurance, peacefulness, and confidence. They don't question their farming methods. If something goes wrong, they know exactly why, and it is usually that they've not been attentive enough. And if something goes right, they're not surprised.

A BIODYNAMIC MARAICHER

Jean-Luc Daneyrolles calls himself a gardener, and he calls his carefully tended plots of land near Apt, in the Lubéron, a garden. He is correct on one count: He is a market gardener, or *maraîcher*, but what he tends is really a small farm, its rough, rocky land separated into tidy fields by snaking stone walls built during Roman times.

(continued)

M. Daneyrolles came to gardening a bit by accident. Growing up near his grandmother, he spent hours in her vegetable garden. At twenty-two, finished with school and out of work, his one desire was to live in a garden. When he found the land he now works, it was poor, suitable only for olive trees and perhaps grapevines, covered with scrubby growth. Ten years later, it is verdant with lush produce, fragrant herbs, and more than twenty varieties of tomatoes.

M. Daneyrolles gives much credit for bringing life from the soil to the way he's learned to control water. "Water is the key," he says. "You have to have it at the right place at the right time."

He also carefully observes the biodynamic farming calendar, which follows the movements of the sun and moon and specifically advises when and how to plant and fertilize.

He buys compost from a nearby goat farm to feed the soil, and is careful about rotating crops. And he's out in his fields all the time, gently working the soil and tending the plants. It's no wonder they grow with such profusion.

M. Daneyrolles calls his gardens *le potager d'un curieux* ("the garden of a curious man") because he's interested in growing uncommon plants. Indeed, his greenhouse offers a who's who of unusual and antique varieties: salad burnet and lovage, copper fennel and anise hyssop, mullein, true lavender, pineapple sage and borage. Half of

another greenhouse is devoted to mesclun (a biting mixture of tiny salad greens), the other half to his collection of tomatoes.

His fields are planted with Jerusalem artichokes, a vegetable called *crosne*, root parsley, and purple potatoes. In another he has flowers, and in yet another a whole salad's worth of greens, from arugula to sorrel.

At one corner of the property is a Roman site, which is protected by the state. Occasionally M. Daneyrolles sits nearby, "to absorb the vibrations of early farmers," he says.

"This land has been cultivated for ten thousand years, that's sure," he says as he surveys his small domain. "When I work on it, I can't help thinking about time, who worked it before me, how beautiful it is because of all the peasants throughout history who have made it that way. When you farm like I do, in a place like this, time is everything. I can't stop thinking about it, and I always learn something from it."

THE FINEST PRUNES

In southwestern France, near the city of Agen, lives Etienne Fuméry, thirty-seven, a spiritual cousin to Jean-Luc Daneyrolles although they don't know each other.

M. Fuméry began farming when he was seventeen years old, following in his father's footsteps. Ten years ago, worried about what he felt were the unhealthy effects of pesticides on a family member, he made a radical shift, to biodynamic farming.

"It was easy for me to change," he says. "I was always the strange one in the family, the artistic one, the one who was vaguely spiritual. Biodynamic farming is very spiritual, and it made so much sense to me."

To farm biodynamically, M. Fuméry believes one must learn to control the elements through emotions. "I can't do it all, of course," he says, laughing. "But if everyone in the world could harness their emotions in a positive way, there's a chance we could harness the elements."

We are standing in the searing sun outside the small stone farmhouse he shares with his wife, Marie, and their six children. His orchards stretched out around us, healthy trees laden with plums that in a few weeks would be fat and purplish blue— unless a freak hailstorm came by to knock them to the ground.

M. Fuméry believes that the biodynamic preparations he puts on the soil make it breathe differently than soil subjected to syn-thetic chemicals. He thinks his soil sends healthy, strong vibrations into the atmosphere, and he doesn't worry much about hail.

"I've seen it," he says. "Storms have come our way and literally bypassed the farm but affected everyone around me. You explain it."

Biodynamic farming is a continual education process. M. Fuméry reads voraciously—mostly spiritual works by farmers and philosophers who have gone before him.

"Biodynamic farming makes you accountable," he says. "You see results. If you let down and don't pay close attention, your crop yield will be affected.

"But the last couple of years I've been one hundred percent attentive and done everything necessary at the right time, and, well, look at the crop. Now my concern is that the trees will be damaged by the weight of all the fruit! It's fascinating."

M. Fuméry harvests the plums and dries them in an electric dryer installed in a hangar in front of the house. Once dried, they are dipped in water, to emerge soft and pliable. The Fuméries package and sell them as *pruneaux d'Agen*, considered the best prunes in France.

Apricot and Red Currant Tart with Almond Cream

Tarte aux Abricots et Groseilles à la Crème d'Amandes

→···←

Apricots and red currants make a stunning pair. Here they are set in a bed of almond cream, which lightly echoes the almond flavor of the apricots. Not only is this delicious, it's a beautiful combination.

If you have a hard time finding red currants, you may use additional apricots and brush the tart lightly with warm diluted red currant jelly instead of a sprinkling of sugar.

You may substitute other fruits for the apricots, of course—think about blackberries, raspberries, plums, even seedless grapes.

A S T U C E . . . .

• *Always place a tart on a baking sheet before sliding it into the oven. It is easier to handle, and should the tart boil over, the drippings will not burn on the bottom of the oven.*

. . . .

FOR THE ALMOND CREAM

⅔ cup (100 g) almonds
¾ cup (150 g) Vanilla Sugar (page 521)
3 tablespoons unsalted butter, at room
    temperature
3 large egg yolks
½ teaspoon vanilla extract

FOR THE TART

One 10½-inch (26½ cm) tart shell, made
    using Homemaker's Pastry (page 509)
    and prebaked
1 to 1½ pounds (500 to 750 g) apricots,
    pitted and cut in half
8 ounces (250 g) red currants, if available
2 teaspoons sugar, or 1 tablespoon
    red currant jelly

1. Preheat the oven to 375°F (190°C).

2. Make the almond cream: Drop the almonds into a saucepan of boiling water for 1 minute; then drain them and slip them out of their skins. Pat them dry. Arrange the almonds on a baking sheet in one layer and place them in the oven just long enough to dry them thoroughly, 5 to 8 minutes. Don't be concerned if they turn a pale golden. They shouldn't, however, turn a deep golden.

3. Place the almonds and 2 tablespoons of the vanilla sugar in a food processor, and

grind until they form a fine powder.

4. In a medium-size bowl, whisk the butter and the remaining vanilla sugar together until blended. Then whisk in the egg yolks, one at a time, until they are thoroughly incorporated and the cream is smooth. Whisk in the vanilla extract and the ground almonds.

5. Make the tart: Spread the almond cream over the bottom of the prebaked pastry shell. Make a ring of apricots, cut side down, around the outer edge of the tart, slightly overlapping the apricot halves. Just inside the outer ring, make a narrow ring of red currants, then another small ring of overlapped apricot halves; place the remaining currants in the center. Sprinkle the tart with the sugar. (If using only apricots, make overlapping concentric rings, then brush with the red currant jelly, which has been diluted with a few drops of water and warmed.)

6. Place the tart on a baking sheet and bake it in the center of the oven until the pastry cream is golden and the apricots are tender, about 35 minutes.

7. Remove the tart from the oven. Remove the sides of the pan and let the tart cool on a wire rack before serving.

One 10½-inch (26½ cm) tart; 6 to 8 servings

Apricots

> • ◄

Soft, velvety, juicy, and sweet, apricots are the divas of summer. The first to arrive on the market are the most highly appreciated, the **rouges de Roussillon.** Orange with a tasteful blush, they are pure and deeply flavored, and they disappear as quickly as they arrive. Apricot jam made with the **rouge de Roussillon** is, as the French say, **une merveille,** a marvel.

If you're in France in late June or July, don't hesitate to buy some **rouges de Roussillon. Their flavor is a combination of sunshine, caramel, and fragrant flowers.**

Fresh Peach Tart
Tarte aux Pêches

This tart was a direct result of a trip to the market one day when peaches were at their best, the cream lady had an abundance of cream in her pot, and the weather demanded a fresh fruit tart, yet something a bit dressy.

If you can't find peaches, use nectarines. And if you have any Peaches in Red Wine (see Index), add a few of those as well.

1 cup (250 ml) plain yogurt (nonfat is fine)

3 tablespoons (firmly packed) light brown sugar

½ to 1 teaspoon vanilla extract, to taste

½ cup (125 ml) Crème Fraîche (page 520), or heavy (or whipping) cream

One 10½-inch (26½ cm) tart shell, made using Homemaker's Pastry (page 509) and prebaked

3 small ripe peaches, peeled, pitted, and thinly sliced

¼ cup fresh red currants or fresh berries, such as raspberries, blackberries, or blueberries

1. In a small bowl, whisk together the yogurt, brown sugar, and vanilla extract. In another small bowl, whisk the crème fraîche until it holds stiff peaks. Fold the crème fraîche into the yogurt mixture.

2. Spread the mixture in the prebaked pastry shell. Arrange the peach slices atop the cream, and sprinkle with the currants. Remove the sides of the pan from the tart and serve immediately.

One 10½-inch (26½ cm) tart; 6 to 8 servings

"Mamie" Leroy's Pumpkin Tart
Tarte au Potiron de "Mamie" Leroy

One Sunday morning I heard a sharp knock on the door. When I answered, there was Agnès Leroy, the mother of a good friend of ours, whom we've come to call Mamie, or Grandma, over the years. Tiny but powerful, she moves with determination in all she does, helping everyone she meets on her path.

There she was on that Sunday, all dressed for church, hat perched on her head, small tart in hand. "I wanted you to try this," she said, both proudly and bashfully. "I just made it and I think it's pretty good. You'll have to tell me what you think."

I immediately tried a slice and fell in

love. It's a wonderful mix of pumpkin, orange juice, raisins, and a touch of cinnamon. A big touch, if you use Mme. Leroy's version, which follows.

Scant ½ cup (60 g) raisins
¼ cup (60 ml) freshly squeezed orange juice
1½ tablespoons unsalted butter
18 ounces (540 g) fresh pumpkin, about ½ small pumpkin, skin and seeds removed, cut into ½-inch (1¼ cm) cubes
1 small tart apple, such as Winesap, peeled, cored, and cut into ½-inch (1¼ cm) cubes
2 large eggs
½ cup plus 1 tablespoon (140 ml) Crème Fraîche (page 520), or heavy (or whipping) cream
6 tablespoons sugar
Generous ¼ teaspoon ground cinnamon
Zest of 1 orange, minced
½ teaspoon vanilla extract
One 10½-inch (26½ cm) tart shell, made using Homemaker's Pastry (page 509) and prebaked

1. Place the raisins and the orange juice in a small saucepan and bring to a boil over medium-high heat. Remove from the heat, cover, and allow to macerate for 30 minutes or as long as several hours.

2. Preheat the oven to 400°F (205°C).

3. Melt the butter in a large heavy saucepan over medium heat. Add the pumpkin and the apple, stir, and cover. Cook until the pumpkin and apple are tender, checking occasionally and stirring to prevent them from sticking to the pan, about 15 minutes.

4. Remove the cover from the pan and continue cooking, stirring occasionally, until all the liquid has evaporated, 5 to 7 minutes. Remove the pan from the heat and transfer the pumpkin and apple to a food processor. Purée until smooth, and let cool to room temperature.

5. In a large bowl, whisk together the eggs, crème fraîche, sugar, cinnamon, zest, and vanilla extract. Whisk in the pumpkin purée, and then stir in the raisins and any remaining orange juice. Pour the mixture into the prebaked pastry shell. Place the tart pan on a baking sheet and bake in the center of the oven until the filling is firm to the touch and cooked through, about 30 minutes.

6. Remove the tart from the oven and let cool slightly. Remove the sides of the pan from the tart and serve warm.

One 10½-inch (26½ cm) tart; 6 to 8 servings

The Riehls of Alsace

=

Trellised Jack-in-the-Beanstalk–like hops shimmer like an oasis in the golden, late-summer land-scape of Alsace. On an umbrella-dotted terrace near the tiny village of Dauendorf, the Riehl family is sitting down to lunch.

Three generations are present at Angèle and Joseph (nicknamed Sepp) Riehl's home, where the terrace overlooks a huge kitchen garden; wheat, rye, tobacco, and sugar beet fields; and hugging the horizon, a long dark stripe that is Germany's Black Forest. They make a jolly group, pouring huge glasses of beer with a deep froth, teasing each other unmercifully. They act as though they haven't seen each other in years, yet the family gathers often. And each gathering is a festival of traditional recipes, home-grown produce, and celebration.

The Riehls have farmed around Dauendorf for generations. Most recently they've become subsistence farmers, supplying themselves with food, holding down other jobs to support their families.

Angèle carries out a platter heaped with *Grumbereknepfl* and its traditional accompaniment, curly endive salad with hot bacon dressing. We all shift dishes, glasses, and plates to make room on the table, which is already laden with Alsatian bounty—platters heaped with fat slices of garden-ripe tomatoes buried in parsley, plates of charcuterie, jars of Angèle's homemade cornichons. It's a veritable summer feast.

There are fifteen family members at this table, ranging in age from seventeen to seventy-five. Of the older generation, Marcel Riehl, who sits at the head, is the only one who didn't farm. He tried it, but after two weeks threw up his hands. "I didn't want to farm," he says now, laughing. Instead, he joined the priesthood and went to Papua, New Guinea, for forty years.

Marcel's nephew, another Joseph,

replaced him on the farm. Now graying and in his sixties, Joseph has also been mayor of Dauendorf for nearly thirty years, long enough for the title to become part of his name. Even his relatives call him "Joseph-le-Maire."

Joseph-le-Maire and his wife, Germaine, farmed potatoes and hops before World War II, along with corn, some wheat, a bit of tobacco, and vegetables they raised for the family. They also had dairy cattle, pigs, and poultry.

Joseph-le-Maire gave up his animals some years ago, but he still farms some acreage just outside Dauendorf, and took us out to see it. Clean and tidy, his corn and hops stretch for a city block, and at the junction of a dirt path through the fields sits a small chapel, its altar festooned with fresh flowers. Built there many hundreds of years ago, it still serves fieldworkers, who visit on a daily basis.

At the table, Joseph-le-Maire reminisces about buying the first tractor in the region in 1954. "What an innovation, everyone wanted one," he says. "So many things changed after that, even the crops. We were

always encouraged to plant new varieties of corn and wheat. The wheat got so bad that bakers refused to use it. Now farmers are getting back to the good, strong varieties. Bread is getting better again."

Sugar beets were introduced after the war, and they completely changed the face of farming in Alsace. As they became more valuable, other crops faded. Now sugar beets blanket the land, a monoculture that everyone hopes will survive, because if it doesn't, Alsace will have an economic crisis on its hands.

Eugénie Riehl, sitting to the right of Marcel, is the matriarch of this cheerful and robust family. Her husband died at an untimely age, and she quickly picked up the reins of their small farm, working it with her three children, Annie, Joseph (yet another one), and Michel. Now well into her seventies, she tends a fruit orchard and huge kitchen garden.

Ironically, not one of her children decided to take over the farm, so she's leased out most of her land.

Why don't they want the farm? Annie and Joseph both laugh heartily. "We worked on the land hard enough when we were children," they say in unison.

Instead, Annie dresses up each day to go to work and keeps a lovely home with a small garden, which is enough property for her. "No one should have to work as hard as we worked," she says. Joseph and Michel both nod.

(continued)

A LOOK TO THE NEXT GENERATION

At Annie's statement and her brothers' concurrence, a brief silence falls over the table. It is palpable with emotion. For the older generation who had no choice but to work the land, who incorporated each innovation as it arose, hoping it would make their workload less, there is regret over the disappearance of active farms. For the middle generation who washed the soil from their hands, and have willed themselves as far away from the hard work and privation of their young lives as they can, there is nostalgia and a measure of guilt. For the younger generation, most of whom know farming through the tales of the elders, there is a flicker of interest, which, if nurtured, might turn them into farmers.

The silent moment passes away as everyone turns to the food on the table. It is all so pure and delicious that we eat until the plates are bare, keeping Angèle and Sepp jumping to serve *Grumbeereknepfl*, which issues in a continuous hot stream.

The talk turns to food, and all agree. Eugénie is the best cook. The mere mention of her sweet cheese tart makes Angèle's eyes shine, and Annie gives a detailed description of the cinnamon bread tart she always eats by the double portion. Eugénie herself waxes poetic over sugared plums and beignets.

As the sun reaches overhead, the parasols come out. We sit at the table and enjoy the cheese tart and Angèle's apple tart.

The Riehl family straddles two worlds, the old and the new, and it seems up to the youngest to determine in which direction it goes. One thing is certain, however. Their heritage is rich. While it would be fitting to see them return to the farm, if all they maintain are the riches of the table, they'll still be far wealthier than most.

Cinnamon Cream Bread Tart

Tarte à la Cannelle

>···<

Though you may find *tarte à la cannelle* in a neighborhood pâtisserie in Alsace, it won't look much like this. This is the old-fashioned precursor to what is now a simple cream tart dusted with cinnamon in a traditional pastry crust.

I much prefer this tender, pillowy version, which I got from Eugénie Riehl. Its basis is the birthright of every Alsatian, buttery-rich kugelhopf dough, which rises until light, then is bathed in a simple mixture of cream and vanilla sugar. Before pouring the cream atop the dough, however, you poke holes in it so the cream can fill them, infusing the bread with its moist richness. Cinnamon, a common spice in Alsace and hardly elsewhere in France, adds just the right touch of flavor.

This is served as dessert in Alsace, which is the way I serve it most often, too. It is also luscious for breakfast, and easily enough made by preparing the dough the night before and letting it rise in the refrigerator overnight. A word of caution: This is so tender and billowy that you may find it serves less people than you expected, because guests will clamor for seconds, and sometimes thirds.

Try to bake this in a round shape, which is much more attractive than a rectangle. A 12½-inch (32 cm) round pan is available at most kitchenware shops.

FOR THE DOUGH

1 package active dry yeast

1 cup (250 ml) milk, heated to lukewarm

½ cup (100 g) sugar

3½ to 3¾ cups (475 to 500 g) unbleached all-purpose flour

1 teaspoon sea salt

2 large eggs

16 tablespoons (2 sticks; 250 g) unsalted butter, cut into small pieces, at room temperature

FOR THE CREAM TOPPING

2 cups (500 ml) Crème Fraîche (page 520), or heavy (or whipping) cream

6 tablespoons Vanilla Sugar (page 521)

1 heaping teaspoon ground cinnamon

1. Prepare the dough: Combine the yeast, the lukewarm milk, and the sugar in a large bowl, or in the bowl of an electric mixer, and mix well. Add 1 cup (135 g) of the flour and the salt and mix well. Then add the eggs, one at a time, mixing well after each addition. Add enough of the remaining flour

so the dough is thick. It will be quite soft and even a bit sticky. Don't add more than the maximum amount of flour, as this is a tender, soft dough and too much flour can make it tough. Knead the dough by slapping it against the sides of the bowl until it becomes quite elastic, about 10 minutes by hand, 5 minutes in an electric mixer.

2. Add the butter, several pieces at a time, mixing until it is incorporated into the dough. Continue kneading until the dough becomes increasingly elastic, about 8 minutes by hand, 5 minutes in an electric mixer.

3. Leave the dough in the bowl, cover it with a damp tea towel, and let it rise in a warm spot (68° to 70°F; 20° to 21°C) until doubled in bulk, about 1¼ hours.

4. Heavily butter and flour a 12½-inch (32 cm) round cake pan or a 12½ x 7½-inch (32 x 19 cm) rectangular baking dish.

5. Lightly flour your hands and punch down the dough so it is completely deflated. Turn the dough into the prepared cake pan, pressing it out until it comes nearly to the edges of the pan. Cover it loosely and let it rise uncovered, in a warm spot until the dough is 2½ to 3 inches high (6½ to 7½ cm) and nearly fills the pan, about 45 minutes.

6. Prepare the topping: In a medium-size bowl, mix together the crème fraîche and the vanilla sugar.

7. Preheat the oven to 400°F (205°C).

8. When the dough has risen, dust three of your fingers with flour and poke holes all over the top of the dough, dipping your fingers into flour occasionally so they don't stick to the dough. Slowly pour the crème fraîche over the dough. Most of it will run into the holes, while some will run over the side. Sprinkle the cinnamon evenly over the top, place it in the center of the oven, and bake until the dough is golden and puffed, 25 to 30 minutes

9. Remove the tart from the oven and let it cool for 5 minutes before serving.

10 servings

Alsatian Cheese Tart
Tarte au Fromage

→•••←

This simple tart is the French version of American cheesecake—with much more flavor and a more interesting texture. In Alsace, where it adorns most pâtisserie shelves, it is made with *fromage blanc,* which resembles a smooth, tangy cottage cheese.

I make it here with a blend of cottage cheese and sour cream, and can vouch for its "authenticity."

3¼ cups (840 g) full-fat cottage cheese
½ cup (125 ml) sour cream
6 tablespoons sugar
1 teaspoon vanilla extract
Zest of 1 lemon, minced
2 large eggs, beaten
1 tablespoon unbleached all-purpose
    flour
One 10½-inch (26½ cm) tart shell,
    made using Homemaker's Pastry
    (page 509) and prebaked

1. Preheat the oven to 325°F (165°C).
2. Place the cottage cheese in a food processor or blender, and purée. Add the sour cream, sugar, vanilla extract, and zest, and mix. Add the eggs and purée until the mixture is thoroughly combined. Then add the flour and process until the mixture is very, very smooth, at least 5 minutes at medium-high speed.

3. Pour the filling into the prebaked pastry shell. Place the tart pan on a baking sheet, and bake in the center of the oven until the filling is set, 30 to 35 minutes.

4. Remove the tart from the oven. Remove the sides of the pan and let the tart cool to room temperature on a wire rack before serving.

One 10½-inch (26½ cm) tart; 6 to 8 servings

Breton Cake

Gâteau Breton

Butter was preserved in Brittany to make cakes like this one, which tastes like a great big butter cookie. It's long been a favorite of mine, and when I worked at a cooking school in Paris, I made it over and over, varying it in every way I could think of, I liked it so much.

This is Germaine Plassart's recipe, which I now follow slavishly. It looks simple, and indeed it is, yet there is a *tour de main* involved, which mostly has to do with baking time and temperature. I made this many times before I got it just right. Now, it works perfectly each time in my oven, but it may take experimenting with time and temperature in another. So follow the baking directions, but check the cake halfway through. If you think it's getting too brown on the edges, refer to the Astuce below.

A true *gâteau breton* is good and golden on the edges, however, almost with a crust. It tastes, simply, of butter and eggs. Sometimes I add vanilla extract or make it with vanilla sugar, and occasionally I add lemon zest. But the way it's best is the way that's most traditional. You'll see.

A S T U C E . . . .

• *If you fear the edges of a cake are cooking too quickly, wet a cotton tea towel and tie it around the pan. It will insulate the cake from the heat, allowing it to bake evenly without getting too brown.*

. . . .

> *7 large egg yolks*
> *2 teaspoons water*
> *1¼ cups (250 g) sugar*
> *16 tablespoons (2 sticks; 250 g) lightly salted butter, melted*
> *½ teaspoon vanilla extract (optional)*
> *2 cups (265 g) unbleached all-purpose flour*

1. Preheat the oven to 325°F (165°C). Butter and lightly flour a 9-inch (23 cm) cake pan.

2. In a small bowl, whisk one of the egg yolks with the water. Set this aside for the glaze.

3. In a large bowl, whisk together the remaining 6 egg yolks and the sugar until the mixture is thick and pale yellow; this will just take a minute or two (see Note). Slowly whisk in the butter, and the vanilla extract if

you're using it. Then sift in the flour and whisk until combined. Don't overmix the flour, or the cake will be tough, but be sure it is thoroughly combined.

4. Turn the batter, which will be quite stiff, into the prepared pan and smooth it out. Lightly but thoroughly paint it with the egg glaze. Using the back of the tines of a fork, deeply mark a crisscross pattern in the top of the cake, going three times across it in one direction, then three in the other. (The marks in the cake will fade, leaving just their trace on the top of the cake.)

5. Bake in the center of the oven until the cake is deep golden on the top and springs back slowly but surely when it is touched, 50 to 55 minutes. Using a knife or cake tester isn't recommended as it always comes out looking slightly damp because of the amount of butter in the recipe.

6. Remove from the oven, transfer the cake to a wire rack, and let it cool thoroughly before serving.

One 9-inch (23 cm) cake; 8 servings

N O T E : You don't need to bother with an electric mixer here. In fact, it's best not to use one because it makes the mixture too light, changing the nature of the cake. I whisk all the ingredients together, whisking from the top to the bottom of the bowl, rather than in a circle, to incorporate just the right amount of air.

Breton Memories

>・<

*R*ecently, when I visited Brittany, I had the good fortune to stay at the home of Germaine and Jean Plassart. Both natives of Brittany, both raised on farms in the beginning of the century, their memories of foods that sustained them as youths were strong. The last day of my visit, baking in the oven was a gorgeous, golden gâteau breton (see page 459). "This is the only cake we knew when we were young," Germaine said. "There wasn't another that I remember."

It makes sense. Butter—always lightly salted with sea salt—and eggs were plentiful on all farms in Brittany, which is still noted for its high-quality butter. And Bretons have hearty appetites and a penchant for good, satisfying desserts.

Breton chickens also seem to have special powers, for their yolks are yellower than most, and this cake is the color of a daffodil.

"I've baked this gâteau for you to take home," Germaine said. "I use the exact recipe my mother did, and this cake is the same kind she made for me."

She carefully cut it in quarters and wrapped it in two separate packages, one for her niece, who is a friend of mine. I drove off with them carefully balanced atop the sea salt, oysters, buckwheat flour, and other Breton bounty I had with me. The cake sent an incredible aroma into the car and I wondered if I'd be able to resist it on the long journey home.

I did, and served it that night. It was rich, buttery, and sumptuous. The next day it was almost better, a little drier, perfect for dipping in coffee.

Lemon Cake with Strawberries
Gâteau au Citron et aux Fraises

>・・・<

*M*mm! Tangy with lemon, rich with almonds, this cake is a sure winner, one that should find its rightful place on the dinner table, the dessert tray, even for breakfast. Not too terribly sweet, it is tender and seductive. It comes from a farmer in Provence who loves to cook but doesn't like to spend her life in the kitchen, and it fits the needs of every busy cook!

Serve the cake with strawberries, as suggested, or with raspberries. (If you are serving it with raspberries, there is no need to macerate them in sugar.)

ASTUCE . . . .

• *I always grind nuts with at least 1 tablespoon of sugar. The sugar will prevent them from turning to a thick paste.*

. . . .

1 pound (500 g) strawberries, hulled

¾ cup (150 g) plus 1 tablespoon Vanilla Sugar (page 521)

½ cup (65 g) almonds, peeled and dried (see Note)

1 cup plus 1 tablespoon (150 g) regular (not unbleached) all-purpose flour

½ teaspoon sea salt

3 large eggs

10 tablespoons (1¼ sticks; 150 g) unsalted butter, melted and cooled

Zest of 1 lemon, minced

¼ cup (60 ml) freshly squeezed lemon juice

¾ cup (185 ml) Crème Fraîche (page 520), or heavy (or whipping) cream

½ teaspoon vanilla extract

→ • • • ←

"Butter is the spirit of milk."

—Jean Rostand, biologist

→ • • • ←

1. Preheat the oven to 350°F (175°C). Butter and flour a 9-inch (23 cm) springform pan.

2. Cut the berries lengthwise into thin slices and place them in a medium-size bowl. Add the 1 tablespoon vanilla sugar, toss, and let macerate for at least 1 hour.

3. Place the almonds and 1 tablespoon from the ¾ cup vanilla sugar in a food processor, and process until finely ground.

4. Sift the flour and salt together into a bowl. Place the eggs in a large bowl or the bowl of an electric mixer, add the remaining vanilla sugar, and whisk until the mixture is pale yellow, light, and fluffy. Whisk in the butter, the zest, and the lemon juice. Then add the ground almonds and the flour, mixing just until blended.

5. Pour the batter into the prepared pan, place the pan on a baking sheet, and bake in the center of the oven until the cake is golden and puffed, and springs back when touched with a finger, 35 to 40 minutes. Remove the cake from the oven and let it

cool for 10 minutes on a wire rack. Then run a knife around the edges of the pan, remove the sides of the pan, and let the cake cool thoroughly on a wire rack.

6. Right before serving the cake, whip the crème fraîche with the vanilla extract just until it holds soft peaks (not until it is stiff).

7. Remove the cooled cake from the pan bottom to a serving platter, and serve it with the berries and cream alongside.

One 9-inch (23 cm) cake; 6 to 8 servings

NOTE: For instructions on blanching and peeling almonds, see page 450, step 2.

About Flour

French flour comes in a variety of types, which are labeled according to their stage of refinement.

The most commonly used flour in the French household is either "type 45" or "type 55," both similar to our all-purpose bleached flour. They are highly processed, and are part of the reason for the renowned lightness of French cakes and pastries.

Flour is not a big item for the French home cook, however. Most French families depend for their baked goods on the plethora of bakeries and pastry shops that line the streets of even the most hidden country towns.

A bit of flour might be needed to thicken a sauce or to make a béchamel, of course, which is why a recent innovation from one of France's largest flour companies, Francine, has been so welcome: Instead of marketing flour in 2-pound (1 kg) bags, it came out with a tiny 1-pound (500 g) bag.

For an American used to baking everything from brownies to bread, buying flour by the 2-pound bag seems, well, ridiculous. Buying it by the single pound seems unthinkable. But one gets used to everything, including loading the shopping cart with 2-pound bags of flour.

The recipes in this book have all been tested with French and American flours, in France and in the U.S. Adjustments have been made and duly noted so that the results you get in your kitchen are as close as possible to those enjoyed on the farm.

Walnut Bread

Pain aux Noix

→•••←

Dany Dubois makes this walnut bread often, using walnuts she picks right across the street from her kitchen window in the village of Peyrenègre, in the Dordogne. Very simple, unencumbered by any flavor but that of walnuts, it exudes their buttery, nutty essence. Because the ingredients are simple, the kind most of us have on hand, it can be whipped together with little forethought—never a small consideration. And yes, the recipe is correctly written: there is no butter, no additional fat at all.

Dany bakes her walnut bread in a long narrow pan and presents it on an elegant white platter, usually for dessert along with Bachelor's Confiture (see Index). It's wonderful for dessert, but we almost prefer it at breakfast, lightly toasted and spread with fresh goat's- or cow's-milk cheese or a thin veil of butter.

Actually it's delicious at any time. At our house a loaf rarely lasts longer than a day.

The baking method for this bread is rather unconventional, but you'll see that the results are wonderful, for it emerges from the oven with a firm sweet crust and a tender, even-textured interior.

2¼ cups (300 g) all-purpose flour

2 teaspoons baking powder

½ teaspoon sea salt

⅔ cup (155 ml) milk

1 large egg

¾ cup (150 g) sugar

1½ cups (170 g) walnuts,
*   coarsely chopped*

1. Preheat the oven to 325°F (165°C).

2. Butter and flour an 8½ x 4½ x 2½-inch (21 x 11½ x 6½ cm) loaf pan.

3. Sift the flour, baking powder, and salt together onto a piece of waxed paper.

4. Whisk the milk and the egg together in a large bowl. Then whisk in the sugar. Using a wooden spoon, quickly stir in the dry ingredients, giving the mixture a good, short beating so all the ingredients are thoroughly combined. Add the walnuts, mixing just until they are combined, and turn the batter into the prepared pan.

5. Bake in the center of the oven until the bread is puffed and beginning to turn golden, 45 minutes. Increase the heat to 375°F (190°C) and continue baking until the bread is deep golden and cooked through, another 15 minutes.

6. Remove the bread from the oven, turn it out onto a wire rack to cool, and serve it at room temperature.

1 loaf; 8 to 10 servings

Traditional Provençal Christmas Bread

Pompe à l'Huile

>...<

This simple cake, which is almost closer to a sweet, firm bread or even a tender biscotti, is a well-loved part of the Provençal *treize desserts*, the thirteen desserts of Christmas Eve. The traditional recipe is flavored simply with orange-flower water, which is haunting and subtle. I love it that way, but I dress it up a bit more for my own pleasure. Here the cake is flavored with anise seeds and brightened with candied fruit. The orange-flower water provides a gentle aromatic background.

I love this dough, which is made with olive oil, because it is easy to work, requires practically no kneading, and results in an unusually satisfying pastry. The *pompe* is wonderful the day it is made, and almost more delicious after a day or two of aging.

I make this often during the Christmas season because it is so much less sweet than many Christmas specialties. It goes well after supper, particularly with Anise Ice Cream (see Index), is fantastic with early morning coffee, and wonderful with afternoon tea.

1½ teaspoons active dry yeast

2 tablespoons orange-flower water

3¾ cups (500 g) unbleached all-purpose flour

¼ teaspoon sea salt

4 large eggs, lightly beaten

¾ cup (150 g) sugar

6 tablespoons olive oil

Zest of 1 lemon, minced

½ teaspoon anise seeds

¼ cup (60 g) candied fruit, diced

1. In a small bowl, stir the yeast into the orange-flower water. Let it sit until dissolved, about 5 minutes.

2. Sift the flour and salt into a large bowl. Make a well in the flour and add the eggs, sugar, oil, and the yeast mixture. Mix the liquid ingredients together, using your fingers, until blended. Add the zest, anise seeds, and candied fruit.

3. Gradually incorporate the flour into the liquid mixture, mixing just until it is all combined. Then knead four or five times. The dough will be quite sticky; lightly dust the work surface with flour and use a plastic dough scraper to help you knead.

4. Form the dough into a ball and place it in a bowl. Cover the bowl with a damp cloth and let it sit in a warm spot (68° to 70°F; 20° to 21°C) until it has risen by half, about 2 hours.

5. Preheat the oven to 350°F (175°C). Lightly oil two baking sheets.

6. Punch down the dough and divide it in half. Knead both batches slightly on a well-floured work surface (use no more than 3 tablespoons flour to dust the work surface) to remove any air pockets. Roll each half out between two sheets of parchment paper to form a 12 x 8-inch (30 x 20 cm) oval that is about ¼ inch (½ cm) thick, and transfer them to the prepared baking sheets. (To do this, peel off the top piece of paper, flip the bread over onto the baking sheet, and remove the second piece of paper. Or roll the dough over a rolling pin, then unroll it on the baking sheet. The soft dough will stretch some, but don't be concerned.)

7. Make a design on each loaf: Working quickly and using a sharp knife, cut a 2½-inch (6½ cm) diameter circle in the center, cutting all the way through the dough but leaving the circle in place. Then cut five rays out from the circle so the design resembles a sun. Let the dough sit in a warm spot (68° to 70°F; 20° to 21°C) until it has risen slightly, about 30 minutes.

8. Bake the *pompes* in the center of the oven until they are golden and puffed, and have developed a scattering of small bumps on their surface, about 25 minutes.

9. Remove from the oven and transfer the *pompes* to wire racks to cool. Serve at room temperature.

2 pompes; about 10 servings

Brioche French Toast with Caramelized Apples

Pain Perdu à la Brioche et aux Pommes

→ ··· ←

Pain perdu. Lost bread. The mere idea is significant, for on the farm, in the homes of those who raise their own food and sustain themselves by their own labor, bread is never lost but is transformed into something else. Those chunks of bread that harden, that are now considered good only for the animals, were once jealously hoarded and transformed to fill the stomachs of hungry, hardworking farm families. The dish they were turned into, no matter what its composition, was always called *pain perdu.* This version is wonderful after a meal, for it is light and satisfying. I like to make it for breakfast, too.

I found this on a cool fall day when I was visiting L'Espérance, a three-star restaurant in Vézeley, Burgundy. Attracted by Marc Meneau's large garden and orchard (I'm aways intrigued by chefs who attempt to control the products they use by raising them themselves), I was anxious to see how this Burgundian star, who was raised in a simple country family, tended his crops.

We walked over a lush lawn, where fruit trees were interspersed with comfortable garden chairs for guests. The herb garden was tucked behind a large hedgerow, a small sanctuary of fragrance and color. A series of heaped beds designed to accommodate as many plants as possible in a limited space, it nonetheless hardly looked prolific enough to supply a restaurant the size of L'Espérance.

M. Meneau didn't hide the fact that his gardens, which had once been large and extended, were now more symbolic. "This is probably the most expensive produce you'll ever see," he said, laughing. "I employ a number of people to care for the garden and the trees, but of course we can't supply the restaurant. I tried that, and it's just too expensive. Now I order from farmers, and I feel it's more important that they do their work and I do mine."

His garden has a use other than ornamental, however, for it serves as a calendar, and M. Meneau walks in it every day to check the progress of different vegetables and fruits, so he knows when to change his menu, when to begin looking for new seasonal produce.

"I have farmers on both sides of me from whom I buy, and their produce is ready at different times," M. Meneau said. "When I see what's ready in my garden, I know whom to call.

"Perhaps it's an expensive way to keep abreast of the seasons," he added as he pinched a sage leaf and inhaled its aroma, "but it's also a place for me to wander and contemplate what I'll cook, a place of inspiration."

ASTUCE . . . .
• *The soaking mixture for the bread is mostly milk, and very light. When you fry the rounds of brioche, the milk will spread, causing little spatters. Don't be concerned, and above all don't be tempted to add another egg to the batter, for it will spoil the lightness of the dish.*

. . . .

FOR THE APPLES
2 tablespoons unsalted butter
4 medium-sweet to sweet-tart apples, such as Idared, Jonagold, Gravenstein, or Golden Delicious, peeled, cored, and cut into thin slices
¼ cup (50 g) sugar

FOR THE PAIN PERDU
1 large egg
1¼ cups (310 ml) milk
1 teaspoon sugar
1 loaf Quick Brioche (page 325)
2 tablespoons unsalted butter
Heaping ¼ teaspoon ground cinnamon

FOR SERVING
½ cup (125 ml) Crème Fraîche (page 520), or heavy (or whipping) cream (optional)

1. Cook the apples: Melt the butter in a large skillet over medium-high heat. Add the apples and toss so they are coated with butter. Then sprinkle with the sugar and continue cooking, shaking the pan and flipping the apples by sharply jerking the pan, or by stirring them with a wooden spoon, until they are tender and golden, 10 to 15 minutes. Remove the skillet from the heat and keep warm.

2. Prepare the *pain perdu:* Whisk together the egg, milk, and sugar in a large shallow bowl until thoroughly combined. Slice eight ¾-inch-thick (2 cm) slices from the brioche, discarding the end piece. Cut out a 3-inch (8 cm) round from each slice.

3. Soak 4 rounds of the brioche in the egg mixture, turning them if necessary, until they are saturated but not falling apart, 3 to 4 minutes.

4. Melt the butter in a large skillet over medium-high heat. Add the soaked brioche rounds and cook until they are golden on one side, about 3 minutes. Turn and cook on the other side until they are golden, 2 to 3 minutes. Transfer them to a warmed serving platter. Continue soaking and sautéing the remaining rounds of brioche. Sprinkle the rounds lightly with the cinnamon.

5. To serve, arrange the apples on top of the rounds of brioche on the platter. Or make individual servings by placing two rounds of brioche on each of four warmed dessert plates, and top each with an equal amount of apples. Serve the crème fraîche alongside, if you like.

4 servings

Peaches and Blueberries with Spice Bread

Pêches et Myrtilles au Pain d'Épices

→•••←

This will send you right over the moon. Peaches and blueberries are already a preordained marvel—why else would they ripen at the same time? Add a thin slice of *pain d'épices* and a touch of crème fraîche, and you have a dessert made for the gods.

The sweet spiciness of the *pain d'épices* echoes the fruit flavors and precludes the need for additional sugar.

1½ cups (180 g) fresh or frozen blueberries
¼ cup (60 ml) water
4 thin (¼ inch; ½ cm) slices Babette's Spice Bread (page 388)
4 peaches, each cut into 8 wedges
¼ to ½ cup (60 to 125 ml) Crème Fraîche (page 520), or heavy (or whipping) cream
Fresh sage leaves, for garnish (optional)

1. **Combine** the blueberries and water in a small heavy saucepan over medium heat and bring to a boil. Reduce the heat to medium-low and simmer just until the berries are hot through and have lost some of their shape, about 10 minutes. Remove from the heat and keep warm.

2. **Cut** each slice of bread in half vertically, and arrange two halves, slightly at an angle and overlapping, on each of four dessert plates.

3. **Arrange** 8 peach wedges atop the bread on each plate, and top the peaches with equal amounts of blueberries and their juice.

4. **Top** each plate with a dollop of crème fraîche, and garnish with 2 or 3 sage leaves, if desired. Serve any remaining crème fraîche separately.

4 servings

Sautéed Beignets with Sugared Plums
Beignets aux Prunes

→···←

This Alsatian dessert is one to dream about. It's about as simple as they come—nothing more than an egg-rich dough deep-fried into golden bubbles, which are then sautéed in cooked plums just long enough to absorb their flavor. But its simplicity belies a rich depth of flavor. In Alsace, it makes use of the abundant *quetsche*, the small purple damson plum. Here I use Italian prune plums, which give a similar deep and sweet/tart result.

I love to serve this dessert, not only because its flavor is incomparable but also because its looks are unparalleled, at once hearty and appealing. I recommend placing a bowlful of crème fraîche alongside, but that's up to you.

FOR THE DOUGH
½ cup (125 ml) lukewarm milk
1½ teaspoons active dry yeast
¼ cup (50 g) sugar
2 cups (265 g) unbleached all-purpose flour
2 large eggs
½ teaspoon sea salt
6 tablespoons (¾ stick; 90 g) unsalted butter, at room temperature

FOR THE PLUMS
2 pounds (1 kg) Italian prune plums, pitted and cut in half lengthwise
¼ cup (50 g) Vanilla Sugar, (page 521)

FOR THE BEIGNETS
6 cups (1½ l) mild cooking oil
¼ cup (50 g) Vanilla Sugar (page 521)

Crème Fraîche (page 520), for serving (optional)

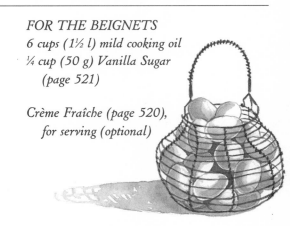

1. Prepare the dough: Combine the lukewarm milk, yeast, and sugar in a large bowl, or in the bowl of an electric mixer, and stir well. Add 1 cup (135 g) of the flour and mix well. Then add the eggs one at a time, beating well after each addition. Slowly add the remaining 1 cup (135 g) flour and the salt, and mix well. The dough will be quite sticky. Continue mixing by slapping the

Prune I.D.

⇥·⇤

*T*he **reine-claude,** *a small green plum with a dusty-blue blush that tastes like tart honey and is considered one of the best in France, was named for the well-loved Queen Claude, the wife of François I.*

Other prunes that delight the French include the small, golden, sweet **mirabelle,** *which is luscious fresh or used in jams and pastries; the succulent purple* **prune d'Agen,** *which is grown in southern France and is best known in its dried form, as* **pruneaux d'Agen;** *and the* **quetsche.**

dough against the sides of the bowl until it becomes slightly elastic, about 10 minutes by hand or 5 minutes by machine. Add the butter bit by bit, mixing until the dough is smooth and comes cleanly off the sides of the bowl, another 5 minutes by hand, 2 to 3 minutes by machine. Loosely cover the bowl and set it in a warm spot (68° to 70°F; 20° to 21°C) until it has doubled in bulk, 1 to 1½ hours. Punch the dough down, then let it rise again just until it begins to expand slightly, about 15 minutes.

2. While the dough is rising, prepare the plums: Combine the plums and the vanilla sugar in a large heavy skillet. Cook over medium heat, stirring occasionally, until the plums soften and give up much of their juice, about 10 minutes. Continue cooking until the juice thickens somewhat, another 4 to 5

minutes. Remove the skillet from the heat and set it aside.

3. Prepare the beignets: Heat the cooking oil in a Dutch oven or deep-fryer until it reaches 365°F (185°C). Lightly sprinkle a large work surface with flour. Line two wire cooling racks with double layers of paper towels.

4. Pinch off tablespoon-size pieces of the dough and place them on the prepared work surface, using up all of the dough. Shake off any excess flour from the pieces of dough and drop them, a few at a time, into the hot oil, making sure not to crowd the pan. Fry the beignets, turning them frequently so they brown evenly, just until they are golden on the outside and cooked through, 3 minutes. Remove them from the oil and set them to drain on the cooling racks. Repeat with the remaining dough.

5. When all the beignets are cooked, reheat the plums over medium-high heat until they are simmering. Add the beignets, and sprinkle with the vanilla sugar. Sauté the beignets just until they have absorbed some of the plum juice, and they and the plums are hot through, 4 to 5 minutes.

6. Serve the beignets right from the pan, transfer them to a warmed serving platter, or divide them among eight warmed dinner plates. Serve crème fraîche alongside if you like.

8 servings

Precious Memories

→·←

Patrick Jeffroy, a gifted young chef in Brittany, shops weekly at the farmers' market in Morlaix, where he grew up and where he is well known by all the farmers, some of whom met him first when he was a young boy. "I remember Patrick coming and tickling the ears of my donkey," reminisced a farmer who used to transport his produce in a donkey cart. "I remember that, too," said M. Jeffroy. "I used to get carrots from another farmer to feed to his donkey."

M. Jeffroy's grandmother lived on a farm, and he spent many a happy afternoon rummaging through her vegetable garden and cooking next to her in the kitchen. "Ever since I was tiny, I'd cook with my grandmother," he said.

"I remember when we'd make baked apples," M. Jeffroy said. "I loved the moment when we went to get the cassis. She made her own and she kept it in her linen cupboard. She'd get the key from a hiding place and slowly open the door. I was so excited—first I'd see the shelves of clean linen, then the shelf of bottles where she put all her homemade liqueurs. She'd hand me the cassis and I'd carefully carry it to the kitchen. It was so precious, I was always afraid I'd drop it.

"Those memories of flavors and experiences from childhood," he said, "they're what keep me in the kitchen, and keep me honest."

Patrick Jeffroy's
Baked Apples
Pommes au Four

→···←

This simple yet elegant dessert is a favorite of Breton chef Patrick Jeffroy's, and the addition of cassis is inspired. Be sure to use tart cooking apples such as Winesaps. When you core the apples, leave a thin wall of apple at the base so the filling will stay inside.

4 tart medium baking apples, peeled and
   cored (leave the base intact)
1 cup (250 ml) hearty red wine
2 strips orange zest, each 2 x ½ inches
   (5 x 1¼ cm)
½ teaspoon ground cinnamon
4 teaspoons apricot jam
2 teaspoons sugar
2 teaspoons unsalted butter
4 teaspoons crème de cassis liqueur
Mint or lemon verbena sprigs, for garnish

1. Preheat the oven to 400°F (205°C).
2. Arrange the apples in a baking dish with 2-inch (5 cm) sides. Pour the wine around them. Add the zest to the wine, and sprinkle the cinnamon over all.

3. Place 1 teaspoon of the jam in the hollow of each apple, then top with ¼ teaspoon of the sugar and ½ teaspoon of the butter. Place the dish in the center of the oven and bake until the apples are tender but still have some texture, about 45 minutes. Remove from the oven, and pour 1 teaspoon of the crème de cassis over each apple.

4. To serve, place each apple in the center of a warmed shallow bowl, and pour the cooking liquid around it. Garnish with the mint or lemon verbena sprigs, and serve immediately.

4 servings

Apple Compote
Compote de Pommes

Classically, the term *compote* denoted fruit cooked whole, or in large pieces, in a sugar syrup. This dish, however, is typically what passes for a compote.

In Normandy, once apples are large enough to be plucked from the tree, the entire populace seems to turn its attention to compote. The air is rich with its aroma. Pastry shops fill everything they can think of with it. Walk into any farm kitchen from October through February, and if there isn't a pot of compote simmering on the stove, there will be a dish of it sitting on the table. Lightly sweetened, seasoned with lemon juice if the apples are very sweet, it is a simple regional dessert, usually served plain. Try it with Butter Cookies from Normandy, on its own, stirred into yogurt, or with a dollop of Crème Fraîche (see Index for recipes).

2½ pounds (1½ kg) tart cooking apples, or
    a mixture of tart and sweet apples, such
    as Gravenstein, Jonagold, Idared, and
    McIntosh, peeled, cored, and cut into
    large pieces
2 tablespoons water
1 to 2 tablespoons light brown sugar,
    loosely packed
2 to 4 teaspoons freshly squeezed lemon juice

1. Place the apples and the water in a medium-size heavy saucepan over medium-high heat. Cover, and when the liquid boils, reduce the heat and stir the apples. Cook, covered, until they are tender through but still in chunks, about 25 minutes. Add the brown sugar and lemon juice to taste, cover, and cook until the seasonings have blended into the apples, an additional 5 to 10 minutes.

2. Remove from the heat and either serve immediately or let cool to room temperature.

About 3 cups (750 ml)

Annie's Peaches in Red Wine
Pêches au Vin Rouge d'Annie

When the heat of the day wanes but the evening is still warm, this chilled fruit dessert makes a fine aromatic end to a meal. The peaches absorb the spiced wine yet retain their own perfumed flavor.

Simple and light, this must be made at least a day in advance so the peaches have time to absorb the wine syrup, says Annie Grodent, who gave me the recipe. If there is syrup left over after you've served the peaches, add more peaches, or apricots or nectarines, for the following day. The fruit will keep in the syrup for 2 to 3 days.

I like to serve *pain d'épices* (see Index for Babette's Spice Bread) or Butter Cookies from Normandy (see Index) alongside this dessert, or to serve the fruit atop ice cream.

ASTUCE . . . . .

• *Don't peel the peaches. The peel helps them hold their shape and texture.*

· · ·

2 bottles (each 750 ml) simple red wine, such as a Côtes du Rhône or a lighter red Sancerre
½ cup (100 g) sugar
Zest of 1 orange, in strips
¼ teaspoon cardamom seeds
1 cinnamon stick
7 whole cloves
4 black peppercorns
4 medium-size peaches
Handful of fresh mint leaves, for garnish

1. Combine the wine, sugar, zest, and spices in a nonreactive medium-size saucepan over medium-high heat. Bring to a boil, reduce the heat so the liquid is simmering merrily, and reduce by half, about 15 minutes. Remove from the heat and let cool to room temperature.

2. Cut the peaches into ½-inch-thick (1¼ cm) slices, and place them in a shallow bowl. Strain the cooled wine syrup over them, cover, and refrigerate for at least 24 hours.

3. To serve, place the peaches in shallow dessert bowls, ladle as much syrup as you like over them, and garnish with the mint leaves.

6 to 8 servings

Farmhouse Crème Caramel

Tian au Lait

> ❖•••❖

Nicole Vallortigara, who grew up on a farm, but who now lives in a tiny hilltop village in Provence, calls this simple farm dessert *tian au lait*, a Provençal name for what is elsewhere called *crème aux oeufs*. One of the most common and best loved farm desserts, it is made throughout the country. I've eaten it in Burgundy, in Brittany, in Provence, and in Normandy—anywhere there are chickens in the *basse-cour* and cows in the field.

You may notice that at one point during cooking the *tian* boils alarmingly, which seems highly inappropriate but actually has no negative effect. There will be some small holes in the bottom third of the custard, and a slight skin on top, but these are both considered desirable. I've baked this at every possible temperature to avoid the boiling, but the temperature and time specified here turn out a perfect farmhouse *tian*.

ASTUCE . . . .

• Don't panic when making caramel, for it is simple. Watch the sugar carefully and don't let it burn. Don't get excited, either, if it turns very dark brown at the edges while the rest of the sugar isn't fully melted—simply swirl the pan so that the sugar blends in. Don't stir the caramel, or it may become lumpy, and those lumps are nearly impossible to get rid of. Some caramel will remain in the mold when you unmold the tian, *no matter how long you leave it in there. Don't be concerned; the dessert will have enough without it.*

. . . .

FOR THE CARAMEL
½ cup (100 g) sugar

FOR THE CUSTARD
1 quart (1 l) whole milk
1 vanilla bean, split down its length
6 large eggs
½ cup (100 g) Vanilla Sugar (page 521)

Edible flowers, for garnish (optional)

1. Preheat the oven to 350°F (175°C).
2. Make the caramel: Place the sugar in a small, heavy saucepan over medium heat. As it begins to melt around the edges, shake the pan regularly, but not constantly, so it melts evenly. It may begin to turn golden before all of the sugar has melted. Do not stir the sugar, but shake the pan regularly so

it caramelizes thoroughly. When it is completely liquid and a dark tea-brown, pour it into a 6-cup (1½ l) soufflé dish, and swirl it around so it completely covers the bottom of the mold. Lightly butter the sides of the mold.

3. Prepare the custard: Heat the milk with the vanilla bean in a medium-size heavy saucepan over medium heat until the milk is steamed and tiny bubbles form around the edges. Immediately remove the pan from the heat, cover it, and let the milk infuse for 10 minutes. Remove the vanilla bean (rinse and save it for making more vanilla sugar).

4. Whisk the eggs until they are broken up but not foamy. Continuing to whisk, very slowly add the hot milk, ¼ cup (60 ml) at a time, until it is incorporated into the eggs.

5. Strain the mixture through a fine-mesh sieve into another bowl, and whisk in the vanilla sugar until it is dissolved.

6. Pour the custard into the prepared mold, and set it in a baking pan with sides that are at least 2½ inches (6½ cm) high. Pour cold water around the mold until it is nearly to the top of the baking pan, and place the pan in the center of the oven. Bake until a sharp knife thrust into the center of the custard comes out clean, about 1 hour.

7. Remove the pan from the oven, and remove the mold from the water bath. Let it cool thoroughly before unmolding. (You may refrigerate the *tian* overnight in the mold and turn it out the following day.)

8. Run a knife around the edges of the mold, being careful not to cut into the *tian*. Place a large shallow bowl, or a serving plat-

ter with a substantial lip, on top of the *tian*, and quickly flip it over. The *tian* will come out with a sucking sound. A great deal of caramel will seep out as well, though a bit will remain in the mold. Garnish the *tian* with edible flowers if you like, and serve.

6 to 8 servings

Cinnamon Rice Pudding
Teurgoule

→ ··· ←

We were served this incredibly luscious dessert at Bernard and Paulette Petit's *ferme-auberge* in Normandy. Traditionally, *teurgoule* is made with raw milk. I've tried it with raw and pasteurized, and though there is a difference, it is fine made with pasteurized. It must be made with whole milk and short-grain rice, however, to achieve the required smooth richness.

You'll need to make this rice pudding in an earthenware bowl—the taste isn't as rich and deep when made in glass or enamelware. Find a big (lead-free) mixing bowl, place the ingredients in it, put it in the oven, and then pretty much forget about it.

Mme. Petit, who gave me this recipe, insists that *teurgoule* must be made with sugar cubes. I've tried it with cubes and with regular granulated sugar, and can honestly find no difference whatsoever.

¾ cup (180 g) short-grain rice, rinsed
¾ cup plus 2 tablespoons (175 g) sugar
¼ teaspoon sea salt
1 teaspoon ground cinnamon
8 cups (2 l) cold whole milk

1. Preheat the oven to 375°F (190°C).
2. Place the rice in a large earthenware mixing bowl. Add the sugar, then sprinkle the salt and cinnamon over all. Pour in the cold milk, and place the bowl in the center of the oven. (You may want to put the bowl on a baking sheet, just in case the *teurgoule* boils over.)
3. Cook the *teurgoule* for 1½ hours. Then reduce the oven temperature to 215°F (about 100°C). Continue cooking for 2 hours.
4. Remove the *teurgoule* from the oven and let it cool for 10 minutes before serving. Right from the oven it is too blisteringly hot to dig into.

6 to 8 servings

La Teurgoule

→·←

*I*n Normandy, sweets run to billowy cream confections, buttery chaussons, turnovers filled with apple compote, whole pears and apples wrapped in puff pastry. It was with some surprise, then, to discover **teurgoule**, a sumptuous but simple cinnamon-laced rice pudding.

What, I wondered, was it doing in Normandy? There isn't a rice paddy anywhere in France except the Camargue, way down south, and there they don't grow white round rice. Cinnamon isn't a French spice, either.

To get to the bottom of the **teurgoule** story, I had to go to Houlgate, where I found a group called the **Confrérie des Gastronomes de la Teurgoule de Normandie**, which is dedicated to saving **teurgoule**. I spoke with the **Grand Maître**, or president, of the group, who recounted a tale of famine and generosity.

"It was back in the eighteenth century that **teurgoule** was introduced to Normandy," said M. René Délivet. "The wheat crops were bad. There was nothing to eat in Normandy. The king directed his soldiers to bring rice into the region and distribute it to the peasants. We've never quite figured out where they got the rice.

"The king was a good man," continued M. Délivet. "It wasn't enough that he thought of rice. He wanted to be sure the people knew how to use it, so he sent along a recipe." M. Délivet conjectured that the recipe came straight from the royal kitchens.

The king's men plastered the recipe on walls, windows, and barns throughout the countryside, the equivalent of printing it in the daily paper.

As for the cinnamon, M. Délivet had the explanation for that, too.

"Honfleur, which is just down the road, harbored boats from all over the world," he said. "During battles, the French ransacked British boats, and among the wealth was cinnamon."

It became part of the local cuisine, presumably not always procured by ransacking. It is still found today in pastries and desserts of coastal Normandy.

Teurgoule saved the peasantry of Normandy. It became a dish of sustenance, what they lived on every day. They prepared it at home and took it to bake in the village baker's oven after he'd removed the bread. Traditionally they ate it with **gallu**, a poor man's brioche.

"There you have all the history about **teurgoule** that we know," M. Délivet said. "Of course, it may have existed well before that, somewhere else."

Today it is a dessert that brings a smile of recognition to coastal Normans, for it is little known outside a small part of the region. There, it is a valued and luscious part of the local cuisine.

Mme. Roulleau's Chocolate Mousse
Mousse au Chocolat de Mme. Roulleau

➤ • • • ✦

What would a cookbook from the French countryside be without a recipe for chocolate mousse? Incomplete, for it remains a favorite dessert on the farm, for all ages, in all situations.

This is one of the best chocolate mousses I've ever tasted, and I thank a neighbor and fine cook, Mme. Roulleau, for it—she dropped the recipe in my mailbox one day after I'd asked her for it, and I made it immediately. It came out just as light yet substantial as hers, and not too sweet. I understand why it's a standby on the farm, for it goes together quickly and offers a rich, satisfying end to a meal.

*3 ounces (90 g) best-quality bittersweet
    chocolate, such as Lindt, Caillebaut,
    or Tobler*
2 tablespoons water
2 tablespoons unsalted butter, softened
3 large eggs, separated (see Note)
Pinch of salt
*2 tablespoons confectioners' sugar,
    sifted*

1. Combine the chocolate and water in a large heatproof bowl set over a saucepan of simmering water. When the chocolate is melted, whisk it until it is smooth, then add the butter, continuing to whisk until the mixture is a silky cream, with no lumps. Remove the mixture from the heat and whisk in the egg yolks one at a time.

2. In a medium-size bowl, whisk the egg whites with the salt until they are white and foamy and hold light peaks. Continuing to whisk vigorously, sprinkle in the confectioners' sugar until the whites hold stiff peaks. Fold the egg whites into the chocolate mixture, and turn into an attractive serving bowl or individual serving dishes. Refrigerate until the mousse is set (it will not get very, very firm, but it will set and hold its shape), at least 2 hours. You may make this up to 4 hours before serving.

4 to 6 servings

NOTE: This delicious chocolate mousse includes eggs that remain uncooked once the dessert is completed. Like me, you should use only the best-quality, farm-fresh eggs to make the mousse. If you are unsure of the quality of the eggs available to you, it is best to avoid recipes that include them uncooked.

Alsatian Bread Pudding
Bettelman

→···←

This classic Alsatian dessert is a cross between bread pudding and *clafoutis*—and to my mind, better than both. Puffed and lightly sweet and fresh, it is best with ripe-from-the-tree Bing cherries. Canned or fresh Royal Annes are an excellent alternative, however. (Do not use canned tart pie cherries—they're way too puckery for this!) If you are using canned cherries, be sure to drain them well.

After baking there may still be a bit of juice at the bottom of the baking dish. If this bothers you (it will be an aesthetic objection rather than a gastronomic one), serve the dessert with a slotted spoon.

The *Bettelman* falls as quickly as a soufflé, so present it immediately. Leftovers, though fallen, are delicious when served the next day.

2 cups fresh Bing or Royal Anne cherries, pitted

4 tablespoons (½ stick; 60 g) unsalted butter, at room temperature

12 thin slices (⅜ inch; 1 cm) firm white bread, such as Pepperidge Farm sandwich bread

4 large eggs

¾ cup (150 g) sugar

3½ cups (875 ml) milk

2 tablespoons kirsch, or other fruit-based liqueur

Zest of 1 lemon, minced

½ teaspoon ground cinnamon

1. Place the cherries in an even layer in an 11 x 9-inch (28 x 23 cm) oval baking dish.

2. Spread the butter evenly over one side of each slice of bread. Cut the slices in half lengthwise, and arrange them, buttered side up, on top of the cherries, overlapping them in concentric ovals so they fit in a single layer.

3. In a large bowl, whisk together the eggs and sugar until foamy. Then whisk in the milk, kirsch, zest, and cinnamon. Pour the mixture over the bread slices, and press gently on the bread so it is thoroughly moistened. Set the dish aside for 2 hours. Press the bread down into the milk mixture occasionally so it remains moist.

4. Preheat the oven to 350°F (175°C).

5. Place the baking dish on a baking sheet (to catch any drips) and bake in the center of the oven until the *Bettelman* is puffed and a rich golden brown, about 1 hour and 5 minutes.

6. Remove from the oven and serve immediately.

6 to 8 servings

The Sugar of Intelligence

I am astounded at the amount of sugar children ingest in France. Snacks are always sweet, candies are offered at every turn, even water is sweetened with fruit- or herb-flavored sirops.

When I have refused to allow my son sugary treats (he is allergic to sugar), the reaction has been negative, at times hostile. One person was so disquieted by our regimen that she took me aside and said, "Mme. Loomis, have you never heard of le sucre d'intelligence? Your son needs it for his brain; he needs it to grow properly."

Her disquiet was so profound that I didn't counter. When I mentioned this episode to some friends, they told me that many years ago there had been a publicity campaign that had something to do with le sucre d'intelligence. I called the sugar manufacturers' union to hunt it down.

Indeed, in the 1960s a publicity campaign had extolled the healthful virtues of sugar. The advertisements they sent me featured an illustration of a person on the run and the following copy:

"Sugar, it's the shortest route to energy. Muscles, brain, and nerves need a rest from the stress put upon them, and not only does sugar wipe out fatigue but it feeds the nerve cells."

"Two for the flavor, one for health . . . instead of automatically using two sugar cubes, I consciously use three."

One ad depicted a pilot at the controls with a teacup in his hand: "A pilot . . . is aware of the energy he gets from that hot, sweet drink. Obviously, drinking a cup of tea with two sugar cubes isn't enough to safely land a Boeing. But, when you're driving planes all day it certainly is useful."

The ads explained everything. Now I understand why attempts to limit sugar intake are regarded with incredulity. And I stand in awe of the power of a publicity campaign that has never quit working, at least in the countryside.

Floating Island
Ile Flottante

→ • • • ←

Amore heartwarming combination of farm ingredients can't be found—golden-yolked eggs and fresh, rich milk. Add a little sugar, a few sugared almonds, and you get one of the best desserts ever created!

Usually this dessert is made with *pralines rosées*, bright red, sugar-coated almonds. They can be purchased at a bakery or *épicerie fine* (specialty shop), but the homemade kind here are far superior.

FOR THE PRALINE
¼ cup (35 g) whole almonds
   (unblanched)
¼ cup (50 g) sugar

FOR THE CREME ANGLAISE
3 cups (750 ml) milk
2 vanilla beans
6 large egg yolks
6 tablespoons sugar

FOR THE "ISLAND"
6 large egg whites
Pinch of sea salt
6 tablespoons sugar

1. Preheat the oven to 350°F (175°C). Lightly butter an 8-cup (2 l) soufflé dish or ovenproof bowl, and dust it with sugar. Lightly oil a baking sheet for the praline.

Place a fine-mesh sieve over a clean medium-size bowl for the crème anglaise.

2. To make the praline: Combine the nuts and the sugar in a small heavy saucepan over medium heat. Cook, shaking the pan occasionally, until the sugar begins to melt. Continue to stir as the sugar melts and begins to color. The sugar will crystallize and cling to the almonds; keep stirring. Then the sugar will quickly begin to melt, turn a dark color, and foam up, covering the almonds which will crackle and pop. If the sugar is coloring too quickly without entirely melting, remove the pan from the heat and continue to stir. Replace it over the heat if the sugar hasn't finished melting. When the sugar is completely melted, pour the mixture out onto the oiled baking sheet and let it cool. (From the time the sugar begins to melt to the pouring of the praline onto the baking sheet will take 5 to 7 minutes.)

3. Make the crème anglaise: Using the milk, vanilla beans, egg yolks, and sugar, prepare a custard according to the directions in "Making a Custard," on page 484, letting the

vanilla beans steep in the scalded milk for 15 minutes before proceeding.

4. After the custard is strained, return the vanilla beans to it and let the mixture cool, removing the vanilla beans just before serving.

5. When the praline is completely cool, grind it in a food processor until it is fine, like sand. Measure out ¼ cup (35 g) of the praline powder and set it aside. You will not need the rest of the praline powder for this recipe (see Note).

6. Make the "island": Using an electric mixer, beat the egg whites and the pinch of salt in a large bowl at medium speed until they are white and foamy. Increase the speed to high, and when the whites begin to firm up, slowly sprinkle the sugar over them, whisking until they become firm and shiny and hold stiff peaks. Slowly pour in the reserved ¼ cup (35 g) praline powder and whisk just until it is mixed into the meringue.

7. Turn the meringue into the prepared mold, lightly packing it in so there are no air spaces, and smoothing the top. Using your thumbnail, make a shallow indentation all the way around the top edge, plopping any meringue remaining on your thumb in the center. The ridge you created with your thumbnail will help the meringue rise evenly.

8. Set the mold in a larger baking pan with sides that are at least 2½ inches (6½ cm) high, and pour boiling water around it, nearly to the top of the baking pan. Place the pan carefully in the center of the oven and bake until the mixture is puffed and evenly golden, 20 minutes. To test if it is cooked through,

stick a sharp knife right down through the center; the knife should come out clean.

9. Cut down around the edges of the "island" with a sharp knife, and immediately invert a large, shallow serving bowl over the mold. Invert the mold and bowl and gently shake the "island" out into the bowl. Some of the caramel from the praline will have melted, making a drizzle of sauce on top.

10. To serve immediately, while the "island" is still puffed and hot, pour as much crème anglaise around it as the dish will hold, and serve the rest separately. Or you may let the "island" cool and chill it slightly in the refrigerator (for about 1 hour) before serving, if you like (refrigerate the crème anglaise as well). It loses some of its height, but will still be delicious.

4 to 6 servings (depending on how gluttonous the eaters are!)

NOTE: It is difficult to make praline powder with fewer almonds and sugar than called for in this recipe, which is why there is a surfeit of powder. Keep what is left in an airtight container, and sprinkle it on buttered toast or over ice cream, or add it to pancake or cake batter or cookie dough.

Making a Custard

1. Rinse out a medium-size saucepan with water, which will prevent milk from sticking to it after scalding. Add milk (plus cream or crème fraîche, and any flavoring, such as vanilla beans). Over medium heat, scald the mixture—heating it to just below a simmer, when it steams and tiny bubbles begin to form around the edges. Remove from the heat at once; steep any flavorings for as long as directed in an individual recipe.

2. Whisk or beat the egg yolks and sugar in a medium-size bowl until the mixture is pale yellow and falls from the whisk or beater in a thick ribbon. Pour the scalded milk (strained if necessary) into the yolk mixture very slowly about ¼ cup (60 ml) at a time, to avoid cooking the yolks, whisking all the while. When the mixture is blended, pour it back into the saucepan.

3. Have ready a fine-mesh sieve set over a clean bowl. Place the saucepan with the custard mixture over medium-low heat and cook, stirring constantly with a wooden spoon, until the custard begins to thicken. As you stir, move your spoon in a constant figure-eight pattern, which will keep the custard moving across the bottom of the pan, preventing it from getting too hot and curdling. If after 7 or 8 minutes the custard is not thickening, increase the heat slightly, continuing to stir. Once you feel a drag on the spoon near the bottom of the pan, and a finger drawn through the custard coating the back of the spoon leaves a distinct track, the custard is ready.

4. Remove the saucepan from the heat and immediately pour the custard through the sieve into the bowl. Let the custard cool at room temperature.

Eggs in the Snow
Oeufs à la Neige

There are several desserts in this book that are as typical of the French farm as chickens in the courtyard and a cow in the barn. *Oeufs à la neige* is one, and it's a dessert I've eaten on just about every farm I've ever visited. Sometimes it comes to the table with the gently floating eggs so perfectly egg-shaped they look sculpted. Most often, however, the eggs are free form and riotous, sweet white puffs that melt in the mouth.

This dessert is so uncomplicated and pure it can make even the most stern, uncommunicative person soften, for it speaks of childhood and the good life, of vacations on the farm and the *oeufs à la neige* made by Mamie, or Grandma.

I find myself making it regularly, for the farm eggs I get at the market are so flavorful and delicious that they practically beg to be turned into this simple, elemental dessert.

FOR THE CREME ANGLAISE
3 cups (750 ml) milk
2 vanilla beans
6 large egg yolks
6 tablespoons sugar

FOR THE "EGGS"
6 large egg whites
Pinch of sea salt
6 tablespoons Vanilla Sugar (page 521)

1. Make the crème anglaise: Using the milk, vanilla beans, egg yolks, and sugar, prepare a custard according to the directions in "Making a Custard," opposite, letting the vanilla beans steep in the scalded milk for 15 minutes before proceeding.

2. After the custard is strained, return the vanilla beans to it and let the mixture cool, removing the vanilla beans just before serving.

3. Make the "eggs": While the crème anglaise is cooling, whisk the egg whites and the pinch of salt in a large bowl until they are foamy. Continue whisking the whites until they begin to turn white, then slowly add the vanilla sugar, continuing to whisk until the whites hold soft peaks.

4. Fill a medium-size saucepan with water to a depth of at least 4 inches (10 cm); bring to a boil over medium-high heat. Reduce the heat so the water is simmering. Using a large spoon, scoop out some of the egg white and set it gently in the water to cook. Repeat until the "eggs" fill but don't crowd the pan. Poach until the egg whites turn slightly more white and appear more solid underneath, where they are in contact with the water, which will take about 3 minutes. Flip them over with the spoon and poach for another 3 minutes. Transfer the "eggs" to a plate covered with a cotton or linen tea towel, to drain. Repeat with any remaining egg white. (You can make the "eggs" up to 3 hours ahead of time. They do not need to be chilled.)

5. To serve the *oeufs à la neige*, remove the vanilla beans from the custard (see Note). Pour the custard into a wide shallow serving dish, and float as many "eggs" on top as will comfortably fit. Reserve any extra "eggs" for the inevitable requests for more.

Serves 6 to 8

N O T E : Rinse the vanilla beans and let them dry. Use them to make more vanilla sugar.

The Shepherd of the Pyrénées

François Poineau, a shepherd, lives at the end of a rutted road that snakes along a fold in the Pyrénées mountains. I approached it from the route between Larrau and Tarretts, near St.-Jean-Pied-de-Port, led on by a nicely etched sign that read "Ossau-Iraty," and an arrow pointing up the mountain.

"Ossau-Iraty" is the commercial name for *ardi gasna*, the sheep's-milk cheese made by Basque and Béarn shepherds, and signs posted along mountain roads indicate production sites.

I followed the road, avoiding craters and streams, hoping I wouldn't end up with my rental car on my head. It was much steeper and farther than I'd expected.

I was following a small truck, and when it stopped to discharge passengers, I stopped too. One of the disembarked passengers came up and knocked on my window. "Can you give me a lift up to my fields?" he asked cheerily.

As we drove, he pointed out the ridge between mountains I needed to go over to get to my destination, telling me not to get discouraged with the state of the road. "It's probably too much for a little car like this,

though," he said when he got out, waving goodbye. "Just don't go through the second stream you come to, because it's as deep as your car."

The second stream circuitously negotiated, I followed the road, which now had become a beaten path through a meadow. The Pyrénées stretched before me. Brilliant green, sculpted for the past 2,000 years by the constant grazing of sheep, horses, and cattle, they presented a spectacular tableau.

A hairpin turn and I'd reached Akdakotxi, François Poineau's *cayolar,* or cabin. He and his flock of 560 sheep were waiting.

He greeted me, then excused himself. "I've got to get them back to pasture," he said. "I won't be a moment." With that, he and his dog, Diego, leapt over the edge of the steep slope down to the pasture and into the midst of the flock. Running down the hill, M. Poineau balancing with a carved walking stick and Diego yapping and weaving in amongst the sheep, they went over a rise, leaving nothing but the tinkling of bells in their wake.

When M. Poineau came back, he turned to a small vat of fresh sheep's milk.

He put it on a burner in the corner of the *cayolar,* and just before the boiling point, he added rennet and a small amount of bacteria mixed with milk, and took it off the heat. We talked while we waited for the curd to form.

M. Poineau became a shepherd and cheesemaker through his objection to compulsory military service. In France, conscientious objectors must perform a civil service for two years, and he headed for the Pyrénées, where other CO's had gone before him. He worked for an elderly shepherd renowned for the quality of his cheese, and fell in love with the profession and the country.

"I learned a craft," he said, "and at the same time I had the impression I was helping someone. It was a wonderful experience. After working with that old man, I decided to make my mark in this profession through quality."

Once the milk was curdled, he cut the curds into small squares, which sat for a half an hour until all the whey rose to the surface. Then he slowly heated them again, stirring it with his hand to break up the curds into pieces no larger than a corn kernel, a long process.

"This is the secret to good cheese: slow heating so it naturally gives up the whey," he said.

I looked around the *cayolar* as M. Poineau worked. Humble, tiny but efficient, it was divided into kitchen and dining area, which was also the cheese "laboratory," a sleeping loft, and a good-size *cave,* for aging the cheese.

This is home for M. Poineau every year from May, when he leads his flock up the mountain, until October, when they head down to their winter home. He doesn't own the *cayolar,* but it is his as long as he leases the pasture on which it sits. He can improve it as he likes, but it will never be his. It belongs to the government, which will give it to the next shepherd when M. Poineau moves on or retires. But part of the shepherd's life is lack of belongings. "I own my sheep—nothing else," he said. "That's how I like it."

During summer, the sheep spend all day outside grazing on sweet mountain grasses and flowers. M. Poineau and Diego retrieve them at night and return them to pasture after the morning milking.

Summer life for the shepherd is reduced to its simplest elements. He milks and makes cheese twice daily until the sheep run dry toward the end of July. Then he watches his flock, tends his cheeses, which need turning and wiping on a regular basis, and

(continued)

works on his *cayolar*. The sheep begin to give milk again in the fall, and the cycle begins anew.

Life is more complicated for M. Poineau, however, for he is president of the Basque and Béarn sheep's-milk cheese union, as well as a member of the Confédération Paysanne, a union of French farmers committed to keeping working farmers on the land.

"When I joined this profession ten years ago, many people had left it, and the cheese was little known outside the Pays Basque," he said. "We've made an effort to publicize it, first by coming up with the name 'Ossau-Iraty' so it's easily identified. Now we're about to launch a television campaign."

Ossau-Iraty has an Appellation d'Origine Contrôlée, a quality label that limits its area of production to the Béarn and Basque areas of the Pyrénées. It can only be made with raw milk from sheep referred to as "Basco-Béarnaise," or *tête-rousse* or *tête-noir* ("red-heads" or "black-heads"). Certain fabrication and aging techniques must be respected.

The curds painstakingly broken into pieces, François stood and leaned over the vat. He put in both hands up to his elbows to gather all of them into a ball, an operation which took more than fifteen painstaking minutes. When he had finished, there wasn't a single kernel floating in the whey.

He cut the ball into four pieces, put each into a mold, and set it on a table fitted with weights. Until several years ago, shepherds pierced their cheeses with wooden sticks that looked like knitting needles so the whey would drain out.

The weights are not the only innovation he uses.

"The old man would shudder if he saw me cut my cheese like this," he said. "It isn't the old way. But I'm careful and I find there isn't a quality difference."

His cheeses rest overnight in the press, go into a brine for forty-eight hours, and then move onto a wooden shelf to age. M. Poineau will sell them after three to four months, though he prefers to wait five. But when someone knocks on his door, as a trio of backpackers did while I was there, he obliges them with a younger cheese if that is all he has.

"I sell two tons of cheese a year," he said, "seventy percent of it from right here."

He cut into a gorgeous golden round for me, so I could taste its rich, buttery, distinctive flavor. But first he took a bite. "Well, it's good, but it should really wait a day," he said. "You take home a cheese and cut into it the day before you want to serve it. When it waits a day to be eaten, its flavor is perfect."

In late afternoon I reluctantly left the *cayolar*, sent off with a firm handshake, a four-pound cheese, and one of M. Poineau's lamb sausages. "Come back again," he said with a smile. "And if you need more cheese, I can always make sure you get some."

Chocolate and Cheese Taluas
Taluas au Fromage et au Chocolat

❖ ∙∙∙ ❖

Taluas are large, yeasted pancakes that, when wrapped hot around cheese and dark chocolate and set by the fire (or placed in the oven) become an astonishingly delicious pastry. You have to try this dessert to believe it. Even the most skeptical of people have eaten it at my house and loved every bite. I will say no more! Try it.

*3 ounces (90 g) sheep's-milk cheese, or
  Gruyère, thinly sliced*
6 Basque Pancakes (recipe follows)
*3 ounces (90 g) best-quality bittersweet
  chocolate, such as Lindt, Caillebaut,
  or Tobler*

1. Preheat the oven to 350°F (175°C).
2. Place equal amounts of cheese on one half of each of the *taluas*. Top with equal amounts of chocolate. Fold the empty half of the *talua* over the filled half, and place on a baking sheet. Warm in the oven until the cheese and the chocolate are melted and the *talua* is hot through, about 5 minutes. Serve immediately.

6 servings

Basque Pancakes
Taluas au Blé

❖ ∙∙∙ ❖

I have never heard anyone wax more enthusiastic about a dish than the Basques I met who spoke of *taluas*. I think I know why. First, *taluas* taste good. They resemble a fat flour tortilla, and they're delicious when filled with whatever you like, but especially a freshly fried egg and a slice of sautéed ham or for dessert, chocolate and cheese.

Marie-Agnès Carricaburu, who lives just outside Esterençuby in the Pyrénées, is a *talua* fanatic. She has many brothers, sisters, cousins, aunts, and uncles, and several times a year they go up into the mountains to her father's *cayolar*, or shepherd's cabin, for a family gathering. There the women make *taluas* and everyone eats, drinks cider or the local grapey Irouléguy wine, and makes a night of it.

"I don't eat that much, but when we have *taluas* I eat two, and I still have room for dessert," says Marie-Agnès, her eyes shining at the thought.

And she saves room for good reason, for dessert *taluas* are something special.

ASTUCES . . . .

• *The amount of filling for* taluas *will vary depending on how many you are and how many pancakes you reserve for dessert. In our home, this recipe easily feeds ten, with enough* taluas *left over for dessert. (Either some people will have two desserts or there will be leftover* taluas, *which isn't a bad thing. They are delicious the next day, filled with whatever you like.) If making them for a meal, count on 1 slice of meat and 1 egg per person.*

• *To cook fried eggs for a crowd, heat a large baking pan in a 400°F (205°C) oven. When it is hot, brush it with olive oil, and break 6 to 8 eggs into it. Return it to the oven and bake until the eggs are set, 7 to 10 minutes. Season the eggs after removing them from the oven.*

. . . .

8¼ cups (1 kg, 110 g) unbleached
    all-purpose flour
½ teaspoon sea salt
2½ cups (625 ml) lukewarm water
1 scant tablespoon (1 package) active dry
    yeast
1½ cups (375 ml) bland vegetable oil,
    such as safflower, for frying

1. Place the flour and salt in a large bowl or on a clean, smooth work surface. Make a well in the middle and add ½ cup (125 ml) of the lukewarm water. Mix the yeast into the water, then add the remaining 2 cups (500 ml) lukewarm water. Slowly incorporate the flour, bit by bit, until all the flour is blended into the water.

2. Remove the dough to a lightly floured work surface and knead it until it is smooth and no longer sticks to your hands, 10 to 15 minutes by hand, about 5 minutes by machine.

3. Place the dough in the bowl, cover with a tea towel, and let rise in a warm spot (68° to 70°F; 20° to 21°C) until it has doubled in bulk, about 1 hour. Punch down the dough and divide it into 34 portions, rolling them into balls.

4. Heat the oil in a large heavy skillet until it is hot but not smoking. (To test the oil, sprinkle tiny drops of water into it. They should sizzle merrily.)

5. On a lightly floured surface, roll out a ball of dough to as thin a circle as you possibly can. Dust the excess flour from the dough and transfer it to the hot oil, carefully slipping it in. The dough will immediately

bubble and crackle. Press it gently into the oil and cook until it is ivory colored and bubbled on both sides, about 30 seconds per side. The *talua* should not get too crisp (if it does, the oil is too hot, so reduce the temperature just slightly). It should be ivory in color, and pliable. Transfer the *talua* to a plate covered with plain brown paper or paper towels, and continue with the remaining dough. As they are made, stack the *taluas* one on top of the other.

About 34 pancakes

Goat Cheese in Red Wine
Fromage de Chèvre au Vin Rouge

This recipe is very specific to Provence, where goat cheese was the only kind the region knew in ancient times—and where it is still the regional favorite.

Goat cheese made in Provence has a special flavor, a sweet tang that comes from the wild herbs that provide forage for the goats on the rocky hillsides.

I encountered this dish at Les Remparts, a restaurant in the tiny hilltop town of Venasque, where chef Pascale Engasser offers a typical Provençal menu. This is its star dessert.

"Everyone here makes this," he said. "I adapted it to my taste, but it is essentially the same wherever you eat it, with only slight variations."

In the old days, each farm had its patch of vines and its goats, its beehives. That this is one result of the combined fruits of their production is only logical.

The candied lemon zest is an option, and a very good one.

> 1 bottle (750 ml) hearty red wine,
>   such as a Côtes du Rhône or
>   Côtes du Ventoux
> 6 tablespoons sugar
> 3 tablespoons mild honey,
>   such as spring wildflower
> 3 fresh plain, soft goat cheeses
>   (each 6 to 8 ounces; 180 to 250 g)
> *Tiny mint leaves, for garnish*
> *Candied Lemon Zest (page 408),*
>   *for garnish (optional)*

1. Before starting this step, be sure to read the safety precautions in "Flambéeing," page 242. Heat the wine in a medium-size heavy saucepan over medium-high heat until it boils. Then reduce the heat and simmer just until it has reduced slightly, about 5 minutes. Remove the pan from the heat. Carefully flame the wine (to remove any excess alcohol) by passing a long match over its surface. The flames will flare somewhat, then die down almost immediately. Add the sugar and the honey, and stir with a wooden spoon until dissolved. (You may make the recipe up to this point several days in advance, and refrigerate it.)

2. Cut the goat cheeses in half horizontally, and place one half in each of six shallow dessert bowls. Return the wine mixture to a boil, remove it from the heat, and carefully ladle the wine around the cheeses. Serve immediately, garnished with the mint, and the candied lemon zest, if desired.

6 servings

Fresh Cheese and Sugar
Fromage Blanc au Sucre

→ • • • ←

Fromage blanc au sucre is dear to every French person, and nowhere is it better than on the farm. It is generally served as part of the cheese course, which is how I serve it as well. A simpler version is just *fromage blanc* and sugar, a favorite after-school snack.

2 cups (500 ml) Fromage Blanc
   (page 93)
1 cup (250 ml) Crème Fraîche (page 520),
   or heavy (or whipping) cream
½ cup (100 g) Vanilla Sugar (page 521)

Evenly divide the *fromage blanc* among four dessert dishes. Serve the cream and the sugar separately alongside.

4 servings

Coffee Ice Cream on Spice Bread

Glace au Café sur Pain d'Épices

>•••<

There I was one day, with a gorgeous, golden loaf of *pain d'épices* sitting before me. I made myself some coffee, sliced some *pain d'épices*, and nibbled and drank a fifteen-minute respite away. The combination was sublime, and it led, most naturally, to this dessert. The spices and the coffee go perfectly together.

Do use finely ground, freshly roasted coffee, either with or without caffeine.

ASTUCE . . . .

• *Make the base for the coffee ice cream the night before so it can cool and the flavor can ripen; then freeze it right before you plan to serve it.*

. . . .

FOR THE ICE CREAM
2 cups (500 ml) milk
2 cups (500 ml) heavy (or whipping) cream
3 tablespoons very finely ground coffee
1 vanilla bean
4 large egg yolks
½ cup (100 g) Vanilla Sugar (page 521)

TO ASSEMBLE THE DESSERT
10 very thin (less than ¼ inch; ½ cm) slices Babette's Spice Bread (page 388), cut in half

1. Make the ice cream: Using all the ingredients, prepare a custard according to the directions in "Making a Custard," page 484, letting the coffee and vanilla bean steep in the scalded milk mixture for 1 hour before proceeding (see Note).

2. After beating the egg yolks and sugar, strain the milk mixture through a cheese-cloth-lined fine-mesh sieve and return it to the washed-out saucepan; reheat over medium heat just until steaming. Remove from the heat and add to the yolk mixture as directed.

3. After cooling the custard, refrigerate, covered, overnight to develop the flavors.

4. The following day, freeze the custard in an ice-cream maker according to the manufacturer's instructions.

5. Assemble the dessert: Fan three half-pieces of the bread out on each of six dessert plates. Cut each remaining half piece into three triangles, each with a very fine point.

6. Place a scoop of ice cream on the pieces of the bread, toward the bottom of the fan. Stick two bread triangles into the ice cream and serve immediately.

6 servings

N O T E : Once you're finished using the vanilla bean, rinse it off and let it dry. Use it to make more vanilla sugar.

Calvados Ice Cream with Apple Calvados Compote

Compote de Pommes à la Glace au Calvados

Normandy is the land of apples and cream, and here they are combined to take advantage of both. Apple compote is commonly served for dessert in Normandy, particularly from September to Christmas, when the apples are crisp and fresh. It can be eaten by itself, but it is also delicious, warm from the stove, with this fresh ice cream.

FOR THE ICE CREAM
¼ cup (60 ml) Calvados
⅔ cup (135 g) sugar plus 1 tablespoon
2 cups (500 ml) whole milk
1½ cups (375 ml) heavy (or whipping) cream
6 egg yolks
¼ teaspoon almond extract

FOR THE COMPOTE
1 tablespoon unsalted butter
2 pounds (1 kg) tart apples, such as
    Macoun, Winesap, or Northern Spy,
    peeled, cored, and cut into 1-inch
    (2½ cm) pieces
½ cup (100 g) sugar
¼ cup (60 ml) Calvados
½ teaspoon vanilla extract

Additional Calvados, for topping
    (optional)

1. Prepare the Calvados for the ice cream: Stir the 1 tablespoon sugar into the Calvados, cover, and let stand overnight.

2. The next day, make the ice cream: Using the milk, cream, egg yolks, and ⅔ cup sugar, prepare a custard according to the directions in "Making a Custard," on page 484.

3. After cooling the custard, stir in the Calvados mixture and the almond extract; then refrigerate, covered, until it is well chilled, 2 to 3 hours.

4. Freeze the custard in an ice-cream maker according to the manufacturer's instructions.

5. Make the compote: Melt the butter in a medium-size heavy skillet over medium-high heat. Add the apples and sugar, and cook, stirring frequently, until the apples have caramelized slightly, about 15 minutes. Reduce the heat to medium-low, add the Calvados and vanilla extract, and cook until almost all the liquid has been absorbed, 7 to 8 minutes.

6. Place two small scoops of ice cream in each of six shallow dessert bowls, surround them with the compote, and drizzle with additional Calvados if you like. Serve the dessert immediately.

6 servings

The Seven Rounds of Calvados

→•←

In the past, when a Norman farmer entertained "correctly," he followed a well-established ritual at the end of the meal. Reserved for the men at table, it involved seven rounds of Calvados, which left the male company in a rich, apple-scented fog (and the women with a pleasant sense of liberty).

Round 1. Le café calva (Calvados poured into the coffee)
Round 2. La rincette (the little nip)
Round 3. La sur-rincette (another little nip)
Round 4. Le Gloria (yet another)
Round 5. L'Alléluia (and another)
Round 6. Le coup de pied au cul (the kick in the ass)
Round 7. Le coup de l'étrier (the kick in the stirrup—in other words, the kick out the door and onto the horse)

The Calvados King

=

Jacques Serre stands amidst his apple trees in the Risle River valley, in the heart of Normandy. His eyes, set deep in his wind-burned face, sparkle against the backdrop of tree limbs bowed under the weight of fruit. He stretches his arms wide and says with satisfaction, "These trees—look what they've done this year."

M. Serre, known locally for his Calvados (apple brandy), hard cider, and a local apéritif called *pommeau* (apple juice mixed with Calvados), planted each of his 1,100 trees by hand thirteen years ago. He chose sixteen different varieties, most of them old and traditional with names like Binet Rouge, La Marie Mesnard, and Clos Renault. A blend of sweet and acid, they give a dry, fruity cider that rocks gently on the palate, a warm, rich Calvados that slides smoothly over the tongue, a sweet, velvety *pommeau.*

M. Serre learned Calvados distilling early. He and his father traveled the region with a wood-fired still, stopping in village squares to distill Calvados for local farmers. "I learned to love cider early, too," he says, laughing. "A traditional children's drink was cider mixed with water, and that's what I always drank at mealtime." He's completely passionate about apples, and every day of his life eats at least six.

Using the same still—which was built in 1937 and looks like a quaint home boiler—M. Serre and his son, Frank, follow the same circuit twice a year. "We make appointments with villagers and distill their cider as they bring it," he says. "Each farmer has his own uniquely flavored cider. We do small batches and carefully clean the still each time." It takes about an hour and a half to distill ten liters (about 2½ gallons) of alcohol, the amount an apple grower can legally make for his own use without having to pay taxes on it.

M. Serre has worked with newer gas- and oil-powered stills, but he much prefers a wood fire. "The heat is soft and gentle, so all the aroma and flavor of the apples stays with the Calvados," he says. He uses the same still for his own Calvados, and it's the wood fire, along with his proven techniques, that makes it among the best in Normandy.

The apple harvest crests at the end of September, and literally tons of apples are stored for two months in large wooden crates under cover, so they can fully ripen. "The old guys always stored their apples in the attic," says M. Serre. "It's a secret of the ancestors, and I'm doing the same thing, only I don't have to carry them upstairs."

Indoor storage makes a difference because the apples can develop off-flavors if they are exposed to the elements. "The only flavor I get in the apples is their own perfume," M. Serre observes.

His state-of-the-art apple press, which is in direct contrast to his clanking still, hums nonstop during the month of November. A percentage of the juice undergoes limited fermentation before being bottled as cider, and a small portion is blended with Calvados for *pommeau.*

The rest is for Calvados, more familiarly called *calva* in Normandy. It goes into wooden barrels to ferment into pure alcohol. The fermentation takes about six months—by April it is ready for the still.

M. Serre can distill about a hundred gallons an hour. As the fermented juice heats, the steam condenses and the crystal-clear condensation is raw alcohol, which needs slow aging. M. Serre, pours it into oak barrels which he stores in a small cellar, or *cave,* built into a hillside on his farm.

Entering the *cave* is like walking into a Calvados aromatherapy treatment, for the air is permeated with a sharp apple aroma. As the Calvados ages, a process that takes seven to ten years, some of the alcohol evaporates, the flavor ripens, it turns a buttery golden color.

The Calvados doesn't just make itself, however. M. Serre frequently tastes and blends, nursing it to its optimum flavor. Most of the year he willingly dedicates up to fifteen hours a day, seven days a week, to his work. During winter, which would normally be considered his vacation, his favorite thing to do is to walk in his orchard. "Why would I want to do anything else?" he says.

I understand, as I stand in the cellar sipping ten-year-old Calvados. Nothing but passion, dedication to time-honored methods, and sheer will to make the best could give such a result.

Anise Ice Cream
Glace à l'Anis Vert

→…←

Yum. Anise has a wonderfully clean, fresh flavor that makes me think of the warm sun and richness of Provence. I was eating *pompe à l'huile*, Traditional Provençal Christmas Bread (see Index), one day and thought how good a scoop of anise ice cream would be with it. I came up with this recipe, made another batch of *pompe*, and a new tradition was created in our home.

Around Christmastime, when *pompe* is a regular offering for either dessert or breakfast, I make this ice cream often. No, we don't eat it for breakfast, when coffee or tea makes an ideal companion, but it's always there for dessert, along with *pompe*.

If you like the sweet, pungent flavor of anise, you'll want to serve this often. Try it along with Butter Cookies from Normandy or even Walnut Butter Cookies (see Index).

2 tablespoons anise seeds
3 cups (750 ml) whole milk
½ cup (125 ml) Crème Fraîche (page 520),
    or heavy (or whipping) cream
4 large egg yolks
½ cup (100 g) sugar

1. Grind the anise seeds to a coarse powder either in a hand mill or in a spice grinder.

2. Using the remaining ingredients, prepare a custard according to the directions in "Making a Custard," page 484. Add the ground anise seeds to the milk and crème fraîche before scalding, then let them steep in the scalded mixture for 10 minutes; strain out the seeds before proceeding.

3. After cooling the custard, refrigerate it, covered, until well chilled, 2 to 3 hours.

4. Whisk the mixture and freeze it in an ice-cream maker according to the manufacturer's instructions.

4 to 6 servings

Peach Ice Cream
Glace à la Pêche

❖ • • • ❖

This tastes the way peach ice cream should: rich, creamy, full of the essence of peach flavor. In France I use either white-fleshed peaches, which have a haunting sweetness, fine-textured flesh, and prodigious amounts of juice; yellow peaches, which are full and perfumed; or seductive *pêches de vignes,* an old-fashioned smallish, but intensely flavored peach that arrives in the market in August. Use whatever peaches in your area have the most perfume and flavor.

Serve this freshly made, with sliced fresh peaches on top.

A S T U C E . . . .

• *Cutting a vanilla bean down its length allows the tiny black seeds to emerge and flavor the milk.*

. . . .

FOR THE CUSTARD
2 cups (500 ml) whole milk (see Note)
1 cup (250 ml) Crème Fraîche (page 520), or heavy (or whipping) cream (see Note)
1 vanilla bean, split down its length
4 large egg yolks
½ cup (100 g) sugar

1 pound (500 g) ripe, fragrant peaches, peeled and pitted
¼ teaspoon freshly grated nutmeg

1. Using all the custard ingredients, prepare the custard according to the directions in "Making a Custard," page 484, letting the vanilla bean steep in the scalded milk mixture for 15 minutes before proceeding.

2. After cooling the custard, refrigerate it, covered, until it is well chilled, 2 to 3 hours.

3. Just before you plan to make the ice cream, purée the peaches in a food processor. Add the purée and the nutmeg to the custard, and whisk until blended. Then freeze in an ice-cream maker according to the manufacturer's instructions.

6 to 8 servings

N O T E : If you prefer a richer ice cream, increase the amount of crème fraîche, and decrease the amount of milk.

Rhubarb Ice Cream with Strawberry-Rhubarb Compote

Glace à la Rhubarbe et à la Compote de Rhubarbe et de Fraises

>···←

If you love the tang of rhubarb and the custardy richness of ice cream, you'll swoon over this. Inspired by the lush green and red rhubarbs that brighten up the market come May and June, it is cool, refreshing, singular.

The compote that accompanies it is purposely tangy as well. Add more sugar if you like, to balance the ice cream.

FOR THE ICE CREAM
3 cups (750 ml) whole milk
½ cup (125 ml) Crème Fraîche (page 520),
*   or heavy (or whipping) cream*
4 large egg yolks
½ cup (100 g) sugar
1 pound (500 g) rhubarb stalks, trimmed

FOR THE STRAWBERRY-RHUBARB COMPOTE
14 ounces (420 g) rhubarb stalks,
*   trimmed, peeled, and diced*
1 tablespoon water
¼ cup (50 g) Vanilla Sugar (page 521)
6 ounces (180 g) ripe strawberries,
*   hulled*
Copper fennel fronds, for garnish
*   (optional)*

1. Make the ice cream: Using the milk, crème fraîche, egg yolks, and sugar, prepare a custard according to the directions in "Making a Custard," on page 484.

2. After cooling the custard, refrigerate it, covered, until it is well chilled, 2 to 3 hours.

3. Cut the rhubarb in large chunks, place them in a food processor, and process until they make a chunky mixture—not quite a purée, but as close as you can get to that. Moisten a cotton tea towel, and place it in a bowl with the edges hanging over the sides. Transfer the rhubarb to the bowl, and bring the ends of the towel up and around it. Squeeze the rhubarb to extract 1 cup (250 ml) of juice. Discard the rhubarb.

4. Remove the custard from the refrigerator and whisk in the rhubarb juice. Freeze the mixture in an ice-cream maker according to the manufacturer's instructions.

5. While the ice cream is freezing, pre-

pare the compote: Place the diced rhubarb, the water, and the vanilla sugar in a medium-size heavy saucepan over medium-high heat. Cover and bring to a boil. Reduce the heat to medium so the rhubarb is cooking gently but consistently, and cook until it is completely tender, stirring once or twice, 10 to 15 minutes. Remove from the heat.

6. Cut the strawberries lengthwise into thin (⅛ inch; ¼ cm) slices, and add them to the rhubarb. Shake the pan to distribute them, and let the sauce cool to lukewarm.

7. To serve, divide the ice cream among six bowls. Spoon the compote around the ice cream, and garnish with the fennel fronds if desired.

6 servings

Walnut Ice Cream with Caramel Sauce

Glace aux Noix, Sauce Caramel

>•••←

Inspired by a farm dessert from the Dordogne, where walnut trees grow wherever there is soil to support them, this ice cream is rich, nutty, and satisfying. It is simple to make, and the addition of a caramel sauce enhances the flavor of the lightly toasted walnuts.

A S T U C E . . . .

• *Making caramel sauce is a snap, but you must watch it very carefully once the sugar begins to caramelize. If it is caramelizing too fast around the edges, swirl it around in the pan (avoid stirring it, which can cause lumps) and reduce the heat, then work on and off the heat. When you are prepared to whisk in the hot water, you might want to wrap your whisking hand in a cotton tea towel to protect it from any hot caramel that hops out of the pan.*

. . . .

FOR THE ICE CREAM

1 cup (120 g) walnut pieces
½ cup (100 g) Vanilla Sugar (page 521)
3 cups (750 ml) whole milk
½ cup (125 ml) Crème Fraîche (page 520),
   or heavy (or whipping) cream
4 large egg yolks

FOR THE CARAMEL SAUCE

1 cup (200 g) sugar
½ cup (125 ml) hot water

1. Preheat the oven to 325°F (165°C).

2. Toast the walnuts: Place the nuts in a single layer in an ovenproof baking dish and toast them in the oven until they are pale golden, about 10 minutes. Remove from the oven and let cool.

3. Place the cooled walnuts in a food processor with 2 tablespoons of the sugar, and process until they are finely ground. Set them aside.

4. Using the remaining ice cream ingredients, prepare a custard according to the directions in "Making a Custard," page 484.

5. After cooling the custard, refrigerate it, covered, until it is well chilled, 2 to 3 hours.

6. Whisk the walnuts into the custard mixture, and then freeze in an ice-cream maker according to the manufacturer's instructions.

7. Once the ice cream is frozen, make the caramel sauce: Place the sugar in a small heavy saucepan over medium-high heat. Shake the pan occasionally to be sure the sugar isn't burning on the bottom, and watch the sugar carefully, shaking and swirling it often so it caramelizes evenly. This will take from 8 to 12 minutes, depending on the depth of caramel flavor and color you want. If it is turning too dark too quickly, work on and off the heat or reduce the heat slightly. (I like a dark, slightly bitter caramel for this sauce, but you may prefer blond caramel.) Watch it, and remove it from the heat once the sugar is completely dissolved and is the color you prefer. Slowly whisk in the hot water, being *very* careful not to add too much too fast, because the caramel will sputter, boil, and behave ominously. Continue whisking until the water is completely incorporated into the caramel.

8. To serve, scoop or spoon the ice cream into shallow dessert bowls or plates. Drizzle a generous amount of caramel sauce over the ice cream, and pass the remaining sauce separately.

6 to 8 servings

LES BASES
The Basics

What makes a soup or sauce so special, a tart shell so crisp, a pizza crust so tender? The basic recipes most farm cooks have in one place and one place only: their heads.

I gleaned the recipes in this chapter from that source, working alongside those farm cooks as they gave me proportions, told me *astuces*, made me touch and taste until I'd gotten each recipe firmly in my mind, and on my palate.

Here you will find the most basic, and the most important, of French farm recipes. Use them, learn them—they will serve you often and well.

Chicken Stock

Fond de Volaille

>···<

Every farm cook has her own recipe for chicken stock. This is the one I always have on hand, the one I make the most frequently. It's rich in flavor yet light and pure. You can adjust the sweetness of it by varying the amount of carrots. Some don't like even a hint of sweetness, and if you're of that opinion, leave out the carrots entirely.

Taste the meat of the chicken when you strain the stock. If you used a good, fresh chicken, it will have flavor left in it and will be ideal to use in soup (see Index for Pascale's Endive Soup) or even on a sandwich.

ASTUCES . . . .

• *Browning onions to near blackness on their cut side gives a rich, almost caramel-like depth to the stock. If you have a gas stove, pierce the uncut side of the onion with a fork and hold the cut side over the flame until the onion turns black. Or if you're more relaxed about these things, balance the onion on the burner and leave it until it turns nearly black, which will only take a minute or so. If you don't have a gas flame, brown the onion under the broiler, placing it as close as you can to the heat. You don't want the onion to cook, you just want it to sear on the surface.*

• *Note that there is no salt in this recipe. Chicken stock should be full-flavored but neutral when it comes to salt, for you may end up reducing the stock further, which would concentrate the salt and negatively affect the flavor.*

. . . .

1 medium onion, cut in half

2 whole cloves

1 chicken (3½ to 4 pounds; 1¾ to 2 kg)

1 medium carrot, trimmed and cut in half lengthwise, then in ¼-inch (½ cm) half-rounds

2 leeks, trimmed 2 inches (5 cm) above the white part, well rinsed and cut into ½-inch (1¼ cm) rounds

1 bouquet garni (5 parsley stems, 3 imported bay leaves, 2 green leek leaves, 12 sprigs fresh thyme, tied in cheesecloth)

2 cloves garlic, peeled

10 black peppercorns

10 cups (2½ l) water

1. Brown the cut sides of the onion over a gas flame or under the broiler until they are a dark, dark brown color, almost black (see Astuce).

2. Stick 1 clove in the uncut side of each onion half, making a little slit in the onion

first if necessary, so the clove will fit in easily.

3. Place all the ingredients in a large heavy stockpot and bring to a boil over high heat. Reduce the heat to medium so the stock is boiling gently but steadily, and cook for 2½ to 3 hours. Leave the stockpot just partially uncovered so the liquid doesn't evaporate.

4. Strain the stock (reserve the chicken for another use, if you like) and discard the vegetables. Allow the stock to cool, and then refrigerate it. The following day, remove the layer of fat on top of the stock and discard it.

About 6 cups (1½ l)

Duck Stock
Fond de Canard

Make this stock with any available duck parts or bones plus the gizzard and the heart. Keep it on hand for cooking vegetables, soups, and sauces. It will keep for a week in the refrigerator or for several months in the freezer.

If you add salt to the stock, just add a touch, as it will concentrate while the stock cooks.

Wings, backs, breastbone, neck and
giblets from one 3½- to 5-pound
(1¾ to 2½ kg) duck
1 large onion, peeled and cut into eighths
1 whole clove
1 bouquet garni (6 parsley stems,
2 imported bay leaves, 6 sprigs fresh
thyme, tied in cheesecloth)
1 large carrot, peeled, trimmed, and cut
into ½-inch (1¼ cm) rounds
6 black peppercorns
6 cups (1½ l) water, or more if needed
Sea salt (optional)

1. Place the duck parts and giblets in a large heavy saucepan. Pierce one section of the onion with the clove. Add the onion, bouquet garni, carrot, and peppercorns to the saucepan. Then cover with the water and bring to a boil over high heat. Reduce the heat to medium and simmer, skimming occasionally, for 45 minutes (add more water if necessary to keep it at the same level). Season to taste with salt if desired. Remove from the heat and let cool.

2. Strain the stock, discarding the bones and vegetables. Refrigerate. Skim off any fat before using.

About 4 cups (1 l)

Les Bases • The Basics

Beef Stock

Fond de Boeuf

→ ••• ←

I always have a reserve of beef stock in the freezer for enriching a stew, making a sauce, creating a soup. I think of it as money in the bank, gastronomic security.

The secrets to a good, rich stock are a mix of marrow and regular bones, long slow cooking, and keeping the water level just above the bones and vegetables but no higher. Browning the bones and vegetables gives the stock an edge, a depth.

A note about sweetness: The more onions and carrots you add, the sweeter the stock will be. If you prefer a stock that is not sweet, add a minimum of carrots and onions—instead, increase the herbs, celery, and fennel (which will give its own distinct flavor)—and make up the weight difference with more bones.

ASTUCE . . . .

• *Freeze some of the stock in ice cube trays, and then store the cubes in a plastic bag. They'll be handy to add at the last minute to a soup or a sauce.*

. . . .

4 pounds (2 kg) beef or veal bones, cut into 2-inch (5 cm) lengths (ideally a mix of marrow and other bones; see Note)

3 large onions, peeled and cut in half

4 medium carrots, peeled and cut into chunks

10 ounces (300 g) celery root, peeled and cut into chunks

4 ribs celery, trimmed and cut into chunks

1 fennel bulb, trimmed and cut into quarters

4½ to 5½ quarts (4½ to 5½ l) water

1 large bouquet garni (5 parsley stems, 3 imported bay leaves, 2 green leek leaves, 12 sprigs fresh thyme, tied in cheesecloth)

20 black peppercorns

5 cloves garlic, peeled

1. Preheat the oven to 450°F (230°C).

2. Place the bones in an ovenproof dish large enough to hold them in a single layer. Lightly oil a baking dish that is large enough to hold the vegetables in a single layer, and place them in it.

3. Place the dish of bones in the center of the oven, and roast for 15 minutes. Then add the dish of vegetables to the oven. Roast until the vegetables and the bones are browned, and the bones have given up most of their fat, about 45 minutes more.

4. Place the bones (leaving the fat behind) in a large stockpot. Add 2 cups (500 ml) of the water to the vegetables to help disengage them from the dish, and scrape up any browned bits. Add the vegetables and any juices to the stockpot. Add the bouquet garni, peppercorns, garlic, and enough water to cover the bones and vegetables (at least 4 quarts, possibly as many as 5).

5. Bring to a boil over high heat, and skim any impurities that foam to the surface. Reduce the heat and simmer, partially covered, until the liquid looks rich and brown, 4 to 5 hours. You may want to taste the vegetables and look closely at the bones. If the vegetables have no flavor, they will contribute nothing more to the stock. If the bones look as though they've given their all, then it's probably time to stop the cooking. However, it won't hurt the stock to continue cooking all day long, and you can even add more vegetables or bones as it cooks—all will contribute to its richness. If the liquid level drops below the bones, add water to keep them covered.

6. Let the stock cool slightly and then strain it. Discard the bones and vegetables and taste the stock. If it isn't quite as intensely flavored as you'd like, return it to the stockpot to cook further, reducing it and concentrating its flavor.

7. Let the stock cool completely, and then store it in the refrigerator overnight. The next day, remove and discard the layer of fat that has formed on the surface, and either use the stock or freeze it for future use.

About 6 cups (1½ l)

NOTE: For richer stock, add any beef scraps or bones you may have. If you get into the habit of making stock, save and freeze bones until you have a good quantity, then turn them into stock.

Court Bouillon

➤•••❮

A court bouillon is the ideal vehicle for poaching fish. There are as many different recipes for it as there are fish in the sea, but I like this one because it is highly aromatic and almost sweet with the flavor of fennel. It lends a fullness of flavor, an added dimension, to fish and shellfish.

ASTUCE . . . .

• *Make this broth when fennel is in season and freeze it for future use. Freeze it in carefully measured quantities, and even freeze some in ice cube trays so that you can have a touch to add to a sauce or soup.*

. . . .

1 medium onion, peeled and thinly
   sliced
2 imported bay leaves
10 black peppercorns
5 sprigs fresh thyme, or ¼ teaspoon dried
   leaves
1 fennel bulb (about 1 pound; 500 g),
   trimmed and cut into thin slices
2 cloves garlic, unpeeled
2 cups (500 ml) dry white wine, such
   as a Sauvignon Blanc or an Aligoté
Zest of 1 orange, in wide strips
6 cups (1½ l) water
1 teaspoon sea salt, or to taste

Place all the ingredients in a large heavy saucepan, cover, and bring to a boil over high heat. Reduce the heat to medium and simmer for 15 minutes. Remove from the heat and let cool. Strain, and refrigerate or freeze.

About 6 cups (1½ l)

Herb Broth
Bouillon d'Aromates

→ • • • ←

It's nice to have an alternative to chicken stock for those recipes that need just a light breath of flavor. I use this herb broth, which can also be the base of a soup (see Index for Herb and Pasta Soup). It is ready to use in 15 minutes, and the light herbal flavor is delicious.

You can also make this into a soup by pouring it over a piece of toasted bread that's been rubbed with garlic. Use it as a tonic, as well, if you're under the weather. If your herbs are seasonal, make a quantity of the broth when they're in season to freeze for later use.

20 sprigs fresh thyme, or 1 teaspoon dried
    leaves
1 sprig fresh sage (10 leaves), or
    2 teaspoons crumbled dried
2 imported bay leaves
4 cloves garlic, unpeeled
½ teaspoon sea salt
6 cups (1½ l) water

1. Place the herbs, garlic, salt, and water in a large heavy saucepan over medium-high heat. Cover and bring to a boil. Reduce the heat and simmer for 15 minutes.

2. Strain the broth and use immediately or freeze for future use.

About 5 cups (1¼ l)

Homemaker's Pastry
Pâte de Ménagère

❖•••❖

*P*âte brisée, French short-crust pastry, is a funny creature—it can be light and buttery or as hard as cardboard. It is not a pastry with a high butter-to-flour ratio, so finding the secret to lightness is not obvious at first. However, thanks to the advice of my friend Nadine Devisme, I did discover how to make perfect *pâte brisée*.

I was describing a certain difficulty I had with it and she said, without skipping a beat, "You need to add more water." Now, I learned to make pie pastry at my grandmother's elbow. And I learned to make *pâte brisée* years ago at cooking school in Paris.

Both schools taught me that water was anathema to flaky, tender pastry.

But I did as Nadine suggested, got excellent results, and never looked back.

This recipe comes from Mme. Odile

Plassart, who was raised on a farm, cooks as naturally as most of us breathe, and makes each meal a celebration of what is best and seasonal. One of her specialties is fruit tarts, and her daughter, Annie Grodent, who is a friend of ours, kept telling me about her mother's pastry.

One day she invited me to have lunch at her parents' home. We had a meal that went on for hours and consisted of all that was best and freshest from the market. I finally got the coveted recipe, and once I read it, I knew it would be a success. I tried it, using the new information I'd gotten from Nadine, and there it was, perfect *pâte brisée*—or, as I prefer to call it here, *pâte de ménagère*.

Here the pastry is treated like puff pastry and folded to develop a multitude of layers—"the way French housewives do it," as Mme. Plassart said.

You may fold it or not. Folding substantially increases its flakiness because as it cooks, the butter creates bubbles between the layers of flour. If you're short on time, however, you can omit the folding and you'll still be very satisfied.

1½ cups (205 g) unbleached all-purpose flour
¼ teaspoon sea salt
7 tablespoons (105 g) unsalted butter, chilled and cut into 7 pieces
5 to 6 tablespoons ice water

1. Place the flour and the salt in a food processor and process once to mix. Add the butter and process until the mixture resembles coarse meal, pulsing five to eight times. Add the 5 tablespoons ice water and pulse just until the pastry begins to hold together, not more than nine to ten times. Add the remaining 1 tablespoon water if the pastry seems dry.

2. Transfer the pastry from the food processor to your work surface and form it into a flat round. Let it rest on a work surface, covered with a tea towel, for at least 30 minutes and as long as 1 hour. The pastry is now ready to be used (see step 4). For flakier pastry, however, proceed with step 3.

3. Lightly dust the work surface with flour. Roll out the pastry to form an 8 x 4-inch (20 x 10 cm) rectangle, and fold it from one short end into thirds, as for a business letter. Turn the pastry so the fold is to the left, like a book, and repeat the rolling out and folding. Let the pastry sit, covered, at room temperature for 15 minutes. Repeat the rolling out and folding. Let it rest another 15 minutes. Repeat the rolling out and folding once more, and then let the pastry sit at room temperature for 30 minutes before rolling it out to fill a tart pan (see Note). Dust the work surface with more flour as needed.

4. If an individual recipe calls for a pre-baked tart shell, follow the directions in "Prebaking a Tart Shell" (this page) for rolling out and baking.

Pastry for one 10½-inch (26½ cm) tart

N O T E : Be sure to let pastry dough rest before you roll it out the final time. French farmwives let it sit at room temperature for 1 hour.

Prebaking a Tart Shell

→•←

1. Roll out the pastry on a lightly floured work surface to form an 11½-inch (29 cm) round, to fit a 10½-inch (26½ cm) tart pan with removable bottom.

2. Transfer the pastry to the pan, fitting it against the bottom and sides. Refrigerate the tart shell for 1 hour.

3. Preheat the oven to 425°F (220°C).

4. Remove the tart shell from the refrigerator. Prick it all over with the tines of a fork, and line it with aluminum foil. Fill the foil with pie weights or dried beans, and bake the tart shell in the center of the oven until the edges of the pastry begin to turn golden, 10 to 15 minutes. Remove the foil and the weights, and continue baking until the pastry is cooked through and golden, another 10 to 15 minutes. Remove the tart shell from the oven and let cool slightly before proceeding with the individual recipe.

Double-Crust Pâte Brisée
Pâte Brisée pour une Tourte

→•••←

In France, a double-crust tart is called a *tourte*. Long ago, *tourtes* were very fashionable on the French table. Now, though still popular, they are generally considered part of *la cuisine paysanne*, the cooking of the countryside.

Tourtes are generally savory and can include anything from mixtures of fruit and vegetables to meats to seafood. What distinguishes them, apart from their heartiness and flavor, is that the top pastry is not pricked to allow steam to escape. Instead, it is left whole so the ingredients inside steam gently as they cook.

This pastry is very buttery and easy to work. Don't be surprised at the amount of water—it's the secret to success.

> 2 cups (265 g) unbleached all-purpose
>   flour
> Generous ¼ teaspoon sea salt
> 9 tablespoons (135 g) unsalted butter,
>   chilled and cut into several pieces
> ⅓ to ½ cup (80 to 125 ml) ice water

Place the flour and the salt in a food processor and process once to mix. Then add the butter and pulse just until the mixture resembles coarse meal, three to five times. Add the ⅓ cup (80 ml) water and pulse just until the pastry begins to hold together, not more than nine or ten times. If the pastry is dry, add more water, 1 tablespoon at a time, until it begins to hold together. Transfer the dough from the food processor to your work surface and form it into a flat round. Let it rest, covered with a tea towel, for at least 30 minutes and up to 2 hours. The pastry is now ready to be rolled according to whichever *tourte* recipe you are following; however, you can make the pastry very flaky by a procedure of rolling and folding as described in step 3 of Homemaker's Pastry (page 510).

Pastry for one double-crust 10½-inch (26½ cm) tart

Puff Pastry
Pâte Feuilletée

→•••←

Although frozen puff pastry is available at supermarkets throughout France, it is still commonly made from scratch in farm kitchens. When you use this recipe you'll see why, for it is simple to prepare and simple to work with. Follow the tips in the accompanying box, and you'll know all you need for successful puff pastry.

1¾ cups (235 g) all-purpose flour

1½ teaspoons fine sea salt

5 tablespoons (75 g) unsalted butter,
   melted and cooled

6 tablespoons ice water

10 tablespoons (150 g) unsalted butter,
   chilled

1. To make the dough, place the flour and the salt in a food processor and process to blend. With the processor running, add the melted butter, then the ice water, and process just until the dough comes together. It will be soft, but it should not be sticky. Form the dough into a flat round about 4 inches (10 cm) across, wrap it well in parchment paper (or waxed paper) and then in aluminum foil, and refrigerate for 30 minutes.

2. Form the chilled butter into a 4½-inch (11 cm) square.

3. Roll out the pastry on a lightly floured surface to form a 9-inch (23 cm) round that is slightly thicker in the center than at the edges. Set the chilled butter square in the center of the dough, and fold the dough over the butter on all four sides, as if you were forming an envelope. The edges of the dough will overlap slightly. You now have a square of pastry. Brush the flour from the dough, and using a rolling pin, press gently but firmly on the "seams" to close them.

4. Turn the dough over onto the seamed side. Press down firmly about ½ inch (1¼ cm) from the top and bottom edges of the square, to encourage the pastry to keep its shape, and roll it out to form a 14 x 6-inch (36 x 15 cm) rectangle.

Making Puff Pastry
✦•✦

• *Roll out all pastry on a cool surface. Marble is ideal, but linoleum, granite, and concrete are all good as well. If your work surface feels warm, cool it down by setting a large baking pan filled with ice on it. Do this as often as necessary to keep the work surface cool.*

• *The dough, also called* détrempe, *and the butter should be the same consistency. If the dough is too soft or the butter too hard, they will not combine easily.*

• *To soften chilled butter, tap it firmly and quickly with a rolling pin, twisting the rolling pin as it hits the butter to prevent it from sticking.*

• *Using a pastry brush, brush any excess flour from the pastry before folding it and before using it. This will allow finer, more delicate layers to form.*

• *When rolling the puff pastry, use careful, even pressure. If you press hard on the edges or the ends, you may smash the butter and pastry together, which will prevent them from layering and becoming crisp. Uneven uncooked pastry will result in uneven cooked pastry.*

5. Brush any excess flour off the dough, and fold the rectangle from one short end into thirds, as for a business letter, brushing flour off each surface as you fold. Turn the dough so the fold is to the left, like a book,

and repeat the rolling out and folding two more times. This is one "turn." Mark the dough by pressing it with a finger, to remind yourself how many times you've "turned" it. Wrap the dough well in waxed paper and refrigerate it for 30 minutes.

6. Repeat step 5, marking the dough with two fingers. Then repeat the "turn" again, marking it with three fingers.

7. At this point the dough will keep, well wrapped, in the refrigerator for up to 1 week. It can also be wrapped airtight and frozen. If you'll be using the pastry for tarts, divide it into 4 pieces and wrap each piece individually before freezing.

8. For one 10½-inch (26½ cm) tart, use one fourth of the pastry. Roll it out to fit a 10½-inch (26½ cm) removable-bottom tart tin, prick the bottom of the pastry with the tines of a fork, and refrigerate the pastry shell for 1 hour before baking. Reserve the remaining dough for other uses.

Pastry for four 10½-inch (26½ cm) tarts

Sweet Pastry

Pâte Brisée au Sucre

This pastry makes a wonderful crust for a sweet tart—or you can roll it out, cut it into squares, brush it with an egg wash, and bake it as cookies. It's very versatile, and it's simple to make. Be sure to work quickly, as with all pastry, so the results will be tender.

A S T U C E . . . .

• *The less you touch pastry, the lighter and flakier it will be. If you make pastry by hand, work quickly and lightly, doing most of the work with your fingertips. If you use a food processor, touch the pastry as little as possible once it is blended. Use a minimum of flour when you're rolling out the pastry, and dust it off with a pastry brush reserved for that purpose before proceeding.*

. . . .

2 cups (265 g) unbleached all-purpose flour
Pinch of sea salt
1 tablespoon sugar
8 tablespoons (1 stick; 120 g) unsalted
*   butter, chilled, cut into pieces*
3 to 4 tablespoons ice water

1. Place the flour, salt, and sugar in a food processor and process once to blend.

Add the butter and process until the mixture resembles coarse cornmeal. Add 3 tablespoons of the ice water and process, pulsing, just until the pastry begins to form larger clumps. Press a bit of the pastry between your thumb and forefinger; if it doesn't hold together, add the remaining 1 tablespoon water and process briefly.

2. Turn the pastry out onto a lightly floured work surface and gather it together into a ball; then form it into a flat round. Wrap it in waxed paper and refrigerate for 1 hour before using in an individual recipe.

3. If an individual recipe calls for a prebaked tart shell, follow the directions in "Prebaking a Tart Shell" (page 511).

A Little Pinch'll Do You

➤•←

*A*s my friend Dany Dubois says, always but always put a pinch of salt in whatever pastry dough you are making. Even a tiny amount of salt heightens and cleans up the flavor, lifting what might be bland into the realm of the well-balanced and delicious.

Pastry for a 10½-inch (26½ cm) tart

All-Purpose Tomato Sauce
La Sauce Tomate qui Répond à Tous les Besoins

➤•••←

In the summer, Dany Dubois makes gallons of this tomato sauce with her garden tomatoes. She preserves it in jars to store in her *cave*. All year it serves as the basis for soup, a topping for pizza, a sauce for meat, pasta, or couscous.

I like to serve this sauce along with roast chicken or duck, and I always make sure to have plenty of bread on hand to sop up every last drop.

ASTUCE . . . .

• *The longer you cook tomatoes, the heavier their flavor becomes. They retain much more of their garden-fresh flavor when cooked just until they lose their shape, as in this recipe.*

. . . .

1 tablespoon rendered duck or goose fat
  (see page 142), or olive oil
2 medium onions, peeled and thinly sliced
3 pounds (1½ kg) tomatoes, peeled, cored,
  and cut into chunks
2 imported bay leaves
½ cup fresh sage leaves, or 1 tablespoon
  crumbled dried
1 tablespoon fresh rosemary leaves, or
  ½ teaspoon dried
Sea salt and freshly ground black pepper

1. Heat the fat in a large heavy skillet over medium heat. Add the onions, stir, and cook until they become translucent and limp, about 10 minutes.

2. Add the tomatoes and herbs, and season lightly with salt and pepper. Cook until the sauce has thickened and the tomatoes have lost their shape but still retain their bright red color, about 40 minutes.

3. Remove the bay leaves and adjust the seasoning. This sauce is now ready to use. It

---

La Tomate

→ · ←

The French began eating the tomato right after the Revolution, when apparently it was introduced into the country by a batallion of soldiers from Marseilles. They had picked up the odd and seductive fruit from their neighbors in Italy.

Chefs brave enough to use the tomato cooked it long and slowly, for sauces. As late as the end of the 19th century, French cookbooks followed their lead, insisting it be cooked for at least three hours or it would be indigestible, possibly toxic!

---

will keep in an airtight container in the refrigerator for 5 days, or frozen for up to 2 months.

4 to 6 servings

Basic Vinaigrette
Vinaigrette de Base

This is the vinaigrette that dresses salads throughout France, in the neighborhood bistro, at the mayor's house, on the farm tucked way back in *la France profonde*.

A S T U C E . . . .

• *Make an extra quantity of this dressing and store it in a tightly capped mason jar (or other container). When you need the dressing, shake the jar vigorously and pour the desired amount into your salad bowl. Season it with salt and pepper, and then add garlic, shallots, or whatever you like to complement your salad before adding greens and tossing.*

. . . .

1 tablespoon best-quality red wine vinegar
Sea salt to taste
1 teaspoon Dijon mustard (optional)
¼ cup (60 ml) extra-virgin olive oil

In a small bowl, whisk the vinegar, salt, and mustard to blend. Then slowly add the olive oil in a thin stream, whisking steadily until the mixture emulsifies.

About ⅓ cup (80 ml); enough for 8 to 10 cups salad greens

Dordogne Hachis
Hachis de la Dordogne

Hachis is essential to seasoning in the cuisine of the Dordogne, if you listen to Dany Dubois. She always has a tub of this aromatic mixture in her refrigerator, and it goes into everything from her signature dish (see Index for Dany's Potato Galette) to soups and stews. I follow her lead in this and keep some on hand, too—it's a blast of flavor in a jar.

Dany makes her *hachis* with a blend of fats, mixing fat from her own cured ham, duck fat, and the pure white fat from the pork she buys nearby. The result is a deep, rich flavor that I've re-created here.

Use *hachis* to taste in dishes where you'd like some extra flavor—you can even stir a touch into an omelette and be amazed by the wonderful flavor it gives!

Hachis will keep for several months in the refrigerator if tightly covered.

Les Bases • The Basics

24 cloves garlic, peeled and green germ
   removed
5 cups (loosely packed) flat-leaf parsley leaves
1 cup (250 g) fat, such as lard, rendered
   duck or goose fat (see page 142), or a
   mixture of all three

1. Coarsely chop the garlic cloves with

the parsley, then place them in the food processor and process, using pulses, until they are evenly minced. Add the fat and process until the mixture is thoroughly blended.

2. Refrigerate, tightly covered.

About 1½ cups (375 g)

Bouquet Garni

T ypically, a bouquet garni is a little bundle of aromatic herbs, specifically parsley, thyme, and bay leaf, often wrapped in the green leaf of a leek and then tied with string. Depending on the dish and the desire, however, bouquets garnis can be made of highly aromatic herbs such as tarragon, chervil, celery leaves, hyssop, or whatever is locally available and popular.

When a recipe calls for a bouquet garni, generally it refers to the traditional version. But if you want to experiment, do so by adding sprigs of your favorite herb.

A bouquet garni is useful in any soup or stew, lending it a gentle herbal flavor. You'll find it soon becomes indispensable.

5 parsley stems
3 imported bay leaves
12 sprigs fresh thyme
2 green leek leaves, rinsed well

Make a small bundle of the herbs and either enclose them, with the leek leaves, in

cheesecloth and tie with string, or place them lengthwise inside one of the leek leaves. Cover with the other leek leaf to enclose the bundle. Gently but firmly tie string around the leek leaves, wrapping it several times around the middle of the bundle. Use as called for.

1 bouquet garni

Quatre Epices

>…<

This subtle blend of spices is used frequently in France, particularly in meat dishes such as pâtés or terrines. It adds a touch of the exotic, an aromatic softening to robust flavors. Once you've tried it, you'll find many uses for it.

I like to mix up this quantity at a time, for I use it often. If you think, however, that you won't use it frequently, mix up just what you need, for it loses its freshness quickly.

A S T U C E . . . .

• *Whenever possible, buy spices in seed form. They stay fresh and keep their flavor many times longer than those already ground. Buy a small electric or hand coffee grinder for grinding the spices. Be sure to brush it out between batches of spices so the flavors don't linger.*

1 teaspoon freshly ground cinnamon
1 teaspoon freshly ground nutmeg
1 teaspoon freshly ground cloves
1 teaspoon freshly ground allspice

Mix the ground spices together in a small bowl, and store in an airtight glass jar, preferably in a dark spot.

4 teaspoons

Clarified Butter
Beurre Clarifié

>…<

Clarified butter has a single advantage over ordinary melted butter. Because the milk solids are removed, the pure butter that remains has a very, very high burning temperature, which makes it ideal for sautéing or cooking at high temperatures, such as for crêpes. It also has a purer flavor.

8 tablespoons (1 stick; 120 g) unsalted butter

1. Place the butter in a small heavy saucepan and melt it over medium-high heat. It will froth and bubble, which is what you want. Watch it carefully, and when it has melted, remove it from the heat and skim off and discard all the froth.

2. Strain the butter that remains through a fine-mesh sieve lined with a double thickness of cheesecloth, and use as required. Clarified butter will keep, tightly covered and refrigerated, for up to 2 weeks.

6 to 7 tablespoons

Crème Fraîche

Crème fraîche is to northern French cooking what olive oil is to southern. It smooths, it silkens, it enriches. In Normandy, where I live, it is available fresh at local markets where farm women—and occasionally men—scoop it gracefully out of large tubs.

Fresh crème fraîche is quite unlike the many brands available at the grocery store. Crème fraîche from the farm market, which comes straight from the cow, changes color with the seasons—from ivory in the winter, when the cows are eating grains and hay, to a golden yellow in the summer, when they graze in the pasture. Its flavor is soft and ultra-creamy. Supermarket crème fraîche is pure white and has a sour tang. Homemade crème fraîche will develop a tang, too, after several days. It's a taste that takes getting used to, and not one I look for. I prefer my cream thick, fresh, and almost buttery.

To approximate fresh crème fraîche, get top cream from milk that has just come from the cow. (I believe Maine is the only state

where such milk is commercially available.) Barring that, get the best cream you can and follow this recipe for a close and very respectable second.

2 cups (500 ml) heavy (or whipping)
cream (preferably not *ultra-pasteurized)*
3 tablespoons cultured buttermilk

1. Whisk the cream and the buttermilk together in a medium-size bowl. Cover with a cotton tea towel and let stand in a warm spot (on top of the refrigerator or on top of a gas stove with a pilot light) until it thickens, 8 to 12 hours depending on the temperature.

2. Cover the crème fraîche, and refrigerate it for several hours until thickened. Tightly covered, it will keep in the refrigerator for 1 week.

2 cups (500 ml)

Vanilla Sugar
Sucre Vanille

In France, vanilla sugar is sold in pretty little packets at the grocery store. It isn't really like granulated sugar, but is rather a cross between granulated and confectioners'. This vanilla sugar works just as well. I always have at least 5 pounds on hand, and I use it in most of my pastries. It's a good way to use your vanilla beans after they've served to flavor milk or custard—just make sure they are dry before you add them to the sugar.

8 cups (3½ pounds; 1¾ kg) sugar
2 fresh vanilla beans, or 4 used vanilla beans

Pour the sugar into an airtight container, and push the vanilla beans down into the sugar. Cover and let ripen for at least 1 week. Replenish the sugar as you use it, pouring out the sugar that is already flavored, adding new sugar to the container, and topping it with the flavored sugar. Replace the vanilla beans once every 2 months.

8 cups (3½ pounds; 1¾ kg)

Visiting the Farm

>···<

I stayed on all of the following farms when I was researching *French Farmhouse Cookbook*, and I recommend each highly. While they are not luxurious, they are always comfortable and homey. What is more important is that they offer a simple and unadorned experience with sincere, friendly, hardworking people. Often, when meals are served, the food is better than one could ever get in a local restaurant, and when the family eats with guests it is always, at least in my experience, fun and warm. One leaves wishing to return, and I think there is no better recommendation.

Tips for staying on the farm:

• Call to reserve a room, and specify when you will arrive. Farmers will generally plan their time around you. If they ask that you arrive at a certain time (so they can do their farm chores and still be available to greet you), respect their request.

• Have cash on hand to pay for your stay. It is extremely rare to find a farm that accepts anything but local checks or cash.

• Travel with soap and other toilet articles—they are rarely supplied.

If you don't speak French, have a French dictionary on hand—it will help!

BRITTANY
Jean and Annick Larhentiec
"Kerviniou"
29610 Plouigneau
Tel: 98.79.20.58

Marceline and Francois Grall
"Kernevez"
29233 Cleder
Tel: 98.69.41.14

AUVERGNE
Monique and Marcel Pelisse
"Jalasset"
43370 Bains
Tel: 71.57.52.72

NORMANDY
Alain and Françoise Petiton
"La Suhardiere"
Livry

Paulette and Herve Marie
La Ferme de la Rivière
14230 St. Germain-du-Port
Tel: 31.22.72.92

Brigitte and Roland Etienne
"La Rosière"
14117 Tracy-sur-Mer
Tel: 31.22.33.88

Bernard and Paulette Petit
La Ferme du Loucel
14710 Colleville-sur-Mer
Tel: 31.22.40.95

Nadine and Christian Devisme
Hameau de Boos
27400 Heudeville-sur-Eure
Tel: 32.50.23.02

PAYS BASQUE
Marie-Agnès and
Michel Carricaburu
L'Auberge Etchegoyen
64220 Esterencuby
Tel: 59.37.09.77

This isn't a farm, but a small hotel in the heart of sheep-herding country, and it offers many of the qualities of a farm, including conversations with the delightful couple who run it, who are farmers as well.

DORDOGNE
Dany and Guy Dubois
Peyrenègre
La Dornac 24120
Tel: 53.51.11.22

Index

➤•••◄

N

O

Susan Herrmann Loomis
specializes in writing about food from
the ground up. She joined the crews of
fishing boats while researching
"The Great American Seafood Cookbook,"
and traveled 20,000 miles
through America for the
"Farmhouse Cookbook."
She and her family live in the tiny
village of Louviers, in Normandy.